Rebecca Whisnant received her doctorate in philosophy at the University of North Carolina at Chapel Hill, and is visiting Assistant Professor of Philosophy at the University of Dayton. In addition to teaching and publishing in ethics and feminist theory, she is an anti-pornography educator and peace activist who has done public speaking on topics ranging from same-sex marriage to the US wars on Afghanistan and Iraq. Her current work focuses on intersections and tensions between feminist theory and the philosophy of non-violence.

Christine Stark is a feminist writer, artist, speaker, and activist of American Indian and European ancestry. She has spoken nationally and internationally on issues of rape, race, poverty, home-lessness, prostitution, and pornography and organized many community events, including *Amerika: Land of Rape and Genocide*. Her writing and art have been published in numerous periodicals and anthologies and she has appeared on National Public Radio and various television and radio shows. She was interviewed for *Dirty Little Secret*, a documentary on sexual violence. She is a member of the Minnesota Indian Women's Sexual Assault Coalition and completing her MFA in Writing from Minnesota State University. Christine is a survivor of incest and a racist prostitution and pornography ring.

NOT FOR SALE: FEMINISTS RESISTING PROSTITUTION AND PORNOGRAPHY

Edited by Rebecca Whisnant and Christine Stark

Spinifex Press Pty Ltd
504 Queensberry Street
North Melbourne, Vic. 3051
Australia
women@spinifexpress.com.au
http://www.spinifexpress.com.au

Edited by Kerry Biram, Melbourne
Cover design by Deb Snibson
Typeset by Claire Warren, Melbourne
Printed and bound by McPherson's Printing Group

National Library of Australia
cataloguing-in-publication data:

Not for sale : feminists resisting prostitution and pornography.

   Bibliography.
   Includes index.
   ISBN 1 876756 49 7.

   1. Pornography – Social aspects. 2. Sex oriented businesses.
   3. Women – Social conditions. 4. Prostitution.
   I. Stark, Christine. II. Whisnant, Rebecca.

305.42

For all survivors of male violence, and for my students.
                                                          RW

For Andrea Dworkin and for the women in my family.
                                                          CS

Contents

Permissions

We are grateful to the following individuals and organisations for their generosity in allowing us to reproduce the following texts:

'Blow bangs and cluster bombs: The cruelty of men and Americans': First published in *Feminista!* volume 5 number 1.

'The use of new communication technologies for sexual exploitation of women and children': © 2002 by University of California, Hastings College of the Law. Reprinted from *Hastings Women's Law Journal*, volume 13 number 1, Winter 2002, 127, by permission.

'How prostitution works': An earlier version was published on Melissa Farley's website (Prostitution Research and Education) at http://www.prostitutionresearch.com/parker-how.html.

'Sex and feminism: Who is being silenced?': First appeared in *Said It*, volume 3 number 3: http://www.saidit.org/archives/jul01/mediaglance.html.

'Strategies of connection: prostitution and feminist politics': This is an edited version of article that appeared originally in the *Michigan Journal of Gender and the Law* 65 (1993).

'Pornography and international human rights': Copyright © 1992 by John Stoltenberg. Reprinted by permission of the author.

Some of the papers in this anthology have been previously published (in some cases in different forms) in other publications.

In some instances it has proven to be impossible to contact copyright holders. Any copyright holders not acknowledged here, or acknowledged incorrectly, should contact the publishers.

Rebecca Whisnant and Christine Stark

Introduction

Prostitution is a multi-billion dollar global industry that includes adult and child pornography, bartering sex for food and shelter, massage parlors, prostitution rings, stripping, saunas, live sex shows, street prostitution, escort services or outcall, ritual abuse, peep shows, phone sex, international and domestic trafficking, mail order bride services, and prostitution tourism.[1] The prostitution industry is an enormously powerful and pervasive cultural presence. The religious right loudly condemns pornography and prostitution, especially railing about the immorality of prostituted women; at the same time, those who consider themselves liberal often regard the sex industry as a hip, cutting-edge, and liberating force. Although the two sides appear to be involved in a battle over the morality of prostitution, in reality men of all political persuasions buy and sell women and children in prostitution.

In contrast, since the 1970s, many feminists have been actively resisting prostitution and pornography as systems of exploitation and violence against women and children.[2] These feminists emphasize that the harms of prostitution have nothing to do with the morality of those who are used within it, and everything to do with the choices and behavior of those who do the using—both the pimps who profit from selling women and children, and the millions of men who feel entitled to exchange money for sexual access. As a result of feminist analysis and activism, it has become more difficult for public discussion of these issues to avoid at least mentioning the feminist view of pornography and prostitution as matters of harm rather than offense, of women's human and civil rights rather than of religiously defined 'morality'.

There are now at least two generations of feminists who clearly understand the damage of prostitution and pornography to all women's safety and civil status, who passionately oppose their steady encroachment on our economy and public life, and who possess the insight, skills, and

---

1 As the foregoing list makes clear, we define pornography as a form of prostitution; thus when we refer to 'prostitution' or 'the prostitution industry', we mean this to include pornography.

2 As Sheila Jeffreys has shown, contemporary feminist work against prostitution has important historical antecedents. See Jeffreys' *The Spinster and Her Enemies: Feminism and Sexuality 1880–1930* (Spinifex Press, 1997) for a useful account of such work by feminists in the late nineteenth century.

experience to lead a renewed movement against pornography and prostitution. Women and men around the world are engaging in courageous and inspired activism, employing novel legal strategies against pornographers and other pimps, and producing new research and analysis. *Not For Sale* is our attempt to help disseminate this body of work, and to connect a radical feminist critique of pornography and prostitution with a broader social justice agenda.

The idea for this anthology originated in 1999 in response to a speech given by feminist author and activist Andrea Dworkin at the University of Minnesota. The Minnesota Coalition Against Prostitution and other groups had organized Dworkin's speech in conjunction with an art show by survivors.[3] During the question and answer period, Dworkin was discussing the watershed legal work—initiated in Minneapolis by herself, Catharine MacKinnon, and others in the early 1980s—that defined pornography as a violation of women's civil rights.[4] Acknowledging the fact that their anti-pornography civil-rights ordinance, although enormously influential, had ultimately failed to become law, Dworkin observed that 'when something ends, something new must begin'. In response to this challenge, Christine developed the idea of an anthology—a lasting body of work to demonstrate that, despite frequent misrepresentation and censorship, feminist work against prostitution and pornography is strong and growing; that it involves activists associated with a broad array of progressive issues; and that it is often organized by survivors of prostitution and pornography. This anthology serves notice: there is a whole new generation of feminists who are resisting the sex industry. We're working alongside the older generation of feminists who laid the groundwork. Many of us are survivors. Something new has begun.

In the summer of 2001, Christine had just begun work toward an MFA in Writing. She was also heavily involved in organizing against prostitution and pornography locally and nationally—work she had been doing for twelve years as an activist, speaker, visual artist, and writer. Christine emailed Rebecca after reading her essay on teaching radical feminism in the university, written for the online feminist journal *Said It*. Rebecca was in the final throes of her PhD work at the University of North Carolina at Chapel Hill, where she had also done several years of feminist anti-pornography

---

3   The groups that brought Dworkin to speak included the Minnesota Coalition Against Prostitution (whose membership included survivors and allies), women in a south Minneapolis neighborhood group against prostitution, the Program Against Sexual Violence at the University of Minnesota, and other Minneapolis activists.

4   Dworkin and MacKinnon's explanation and defense of their proposed legislation, originally published in their book *Pornography and Civil Rights: A New Day for Women's Equality* (Minneapolis: Organizing Against Pornography, 1988), can now be read online at
http://www.nostatusquo.com/ACLU/dworkin/other/ordinance/newday/TOC.htm.

activism, primarily in the form of presenting slideshows and lectures to classes, conferences, and organizations.

We agreed to collaborate on a new anthology that we hoped would help strengthen feminist sentiments and revitalize feminist activism against pornography and prostitution, while offering a supportive platform for a growing number of survivors to tell their stories and articulate their analyses. We wanted to inspire and connect people who were already doing vital research and activism on these issues, as well as to draw new energy to the movement by showing readers that their existing commitments to social justice in other areas provide fertile ground for extending their concern to prostitution and pornography.

Producing the book has been a long process, with many fits and starts as one and then the other of us moved, started new jobs and new graduate programs, bought houses, weathered family crises, and so on. One thing we certainly learned, as novice editors, is that producing an anthology is an enormous amount of work. We received many contributions that, in the end, we were unable to use. The experiences and voices of these writers expanded our understanding of the issues and fueled our commitment to the project. Hundreds of emails (and one visit) later, after three years of collecting articles from all over the world and countless discussions on content, editing, and style, *Not For Sale: Feminists Resisting Prostitution and Pornography* is in print.

In undertaking this project we hoped, among other things, to create and occupy some new ground in what are sometimes called the 'feminist sex wars'—the ongoing disputes between feminists who defend prostitution and pornography as legitimate and potentially empowering 'sex work', and those who see them as systems of male exploitation and violence against women and children. As those familiar with the debate know, this disagreement typically accompanies additional disagreements over sadomasochism and other sexual practices that are seen by one side as legitimate, even liberating, and by the other side as oppressive and anti-feminist. For these reasons, the two sides are often called 'pro-sex' and 'anti-sex'. (The tendency to label the latter position 'anti-sex' betrays, in our view, a regrettably limited vision of what sex is and can be.) As will be clear, we stand unequivocally on one side of that debate as it is typically framed: we believe that feminists who defend pornography and prostitution are mistaken in their analyses, and that their political positions and alliances are harmful to women, to feminism, and to the cause of social justice. However, we also want to help expand and reframe this debate. While building on the indispensable analyses of radical feminists such as Andrea Dworkin, Catharine MacKinnon, and Kathleen Barry, we felt the need to connect radical feminist perspectives on the sex industry more explicitly and extensively with radical critiques of racism, militarism, and unbridled corporate capitalism, as well as to show how the harms of pornography and prostitution are amplified and extended by contemporary technologies of mass communication. While only sometimes addressing our feminist adversaries primarily and directly, we hope that the alternative analyses collected here will provide a clear and compelling counterpoint to the 'pro-sex' point of view.

As our authors make clear, there is far more to this issue than simple claims of being 'pro-sex' or 'anti-sex'. Prostitution and pornography both reflect and anchor larger systems of male dominance, as well as other oppressive institutions and structures such as racism, imperialism, militarism, and global corporate capitalism. The industries of sexual exploitation do devastating harm to the women and children within them. Sexually exploited persons are subject to massive physical and psychological violence as well as poverty, drug addiction, racism, and homelessness. Prostitution and pornography also undermine all women's safety and dignity by legitimizing the objectification of women, and by training men and boys to desire and expect compliant sexual servicing from women and girls. We hope that the book will become a resource for people involved in various movements for social justice—such as those against racism, globalization, and war—as well as for those who identify themselves primarily as feminists.

Organization and contents

We have divided the essays into three sections. Because of the richness and wide range of many of these essays, our placement of them in particular sections was in some cases somewhat arbitrary.

The opening section, 'Understanding systems of prostitution', includes informative and analytical overviews of what we are up against when we take on the sex industries. Joe Parker summarizes how prostitution works—the customers' motivations, the pimps' methods, and the effects on the women, children, and men who are used. Rebecca Whisnant addresses some basic conceptual issues about pornography, arguing that it is a form of technologized and documented prostitution and that questions about coercion and consent in the industry are both more and less central than feminist discussions have sometimes suggested. Robert Jensen's article powerfully connects pornography with the militarism of empire, showing that both rest on contempt for others and a repudiation of our common humanity. Donna Hughes explains how new technologies of mass communication extend and facilitate the abuse of women and children through the sex industry, making clear in the process the extent to which new technologies blur whatever distinction may have once existed between prostitution and pornography. Taylor Lee discusses her experiences working in strip clubs, what led her into the industry and what helped her get out of it. Throughout her paper she analyzes stripping as an integral element of the system of prostitution. Seiya Morita places the enormous Japanese sex trade in context, arguing that its expansion correlates with an increase in sexual violence and describing various other concrete harms that accompany it. Gail Dines and Vednita Carter both offer analyses of pornography's vicious racial stereotyping, and Chong Kim's recollection of her experience as an Asian American woman in prostitution makes it clear that racism pervades all levels of the sex industry. Melissa Farley and Jacqueline Lynne describe their research on the impact of racism and colonization on prostituted First Nations women in Vancouver, and Samantha Emery discusses how connecting with her Anishinaabe identity and culture aided her leaving and recovering from prostitution and drug addiction. The section ends with Andrea Dworkin's call for a renewed commitment to the politics of feminism and for activism in solidarity with prostituted women.

The book's middle section, 'Resisting the sexual new world order', opens with D.A. Clarke's far-ranging exploration of connections between the sex trade, neoliberal dogma, trends in pop culture, and geopolitics. (A late addendum addresses the implications of 'war porn' and the Abu Ghraib scandal.) Joyce Wu describes an attempt to intervene in the discourse of leftists who legitimize and celebrate the buying and selling of women in pornography. The women of Vancouver Rape Relief and Women's Shelter analyze current regressive economic/political trends in Canada and their impact on women and girls who suffer sexual violence both within and outside of prostitution. Their experience and analysis remind us once more that wherever there is poverty and hunger, women and girls are driven into prostitution. The remaining essays in this section further expose the dangerous hypocrisies of the political left with respect to the traffic in women. Mary Sullivan critiques the crippling inadequacy of the 'sex work' perspective as it applies to the health and well-being of women in Australia's legalized brothel prostitution. Adriene Sere reveals the alliance of left/liberal media outlets with the 'pro-sex' point of view and their erasure and distortion of radical feminist perspectives. Kirsten Anderberg recounts her disillusioning encounter with a group of 'pro-sex' individuals who celebrate pornography while ridiculing her discomfort and stifling her dissent. Christine Stark takes to task 'sex radicals' such as Patrick Califia, Carol Queen, and Annie Sprinkle, questioning the legitimacy of their claim to radicalism.

The essays in the third and final section, 'Surviving, conceiving, confronting', both document and advocate for creative thought and committed action against prostitution and pornography. Some describe various modes of social change or activism on behalf of prostituted women: for example, Carol Davis's account of activist theater in Nepal, Leslie Wolfe's call for specific legal changes targeting traffickers, and longtime activist Ann Simonton's conversation with former porn actress Carol Smith regarding her plans to educate young people about the pornography industry and her planned lawsuit against the pimps who continue to exploit her name and image. Sherry Lee Short draws on her own experience resisting the encroachment of strip bars in rural areas, offering analysis of why the stripping industry flourishes in such communities and concrete advice on how to stop it. Other essays in this section emphasize new conceptual approaches to, and arguments against, pornography and prostitution. Rus Funk recounts his own evolution from porn user to anti-porn activist, urging men to join the movement based on their commitment to justice and equality, rather than on their own self-interest. Sheila Jeffreys proposes regarding prostitution as what the United Nations calls a harmful cultural (or traditional) practice, and draws our attention to Western bias as a partial explanation for the United Nations' failure (so far) to treat it as such. John Stoltenberg argues that pornography must be treated in the international arena as a human and civil rights issue rather than as a trade issue. Margaret Baldwin's article moves easily and productively between theory and practice, describing her work bringing about progressive legal changes regarding prostitution in Florida while challenging the continuing tendency, even within feminism, to distance ourselves from prostituted women. Jane Caputi's essay nurtures our imagination, reminding us of the profound distance between pornographic and truly radical, life-affirming ways of thinking and talking about sex, bodies, and women.

Acknowledgements

Working on this book has reminded us once again of the importance of bringing diverse perspectives and gifts to the movement against sexual trafficking and exploitation. Above all, we want to thank our contributors, who took time from their activism, research, and/or service to share their analyses and their hard-won wisdom. We especially thank those contributors who are survivors, who were willing to revisit and expose painful parts of their lives as part of the work. We deeply appreciate their courage and dedication.

We would like to thank Susan Hawthorne of Spinifex Press for her commitment to the book and for her patience, both in awaiting the finished manuscript and in answering the many questions of novice editors. Gratitude is also due to Kerry Biram for her careful and sensitive copyediting. In addition, we owe a debt of thanks to the online journal *Said*

It, the *Hastings Women's Law Journal*, and Sage Publications for granting reprint permissions.

Christine: I want to thank Andrea Dworkin and Catharine MacKinnon, without whose support over the past fourteen years I would not be doing this work and might not be alive. Miigwech to Samantha Emery, Rose Kramer, Earl, Kathy, Carol, Rhonda, and Skip for their guidance. Also, thanks to Lindsay and Amanda Kaylor-Brice, Don Town, Millie Smith, Rene Simon, Claudine O'Leary, Nayiree Roubinian, Garine Roubinian, Yoshi Bird, and Jennifer Reed. A special thanks to my co-editor, Rebecca Whisnant, for putting together the manuscript when my mother died three weeks before it was due.

Rebecca: Working on this book has reminded me often of the 'posse' of feminist friends and colleagues with and from whom I learned about pornography during my graduate student years in Chapel Hill. I want to thank Jane Reid, Mary MacLeod, Lori Alward, Shelby Weitzel, Cindy Stark, and Vicki Behrens for the many hours of discussion and mutual education that formed—and continue to influence—my radical feminist perspective. Thanks also to the philosophy departments at the University of Southern Indiana and the University of Dayton for supporting my research, and to my family for their pride and encouragement. For diligent and thoughtful reading and discussion, as well as tireless love and support, I thank Marty, my partner in all things.

PART ONE

Understanding Systems of Prostitution

Joe Parker

How prostitution works

Introduction

Prostitution, pornography, and other forms of commercial sex are a multi-billion-dollar industry. They enrich a small minority of predators, while the larger community is left to pay for the damage. People used in the sex industry often need medical care as a result of the ever-present violence. They may need treatment for infectious diseases, including AIDS. Survivors frequently need mental health care for post-traumatic stress disorder, psychotic episodes and suicide attempts. About a third end up chronically disabled and on Social Security. The sex trade plays an active role in promoting alcohol and drug problems. Pimps also use prostituted women in forgery and credit card fraud. The community must pay for chemical dependency treatment, insurance costs and incarceration. In addition to these costs, the community loses the contributions which might have been made to legitimate community productivity by those used up in the sex industry. The operators of sex businesses not only do not pay for these expenses; many manage to avoid paying taxes at all.

The johns

No business can afford to create a product for which there are no buyers. The first step in understanding the sex industry is to understand the customers, the johns.

Real sexual relationships are not hard to find. There are plenty of adults of both sexes who are willing to have sex if someone treats them well, and asks. But there lies the problem. Some people do not want an equal, sharing relationship. They do not want to be nice. They do not want to ask. They like the power involved in buying a human being who can be made to do almost anything.

The business of prostitution and pornography is the use of real human beings to support the fantasies of others. Anyone working in prostitution who tells a john too much about who they *really* are interferes with the fantasy. They risk losing a customer, and may get a beating as well. In real relationships with real people, you are stuck with the limitations of who you are, who your partner is, and what you can do together without hurting each other.

Some people do not want real relationships, or feel entitled to something beyond the real relationships they have. They want to play 'super stud and

3

sex slave' or whatever, inside their own heads. If they need to support their fantasies with pictures, video tapes, or real people to abuse, the sex trade is ready to supply them. For a price, they can be 'a legend in their own minds'.

The most common type of prostitution customer is the **user**. He is quite self-centered, and simply wants what he considers to be his needs met. The user would deny any intent to harm anyone, and might even claim some empathy for the sex workers he uses. However, his empathy does not extend to discontinuing his using behavior, nor to helping anyone escape from the sex industry. He does not care whether the person he is using is unwilling or unusually vulnerable. He simply feels entitled to whatever he wants, whenever he wants it. If someone is hurt, that is not his problem. He feels that the fee he pays covers any damages. He sees himself as a respectable person, and works to protect that appearance. Users provide a large, safe, and steady income for the pimps and other 'businessmen' of the sex industry.

Sadists are people who have the ability to take pleasure in another person's fear, pain, or humiliation. They constitute about ten percent of the population. Sadists vary in severity, ranging from those who just make you feel bad, to those who do torture murders. There is a definite practice effect. If they are allowed to hurt people often, their sadism gets worse. Physical, sexual, and emotional abuse by sadists drives their child victims from their homes into the street, trying to escape. The pimps and 'chickenhawks' take it from there.

Sadists are attracted to prostituted women and children because they are willing to get into a car or come to a place where the sadist can be in control. Sadism is about control. Hurting people who cannot stop them is their most intense and pleasurable form of control. Sadists play close attention to matters of power. They are most brutal with small women and children, and are more careful with larger women and men. They avoid people who may have someone to protect them, or someone who may take revenge on the victim's behalf. There are pimps who specialize in supplying victims to sadists, and who base their fees on the amount of damage done to the victim. Sadists are found at all levels of society, including the respected and powerful. They often use this position of respect or power by saying, 'You are just a whore; nobody is going to believe you.' If they do kill someone, they are very aware that, to some extent, the effort society puts into finding the killer will reflect the value placed on the victim. People working in prostitution are safe victims.

Necrophiles are people who can take pleasure in filth, degradation, and destruction. They are the users of the sick, the old, the psychotic, the brain damaged, the 'tracked' and tattooed casualties of the sex industry who are in the end stages of their lives. For necrophiles, broken bodies and broken minds are a turn-on. They glory in their superiority over ruined human beings, and feel entitled to express their contempt in every way. Necrophiles must keep their perversion secret from their friends and families, both to protect their social standing, and to protect their fantasies of superiority. Normal people just would not understand.

Child molesters participate in the sex industry in several ways. Some have been aware of a sexual attraction to children, often of a particular age and sex, from some time in late childhood. They then make the choice to act on it. Some have sadistic characteristics. Children are easier than adults to control. The molester's own children, in his own home, are the easiest of all to control.

Necrophilic child molesters enjoy the knowledge that, when the molesters are finished with them, the children's lives will never be the same. They enjoy the fact that the children may later self-destruct in addiction, prostitution or suicide. It proves that they were right.

Sex offenders against children operate with varying degrees of sophistication. Some do careful 'grooming'. They use pornography to break down resistance, and supply drugs, alcohol, and money. Others just start out with forcible rape. Many claim unusual 'love' for children. They claim that sex between adults and children is not harmful, and should be legalized. Pedophiles actually teach children that they are helpless, hopeless, worthless, and only good for sex and hurting. A large portion of workers in the sex trade started out as sexually abused children. Some were even 'broken in' by being shared with or rented out to others by their own families.

There are specialist pimps who provide children to johns. The fees vary depending on the age, sex and appearance of the child, as well as the amount of damage the child has already incurred. When caught, the pimps and johns claim not to have known the child's real age. There is a market for small adults made up to look like children, both for direct sex and for pornography. But the truth is in the fees: real children sell for more than fake ones.

Prostitution buffs

Prostitution buffs are like police and fire buffs, that is, they are people with an intense interest in those occupations even though they do not belong to them. Prostitution buffs are people with a morbid fascination for or obsession with prostituted persons and their activities. Some characterize themselves as 'researchers', and amass hundreds of pages of notes and photographs that somehow are seldom published.

Others claim to be intent on religious redemption of 'sinners', and spend huge amounts of time in vice areas, but never quite manage to offer anyone any practical help.

A third group consists of 'community livability' activists, who blame the people being prostituted for the behavior of the johns, pimps, and drug dealers.

As with any obsession, with some people it may get out of control. Police buffs may take unlawful police action, and some fire buffs eventually set fires. Each type of prostitution buff strongly believes in their own rationalizations for their activities, and would vehemently deny any personal sexual interest. The trouble is, it is obviously there. They show a lot of subtle signs which may indicate to someone working in prostitution that they may be potential customers.

When a prostituted person approaches the buff to offer their services, the response may be unpredictable and dangerous. Sometimes the buffs will accept their services, and the worker may never realize that they are anything but a normal trick. At other times, they will be met with rage, as if they are making a heterosexual or homosexual attack on the buff. They may be beaten, knifed, or thrown out of a moving vehicle.

Most of the 'research' and 'religious' buffs are men, and they spend enough time studying their subject so that their identifications of who is and who is not prostituting are fairly accurate. Many of the 'community livability' activists are women. Some may use pepper spray or draw weapons on young people who are in no way involved, but who fit whatever stereotype the activist has created of what a prostitute should look like.

Customer streams

Three forces generate streams of customers for prostitution: isolation, sexual abandonment, and unusual interests. Prostituted people are used to service populations that are physically isolated from the life of their communities. These customers come from such sources as military bases, logging or mining camps, and farm labor camps. Operators of these facilities are often involved in arranging prostitution services through local pimps.

Other customers are isolated by travel, such as seamen, truckers, and traveling businessmen. Hotels, motels, bars and other businesses which provide support services for travelers often also participate in arrangements for sexual services.

In some religious cultures, and some individual family cultures, sex is regarded as an unpleasant duty of marriage, and once the childbearing years are over, one partner may cut the other off from sexual activity. The sex industry does not reach out to middle-aged women, so their only choice is to have affairs. This may be morally unacceptable to them, or eligible partners may not be available. For them, there may be no solution.

For men, prostitution is quite available, and many men may see it as less wrong than having affairs, or as requiring less effort. These men provide a large and steady income for the sex industry; most of these johns would be classified as 'users', and an unclear proportion of them might not be prostitution customers if they were not isolated.

Customers who remain in or near their home communities are more likely to use prostituted people due to unusual interests, such as sadism, pedophilia, or sexual addiction. They are isolated by the nature of their desires, rather than their location. For example, men who prefer sex with boys, but who do not view themselves as homosexual, support a whole segment of the industry involving prostituted males. It is unclear whether local law enforcement efforts, or the openness and aggressiveness with which the sex industry is allowed to operate in a community, affects the stream of 'special interest' customers.

A large portion of prostituted people are also used in and around the communities where they grew up. The fact that survivors often meet previous tricks in local grocery stores and other random places can be a considerable problem for their recovery.

For those whose special interests place them at serious legal risk in their own community, there is sex tourism. Some cities in the US are well known to run more 'wide open' than others, that is, there are fewer and weaker laws on the books, and police and other officials are discouraged from enforcing them. These conditions are often the result of cooperation between business and elected officials, who are repaid by the sex industry in various ways.

The pimps

No one really wants to have sex with five, ten, or twenty strangers a day, every day. Besides coping with the sheer numbers of sex acts involved, some of those strangers are going to use a person in ways that are bizarre, painful, disgusting, and occasionally fatal. When people who have worked in prostitution say that they have been subjected to repeated rape, they are not exaggerating or being 'hysterical'; they are being legally precise. Rape is sexual intercourse against the will of the victim, carried out by threat or force.

In prostitution, the john performs the sex act with the unwilling victim, but subcontracts the intimidation and violence to another man, the pimp. The john would like to believe he is paying for sex, but the person he has sex with gets little or none of the money. The money goes to the pimp to pay for the force needed to keep prostituted women and children working. It goes to the drug dealer who provides whatever it takes to keep the workers from becoming psychotic or committing suicide. It goes to pay the businessmen who provide the real estate, support services, and legal protection for the trade.

Pimps come in three general types. **Media pimping**, like other kinds, involves selling fantasies that ultimately hurt people. Two of their central lies are that women are only good for sex, and men are only good for violence. They claim that they produce sex and violence because that is all that sells. In fact, many other things sell as well or better. (For example, Walt Disney and

Steven Spielberg productions often are very successful.) Media pimps often have a tremendous sense of superiority over 'common' people, yet lack the intelligence and creativity to do high quality work. They enjoy their alternative, selling a degraded view of the human race.

Advertisers often implicitly promise that buying their products will bring happiness, power, and sexual success. After spending their money, the victims of this 'bait and switch' scam find that they get only a pack of cigarettes, a bottle of shampoo, or a magazine full of dirty pictures. They are just as lonely and unhappy as before, but their money is gone.

Media pimps perform another 'bait and switch' function, in cooperation with business-level pimps. They attract young people hoping for fame and fortune in the legitimate entertainment business, and manipulate them into the lower levels of the sex industry. They degrade ordinary people living ordinary lives by showing only idealized characters with perfect bodies, high-powered jobs, and plenty of money. The characters' problems are always solved in an hour or two, and always with a liberal application of sex and violence.

Real people, whose lives cannot hope to measure up to these 'ideals', are made to feel inferior and worthless. The media pimps work to divert people from the ups and downs of real life into dependence on the fantasy worlds that they sell. The sex industry, above all, sells fantasy regardless of who gets hurt.

The media pimps have a *lot* of money. They own magazines and news-papers, and produce movies and television programs. They can afford to hire law firms and advertising agencies to further their interests. Their money can buy access to political officials, and special treatment for their businesses. In return they offer favorable media exposure and large campaign contributions. Their money often goes to support various front organizations which work to direct public discussion toward 'free speech rights', and away from the damaging effects of the sex industry on the women and children used in it.

Business-level pimps extract profits from the sex industry in ways that minimize the risk of public exposure or criminal prosecution. They own the bars and strip clubs which attract concentrations of potential johns. They offer jobs as dancers and hostesses to vulnerable young people who are potential candidates for more direct use in the sex trade. They own the adult book stores, massage parlors, motels, and legal brothels. They posture as legitimate businessmen, conceal their ownership behind corporations and front men, and deny knowing that their property is being used in the sex industry. They charge sex businesses far higher rents and fees than they could get from legitimate tenants, which indicates that they know what the businesses are doing.

Through contacts in the business community, they arrange for sexual services for visiting businessmen, politicians, celebrities, and sports teams. By keeping these arrangements secret, business pimps ensure a degree of protection for their other activities from their customers in high places.

Business-level pimps separate themselves from the 'dirty workers' of the sex trade by treating them as independent contractors rather than as employees. This enables them to avoid having to pay taxes, overtime pay, health insurance, and workers' compensation. If one of the workers is arrested, the businessman is protected from any legal involvement. They subcontract any violence needed to the street-level pimps.

With support from elements of the 'legitimate' entertainment industry as well as from street-level pimps, they produce and distribute commercial pornography. They support and have the support of 'civil liberties' advocates who oppose censorship regardless of the harm done to the people used in *making* the pornography. They disclaim any responsibility for the actions of potentially violent sex offenders who use pornography to 'fuel' their fantasies until they are ready to commit actual violence.

Business pimps often join civic organizations, make highly public contributions to charity, and play a role in local politics. They continually assert their identity as legitimate businessmen. When threatened, they call on the support of the *real*, legitimate, non-sex business community, often successfully.

Unlike street-level pimps, the businessmen usually manage to hold onto their profits. They have investment skills, can afford lawyers, are seldom addicted, and rarely take the risks involved in more basic levels of crime. Often the greatest danger they face is from the Internal Revenue Service, not from the police.

Street-level pimps are the foot soldiers of the sex industry. Typically, they are small-time criminals who have a high need for sadistic gratification, and are heavy users of drugs and alcohol.

The johns and business-level pimps subcontract to these men the brainwashing, terror, beatings, and the occasional murder needed to keep prostituted women and children working.

Pimps are part of the business even where prostitution is legal. Brothels do not run employment ads. The brothel owners require that any new 'employee' be 'referred' by someone ready to supply whatever force is necessary to control the woman. The brothel operators often 'help' by calling the pimp when a woman leaves work, and telling him exactly when she left, and exactly how much money she had.

Street pimps learn the business from friends and relatives already in the business, from other criminals in jails and prisons, and from other pimps they meet hanging out in the bars and clubs. Occasionally, someone especially talented in greed and cruelty learns the trade solely by practicing on available victims.

Pimps tend to avoid identifying themselves as such, except to other pimps. They like to present themselves as husbands, boyfriends, or protectors. When caught in acts of violence, they try to prevent outside interference by claiming that it is 'only a domestic matter'. In fact, the pimps themselves are the greatest danger to those they exploit; the johns and the police are lesser hazards.

Street pimps pride themselves on their finesse, on controlling their victims by psychological manipulation. They claim that prostituted women and children give their money to the pimps because they 'love' them. (In criminal language, 'She loves me' means 'I can control her'.) Street pimps try to play down their use of threats and violence, despite the fact that it is their biggest contribution to the sex industry.

Throughout human history there has been the kind of greed that takes the form of wanting to own other human beings. Slavery died out in most areas because it was unprofitable compared to more modern methods of production. The one trade where the would-be slaver can still find success is in the sex industry. For many pimps, the gratification of owning slaves is as important as the drugs and the money.

Contrary to the images in the media, most pimps exploit members of their own race. Many are nearly the same age as their victims.

Most pimps are male, but women are becoming more and more involved as active operators in the sex industry. Some are involved in helping a male pimp to control his 'stable', or act as madams in brothels owned by someone else. Some run 'escort' or out-call services themselves, but maintain relationships through which they can call on male enforcers when needed.

Occasionally women are involved in supplying their own children to pedophiles, pornographers, or others in the sex industry. The mother's own addiction is the usual cause. Plain greed for money, and the mother's own sexual perversity are other motivations.

Street-level pimps usually spend their money on clothes, jewelry, cars, and especially on their own addictions. They are often involved in other types of crime, especially drug dealing, and may go to prison for those offenses. Successful prosecution for pimping itself is quite unusual. It is rare for a street pimp to hold onto his money and make the transition to a business-level operator, but there are always a few at the business level who started as street pimps.

Where the workers come from

The sex industry ultimately is about **power**. This is best demonstrated by the care which the industry takes to ensure that those it uses are powerless. The predators are neither irrational nor stupid. They watch carefully for a kind of 'victim profile', and avoid anyone who may be uncontrollable or dangerous.

They focus on young people coming out of families that are abusive, disorganized, or non-existent. One fundamental function of the family is protection of its members, especially its children. The family is also a team in which all players must do their jobs. If a member is lost or disabled, others in the extended family or community must step in to carry on. When one or more adults in a family are absent, addicted, mentally ill, or severely demoralized, the children are in danger.

When the family is poor, or is part of a devalued minority group, and where opportunities for education and good jobs are limited, some members of those families may be willing to take risks. If the young people are being terrorized, beaten, or sexually abused by the very people who should be protecting them, many are going to take their chances on the street. For some, nude dancing or even prostitution may look better than their previous life. If they are under age, have no address, or cannot afford to have their parents involved, most social service agencies will not help them. In some jurisdictions children are still treated as some adult's property.

The juvenile system has little interest in non-criminal runaways or 'throwaways'. There are minimum age requirements for normal jobs, usually between 14 and 18 years of age. The very young are practically forced into the sex industry, even before the pimps and johns get involved. They may have to do prostitution from the age of 12 or 14 until they turn 18, and can get a 'better job' such as nude dancing.

There are three general patterns for 'breaking' someone into prostitution. In **slave-taking**, a young male predator 'befriends' a victim long enough to be sure she herself is not dangerous, nor protected by anyone who is. He manipulates her into a situation where she can be kidnapped and held in isolation in a place the slaver and his friends control. Over a prolonged period, she is terrorized, tortured, and gang-raped. She is threatened with her own death and that of anyone she loves.

Once she is convinced that her only chance of survival is to do exactly as she is told, she is 'turned out'. Her first 'trick' may in fact be a member of the prostitution organization, in a set-up to make sure she performs as directed. After she has been properly 'seasoned', she is put to work for her captors, or sold to another pimp.

The **domestic violence transition** targets young people coming out of abusive homes who are emotionally needy, and have no real idea of what a normal loving relationship is like. They become involved with a 'boyfriend' who initially treats them better than they have ever experienced before. The boyfriend gradually becomes extremely controlling, and eventually violent. He introduces commercial sex in terms of his pressing need for money, and claims 'If you love me, you will do this'. He quickly transitions from 'Just this once' into 'You are just a whore—my whore!' and requires daily prostitution. He continues controlling the victim with alternating emotional manipulation and explosive violence, while living on her earnings, for as long as she lasts.

The **grooming** process is used by older and more sophisticated predators, and is especially used on younger children. These perpetrators become adept at identifying abused, neglected, and depressed children, and 'befriending' them. They develop a 'special' relationship, one that isolates the child from others, and makes the child feel indebted to the groomer. Slowly, resistance is broken down, using gifts, money, alcohol, drugs, and pornography. In the sex industry, pornography is not only a profitable product; it also is a working tool.

They engage the child in progressively more direct sex, and begin to merge the abuse into the child's identity: 'You want this', 'You like this', 'You make it happen', 'Now you are dirty, perverted, queer'. These predators are often only interested in children of a specific age or appearance. When the children develop beyond that, they may be passed off to pedophiles interested in older children. Being suddenly 'dumped' for no understandable reason often causes great emotional damage to the child.

Over a lifetime these predators may victimize an incredibly large number of children. The emotional damage they do leaves a child even more isolated and vulnerable to further involvement in the sex industry.

Gender differences

The experience of prostitution is remarkably similar for males and females, but there are some differences. Most young men used in prostitution are heterosexual. They are drawn into the sex industry by many of the same forces as apply for women except that pimps are less commonly involved. Many johns consider themselves straight, and claim that only the prostituted young male is gay. Those used in male-on-male prostitution are often left with tremendous confusion about their actual sexual orientation. When trying to escape 'the life', they may encounter all the prejudices encountered by gays, in addition to the stigma of prostitution. They are at higher risk of HIV than prostituted women.

Rape and sexual slavery are common in jails and prisons. There is considerable public support for it as a normal part of the punishment. Some of those who run institutions do their best to maintain a safe and controlled environment. They may be hampered by outdated buildings that are hard to supervise, and by a lack of staff. Others may care very little about what inmates do to each other. Inmates who go to staff for protection often end up in protective custody, which is practically the same as disciplinary isolation. The response of convicts toward 'snitches' ranges from abusive to deadly.

Almost all of these traumatized men are eventually released. Many dissolve into dependence on alcohol and drugs, or are disabled by psychological symptoms. Others wander the streets, intoxicated, armed, and ready to react explosively to any threat of harm or humiliation.

Women used in prostitution usually have children sooner or later. Mothers who cannot protect themselves can rarely protect their children. In the endless whirl of sex, drugs and violence, the children may be neglected, traumatized, or even become merchandise in the sex industry themselves. One of the most painful events in the life of a prostitute is losing custody of children, regardless of how good the reasons for that loss may be. Most prostituted women very much want to be good mothers, often trying to give their children the love and care they never received themselves. The birth of a 'trick baby', that is, one fathered by some unknown john, produces very complicated feelings. Some mothers can separate their feeling for the baby from the anger at the way the baby was conceived, but others cannot. Some 'trick babies' are given up for adoption by mothers who fear that they otherwise may abuse them.

If the baby was fathered by a pimp, or in official records is at least claimed to be, the courts may fail to recognize, or ignore, the real nature of the relationship. The pimp may be given visitation rights or even custody. This gives the pimp a new person to threaten and a new means of controlling the mother. It makes escaping from the sex industry even harder than it already is.

Both male and female survivors of prostitution usually develop a tremendous hatred of men, especially those in authority. They hate men both for the actual harm done, and for the help that was not given when it was terribly needed.

Society's role

Society at large provides the pimps with a very powerful weapon. It makes prostitution an **identity**, not an occupation. Once you have taken money for sex, you are a prostitute. Society does not allow an expiration date on that identity, nor a way to be publicly accepted as something else. Society offers help to people in trouble largely based on the value set on that person. It is much easier to get help for a married, middle-class victim of domestic violence than for a refugee from the sex industry trying to escape from a pimp.

Many people prefer to view prostitution as a 'lifestyle choice', or even as an 'addiction' to a lifestyle. They think that most people in the sex industry are there to support their drug habits, when actually the drugs are used to cope with what is happening to their lives. Society assumes that nothing can be done to help them, so there is no need to try; the pimps count on it.

Being trapped, under the control of violent and merciless men, without hope of outside help, sets the stage for Stockholm Syndrome. When the victim cannot successfully fight or flee, she may try to form a protective relationship with her captor. She hopes that if she can prove her love and loyalty to the pimp, she can 'love' him into being good. This can become such a desperate attachment that she actually believes she loves him, and passes up chances to escape. Stockholm Syndrome is often the real reason for what others see as the 'choice' to stay in the sex industry.

Prostitution and the drug trade go hand in hand. Customers for sex are also often buyers for drugs. Many pimps are supporting their own habits, and dealing drugs as well. The pimps consider drugs and alcohol a cost of doing business, as without the chemicals, their 'livestock' may become psychotic or commit suicide. In addition to the brainwashing and violence, addiction provides a form of control. Drugs also produce isolation from people who otherwise might try to protect a victim or help her escape. The only creature less worthy of help than a prostitute is an addicted prostitute.

The health effects of prostitution are devastating. Prostitution, especially in childhood, is at least as effective as war in producing post-traumatic stress disorder. Survivors usually have some combination of depression, anxiety, and dissociative disorders. Brain damage, psychosis, and suicide are common. Long-term psychiatric disability, serious medical illness, and the effects of accumulating injuries shorten lives.

Conclusion

People who have had luckier lives, as well as those who profit from the sex industry in some way, frequently refer to prostitution and pornography as 'victimless crimes'. They point to a tiny fraction of sex workers who actually might be involved by choice. They selectively read history to find some tiny minority, somewhere, at some time, who gained something in the sex business. The very selectiveness of their attention indicates that, on some level, they *know* that for *almost everyone*, involvement in the sex industry is a terrible misfortune. As many an old cop will say, 'Anyone who thinks prostitution is a victimless crime hasn't seen it up close.'

References

Herman, Judith Lewis. (1992). *Trauma and Recovery*. New York: Basic Books.

Jarranson, James M. and Michael K. Popkin (eds). (1998). *Caring for Victims of Torture*. Washington, DC: American Psychiatric Press.

Rebecca Whisnant

Confronting pornography:
Some conceptual basics

Porn takes over

There can be no doubt, at this moment in history, that pornography is a truly massive industry saturating the human community. According to one set of numbers, the US porn industry's revenue went from $7 million in 1972 to $8 *billion* in 1996 . . . and then to $12 billion in 2000.[1] Now I'm no economist, and I understand about inflation, but even so, it seems to me that a *thousand-fold* increase in a particular industry's revenue within 25 years is something that any thinking person has to come to grips with. Something is happening in this culture, and no person's understanding of sexuality or experience of relationships can be unaffected.

The technologies of pornography are ever more dynamic. Obviously, video porn was a huge step up from magazines and even from film. Not only was it cheap to rent and watch in privacy and anonymity, it was also easier and cheaper to make, thus opening up a huge amateur market. In the mid-1990s, *Playboy* ran a feature story on how to make your own amateur pornography, including tips and tricks on coaxing a reluctant female partner into participating.

Video is now old hat, of course; more recent developments include not only standard-issue web porn, but also elaborate and 'realistic' porn video games, websites where the consumer can cross-index porn stars with the kinds of sexual acts he wants to see them perform, and porn DVDs that enable the viewer to control the action and inject himself into it. One might expect that the advent of the web and internet porn would reduce the market for video porn rentals; instead, the relevant period of time saw rentals multiply nearly tenfold, from 75 million in 1985 to 721 million in 2000.[2]

Meanwhile, pornography has become so merged with big business that the two are hardly distinguishable. GM (via its subsidiary, DirecTV) now sells more porn films than Larry Flynt (Egan 2000). AT&T offers broadband cable

---

1   These numbers come from the companion website to a Court TV documentary entitled *Adults Only: The Secret History of the Other Hollywood*. See 'Porn Industry Facts' at http://www.courttv.com/archive/onair/shows/mugshots/indepth/hollywood/index.html (last accessed March 18, 2004).
2   See 'Porn Industry Facts,' cited in note 1.

subscribers a hardcore porn channel, and also owns a company that sells porn videos to nearly a million hotel rooms (Egan 2000). According to *Forbes* magazine, the contemporary legal pornography business is a $56 billion global industry (Dines 2003). Those who fear a government crackdown on pornography can rest easy: too many Fortune 500 companies are making megabucks from it for the US government to dream of getting in the way.

These depressing developments give us at least a ballpark estimate of the size and impact of the industry. However, as many commentators have pointed out, it is difficult to get a clear picture of the industry's size. On the one hand, much of the material is illicit and not measured in official numbers, and a great deal of it is free. On the other hand, there is always the risk that the industry's own numbers are inflated. Thus, it as (as always) useful to supplement statistics with an appeal to experience and common sense.

During my 15 to 20 years as an adult, the visibility of pornography in everyday life has exploded. One cannot avoid it. It pops up on the computer screen unbidden and screams out ads for itself in one's personal email. Larry Flynt advertises his Hustler stores on highway billboards, after being lionized as a hero of free speech in a major Hollywood movie. Meanwhile, glancing over into the next car while sitting at a red light may get you a look at a porn movie playing on the backseat DVD player (AP 3/10/04).

Sniggering jokes about porn in mainstream sitcoms and other TV shows are as common as dirt. Girls of ten and twelve know how to mimic the poses and conventions of the industry, having watched shows like *Can You Be a Porn Star?* on cable TV. Pornography has become the ultimate cool—quotidian and yet thrillingly audacious. Constant pop cultural references teach us that men's pornography use is both inevitable and completely legitimate, and that the way to be a cool, modern, liberated woman is to not only tolerate it but join in.

Take, as but one example, a subplot on a recent episode of the hugely popular sitcom *Friends*. Monica walks in on her husband Chandler masturbating to pay-per-view pornography in his hotel room—but due to his last-minute switch to the nature channel, she mistakenly assumes that he's into 'shark porn'. She's appalled but, like a good girl, she decides to play along and support his fetish—renting him nature videos about sharks, and offering to 'thrash around in the tub' for his sexual entertainment. When she realizes that he's just into regular porn—'just good old-fashioned girl–girl action', as he helpfully clarifies—she is thrilled and relieved. Meanwhile, he congratulates her as the 'best wife ever' for having been willing to play along with even a profoundly disturbing fetish. Lesson learned, roll credits.

'It looks like violence but it's not'

It's common for well-intentioned people to respond to feminist critiques of pornography by quickly intoning 'Well, of course I'm against the violent stuff'. While the attempt to distinguish the "violent stuff" from the rest of it was always a dicey proposition, ongoing changes in the content and emphasis of pornography have rendered the violent/nonviolent distinction almost entirely obsolete. This distinction is far too coarse to take account of what we perceive in contemporary pornography.

Some things in pornography never change: the body fragmentation, photographically cutting up women's bodies into isolated and fetishized parts; the sexualizing of childhood and the infantilization of adult women; the contemptuous and mocking cartoons; the bondage; the rape myths; the vacant, taken-aback, and/or fearful expressions on the women's faces. The precision of pornographic conventions, and their lack of fundamental variation, gives the lie to any suggestion that we are simply talking about any old descriptions or images of 'sex'.

At the same time, the industry is dynamic, both creating and responding to the cynicism and ennui of its consumers by constantly upping the ante. Martin Amis's 2001 *Guardian* article 'A Rough Trade', despite its generally sneering tone, nonetheless delivers some important information on changes in the industry and its effects on the women who participate in it. As Amis makes clear, the direction of the industry is toward 'gonzo', or pure and plotless succession of sex acts, with an emphasis on more 'extreme' activities. There is enormous pressure on women to engage in anal sex, double penetration (having her vagina and anus penetrated simultaneously), and even 'double anal' (having more than one penis penetrate her anus at once). A woman doesn't 'have' to do these things until her status in the industry has started to decline (which happens very quickly); at the same time, engaging in these acts lowers her status still further. Amis quotes Jonathan Morgan, a 'performer turned director', who explains it as follows:

> The girls could be graded like A, B, and C. The A is the chick on the boxcover . . . Here you have a borderline A/B doing a double anal. Directors will remember that. She'll get phone calls. For a double anal you'd usually expect a B or C. They have to do the dirty stuff or they won't get a phone call. You've had a kid, you've got some stretchmarks—you're up there doing double anal. Some girls are used in nine months or a year. An 18-year-old, sweet young thing, signs with an agency, makes five films in her first week. Five directors, five actors, five times five: she gets phone calls. A hundred movies in four months. She's not a fresh face anymore. Her price slips and she stops getting phone calls. Then it's, 'Okay, will you do anal? Will you do gang-bangs?' Then they're used up . . . The market forces of this industry use them up.

Amis's remarkably candid interviewees also make clear that mainstream pornography increasingly merges sex with violence and degradation, from spitting and choking to 'assbusting' and 'gangbanging', as well as of course the ever-essential 'facial' (in which the man ejaculates in the woman's face). Porn director John Stagliano, in discussing Rocco Siffredi, one of his favored male stars, observes that:

> Together we evolved toward rougher stuff. He started to spit on girls. A strong male-dominant thing, with women being pushed to their limit. It looks like violence but it's not. I mean, pleasure and pain are the same thing, right? Rocco is driven by the market. What makes it in today's market place is reality.

In other words, today's porn consumers are no longer satisfied with regular old ordinary male-dominant sexuality; there has to be an extra kick, an extra charge, and that comes from 'women being pushed to their limit'. And of course, note Stagliano's chilling recognition that this is, in fact, not mere fantasy but 'reality'.

Feminists who work against pornography know that, at a certain basic level, this material defies description—the depths of its hatred and erasure of women must be experienced to be believed. It is clear, however, that despite surface variations in the level of violence and contempt being openly expressed in different pornographic materials, the industry functions as a mutually reinforcing whole. As a whole, it is a form of hate propaganda, whose effects are especially powerful because it bypasses rational thought and goes straight for the jugular, as it were, conditioning the consumer to respond sexually to a fascistic sexual ideology.

I want to close this section by describing two pornographic images that, to me, capture the core of pornography's contempt for and endangerment of women. I am describing them from memory (thus without specific citation) because these are images that have stayed burned in my mind over a number of years since I actually saw them. Both are from pornographic magazines that students gave me some time in the 1990s when they knew I was doing feminist research and writing about pornography.

The first is from one of the thousands of relatively interchangeable porn magazines that line the shelves of adult bookstores across the country. I don't remember its title—nothing famous. In one of the numerous 'pictorials' was a photo of a woman's backside leaning over a chair in what looked like an ordinary living room. The photo shows only this one body part, more or less in close-up. The woman's anus is gaping and distended, misshapen, a black hole around an inch in diameter. It leaps off the page—something is horribly wrong. Anuses don't look like that. What has been done to her? How did it get like that? How does she feel about having this damaged, mutilated, ravaged bit of her anatomy displayed for men to jerk off on, about, into? We don't know—her face is hidden, gone, not relevant, not part of the picture. Her pain and humiliation, the damage already done to her, is front and center. A bulls-eye—here's where to hit, here's where to push. It doesn't matter— she's already broken. Her physical integrity is gone, the boundary of her body completely demolished. I cannot forget this picture.

The other is a cartoon sequence from an issue of *Hustler*, titled 'Why We Hate Women'. Each panel depicts some contemptible or objectionable female habit, like asking men to do laundry, whining about ill treatment, that sort of thing—I don't recall exactly. The panel I remember is the last one in the sequence. Its caption is 'they always want to cuddle after you fuck them'. The drawing is of a woman sitting up in bed, her face startled and hurt, taken aback. She is covered in ejaculate, literally drenched and dripping, as if a bucket of it has been emptied over her head. I cannot forget her expression.

This is where we are. This is 'reality'. We live in, and live out, the sexual reality that this material both constructs and reflects. From here on, I want to offer some reflections and suggestions about how we can think about it.

Conceptual basics

So many confusions surround our talk about pornography that it can be useful to introduce some elementary distinctions and conceptual clarifications. (Some of these points I will just touch on, since they have been made repeatedly and well by other authors; others have received less attention and so bear a bit more discussion here.)

Prostitution and pornography

It's common in everyday parlance to distinguish sharply between pornography and prostitution. Beyond the obvious fact that we use two different terms to refer to the two practices, many men who would regard patronizing a prostitute as beneath them see nothing wrong, pathetic or shameful in their use of pornography. Finally, of course, the legal status of prostitution—in the US at least—is very different from that of pornography. It is illegal (except in parts of Nevada) to purchase sex from a prostitute 'in person', as well as to be the one selling it; whereas the production and distribution of most pornography is legal. This legal difference, again, reflects a widespread public perception that prostitution and pornography are two very different things—and that pornography is either perfectly acceptable or, at least, 'less bad' than prostitution.

It is way past time to challenge this distinction. Pornography is the documentation of prostitution. It is a technologized form of prostitution— prostitution at one remove.

To see the point, consider an example. Suppose that Fred is making money by selling Gertrude's sex act to Harvey and reaping part or all of the proceeds. In short, Fred is a pimp. It then occurs to him that with this new technological innovation called the camera (or video camera, or webcam, etc.), he could sell Gertrude's sex act not just once, to Harvey, but many thousands of times, to many thousands of different men. In this way, he can make a great deal more money from this one sex act than he is making now. So Fred is happy. Meanwhile, Harvey will almost certainly pay less for his magazine or DVD or web site access than he would have paid for the act 'in person', so Harvey is happy. Everybody wins . . . oh yes, except Gertrude. She will probably not make any more money this way; she might well make less, even though her sex acts are now being sold far and wide, at enormous profit to the pimp and with enormous potential damage to her own privacy and safety.

The structure, logic, and purpose of Fred's activity have not changed. He is still a pimp. He has simply become more savvy and enterprising than he was back in his days as an ordinary street pimp. The basic elements of Gertrude's experience, similarly, have not changed: she is still exchanging sex acts for money. The only member of our original trio now having a significantly different experience is Harvey, who now has his sexual experience 'with' (at, on) Gertrude at some technological remove. He may like it this way or he may not, but keep in mind that he is getting the goods at a much lower price, with greater anonymity, and with the added benefit of not having to see himself as a john. Plus, if all that isn't enough for him, he can still seek out 'in-person' experiences with prostitutes if he wishes. So really, from his point of view, what's not to like here?

There is one other difference: namely, that the man onscreen actually performing the sex act (or having it performed on him) is being paid rather than doing the paying. So essentially, a male prostitute has entered the scene and is now participating alongside the female prostitute. But what of it? The basic structure of pimp, prostitute, and customer remains intact. (Changing the gender of one or more participants, of course, also would not change the basic structure.) Again, the transaction has simply become immensely more profitable for the pimp, while becoming cheaper, legally safer, and more anonymous for the customer.

Pornography *is* prostitution.[3] Our usual failure to see it this way is striking. Whose interests does that failure serve? Again, it benefits the pimps and johns, both of whom get to see their pornography-related activities as relatively

---

3   An exception to the analysis of pornography as prostitution will, of course, be the case of pornography that is merely written or drawn, rather than using the actions and images of actual living human beings.

respectable, rather than as mass-produced prostitution.

In this respect my analysis converges with those on the pro-pornography side who emphasize the connections and commonalities among different forms of 'sex work', from stripping to escort services to pornography to paid phone sex. Of course, their objective is to take this insight in the opposite direction: in their view, since pornography is both legal and widely regarded as innocuous, then so too should prostitution be. While I strongly disagree with that conclusion, perhaps we can all agree that it is time to start asking the question openly: if you think that there is a real dividing line between pornography and prostitution, such that the legal status quo makes sense, then how do you defend that position? What are the relevant differences between the two?

Even if we initially accept the distinction between pornography and prostitution, it soon starts to get blurry as we consider examples. If a man pays to access a website where he can instruct far-away women to perform particular acts for him via live webcam, is that pornography or prostitution?[4] Come to that, what about good old-fashioned 'live sex shows' and private dances in strip clubs? Here again, the man is paying to watch, rather than to actually do something or have it done to him. Often enough, even men who hire prostituted women in private want to *watch* them do something (sometimes with each other). Which is that—pornography or prostitution? Shall we say that something is prostitution if the woman is in the same room with the buyer, and otherwise it's pornography? What kind of pointless distinction is that?

It is perhaps also worth pointing out that the pornography industry shows a nearly inexhaustible capacity to blur the distinction between pimps and johns, turning one into the other with dizzying speed and regularity. The burgeoning market of 'amateur' porn is the direct descendant of time-honored traditions such as *Hustler*'s 'Beaver Hunt' feature, in which 'readers' are urged to send in 'beaver shots' of their wives and girlfriends, thus pimping the women in their lives. (It's impossible to know how many of these women were even aware of where these pictures were going—one risk that's less endemic to 'live, in person' prostitution than to pornography.) While the question of whether pornography causes rape is a perennial and important one, what definitely seems clear is that pornography 'causes'—that is, encourages and legitimates and inspires—pimping.

Not surprisingly, rape, pimping, and pornography sometimes converge in profoundly ugly ways. In *Our Guys*, Bernard Lefkowitz's fine book on the 1989 gang rape of a young retarded girl, he reports that the teenaged male

---

4   Donna Hughes's article in this volume makes clear how various new technologies continue to erode whatever rough-and-ready distinction may have once existed between prostitution and pornography.

perpetrators were in the habit of getting together in one of their basements to watch video pornography. After committing the gang rape, they planned to lure the victim down to the basement again so that this time they could videotape the assault.

Offense, harm, and coercion
Feminists have had some limited success in getting across that our problem with pornography concerns the harm it does, rather than the offense it causes. Offense, we have repeatedly stressed, is a way of feeling bad, which can usually be avoided or ended by avoiding the stimulus that triggers the bad feeling (hence the familiar refrain that 'anyone who doesn't like pornography doesn't have to look at it'). Harm is different. It is an objective condition, not a way of feeling; to be harmed is to have one's interests set back, to be made worse off, to have one's circumstances made worse than they were or than they would be in the absence of the thing that's doing the harm. Whether a person is harmed or not does not depend on how she feels. In fact, she can be harmed without even knowing about it—say, by having vicious lies about her spread behind her back, thus damaging her reputation and diminishing her opportunities. In contrast, no one can be offended without knowing about it, because offense is something that happens in one's head.

Feminists have claimed that the mass production and consumption of pornography harms women in general—by contributing to violence and discrimination against women, and by conditioning its users to respond sexually to women as inferiorized, fetishized objects who crave humiliation and degradation. We have also claimed that the pornography industry harms many, if not all, of the women who participate in it. Coercion and abuse is rampant in this industry—from the literal enslavement often associated with international sex trafficking, to women and girls who get filmed without their knowledge (remember those ubiquitous and slyly salacious pop-up ads for the tiny, easily hidden 'X2' video cameras?), to women whose husbands or boyfriends tell them that the pictures or videos being made of their sex life are 'just for us', when in fact he's uploading them to the internet (or does so later, after they break up).

In a sense, pornography critics have suffered from too much success in conveying this latter argument, in that now many people's only response when confronted with feminist critiques of the industry is 'but what about the women who *choose* . . .?' That is, by emphasizing the extent of coercion into the industry, we may have inadvertently made this seem to be the only issue of concern. And in a media environment where we all see breathless press accounts of women lining up eagerly to get into *Playboy* and *Penthouse* shoots, the coercion argument alone simply won't suffice.

I want to suggest that the issue of choice, consent, and coercion is at once both more and less central than we in the feminist anti-pornography movement have tended to make it. It is more central, in that coercion really is different from, and worse than, non-coercion; we need to avoid implying that there is no important difference between doing something voluntarily and being forced to do it. It is less central, in that we need to emphasize even more clearly that consent is not the *only* important issue. Let me now address these two points in turn.

Often, when confronted with critics who point out that 'some women choose' (and who myopically assume that this is a debate-settler), our response has been to question the very possibility of 'choice' or 'consent' under pervasive conditions of sexual (and sexualized) inequality, or sometimes even to imply that consensual prostitution is no better than prostitution that is outright forced. Such responses are neither necessary nor plausible. Choice and consent are not everything, but neither are they nothing. Typically, and other things equal, something consensual is *better* than that same thing non-consensual. That doesn't mean that it's good or even that it should be allowed, let alone encouraged—but it's at least somewhat less bad.

Granted, there are plenty of circumstances in which it's not clear whether consent is present or not. Consent is not a simple on/off switch, and it is important to be aware (and to make others aware) of the sexist social pressures, abuse histories, economic needs, and other factors that constrain and influence women's and girls' participation in the sex industry. If women's participation exists on a kind of continuum, with one end being 'fully free choice from a range of meaningful alternatives', and the other end being 'outright coercion and force' (say, having a gun to one's head), then probably most women in the industry are located somewhere in between these two extremes. Nonetheless, each of these endpoints is very different from the other one, and even from most of the midpoints. Choices made in the absence of better economic alternatives, or in the grip of pernicious ideologies, or even as a result of traumatic dissociation, are still choices, and are still significantly different from being forced.

Rather than always putting 'choice' and 'consent' in scare-quotes, we need to clarify what does and does not follow from the observation that something is a choice, or is consensual. That something is chosen or consensual is perfectly consistent with its being seriously oppressive, abusive, and harmful—to oneself and/or to a broader group of which one is a member (e.g. women).

What I am saying is that we need to think and talk somewhat differently about women who participate in the sex industry. Yes, many are coerced. Many are not coerced, but their choices to participate are made under far less than ideal conditions and result in significant harm to themselves. Finally, there may be some women (a relative few, to be sure) who choose participation in the sex industry from a meaningful range of options and who experience that participation as at least tolerable, and at best empowering. Certainly there are women who report this to be true of them, and while we may often suspect that a level of denial is operative, we need not assume a priori that denial or dissociation explains every such case. Rather we can grant, at least for the sake of argument, that such cases exist. The next question is, what of it? In particular, it seems to me that a useful next question would be this: on whose backs are they having this tolerable-to-empowering experience? What are the costs to women in general, and to the overwhelming majority of prostituted women in particular, of allowing this opportunity to those few (by definition relatively privileged) women who might freely and sincerely choose it for themselves?[5]

Many of those who enter and remain in the industry *voluntarily* are also grievously harmed by their participation in it. Coercion is only one kind of harm; there are others, and we need to explain what they are and why they are worthy of our serious attention.[6] As in other forms of prostitution, the rates of addiction (to both illegal street drugs and prescription drugs) are very high as women numb themselves to the continual objectifying intimate use of their bodies. Rates of sexually transmitted diseases are astronomical as well, with minimal health and safety protections for people working in the industry (Huffstutter 2003). Women in the industry report devastating effects on their capacity for intimate relationships: one 21-year-old interviewed by Martin Amis says, 'I don't have relationships any more. They make life unstable. The only sex I have is the sex on screen.' Again, recall that most women in this industry are very young. Women in their early twenties are likely to be washed-up, considered too old for 'Just 18' or 'Teen Sluts'. However they got where they are, the fact remains that (as Gail Dines puts it) 'No woman was put on this earth to be hurt or humiliated in order to facilitate male masturbation' (Dines 2003, p. 314).

Furthermore, we need to make clear—loudly and consistently—that pornography's broader social harms of gender subordination, commodified sexuality, and eroticized dominance *do not depend* on whether the persons

---

5   This point is especially important to make in response to those who point out that some women gain significant power in the industry by becoming producers themselves, rather than 'actresses'. Such women have become pimps, and need to be held accountable for the effects of their choices on other women—especially those they are pimping.

6   For example, go back to the picture I described earlier of the woman's damaged anus. Ultimately, what is the importance of knowing whether she 'consented' to take part in the industry, or even to the specific acts which led to that kind of bodily harm? In some sense we can hope that she wasn't forced, but whether she was forced or not, her body and no doubt her spirit are damaged beyond recognition.

depicted are participating voluntarily. That is, when we are asked, 'What about the women who choose?', we need to be less quick to respond, 'But do they *really* choose?', and more ready to explain why their choice (or lack thereof) is only one of many morally and politically relevant features of the situation. We also need to emphasize, continually, that the pornography industry—like prostitution more generally—does not ultimately exist because of women's choices. Rather it exists because men, as a class, demand that there be a sub-class of women (and children, and men, and transgender people—but mostly women) who are available for their unconditional sexual service.

It's bad to deceive, coerce, or force women (or men) into pornography. It's also bad to harm, objectify, and use up women (or men) who are not being deceived or coerced. And it's bad to use women (or anyone) in an industry that harms *other* women and that contributes to keeping women as a class subordinate to men—even if the particular woman being used is as free and fulfilled in her pornography career as anyone could possibly desire to be. No matter how implausible we may find the latter scenario, we still need to be clear that our analysis and critique of the industry do not depend on denying it.

'What can we do?'

To confront pornography and listen to the women hurt in it and by it, and still to cast pornography as merely a free speech issue, or as merely a matter of who feels offended by what, requires a stunning exercise of deliberate blindness, an extraordinary numbing of one's basic capacities of sympathy, moral identification, and outrage. It indicates that privilege is being defended with all the perceptual and conceptual resources at one's disposal—the privilege of being a man, yes, but also the relative comfort of being a woman who believes it cannot and will not happen to her.

Those of us who do understand the harms of pornography often wonder what we can do to fight against this powerful and ubiquitous industry. Beyond the usual (and important) responses about joining with others to resist the industry politically, I'd like to close with some additional suggestions about fending off pornography in our own lives.

Men: don't use pornography. Throw it away and start dreaming your own dreams about sex, women, men, and joy. Don't let this vicious industry lead you around by your dick. Don't kid yourself by saying, 'Well, I don't look at the really bad stuff. The woman doesn't look abused. Look, there she is having an orgasm.' Take yourself, and her, more seriously than that.

Also, don't let your friends use pornography without challenging them. You don't have to deliver a long feminist declamation—just let them know that you don't like pornography and don't want to be a part of seeing it or having it around. Let them call you pussy-whipped—you know better, and if you let them intimidate you by calling you names, then who is it that's really got you whipped? . . . As men, you have a lot of power to challenge pornography, because things you say (especially about gender-related issues) are taken to be more important and more likely to be true simply because you say them. This is sad and unfair, but you can use it in the service of justice. Let what you say matter. Allow yourself to make a difference.

Women: don't lie to yourself and say that this issue has nothing to do with you or your friends. Have the courage to recognize the truth of your vulnerability to violence and degradation. This is not 'victim feminism'. Having the courage to look at the truth and pass it on to others does not make you weak; it makes you strong.

And here's another challenge: demand that your intimate relationships be free from the polluting influence of pornography. This is a hard one, especially for straight women. It narrows the field of men for you to relate to a whole lot. It introduces the possibility, indeed the near-certainty, of conflict into the intimate relationships that you do have. It raises the specter of loss, of rejection, of being called every misogynist name in the book by men outraged at the affront to their masculine birthright. And every woman has to decide for herself what her own tolerance level will be, what compromises she will make with this industry that chews other women up and spits them out, to what extent she will put up with having the most intimate spaces of her relationship invaded by the pornography in her own lover's head. But I can't help fantasizing about a *Lysistrata*-like resistance[7] of heterosexual women saying, *en masse*, 'We will not date, marry, or have sex with men who use pornography. It's us or the dirty pictures—you pick.'

Regardless of the form(s) one's resistance takes, it is not easy to stand up against this powerful and pervasive industry—particularly since the industry and its supporters have polluted public discourse in ways that make it almost impossible to think clearly about it. The more we can keep the relevant concepts and issues clear in our own heads—including some of those I've discussed here—the less easily we can be manipulated and shut down.

As in all radical movements, it can also help to keep imagining what the justice we seek to create would look and feel like. Pornography as we know it, and the sexuality that it teaches us, is no more natural or inevitable than super-size fries and 60-inch TV screens. What would it be like to be free in our minds and in our relationships—free to create our own versions of sex, our own ideas about what it means to be a man or to be a woman? 'When equality is an idea

---

7   In *Lysistrata*, a comedic play by the Greek dramatist Aristophanes (c. 447–385 BCE), women from different states unite to end the Peloponnesian war by withholding sex from their husbands until the men agree to lay down their weapons.

whose time has come,' writes John Stoltenberg, 'we will perhaps know sex with justice, we will perhaps know passion with compassion, we will perhaps know ardor and affection with honor' (Stoltenberg 1990, p. 135). Could this time be tomorrow, or next week, or next year? What can each of us do *today* to bring it closer?

References

Amis, Martin. (2001). 'A rough trade'. *The Guardian*, March 17, 2001. Available at http://www.guardian.co.uk/weekend/story/0,3605,458078,00.html (last accessed March 18, 2004).

Associated Press, 'Call It Drive-By Porn'. March 10, 2004. Available at http://cbsnewyork.com/water/watercooler_story_070144339.html (last accessed March 18, 2004).

Court TV. *Adults Only: The Secret History of the Other Hollywood*. (TV documentary).

Court TV. 'Porn Industry Facts'. Available at http://www.courttv.com/archive/onair/shows/mugshots/indepth/hollywood/index.html (last accessed March 18, 2004).

Dines, Gail. (2003). From Fantasy to Reality: Unmasking the Pornography Industry. In Robin Morgan (ed.) *Sisterhood is Forever: The Women's Anthology for a New Millennium*. New York: Washington Square Press.

Egan, Timothy. (2000). 'Wall Street Meets Pornography'. *New York Times*, October 23, 2000. Available at http://www.nytimes.com/2000/10/23/technology/23PORN.html?ex=1079845200&en=1f5417e5ec2e83db&ei=5070 (last accessed March 18, 2004).

Huffstutter, P.J. (2003). 'See No Evil'. *Los Angeles Times*, January 12, 2003. Available at http://www.latimes.com/features/printedition/magazine/la-tm-pornjan12.story (last accessed March 18, 2004).

Lefkowitz, Bernard. (1998). *Our Guys*. New York: Random House.

Rich, Frank. (2001). 'Naked Capitalists: There's No Business Like Porn Business'. *New York Times Magazine*, May 20, 2001.

Stoltenberg, John. (1990). *Refusing to Be a Man: Essays on Sex and Justice*. New York: Meridian.

Robert Jensen

Blow bangs and cluster bombs:
The cruelty of men and Americans

During the Gulf War, the US military kept tight control of journalists to make sure that an already timid news media had no room to move. Copy had to be cleared by military censors, allegedly for security reasons, though the main fears of politicians and military officers concerning journalists are always political, not military.

One of the facts initially censored from a journalist's report during that war was that on the USS *John F. Kennedy*, pilots watched pornographic movies before flying missions, apparently to help get them pumped up to drop bombs. The censor told the journalist that the facts were too embarrassing to allow to be published (Kurtz 1991).

Embarrassing, but instructive: pornography and war are not the same endeavor, but the mass-mediated misogyny of modern pornography and the high-tech brutality of modern war share a common cruelty. Men pop a tape in a VCR. Men pop into jet planes. Men ejaculate onto women's faces. Bombs fall to the ground. Aggression is normalized.

My political life for the past dozen years has been anchored in resistance to the pornography of men and the wars of the United States; this is the struggle against patriarchy and empire. That means my life has been saturated with images of cruelty, from the intimate to the global.

Blow bangs

Blow Bang #4 is a videotape made and sold in America. It is a videotape that American men watch and masturbate to. It consists of eight different scenes in which a woman kneels in the middle of a group of three to eight men and performs oral sex on them. At the end of each scene, each of the men ejaculates onto the woman's face or into her mouth. The copy on the video box describes it this way: 'Dirty little bitches surrounded by hard throbbing cocks—and they like it.'

In one of these scenes, a young woman dressed as a cheerleader is surrounded by six men. For about seven minutes 'Dynamite' (the name she gives on tape) methodically moves from man to man while they offer insults such as, 'You little cheerleading slut.'

'—and they like it.'

28

For another minute and a half, she sits upside down on a couch, her head hanging over the edge, while men thrust into her mouth, causing her to gag.

'—and they like it.'

She strikes the pose of the bad girl to the end. 'You like coming on my pretty little face, don't you,' she says, as they ejaculate on her face and in her mouth for the final two minutes of the scene. Five men have finished. The sixth steps up. As she waits for him to ejaculate onto her face, now covered with semen, she closes her eyes tightly and grimaces. For a moment, her face changes; it is impossible to know exactly what she is feeling, but it looks as if she is going to cry.

'—and they like it.'

After the last man ejaculates, she regains her composure and smiles. The off-camera narrator hands her the pom-pom she had been holding at the beginning of the tape and says, 'Here's your little cum mop, sweetheart—mop up.' She buries her face in the pom-pom. The screen fades, and she is gone.

I watched *Blow Bang #4* as part of a project to analyze the content of contemporary pornographic videos. After several months, most of the images from those videos had faded from my mind. The one image I could not get rid of was 'Dynamite's' face right before Man #6 ejaculates onto her face.

Blow Bang #4 is one of about 11,000 new hardcore pornographic videos released in 2001, one of 720 million tapes rented in a country where total pornographic video sales and rentals total about $4 billion annually. When I watched #4, there were six tapes in the *Blow Bang* series. Ten months later, as I write this, there are 15. Why so successful? 'If you love seeing one girl sucking on a bunch of cocks at one time, then this is the series for you', a reviewer says. 'The camera work is great.'

Cluster bombs

The CBU-87, or cluster bomb, is made in America. It is a bomb that US pilots have dropped from US planes over Southeast Asia, Iraq, Yugoslavia, and Afghanistan.

Each cluster bomb contains 202 individual bomblets (BLU-97/B). The CBU-87s are a combined effects munition; each bomblet has an anti-tank and anti-personnel effect, as well as an incendiary capability. The bomblets from each CBU-87 are typically distributed over an area roughly 100 × 50 meters, though the exact landing area of the bomblets is difficult to control.

As the soda can-sized bomblets fall, a spring pushes out a nylon parachute (called the decelerator), which inflates to stabilize and arm the bomblet. The BLU-97 is packed in a steel case with an incendiary zirconium ring. The case is made of scored steel designed to break into approximately 300 preformed thirty-grain fragments upon detonation of the internal explosive. The fragments travel at extremely high speeds in all directions; this is the primary anti-personnel effect of the weapon. 'Anti-personnel' means that the steel shards will shred anyone in the vicinity.

The primary anti-armor effect comes from a molten copper slug. If the bomblet has been properly oriented, the downward-firing charge travels at 2570 feet per second and can penetrate most armored vehicles. The zirconium ring spreads small incendiary fragments. The charge has the ability to penetrate five inches of armor. The tiny steel case fragments are also powerful enough to damage light armor and trucks at 50 feet, and to cause human injury at 500 feet. The incendiary ring can start fires in any combustible environment.

Human Rights Watch, the source for this description (Human Rights Watch 2001), has called for a global moratorium on the use of cluster bombs because of the unacceptable civilian casualties the weapons cause. Those casualties come partly in combat, because the munitions have a wide dispersal pattern and cannot be targeted precisely, making them especially dangerous when used near civilian areas.

But even more deadly is the way in which cluster bombs don't work. The official initial failure-to-explode rate for the bomblets is five to seven percent, though some de-mining workers estimate that up to 20 percent do not explode. That means that in each cluster bomb, from 10 to 40 of the bomblets fail to explode on contact, becoming landmines that can be set off by a simple touch. Human Rights Watch estimates that more than 1600 Kuwaiti and Iraqi civilians have been killed, and another 2500 injured, by the estimated 1.2 million cluster bomb duds left after the 1991 Persian Gulf War.

What does that mean in real terms? It means that Abdul Naim's father is dead. The family's fields in the village of Rabat, a half hour from Herat in western Afghanistan, were sown with cluster bombs, some of the 1150 reportedly used in Afghanistan. Some of the farmers tried to clear their fields; some of them died trying. Naim told a reporter that out of desperation his father finally decided to take the chance. Using a shovel, the farmer cast three bomblets aside successfully. The fourth exploded. The shrapnel caught him in the throat (Goldenberg 2002).

Or consider this testimony from a 13-year-old boy in Kosovo:

> I went with my cousins to see the place where NATO bombed. As we walked I saw something yellow—someone told us it was a cluster bomb. One of us took it and put it into a well. Nothing happened . . . We began talking about taking the bomb to play with and then I just put it somewhere and it exploded. The boy near me died and I was thrown a meter into the air. The boy who died was 14—he had his head cut off.

The 13-year-old lived, but with both his legs amputated (Norton-Taylor 2000).

Why does the US military continue to use cluster bombs? According to General Richard Myers, Chairman of the Joint Chiefs of Staff: 'We only use cluster munitions when they are the most effective weapon for the intended target.'

Patriarchy and empire

What do blow bangs and cluster bombs have in common? On the surface, very little; pornography and war are different endeavors with different consequences. In pairing them, I am not making some overarching claim about the connection between patriarchy and empire. But I can say this: To be effective, contemporary mass-marketed pornography and modern war both require cruelty and contempt. The pornography I watched in the summer of 2001 was about the cruelty of men, and men's contempt for women. The war I watched in the fall of 2001 was about the cruelty of Americans and Americans' contempt for people in other parts of the world.

Although I have been involved in intellectual and political work around both issues for more than a decade, I was surprised at how strong my emotional reactions were to both the pornography and the war, and how similar they were, and just how deep the sadness went.

Pornography and war

Pornography and the wars of the US empire both depend for their success on the process of rendering human beings less-than-fully-human so they can be hurt—in the case of pornography to provide pleasure for men, and in war to protect the comfort of Americans. Women can be denigrated to provide sexual pleasure for men. A few thousand Afghan civilians can be sacrificed to protect the affluence of Americans.

I am against pornography and against the wars of empire. This confuses some of my left-wing allies, who also oppose the war but think pornography is about sexual freedom, and therefore wonder if I am a closet conservative. It also confuses some of my right-wing opponents, who cheer on the war but think all lefties are pro-pornography, and therefore wonder if I am a closet conservative. I am not a conservative, closeted or otherwise. I simply do not accept the liberal/libertarian assertion that pornography is about sexual freedom, nor the conventional wisdom that the United States goes to war for freedom.

A more compelling explanation of contemporary mass-marketed pornography is the radical feminist critique, which emerged from the wider movement against sexual violence in the late 1970s. The previous moral debate about obscenity between liberals and conservatives had pitted the critics of 'dirty pictures' against the defenders of 'sexual liberation'. The feminist critics shifted the discussion to the ways in which pornography eroticizes domination and subordination, how it reflects and helps maintain the second-class social status of women.

A more compelling explanation of the war in Afghanistan is the critique of the US empire. Terrorism is a serious problem, one that deserves serious attention from US policymakers, but the conflict in Afghanistan is not primarily a war on terrorism. A serious attempt to solve the problem of terrorism would be multilateral and sophisticated, attending to the need to bring terrorists to justice through legal means and also the need for a more just US foreign policy to make future terrorism less likely. Instead, the policy of the Bush administration, with the support of most of Congress, is unilateral and crude. It will not eliminate terrorist networks nor change the conditions in which terrorism breeds. It is, instead, an attempt by the most powerful nation on earth to extend and deepen its dominance in the world, toward the goal of guaranteeing that a small segment of the population can continue to enrich themselves and a larger segment can continue to live in relative affluence (Mahajan 2002, 2003).

Choices

A common rebuttal to these positions is that sex is natural and conflict is inevitable. That is true enough, and beside the point. Sexuality and conflict are unavoidably part of being human. But blow bangs and cluster bombs are not. Those are choices about how to deal with sexuality and conflict. Blow bangs and cluster bombs are neither natural nor inevitable.

It is true that both blow bangs and cluster bombs—pornography and the wars of empire—work. That is, they achieve certain results. Pornography produces sexual pleasure. Wars of empire protect the affluence of the empire. It is unclear how long they can work, whether sexual pleasure through pornography or affluence through the wars of empire can be sustained indefinitely. But that they work in the short term is undeniable. Men watch pornography and masturbate to orgasm. The United States fights wars and maintains its economic dominance.

But at what cost? The radical feminist critique of pornography has identified the cost of pornography to women and children, including the harm to the women and children who are used in the production of pornography, who have pornography forced on them, and who are sexually assaulted by men who use pornography. More generally, there is the harm that comes from living in a culture in which pornography reinforces and sexualizes women's subordinate status.

Right now, law ignores most of those harms and attempts to address others. But the realities of power and male dominance mean that even the laws that exist do very little in practice to stop the systematic abuse of women and children.

The costs of war are even more obvious, as we see the images from the battlefield on television and in the newspapers. We should also understand that war not only brings immediate death but a more widespread suffering long after the battles are over. The combination of high-tech weapons, television, and Pentagon PR has allowed Americans to ignore the obvious, and to believe that the suffering in war is limited. So, the United States can violate the Geneva Conventions with impunity—officials illegally target civilian infra-structure (such as they did in Iraq in 1991, destroying water and sewage treatment facilities and electrical stations, the direct cause of tens of thousands of deaths during the war and in the few months after its end) and use indiscriminate tactics and weapons (such as depleted-uranium weapons in Iraq and Yugoslavia, the long-term health effects of which remain unknown). For this, the officials are applauded in the mainstream for their humanitarianism.

Men who use pornography want to believe that pornography is natural and inevitable so that they don't face the obvious question: By what right do I gain pleasure at the expense of others? Americans protecting their affluence want to believe that the wars of empire are natural and inevitable so that they don't face the obvious question: By what right do I live so comfortably at the expense of others?

Sexuality is natural and conflict is inevitable. How we deal with sexuality and conflict involves choices. We could choose to create a sexuality rooted in an egalitarian ethic of mutuality and respect. We could choose to create a world order rooted in an egalitarian ethic of mutuality and respect. In such a world, blow bangs and cluster bombs would not exist.

Other choices

The costs of pornography and the wars of empire are borne mainly by those in the subordinated position. But there is a cost to those of us in the dominant position, not on the same scale, but a cost all the same.

When men make the choice to acquire sexual pleasure through blow bangs, we forgo part of our humanity. When Americans make the choice to protect our affluence through cluster bombs, we forgo part of our humanity.

Both of those claims are based on specific ideas about what it means to be a human being, ideas that are very much at odds with patriarchy and the empire.

Not blow bangs

In the sexual sphere, I am suggesting that being human is about something more than physical pleasure.

This is not an argument for self-denial or for some traditional notion of sexuality within conventional heterosexual relationships. I am neither a sexual ascetic nor a sexual fundamentalist. I do not believe there is anything wrong with physical pleasure, nor do I believe that physical pleasure can properly be experienced only between two people of the opposite sex who are married.

But I do believe that sexuality can be about more than pleasure. It can be about finding pleasure and intimacy through connection. I use the metaphor of heat and light. There is a cliché that when an argument is of little value, it produces more heat than light. One of the ways this culture talks about sex is in terms of heat: She's hot; he's hot; we had hot sex. Sex is bump-and-grind; heat makes the sex good.

But what if our embodied connections could be less about heat and more about light? What if instead of desperately seeking hot sex, we searched for a way to produce light when we touch? What if such touch were about finding a way to create light between people so that we could see ourselves and each other better? If the goal is knowing ourselves and each other like that, then what we need is not heat but light to illuminate the path. How do we touch and talk to each other to shine that light? There are many ways to produce light in the world, and some are better than others. Light that draws its power from rechargeable solar cells, for example, is better than light that draws on throw-away batteries. Likewise, there will be many ways to imagine sex that produces that light. Some will be better than others, depending on the values on which they are based.

So, here's my pitch to men: Even if we have no concern for anyone else, the short-term physical pleasure we gain through pornography is going to cost us something: we lose opportunities for something more. Heat is gained, but light is lost.

I believe men—even the most boisterous macho men posturing about sexual conquests—understand that at some level. We understand that the acquisition of that kind of physical pleasure at the expense of women also comes at the expense of our own humanity. I am not just generalizing from my own experience; this is a consistent theme in my exchanges with men, both in formal research interviews and informal conversation. When most of us strip away our sexual bravado, there is a yearning for something beyond the quick pleasures of the pornographic.

During a discussion of sexual experiences, I once heard a man say, 'There is no such thing as a bad orgasm.' I assume that he meant getting off was getting off; no matter what the circumstances or methods, it was always good. But I want to believe that underneath that flippant remark, he knew better. That is to say: I believe we men can be human beings, too.

Not cluster bombs

In the social sphere, I am suggesting there is something more to being human than protecting affluence.

Most people in the United States take for granted a standard of living that the vast majority of the world can barely imagine and can never expect to enjoy. Most of us can recite the figure that the United States has about five percent of the world's population yet we consume about 25 percent of the world's oil and 30 percent of the gross world product. But relatively few want to understand the relationship between that affluence and foreign policy and military intervention.

A clear statement of the connection came in February 1948 in a top-secret US State Department document, Policy Planning Staff memorandum 23, which defined US post-war policy in Asia, focusing in particular on Japan and the Philippines. George Kennan, the first Director of the State Department's Policy Planning Staff, wrote:

> We [Americans] have 50 percent of the world's wealth but only 6.3 percent of the population. This disparity is particularly great between ourselves and the peoples of Asia. In this situation, we cannot fail to be the object of envy and resentment. Our real task in the coming period is to devise a pattern of relationships which will permit us to maintain this position of disparity without positive detriment to our national security (Policy Planning Staff 1948).

For Americans to live our level of affluence, people around the world (and an increasingly large number of people in the United States) must suffer some level of deprivation. There is no other way to maintain the position of disparity.

Yet all the while that we are living that affluence and accepting the imperial system that guarantees it, we are also talking about how materialism is negatively affecting our lives. People can see themselves trapped in the endless cycle of making money to finance a lifestyle that gives them the luxuries to make bearable the work they do to earn the money to maintain the lifestyle. Parents give their children every possible electronic amusement device, and then lament their children's lack of interest in something beyond the screen. We accept a consumer culture that produces households that eliminate the possibility of meaningful interaction among members of the household, and then we wonder why our houses, full of so many products, feel so empty.

So, here's my pitch to Americans: Affluence has made us comfortable. It also has cut us off from certain kinds of experiences; it has enriched us in one sense while impoverishing us in a much more important way. What we have gained in the short run will be balanced by a catastrophic loss in the long run.

I believe that Americans—even people who claim to love their wealth and status without question—understand that at some level. We understand that the truism 'money can't buy happiness' is indeed true, and when we deny that, not only do vulnerable people around the world suffer, but we lose something as well. If we are willing to accept that suffering simply to indulge and insulate ourselves, we lose our humanity.

After a talk I gave about US policy in the Middle East, a man came up to argue. He said bluntly that he thought the United States should dominate the region to make sure that we would always control the world's oil supplies. I asked what he was willing to do to ensure that—would he be willing to use massive force? 'Nuke 'em,' he said. I assume that he meant that, in the end, force was the only way to protect affluence, and affluence had to be protected. But I want to believe that underneath that flippant remark, he knew better. That is to say: I believe that we Americans can be human beings, too.

Justice and self-interest

I think there are clear arguments from justice for rejecting mass-marketed pornography and the wars of empire. But I know that such arguments are not persuasive for everyone, which is why I also am suggesting there are compelling arguments from self-interest—if we can go beyond very narrow understandings of self-interest and embrace a fuller and richer conception of our own humanity. When I say that we men and Americans can be human beings, that is what I mean—for people with power and privilege to become fully human, we must imagine a different kind of self-interest. The traditional traits associated with masculinity in this culture are domination, toughness, hyper-competitiveness, emotional repression, aggressiveness, and violence. That also describes the posture of the United States in the world. In both cases, there is sometimes a veneer of kindness. In gender relations it is called chivalry. In world affairs it is called humanitarianism. In both cases, it is a cover for maintaining control. In both cases, we must abandon the veneer and honestly face a simple question: What kind of people are we when we allow pleasures and comforts not only to trump the cries of others but also to drown our own humanity?

The paradox is that those of us in positions of privilege and power—those who may seem most likely to want to keep the systems as it is—have the material resources to create the conditions under which truly progressive change can happen. We can refuse to continue to exercise that power in unjust ways and resist those who exercise that power in our name.

Here, again, is the pitch: letting go of power and privilege—forgoing some of the material rewards that come with them—offers other rewards. Letting go of blow bangs creates the space in which a new intimacy and sexuality can flourish. Letting go of cluster bombs creates the space in which we can rethink our own affluence and allow new relationships between people to emerge. In both cases, the rejection of domination also has an intrinsic reward at the moral level. That reward is routinely ignored or laughed off as being ridiculously idealistic. When such rewards are talked about at all in the dominant culture, they are usually framed in terms of an afterlife, in a spiritual realm. But they are very much the rewards of this earth, rewards of mind and body, and if they are to be enjoyed they must be made real here and now.

Pornography and the wars of empire are based on the idea that domination is natural and inevitable. I am anti-pornography and anti-war because I believe that domination is a choice, the rewards of which are seductive but in the end illusory. I believe that love, compassion, and solidarity can anchor our lives at every level, from the intimate to the global.

I also believe that to build a world based on love, compassion, and solidarity, we who have privilege and power must be ruthlessly honest with ourselves and each other, in ways that will undoubtedly seem harsh and cause us great pain. We may wish there was another way out, but the lesson of my life is that there is no other path. The most important choice we have to make is to step onto that path, understandably afraid of where it may lead but safe in the knowledge that along the way we can find our own humanity.

References

Goldenberg, Suzanne. (2002). 'Long after the Air Raids, Bomblets Bring More Death,' *Guardian* (UK), January, 28, p. 12.

Human Rights Watch. (2001). 'Cluster Bombs in Afghanistan'. Available at http://www.hrw.org/backgrounder/arms/cluster-bck1031.htm (last accessed May 7, 2004).

Kurtz, Howard. (1991). 'Correspondents Chafe Over Curbs on News; Rules Meant to Protect Troops, Officials Say'. *Washington Post*, January 26, p. A-17.

Mahajan, Rahul. (2002), *The New Crusade: America's War on Terrorism*. New York: Monthly Review Press.

Mahajan, Rahul. (2003). *Full Spectrum Dominance: US Power in Iraq and Beyond*. New York: Seven Stories.

Norton-Taylor, Richard. (2000). 'Cluster Bombs: The Hidden Toll,' *Manchester Guardian* (UK), August 2.

Policy Planning Staff. (1948). 'Review of Current Trends/US Foreign Policy.' *Foreign Relations of the United States* 1948, Vol. 1, Part 2, pp. 524–525.

Donna M. Hughes

The use of new communications and information technologies for sexual exploitation of women and children

Introduction

New communications and information technologies have created a global revolution in communications, access to information, and media delivery. These new communications and information technologies are facilitating the sexual exploitation of women and girls locally, nationally and transnationally. The sexual exploitation of women and children is a global human rights crisis that is being escalated by the use of new technologies.[1] Using new technologies, sexual predators and pimps stalk women and children. New technical innovations facilitate the sexual exploitation of women and children because they enable people to easily buy, sell and exchange millions of images and videos of sexual exploitation of women and children.

These technologies enable sexual predators to harm or exploit women and children efficiently and anonymously. The affordability and access to global communications technologies allow users to carry out these activities in the privacy of their home.

The increase of types of media, media formats, and applications diversifies the means by which sexual predators can reach their victims. This paper will not attempt to categorize all the types and uses of this new technology; however, it will describe the most common and newest of these technologies, and how they are used for the sexual exploitation of women and children.[2]

---

1 For the purpose of this paper, I use the term 'sexual exploitation' to refer to trafficking for purposes of sexual exploitation, commercial sex acts, such as prostitution, pornography, and live sex shows, stalking for purposes of sexual assault or abuse, and all forms of child sexual abuse.

2 This paper is not about strict legal definitions, nor is it about the law. In fact, many experiences of women and children fall into gray areas, rather than conform to existing definitions. Also, much of the research on sexual exploitation and the internet focuses on images, and the people in the images are rarely available for interviews to describe their experiences, their consent or coercion, their freedom or slavery. The extent to which the experiences of these women and children meet existing legal criteria for crimes is beyond the scope of this article.

New and old technologies combined

Older technologies, like television and cable, are now combined with modern technologies to create new ways of delivering information, news, and entertainment. Web TV combines the television with the internet. New cable networks use satellite transmission to deliver hundreds of channels, and pay-per-view delivers content on demand (Hughes 2001).

Presently, there is a high demand for pornographic videos through mainstream communication networks such as cable TV (Li 2000). Only one of eight major cable companies in the United States does not offer pornographic movies (Rich 2001, p. 51). Satellite and cable companies say that the more sexually explicit the content, the greater the demand. Adult Video News reports that pornography offerings on TV by satellite or cable are increasing video store sales and rentals, not decreasing them, as might be expected. The explanation is that pornography on TV is advertising pornography and finding new buyers. The mainstreaming of pornography is increasing the exploitation or abuse of women and children used in making pornography. According to Paul Fishbein, owner of Adult Video News, anything sells:

> There are so many outlets [for the videos] that even if you spend just $15,000 and two days—and put in some plot and good-looking people and decent sex—you can get satellite and cable sales. There are so many companies, and they rarely go out of business. You have to be really stupid or greedy to fail. (Rich 2001)

Another producer said:

> [A]nyone with a video camera can be a director—there are countless bottom feeders selling nasty loops on used tape. Whatever the quality or origin of a product, it can at the very least be exhibited on one of the 70,000 adult pay Web sites, about a quarter of which are owned by a few privately held companies that slice and dice the same content under different brands. (Rich 2001)

As a result of the huge market on the web for pornography and the competition among sites, the pornographic images have become rougher, more violent and degrading. One producer claimed that there were 'no coerced' performances in pornography videos, although she immediately acknowledged that 'there are little pipsqueaks who get their disgusting little (misogynistic) videos out there' (Rich 2001). The 'misogynistic porn' this producer refers to involves degrading images, such as ejaculation on the woman's face, real pain, and violence against women that results in physical and emotional injuries (Amis 2001).

In the last ten years, some American and European pornography producers have moved to places such as Budapest in Hungary because of the availability of cheap actors from Eastern and Central Europe (Singer 2001). Budapest is a destination and transit city for women trafficked from Ukraine, Moldova, Russia, Romania, and Yugoslavia (Lukyanov n.d.). There are hundreds of pornographic films and videos produced each year in Budapest (Singer 2001). Budapest is now the biggest center for pornography production in Europe, eclipsing rivals such as Amsterdam and Copenhagen.[3] Most Western European producers of sex videos use Eastern European actors whenever possible. An executive at Germany's Silwa production company explained: 'They cost less and do more. Even excruciating or humiliating acts usually cost only two or three hundred dollars.'[4]

The postal service, traditionally the most anonymous and popular way to transmit pornography, is still used by collectors and producers of child pornography to distribute the pornography. Now, sending materials through the mail is combined with internet technology. Raymond Smith of the US Postal Inspection Service, who handles hundreds of cases of child pornography, has found that the rise in internet use by sexual predators has also increased their use of the US mail service.[5] He said that from the time they first started investigating child pornography in the early 1980s until five years ago, they had almost eliminated the distribution of child pornography. But since the internet became publicly available, the number of cases connected to the internet has steadily increased. In 1998, 32 percent of cases were related to the internet. In 1999, 47 percent were internet-related, and in 2000, this had risen to 77 percent.

Producers of child pornography advertise their videos on the internet and distribute them through the mail. Men in chat rooms trade small files, still images and short movie clips on the internet, but longer movies are sent by mail. Stalkers talk to children in chat rooms, ask them to take pictures of themselves, and send them through the mail. When stalkers convince children to travel to meet them, they send them bus and plane tickets through the mail.

McLaughlin (2000) states that scanners and video digitizers are used to turn old pornographic images, films, and videos into electronic formats that can be uploaded to the internet. About half of the child pornography online is old images from films and magazines produced in the 1960s and 1970s. Digital cameras and recorders enable the creation of images that do not need professional processing, thereby eliminating the risk of detection. These new types of equipment also make it technically easier for people to become

---

3   'To Its Buyers and Sellers, The Sex Trade is Just Another Busine$$'. Available at http://www.pirko.de/Englisch/lustig/Sex.html (last accessed March 23, 2002).

4   'The Sex Industry: Giving The Customer What He Wants', *The Economist*, February 14, 1998, p. 21.

5   Interview with Raymond Smith, Fraud, Child Exploitation and Asset Forfeiture Group, Office of Criminal Investigations, US Postal Inspection Service (May 7, 2001).

producers of pornography. Digital media formats are neither static nor independent. One format can be quickly converted into another (Hughes 1999). Videos are still the primary production medium for child pornography, and the still images for the internet are produced from video captured images (Taylor 2001). From one video, 200–300 still images can be captured, and then uploaded to a newsgroup or to a website. According to the COPINE (Combating Paedophile Information Networks in Europe) Project, production of child pornography still combines older methods of production, while using new internet technologies for distribution.

> It is safe to say that the number of manufactures [sic] [producers of child pornography] has increased over the years with the availability of new medium [sic]. Home development of black-and-white 35mm film, self-developing Polaroid film, video cameras, camcorders, computer scanners, CU-SeeMe technology [live video and audio transmission] and now computer cameras (including video) have made child pornography easier and easier to produce and reproduce. (McLaughlin 2000)

One police analyst noted that prior to the internet the majority of collectors of child pornography were not distributors because duplication technology was not readily available. Now, making copies of image files 'involves a few clicks of any computer mouse allowing for effortless distribution' (McLaughlin 2000). Therefore, collectors of child pornography have quickly and easily become distributors.

New technologies for sexual exploitation

Digital Video Disk (DVD)

One new technology is Digital Video Disk (or Digital Versatile Disc; DVD), which provides high quality videos and interactive capabilities for the viewer. While making the videos, scenes can be shot from multiple angles, and all points of view can be added to a CD-ROM. The viewer can then choose the version, point of view, or camera angle he/she prefers. Viewers can watch the movie in chronological order, moving from one character to the next, or watch the movie from one character's point of view. Viewers can interact with DVD movies in much the same way they do with video games, giving them a more active role (Kaplan 2001). According to one producer:

> If a viewer wants something different, we give it to him. The viewer can go inside the head of the person having sex with [name deleted], male or female. He can choose which character to follow. He can re-edit the movie. It's a great technology. (Rich 2001)

The following is a description of a recent pornographic movie recorded on DVD:

Chasing Stacy from VCA Labs, is a choose-your-own-adventure flick that follows Stacy the porn star as she signs autographs, drinks coffee, works out at the gym and takes a shower. At various points, a small green icon appears in the corner of the screen and Stacy looks straight at the camera. That's when viewers get the chance to ask Stacy out on a virtual date by pressing the Enter button on the DVD remote control. The date scenes are filmed so that the viewer feels like he's sitting directly across a glass table from Stacy, who provides insights into her personal life. Later, the viewer can select whether to take Stacy back to her house, to her office, or to another locale for a tryst. With the remote control, the details can be chosen as the action unfolds. (Kaplan 2001)

The pornography producer, VCA, released this DVD in July 2000 and sold more than 12,000 copies by January 2001, making it their fastest-selling title (Kaplan 2001).

Although technologies like this have many applications and enable creativity and interactivity, when used in pornographic films, these raise the question of the impact on people, their relationships, and expectations about relationships. A portion of men who use pornography and seek out women in prostitution do so either because their lack of social skills or their misogynistic attitudes prevent them from establishing relationships with their peers (Parker 2002). Technology such as this may further distance and alienate some men from meaningful and realistic relationships (Hughes 2001).

There are a number of venues and media formats with different technologies for the transfer of files and communications, including Usenet newsgroups, World Wide Web, email, live synchronous communication (text and voice chat), bulletin or message boards, Web cams for live transmission of images or videos, live video conferencing (live video chat), streaming video, peer-to-peer servers, and file sharing programs (Hughes 2001). All forums and applications offer ways to engage in the sexual exploitation of women and children (Hughes 2001).

How each is used for sexual exploitation depends on the legality of the activity, which varies from country to country, the techniques adopted by the sex industry or individual users, and the level of privacy or secrecy attempted by the users (Hughes 2001). Perpetrators have taken advantage of new technologies and applications to stalk victims, transmit illegal materials, and avoid detection by law enforcement (Hughes 2001). According to one official: 'If it can be done, they're doing it.'[6]

---

6   Interview with Glenn Nick, US Customs Smuggling Center (May 17, 2001).

Newsgroups
Usenet newsgroups are still popular sites for the exchange of information on how to find women and children for sexual exploitation (Taylor *et al.* 2001). Although much media attention is given to child pornography rings that use sophisticated technologies to keep their activities secret, such as the Wonderland Club that used a Soviet KGB code to encrypt all its communications, the older public newsgroups are still commonly used to upload and download child pornography (Miller 1998). The COPINE Project reports that over 1000 child pornographic images are posted on newsgroups each week (Taylor *et al.* 2001).

Websites
Websites are used in various ways to assist in the sexual exploitation of women and children. Websites are the most popular venue for the distribution of pornography online. Large legal sex industry businesses have sophisticated websites with subscription fees that bring in millions of dollars per year. There are also tens of thousands of free pornography sites that are maintained by amateurs or someone making a relatively small amount of money from advertising banners for larger sites and businesses. Websites offer streaming videos that can be viewed with web browser plug-ins (Taylor *et al.* 2001). The most recent versions of web browsers (e.g. Internet Explorer, Netscape) come packaged with these plug-ins (Hughes 2001).

Pimps and traffickers use the web to advertise the availability of women and children for use in making pornography (Hughes 1999). One example includes prostitution tourists and Western producers of pornography who have been traveling to Latvia since the early 1990s to find vulnerable children and young adults to sexually exploit in their videos.[7] In August 1999, the vice police in Latvia initiated criminal proceedings against the owners of Logo Center, a 'modeling agency', for production of pornography and the use of minors in the production of pornography. The two managers of the Logo Center provided women and children to foreign prostitution tourists and foreign pornography producers. They had several websites with pornography, information about minors, and photographs of their 'models' in different sex acts.[8] (Websites: logosagensy.com, pronorussian.nu, marige.nu, and logosagensy.nu; these websites are no longer available on the internet, but are on file with the author.) During the time these pimps operated they exploited approximately 2000 women, men, girls and boys, resulting in 174 juveniles relying on prostitution for their basic livelihood.

---

7 Personal communication with Valdis Pumpurs, Head of the Criminal Police of Latvia (May 2001).
8 Personal communication with Valdis Pumpurs.

The Logo Center supplied women and children for pornography production in other countries. In one case they supplied 'porno models' to a Swedish pornography producer who made videos in Finland. The Logo Center website had links to other sites with bestiality and child pornography. After being arrested, the two owners were charged with distribution of child pornography.

Pimps also use websites to advertise their brothels or escort services directly to men (Hughes 1999). These sites are often used to attract foreign businessmen or tourists (Hughes 1999). The following is from a website in Prague in the Czech Republic:

> Would you like to spend an exciting night in Prague with a beautiful young girl? She will do everything for your pleasure. She will make you happy with kissing you on your mouth, French sex and sexual intercourse. During your stay, you can visit the 'Golden City' with your girl. The girls are pupils and students, who are financing their education.[9]

Increasingly, prostitution websites include photographs of the women, sometimes nude. This practice exposes women, identifying them to the public as prostitutes. Many of the photographs look like modeling photographs, and the women may never have intended for those photographs to be used to advertise them as prostitutes. Some of the women may not even know their photographs are on websites. Women suffer from the stigma placed on them for being in prostitution.[10] This public display and labeling further harms women in prostitution (Hughes 1999).

Web-based message boards and bulletin boards are increasingly popular for an exchange of information by perpetrators of sexual exploitation. They are used in much the same way as newsgroups, but can be private and protected by passwords. Using these applications, men can book sex tours and 'appointments' with women through the web, email and chat rooms (Hughes 2001).

Message boards on brothels' websites enable men to post 'reviews' of the women for other men, and communicate with pimps about the women's appearances and 'performances'. On sites where the women's photos are displayed, men can evaluate the women:[11]

---

9   'Milas Holiday and Escort Service in Prague', http://www.prag-girls.de/frame-hallo.htm (last accessed April 21, 2001; no longer available online, but on file with author).

10 See generally *Coalition Against Trafficking in Women, Making the Harm Visible: The Global Sexual Exploitation of Women and Girls* (Donna M. Hughes and Claire M. Roche (eds), (1999)).

11 'Milas Holiday and Escort Service in Prague'.

Alina's new photos indicate that she has gained some extra weight!! Please advise what is her weight currently. Thanks and regards . . .

Another example includes:

Dear Milla:
What happened to Alina? She seems that she gained some weight since the last time she was with you. She must not be 52kg as written on her page. Please advise her exact weight.

Men use message boards to make reservations for their upcoming visits. A website for a brothel in Prague in the Czech Republic had the following message and request:

Hallo Mila!
I found your page on the internet. I'm going to Prague this summer and probably will visit your establishment. How long time before do one have to make reservations? Could you please put out som more photos of the girls. Is there also possible to have analsex with the girls if you stay overnight ? See you ! /Peter

Another posting included:

I understand from our talk, by telephone you have, 6 girls our more, ATT the time, girls are from Ukraine. I will be in Praha, late August 2000, So I will arrive to Praha, late at night, if I remember rite, me flights is from Iceland to Copenhagen and from Copenhagen to Praha. do you have some taxi our pick up from the airport? I wold like to stay in your house the first 2 nights when I am testing your girls after that I will know which of your girls I like. I will chosen one of them to stay in me hotel four 2 nights, so I will have one of your girls, one hour at the time in your house before I chosen which one I chosen to stay with me in me hotel, is that ok with you? I understand you have 6 girls, I wold prefer to have sex with all of them, and then chosen one of the to stay in me hotel four 2 night after thatch, is thatch ok with you? Are your girls shaved? Ragnar . . .

Websites are also used to market images and videos of rape and torture (Hughes 1999). Slave Farm, a website registered in Denmark, claims to have the 'world's largest collection of real life amateur slaves.'[12] Men are encouraged to 'submit a slave to the picture farm'. The images include women being subjected to sexual torture, bondage, and fetish sadism. Descriptions of images include: 'needle torture', 'hot wax', 'extreme hogtie', 'hanging bondage', 'tits nailed to board', 'drunk from the toilet', and 'pregnant bondage'. Live chat is available where men can 'command the bitches'. A

12 'Slave Farm', available at http://www.slavefarm.com ('the world's largest amateur BDSM site') (last accessed March 19, 2002).

number of images are available free, but full access requires payment of a subscription fee. The women in the images and videos are visibly injured, with cuts, burns, bruises, welts, and bleeding wounds.

Another website registered in Moscow advertises itself as 'the best and most violent rape site on earth'.[13] It claims to have 'Several Hunders [sic] of rape pics.' Subscribers are offered 30,000 hardcore porn images, 500 online video channels, and 100 long, high-quality videos. There are images and videos of 'violent rapes, ass rapes, mouth rapes, gang rapes, nigger rapes, torn vaginas, and tortured clits'. A free 13MB video and audio movie can be downloaded in 12 segments, each about 1MB. The film shows a hooded perpetrator raping a woman in an office.

Previously, few people had access to such extreme material. As one consultant explained:[14]

> [f]ormerly men used to have to remove themselves from their community by three levels [to find extreme, violent pornography]. First, they had to go somewhere, physically, then know where to go, and then know how to find it. The Web makes it very easy to get that far removed very quickly.

The resurgence of child pornography through the internet is a priority for some law enforcement agencies, resulting in unparalleled international cooperation to break up the rings (Hughes 2001). In contrast, the pornography of adults and post-adolescent teens has been ignored (Hughes 2001). In the United States and Europe there are very few cases of prosecution of producers of adult and post-adolescent teen pornography.

A lot of the pornography is extremely misogynistic, with women portrayed as seeking and enjoying every type of humiliation, degradation, and painful sex act imaginable (Hughes 2001). Women and children are harmed physically, sexually, and emotionally in the making of pornography.[15] Although there is less information about women in pornography, it is likely that many women are coerced into making pornography just as they are coerced into prostitution. In addition, by filming the violence and sex crimes

---

13 http://www.borov.com (last visited February 26, 2001; web-site no longer links to this material; on file with author).

14 Interview with Jeff Middleton, *Computer Focus* (May 17, 2001).

15 Liz Kelly and Dianne Butterworth, address at the *Journal of Information Law and Technology*'s event entitled 'Policing the Internet: First European Conference on Combating Pornography and Violence on the Internet' (February 14, 1999). (For a description, see Yaman Akdeniz, 'Policing the Internet' (Conference Report), *The Journal of Information, Law and Technology* (1999, (1). Available at http://elj.warwick.ac.uk/jilt/Confs/97_1pol/akdeniz.doc). See also *In Harm's Way: The Pornography Civil Rights Hearings*, pp. 39–199 (Catharine A. MacKinnon and Andrea Dworkin (eds). (1998)) [hereinafter *In Harm's Way*].

against women and post-adolescent teens, thereby turning it into pornography, images of these violent crimes can be distributed publicly on the internet with no consequences to the perpetrators (Hughes 2001).

The percentage of degrading, violent, misogynistic pornography continues to increase, and the images and videos become more readily available.[16] However, there doesn't seem to be anything new in the content of pornography: perpetrators have always raped and tortured women and children in the making of pornography (Hughes 2001). What *is* new is the volume of pornography produced and the fact that an average person with a computer, modem and search engine can find violent, degrading images within minutes, a search that could have taken a lifetime just fifteen years ago. The increase in video clips with audio and streaming video makes the action and harm come alive (Hughes 2001). New techniques, such as shockwave flash movies, enable the creation of animated videos. Skilled amateurs can create snuff films for distribution on the web. One person I interviewed said:

> [w]ith virtual film, it is possible to produce a snuff film from animation, but very difficult to tell it is not real. Now, we are limited only by our imaginations. There is nothing that can't happen on the Web.[17]

Chat rooms

Real time synchronous communication, or 'chat', is a popular means of communication on the internet.[18] Chat is available through Internet Relay Chat (IRC) channels, instant messaging, such as ICQ, web-based chat sites which are accessed through browsers, Multi-User Dimension (MUD) or Multi-User Simulated or Share Hallucination (MUSH) programs. There are over 100,000 chat rooms available to users worldwide. Some of these formats and the 'rooms' users create are open to the public, some are private and require passwords, and others are used for one-to-one communication. No messages are archived or stored and no log files are maintained, as is done with emails or web accesses, so stalkers use them to look for victims without the danger of being traced by law enforcement authorities. There have been numerous cases in the US and the UK, where predators contact children for both online and physical meetings. Often, during these meetings, the children are emotionally and sexually abused.[19] There have also been numerous cases of online stalking

---

16 See generally *In Harm's Way*.
17 Interview with Jeff Middleton.
18 'Internet Crime Forum, Internet Relay Chat Sub-Group, Chat Wise, Street Wise: Children and Internet Chat Services' (March 2001), at http://www.internetcrimeforum.org.uk/chatwise_streetwise.html (last accessed March 23, 2002) [hereinafter 'Internet Crime Forum'].
19 'Internet Crime Forum'.

of adults that began with conversations in chat rooms, which led to physical meetings that turned into sexual assaults.[20]

In chat rooms, perpetrators engage children in sexual conversation or expose them to sexual material, including adult and child pornography. Predators sexually exploit children online through this sexual talk. Perpetrators ask children to send them pictures or sexual images of themselves or their friends. They may encourage the children to perform sex acts on themselves or friends for the stalker's sexual satisfaction. Stalkers use these activities as part of a 'grooming' process to entice children into more direct contact such as telephone conversations and eventual physical meetings.

When the child stalkers use voice chat, the predators and stalkers encourage the children to get headphones to reduce the risk of someone else in the house hearing the voices. They suggest that children get web cameras for their computers and move their computers to their bedrooms where the stalker can encourage sexual touching and masturbation while they watch via a web cam.

> A typical ruse employed by paedophiles is when the predator asks the victim what she is wearing. This is usually followed by asking her to take some clothing off such as her underwear. The more cunning paedophile will say something more innocuous like, 'do you enjoy taking showers?', swiftly followed by, 'do you touch yourself in the bath?'. It is also commonplace to ask the girl if she has pubic hair in order to build up a mental picture of her level of physical maturity. The intention of most paedophiles is to engage the girl in cybersex activities.[21]

In one transnational case, Franz Konstantin Baehring, a 37-year-old German man living in Greece, contacted a 14-year-old girl from Florida in a chat room.[22] He followed his internet communication with letters by mail and telephone calls. After a year of corresponding, he convinced the girl to run away from home and travel to Greece. To assist the girl in leaving her home, Baehring contacted a woman at a mobile phone store and convinced her to assist an 'abused girl in leaving home'. The woman met the 14-year-old, gave her a programmed cell phone and drove her to a local airport. The girl flew to Ohio, where Robert Arnder, a convicted child pornographer and one of Baehring's contacts, assisted the girl in getting a passport and leaving the United States. Baehring paid Arnder $2000 for his assistance. Police were able to trace the girl's travels and her contacts by examining the email messages left on her computer at home. When police investigated Robert Arnder, they

---

20 Karamjit Kaur, 'More internet Date Rapes', *Straits Times* (Singapore), February 28, 2001; Tom Gardner, *Associated Press*, February 19, 2001; Conal Urquhart, 'Killer Spread his Rape Fantasies on the Internet', *The Times* (London), October 4, 2000.

21 'Internet Crime Forum'.

22 Interview with April Hindin, Postal Inspector, Tampa, Fla. (May 15, 2001).

found that he had pornographic images and videos of his own 13- and 17-year-old daughters on his home computer.[23] He had sexually abused his daughters for at least five years. Arnder has since been indicted on 147 counts of rape, 145 counts of sexual battery, two counts of compelling prostitution, six counts of pandering obscenity involving a minor, four counts of pandering sexually oriented material involving a minor, three counts of child endangerment and one count of interference with custody.

In Greece, Baehring kept the 14-year-old girl under control by locking her in an apartment in Thessaloniki (Greenwood 2001, p. 12). She was not permitted to answer the phone or the door. The girl's friends received email messages sent from internet cafés in Athens and Thessaloniki saying that she was happy. Baehring told his mother that he felt pity for her because she suffered from leukemia and he was trying to make her happy. He told the girl that he was a child psychologist who specialized in hypnotherapy and ran a youth center.[24]

When authorities found Baehring, he was charged with abduction of a minor with malicious intent, sexual assault and exposing a minor to improper material. Investigation of Baehring's home revealed child pornography of other girls.[25] He is suspected of involvement with pornography rings on the internet.[26] The girl suspects that Baehring may have had other girls under his control and used them in making pornography.[27]

The international effort to find the missing girl involved the Polk County Sheriff's Office in Florida, the US State Department, the US Customs Department, US postal inspectors, the FBI, Interpol, the US Embassy in Greece, the Greek Consulate and the police in Greece (Hughes 2001). The international cooperation has been praised, but the intensity of these efforts also highlights the resources needed to find one girl; there are thousands of girls missing each year from parts of the world where such resources and cooperation don't exist (Hughes 2001).

File Transfer Protocol (FTP)
Although File Transfer Protocol (FTP) is one of the oldest ways of exchanging files on the internet, it is still popular with child pornography collectors for one-to-one exchange of child pornography. FTP allows users to have direct

---

23 'Man faces 308-Count Indictment Related to Alleged Sex Acts With Teens', *Associated Press*, January 24, 2001.
24 'Missing Teen Found, Says She Doesn't Want to go Home', *Athens News*, February 2, 2001.
25 'German Man Charged With Luring Florida Girl Overseas', *Associated Press*, February 3, 2001.
26 'German Suspected of Links With Pornography Rings', *Athens News*, February 6, 2001.
27 'Missing Teen Found'.

access to another person's computer hard drive to upload and download files. This technique of file exchange is more likely to occur between child pornography collectors who have met in other venues and have come to trust each other (Hughes 2001).

Live video chat
Every venue on the internet is used to transmit images of sexual exploitation. The number of video clips is increasing and streaming video is available for those with high-speed internet connections. Live web broadcasts have become common (Hughes 2001).

In 2000, a case of human smuggling and trafficking was uncovered in Hawaii, in which Japanese women were trafficked into Honolulu to perform live on the internet for audiences in Japan.[28] Due to more restrictive laws concerning pornography in Japan, the men decided to operate their website from Hawaii and broadcast the live shows back to Japan.[29] The Japanese men in Hawaii placed ads in Japan for 'nude models'. Upon their arrival in Hawaii, the women were used to make pornographic films and perform live internet sex shows. The entire operation was aimed at a Japanese audience. The website was written in Japanese. The women performed strip shows by web cam and responded to requests from men watching in Japan. They used wireless keyboards for live sex chat with the men at a rate of $1 per minute. The Japanese men, operating as Aloha Data, used digital cameras to capture the live video chat, then transmitted it to a server in California run by a 'not respectable, but not illegal' internet service provider called Lucy's Tiger Den. Japanese viewers accessed the performance through the California server.

The US Immigration and Naturalization Service pursued the case, not because of the pornographic content of the broadcast or the sexual exploitation of the women, but because of immigration violations (Hughes 2001). This case offers some twists in crime, human smuggling or trafficking and new technologies. James Chaparro, Director of the Anti-Smuggling and Trafficking Unit, US Immigration and Naturalization Service, characterized the case in this way: 'The Japanese men violated US immigration law by smuggling/trafficking Japanese women into the US in order to circumvent the Japanese law against pornography.'[30] Omer Poirier, US Attorney in Honolulu, who handled the case, described it in this way: 'Japanese men were smuggling women into the US from Japan to provide services for men in Japan.'[31]

---

28 'Immigration Raid Closes Internet Porn Site', *Associated Press*, January 15, 2000.
29 Interview with Omer Poirier, US Attorney, Honolulu, HI (May 1, 2001).
30 Interview with James M. Chaparro, Director of the Anti-Smuggling and Trafficking Unit, US Immigration and Naturalization Service (May 1, 2001).
31 Interview with Omer Poirier.

Peer-to-peer networks and file swapping programs
In the last five to six years, a new technology has been developed and released as freeware that can create a network of peer computers. The result is an open, decentralized, peer-to-peer system. File swapping programs are used to find files on the network. Using the program the user designates one directory on his/her computer that will be open to the public and another for downloaded files. When the user logs onto the internet, he/she is automatically connected to all other people running the same program. All available files are indexed into a large searchable database. When keywords are entered, the request moves from one computer to the next returning links to files. At that point, the program can download the requested files from other members' network computers.[32] It is touted as a revolution in how computers and people communicate with each other on the internet. Examples of these peer-to-peer networks include Napster, Scour Exchange, Gnutella, Freenet and Imesh (Hughes 2001).

These programs create a decentralized system, meaning there is no central server through which all communications pass. Consequently, there are no logs of transmissions, and transmissions are not traceable because each site can only trace the connection back one level (Hughes 2001). You can enter the public network or create a private one of your own (Harris 2000). These are the features that make this new information technology so attractive to perpetrators (Hughes 2001).

> [S]oftware that turn[s] your PC into both a client and a server. They'll create a true Web by allowing users to easily connect directly to each other . . . Download Gnutella and you can trade any type of file, pirated or not, with anybody else on the Gnutella network in virtual anonymity. (Berst 2000)

Gnutella has a monitoring feature that allows users to monitor the searches of others to see what people are searching for (Berst 2000). According to Glenn Nick, of the US Customs Cyber Smuggling Center, 'most searches on these networks are for adult and child pornography'.[33]

Technologies for anonymity and disguise

For those engaging in criminal activity or sexual exploitation, anonymity and disguise are critical. Criminals in general are using new communications technologies such as mobile phones to avoid police tracing of their phone calls. Mobile phone services often offer free or cheap phones for signing up for their

---

32 See generally Gnutella, available at http://welcome.to/gnutella (last visited May 1, 2001).
33 Interview with Glenn Nick, US Customs Cyber Smuggling Center (May 17, 2001).

services. Criminals use these phones for a week, and then discard them. Pre-paid phone cards enable anonymous use of landline telephone systems. Users of cellular and satellite phones can be located far away from their home bases and still be able to use their phones. Mobile phones can be programmed to transmit false identification (Davis 2000). Those engaging in international sexual exploitation use new technologies for ease of communication and to avoid detection (Hughes 2001).

Criminals can avoid being traced by sending their communication through a series of carriers, each using different communication technologies, such as local telephone companies, long distance telephone companies, internet service providers, wireless networks, and satellite networks. They can send the communication through a number of different countries in different time zones. This complicated routing of communication makes it difficult to trace the perpetrator.[34]

In addition, criminals can avoid identification by transmitting their messages over the internet through a series of anonymous re-mailers that strip off identifying headers and replace them with new ones (Hughes 1999). One re-mailer service removes identifying features from the header, holds all incoming message until five minutes after the hour, and then resends them in random order to make tracing an individual message more difficult (Denning and Baugh 1999). Messages can pass through up to 20 other re-mailer services, with at least one located in a country known for its lack of cooperation with the global community and law enforcement (Denning and Baugh 1999).

Perpetrators can also utilize technologies that do not save incriminating evidence. New technologies like Web TV, in which web communications are displayed on a TV, do not have a file cache, like browsers installed on a computer (Taylor *et al.* 2001). Therefore illegal material is not accidentally left in the cache to be discovered by the police (Hughes 2001).

Encryption is a technology used to disguise the content of either text or graphics files. Currently, there is a debate among lawmakers around the world about whether law enforcement agencies should be provided with encryption keys so they can decode messages if there is evidence of its use in committing a crime (Denning and Baugh 1999). Several law enforcement officials in the UK and the US indicated that at this point the capabilities and threat of encryption seem to be talked about more than they used to be for cases of trafficking and sexual exploitation (Hughes 2001). Encryption programs are

---

34 See generally 'President's Working Group on Unlawful Conduct on the Internet, The Electronic Frontier: The Challenge of Unlawful Conduct Involving the Use of the Internet' (Mar. 2000). Available at
http://www.usdoj.gov/criminal/cybercrime/unlawful.htm.

not easy to use, and other methods of hiding activity or content are more popular and easier to manage (Hughes 2001).

Technologies of cyber hijacking

The sex industry uses techniques such as 'page jacking' to misdirect or trap people on pornographic websites as page after page of pornography opens up. Page jacking is a technique the sex industry uses to misdirect users so they mistakenly come to their websites (Hughes 2001). The websites include false key-word descriptions so that the search index will bring these individuals on to pornographic websites (Hughes 2001). The users will then click on the link of their chosen topic, only to find themselves on a pornographic website (Hughes 2001).

Another technique used by the sex industry is called 'mouse-trapping'. 'Mouse-trapping' occurs when the sex industry web page designers disable browser commands such as 'back' or 'close' so that viewers cannot leave a pornographic site (Hughes 2001). Once intended or unintended viewers are on these sites, they are trapped on them because the 'back' or 'close' buttons/icons are disabled; when these buttons are clicked, another pornographic website opens up, resulting in an endless number of web pages opening up on the viewer's screen (Hughes 2001). In addition, pornographic websites can change the default homepage setting on a web browser, so that the next time the user opens the browser he/she is taken directly to the pornographic site (Hughes 2001). Furthermore, the sex industry has no idea whom they are trapping on their websites, whether they are children or adults who fervently do not want to view pornography (Hughes 1999).

Pornographers are very aggressive about using popular current events and search subjects to misdirect viewers (Hughes 1999). The sex industry has exploited just about any topic on the web to trap people onto its websites (Hughes 1999). Pornographers will even exploit the arrests of other pornographers. For example, when a research assistant performed a computer search for news reports about the break-up of a child pornography ring in Russia, she found that entering the case-related keywords directed her to websites containing child pornography.[35]

Conclusion

The use of new communication and information technologies for the sexual exploitation of women and children is creating a crisis for women's and children's status, rights, and dignity all over the world. Pimps, traffickers,

---

35 Personal communication with Amy Potenza, Research Assistant, University of Rhode Island (May 24, 2001).

stalkers, and users of pornography and women and children in prostitution have adopted new technologies to further their abuse and exploitation of women and children.

The use of new communications and information technologies in the sexual exploitation of women and children continues to grow with the increased number of users on the internet. Internationally, there have been governmental and law enforcement responses to distribution of child pornography, and in the US and UK there have been official responses to child stalkers in chat rooms. However, there is little governmental intervention to stop the sexual exploitation of adult women.

References

Amis, Martin. 'A Rough Trade'. *Guardian Unlimited*, March 17, 2001. Available at http://www.guardian.co.uk/Archive/Article/0,4273,4153718,00.html (last accessed March 22, 2002).

Berst, Jesse. 'How Napster and Friends Will Turn the Web Inside Out'. *ZDNet*, April 24, 2000. Available at http://www.zdnet.com/anchordesk/stories/story/0,10738,2554369,00.html.

Davis, Richard. (2000). 'New Technology: What Impact Will This Have On How Criminals Manage Their Business?' Address at the Wilton Park Conference entitled *Organised Crime: The Dynamics of Illegal Markets*, West Sussex, UK (March 1, 2000).

Denning, Dorothy E. and William E. Baugh, Jr. (1999). 'Hiding Crimes in Cyberspace'. *Information, Communication, and Society*, September 1, 1999.

Dworkin, Andrea and Catharine A. MacKinnon (eds). (1998). *In Harm's Way: The Pornography Civil Rights Hearings*. Cambridge, MA: Harvard University Press.

Greenwood, Jill King. (2001). Missing-Girl Case Points to Greece; 2 Suspects Charged. *Tampa Tribune*, January 27, 2001.

Harris, Ron. (2000). 'Gnutella Gives Copyright Holders Headaches'. *Associated Press*, April 10, 2000.

Hughes, Donna M. (1999). *Pimps and Predators on the Internet—Globalizing Sexual Exploitation of Women and Children*. Available at http://www.uri.edu/artsci/wms/hughes/pprep.htm.

Hughes, Donna M. (2001). *The Impact of the Use of New Communications and Information Technologies on Trafficking in Human Beings for Sexual Exploitation: A Study of the Users*. Report submitted to the Group of

Specialists on the Impact of the Use of New Information Technologies on Trafficking in Human Beings for the Purpose of Sexual Exploitation, Committee for Equality Between Women and Men, Council of Europe, May 2001.

Kaplan, Karen. (2001). 'Pushing Porn on DVDs'. *Los Angeles Times*, January 9, 2001.

Li, Kenneth. (2000). 'Silicone Valley: Porn Goes Public'. *The Industry Standard*, November 6, 2000. Available at http://www.thestandard.com/article/display/0,1151,19696,00.html (last accessed March 22, 2002).

Lukyanov, Fedor. '"Alive Goods" Is Flow From the East'. *Rossiyskaya Gazeta*. Available at http://www.rg.ru/english/eco_soyuz/03_11_1.htm (last accessed March 23, 2002).

McLaughlin, James F. (2000). 'Cybersex Child Sex Offender Typology'. The Regional Task Force on Internet Crimes Against Children for Northern England, available at http://www.ci.keene.nh.us/police/Typology.html.

Miller, Stuart. (1998). 'Technological Level of Wonderland Network Shocked All Investigators'. *Irish Times*, September 3, 1998.

Parker, Joe. (2002). 'How Prostitution Works'. Available at http://www.prostitutionresearch.com/parker-how.html (last accessed March 23, 2002).

Rich, Frank. (2001). 'Naked Capitalists'. *New York Times Magazine*, May 20, 2001.

Singer, Natasha. (2001). 'Blue Danube'. Available at http://www.nerve.com/Photography/Plachy/BlueDanube/ (last accessed February 25, 2001) (on file with author).

Taylor, Max *et al.* (2001). 'Child Pornography, The Internet and Offending'. *Isuma: Canadian Journal of Policy Research*, Summer 2001.

Taylor Lee

In and out:
A survivor's memoir of stripping

Slow suicide

> The silence is stifling; a slow suicide that can only be stopped by voice and truth.
> Each time I conquer my fear for a moment and let my thoughts take form in words,
> I fight death. Each time I expose my wounded soul, I sign a contract to live another
> day and encourage others to do the same.

I originally intended to write a chapter rich with psycho-social theory and
analysis of stripping. Writing a research paper, analyzing others' experiences
and theorizing about them is easier than processing and explaining your own
experiences. Yet facts, abstract and removed from immediacy and emotion, do
not change the world. In addition, silence equals a slow suicide for those of us
who have gotten out of the sex industry. So I have decided to base this chapter
on my personal story. My story shows how a woman enters prostitution, why
she stays in prostitution, and how she gets out, if she does. Although my
experience is not representative of all women in prostitution, many elements
of it are common among the population that I have worked with, both in the
sex industry and then in social service as an advocate for prostituted women.
Many of the poems and journal entries in this chapter were scribbled
during the middle of the night, during my second and third years after leaving
stripping, in a notebook that I kept at the head of my bed. Some entries seem
foreign; I do not remember writing them. Apparently my thoughts and
feelings demanded expression; in fact, journaling served as a conduit for
emotional and psychic catharsis as it connected thought with affect and past
with present. Without this form of release and the processing that followed,
I believe that I would still be stuck. I would have either returned to the life
or lived miserably outside of it.
'Women of the night' are wanted out of sight. If they are not heard, they do
not have to be acknowledged. When a woman does get out of the sex industry,
shame encourages her to be silent. So, many women stay in prostitution and
their lives are swallowed by guilt, shame, drugs, and violence. The women are
afraid that there is nothing else for them, that they deserve no better. This
is wrong.

Stripping as prostitution

This chapter is largely about stripping in adult entertainment clubs. However, I do not see stripping as a discrete entity, but as a component of the much larger system of prostitution. Accordingly, I use the term 'prostitution' to illuminate the true nature of strip clubs that is often concealed by euphemism, strategic presentation, and market positioning. Identifying stripping as a form of prostitution—and strippers as prostituted women—fights the glamorization and mystification of stripping. Stripping is simply the sale of sexuality: sexual contact for money, shopping trips, expensive dinners, and/or drugs. The sale of sexuality through stripping also leads to the customer's impression that he has bought the right to touch, grab, slap or otherwise violate, degrade, or devalue the woman stripping.

The connection between prostitution (including stripping) and money is often acknowledged, but the role of economics and power is often misunderstood or unexamined. Many believe that women profit from prostitution, when in fact the largest portion of the profits goes to pimps, clubs owners, and other businessmen. Many also believe that the women possess the power in stripping. Actually the managers, owners, and investors are the ones in power, even though stripping may feel empowering to the individual woman. For example, club rules forbid dating customers, as the clubs consider such interaction prostitution—but the club's management, investors, lawyers, and friends are different, of course. The clubs are clearly not concerned with abolishing prostitution, but rather with controlling it. Pleasing the higher-ups is good for business, but taking business out of the club with regular customers is bad for business. The terms 'prostitution' and 'sex industry' address this reality and highlight the true position of women in stripping as that of commodity.

Then and now

> Go gently into the night? I cannot.
> Trying, death would be hastened, but gruesome.
> All the ways I have tried to silent the driving voice have failed.
> The whisper has turned to an urgent scream.

I found this writing months after it had been written and wondered who wrote it. Later I remembered dreaming it. This entry is powerful because it was written at a time when I was trying to walk away from my past but found that I was bound by it.

I spent six years in the sex industry. For most of that time, I was dancing in adult entertainment clubs and traveling throughout the country. The chronology is unclear and events are foggy.

Although the years I spent in the sex industry seem cut off from the rest of my life, a closer analysis reveals clear ties between that time and my earlier experiences. The connection is subtle but profound. My training began in childhood, when I lived in a neighborhood with boys who spent many hours educating the girls on the block about sex. The boys demonstrated how our body parts could be used. Perhaps it was just child's play, but I had been alive less than a half dozen years (not long enough to know this was not typical), and some of the boys had been alive over a dozen years (clearly long enough to know that this was inappropriate). In any case, I learned then exactly what girls are for.

Afterwards, I only had to turn on the television to learn more about women's roles. I saw women serving men, existing in the shadow of men, being beautiful, being thin, and loving their lot in life. I only had to read magazines to learn still more: how to be sexy for men, 20 ways to get a man, 10 ways to keep a man, diet to be beautiful. I developed early and was overjoyed. I was becoming what I was supposed to be—thin but curved, cute and young but able to be sexy. The first time I had sex, I was raped by someone close enough to my family to call my mother 'mom'. Now, I was sure what I was for. I knew that my greatest asset was my sexuality and knew how badly it was desired. I also realized that I had little control over my sexuality, that it could be taken at will. It was easy to give it for profit; at least then I was in control.

For most women I know, it is not hard for them to see where their work in prostitution began. I have heard more versions of my own story than I ever imagined I would. Nearly all the stories tell of abuse. Each story ends with entry into work where they profit from the sale of their bodies or sexuality, because they can, and in some cases they must, in order to attain some sense of control in their lives. Funny, I thought I was the only one. I felt isolated and crazy. No one told me, 'Hey, I've been there too. I understand'. So I do— I tell others. Unfortunately, I must be cautious in both personal and professional domains, as many will still cast stones.

Because many women who have worked in the sex industry have difficult histories, they have developed elaborate defense mechanisms and coping strategies. Compartmentalization is commonly used by prostituted women as a means of protection. By compartmentalizing different experiences, a woman is able to have separate arenas of thought and action. In one arena she may be a caring, attentive mother who would do anything for her children, while in another compartment she may be a drug addict who will do anything with anyone for money or a high. Perhaps she is a successful student during the week and a sexy stripper each weekend. Regardless of the details, there are distinct compartments that are conveniently separate. Compartmentalization ensures that the woman does not have to face the inherent cognitive dissonance of being a 'Madonna' *and* a 'whore'. Women in the sex industry frequently display selective memory or some type of mental block. The purpose of the denial is to protect oneself from painful experiences like rape or abuse and/or from looking at some of one's behaviors, like having sex with strangers and pretending to enjoy it.

Both compartmentalization and memory alteration are dissociative processes that illustrate the presence of trauma before and/or during sex work. As a woman leaves prostitution, she often tries to forget the past and deny any components of her life that are connected to prostitution. She actually needs to recognize that she is the sum total of all her experiences. The guilt and shame of the past can trap a woman and make getting out of prostitution impossible. Re-framing the past, recognizing one's strengths and gains, is necessary to reduce the shame and guilt enough so that they are no longer stumbling blocks to exiting the life.

Selling my Self

What does it matter that they see my body unclothed, masked in make-up and costume? It is no longer my own. Virginity stolen. Body desecrated. Why hide it? Why not profit from the very thing that may be taken again at any time? My body is not my Self. Long ago the ties were severed, leaving my body as a vessel for, but disconnected from, my soul.

This piece addresses the often-asked question, 'How can you sell your Self?' It is not difficult. Once a woman is abused, as a majority of women in the sex industry have been, she gains the powerful skill of dissociation. Once a woman's ownership rights over her body are stolen, the body becomes foreign, separated from Self. The body becomes a tool, a weapon, a burden to drag around. The body can then be used for profit or further abuse. Some victims feel betrayed by their bodies and turn to punishing them. The body can be abused with alcohol, food, starvation, self-mutilation, and even death. The victim of abuse is left to frantically seek ways to regain her control (by abusing herself) and ways to increase her power (by abusing others). Promiscuity and prostitution fit here, for if you give sex away it cannot be taken and if you profit economically you are gaining power in this society. It is not difficult at all.

Women often enter the sex industry in attempts to gain power in their lives and control over themselves. Unfortunately, by the time a woman heals and sees what is happening, she is often stuck. Addiction to the lifestyle is the norm. As I left my last club for the final time, a manager looked at the evening gowns and locker contents in my hand and with a knowing smile and full frontal hug said, 'That's OK, honey. We'll be waiting for you when you come back.' I was furious with him, but even more with the fact that what he said is reality for so many women—as if through a revolving door, women leave and return to the sex industry time and again. Addictions bring them back. The addictions include fast money, power, drugs, alcohol, adrenaline, attention, love. Rarely is it a single addiction. Many women don't even attempt to leave, as they are aware of what they must give up and know that they cannot.

Getting out

The question that has not been clearly answered is what enables or forces a woman to get out? For each woman it is different. I remember looking around me on my last night of work in a strip club, and I was afraid. Every way I turned I saw zombies, the living dead, pastel people. I realized I was one of them. The lights, the noise, the money, the drinks, the beauty were all distracting mirages. I could not hear my Self, yet I knew I was not the image that others saw. I realized why I had spent so many years in clubs. The commotion outside of me allowed me to exist without looking inside. I did not have to see the confusion or feel the pain within me. As I looked around me that night, I realized that time had healed old wounds. I did not need the distractions to avoid them. In fact, I wanted to hear my inner voice again. I needed to feel again before I disappeared, as I knew I would if I stayed.

> Pastel people, you have attained serenity on the surface. Nothing truly excites or agitates. The surges and pulses of creation run deep and muffled. Slough off your social mask. Rejuvenate. Renew the spirit that is life. Soon vibrancy returns; the colors of gemstones and night and light emerge. And with it, passion, rage, true tranquility.

It is simple. As long as a woman has one reason why prostitution is not so bad, as long as she has one benefit to cling to, she is able to continue sex work. On my last day, I saw clearly: No, they are not just lonely guys looking for a friend. No, I do not love existing for their pleasure. No, the money is not making me happy. No, I will not talk to and dance for whoever pays me the most even if I want to spit in his face. I left because I knew that I could. Although I could no longer afford the house I rented, I had friends to stay with. I could not pack and move my things by myself, but I had a family who helped me. I could not get financial aid and I could not afford school, but my family lent me money until I could sell my car. I was afraid of all the changes. I felt stigmatized and was certain others would know and judge me. In the back of my mind, a little voice whispered something that I heard often as I grew up, 'You can be and do whatever you set your mind to.' My mind was set. Nine years later I have a family, a master's degree, a socially acceptable job, and a future.

As happy as I am on some levels, I am troubled on others. One question haunts me: could I have done it alone? Most of the women I worked with in the sex industry and in social service could not do the same. They did not have the support. They were not read bedtime stories every night while growing up. While I got out through privilege, many women in prostitution have no other options.

Staying out

> For too long my skin has been my passport, my body my résumé. How easy for a woman to do. Sexuality disguised as power and liberation soon entraps and limits expression. The remedy: discontinuation of a hyper-sexual identity. Learn how to be in the world, how sexuality can be beautiful, and how to stop allowing sexuality to overshadow all components of identity. Becoming more than parts, or the sum of parts, heals the soul and promises new life. Transition is a difficult necessity.

A woman is on shaky, new ground when she leaves prostitution. It is not difficult to understand why many women return to the sex industry soon after they try to 'get out' (funny that we use that term, as if they are imprisoned). In prostitution, one relies on sexuality as the core of one's being. Emotions are polluted; relations are clouded; the self is sacrificed for a repertoire confined to the realm of sexuality. Through limited possibilities and limiting expectations, identity is lost. Once the focus shifts and these roles are cast away, the world is strange and unwelcoming. The path is rough and uncharted. Relations seem empty and drab.

I, like most women in the sex industry, had become a character. I had a stage name, a sexual persona, a second identity. Club managers are smart. They encourage this process and help each new recruit dissociate by insisting that she wear costumes and have a stage name and create a 'bio': she can become anyone she wants to be. After years, my real name was as foreign as my stage name was familiar. My sexuality had become my most important feature and most valuable trait after years spent earning a living by magnifying it. When I left the sex industry, I realized that I was out of balance. Like a child, I had to relearn how to have friends based on personality, how to think as an intelligent woman, how to love with my heart. Above all, I had to take time to discover who I am, what I like, what I want. It is hard. It is scary. It is worth it.

After becoming accustomed to daily life outside of prostitution, I realized that things are not so different. The discrimination and devaluing that I faced as a stripper were also present in academia and the rest of the 'outside' world. It became obvious that the problem is not only prostitution. The problem is the treatment of and expectations placed on women. The environment and events may vary, but the story is the same for women everywhere. Women have limited options and face constricting gender role expectations. We are bombarded by images of what we should be. Some insist that women have come a long way. I don't think so. Oppression has become more subtle, more dangerous, since it is hidden.

Free to choose

I freely choose to sell my body for money, for fame.
I freely choose to work as a sex machine, a walking candy store.
I freely choose to diminish my self with each look, with each touch.
I freely choose to reduce myself to parts for others' pleasure.
Only they can value the flesh I abhor, the flesh that betrayed me,
   the flesh that defines me.
The connection between my body and my soul is long gone with sex
   I did not choose.
So now, I am free to choose.

Some proclaim that women are free to choose or resist work in the sex industry. Through my writing, research, and work on the issue I have a different understanding of prostitution. Choice is not so clear any more. Can a woman freely choose to work in the sex industry? In cases where kidnapping, torture and/or mind control are used to force a woman into prostitution and to keep her there, clearly choice is not applicable. Certainly coercion and exploitation of economics, abuse, and naiveté also need to be taken into account.

My experiences don't include forced sex work such as sex rings and sexual slavery. I did not get kidnapped or answer to an abusive pimp; there was choice on some level. This allowed me the delusion that I was in control of my destiny. I did not see the connection between my 'choice' to enter the sex industry and my past. I did not see that I was primed for this choice through earlier experiences resulting in my Self being severed from my body, in my awareness that my sexuality/body was my most valued asset, and in my finding power only through sexuality. I was not conscious of the manipulation and coercion that occurred on a personal and societal level.

In retrospect, manipulation and coercion led to my entry into the sex industry and then to my remaining there. Manipulation was subtle. Initially, club managers/pimps assured me that I never had to do anything that I did not want to do; however, they frequently played the 'friend card' and requested favors (personal ones or ones 'for the good of the club') such as entertaining associates, investors and the like. Further, economic rewards and social acceptance (in that arena) were directly connected to my popularity and what I was willing to do. The terms 'stripper' and 'prostitute' were replaced with 'adult entertainer' and 'escort' to separate us hard-working, ethical professionals from the sleazy type (the difference being the wardrobe and environment, not the function or dynamics). The coercion I faced did not involve physical force. Instead the coercion was emotional and psychological in nature. This included socialization as a sex object, fear of never being accepted in the straight world after being a 'whore', induction into the sex world 'family' (one that accepts those not accepted elsewhere, and a closed system that is difficult to leave), and knowledge that I could not make ends meet and that I would never make the same amount of money (even with a PhD).

Moving on

Early in 1995, I ended my six-year career in the sex industry. The road out of prostitution has been long and tough. I have gone through stages of stabilizing, normalizing, forgetting the past, hiding the past, then processing, accepting, and finally integrating past, present and future into my Self. Simply regaining relative physical and mental health was a year-long process. Normalizing—becoming a part of the day world, living day-to-day, becoming a human being rather than a facade—took additional time and required resisting the temptation to return to the life. At first, the daily grind was devoid of the excitement, the chaos, the adrenaline rush, and the drug or alcohol high of the night world.

For a time, I believed that forgetting the past would lead to happiness. Later, I realized that forgetting was impossible, and that in my attempts to do so I was fragmenting my Self and denying a portion of my Self—the effect being psychological imprisonment. Through my writing and through social service work with other women in the sex industry, I have been able over time to accept my past experiences. Still, integrating these experiences into a complete Self is difficult because in retrospect the experiences seem so foreign.

I have been out of the sex industry long enough for it to feel like a lifetime ago. I am certain that we need to fight the system of prostitution and we need to do so without shaming the women used in the system. Chances are good that their lives have been difficult enough.

Seiya Morita
(for the Anti-Pornography-&-Prostitution Research Group)

Pornography, prostitution, and women's human rights in Japan

The last ten years in the 20th century, from the viewpoint of female human rights and sex equality, were paradoxical for Japan. Although Japan is very backward in the field of sex equality, at last a series of basic laws protecting the human rights of women came into being, the plaintiff women in sexual harassment trials gained victories one after another, and the social perception of violence against women progressed little by little. However, during the same period, sex work theory has spread, and the argument has swept over the media that nothing is wrong with pornography or prostitution because consent has been given by the persons concerned. Pornography and prostitution became more epidemic in Japan during the 1990s, and serious crimes associated with them took place more frequently.

Progress

Social consciousness about sexual harassment and domestic violence progressed rapidly in the 1990s. Sexual harassment became recognized as a problem in Japan only in the second half of the 1980s, more than 10 years behind the United States. A women's group played a major role in introducing and spreading the concept of sexual harassment in Japanese women's movements when it translated and published a US guidebook about sexual harassment in 1988. This group then carried out a questionnaire targeting 10,000 women to make clear the actual prevalence of sexual harassment in Japan. In 1991 this group published the results as a book, which clearly showed the pervasiveness of sexual harassment in Japan.

But in the beginning of the 1990s, most Japanese people still assumed that sexual harassment involved only love affairs in the workplace. However, such recognition changed significantly in the 1990s, due to the serious and steady efforts of the female researchers, lawyers and activists, and due to the struggles of the courageous women who took legal action against sexual harassment in the workplace. An important breakthrough occurred when two female victims who suffered sexual harassment brought suits in Fukuoka and Numazu at the end of the 1980s. The cases became the first full-fledged sexual harassment lawsuits in Japan. The trial in Numazu was settled in 1990. The court decision condemned the defendant's acts, saying that '[the defendant] exploited the position of a superior official, and didn't look upon her as a human being with personality, thinking of a woman only as an object for pleasure and play', and passed judgment in favor of the complainant. As for the trial in Fukuoka, Fukuoka District Court also decided completely in favor of the plaintiff in 1992. These two victories in the beginning of the 1990s played a decisive role in raising social consciousness about sexual harassment (Nagai, 1994).

After that, sexual harassment trials were raised frequently. Some disadvantageous judgments for complainants were handed down during the first few years, but victory for the complainant became more common as sexual harassment came to be recognized socially. Even if a plaintiff lost the case in the first trial, she almost always won her case in an appeal hearing. Moreover, the pernicious sexual harassment committed by the director of the Institute of Southeast Asia Studies of Kyoto University in 1997 highlighted the serious issue of sexual harassment in universities, and formed the basis for developing measures against sexual harassment in universities.

Domestic violence also came to be recognized as a serious problem in Japanese society in the 1990s. As in many other countries, the status of the Japanese woman in the home has been very low, and a husband's violence against his wife has not been considered a criminal act. Even when a wife petitioned for a divorce because of her husband's violence, the members of the Mediation Committee of the Family Court, irrespective of their gender, very often showed sympathy to the battering husband and counseled her to be patient. Moreover, in preceding cases marital rape had not been recognized as rape until recently.

A grass-roots women's group played a major role in changing these conditions. In the beginning of the 1990s, a researcher, a lawyer, a counselor, a social worker, a journalist and others—all women—came together to form the Domestic Violence Research Group, and carried out a nationwide survey about domestic violence. The results showed that about 80 percent of the respondents had suffered domestic violence in some form (physical or mental). After that, women's movements against domestic violence spread rapidly in the second half of the 1990s, and many books, reports and newspaper articles were published on the subject. The local and national governments also started to carry out official investigations from the late 1990s. For example, according to a national investigation (published in February 2000) by the Gender Equality Bureau of the Cabinet Office, the women who had experienced such serious acts as 'sustained life-threatening violence' and 'sustained violence severe enough to warrant medical treatment' each constituted about 5 percent of the respondents. As an important result of such efforts, the *Law for the Prevention of Spousal Violence and the Protection of Victims*, although inadequate, was finally enacted in 2001.

In other fields, we have also seen progressive changes to protect the human rights of women and children. For example, the *Basic Law for a Gender-equal Society* was instituted in 1999. The law sets as its principal purpose to promote 'respect for individuals' and 'equality under the law' stipulated under the Constitution of Japan, and declares 'no gender-based discriminatory treatment of women or men' and 'the securing of opportunities for men and women to exercise their abilities as individuals', among other measures. It charges the state and local governments with 'the comprehensive formulation and implementation of policies related to promotion or formation of a Gender-equal Society (including positive action).' In the same year, child pornography and child prostitution, which had been nearly uncontrolled until then, came to be legally banned. As is well known, Japan had a shameful history in providing the world with a great deal of child pornography until this law was established. Even now, prostitution of high school students is spreading extensively, and Japanese men travel to other Asian countries in groups to take advantage of child prostitution. In 2000, after a series of murders by male stalkers, the *Law for Preventing Stalking* was enacted. In addition, in the same year, the *Criminal Procedure Act* was revised to abolish the time limit (six months) for bringing charges of rape.

Of course, these progressive changes were brought about not only by the efforts of the domestic women's groups, but also by the strong pressure of international public opinion. Above all, the success of the United Nations Fourth World Conference on Women in Beijing in 1995 played a major role in establishing some laws about the human rights of Japanese women in the years that followed.

Needless to say, each of the achievements mentioned above is insufficient. The punishments handed down to perpetrators are so light, and compared with Western countries, there are very few official or civil organizations and facilities supporting the victims and survivors in Japan. Although some progressive laws have been enacted, the Japanese government keeps financial support for them at a low level, using the excuse of financial difficulty.

In addition, as I will mention later, the law punishing acts related to child prostitution and child pornography allows child pornography in the form of drawings, paintings, animations, computer graphics, etc. to continue without regulation. This kind of child pornography makes girls into the objects of rape, gang rape, and abuse in confinement.

In spite of the legal progress on many fronts, we still find anachronistic situations in the field of women's human rights. For example, rape is defined very narrowly in the clauses of the Criminal Law established under the totalitarian Mikado government of prewar days. It is even more narrowly interpreted in court; the highest penalty for rape is less than that for theft. Moreover, the 'victim's fault' theory, based on the anachronistic idea of 'female chastity', even now has a big influence in trials, and harms female victims seriously. As Japan has no comprehensive law to prohibit and punish all forms of violence against women, many sexual assaults which don't adequately fall into the frame of the existing laws are under no legal regulation.

Nevertheless it is epoch-making that in this Japan where women are still oppressed, sexual harassment, domestic violence, and child pornography and child prostitution were recognized as crimes, and distinct legal and administrative frameworks were formed to cope with them.

Counter flow

However, on the other hand, the ideology of sexual liberalism and 'sex work' theory has spread in the 1990s in Japan. This ideology says that there is nothing wrong with pornography and prostitution because the persons concerned agreed to engage in them, and that sex work is work just like all other occupations, so there is no sex discrimination nor the violation of women's human rights involved in either. This ideology, which came into circulation in Europe and the US in the 1980s, made its way into Japan in the 1990s and spread quickly. The translation and publication in Japan in 1993 of *Sex Work: Voices of Women Who are Engaged in the Sex Work Industry* (Priscilla Alexander and Frederique Delacoste (eds)) became an important motivator for this theory. This book had a big impact on feminist movements and leftist groups in Japan, and the following discourses soon became dominant: prostitution is not a system of male dominance, therefore by regarding it as a form of work—fully legalizing it and wholly exempting it from punishment (i.e. exempting pimps and johns from punishment)—we could do away with discrimination against prostitution and eliminate violence and injuries from the sex industry. Post-modernist theory, which came to be dominant in Japanese sociology in the 1990s, also functioned to undermine feminism, and led many leftist intellectuals to accept prostitution, sadomasochism, and pornography as various forms of human sexuality.

Moreover, opportunities to use and exploit women sexually in the media and in everyday life increased substantially. For example, many TV commercials and advertisements use women and children sexually, and a large amount of pornography is placed in convenience stores (7-Eleven, Lawson and so on). The Japanese convenience store is a kind of general grocery store, which children as well as adults use daily in almost every city, stocking cosmetics, stationery, food, books and magazines, etc. Many pornographic magazines, which display female nakedness and make rape an amusement, are available in the magazine corner, and even pornographic comics, which openly display child rape, are located in this area. Moreover this area isn't separated from the rest of the store in any way, schoolchildren can and do read these materials easily.

Pornographic images, materials, and works penetrate the world of videos, DVD, the internet, CATV, PC games and so on. New communication technology always provides new means and opportunities for pornography, thus promoting the daily sexual objectification of women more and more. In Japan, 30,000 titles of pornographic videos are made and released onto the market every year. Moreover, the explosive spread of cellular phones and the expansion of the internet enable people to sell and buy female sexuality more easily, and to make the situation of prostitution in Japan more serious. In spite of the legal ban on prostitution targeting children under eighteen, child prostitution using 'meet-a-mate' sites on the internet and cellular phones has not disappeared, but rather increased.

Reported incidents of sexual abuse against children, of sexual crimes by teachers, policemen and legal professionals, and of rape and indecent assaults (that is, sexual assaults without penis insertion) have all increased in recent years. Here, we shall consider the recent seven-year study of the reported number of indecent assault and rape cases.

Table 1   The reported incidents of indecent assaults and rapes in the past 7 years

Year	Reported incidents of indecent assault	Reported incidents of rape	The total
1996	4025	1483	5,508
1997	4398	1657	6,055
1998	4251	1873	6,124
1999	5346	1857	7,203
2000	7412	2260	9,672
2001	9326	2228	11,554
2002	9476	2357	11,833

Source: National Police Agency's homepage (http://www.npa.go.jp/english/index.htm)

The total number increased consistently over the last seven years, and increased by a factor of two between 1996 and 2002. According to the 'Survey on Violence Between Men and Women' by the Japanese Cabinet Office in 1999, only about 10 percent of victims of rape and indecent assault reported their sexual injuries to the police, or consulted them about the assault. The number of violent sexual crimes (rape and indecent assault) amounted to approximately 120,000 in 2002. Moreover, the fastest-growing group of indecent assault victims during these same years were those between 13 and 19 years old. Comparing 1996 with 2000, in the age group of 20 years of age or more, victims of sexual crime increased 1.16 times for these 4 years, whereas in the age group of 13–19-year-olds, the numbers of victims of sexual crime increased by 1.4 times.

Thus, on the one hand, in the last ten years of the 20th century and the first years of the 21st century, Japanese women's movements have achieved important progress in the fields of law, trials, etc.; however, with the spread of pornography and prostitution, the tendency to undermine such achievements and to promote the sexual objectification of women and girls became even more powerful.

The harms of pornography in Japan

Many people say that pornography is 'victimless', like prostitution. Is that true? The many books and articles of Catharine A. MacKinnon and Andrea Dworkin teach us that such a discourse is a lie. In fact, all five of the key harms of pornography—those that they described, and tried to make legally actionable in their *Anti-Pornography Civil Rights Ordinance*—are prevalent in Japan. These harms are described in MacKinnon and Dworkin (2002) as follows: (1) coercion into pornography; (2) forcing pornography on a person; (3) assault due to pornography; (4) defamation through pornography; and (5) trafficking in pornography.

Coercion
Coercion into pornography can be divided into four categories:
1-1   A person may be coerced to appear in pornography by threats, deception and/or the use of violence.
1-2   Even when a person has agreed to perform in pornography, she may be coerced to perform acts to which she has not consented.
1-3   A person may be secretly photographed or filmed while undressing, bathing, or using the toilet, and the results may be exhibited as pornography.
1-4   Finally, even when a person has agreed to be photographed naked or performing sexual acts for personal pleasure, these pictures may be made public later as pornography without her permission.

Firstly, in the case of 1-1, because most victims take no legal action from fear of retaliation or because of severe mental distress, these harms have almost never come to the surface. However, as far as we can know directly, such cases take place frequently. A common pattern is that pornographers deceive a woman by saying it is merely a swimsuit or underwear shot that is going to be taken, and then bring her to a back room for video-recording. Men waiting in the room rape her by using threats and violence, and the pornographers video-record the scene. The resulting 'works' are found not only in underground porn videos but also in legal pornographic videos sold or rented openly in ordinary video shops. The assailants are often members of (or persons related to) Japanese gang organizations, so most victims are compelled to keep the matter to themselves and/or are pushed into suicide. (We know about this worst case from an ex-porno actor.)

Some recently reported criminal incidents in Japan show that men who commit sexual crimes often take pictures or videos of the naked bodies or sexual acts of the victims to later enjoy them as private pornography. For example, according to a press release, a suspect arrested and prosecuted for 10 rapes with murder in October 2000, repeatedly raped white women by using sleep-inducing drugs, and recorded the rape scenes in more than 100 videos. In September 2001, another suspect, a junior high school teacher, was arrested for confining a junior high school girl in handcuffs in his car and causing her death. He planned to bring the girl to a hotel room and video-record the rape scene; he had already raped and video-recorded a high school girl in June in the same year. A suspect arrested for the sexual assault and rape of 11 girls aged 5–10 in August 2002 (again, according to the news release) committed sexual assault against more than 100 girls aged 5–10, and the videos, in which he had recorded sexual acts and the naked bodies of about 45 girls, were seized from his home by the police. Finally, in April 2002, a 30-year-old man was arrested for violating the Child Welfare Law. The release says that the man took nude photographs of a junior high school girl with whom he had become acquainted through a meet-a-mate site on the internet. He then threatened her, saying that if she betrayed him he would distribute these photographs. He forced her to engage in sexual acts with him, and he shared the photographs of her with his friends via the internet early in August 2000.

As for 1–2, not a few testimonies of the actual victims are available. For example, in interviews with three pornography actresses carried out by the magazine *Sukola* in their issue dated 25 February 1999, the women testified bluntly that violent sexual acts, different from what they had initially agreed to, were forced on them by the staff. In an interview with a former pornography actor printed in our publication, he vividly testified that he had suffered sexual abuse beyond his prior consent on the set (Anti-Pornography-&-Prostitution Research Group, 2001).

In some pornographic videos currently massively rented or sold as legal, women are compelled to 'perform' by violence and/or threats. For example, in the videos in the series 'Nyo-han' (Woman Fucking) directed by Baksheesh Yamashita, a young woman around 20 is repeatedly beaten, punched, and kicked, and suffers filth, gang rape, and being dragged around by her hair by several men. The woman's appearance of desperately resisting, trying to run away, and screaming with desperation clearly suggests that she isn't just play-acting. Indeed, a woman who appeared on another video in the same series confessed to a woman who supported her that it was not acting at all. Moreover, in his book, *The Sex Disabled People*, Baksheesh Yamashita wrote boastfully about his 'technique' that he doesn't talk to an actress in advance nor in detail about what is to be done, and he video-records the rape scene without any rehearsal, so that the actress really experiences the fear of being raped.

Similarly, in a pornographic video in the series 'Mito Gohmon' (Torture and Agony) directed by Katsuyuki Hirano, he commits various abusive acts against an actress, such as beating and punching her tens of times, making her appear on a public street, covering her face with filth, having her eat large amounts of food and then vomit on the road from the window of a moving car, and sprinkling a shower of sparks from fireworks on her naked body. In all of these acts she cries and screams desperately and shows a furious refusal and hateful attitude to these practices.

As for 1–3, we can find some cases in recently reported incidents which were prosecuted using existing laws. For example, in one case, the president of a video production company edited and sold nationally as pornography a video in which three women, aged in their twenties, had been video recorded in secret while they were bathing. In this case, the guilty verdict came out from the Tokyo District Court on 14 March 2002, and the man was sentenced to two years in prison for defamation (with a probationary period of four years). Needless to say, this case is the tip of the iceberg, and there is no doubt that most of the countless 'sneak shot' videos currently sold or rented were really shot by setting up videos secretly in such places as public lavatories, the dressing rooms of public bathhouses, and the bathrooms of female dormitories. Yet these crimes rarely become criminal or civil cases, because most victims don't become aware of them, or don't take action even if they are aware.

As for 1–4, one of the cruelest cases is the murder of a female office worker in 1997. After her murder, Japanese weekly magazines or sports papers for salaried men published many 'entertainment' articles about the personal life of the victim, and they carried on their pages a nude photograph of the victim when alive (provided by a certain man who was familiar with her) as a kind of pornography. Moreover, recently the scale of this kind of damage has increased progressively as the use of the internet spreads. Innumerable websites exhibit vast numbers of photographs and moving images of nudes, and sexual acts of 'amateurs', and it is very probable that these sites contain many photographs or moving images of women who didn't agree to have their images publicly exhibited.

Forcing pornography on a person

This harm can be divided into two principal categories:

2–1   A person may be unwillingly exposed to pornography in the home and/or in the workplace.

2–2   A person may be forced by one's husband or lover to do sexual acts as pictured in pornography.

Addressing category 2–1, various investigations of domestic violence by public institutions show that a considerable number of such cases exist. For example, in the national investigation (published in February 2000) of the Gender Equality Bureau of the Japanese Cabinet Office, those who answered that they 'have been shown pornography they did not want to see' are no less than 5.3 percent of 1464 respondents (all women). As for pornography in the workplace, in the Sexual Harassment Investigation of the Government Officials by National Personnel Authority in 1997, 36 percent of women reported that they had suffered sexual harassment by 'the presentation of a poster of a naked or bathing woman'.

As for category 2–2, unfortunately no clear investigation results currently exist in Japan. In order to fill the vacuum, we are now carrying out a questionnaire that investigates this kind of harm as well as other damage resulting from pornography.

Assault due to pornography

Some previously mentioned sexual crimes also suggest the causal relation between pornography and sexual crimes. The criminals who video-recorded their rape scenes are in most cases strongly influenced by violent pornography; indeed a lot of pornographic videos were seized from their homes. For example, in one recently reported case, a salaried man was arrested for confining a 20-year-old woman in his home for two weeks in April 2002. More than thirty titles of pornographic computer games with themes of confinement, rape, and slave training of women were seized from his home. As the press release said, the victimized woman testified that she had been forced to perform the same acts as were seen in the computer games, such as wearing a dog collar.

As in all other countries, in Japan too, apologists for pornography maintain that there is no causal relation between the spread of pornography and sexual crimes, and that pornography is useful in preventing sexual crimes because pornography has a cathartic effect. However, graphs of the spread of pornographic videos in Japan and the reported incidence of violent sexual crime (rape and indecent assault), show that there is a clear correlation between the two (cf. Figure 1). Figure 1 shows that until the middle of the

1980s, when pornographic videos began to be distributed, the reported number of violent sexual crimes had decreased, as had that of general violent crimes. After the mid-1980s the downward trend in violent sexual crimes became weaker, and there was a clear upward trend in the 1990s, in contrast with the continuing downward trend of reported incidents of general violent crimes.

Figure 1   *Index of violent sex crimes and of general violent crimes, and annual number of titles of pornographic videos examined by Video Moral Examination Committee*

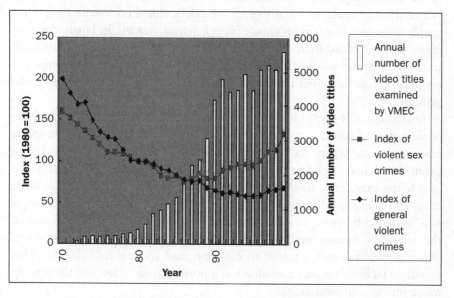

Source: Crime Statistics, National Police Agency

Note: Video Moral Examination Committee (VMEC) is a self-censorship organization of the pornographic video makers.

In a nationwide survey carried out from October 1997 to the end of January 1998, covering persons suspected by police in rape and indecent assault incidents, 33.5 percent of all respondents answered in the affirmative that 'when watching a pornographic video, you also had wanted to do the same thing'. When the suspected persons are juveniles, about 50 percent answered in the affirmative (Tsunoda 2001). Only the most bigoted person can believe that sexual crimes are unrelated to the spread of pornographic videos which eroticize any and all sexual crimes (rape, gang rape, sexual harassment, molestation, sneak shot, confinement of women, etc.) and make them entertainment for men.

Defamation through pornography

The harm of defamation through pornography can be divided into two categories:

4–1   A female face shot is combined with a nude photograph or image of another woman and exhibited as pornography.

4–2   A certain woman's personal characteristics (e.g. her name, elements of her face, or her personal life history) are used in pornographic contexts in public.

In relation to instances of category 4–1, in Japan, a kind of pornography called 'idol collage' is spreading explosively on the internet. The 'idol collage' is a composite image of a pornography model's naked body with the photograph of the face of a famous female (singer, actress, model). In Japan, there are many sites exhibiting many composite images (or moving images) of this kind. In most cases the administrators of these sites indicate they are 'composite images,' but in the worst cases, the administrators declare the images to be genuine.

In the case of 4–2, pornographic novels making free but unauthorized use of the names of famous actresses, singers and models are often carried in sports newspapers in Japan. In addition, demeaning sexual cartoons featuring prominent female politicians and other female leaders are very often found in a leftist magazine, *Uwasa No Shinso* (The Truth of Rumors). The most cruel and savage case is one in the 1980s, when a female high school student was snatched by some boys, confined over a long period of time in one of the offenders' homes, and repeatedly raped and violently abused by them. She was finally killed, encased in concrete, and thrown into the sea. This appalling incident became the subject of a pornographic video and the tragedy made into sexual amusement.

Trafficking in pornography

The trafficking of pornography occurs on a vast scale in Japan. As already stated, about 30,000 titles of pornographic videos are made every year and thousands of copies of each are put on the market. Likewise, more than 400 titles of pornographic games for personal computers are put on the market every year. Child pornography is legally prohibited, but virtual child pornography such as cartoon, animation and computer graphics overflows in Japanese media, from major comic magazines to the internet. The content of this kind of child pornography is, in most cases, the rape, confinement, and abuse of virtual girls; many virtual girls are described to be abused in a variety of ways and to be thoroughly made into sexual slaves. Virtual child pornography can be seen at convenience stores, available to anyone, and anyone also can get it through the internet and obtain it in PC shops. There is no doubt that the trafficking of pornography significantly reduces the status of females in Japan, distorts men's views of women, and infringes upon the equal and personal rights of women.

The harms of prostitution in Japan

As most people know, Japan is a major country for prostitution as well as for pornography. The so-called 'ejaculation industry' (that is, prostitution in forms other than vaginal intercourse) as well as prostitution in the strict sense of inserting a penis into a vagina in exchange for money, have become quite mundane. In the Japanese corporate community, it is common for older men in the company to bring freshmen to the sex entertainment industry—for instance, to a massage parlor (called 'soap land'). In a 1997 survey of 2500 men, more than 50 percent of respondents answered that they have bought sex one or more times (Thinking Group on Prostitution and Men 1998). The percentage of Japanese men who have bought sex is very high compared with men in other countries. For example, according to the HIV and Sex in Japan Survey, 2000 carried out by the Ministry of Health and Welfare (currently the Ministry of Health, Labour and Welfare), the percentage of men who have bought sex in the past year is 1.1 percent in France, 0.6 percent in Britain, 1.8 percent in Norway, 2.8 percent in the Netherlands (where prostitution is even legalized), whereas the percentage in Japan is 13.6 percent. Japan is the highest by a substantial margin, the second highest being Spain at 11 percent.

As in all other countries, in our country, dominant men and 'sexual liberals' maintain that prostitution is based on the free will of the persons concerned and there are no victims in it. However, just as with pornography, this claim is not true.

The harms of prostitution can be divided into at least the following four categories:

1 coercion into prostitution (by violence, threat, and/or deception, or by using economic force or social power relations);
2 various harms that prostitutes suffer in the act of prostitution (e.g. being forced into acts not agreed to);
3 secondary harm brought about by men whose sexuality is distorted by prostitution, and
4 the decline in the status of women through the spreading of prostitution.

Coercion into prostitution
Until the beginning of the 1960s, cases were seen where girls in farming villages were sold by their parents to pimps because of poverty. Thus thousands of girls became victims of 'human trafficking' every year. As Japan became an 'affluent society' through the high-speed economic growth in the

1960s and 1970s, the main victims of 'human trafficking' in Japan became the women and children of the Third World, especially South-east Asia. Some researchers estimate that thousands of foreign women and children are illegally brought into Japan every year, and forcibly made to engage in the sex industry by pimps. The profit generated by this 'forced labor' is equal to about 33 billion dollars. Today, more than 70,000 foreign women are forced to engage in prostitution in a state of confinement or semi-confinement, and since Japanese gang organizations started to participate in the human trafficking business in the early 1980s, it can be estimated that from 500,000 to a million women have been brought into Japan as sex slaves (Suzuki, 2000). Living under miserable conditions, many foreign women committed suicide or were murdered in Japan. Of course, the victims of forced prostitution are not only foreigners. Japanese women are often also brought into forced prostitution for debt repayments, or by the coercion of their boyfriends or husbands, or when still children by their parents. As the scale of prostitution in general increases, so too does the scale of forced prostitution or human trafficking.

Considering the social and economic contexts of prostitution, we can also say that much prostitution is in some sense coerced. Women possess low economic, social, and political status compared with men, and prostitution (including performance for pornography) is almost the only activity for which women can get incomes higher than men. Additionally, systematic power structures in contemporary society where women are sexually objectified tend to direct women strongly towards treating their own sexuality as a commodity. Taking all this into consideration, we should say that 'free prostitution' in the truest sense of the word does not exist in our society.

Harms in the act of prostitution
This kind of harm can be divided into two main categories:

2–1   Being forced by johns into acts not in prior contracts or forced to perform unwanted and humiliating acts in prostitution.

2–2   Being prostituted under unsanitary or dangerous conditions.

The damage caused in cases of type 2–1 hardly ever becomes a criminal or civil case, but many testimonies by prostituted women themselves are available in various forms. For example, in *The Experiences of 50 Prostituted Women* the Study Group of Contemporary Prostitution informs us that in prostitution, johns very often coerce on prostitutes acts that are not in contracts, and that such experiences inevitably accompany this work. The Ikebukuro incident in 1987—in which a call girl desperately resisted a john's violence and abuse, killing him with his own knife, which he had picked up to threaten her—showed clearly the risky conditions in which women prostitute. Although the female defendant asserted legitimate self-defense, the court found that the degree of violation to the defendant's sexual and physical freedoms was considerably reduced compared with ordinary women, on the grounds that the defendant had made a contract of prostitution and received payment of a large sum. The defendant's conduct was deemed excessive self-defense and she was found guilty.

Women are also prostituted under unsanitary and dangerous conditions. The aforementioned HIV and Sex in Japan Survey, 2000 asked women in sex shops the question, 'Can you give your service by attaching a condom?' Sixty-one percent of these women (in the Kanto district) answered that using a condom was 'generally impossible'. Only 6.8 percent answered that using a condom was 'fully possible'. Because of such conditions, serious effects such as unwanted pregnancy, venereal disease and AIDS infection frequently occur in the sex industry. Moreover, a fire that occurred in September 2001, at Kabuki town in Shinjuku ward, clearly showed the very bad conditions under which women engage in the sex industry. Many female employees of the sex shop in the multi-tenanted building were forced to give sexual service to men in a very narrow room with fully sealed windows. When the fire occurred at the stairs of the building, there was no escape from the fire, and all the women died of carbon monoxide poisoning. We can assume that this is a common and normal situation in many sex shops.

Secondary harms of prostitution

Prostitution allows men to imitate and practice sexual violence and sexual assault. It functions as a field exercise in which men learn rape and other abusive sexual practices by doing them (Sugita 1999). During World War II, Japanese soldiers raped and killed countless Chinese women in China; they had already learned to treat women as sexual instruments through the military comfort-women system.

If pornography strengthens the male view of a woman as a 'sexual object' and a 'sexual amusement', prostitution creates a sexist form of male sexuality in an even more practical and active sense by allowing a man the direct use of a real woman. Men, as it were, somaticize an objectifying and misogynist sexuality through prostitution. Men who have sexist sexuality see all women as latent sexual commodities or potential whores. Men often impose sexual acts on prostituted women that they can't impose on their wives or girlfriends; at the same time, some men do impose sexual acts learned through prostitution on their wives, girlfriends, or sometimes even on their children. In addition, the prevalence of prostitution leads to the spreading of various forms of sexual harassment, and also reinforces the foundation of sexual harassment socially. After all, sexual harassment is a form of prostitution in a broad sense—seeing a woman as existing to sell her sexuality and to please men.

Decline in women's status due to prostitution

The broad existence of prostitution is itself an indictment of the remarkably low status of women, and of women's remarkably low wages (the average wage of Japanese women is still half that of men). At the same time, prostitution consolidates the low status and the low wages of women in general. Women are low-priced in the general labor force, but highly priced as sexual commodities, and these situations mutually reinforce each other. As with pornography, prostitution further promotes and consolidates the sexual objectification of women and the identification of women with sexuality. Prostitution is a symptom of sexual discrimination, but at the same time, it actively produces and reproduces sexual discrimination.

Legal approaches

The traditional legal approaches to pornography and prostitution in Japan are little different from those in the United States. Pornography is a subject of criminal regulation based on 'obscenity'; it is not recognised as conflicting with the human rights and equality of women. Therefore a great deal of sexist and violent pornography is in the mass marketplace without any regulation.

Prostitution in a narrow sense (accompanied by penile insertion) is a subject of 'prevention' from the viewpoint of 'the disorder of sexual morals and manners' under the Law Preventing Prostitution. Johns are fully exempted from criminal punishment. Prostitution itself is not a subject of criminal punishment, but many prostituted women are arrested under the provision against 'solicitation'. The broader ejaculation industry (prostitution in a broad sense, not accompanied by penile insertion) has a legitimate position and some legal controls under the Law Regulating Adult Entertainment Businesses. Neither form of prostitution is recognised as conflicting with the human rights and equality of women.

Sexual liberals draw attention to the right to work and human rights of women engaging in the sex industry, but in alleging that sex work is 'just work' and that women voluntarily engage in it with free will, they give legitimacy and authority to male dominance and the whole sex industry. Their 'cares' for the human rights and security of 'sex workers' are somewhat akin to the 'cares' of white slave owners for the Black slaves working healthily and contributing to the harvest of cotton. They insist on abolishing the Law Preventing Prostitution and achieving the full legalization of prostitution, exempting all involved (including pimps) from criminal punishment. They say that doing this will eliminate discrimination against prostitutes and improve their working conditions. However, this could only lead to a grotesque, sexist society where people trade and traffic openly and legally in female sexuality.

'Sexuality' should be protected more strongly than as simply 'work' or 'labor', because it concerns the personality (or personal integrity) and privacy of human beings more deeply than work does. So to identify sexuality with work results in sanctioning many practices that violate sexuality. For example, consider the case where a male boss orders a female subordinate to perform a sexual service for him in exchange for promotion or an increase in wages. In our usual understanding, this is considered to be vicious sexual harassment. However, if sex is just another form of work, this sexual request would be no different from the boss ordering her to put his documents in order in exchange for extra wages.

In addition, if a system of dealing in female sexuality is justified as a whole, it would become much more difficult to charge individual violating acts in such a system. As an example, take the judgment in the Ikebukuro self-defense case mentioned above. The judgment is in fact based on the assumptions of 'sex work' theory. The standpoint of this judgment is that, because the defendant engaged in special 'work' for an expensive reward, knowing that it was accompanied by some risk, the degree of the infringements she suffered should be estimated as less than it would be for ordinary women. If the sex work theory prevails, it would generalize judgments such as the Ikebukuro precedent. If you make a choice to engage in 'sex work', you should accept the risk in it. Needless to say, this point of view falls in well with the currently prevalent neo-liberal concept of the individual.

Furthermore, if the system in which female sexuality is sold and bought openly has a fully legal status, then illegal practices (above all, human trafficking) will increase extraordinarily on the fringe of the system, because it is impossible to judge by appearances whether women in prostitution are there of their own free will or as a result of human trafficking.

In this way, the legal 'solutions' defended by the sex work theorists would accomplish little of the goal they set out so proudly to achieve (that is, to protect the rights of sex workers). Rather they would impose the responsibility for the harms of prostitution on the sex workers themselves, the women in pornography and prostitution who are the victims of the system. Nothing could be more unjust. It is the same as the responsibility for sexual harassment being turned over to its victim.

We don't accept this position. It is not because prostitution in a narrow sense is illegal that many violations of female human rights have emerged in the sex industry. If that is true, why don't the violations of human rights decrease at all in prostitution in a broad sense (without insertion) or in pornography, both of which are already legalized?

We need a new legal approach, one which recognizes both pornography and prostitution as systems of female discrimination and male domination, and which aims to abolish them in the future (that is, to realize a society where no woman needs to sell her sexuality) while at the same time protecting the human rights of women who are currently in these industries, and enabling them to get out. Of course, we can and will cope with the various harms in pornography and prostitution by using the inadequate current laws (Tsunoda 2001) however, it is also certain that under the existing laws women have often no remedy for the violation of their human rights.

We believe that the right concepts to serve as a key to such a new legal approach in Japan are 'seiteki-jinkaku-ken' (sexual personal right)[1] and 'seiteki-byodo-ken' (sex equality right).

The concept of the 'sexual personal right' is based on a modern principle: 'sexuality is an essential part of personhood' (Sugita 1999). That is, 'sexuality' is a core aspect of the human personality or personal dignity, and is one of the most important components of personal rights. The sexual personal right is

> based on freedom from the state, as negation of the wrongful intervention by the state into sexual and reproductive areas, however at the same time it requires freedom through the state in order to realize freedom from male sexual violence in all social fields, and from sexual dealings in women through market mechanism (Nakasatomi 2000, p. 31).

Second, on the basis of the 'sexual personal right', the concept of 'sex equality right' recognizes that sex equality between men and women as genders is one of the most important human rights, and it requires the eradication of the gender power relations of domination and subordination.

From the second half of the 1980s to the first half of the 1990s in Japan, the concept of a right of sexual freedom or right of sexual self-determination has made significant contributions to protecting the human rights of women. The concept completely reformed the old legal interpretations of sexual crimes, which had been formerly judged on the basis of 'chastity' or 'sexual morals'. So the newer concept had positive effects in the cases of rape and sexual harassment. However, when it comes to more subtle sex discrimination such as pornography and prostitution, which are supposed to be formally based on the consent of the parties involved, sexual liberals often use the sexual freedom right to legitimize pornography and prostitution. Here, most of the sexual infringements take place in the vast gray zone between 'consent' and 'dissent'. In this area, then, the narrow concept of 'right of sexual freedom' or 'right of sexual self-determination' is inadequate.

On the contrary, the concept of sexual personal right is a broader concept

---

1   The Japanese word 'jinkaku ken' is directly translated from the German word 'Personlich-keitsrecht'. It is difficult to translate this word exactly into English, so in this paper we describe it as 'personal right', meaning the right to integrity of the person, or the right to dignity as a person.

which includes 'sexual freedom right' and/or 'the right of sexual self-determination', but should not be reduced to them. Even cases which can't be strictly classified into either 'with consent' or 'without consent' can often be recognized as violations of the sexual personal right. Furthermore, the concept of 'the personal right' has been widely accepted in Japanese judicial precedents.

The new legal concept of the sexual personal right can be especially helpful in powerfully articulating the violation of human rights in pornography and prostitution. For example, pornographers often shoot films in very bad, dangerous, and unsanitary conditions, and in the pursuit of excessiveness and reality, they have abused the performing woman in the following ways, among others: splashing filth and semen on her face or making her eat them; making her expose herself or her breasts in public; kicking her; hitting or punching her; tying her up and hanging her; ejecting semen into her vagina without contraception. Even if these actions are based on prior formal 'consent' of the woman, they obviously violate the sexual personal right of that woman. If the concept of the 'sexual personal right' is confirmed legally, and the legal redress system of protecting the right is properly established, then, even when the performing woman formally 'agreed' to some of the acts, if she in fact felt humiliated and abused in the process of shooting, she could later take legal action against those who imposed them on her, for the violation of her sexual personal right. The same can be said for various daily acts in prostitution.

Furthermore, to impose sexual acts on a woman by exerting economic power over her, or to make her expose her sexual body openly in the context of diminishing her dignity and subordinating her, can be understood as the violation of her sexual personal right. Also, it can be seen that the many acts done to women in pornography and prostitution are in violation of their sexual personal rights, irrespective of 'consent' (Morita 2001).

The sexual personal right is closely connected to the sex equality right. 'Equality' is above all 'equality of the person'. To 'violate equality' is primarily to disavow 'the personality' (or personal integrity) of the other person and to trample upon it. The making of a woman into a sex object denies her 'personality' or 'integrity as a person' and converts her from 'a person' to 'a sexual thing'. When we recognize that many deeds in pornography and prostitution objectify women and violate the sexual personal rights of women, then it will become clear that these deeds simultaneously violate the sexual equality rights of all women. On the other hand, showing a woman sexually, in the context of violating her 'sex equality right' or intensifying the subordinated and stigmatized status of the gender that she belongs to, can be also recognized as an even more serious violation of her sexual personal right.

Japan has no proper system of legal redress for the violation of collective rights based on race, ethnicity, gender, etc., and has no equality law equivalent to the civil rights laws or *Violence Against Women Act* of the United States. The 14th article of the Japanese Constitution advocates the high ideal that 'there shall be no discrimination in political, economic, or social relations because of race, creed, sex, social status, or family origin', but Japan still has no comprehensive law which effectively embodies and enforces this ideal.

Finally, in April 2002, the government of Japan submitted to the Diet a bill for a Human Rights Protection Law, which forbids discrimination by 'race, ethnicity, creed, sex, social status, family origin, disability, illness, and sexual orientation', and enables the victims of discrimination to appeal to the Human Rights Committee for remedy. However, the bill was drafted by the conservative government which has been indifferent to the protection of human rights, and has many deficiencies. For example, there is a low degree of independence of the Human Rights Committee from the government, and the preclusion of remedies for discrimination in employment, etc. It is not clear whether we could use this law to protect the human rights of the victims of pornography and prostitution, so in order to utilize it effectively, we need to give more concrete shape to a new legal approach.

These two rights' implications for pornography and prostitution will enable us to protect the human rights of women in these industries in the present, and also to promote the elimination of pornography and prostitution in the future. In addition, these concepts will give a reliable means of legal redress for women who are coerced into pornography or prostitution.

A new movement

What is most urgent is to set about the theoretical and analytical work of promoting the sexual personal rights and sex equality rights of women. Above all, it is vital to investigate further the harms connected to pornography and prostitution in Japan and to present a theoretical and practical direction for overcoming them socially. Social consciousness about sexual harassment and domestic violence has recently been progressing and some measures (though still inadequate) have been taken against them; but pornography and prostitution are still protected in the name of freedom of speech and the right to self-determination, and efforts against them by women's movements lag behind significantly.

With the abovementioned concerns in mind, experts and activists in various fields gathered together and in December 1999 organized the Anti-Pornography-&-Prostitution Research Group. As a group for research, criticism, and abolition of both pornography and prostitution, our group is a pioneer in Japan. We understand that both pornography and prostitution have a common social structure and logic, that they conceal the real situations under the ideology of 'consent', and that they promote sex discrimination and male dominance in the name of 'sexual freedom'. We are clearly based on feminism, not on a conservative moral stance. Furthermore, we consciously take an opposite standpoint to that of 'sexual liberals' and those who support 'sex work theory'.

As our first step, in February 2000 we published the first issue of our publication, *Articles and Documents*, including articles written by our members, translations of important English articles on pornography, and many clippings of Japanese newspapers on the matter.

Next, funded by the Tokyo Women's Foundation, our group began studying the violation of females in violent porno videos. In this project we analyzed violent pornographic videos made by popular directors such as Baksheesh Yamashita and Katsuyuki Hirano, and tried to make clear what was done to women in them, how women were portrayed, and what effects were brought about in the viewers of these videos. To report the results, we organized a conference entitled 'Image and Violence: On Porno Videos and Human Rights', which was held on 20 May 2001 at Women's Plaza in Tokyo. This conference was very successful, with more than 80 people participating. On the same day, we published a report of the same name (*Articles and Documents No. 2*), which includes analyses and reports of our members on the violent pornographic videos, a interview with a former porn actor, and a translation of *Pornography and Civil Rights* by C. MacKinnon and A. Dworkin.

In 2002, in order to make clear a more complete picture of the harms of pornography, our group carried out a nation-wide questionnaire targeting members of women's consulting offices, female lawyers, and feminist counselors about whether they have received consultations on the harms of pornography, and what the contents of these consultations were. We published the results and analyses of this investigation in 2003. We will translate them into English and upload them onto our internet site (http://www.app-jp.org/) at some future time.

Furthermore, we are investigating the legal regulation of pornography in other countries and exploring how to make legislative provision for the redress of victims of pornography. We sincerely hope you will give us your help and cooperation.

References

Anti-Pornography-&-Prostitution Research Group (ed.) (2001). *Image and Violence: On Porno Videos and Human Rights.* Tokyo: Anti-Pornography-&-Prostitution Research Group.

MacKinnon, Catharine and Andrea Dworkin. (2002). *Pornography and Sex Discrimination.* Tokyo: AOKI Books.

Morita, Seiya. (2001). 'A Comparison and Analysis of Yamashita's and Hirano's Porno Videos'. In Anti-Pornography-&-Prostitution Research Group (ed.). *Image and Violence: On Porno Videos and Human Rights.* Tokyo: Anti-Pornography-&-Prostitution Research Group.

Nagai, Chieko. (1994). 'The Right to Work and Sexual Harassment'. In Kazuko, Watanabe Chieko (ed.) *Women, Violence, and Human Rights.* Tokyo: Gakuyo Books.

Nakasatomi, Hiroshi. (2000). 'Sex Dominance and Human Rights'. *Ho No Kagaku (Science in Law)*, 29.

Study Group of Contemporary Prostitution. (1995). *The Experiences of 50 Prostituted Women.* Tokyo: Datahouse Co.

Sugita, Satoshi. (1999) *The Androarchal Sexuality: A Critique of Apologetics of Pornography and Prostitution.* Tokyo: Aoki Books.

Suzuki, Yoshio. (2000). 'Women Sold into the Japanese Sex Industry: The Real Situations of the Modern Sexual Slavery'. *Women's Asia*, 21.

Thinking Group on Prostitution and Men (ed.). (1998). *Survey of the Male Attitude Towards Prostitution.* Tokyo: Thinking Group on Prostitution and Men.

Tsunoda, Yukiko. (2001). *Sex Discrimination and Violence*, Tokyo: Yuhikaku.

Yamashita, Baksheesh. (1995). *The Sex Disabled People.* Tokyo: Ota Publishing House.

Vednita Carter

Prostitution and the new slavery

Some time ago I began to look for information on pornography. I was not surprised to find that there was nothing at all specifically about black women and pornography to be found at the public libraries. It is my everyday experience to be made invisible in a white-dominated society. The only place that I knew to go for information about my sisters was the porn stores, where they were not invisible, but rather prominently featured.

Going into the porn stores was not something that I looked forward to doing. As my co-worker and I went into the store, she quickly reminded me not to react to what I would see because the clerks might ask us to leave. In fact, a big sign at the entrance stated that they had the right to ask 'certain customers' to leave.

When we entered, a sense of panic immediately came over me. The place was like a cement bunker. It was one big, dark, dirty room. A musty odor permeated the space. The stale smell of sweat and semen hung in the air. Dusty shelves stretched from corner to corner, ceiling to floor. As I looked around, all I could see was wall-to-wall women.

On one side of the room I saw nothing but bondage magazines. The covers displayed pictures of women tied up, chained up, hung upside down. Some had ball gags stuffed in their mouths. In some, the women's eyes and mouths were taped shut. Some were handcuffed, some shackled to chairs, others locked in cages. All of them had their legs spread—or more often roped—wide open.

Looking in another direction, I saw my sisters—beautiful Black women—nameless and often faceless, plastered on the covers of magazines with titles such as *Chocolate Pleasure*, *Black on Black*, *Black Sugar*, and *Bound Black Beauties*. Many were restrained and all of them were made to appear as if they were 'asking for it'—screaming and moaning with desire.

My heart fell to my feet. All these women exposing their most intimate, private, sacred parts. All of these Black women for sale. As I continued to look, I thought about slavery. I thought about the stories my Grandmother told me about her mother's life under slavery. Even though I never experienced the physical pain of being auctioned off, seeing these Black women shackled, spread-eagle, or hog-tied made it seem as though this part of history—the history of my family's enslavement—was repeating itself all over again.

Looking at the women's faces, I could see they felt shame, embarrassment, hopelessness, and a deep down sorrow. They looked like they were there but yet they weren't there. Many appeared high off of whatever drug they needed to take in order to cope with the brutal exploitation of their bodies.

As I stood in the porn store, my thoughts flashed between the women in the pictures and the pictures that were burned in my memory. As I looked past the contorted masks of sexual desire painted on the women's faces, I could see my own reflection in their deadened eyes. Struggling with feelings of hurt and rage, I thought to myself: What gives anyone the right to exploit another human being to this extent? How can anyone get turned on by dehumanizing another human being? We are living, breathing, feeling people just like the rest of the human race (men).

Pornographic videos and magazines perpetuate the myth that all Black women are whores. A caption under a picture of a Black woman in one porn magazine reads, 'for men who seek hot sex on a regular basis with high performance fuck machines I suggest they try sleeping Black.' Titles like *Big Black Bazoons*, *Big Black Bitch*, *Big Tit Black Milk*, *Black and Kinky*, *Black Whore*, *Black Fantasy*, and *Bitchin Black Ass* portray Black women as ready and willing for anything with anybody.

Everything about African-American women is sexualized in pornography, even our efforts to win civil rights for our people. Another porn magazine 'quotes' a Black woman saying, 'Black power comes in many forms, this is my favorite one: a big juicy chocolate jism stick totally filling my mouth.'

Racist stereotypes in the mainstream media and in porn portray Black women as wild animals who are ready for any kind of sex, anytime, with anybody. Additionally, strip joints and massage parlors are typically zoned in Black neighborhoods, which gives the message to white men that it is okay to solicit Black women and girls for sex, that we are all prostitutes. On almost any night, you can see them slowly cruising around our neighborhoods, rolling down their windows, and calling out to women and girls. We got the message growing up, just like our daughters are getting the message today: this is how it is, this is who you are, this is what you are good for.

Racist/sexist stereotypes of Black women always appeared in rock music. Twenty-five years ago the Rolling Stones reduced us to tasty little mouthfuls called 'Brown Sugar'. Today, a generation raised on pornography is recording music that reflects its ideology that women are things: 'Let a Ho Be a Ho', 'Pimp the Ho', 'Bitches ain't Shit but Ho's and Tricks'. These are just a few examples. How does this affect the way young Black women view themselves? Young Black women who are constantly bombarded with these messages begin to internalize them and accept them as a true definition of who they are.

The sexual exploitation of Black women was one of the greatest harms done to the Black race during slavery. African women were brought to this country against their will. Every time they were raped by the master or overseer, every time they were used as breeders, every time their daughters were raped and assaulted or sold to brothels, they were told what their self-worth was.

After the Emancipation Proclamation in 1863, many slaves fled from the south to the north in search of true freedom. I can imagine what their thoughts might have been: no more worries about mothers and daughters being raped and assaulted or sold off. Little did they know that the white man wasn't going to relinquish their bodies that easily. During this period white men perpetuated the myth that all Black women are wild sex animals in an attempt to excuse and hide their continued sexual exploitation. Up until the 1960s, white men were still invading the homes of Black families in the south, raping mothers and daughters. It wasn't until the civil rights movement that this practice appeared to stop—or at least we didn't hear about it any more. As a result of the systemic abuses Black women have suffered in this country, the lesson sadly passed on from grandmother to mother to daughter in our communities is that sexual exploitation by white men is inevitable. Pornography is just another way that these men can own and control Black women.

Although feminist analyses of pornography address the ways in which it sexualizes racism, no one body of work presents an in-depth analysis of Black women's vulnerability to commercial sexual exploitation or how images of Black women in porn not only perpetuate racist stereotypes but shape the ways in which young Black women view themselves. Feminist analysis must begin to take into consideration the impact of the slavery experience on African-American women. This is the root cause of contemporary sexual slavery in the Black community. The feminist movement must acknowledge that this society has systematically raped Black women over and over again. It must acknowledge how this would cripple Black women as a group – emotionally, psychologically and politically.

The Black community needs to recognize the shackles of slavery that we still have binding us. The African American church needs to recognize that women used in prostitution, porn, and stripping are victims. Black men need to unlearn the lessons of slavery: we are not their bitches, we are not their ho's, any more then we are the bitches and ho's of white men, on the plantation or in the hood. We need to educate ourselves about our history and how it affects who we are now. We need to understand the trickery that has been played on us since the first African was thrown on American shores only to be forced into bondage and sexual slavery. We need to understand how that experience, and the years of racism which followed abolition, shapes our lives and the ways we see each other. Only when we are able to understand this history and start to deprogram ourselves will African American people begin to understand the true meaning of self-worth. Only then will we be able and willing to invite our white allies to join us in the fight to end the dual oppression of racism and sexism.

Gail Dines

King Kong and the white woman: *Hustler* magazine and the demonization of black masculinity*

From the box office success of *The Birth of a Nation* in 1915 to the national obsession with O.J. Simpson, the image of the Black male as the spoiler of white womanhood has been a staple of media representation in this country. The demonization by the media of Black men as rapists and murderers has been well documented by scholars interested in film (Carby 1993; Guerrero 1993; Mercer 1994; Snead 1994; Wiegman 1993; Winston 1982), news (Entman 1990; Gray 1989) and rap music (Dyson 1993; Rose 1994). While this image stands in sharp contrast to the feminized 'Uncle Tom' which was popular in early Hollywood films, both images serve to define Black men as outside the 'normal' realm of (white) masculinity by constructing them as 'other' (Wiegman 1993). Although both the 'Uncle Tom' and the sexual monster continue to define the limits of Black male representation in mainstream media, it is the latter image which dominates, and, according to Mercer (1994), serves to legitimize racist practices such as mass incarceration of Black men, police brutality and right-wing government policy.

Recently, scholars have turned their attention to pornography (Cowan and Campbell 1994; Forna 1992; Mayall and Russell 1993; Mercer 1994) and specifically how the codes and conventions of this genre (re)construct the Black male body, especially the penis, as dangerous and a threat to white male power. The focus of this research tends to be poorly produced hard-core pornography movies which are relegated to the shelves of 'adult-only' stores because of their close-up shots of erect penises, ejaculation and vaginal, anal and oral penetration. What tends to be ignored in these studies is the content of the mass-produced, mass-circulated pornography magazines which, because they can be purchased in bookstores, news stands and airport terminals, have a much larger circulation.

*   This essay was first published in the *Journal of Violence Against Women*, 4 (3), (pp. 291–307). Reprinted by permission.

Of the hundreds of mass-produced, mass-distributed pornography magazines, the three best sellers are *Playboy*, *Penthouse* and *Hustler* (Osanka 1989). While these three magazines are often lumped together, they differ markedly in the type of world they construct. *Playboy* and *Penthouse*, in their pictorials, cartoons, advertisements and editorials, depict a 'whites-only' world, a world so affluent and privileged that blacks are excluded by invisible market forces. Indeed, even the white working-class is invisible in the *Playboy* world of expensive clothes, gourmet restaurants and well-appointed homes. *Hustler*, however, in its pictorials, 'beaver hunts' (explicit snapshots of readers' wives and girlfriends), advertisements and editorials, constructs a world populated by working-class whites who live in trailer homes, eat in fast-food restaurants and wear ill-fitting clothes. While blacks are absent from most sections of the magazine, they appear regularly in caricatured form in the cartoons, where they are depicted as competing with white men for the few sexually available white women. *Hustler* cartoons depict a world filled with seething racial tensions brought about by the Black male's alleged insatiable appetite for white women. The competition between Black and white men and the ultimate victory of the Black male is the source of much 'humor' in *Hustler* cartoons and serves to visually illustrate to the mainly white, working-class male readership what happens if black masculinity is allowed to go uncontained. *Hustler* is by no means the first mass-distributed media to visually depict the ultimate white fear; indeed, *The Birth of A Nation* and *King Kong* (1933) played similar roles, but this time in *Hustler* it is the white man who loses, as evidenced in his failure to win back the 'girl'. This article will examine how *Hustler* draws from past regimes of racial representation and articulates a more contemporary myth where Black masculinity, having been allowed to run amok because of liberal policies, has finally rendered white men impotent, both sexually and economically.

From 'The Birth of A Nation' to 'Black Studs'

Theorists such as Wiegman (1993) and Snead (1994) have traced the beginnings of the image of the Black man as sexual monster back to the late nineteenth century, as the product of a white supremacist ideology which saw the end of slavery as bringing about an unleashing of animalistic, brute violence inherent in African-American men. D.W. Griffith's *The Birth of a Nation* (1915), was, without question, the first major mass circulation of this image in film, and was to become the blueprint for how contemporary mass media depicts Black males.

The notion of the Black male as a sexual monster has been linked to the economic vulnerability that white working-class men feel in the face of a capitalist economy over which they have little power. Guerrero (1993), in his discussion of the emergence of this new stereotype in the novels of Thomas Dixon, suggests that the economic turmoil of the postbellum South served to

undermine the white southern male's role as provider for his family; thus he sought to inflate his depreciated sense of manhood by taking up the honorific task of protecting White Womanhood against the newly constructed specter of the 'brute Negro' (p. 12).

This encoding of the economic threat within a sexual context is, according to Snead (1994), the principal mechanism of cinematic racism and is one of the subplots of the enormously successful *King Kong* movie (re-named *King Kong and the White Women* in Germany). Arguing that 'in all Hollywood film portrayals of blacks . . . the political is never far from the sexual' (p. 8), Snead links the image of King Kong rampaging through the streets of Manhattan with a defenseless white woman clutched to his body to the increasing economic emasculation of white men in the Depression years and the growing fear that black migration from the South had reduced the number of jobs available to working-class whites. King Kong's death at the end of the movie remasculinizes the white man, not only by his conquering of the black menace, but also by regaining the woman. In this way, representations of Black men and white men are not isolated images working independently but rather 'correlate . . . in a larger scheme of semiotic valuation' (Snead 1994, p. 4). Thus, the image of the Black male as sexual savage serves to construct white male sexuality as the protector of white womanhood, as contained and, importantly, as capable of intimacy and humanity.

In her analysis of black and white masculinity in Hollywood movies, Jones (1993) argues that although black and white actors are increasingly portrayed in terms of a violent masculinity, for white actors this violence is tempered by his sexually intimate scenes with a white woman. These scenes assure the audience that for all his violence, the white male is still capable of bonding with another human being and of forming relationships. For black actors, however, this humanizing quality is absent and thus he can only be defined in terms of his violence. The problem with this type of representation is that, according to Jones, 'they suggest that there are fundamental differences in the sexual behavior of black males and white males and are ultimately indicative of the psychic inferiority of the black male' (Jones 1993, p. 250) and the superiority of white masculinity.

Hard-core pornography similarly depicts Black men as more sexually dehumanized than white men. This would seem surprising since in pornography all participants, men and women, are reduced to a series of body parts and orifices. However, studies that compare the representation of white men and Black men in pornography (Cowan and Campbell 1994; Mayall and Russell 1993), have found that it is Black male characters who are granted the least humanity and are most lacking in ability to be intimate. Moreover, in movies and magazines which feature Black men, the focus of the camera and plot is often the size of his penis and his alleged insatiable sexual appetite for white women. Movies with titles such as *Big Bad Black Dicks*, *Black Stallions on Top*, *Black Pricks/White Pussy*, and *Black Studs* draw attention to the black male body and in particular the penis, a rare occurrence in pornography targeted at heterosexual men. Movies such as *The Adventures of Mr. Tootsie Pole* (Bo Entertainment Groups) feature a black male and white female on the cover. The text beneath the picture says 'he's puttin his prodigious pole to the test in tight white pussy'. In *Black Studs* (Glitz Entertainment), three white women are shown having sex with three black men. Above the pictures, the text reads, 'These girls can't get enough of that long black dick.' The penis becomes the defining feature of the Black man and his wholeness as a human being is thus rendered invisible.

The image of the Black male as sexually aggressive is a regular cartoon feature in *Hustler*, one of the best-selling hard-core porn magazines in the world (Osanka 1989). Cartoons which have as their theme the sexual abuse of white women by Black men began appearing in the late 1970s, and by the mid-1980s *Hustler* was running an average of two to three such cartoons an issue. *Hustler* was by no means the first to produce such an image but it is probably the first mass-distributed cultural product (albeit in caricatured form) to visually depict an enormous black penis actually doing severe physical damage to the vagina of a small white woman.

That these types of images have been marginalized in the debate on pornography is problematic, especially in light of the international success of *Hustler* magazine. Much of the analysis of pornography has focused on the ways in which the text works as a regime of representation to construct femininity and masculinity as binary opposites. This type of theorizing assumes a gender system which is race-neutral, an assumption which cannot be sustained in a country where 'gender has proven to be a powerful means through which racial difference has historically been defined and coded' (Wiegman 1993, p. 170). From the image of the Black woman as Jezebel, to the Black male as savage, mainstream white representations of Blacks have coded Black sexuality as deviant, excessive and a threat to the white social order. In *Hustler* sex cartoons, this threat is articulated par excellence in caricatured form and serves to reaffirm the racist myth that failure to contain Black masculinity results in a breakdown of the economic and social fabric of white society.

'F*** you if you can't take a joke': Marketing the *Hustler* cartoon

In the history of American mass media, cartoons have been a major form for the production and reproduction of racist myths. From the prestigious *Harper's*

Weekly of the late 1900s to contemporary Disney cartoons, Blacks have been caricatured as savages, animals and lazy servants. Cartoons, with their claim to humor, have been especially useful vehicles for the expression of racist sentiments which might otherwise be considered unacceptable in a more serious form. Indeed, in his award-winning documentary, *Ethnic Notions* (1987), Marlon Riggs shows how the cartoon image of Blacks has changed little from the beginning of the century to more contemporary versions, while other media forms were forced, in the post-civil-rights era, to encode the racist myths in a more subtle manner.

The *Hustler* cartoons, which have as their theme the Black male as spoiler of white womanhood, are an outgrowth of the portrait caricature which originated in Italy at the end of the sixteenth century. These portrait carica-tures, with their distinctive technique of 'the deliberate distortion of the features of a person for the purpose of mockery' (Gombrich 1963, p. 189), became very popular across Europe and were adapted in the middle of the nineteenth century by cartoonists who used similar methods of distortion against anonymous members of recognizable social groups rather than of well-known individuals. Gombrich (1963), in his celebrated essay on caricatures, argues that the power of this visual technique is that the distorted features come to stand as symbols of the group and are thought to say something about the 'essential nature' of the group as a whole. The black male cartoon character in *Hustler* is caricatured to the point that his penis becomes the symbol of Black masculinity and his body the carrier of the essential nature of Black inferiority.

It is not surprising, therefore, that the only place where Blacks appear with any regularity in *Hustler* is the cartoon. To depict Black men as reducible to their penis in the more 'serious' sections of the magazine might open *Hustler* up to charges of racism as well as the regular criticisms it receives from women's groups regarding the openly misogynist content. Indeed, the cartoon has become the only place where *Hustler*'s claim to being the most 'outrageous and provocative' (*Hustler* July 1984, p. 9) sex and satire magazine on the shelves is realized. Although Larry Flynt (publisher and editor of *Hustler*) regularly criticizes *Playboy* and *Penthouse* for being too 'soft' and for 'mas-querading the pornography as art . . .' (Flynt November 1983, p. 5), *Hustler*'s own pictorials tend to adopt the more soft-core codes and conventions (young, big-breasted women bending over to give the presumed male spectator a clear view of their genitals and breasts), than the hard-core ones which specialize in rape, torture, bondage, bestiality, defecation and incest. However, in the cartoons these hard-core themes appear regularly, together with cartoons which focus on leaking and bad-smelling vaginas, exploding penises, impotent penises, disembodied corpses, bloody body parts being used as masturbation tools, and depictions of Black men raping, mutilating and pimping white women.

One of the main reasons for the hard-core content of the cartoons is that *Hustler* has to be careful not to alienate its mainstream distributors with pictorials or articles that might be classed as too hard-core and thus relegated to the porn-shops, a move which would severely limit its sales (*Hustler's* success is mainly due to its ability to gain access to mass distribution outlets in the US and Europe). On the other hand, *Hustler* also has to keep its promise to its readers to be more hard-core or else it would lose its readership to the more glossy, expensively produced soft-core *Playboy* and *Penthouse*. Toward this end, *Hustler* relies on its cartoons to make good on its promise to its readers to be 'bolder in every direction than other publications' (Flynt July 1988, p. 7), while keeping the pictorials within the limits of the soft-core genre.

Flynt regularly stresses that the cartoons' boldness is not limited to sexual themes but rather also to their political content. Indeed in his editorials, Flynt regularly stresses that, 'We are a political journal as well as a sex publication' (Flynt 1983, p. 5). In an editorial responding to critics of *Hustler* cartoons— titled 'Fuck You if You Can't Take a Joke'—Flynt tells his readers that his critics are not upset with the sexual content of the magazine but rather with his satire which carries 'the sting of truth itself' (Flynt July 1988, p. 7). Flynt continues by arguing that he will not allow his critics to censor what is in effect the political content of his magazine since 'satire, both written and visual, has . . . been the only alternative to express political dissent.'

A strategy that Flynt has used to promote the cartoons to the readers is the elevation of the long-standing cartoon editor of *Hustler*, Dwaine Tinsley, to the status of a major satirist of our day. The creator of the 'Chester the Molester' cartoon (a white middle-aged pedophile who appeared monthly until Tinsley was arrested on child sexual abuse charges in 1989) and some of the most racist cartoons, Tinsley is described by *Hustler* editors as producing '. . . some of the most controversial and thought-provoking humor to appear in any magazine' (*Hustler* November 1983, p. 7), and in some cases cartoons that are 'so tasteless that even Larry Flynt has had to think twice before running them' (*Hustler* November 1983, p. 65). We are, however, reassured by *Hustler* that the 'tastelessness' will continue since 'Larry is determined not to sell out and censor his creative artists' (*Hustler* November 1983, p. 65) because satire 'is a necessary tool in an uptight world where people are afraid to discuss their prejudices . . .' (*Hustler* July 1994, p. 108).

Thus *Hustler* does not position itself simply as a sex magazine but rather also as a magazine which is not afraid to tell the truth about politics. This linking of the sexual with the political makes *Hustler* cartoons a particularly powerful cultural product for the production and reproduction of racist ideology for, as

Snead argues, 'it is both as a political and as a sexual threat that black skin appears on screen' (Snead 1994, p. 8). On the surface, these cartoons would seem to be one more example of *Hustler*'s 'outrageous' sexual humor, the Black male with the huge penis being equivalent to the other sexually deviant (white) cartoon characters. However, *Hustler*'s depictions of Black men are actually part of a much larger regime of racial representation which, beginning with *The Birth of a Nation*, and continuing with Willie Horton, makes the Black male's supposed sexual misconduct a metaphor for the inferior nature of the Black 'race' as a whole.

Black men and white women: The white man under siege

During the 1980s, *Hustler* featured the work of four cartoonists, Collins, Decetin, Tinsley and Trosley. What is surprising is that while these cartoonists had very distinct styles, they all used a similar caricatured image of a Black male with an enormous muscular body, undersized head (signifying retardation), very dark skin and caricatured lips. The striking feature of this caricature is that the 'man' is drawn to resemble an ape, an image which, according to Snead (1994), has historical and literary currency in this country. Pointing to King Kong as a prime example of this representation, Snead argued that 'a willed misreading of Linnaean classification and Darwinian evolution helped buttress an older European conception . . . that blacks and apes, kindred denizens of the 'jungle', are phylogenetically closer and sexually more compatible than blacks and whites' (Snead 1994, p. 20). Black film critics have long argued that the King Kong movie and its sequels played a major role in the sexual demonization of Black masculinity since the ape—the carrier of blackness—was depicted as out of white control; the result being the stalking and capturing of a white woman.

While the original Kong was lacking a penis, the *Hustler* version has as his main characteristic a huge black penis that is often wrapped around the 'man's' neck or is sticking out of his trouser leg. The penis, whether erect or limp, visually dominates the cartoon and is the focus of humor. This huge penis is depicted as a source of great pride and as a feature which distinguishes Black men from white men. For example, in one cartoon, a Black and white man are walking next to a fence with the white male making a noise by dragging a stick along the fence; the Black man is doing the same only he is using his large penis which is much bigger than the stick. The Black male, who is walking behind the white man, is snickering at the white male's stick (*Hustler* February 1989, p. 95).

Black men are depicted as being obsessed by the size of their penis which is one more example of how the dominant regime of racist representation constructs Blacks as 'having bodies but not minds' (Mercer 1994, p. 138). In one cartoon, a large Black male with an undersized head is looking at his newborn son and screaming at the white nurse, 'Never mind how much he weighs, bitch! How long's my boy's dick?' (*Hustler* 1988 December, p. 32). Not only is the Black male depicted as verbally abusive but also as lacking care and interest in his son's health and well-being. This image fits in with the dominant representation of Black men as either abusive or absent fathers who take advantage of the welfare system developed by misguided liberals (see below).

Whereas the King Kong movies left to the imagination what would happen to the white woman if Kong had his way, *Hustler* provides the mainly white readership with detailed images of the violence Black men are seen as capable of doing to white women's bodies. In many of the cartoons, the theme of the joke is the severely traumatized vagina of the white sexual partner. In one cartoon, a naked white woman is sitting on a bed, legs open, and her vagina has red stars around it, suggesting pain. Sitting on the end of the bed is a naked, very dark, ape-like male, his huge, erect penis dominating the image. He is on the phone asking room service to send in a shoe horn. The white woman looks terrified (*Hustler* November 1988, p. 100). In another cartoon, a similar-looking couple are walking down the street. The Black male has his arm around the white female and on his shirt is written 'Fucker'; on hers is 'Fuckee' (*Hustler* May 1987, p. 79). Although the male is clothed, the outline of his huge penis can be seen. The woman's vagina on the other hand is clearly visible since it is hanging below her knees and is again red and sore, a marker of what Black men can and will do to white women if not stopped by the white male protector of white womanhood.

In *Hustler* cartoons, the white male is constructed as anything but the protector of white womanhood. He is a lower-working-class, middle-aged male whose flabby body is no match for the muscular, enormous black body. In stark contrast to the big black penis is the small-to-average white penis which is rarely erect and never threatening to white women. On the contrary, the size of the white man's penis is a source of ridicule or frustration to his sex partner (who is always white). Rather than showing empathy, the woman is constantly poking fun at his 'manhood', searching for it with magnifying glasses or binoculars. One cartoon, for example, has a white couple in bed with the woman under the covers gleefully shouting, 'Oh I found it!' (*Hustler* May 1992, p. 10). The man is clearly embarrassed and covering up his penis. Other cartoons show the white man endlessly searching pornography shops for penis enlargers (presumably the same enlargers which can be mail ordered from the ads in the back of *Hustler*). A cartoon which speaks to the racial differences constructed in the cartoons depicts a Black man with a small penis; the joke is focused on the size since a Black preacher is praying for his penis to grow. The caption reads, 'Sweet Jesus—heal this poor brother! Rid him of his honkie pecker' (*Hustler* March 1984, p. 15).

The size of the black penis is the theme of a full page 'interview' between *Hustler* editors and 'The Biggest, Blackest Cock Ever!' (November 1983, p. 6). The page is in the same format as *Hustler* interviews, but in place of a person is a picture of a large black penis. The subtitle reads: 'A candid, explosive man-to-dick conversation with the most sought after piece of meat in the world'. *Hustler* editors ask, 'Why do women love big, black cocks?' The answer given by the 'cock' (which is of course written by the *Hustler* editors) is '. . . they love the size . . . you know any white guys hung like this?' The editors continue by framing the discussion in clearly political terms by their answer to the question of why Black men prefer white women: 'I likes [*sic*] white pussy best. It's my way of gettin back at you honkies by tearin' up all that tight white pussy . . . I fuck those bitches blind.' Indeed, the cartoons surrounding this interview provide visual 'testimony' of how much damage the black penis can do to white women.

The small penis would seem one of the reasons why white male cartoon characters, in contrast to black male cartoon characters, have trouble finding willing sex partners. His sexual frustration leads him to seek female surrogates in the form of dolls, bowling balls, children, chickens and skulls. The Black man, however, appears to have no problem attracting a bevy of young white women. When the white man does find a willing sex partner, she tends to be middle-aged, overweight and very hairy. The Black man's white sexual partner is, however, usually thin, attractive and lacks body hair. This is a very unusual female image in *Hustler* cartoons and suggests that the Black male is siphoning off the few sexually available, attractive women, leaving the white man with rejects.

The message that white women prefer Black men is the theme of a spoof on Barbie, a doll which represents the all-American female with her blonde hair, tiny waist and silicone-like breasts. The picture is of Barbie dressed in black underwear, on her knees with ejaculate around her mouth. Standing next to her is a black male doll pulling a very large penis out of her mouth. The caption reads '. . . in an attempt to capture the market the manufacturer has been testing some new designs . . . We're not sure, but perhaps this Slut Barbie (with her hard nipples, a permanently wet, open pussy and sperm dripping from her mouth) goes a bit too far' (*Hustler* July 1984, p. 23). The obvious choice for Barbie's sex partner would have been Ken, her long-term boyfriend, but the suggestion here is that Ken, with his white penis, would not have been enticing enough for this all-American girl to give up her virginal status.

Because of the lack of willing sex partners, the white man is often reduced to paying for sex. However, once again, Black men have the upper hand since almost all the pimps in *Hustler* cartoons are black. These Black men have, however, traded in their large penises for big Cadillacs, heavy gold jewelry and fur coats, riches no doubt obtained from white johns. The prostitutes are both black and white but the johns are almost always depicted as white. Many of the cartoons have as their theme the white man trying to barter down the black pimp, with the black pimp refusing to change the price. The power of the Black man is now absolute—not only can he get his pick of attractive white women, he also controls white prostitutes, leaving the white man having to negotiate to buy what he once got for free.

Not only is the Black man draining the white man's access to women, he is also draining his pocket in the form of welfare. The Black male is shown as deserting his family and numerous unkempt, diseased children, leaving the welfare system to pick up the tab. One cartoon features a Black woman surrounded by children saying to a white interviewer, 'Yes, we does [sic] believe in Welfare' (*Hustler* December 1992, p. 47). Another example is a cartoon advertising different dolls. The first doll is called 'Beach Darbie' which is a Barbie look-alike in a bathing costume. The second doll, also Barbie, is dressed in a white jacket and is called 'Ski Darbie'. The third doll is an overweight white female with bedroom slippers and a cigarette hanging out of her mouth; she is called 'Knocked-Up Inner-City Welfare Darbie'. In each hand she has a black baby (*Hustler* December 1992, p. 107).

In *Hustler* cartoons Black men have precisely the two status symbols that white men lack: big penises and money. The white man's poor sexual performance is matched by his poor economic performance. Reduced to living in trailer homes, poorly furnished apartments or tract houses, the *Hustler*'s white male cartoon character is clearly depicted as lower-working-class. His beer gut, stubble, bad teeth and working man's clothes signify his economic status and stand in sharp contrast to the signifiers of power attached to the image of the Black male.

A new ending to an old story

The coding of Black men as sexual and economic threats takes on a contemporary twist in *Hustler* since this threat cannot be easily murdered as in King Kong, but rather is now uncontainable and returns month after month to wreak havoc on white women's bodies and white men's pay checks. This new ending changes the relationship between the binary representations of Black and white masculinity. In his analysis of the racial coding of masculinity in cinema, Snead argues that 'American films . . . have always featured . . . implicit or explicit co-relations between the debasement of blacks and the elevation and mythification of whites' (1994, p. 142). In *Hustler* cartoons, both Black and white men are debased, the former for being hyper-masculine, and the latter for not being masculine enough.

Since the target audience of *Hustler* is white men, it would seem surprising that the cartoons regularly ridicule white men for being sexually and economically impotent and for failing to contain the Black menace. However, when class is factored into the analysis, it becomes apparent that it is not simply white men as a group who are being ridiculed. The debasement of white masculinity in *Hustler* cartoons is played out on the caricatured flabby, unkempt body of the lower-working-class white male, a class that few whites see themselves as belonging to, irrespective of their income. Thus, in between the hyper-masculinity of the Black male and the under-masculinized white lower-working-class male, is the reader inscribed in the text, who can feel superior to both types of 'deviants'. The reader is being invited to identify with what is absent in the cartoons: a 'real man' (*Hustler*'s first issue ran an editorial which introduced the magazine as one for 'real men'), who turns to *Hustler* because it is, according to its editors, 'truly the only magazine that deals with the concerns and interests of the average American' (*Hustler* 1984, p. 5).

The reader, constructed as the average American, is, as *Hustler* is careful about pointing out, not the same as the cartoon characters. In an editorial praising Tinsley, the editors wrote 'Dwaine Tinsley is not a black, a jew, a wino, a child molester, or a bigot. But the characters in his cartoon are. They are everything you have nightmares about, everything you despise . . .' (November 1983, p. 65). Thus, in coded terms *Hustler* provides distance between the reader and the cartoon characters who are either lower-class (black, wino, child molester, bigot) or the elite (jew), by leaving open the 'middle class', the category where most white Americans situate themselves (Jhally and Lewis 1992).

The lower-class, sexually impotent white male in *Hustler* cartoons is thus not an object of identification but rather of ridicule and a pitiful example of what could happen if white men fail to assert their masculinity and allow the Black male to roam the streets and bedrooms of white society. This character thus stands as a symbol of the devastation that Blacks can cause, a devastation brought about by 'bleeding heart' liberals who mistakenly allowed Blacks too much freedom. Just as Gus (the black would-be rapist) in *The Birth of a Nation* was an example of what could happen when blacks are given their freedom from slavery (a dead white woman being the end result), *Hustler*'s Black male is an example of what could happen if Black men are not contained by white institutional forces such as the police and the courts. Whereas *The Birth of a Nation* and King Kong were, according to Snead, the past nightmare visions of the future, *Hustler*'s representation of Black men can be seen as the current nightmare vision of the future, since it 're-enacts what never happened, but does so in an attempt to keep it from ever happening' (Snead 1994, p. 148).

By making the white male the loser, *Hustler* departs from the traditional racial coding of masculinity and provides a different ending to the nightmare vision of Black men taking over. This ending is, however, not simply restricted to the pages of *Hustler*; it is rather articulated in the numerous news stories on 'welfare cheats', 'inner-city violence' and 'reverse discrimination'. The 'white male' is, according to the media, fast becoming the new 'minority' who has to support black families in the inner city; it is he who has to give up his job to an unqualified black person because of past oppression. The white male is under siege and unless he fights back, he will lose his masculine status as breadwinner. The absence in *Hustler* cartoons of elite whites as exploiters of poor whites firmly positions the Black male as the 'other' who is the source of white male discontent. Given the current economic conditions, which include falling wages, downsizing and offshore production, the 'average' white male (along with everyone else who is not a member of the economic elite) is experiencing increasing levels of discontent, and, as in previous periods of economic decline, it is the Black population who are demonized and scapegoated as the cause of the economic woes.

While the racial codings of masculinity may shift according to the socio-economic conditions, from the feminized 'Uncle Tom' to the hyper-masculinized 'buck', Black masculinity continues to be represented as deviant. It is this constructed deviant status which continues to legitimize the oppression and brutality that condemns young Black males to a life on the margins of society and makes them the convenient scapegoat for the economic and social upheaval brought about by global capitalism and right-wing government policies. While this article has placed in the foreground *Hustler* cartoons, the regime of racial representation discussed continues to inform most mainstream media content and contributes to the 'common sense' notion that it is Black culture, not white supremacy, that is the source of racial strife in America.

References

Carby, H. (1993). 'Encoding White Resentment: "Grand Canyon"—A Narrative'. In C. McCarthy and W. Crichlow (eds.). *Race, Identity and Representation in Education*. New York: Routledge. (pp. 236–247).

Cowan, G. and R. Campbell. (1994). 'Racism and Sexism in Interracial Pornography: A Content Analysis'. *Psychology of Women Quarterly*, 18. (pp. 323–338).

Dyson, M. (1993). *Reflecting Black: African-American Cultural Criticism*. Minneapolis: University of Minnesota Press.

Entman, R. (1990). 'Modern Racism and the Image of Blacks'. *Critical*

Studies in Mass Communication, 7. (pp. 332–45).

Flynt, L. (November 1983). 'The Politics of Porn'. *Hustler*. (p. 5).

Flynt, L. (July 1988). 'Fuck You if You Can't Take a Joke'. *Hustler*. (p. 7).

Forna, A. (1992). 'Pornography and Racism: Sexualizing Oppression and Inciting Hatred'. In C. Itzin (ed.). *Women, Violence and Civil Liberties: A Radical New View*. Oxford: Oxford University Press.

Gombrich, E. (1963). *Meditations on a Hobby Horse*. London: Phaidon Publications.

Gray, H. (1989). 'Television, Black Americans and the American Dream'. *Critical Studies in Mass Communication*. 6. (pp. 376–385).

Guerrero, E. (1993). *Framing Blackness: The African American Image in Film*. Philadelphia: Temple University Press.

Jhally, S. and J. Lewis (1992). *Enlightened Racism: The Cosby Show, Audiences, and the Myth of the American Dream*. Boulder: Westview Press.

Jones, J. (1993). 'The Construction of Black Sexuality: Towards Normalizing the Black Cinematic Experience'. In M. Diawara (ed.). *Black American Cinema*. New York: Routledge. (pp. 247–256).

Mayall, A., and D. Russell. (1993). 'Racism in Pornography'. In D. Russell (ed.). *Making Violence Sexy: Feminist Views on Pornography*. New York: Teachers College Press.

Mercer, K. (1994). *Welcome to the Jungle: New Positions in Black Cultural Studies*. New York: Routledge.

Osanka, F. (1989). *Sourcebook on Pornography*. Lexington, MA: Lexington Books.

Riggs, Marlon (producer/director). (1987). *Ethnic Notions* [Documentary film]. San Francisco: California Newsreel.

Rose, T. (1994). *Black Noise: Rap Music and Black Culture in Contemporary America*. Hanover, NH: University of New England Press.

Snead, J. (1994). *White Screen, Black Images: Hollywood from the Dark Side*. New York: Routledge.

'The Biggest Blackest Cock Ever'. (November 1983). *Hustler*. (p. 6).

Wiegman, R. (1993). 'Feminism, "The Boyz", and Other Matters Regarding the Male'. In S. Cohan and I. R. Hark (eds.). *Screening the Male: Exploring Masculinities in Hollywood Cinema*. New York: Routledge. (pp. 173–193).

Winston, M. (1982). 'Racial Consciousness and the Evolution of Mass Communication in the United States'. *Daedalus*. 4. (pp. 171–182).

Chong Kim

Nobody's concubine

....

I am a 29-year-old Asian single mother. I was involved in the sex industry beginning in the early summer of 1994 in Lawton, Oklahoma. I started out as an exotic dancer and worked my way up. My name was Jules when I was in the industry. I am including it here because I want my clients to know what I really felt about them.

Before this turn took place in my life, I was a child who had abuse and ridicule written all over my face. I was abused by my prominent family who went to church every Sunday, followed every rule in the Bible and were excellent hard-working citizens of the United States. Why would anyone want to believe that abuse can exist in such a child's life?

As years went on, I was known as the 'Ugly Duckling'. I would open pages of *Playboy* magazines and wish that I could be as beautiful and powerful as I thought these women were. Unlike most teenage girls, I was a tomboy. I stayed to myself, had very few friends, and I was a virgin. This was one thing I wanted to hang on to, to prove to my family—and especially to myself—that I wasn't this whore they thought I'd turn out to be. I wanted to believe that I was not a 'toy' for men.

In May of 1994 I was everything I should have been: a young girl, not known for cursing in her language, a virgin. Boys weren't a big issue for me. I went to mass when I was told, and most of all I was engaged to the one young man I had loved for nine years, my high school sweetheart.

Things went smoothly up until the evening of June 7, 1994, when a friend of mine encouraged me to do something spontaneous. At that time, my family and I were living in Chickasha, Oklahoma, about two hours from Lawton. That night my friend and I met up with two guys, one of whom was a taxicab driver. I had very low self-esteem, and nobody had taught me about dating. I just took my insights from movies and assumed that men were cordial and respectful. That night, my friend and the guy she left with disappeared on me, leaving me with a man I knew nothing about. It was hot that evening, and he stated that he was going to go to a hotel. As innocent as I was, and with the mind of a twelve-year-old, and knowing nothing about sex, I agreed to stay with him at the hotel, believing that he was not a bad guy.

That evening I was raped. My world, my thoughts, and my self-esteem changed. My boyfriend at the time broke up with me after I mentioned the rape. I was emotionally torn by the betrayal. My family had shut me out when I was abused as a child, and now my boyfriend had decided to shut me out too. I soon came to believe that I was not worth anything anymore.

After the rape, I started out dancing. The power of those men wanting me, the jealousy of other women glaring at me, was a rush—an extreme rush I had never felt before. I became very promiscuous and didn't care anymore. My heart turned cold. I was the woman that every man fantasized about and every woman's nightmare—or so I thought.

In 1995, I was introduced to an escort service after escaping from an abusive boyfriend. My abuser had destroyed my citizenship certificate, so that there would be no proof that I was a legal resident of the US. He also shredded my license and social security card. I had nothing but a Blockbuster card, which didn't help me in finding jobs, welfare, or housing. Without the documents I could not even work at the clubs. What was I to do without a job, home, or money to even survive?

I knew nothing about escort services; I was told it was a dating service, that if an available bachelor who was rich wanted to take a classy lady out to dinner, we'd be the ones to be called. I asked them if we would have to sell our bodies. The agent of the escort service reassured me that this was nothing like prostitution.

After a few calls, the money came in great—until I was raped by a client, and then the agency was angry at me. I went to the police, and they just laughed at me, saying, 'If you got yourself into the escort service, then you can get yourself out.' There was no sympathy there. The agency gave me an ultimatum that if I chose to quit, I'd be back at square one, homeless with no money. I took a good look at myself in the mirror that evening, and I broke down and cried. I was not getting any type of welfare or support, due to having no documents. So the next day I swallowed my pride, and went back to being an Escort Lady.

The more I got in, the more I enjoyed the cash flow, the men, and how I was known as a 'high stakes' girl. Due to the fact that I was Asian, I was worth more than the other girls. The price for the others was $200, and for me it was $275. I began to feel like a 'Million Dollar Bitch'. I loved this new slogan I made for myself.

Narcotics played a big role in my life. That's why I was constantly broke. I couldn't face these clients all on my own. My emotions would have gotten to me, so I had to take something to medicate myself. The clients I was involved with were no strangers, but very prominent men: teachers, lawyers, child psychologists, doctors, priests, and church members as well; you'd be surprised how many more. That's when my trust in society disappeared. These men lived double lives, and the sad part was that no one knew about it, nor did they even care.

After a while, the clients wanted more. They expected me to be the 'Asian Girl' they were told about: a concubine, a woman who would become their sex slave and was willing to endure any kind of pain. So then my occupation changed from being paid to satisfy these men into being a punching bag. Day in and day out I was beat, raped, and stabbed. I had no justice, nor would anyone want to hear. I continued in the industry not to survive or to take care of my kids, but due to the familiarity of being abused, and due to the fact that I didn't feel love in my life. As long as I was in a stranger's arms, I was content with that.

In the spring of 1998, I met my son's father, and it was he who broke me out of the industry. At the time I was residing in Pittsburgh, Pennsylvania. He taught me the true value of beauty, and when it was okay and not okay to dress sexy. He was the man I was searching for. Just having someone no longer hitting me, but touching me with gentle hands, looking at me with admiration instead of those lustful eyes, I knew in my heart I would never forget this moment. In the early fall of 1998, this boyfriend committed suicide and passed away. It tore me apart, and I kept wondering why I had to keep surviving. But a month after his death, when I wanted to kill myself, ending all misery, I was awakened by the knowledge that I was going to be a mother. I sat there and cried. And from that point on, looking back at my history of abuse, I knew it was now my duty to give this child what I never had: love.

Since moving to Minneapolis nearly four and a half years ago, I've been working on improving my life emotionally, financially, mentally, and spiritually. My daughter, who is now six years old, has been adopted in Dallas, Texas, due to my history of prostitution. My four-year-old son is currently residing with my family in Texas due to his health needs. Although I am a recovering cocaine addict, I have been clean and sober since February 22, 2000. During my four years of recovery, I've been able to acquire emotional stability through counseling, groups, and finding a spiritual ground for myself.

Now I speak to organizations and even high schools about prostitution and pornography and how they affect all lives, not just those of women. I'm currently writing a book about my life, called *Silent Cries*. It is dedicated to children who are victims of sexual violence and exploitation. It is my way to speak out loud about the trauma and the pain I went through as a small child, and the courage I had to get to where I am today.

It's not easy being a woman, but being a woman of color is even harder—especially one with heavy cultural expectations from family and society. All my life, not just in prostitution, I have been stereotyped by men of all races—mostly white, but also black, Hispanic, and Asian. Men come up to me and say that they want to date me because I'm Asian. When I ask them why, their response is, 'You can take care of a man better than a white woman.' I find this offensive. They expect me to play the 'submissive' role because of my cultural background. We are here in the US, not in Asia, and I do not like it when people expect me to fit the stereotype of an Asian woman. I am not an Asian woman, but just a woman—not because I have to be, but because I'm proud to be one. Do not treat me like an Asian woman; treat me with humanity. Do not pick me out of a crowd of women because of my race, because I will not come to you. Pick me because I am intelligent, and I am beautiful inside and out.

Melissa Farley and Jacqueline Lynne

Prostitution in Vancouver: Pimping women and the colonization of First Nations

Introduction

The recent history of Canada is the history of the colonization of First Nations.[1] Colonization is a process that includes geographic incursion, sociocultural dislocation, the establishment of external political control and economic dispossession, the provision of low-level social services, and ultimately, the creation of ideological formulations around race and skin colour that position the colonizers at a higher evolutionary level than the colonized (Frideres 1983).

Colonial practices that harmed Canada's First Nations were theft of land, the imposition of private property rights on nations, brutal labor exploitation, and violent conversions to Christianity. In order to recognize the sexual exploitation of First Nations women in contemporary Canadian prostitution, one must first understand how all First Nations women were subjugated by sexist colonial policies. Prostitution requires a devalued class of women (Barry 1995) which Canada produced by means of powerfully oppressive and interlocking forces: the military, the state, the church, and market capitalism.

Canada's First Nations peoples suffered colonial oppression from both the British and the French. Colonization results in a multitude of losses among those who are colonized. Colonized peoples lose their land, often their language and culture, and their health as well. Prostitution can be understood as the colonization of women by men, generally. Since prostitution is hierarchically structured not only by gender but also by race/ethnicity and by class, First Nations Canadian women are often at the bottom of a brutal hierarchy within prostitution itself.

Colonization of Canada's First Nations

Canada's colonizers profited from the prostitution of First Nations women. The following is an early account of colonial procurement and First Nations resistance:

---

1   We use the terms 'Aboriginal', 'First Nations', and 'Native' throughout this paper to refer to nations of people who have lived in Canada continuously for thousands of years.

The . . . Chipewyan Indians complain . . . of the injustice done to them by the Canadians in taking their women from them by force; some of the Canadians keep no less than 3 women . . . [For example, a] Canadian that had 2 women before, went to their tents and took a young woman away by force . . . The old Indian, her father, interfered, he was knocked down . . . all this is encouraged by their masters, who often stand as Pimps to procure women . . . they make great profit, the Masters in the Traffic of the Females for the mens uses. (Philip Turner 1792, cited in Bourgeault 1989, pp. 100–101)

This same pattern is seen globally throughout history.[2]

Much has been written regarding the North American genocide (Churchill 1992; Ryser 1995).[3] The effect of colonization has resulted in 90 percent depopulation of Indian peoples throughout the western hemisphere from 1492 to the 1920s when the population began once again to increase (Ryser 2001). Estimates of the First Nations population of Canada at the time of first contact with Europeans range from 220,000 to two million, with a conservative figure of 500,000 currently accepted by Canada's Royal Commission on Aboriginal Health (RCAP 1996, p. 116). Estimates of contemporary First Nations populations vary. The official 1996 Canadian Census of the First Nations population in Vancouver is 1.7 percent, whereas the estimate from the 1998–1999 Capture/Recapture data cites 7 percent of Vancouver/Richmond's people as First Nations (Healing Ways Aboriginal Health and Service Review 1999).

For its first 100 years, Canada functioned primarily as a military and commercial outpost of Great Britain. The Hudson's Bay Company prohibited European women from emigrating to Canada, thus Canada's first brothels were established around military bases and trading posts. Sometimes First Nations women were traded or purchased by colonists in exchange for alcohol or European goods (Absolon, Herbert and MacDonald 1996).

---

2 For example, in 1909, a Kenyan official described the need for 'home comforts' of Europeans in Nairobi (Leys 1902, cited by White 1988). In 1938, Nairobi's Municipal Native Affairs Officer noted that when indigenous men were trafficked for labor, a population imbalance of one female for every eight males resulted, with 'a demand for a large number of native prostitutes.' Trafficking of Kikuyu girls into Nairobi was 'continually mentioned by the Kikuyu Native Councils urging that steps be taken to stop it.' (St. Davies 1939, cited by White 1988)

3 Estimates of the population of North America in 1492 range from 4 million (Denevan 1992) to 18 million people (Ryser 2001). The smaller the number presumed at first contact, then the smaller the number of those presumed dead from genocide. And the smaller the number of First Nations people today, the smaller the likelihood of funding allocations. A similar slippage occurs in population estimates of US Indians. Primarily a result of improved data collection by the US Census, the recorded population of American Indians and Alaska Natives in the United States increased by 250 percent from 1960 to 2000 (Population Reference Bureau 2000).

Christian ideology provided a moral cover for colonization. 'Health' and 'Christianity' were equated, as were 'traditional' and 'diseased' (Kelm 1998, p. 59; Choney *et al.* 1995). Colonizers viewed First Nations women as breeders of savages who required taming and civilizing. Forced conversions of Native peoples to Christianity devalued women's spiritual role within nations.

The Canadian residential school system was one means of cultural and physical assault against First Nations (Lomawaima 1994; Haig-Brown 1993, p. 15). The schools were run jointly by the Department of Indian Affairs and Christian churches. First Nations youth were removed from their homes, physically controlled in residential schools, and subjected to teaching that ignored or demeaned their cultures. The International Human Rights Association of American Minorities documented great harm against 50,000 Native children in these boarding schools. Children were tortured for speaking Aboriginal languages. Other human rights violations committed by church administrators included murder by beating, poisoning, hanging, starvation, strangulation, involuntary sterilization and medical experimentation. The document also noted that church clergy, police, and government officials were involved in maintaining pedophile rings using children from residential schools (INCITE! 2001).

The Royal Commission report documented the perilous state of First Nations housing in 1996: 84 percent of Aboriginal households on reserves did not have sufficient income to cover housing (RCAP 1996, p. 180). Housing instability increases reserve-to-urban migration, leaving young women extremely vulnerable to prostitution, since homelessness is a primary risk factor for prostitution. When women in prostitution are asked what they need in order to get out, first on their list of needs is housing (Farley *et al.* 1998; 2003).

> Aboriginal people are more likely to face inadequate nutrition, substandard housing and sanitation, unemployment and poverty, discrimination and racism, violence, inappropriate or absent services, and subsequent high rates of physical, social and emotional illness, injury, disability and premature death. (Canada, Royal Commission on Aboriginal Peoples 1996, p. 107)

Colonization resulted in chronic health problems that have been well documented among First Nations in Canada. Among the Sioux in Ontario, for example, health problems include: cardiovascular disease; respiratory disease; renal disease; poor nutrition; cancers; dental caries; ear, nose and throat infections; high-risk pregnancies; birth anomalies; multiple mental illnesses; poisonings and injuries; communicable disease; and tuberculosis (Beardy 1992, cited in RCAP, p. 203).

The transformation of Aboriginal people from the state of good health that had impressed travellers from Europe to one of ill health, for which Aboriginal people were (and still are) often held responsible, grew worse as sources of food and clothing from the land declined and traditional economies collapsed. It grew worse still as once-mobile peoples were confined to small plots of land where resources and opportunities for natural sanitation were limited. It worsened yet again as long-standing norms, values, social systems, and spiritual practices were undermined or outlawed. (RCAP 1996, p. 113)

The physical harms of colonialism cannot be separated from its psychological and spiritual damage. Disconnecting First Nations people from culture and history, 'colonialism is not satisfied merely with holding a people in its grip and emptying the native's brain of all form and content . . . it turns to the past of the people, and distorts, disfigures and destroys it' (Fanon 1963, p. 210).

In 1890, Rizal described the psychological effects of Spain's colonization of the Filipino people. His description applies equally to Canada's First Nations:

. . . little by little they lost their old traditions, the mementos of their past; they gave up their writing, their songs, their poems, their laws in order to learn by rote other doctrines which they did not understand, another morality, another aesthetics different from those inspired by their climate and their manner of thinking. Then they declined, degrading themselves in their own eyes; they became ashamed of what was their own; they began to admire and praise whatever was foreign and incomprehensible; their spirit was dismayed and it surrendered [to] . . . this disgust of themselves. (Rizal 1972, p. 58)

The self-hatred, sense of inferiority, and sluggishness described by Rizal might also include symptoms of malnutrition, despair, depression, substance abuse or all of these. Racism and cultural stereotyping are chronic, insidious traumas that wear away at peoples' self esteem and well-being (Root 1996). In a series of studies, Kirmayer (1994; 2000) documented the psychological consequences of racism and cultural alienation among First Nations youth: high rates of interpersonal violence, depression, suicide, and substance abuse.

Alcohol and drug abuse claim the lives of countless First Nations people. Discussing the role of addictions among First Nations, Summit leader Bill Wilson stated:

When you look at the conditions that [First Nations people] are in, it would be a surprise to me if they did quit drugs and alcohol and stopped committing suicide. We are not dealing with the core problem in all of this. If we had healthy communities that were thriving and had an economy, in all probability, we wouldn't be as interested in doing drugs and alcohol. (Rees, 2001)

Not surprisingly, the suicide rate among First Nations is three times higher than that of other Canadians. It is six times higher for those aged 15–24 (Bobet 1990). According to some observers, suicide rates parallel the destruction of cultures. There is a strong link between alcoholism and suicide (Foster 2001).[4]

Colonization, racism, and prostitution

Theft of land and destruction of traditional ways of life left many First Nations people in a state of extreme poverty that has endured for generations. In 1990, 80 to 90 percent of First Nations women raising children by themselves in urban Winnipeg, Regina and Saskatoon were living below the poverty level. (Statistics Canada 1991 Census, RCAP 1996, p. 171). This overwhelming level of poverty in any patriarchal culture tends to be associated with a high rate of prostitution.

Prior to European invasion, the majority of First Nations women and men lived in relatively egalitarian relationships (Bourgeault 1989).[5] We are not suggesting that prostitution in some form did not exist among First Nations. Sexual exploitation is not exclusive to European culture, and prostitution in Canada cannot be said to have been 'wrought in toto by the white man, by his capitalist relations of production or depraved sexual proclivities . . .' (Hammar 1999, discussing Papua New Guinea prostitution, p. 79). However, with European contact, prostitution of First Nations was institutionalized and greatly expanded.

---

4   Similar health consequences of colonialism on Aboriginal people are seen in health data from the United States. American Indians and Alaska Natives have the second-highest infant mortality rate in USA, and the suicide rate of American Indians is 50 percent higher than the national rate. (US Dept of Health and Human Services 2001, p. 82; US Dept of Health and Human Services 2001a, p. 17)

5   Colonialism inflicted simultaneous race and sex discrimination on First Nations women. First Nations women's traditional roles and status were undermined by colonizers who saw women's position as subversive to the political, social and religious order formulated by Canada's colonists. (LaFromboise, Heyle and Ozer 1990). The Indian Act of 1876 was a legal tool which attempted to assimilate First Nations into European culture, and which specifically disenfranchised First Nations women. '[First Nations] women marrying out was an engine of assimilation and extinction that [First Nations] men marrying out was not.' (MacKinnon 2001, p. 458). First Nations women who married non-status men were forced to leave their parental homes and reserves; their children were not recognized as First Nations, and therefore were denied access to community and financial benefits. First Nations women were excluded from voting, running for political office on band councils, and they could not own land. Cruelly, the Indian Act also held the power to deny a First Nations woman's return to family on the reserve for any reason— even if she was ill, widowed, or divorced. Upon her death, she was denied the right to be buried on a reserve with her ancestors (Jamieson 1978). No such restrictions were placed on First Nations men.

Prostitution is colonization of women, generally. Although infrequently analyzed as such (Lynne 1998; Scully 2001) prostitution is also a specific legacy of colonialism in that it constructs a colonial institution to exploit indigenous women along with the exploitation of other First Nations resources. Prostitution of Aboriginal women occurs globally, in epidemic numbers. Hierarchies within prostitution locate indigenous women at the bottom of a brutal race and class hierarchy (in addition to their being at the bottom of race and class hierarchies in other walks of life).

Colonists supplied First Nations men working as indentured labourers with sexual access to women of their own ethnicity. Thus one aspect of colonial prostitution was colonists' calculated intention to keep white women off-limits to indigenous men (Hunt 1986; Scully 2001). Colonizers used First Nations women as domestic servants (including sexual servants) and as objects to provide sex acts to First Nations men in order to offer incentive to the men to remain in labor bondage. British military officers in Canada acquired 'country brides' in marriage-like prostitution, providing men with exclusive sexual access to First Nations women. Children were often born from this concubinage, although European common law did not recognize these relationships. When European women were later permitted to emigrate to Canada, European men abandoned their First Nations families, preferring the European family (Bourgeault 1989).

First Nations women were considered 'exotic' sexual commodities and were assumed by British and French colonizers to enjoy that status, not only because they were seen as primitive and savage but also because they were female. Yet men's assumption of the right to rape indigenous women is not a new idea. Vespucci, a colleague of Christopher Columbus, wrote that women colonized by the Spanish in 1498 were 'urged by excessive lust, defiled and prostituted themselves' (Small and Jaffe 1991). Colonist Vespucci, like other johns, attributed his own impulse to sexually assault First Nations women to the colonized/prostituted woman herself.

The life and death of Casey Jo Pipestem, a Seminole girl who was prostituted and murdered, is typical of the continued violence against First Nations women who struggle with family violence, cultural conflict, migration, prostitution, and poverty. The conflict between traditional Seminole values and urban street survival was a part of Casey's life from birth onwards. She was raised by her grandmother who taught her traditional ways. At age seven Casey was the youngest Buffalo Dancer in the Seminole Nation. Devastated by her grandmother's death when she was eight, she returned to her mother's home, but was soon on the streets. Casey was close to her stepfather who was murdered when Casey was thirteen, at which time she moved from Oklahoma City to Seminole where she lived with an uncle, a former tribal administrator. Her high school basketball coach recalled Casey's exceptional athletic skill. Although she was described by her uncle as being 'in the process of returning to traditional ways,' Casey still had 'city ways' and did not fit in. Her uncle said that Casey 'didn't wear the same clothes as the other kids, didn't speak the same language, and she didn't have any friends.' At age seventeen, feeling alienated in rural Seminole, she returned to Oklahoma City and to a street life. She met an older pimp who quickly addicted her to drugs and prostituted her. Two years later, she was murdered near a truck stop (Moore 2004).

Prostitution and globalization

Pimps and traffickers take advantage of the subordinate status of women and girls by exploiting sexist and racist stereotypes of women as servants and commodities. The economic dependence of countries on multinational corporations creates conditions for women to sell their own sexual exploitation at far better rates of pay than other forms of labor, thereby promoting prostitution and trafficking (Hernandez 2001). Global economic policies seamlessly weave together sexism, racism, and colonialism via invasions of peoples' lands, causing agricultural and community dislocation and environmental destruction. These devastating events result in poverty and subsequent rural-to-urban migration which produces an urban workforce available for labor exploitation generally, as well as for prostitution of women and children. Promoting prostitution as a reasonable job for poor women, the International Labor Organization euphemistically declared: 'Mobile populations tend to have greater motivation and opportunities for commercial sex' (Lim 1998, p. 34). A current example of this 'motivation' is the situation of some nations in Congo.

Congo has been described from the colonist's perspective as '*too well endowed* with natural resources' (Harden 2001, italics added). The colonist cannot be expected to resist the opportunity to rape either the land or its women. The nations of people in what is now called Congo have been devastated by centuries of colonial assault (primarily by Belgium and the United States, but recently also by Rwanda).[6] At the turn of the twentieth century, Leopold of Belgium plundered rubber and slaves from Congo. The most recent resource to be exploited is coltran, a metal used for superconductor chips in cell phones and pagers. Coltran is found in abundant quantities in the lands of the Ituri people (eastern Congo). When the price of coltran crashed (from $80 to $8 a kilo) as a result of environmentalists' protests, the prostitution that had been instituted to provide coltran miners with 'temporary wives' continued even though the mines were closed down (Harden 2001).

---

6   The World Health Organization estimated that 2001's monthly toll of avoidable deaths in Congo was 72,800 (Harden 2001).

Post-colonial violence among First Nations communities

Imposing a sexist and racist regime on First Nations women, the process of colonization elevated male power within the colonized community (Fiske 2002). The cultural destruction of positive roles for First Nations men, and their subsequent identification with supremacist attitudes, have resulted in astronomical rates of husband violence, incest and rape among First Nations. Freire described this process as 'adhesion to the oppressor' (1994, p. 27). Dworkin has also discussed the harm inflicted on women by colonized men:

> The stigma of the prostitute allows the violent, the angry, the socially and politically impoverished male to nurse a grudge against all women, including prostituted women; this is aggressive bias, made rawer and more dangerous by the need to counter one's own presumed inferiority. (Dworkin 2000, p. 325)

For example, in 2004 the Black Pimp has replaced the Black Panther as role model. 'Gangsta pimpology' in the USA permits the formerly colonized/ enslaved man to vent his fury on the women and girls of his community. The image of the cold, in-charge pimp with his stable of 'ho's' has been accurately described as a 'toxic cultural product' that perpetrates ongoing harm (Abu-Jamal 2001).

Nahanee (1993) wrote of 'the almost total victimization of [Aboriginal] women and children' and noted that:

> Violence against Aboriginal women has reached epidemic proportions according to most studies conducted over the past few years. This violence includes the victimization of women and their children, both of whom are seen as property of their men (husbands, lovers, fathers), or of the community in which they live.

Eighty percent of US Indian women seeking care at one clinic reported having been raped (Old Dog Cross 1982). In Canada, the death rates of First Nations women from homicide were more than four times higher than the rate for all Canadian women, and their deaths from suicide were three times that of Canadian women (Health Canada, Medical Services Branch, unpublished tables, 1995, in RCAP, p. 153).

Prostitution in Canada today

The death rate of women in Canadian prostitution is 40 times higher than that of the general population (Special Committee on Pornography and Prostitution, 1985). One woman (in the Netherlands) described prostitution as 'volunteer slavery', articulating both the appearance of choice and the overwhelming coercion behind that choice (Vanwesenbeeck 1994, p. 149). Yakama Elder Russell Jim (1997) described prostitution as 'self-cannibalization'. Jim's characterization suggests the demolition of the self that occurs in prostitution which paradoxically appears to be a result of the victim's own choices.

Prostitution harms those in it, most of whom began prostituting as adolescents. Nadon *et al.* (1998) found that 89 percent of their interviewees had begun prostitution before the age of 16. In Canada, as elsewhere, the average age of entry into prostitution is adolescence (cited as between age thirteen and nineteen in Lowman 1993).[7] Children enter prostitution because of abusive treatment by caregivers (Lowman, 1993, p. 72) and because they run away from dangerous home environments (Federal/Provincial Territorial Working Group on Prostitution 1998). Boyer and colleagues (1993) interviewed 60 women prostituting in escort, street, strip club, phone sex, and massage parlors in Seattle. All began prostituting between the ages of 12 and 14. Fifty-two percent of 183 Vancouver women turned their first trick before the age of 16, and 70 percent were prostitued before age 18 (Cunningham and Christensen 2001).

The vast majority of those in prostitution have been sexually abused as children, usually by several predators. Currie (1994) reported a 73 percent incidence of childhood sexual abuse of women who were prostituting in Vancouver. One girl prostituting in Seattle said:

> We've all been molested. Over and over, and raped. We were all molested and sexually abused as children, don't you know that? We ran to get away. They didn't want us in the house anymore. We were thrown out, thrown away. We've been on the street since we were 12, 13, 14. (Boyer, Chapman and Marshall 1993)

Cunningham and Christensen (2001) found that 68 percent of women prostituting in the Downtown Eastside of Vancouver had been recently raped, and 72 percent had been kidnapped. Of the women interviewed by Cunningham and Christensen, 89 percent reported that customers refused condoms in the previous year, another type of violence.

Prostitution is one type of domestic violence. Physical coercion, rape, and violence by husband/partner/pimp and john are perpetrated against women in prostitution (Currie 1994; Lowman 1994, Lowman and Fraser 1995; Miller 1995; Stark and Hodgson 2003). Giobbe (1993) compared pimps and batterers and found similarities in their use of enforced social isolation, minimization and denial, threats, intimidation, verbal and sexual abuse, attitude of ownership, and extreme physical violence to control women.

---

7   Victoria and British Colombia surveys found the average age of entry into prostitution to be 14–15.5 years, and a Vancouver survey found the average age of entry into prostitution to be 16.3 years for girls and 15.6 years for boys (Lowman and Fraser 1989).

First Nations gay men, like First Nations women, are in double jeopardy. Comparing Canadian Aboriginal and non-Aboriginal gay men, researchers found that the Aboriginal gay men were significantly more depressed and more likely to be poor, unstably housed, and receiving welfare. They were also more likely to have been sexually abused as children, to have had non-consensual sex, and to have been prostituted (Heath *et al.* 1999).

In order to find out about their experiences in prostitution, what preceded their entry into prostitution, and what their current needs were, we interviewed women prostituting in Vancouver, Canada. This study was a part of a multi-country study of the effects of prostitution (Farley *et al.* 2003).

Interviews with women prostituting in Vancouver

Brief structured interviews of 100 prostituting women and children were conducted in Vancouver, BC. We contacted agencies working with prostitutes and set up collaborative efforts where possible. The second author was a board member of a Vancouver agency that provided services to prostitutes and she was familiar with locations where prostitution commonly occurred in Vancouver. She was known to some of our interviewees in her capacity as a social worker. When possible, interviewers were themselves survivors of prostitution or sexual assault. Interviewers were screened for the ability to establish an easygoing rapport on the street and in occasionally dangerous locations. The women we interviewed were from the Downtown Eastside, Franklin, and Broadway/Fraser prostitution strolls in Vancouver. We attempted to contact any woman known to be prostituting, whether indoors or outdoors. We asked women to let their friends who were prostituting elsewhere (e.g., in other areas or indoors) know that we would return to a certain location at a certain time the next day.

Informed consent included a summary of research goals and participants' rights. Respondents' copies of the consent form included names and phone numbers of local agencies that could be contacted for support and assistance and included the authors' phone numbers and email addresses.

Fifty-two percent of our interviewees were women from Canada's First Nations, a significant over-representation of this group of people, compared to their representation in the population of Vancouver generally (1.7–7 percent). Thirty-eight percent were white European-Canadian, 5 percent were African-Canadian, and 5 percent left the question blank. In response to 'race/ethnic group', the majority of the 52 First Nations women described themselves as Native. Next most often, they described themselves as Metis, a French word which translates to English as 'mixed blood' and is used among those we interviewed to describe people who are of both First Nations and European ancestries. Historically, the two major colonizers of First Nations of Canada were the British and the French, therefore the majority of those called Metis were First Nations/French or First Nations/British.

The First Nations women also categorized themselves as Native Indian, Cree, Cree Native, First Nations, Cree Metis, Ojibwa, Blackfoot/Cree, Aboriginal, and Interior Salish. Unfortunately, fewer than 10 women identified themselves by specific tribal ancestry, so we were unable to compare tribes in our analyses.

Childhood violence

Eighty-two percent of our respondents reported a history of childhood sexual abuse, by an average of four perpetrators. This statistic (those assaulted by an average of four perpetrators) did not include those who responded to the question 'If there was unwanted sexual touching or sexual contact between you and an adult, how many people in all?' with 'tons' or 'I can't count that high' or 'I was too young to remember.' Seventy-two percent reported that as children, they had been hit or beaten by a caregiver until they had bruises or were injured.

Sexual and other physical violence in prostitution

Ninety percent of these women had been physically assaulted in prostitution. Of those who had been physically assaulted, 82 percent had been assaulted by johns. Eighty-nine percent had been physically threatened while in prostitution, and 67 percent had been threatened with a weapon. Seventy-eight percent of these respondents had been raped in prostitution. Sixty-seven percent of those women had been raped more than five times in prostitution. Seventy-six percent of those who reported rapes stated that they had been raped by customers.

Sixty-seven percent of our interviewees reported that pornography was made of them in prostitution, and 64 percent had been upset by an attempt to force them to perform an act that customers had seen in pornography.

Seventy-five percent of the women we interviewed in Vancouver reported physical injuries from violence in prostitution. Many reported stabbings and beatings, concussions and broken bones (broken jaws, ribs, collar bones, fingers, spinal injuries, and a fractured skull), as well as cuts, black eyes, and 'fat lips.'[8]

---

8   Other descriptions of violence included:
   a) '[I have a] long history of physical abuse. I was beaten by my mother's boyfriend, ran away from home to a pimp who beat me, I left him for a man who beat me up, and so on . . .'
   b) A 13-year-old told us she had 'disalignment in my neck, cuts, and scratches, bruises caused by bad dates. Also deafness.'
   c) 'A stalker hit me with his car on purpose.'

Fifty percent of these women suffered head injuries as a result of violent assaults with, for example, baseball bats, crowbars, and having their heads slammed against walls and against car dashboards. Women were regularly subjected to extreme violence when they refused to perform a specific sex act.

Verbal and emotional abuse in prostitution

Verbal abuse in prostitution is socially invisible, just as other sexual harassment in prostitution is normalized and invisible. Yet it is pervasive: 88 percent of our respondents described verbal abuse as intrinsic to prostitution. One woman in Vancouver commented 'Lots of johns are super-nice at first. Then when the sex act starts, they get real verbally abusive.' Johns' verbal assaults in all types of prostitution are likely to cause acute and long-term psychological symptoms. One woman said that over time, 'It is internally damaging. You become in your own mind what these people do and say with you. You wonder how could you let yourself do this and why do these people want to do this to you?' (Farley 2003). The verbal abuse against prostituted women is reflected in the names that all women are called by violent men during sexual assaults. The epithets seem intended 'to humiliate, to eroticize, and to satisfy an urge for self-justification' (Baldwin 1992, p. 60).

Current needs of interviewees

Eighty-six percent of these women in prostitution reported current or past homelessness, with housing being an urgent need. Ninety-five percent stated that they wanted to leave prostitution. Eighty-two percent expressed a need for treatment for drug or alcohol addiction. They also voiced a need for a home or safe place (66 percent), job training (67 percent), health care (41 percent), peer support (41 percent), and self-defence training (49 percent). Fifty-eight percent stated that they needed individual counselling; 32 percent wanted legalized prostitution; 33 percent needed legal assistance; 12 percent needed childcare; and 4 percent wanted physical protection from pimps. This brief list of needs may be seen as an opportunity for program development among service providers.

---

d) 'Date tried to assault me with steel-toed boots because I wouldn't do something he wanted.'
e) 'A bad date hit my head on a wall.'
f) 'I was beaten with stones by a couple of women.'
g) A pimp locked her in a room and beat her 30 times with a baseball bat.
h) 'My boyfriend pushed me downstairs and broke my arm, [I've had] multiple beatings by various boyfriends, broken kneecaps, broken limbs. I'm scared of men.'
i) 'Two years ago, I was beat and raped for 45 minutes.'

Race/ethnic comparisons
We compared First Nations women with European-Canadian women in a number of analyses. Childhood sexual abuse was reported significantly more often by interviewees identifying as First Nations than by those describing themselves as European Canadian. Significantly more First Nations women than European Canadian women also reported childhood physical abuse.

There were ethnic differences in response to a needs assessment. First Nations women indicated a significantly greater need for self-defence training, a greater need for peer support, a greater need for job training, and for individual counselling.

Conclusion

Vancouver's Downtown Eastside, one of the poorest areas in North America, is referred to as the 'urban reserve' by its First Nations residents. Life expectancy is short. A neighbourhood centre in the Downtown Eastside categorizes anyone over age 40 as a senior. The women we interviewed were survivors of conditions that many do not survive. Many were hungry, drug-sick, and almost all had a palpable look of fear in their eyes. Violence seemed to be in the very air they breathed. Our findings document this horrific level of violence.

One woman told us that she was continually raped in prostitution, explaining, 'What rape is to others, is normal to us.' Another woman, 36 years old, described a rape as the 'defining experience' of her life. At age sixteen, she was raped at knifepoint, after which the rapist gave her a gold chain, in effect paying her for the rape and defining her as a prostitute.

A fear of men was pervasive among these women, one of whom told us that being hit and bruised was 'just your common aggressiveness from men'.

The normalcy of living with violence began, for many, in childhood. Eighty-two percent of the women we interviewed had been sexually abused as children. First Nations women in this study almost always reported childhood physical and sexual abuse. A Dené woman interviewed by the second author spoke of communities in which the entire female population had been sexually assaulted by men. She had been threatened with further violence if she attempted to speak out against this (Lynne 1998, p. 43).

Many of our interviewees told us that they knew women who had been murdered in prostitution. In 2001–2002, the international press noted the disappearance of more than 50 women in British Colombia, many from Vancouver's Downtown Eastside, most if not all of the women having been prostituted (Canadian Press 2001; Inwood 2002; Colebourn 2002). The torture/violence that these women were subject to defies the imagination even though torture of women is often documented in pornography. For example, one man, who was arrested for aggravated assault against a Downtown Eastside woman in prostitution, confessed that his attack was a trial run for enslaving and killing prostitutes. He had already constructed a deadbolted dungeon room in his basement for that purpose (Bailey 2002).

Although sex inequality happens across race and class lines, the triple forces of race, sex and class discrimination disparately impact First Nations women. Fifty-two percent of our respondents were First Nations women. The over-representation of First Nations women in prostitution reflects their poverty and their marginalized status within Canada.[9] While almost all of our respondents had migrated, the brutal poverty on Canadian reserves makes migration more crucial for First Nations women's economic survival. The Federal/Provincial Working Group suggested that 'many aboriginal youth who eventually joined the sex trade had left their home communities for urban areas'. The Working Group stated that these First Nations youth were particularly vulnerable to sexual exploitation by pimps and customers because they were doubly alienated in that they were both homeless and in an unfamiliar cultural environment (1998, p. 14).

The violence against these women in prostitution was only one element of a lifetime continuum of violence. Previous research has linked childhood sexual abuse to prostitution. One young woman told Silbert and Pines (1982, p. 488), 'I started turning tricks to show my father what he made me.' Dworkin (1997) described sexual abuse of children as 'boot camp' for prostitution.[10] West *et al.* (2000) found that women were most likely to prostitute if they had experienced sexual abuse as children and were later re-victimized by rape in adulthood. Our respondents were in a state of almost constant re-victimization.

The current state of Aboriginal housing poses an 'acute threat to health'. (RCAP, p. 372). Prostitution is intimately related to homelessness, with 86 percent of our respondents currently or previously homeless. Many women told us that they urgently needed safe housing. One young woman commented, 'The prostitutes in [Canada] are very young and have no place to sleep. They sleep on the streets and this is when the men take advantage of them and rape them' (Youth Delegates of Out from the Shadows, 1998. p. 6).

The ongoing trauma of prostitution, other violence, and homelessness which these women suffered made it likely that some of them minimized childhood violence. To review a history of violence and trauma while in the

---

9 Aboriginal households were 90 times more likely than other Canadian households to be living without piped water supply (RCAP 1996, p. 369).
10 Use of a child for sex by adults, with or without payment, is prostitution of the child. When a child is incestuously assaulted, the perpetrator's objectification of the child, his rationalization and denial are the same as those of the john in prostitution. Incest and prostitution result in similar physical and psychological symptoms in the victim.

midst of ongoing abuse was too painful for some. Some of these women did not categorize juvenile prostitution as sexual violence.[11] Others minimized violence which they had experienced by comparing it to that suffered by friends. For example, one woman said that since she had no broken bones and had not been assaulted with a weapon, her rape and strangulation by a john did not count as much.

Culturally appropriate treatment for those escaping prostitution is a necessity. The Peguis First Nation community in Manitoba found that a combination of traditional and western healing approaches was especially effective for those who suffer from emotional problems, including those related to alcohol and drug abuse, violence, and suicide. (Cohen, cited in RCAP 1996, p. 213.) In New Zealand, use of Maori philosophy to address the harm of prostitution was explained by Strickland:

> I am a Maori community worker addressing the problems of my people who are caught up in this colonized system that has uprooted them from their land, rivers, mountains, forests, their language, and their gods and beliefs. When a nation of people has been stripped of their heritage one can easily become a lost soul—vulnerable and open to manipulation and exploitation. In this instance our women and children have been forced into paid rape (prostitution). Healing from prostitution involves healing of the four cornerstones for my people: Tinana (body), Hinengaro (mind), Wairua (spirit), and Whanau (family). (Strickland 2003)

The Royal Commission Report suggests that a general health strategy for First Nations should involve equitable access to health services, holistic approaches to treatment, aboriginal control of services, and diverse approaches which respond to cultural priorities and community needs (RCAP 1996, p. 110). These four basic strategies are applicable to the healing of those in prostitution. Western medical treatment must be combined with traditional healing practices for urban First Nations women who want to exit prostitution. An approach which addresses prostitution from a public health perspective only ('How can we make sure she does not have STD/HIV so she does not transmit STD/HIV to the customer to take home to his wife/girlfriend?') or from a legal perspective only ('How can we keep prostitution out of my neighbourhood?'), but which fails to address the psychological and spiritual damage to the person in prostitution will not be effective.

---

11 One woman at first answered 'no' to the question, 'before you were 18 years old, did you experience any unwanted sexual touching or any sexual contact between you and a grownup?' Then she thought about it briefly and asked (without interviewer prompt): 'Does this question mean for when I was prostituting underage?' After the interviewer said yes, the young woman said, 'Every time a john touches me, it's unwanted.' She started prostituting at age 12.

The number one issue we have to deal with is violence against women and children, because as long as we destroy ourselves from within, we don't have to worry about anyone else. Sexual violence . . . causes so much shame for survivors and communities . . . Nevertheless, because sexual violence has been one of the most successful avenues of colonization, Native communities cannot prosper until we find a way to eradicate sexual violence and heal from the shame and self-hatred it has instilled in us . . . (INCITE 2001)

Eighty-two percent of the women we interviewed voiced an urgent need for treatment of drug and alcohol addiction. Women in prostitution self-medicate for depression and PTSD with drugs and alcohol.[12] In order to treat addiction, one must also address the reasons for relapse (Shavelson 2001). These include sexual violence, and generally, the harms of colonialism described above. The effect of traumatic events on a person's descent into substance abuse cannot be ignored.[13]

Ninety-five percent of our interviewees said that they wanted to escape prostitution, while at the same time also telling us that they did not feel that they had other options for survival. If we consider 'consent to prostitution' as indicating that these women had viable economic alternatives in their lives, then they certainly did not consent to prostitution, in that meaning of the word.

In order for women to escape prostitution, they must become 'social activists in their own lives' (Lynne 1998, p. 73). We saw humour and vision among these women. In response to a health questionnaire, one woman reported an allergy to country music. Another woman envisioned a future in which she helped 'end abuse to any living breathing thing i.e., people, puppy farms, etcetera, etcetera, ETCETERA.'

It is crucial to understand the sexual exploitation of First Nations women in prostitution today within the context of colonial violence. It is beyond the scope of this paper to discuss what should be done about the historical terrorism conducted by states (such as Canada) against nations (such as Ojibwa, Cree, Blackfoot, Salish). A lack of coexistence between nations and states is at the

---

12 Wayne Christian, director of the First Nations Round Lake Treatment Centre in Armstrong, noted that most of his clients have used drugs and alcohol to 'deaden' the pain of emotional and physical trauma. 'Up to 95 percent of clients at Round Lake reported a history of some kind of trauma, personal trauma, whether it was residential school, sexual abuse, physical violence, abandonment—those types of issues . . .' (Rees 2001).

13 Women in prostitution who are dealing with addictions cannot receive treatment in mixed-gender groups. It is unsafe for them to discuss prostitution in the traditional 12-step setting, since men regularly proposition them as soon as the women are known to have prostituted. Furthermore, confidentiality is a concern in small communities where everyone is either related or knows one another (Rees 2001).

root of social and political crises (Ryser 1995) that ultimately affect First Nations women in prostitution.

Prostituted women are displaced women, in the most profound and pervasive meaning of what displacement is. They are displaced physically, emotionally, socially, and spiritually. Trafficked from reserve to city, the internally displaced in North America are poor, rural and indigenous (Lynne 1998, Cohen and Sanchez-Garzoli 2001). This displacement makes them extremely vulnerable to the sexual exploitation and violence intrinsic to all types of prostitution. In some communities across Canada, Aboriginal youth comprise '90 percent of the visible sex trade'. (Save the Children Canada 2000, p. 7)

In order to address the harm of prostitution, it is necessary to use culturally relevant education, prevention and intervention strategies similar to those dedicated to other forms of gender-based abuse such as rape and intimate partner violence. This understanding of prostitution as violence against women must then become a part of public policy and it must be structurally implemented in public health care, mental health services, homeless shelters, rape crisis centres and battered women's shelters (Stark and Hodgson 2003). Social scientists and feminist activists have begun to address the harms of incest, rape and other family violence. We hope to see a greater focus on prostitution as part of a continuum of violence against women.

Acknowledgements

Thanks to Ann Cotton, Psy.D., Seattle, Washington, who made significant contributions to this paper with her consultation and statistical analysis.

Thanks to Rudolph Ryser, Ph.D., Center for World Indigenous Studies, Olympia, Washington, for invaluable information about geopolitics.

References

Absolon, K., E. Herbert, and K. MacDonald. (1996). *Aboriginal Women and Treaties Project*. Victoria, BC: Ministry of Women's Equality.

Abu-Jamal, M. (2001). 'Stolen Culture'. Available at http://awol.objector.org/mumia/stolenculture.html (last accessed December 12, 2003).

Al-Issa, I. and M. Tousignant. (eds). (1997). *Ethnicity, Immigration, and Psychopathology*. New York: Plenum Press.

American Psychiatric Association. (1994). *Diagnostic and Statistical Manual of Mental Disorders* (4th Ed.). Washington, DC: American Psychiatric Association.

Avina, C. and W. O'Donohue. (2002). 'Sexual Harassment and PTSD: Is Sexual Harassment Diagnosable Trauma?' *Journal of Traumatic Stress*, 15 (1), 69–75.

Bailey, S. (2002). 'Dangerous Sexual Sadist Refused Right To Appeal'. *Vancouver Sun*, March 15, 2002. Available at http://www.canada.com/vancouver/news/story.asp

Baldwin, M.A. (1992). 'Split at the Root: Prostitution and Feminist Discourses of Law Reform'. *Yale Journal of Law and Feminism*, 5, 47–120.

Baldwin, M.A. (1993). 'Strategies of Connection: Prostitution and Feminist Politics', *Michigan Journal of Gender and Law*, 1 (65).

Beardy, N. (1992). 'Executive director, Sioux Lookout Aboriginal Health Authority, Sioux Lookout, Ontario, 1 December 1992'. Cited in Canada. Royal Commission on Aboriginal Peoples. (1996). *Report of the Royal Commission on Aboriginal Peoples*. Ottawa: Minister of Supply and Services Canada.

Benoit, C. with A. Millar. (2001). 'Dispelling Myths and Understanding Realities: Working Conditions, Health Status and Exiting Experiences of Sex Workers'. Available at http://web.uvic.ca/~cbenoit/papers/DispMyths.pdf

Bishop, R. and L.S. Robinson. (1998). *Night Market: Sexual Cultures and the Thai Economic Miracle*. New York: Routledge.

Bobet, E. (1990). *The Inequalities in Health: A Comparison of Indian and Canadian Mortality Trends*. Ottawa: Health and Welfare Canada.

Bourgeault, R. (1989). 'Race, Class, and Gender: Colonial Domination of Indian Women'. *Socialist Studies*, 5, 87–105.

Bownes, I.T.; E.C. O'Gorman and A. Sayers. (1991). 'Assault characteristics and posttraumatic stress disorder in rape victims'. *Acta Psychiatric Scandinavica*, 83, 27–30.

Boyer, D., L. Chapman and B.K. Marshall. (1993). *Survival Sex in King County: Helping Women Out*. Report Submitted to King County Women's Advisory Board. Seattle: Northwest Resource Associates.

Canada. Royal Commission on Aboriginal Peoples (RCAP). (1996). *Report of the Royal Commission on Aboriginal Peoples*. Ottawa: Minister of Supply and Services Canada.

Canadian Press. (2001). 'Vancouver Police Fear Many More Women Missing'. *Halifax Herald*, September 22, 2001. Available at http://www.herald.ns.ca/stories/2001/09/22/f191.raw.html

Choney, S., E. Berryhill-Paapke and R. Robbins. (1995). 'The Acculturation of American Indians: Developing Frameworks for Research and Practice'. In J. Ponterotto, J. Casas, L. Suzuki and C. Alexander (eds). *Handbook of Multicultural Counseling*. Thousand Oaks, CA: Sage Publications. (pp. 73–92).

Churchill, W. (1992). *Fantasies of the Master Race: Literature, Cinema, and the Colonization of American Indians*. Monroe, Maine: Common Courage Press.

Cohen, B. (1994). 'Health Services Development in an Aboriginal Community: the Case of Peguis First Nation', Research Study Prepared for RCAP. Cited in Canada Royal Commission on Aboriginal Peoples (1996) *Report of the Royal Commission on Aboriginal Peoples*. Ottawa: Minister of Supply and Services Canada.

Cohen, R. and G. Sanchez-Garzoli. (2001). 'Internal Displacement in the Americas: Some Distinctive Features'. Brookings-CUNY Project on Internally Displaced Persons. Available at http://www.brook.edu/dybdocroot/fp/projects/idp/articles/idamericas.htm

Colebourn, J. (2002). 'Candles Lit for Missing Women'. *Vancouver Province*. February 10, 2002. Available at http://www.canada.com/vancouver/story.asp

Cunningham, L.C. and C. Christensen. (2001). *Violence against Women in Vancouver's Street Level Sex Trade and the Police Response*. Vancouver: PACE Society.

Currie, S. (1994). 'Assessing the Violence Against Street Involved Women in the Downtown Eastside/Strathcona Community: A Needs Assessment'. Cited in Federal/Provincial Territorial Working Group on Prostitution. (1998). *Report and Recommendations in Respect of Legislation, Policy and Practices Concerning Prostitution-Related Activities*. Canadian Federal/Provincial Working Group on Prostitution.

Davies, E. St. A. (1939). Some Conditions Arising from the Conditions of Housing and Employment of Natives in Nairobi. April, 1939. Kenya National Archives: MD 40/1131, V. 1 cited by L. White. (1988). 'Domestic Labor in a Colonial City: Prostitution in Nairobi, 1900–1952'. In B. Stichter and J. Parport (eds). *Patriarchy and Class: African Women in the Home and the Workforce*. Boulder: Westview Press.

Denevan, W.M. (1992). *The Native Population of the Americas in 1492* (2nd Ed.). Madison: University of Wisconsin Press.

Duran, E. and B. Duran. (1995). *Native American Postcolonial Psychology*. Albany: State University of New York Press.

Dworkin, A. (2000). 'Palestinians/Prostituted Women'. In *Scapegoat*. New York: Free Press. (pp. 275–333).

Dworkin, A. (1997). 'Prostitution and Male Supremacy'. In *Life and Death*. New York: Free Press. (pp. 139–151).

Ekberg, G.S. (2001). Prostitution and Trafficking: the Legal Situation in Sweden. Paper presented at *Journées de formation sur la mondialisation de la prostitution et du trafic sexuel*, March 15, 2001. Association québécoise des organismes de coopération internationale: Montréal, Québec, Canada.

Epstein, J.N., B.E. Saunders, D.G. Kilpatrick and H.S. Resnick. (1998). 'PTSD as a Mediator Between Childhood Rape and Alcohol Use in Adult Women'. *Child Abuse and Neglect*, 22, 223–34.

Estes, R.J. and N.A. Weiner. (2001). *The Commercial Sexual Exploitation of Children in the US, Canada, and Mexico*. Philadelphia PA: University of Pennsylvania School of Social Work.

Farley, M. (2003). 'Prostitution and the Invisibility of Harm'. *Women and Therapy*, 26 (3/4), 247–280.

Farley, M., I. Baral, M. Kiremire and U. Sezgin. (1998). 'Prostitution in Five Countries: Violence and Posttraumatic Stress Disorder'. *Feminism and Psychology*, 8 (4), 405–426.

Farley, M., A. Cotton, J. Lynne, S. Zumbeck, F. Spiwak, M.E. Reyes, D. Alvarez and U. Sezgin. (2003). 'Prostitution and Trafficking in Nine Countries: An Update on Violence and Posttraumatic Stress Disorder'. In M. Farley (ed.). *Prostitution, Trafficking and Traumatic Stress*. Binghamton, NY: Haworth. (pp. 33–74).

Farley, M. and H. Barkan. (1998). 'Prostitution, Violence against Women, and Posttraumatic Stress Disorder'. *Women and Health*, 27 (3), 37–49.

Farley, M. and V. Kelly. (2000). 'Prostitution: a Critical Review of the Medical and Social Sciences Literature'. *Women and Criminal Justice*, 11 (4), 29–64.

Federal/Provincial Territorial Working Group on Prostitution. (1998). *Report and Recommendations in Respect of Legislation, Policy and Practices Concerning Prostitution-Related Activities*. Canadian Federal/ Provincial Working Group on Prostitution.

Freire, P. (1994). *Pedagogy of the Oppressed*. New York: Continuum.

Frideres, J. (1983). *Native People in Canada: Contemporary Conflicts* (2nd Ed.). Scarborough, Ontario: Prentice-Hall; cited in Kelm, 1998 (pp. 295–296).

Haig-Brown, C. (1993). *Resistance and Renewal: Surviving the Indian Residential School*. Vancouver: Arsenal Pulp Press.

Hammar, L. (1999). 'Caught between Structure and Agency: The Gender of Violence and Prostitution in Papua New Guinea'. *Transforming Anthropology*, 8 (1&2), 77–96.

Harden, B. (2001). 'A Black Mud From Africa Helps Power the New Economy'. *New York Times Magazine*, August 12, 2001.

Heath, K.V., P.G.A. Cornelisse, S.A. Strathdee, A. Palepu, M. Miller, M.T. Schechter, M.V. O'Shaughnessy and R.S. Hogg. (1999). 'HIV-associated risk factors among young Canadian Aboriginal and non-Aboriginal men who have sex with men'. *International Journal of STD and AIDS*, 10, 582–587.

Hernandez, T. K. (2001). 'Sexual Harassment and Racial Disparity: The

Mutual Construction of Gender and Race'. *U. Iowa Journal of Gender, Race and Justice*, 4, 183–224.

Houskamp, B.M., and D.W. Foy. (1991). 'The assessment of posttraumatic stress disorder in battered women'. *Journal of Interpersonal Violence*, 6, 367–375.

Hunt, S.J. (1986). *Spinifex and Hessian: Women's Lives in North-Western Australia, 1860–1900*. Nedlands: University of Western Australia.

INCITE! (2001). 'Colonialism and Gender Violence in the Lives of American Indian Women'. Minneapolis: Women of Color Against Violence. Available at at: http://www.incite-national.org/involve/colonialism.html

Inwood, D. (2002). 'No Need for Inquiry Says Mayor'. *Vancouver Province*. Available at http://www.canada.com/vancouver/story.asp

Jim, R. (1997). Remarks at World Congress on Violence and Human Coexistence. University College, Dublin, Ireland. August 20, 1997.

Kelm, M. (1998). *Colonizing Bodies: Aboriginal Health and Healing in British Columbia, 1900–1950*. Vancouver: UBC Press.

Kemp, A., E. Rawlings and B. Green. (1991). 'Post-Traumatic Stress Disorder (PTSD) in Battered Women: A Shelter Sample'. *Journal of Traumatic Stress*, 4, 137–147.

Kirmayer, L.J. (1994). 'Suicide Among Canadian Aboriginal Peoples'. *Transcultural Psychiatric Research Review*, 31 (1), 3–58.

Kirmayer, L.J, L.J. Boothroyd, A. Tanner, N. Adelson and E. Robinson. (2000). 'Psychological Distress Among the Cree of James Bay'. *Transcultural Psychiatry*, 37 (1), 35–56.

LaFromboise, T.D., S.B. Choney, A. James and P.R. Running Wolf. (1995). 'American Indian Women and Psychology'. In H. Landrine (ed.). *Bringing Cultural Diversity to Feminist Psychology: Theory, Research, and Practice*. Washington, DC: American Psychological Association.

LaFromboise, T.D., A.M. Heyle and E.J. Ozer. (1990). 'Changing and Diverse Roles of Women in American Indian Cultures'. *Sex Roles*, 22, 455–476.

Leys, N. (1909). Appendix to the Nakuru Annual Medical Report: An Account of Venereal Disease in the Naivasha District, Kenya National Archives: PC/NZA/2/3. Cited by L. White. (1988). 'Domestic Labor in a Colonial City: Prostitution in Nairobi, 1900–1952'. In S.B. Stichter and J. Parport (eds). *Patriarchy and Class: African Women in the Home and the Workforce*. Boulder: Westview Press.

Lim, L.L. (ed.). (1998). *The Sex Sector: The Economic and Social Bases of Prostitution in Southeast Asia*. Geneva: International Labor Organization.

Lomawaima, K.T. (1994). *They Called it Prairie Light: The Story of Chilocco Indian School*. Lincoln: University of Nebraska Press.

Lowman. J. (1993). 'Canada'. In N.J. Davis. (ed.) *Prostitution: An*

International Handbook on Trends, Problems, and Policies. London: Greenwood Press. (pp. 56–86).

Lowman, J. and L. Fraser. (1989). Street Prostitution: Assessing the Impact of the Law. Vancouver. Dept of Supply and Services Canada. Cited in Federal/Provincial Territorial Working Group on Prostitution. (1998). *Report and Recommendations in Respect of Legislation, Policy and Practices Concerning Prostitution-Related Activities.* Canadian Federal/ Provincial Working Group on Prostitution.

Lowman, J. and L. Fraser. (1995). Violence against persons who prostitute: the experience in British Columbia. Unedited technical report. Department of Justice Canada. Cited in Federal/Provincial Territorial Working Group on Prostitution. (1998). *Report and Recommendations in respect of Legislation, Policy and Practices Concerning Prostitution-Related Activities.* Canadian Federal/Provincial Working Group on Prostitution.

Lynne, J.A.M. (1998). Street Prostitution as Sexual Exploitation in First Nations Women's Lives. Essay submitted in partial fulfillment of Master of Social Work. University of British Colombia, Vancouver. April 1998.

MacKinnon, C.A. (2001). *Sex Equality.* New York: Foundation Press.

MacKinnon, C.A. and A. Dworkin. (1997). *In Harm's Way: The Pornography Civil Rights Hearings.* Cambridge: Harvard University Press.

Månsson, S. and U. Hedin. (1999). 'Breaking the Matthew Effect—On Women Leaving Prostitution', *International Journal of Social Welfare*, 8, 67–77.

Miller, J. (1995). 'Rape myths and violence against street prostitutes'. *Deviant Behavior*, 16, 1–23.

Ministry of Labour in cooperation with the Ministry of Justice and the Ministry of Health and Social Affairs, Government of Sweden. (1998). *Fact Sheet.* Artiklnr, A98.004 pp. 3–4. Stockholm: Secretariat for Information and Communication, Ministry of Labour.
(Tel: +46 8 405 11 55, Fax: +46 8 405 12 98)
Available at http://www.prostitutionresearch.com/swedish.html

Moore, E. (2004). 'Prostitutes' Grim Lives End in Violence Along Interstate'. *Houston Chronicle.* Available at
http://www.chron.com/cs/CDA/ssistory.mpl/front/2457889

Nadon, S.M., C. Koverola and E.H. Schludermann. (1998). 'Antecedents to Prostitution: Childhood Victimization'. *Journal of Interpersonal Violence*, 13, 206–221.

Nahanee, T. (1993). 'Dancing with a Gorilla: Aboriginal Women, Justice and the Charter'. In *Aboriginal Peoples and the Justice System: Report of the National Round Table on Aboriginal Justice Issues, Royal Commission on Aboriginal Peoples.* Ottawa: Minister of Supply and Services.

Najavits, L.M., R.D. Weiss, S.R. Shaw and L.R. Muenz. (1998). 'Seeking

Safety': Outcome of a New Cognitive-Behavioral Psychotherapy for Women with Posttraumatic Stress Disorder and Substance Dependence'. *Journal of Traumatic Stress*, 11 (3), 437–456.

Nasrin, T. (1997). The Role of the State in Men's Violence against Women. Plenary Speech at *World Congress on Violence and Human Coexistence*. University College, Dublin, Ireland. August 21, 1997.

Old Dog Cross, P. (1982). 'Sexual Abuse: A New Threat to the Native American Woman: An Overview'. *Listening Post*. 6 (2) 18.

Ouimette, P.C., R. Kimerling, J. Shaw and R.H. Moos. (2000). 'Physical and sexual abuse among women and men with substance use disorders'. *Alcoholism Treatment Quarterly*, 18 (3), 7–17.

Population Reference Bureau. (2000). *2000 United States Population Data*. Washington, DC.

Ramsay, R., C. Gorst-Unsworth and S. Turner. (1993). 'Psychiatric Morbidity in Survivors of Organised State Violence Including Torture'. A retrospective series. *British Journal of Psychiatry*, 162, 55–59.

RCAP, *see* Canada. Royal Commission on Aboriginal Peoples.

Rees, A. (2001). 'Sedating Poverty'. *The Vancouver Province*. Available at http://www.canada.com/vancouver/news/story.asp

Rimonte, N. (1997). 'Colonialism's Legacy: The Inferiorizing of the Filipino'. In M.P.P. Root (ed.). *Filipino Americans: Transformation and Identity*. London: Sage (pp. 39–61).

Rizal, J. (1972). 'The Indolence of the Filipino'. In Manila: National Historical Commission (ed.). *Political and Historical Writings* 7, 229–259. Rizal's original work was published in 1890, and cited in N. Rimonte (1997) 'Colonialism's Legacy: The Inferiorizing of the Filipino'. In M.P.P. Root (ed.). *Filipino Americans: Transformation and Identity*. London: Sage. (p. 58).

Root, M.P.P. (1996). 'Women of Color and Traumatic Stress in "Domestic Captivity": Gender and Race as Disempowering Statuses'. In A.J. Marsella, M.J. Friedman, E.T. Gerrity and R.M. Scurfield (eds). *Ethnocultural Aspects of Posttraumatic Stress Disorder: Issues, Research, and Clinical Applications*. Washington, D.C.: American Psychological Association.

Ryser, R.C. (1995). 'Collapsing States and Re-emerging Nations: the Rise of State Terror; Terrorism, and Crime as Politics'. In R.C. Ryser and R.A. Griggs (eds). *Fourth World Geopolitical Reader I: International Relations and Political Geography Between Nations and States*. Olympia, WA: DayKeeper Press.

Ryser, R.C. (1997). Chair, Center for World Indigenous Studies; Personal Communication. Olympia, Washington, USA.

Save the Children Canada. (2000). *Year One 1999–2000: Out of the*

Shadows and Into the Light: A Project to Address the Commercial Sexual Exploitation of Girls and Boys in Canada: First Year End Report. Vancouver: Save the Children Canada.

Scully, E. (2001). 'Pre-Cold War Traffic in Sexual Labor and Its Foes: Some Contemporary Lessons'. In D. Kyle and R. Koslowski (eds.). *Global Human Smuggling: Comparative Perspectives*. Baltimore: Johns Hopkins University Press. (pp. 74–106).

Shavelson, L. (2001). *Hooked: Five Addicts Challenge Our Misguided Drug Rehab System*. New York: The New Press.

Silbert, M. and A. Pines. (1982). Entrance into Prostitution. *Youth and Society*, 13 (4), 471–500.

Small, D. and M. Jaffe. (1991). 1492: *What Is It Like To Be Discovered?* New York: Monthly Review Press.

Special Committee on Pornography and Prostitution. (1985). *Pornography and Prostitution in Canada (Vols. 1 and 2) The Fraser Report*. Ottawa: Minister of Supply and Services Canada.

Stark, C and C. Hodgson. (2003). 'Sister Oppressions: A Comparison of Wife Battering and Prostitution'. In M. Farley (ed.). *Prostitution, Trafficking and Traumatic Stress*. Binghamton: Haworth. (pp. 17–32).

Strickland, M.T. (2003). Personal communication. Auckland, NZ.

Sullivan, M. and S. Jeffreys. (2001). *Legalising Prostitution is Not the Answer: The Example of Victoria, Australia*. Victoria: Coalition Against Trafficking in Women Australia. Accessed at http://action.web.ca/home/catw/attach/AUSTRALIAlegislation20001.pdf

US Department of Health and Human Services. (2001). *Mental Health: Culture, Race, and Ethnicity: A Supplement to Mental Health: A Report of the Surgeon General*. Rockville, MD: US Department of Health and Human Services, Public Health Service, Office of the Surgeon General.

US Department of Health and Human Services. (2001a). *Mental Health: Culture, Race, and Ethnicity: A Supplement to Mental Health: A Report of the Surgeon General: Executive Summary*. Rockville, MD: US Department of Health and Human Services, Public Health Service, Office of the Surgeon General.

Vancouver/Richmond Health Board. (1999). *Healing Ways: Aboriginal Health and Service Review*. Vancouver: Vancouver Richmond Health Board.

Waldram, J.B. (1997). 'The Aboriginal Peoples of Canada: Colonialism and Mental Health'. In I. Al-Issa and M. Tousignant (eds). *Ethnicity, Immigration, and Psychopathology*. New York: Plenum Press.

Waldram, J.B., D.A. Herring and T.K. Young. (2000). *Aboriginal Health in Canada: Historical, Cultural, and Epidemiological Perspectives*. Toronto: University of Toronto Press.

130 *Understanding Systems of Prostitution*

Weathers, F.W., B.T. Litz, D.S. Herman, J.A. Huska and T.M. Keane. (1993). The PTSD Checklist (PCL): Reliability, Validity, and Diagnostic Utility. Paper presented at the 9th Annual Meeting of the International Society for Traumatic Stress Studies. San Antonio, Texas. October 27, 1993.

West, C.M, L.M. Williams and J.A. Siegel. (2000). 'Adult Sexual Revictimization Among Black Women Sexually Abused in Childhood: A Prospective Examination of Serious Consequences of Abuse'. *Child Maltreatment*, 5 (1), 49–57.

Youth Delegates of Out of the Shadows: International Summit of Sexually Exploited Youth. (1998). 'Declaration and Agenda for Action of Sexually Exploited Children and Youth', March 12–17, 1998. Victoria B.C. Accessed at http://sen.parl.gc.ca/lpearson/

Samantha Emery

The journey home

(interviewed by Christine Stark)

CS: **When and where were you born?**
SE: I was born on the White Earth reservation in Minnesota back in 1944 and my sister and I were adopted out when I was about three and she was about two. We were raised by Greek people in Minneapolis. It took years to find out why we were displaced.

Growing up, we didn't know that we were Indians. The people I grew up around all had blond hair and blue eyes and even though we had different skin color, it never dawned on us that we were Indian. They used to call me Blackie. The other kids wouldn't play with us because we were too dark. My adopted mom would take us out of the sun because we got way too dark.

CS: **How did your adopted parents treat you in other ways?**
SE: My father didn't know anything because he was away on business. My mom was the disciplinarian and she was mean to us. If you've seen *Mommy Dearest*, that was her. She made us drink Tabasco sauce so we wouldn't lie. She burned our fingers on the stove so we wouldn't steal. She tied us up and put us in a closet. That type of thing. She would come up in our room and if our clothes weren't on the hangers in the right way she would throw them all on the floor and make us get up and hang them up. Sometimes she had temper tantrums and took our clothes and Christmas presents and burned them. We just thought that was the way it was.

CS: **What were your teenage years like?**
SE: I spent most of my teenage years in reform school. It was better than being at home. There were mostly Indians and a few white people at the school. My sister and I didn't know we were Indian then. As a matter of fact, some of my [biological] cousins were at the reform school and they see me now and comment on how they used to know me as Maria. That was my Greek name.

At the school there was a sense of belonging. My sister and I belonged there. There was a sense of love because your friend loved you. Today they call it lesbianism. We didn't know that word then. If there was any love in the family, we never knew it. If there were any hugs, we never got any. We just had to give my adopted mom a kiss on the cheek before bed. We never knew what love was in the family setting.

131

CS: **How did you and your sister find out you were adopted?**
SE: My family came back from Europe one time when I was about eight and that's when my sister and I found out we were adopted. My cousin [from my adopted family] said 'Well, you're adopted'. We said, 'What do you mean?' She said, 'They aren't your parents'. We didn't believe her. She said, 'Your parents were killed in a car accident'. My sister and me, our eyes just locked together.

From that time on it was all payback. We did everything to upset our adopted mom. I was writing bad checks at age nine. I was even taking her pills off the counter. I took two of these, two of them, two of those, and in a few minutes I'd be awfully high. But I didn't know the words 'awfully high', I just knew I would get sick, throw up, and then be on cloud nine. That's how I got started on drugs. I would call a pharmacy and re-order her pills. I look back and I wonder how a pharmacist could accept a refill order from a small voice on the phone.

CS: **How did you get started in prostitution?**
SE: It started when my dad died. I had already had a child. I brought her home for him to see. He took his teeth out and said to my daughter, 'Too bad you have to live in this cruel world'. Then he proceeded to die. When he died, my mom got mad at me and threw all my stuff, all my baby's stuff out on the front lawn. So I called one of my girlfriends who I was in reform school with and I told her what happened and she said she'd be over to get me and my belongings. She got there and said, 'Well, this is what we're going to have to do'. She took me to a strip club and said, 'You watch what I do'. She turned a trick and told me it was a way of making money, paying the rent, and taking care of my baby. That's the way I looked at it for a long time.

After a while, the drugs and the baby became equal. I started blacking out a lot and didn't remember what happened. So I went to jail quite a few times for writing bad checks and prostitution. One of my bosses, the owner of a strip club, set us up with tricks for a 'Finder's Fee'. When I got drunk he would fix me up with four or five tricks and I didn't remember much. My girlfriend would tell me about it the next day. Actually, my first act of prostitution might have been when I was fourteen, but we didn't call it that. My sister and I just let that guy have my body so that we could get money to get a bus trip. We ran away to Chicago. I became an alcoholic then, at fourteen.

CS: **I was wondering if you would talk about how you ended up in prostitution in Los Angeles.**
SE: A guy told me he was going to LA and asked if I wanted to go with him. Of course, it was an escape. I had four or five DWIs [driving while intoxicated] in Minnesota. I had lost custody of my youngest daughter to my crack-addicted husband. My husband told the judge I was nothing but a junkie and since he'd been an employee at the Ford plant for seven years, he won. We'd battle about

our daughter. He'd say, 'Come get your daughter'. Or he'd say 'If you don't have your daughter back in an hour I'm calling the police'. One time I just couldn't deal with it and I caught a ride to Colorado. My leg was in a cast. I didn't stay with those people and a day after I left Colorado the guy shot his wife and then himself. If I'd stayed with them, I'd probably have died. I found my way to California.

In California, I ended up living in a cardboard condo, those cardboard boxes where you put your little blanket. I survived on a lot of soup lines. I rode the buses all night long and caught tricks in between. I was in a cast but the tricks didn't care if I was broken up. I just got them off anyway and got my money. Another time a man held me out a third-floor window by my ankles until I agreed to trick for him. He would beat me all the time if the money wasn't right or if I took too long. If you think Hollywood ain't got prostitution, you're wrong. There are a lot of prostitutes running around the streets all night long because they don't got nowhere else to go. That's all there is. When I was there I'd try to find someone to buy a hotel room so that I had a place to shower and sleep. It's survival. I used to know the Alcohol Commissioner of Los Angeles. He made sure I got into HUD [Housing and Urban Development] housing and he also asked me to turn a trick. I was wearing a size three then, and even that was big. All I knew was to prostitute, smoke crack, and shoot smack. How do you get out of that situation?

When you hang with that kind, you're going to be that kind. Your body gets worse. I've been in half-way house with bad panic attacks and in mental hospitals. I'm messed up now because I've done so much meth. I think I damaged my body. I did a lot of carbo tetrachloride [spot remover] and those brain cells do not rejuvenate. I never worried about my brain then. One time when I was in California I walked by a mirror on the way to a bathroom, looked at myself, thought I saw what I saw and reversed. I could count my ribs. I took all that shit and threw it out the window and went back to drinking.

I lost my eye at a party. We were all drinking and they brought out the crack pipes and I wanted to leave. I went to the door and a guy stood in my way and said, 'You're not leaving'. I said, 'I want to go'. He hit me in the eye. I went home and my eye was hanging out and my roommate said, 'What the hell happened to you?' My eye has been blind ever since. Now I have to ask others for help. I have had to learn to be humble and forgive myself for my past. I used to sell drugs and people died from them. The only way I can make amends is by helping people now. Today I help others by sharing my story.

CS: **I know that getting out of prostitution, off of drugs and alcohol, and getting your life together is a process. Will you talk about that?**

SE: It happened over the years. Never one moment, one night, or overnight. A turning point for me was when I was 27 and in a Minneapolis jail. They told me I was Native American in jail. They asked me what I thought about that. I said I feel like the Indian on the nickel, in other words, I didn't feel anything.

I had the BIA [Bureau of Indian Affairs] open up my records to see how much Indian I was and I was enough Indian to go to college, so I went to Minneapolis Community College. A good friend of mine, Steve, and I sat in his office. When red-heads and blondies and blue-eyed people would walk by I would say, 'Are they Indian?' He said, 'Yes, otherwise they wouldn't be getting financial aid'. He was educating me then. I started watching a lot of movies about how the Indians were shifted from reservation to reservation and how the white people took away the land and our grandparents were sent to the government schools. I went through some Indian treatment centers and worked with some spiritual men.

One time I was in treatment and I screamed in my sleep and they all came running. I had had a vision that my sister and I had been sexually abused when we were still on the reservation. We had been tied up on the couch. It had been blocked out of my mind. I started learning a lot about my culture. I became one of the spiritual men's helpers and he told me what to cook for ceremonial meals and what to put on the table and why we do certain things. I got all that information but I still went back to using because I was not ready yet.

After two years of being sober I met Nick in a treatment center. He was from White Earth and he helped me find my biological family. I said, 'Are you Indian?' He said, 'Yeah. Are you?' I said, 'Yeah. Maybe you can tell me who I am'. He tracked down my family for me. He told me I had a brother and my mother lived in California and my grandma was on the reservation. I met my family members who were living in Minnesota, including a lot of cousins. They took me to Chicago to a pow wow and they took me to the reservation to see my grandma and she was enthused. When I got back to Minneapolis it was Christmas time. The clients at a treatment center passed a hat around for a plane ticket so that I could go to California to meet my real mom. They gave me five days in California and I got to meet my brother and mother.

I met my mom at the airport. When she saw me she said, 'Is that you?' I said, 'Yeah, is that you?' And she said, 'Yes. I wondered what happened to you girls'. I told her my sister was in Minneapolis and I asked her what my clan was and she didn't know. I asked her what tribe we were and she said 'White Earth'. I asked her if she spoke the language and she said 'No'. I asked her what happened to her and she said she drank and one time she left us with some family members while she was out drinking. She stayed drunk for days and her brothers and sisters passed us around. She went to get us and we weren't there and nobody told her nothing. We weren't there. So in order to start a new life without us she caught a ride to California and married a Japanese man. My mom died soon after that and I started to drink again. She died in the streets of alcoholism.

I stayed sober a while and moved to Bemidji [near the White Earth reservation] to live with some cousins. I thought I would stop using after I met my family, but I had a couple of relapses. I'd call my cousin Judy, say, 'Come on down and get me, I'm done drinking'. I'd go with Judy and stay with her for a couple of days at a cabin. My grandma came over, too. I had to deal with me. Sometimes we got snowed in. Sometimes there wasn't any coffee. Sometimes there weren't any cigarettes. And grandma just went out everyday and got a lug of wood and put it by the fire. Toward the evening she'd fix the logs on the fireplace and me and Judy would be sweating, wearing shorts and head bands.

By that time, I'd already been labeled every label in the world—bipolar, schizophrenic, every label. I felt like I couldn't be helped by Western medicine. I met a traditional healer and I've been working with her ever since. She said, 'My girl, you know, the spirits tell me I need to help you'. She asked me some questions and told me about a cleansing ceremony. A few months later, I bought some tobacco and asked the lady for help. I said, 'Hello', and she said, 'Oh girl, it is so good to see you'. I told her, 'I brought you some tobacco for that ceremony you told me about and I think I'm ready'. She said, 'Oh, I don't know if you're ready'. I looked at her with my snappy little eyes and said, 'You want me to have another winter like the last one?' So we had a cleansing ceremony and I was reborn and my past was taken from me. I was given a new life and ever since then I belonged to the lodge. Since that ceremony I've never had a drink and never gotten high.

It's taken many years to get where I am today. After that first healing ceremony I went to another lodge, that was one of the oldest lodges they have, and now that's where most of my healing comes from. I still fight with going to Western medicine because that is what I was used to. We have all these healers here on the reservation and all we have to do is bring tobacco and a gift, or just tobacco, and our healers and the spirits make us well. But some of us still run to the hospital and $15,000 later they give you surgery.

CS: What advice would you give to young girls today?

SE: That's a heavy question. I tell my life story to a lot of groups, including young people who have been adopted out. I tell them that troubled youth should find a mentor, or big sister, of their own race. If you have two nations, I don't know. My niece is Black and Indian and both her people have a lot of heritage and she's going for both, she doesn't want to choose.

My cousin's daughter had her first moon time recently and there were 35 women in that circle. We all gave her advice on what we learned from our life. I told her about my second-oldest daughter, who is still in prostitution and on drugs, and I told her, 'Don't give up your goods. Men will tell you anything, but don't believe them'. And sometimes we believe that money will buy everything. I tell girls not to let that be true in their lives. I say if you're desperate, try to get help. Go to somebody. Go to a shelter. Young Indian people should go to these Talking Circles. I tell adults to be mentors—a big sister or brother.

I also tell people to find their roots. Find their heritage and culture. Learn their language and keep on learning. One spiritual man told me I would never stay sober until I dealt with my first emotional pain and that's what it boiled down to. My first emotional pain was being separated from my mother, and the second one was being taken off the reservation. There were many more to follow after that, but the cleansing ceremony took care of all of that. After I was reborn I didn't have any of that past. Places like the Anishinaabe Cultural Center in Detroit Lakes have people that work with women and people that work with men and they have kids' programs. Indian cultural centers are important for our communities.

I also think it's important for kids in high school to go in and help a single mom. To see what it's like to all of a sudden have a kid to raise while still being a kid yourself. High school kids should be getting credits for going and helping a mom, or helping elders in their homes. They will learn a lot about how hard life can be.

Andrea Dworkin

Pornography, prostitution, and a beautiful and tragic recent history*

In 1983 Catharine MacKinnon and I taught a course on pornography at the University of Minnesota Law School. We had a class of activists, thinkers, people who organized in the community, and students who wanted to be activists and thinkers. Through the activism of the people in neighborhoods organizing against pornography along with students, a grassroots movement grew in Minneapolis. These folks decided that the buying and selling of women was no longer something that would be done with impunity. Catharine MacKinnon and I created a civil-rights law that allowed women harmed by pornography, including the women in it, to sue pornographers and distributors. The law was passed twice in Minneapolis and vetoed twice by its mayor. The mayor, of course, is now running around as a representative of Amnesty International—he deplores torture in places outside of Minnesota.

In 1983 things were different than now. Pornography was being made all over the place but every city in the country, except for New York and Los Angeles, believed it was not being made there. That included Minneapolis and its twin city of St. Paul. When we told the mayor that we knew pornography was being made in Minneapolis he did not care; he remained indifferent to the harm of pornography.

The first time he vetoed the civil-rights bill he claimed that it would violate the constitutional rights of the pornographers, which superseded in importance the speech rights of women and children who were shut up by pornography. Someone takes a woman or child and they tie them up or invade their body, they hurt them, they take pictures of it and they sell the pictures. And, in our system of law, the pictures are speech and the women and children in the photographs are less than nothing. Their only value is what a pimp can get for them in an open market.

The good news is that Minneapolis is a city in which large numbers of people became educated about pornography and prostitution as forms of sexual abuse. Many people came to understand what the cost is to women as citizens, as

---

* This is a slightly edited version of a speech given by Andrea Dworkin in November 1999 at the University of Minnesota.

human beings, on this planet. The bad news is that the 'sex industry'—a euphemism for the sexual enslavement of women—is bigger than it ever has been, including in Minneapolis. More women are for sale; the pornography industry is so huge that no one is surprised anymore when pornography is being made in their town or down the street. Whether the pornography is made out of adult women or children, there is no doubt that the women and children like it—the adult women have made this choice that they want to be hung from a tree, which is what they have been hoping for their whole adult lives; it is their greatest ambition. But virtually all of those adult women were put in pornography as children; they were photographed and prostituted as children. One cannot separate the women and the children just as one cannot untie these two branches on the tree of sexual exploitation and abuse.

In Minneapolis feminist groups from the whole state joined with groups who had never been in coalition with one another before: women of color groups, lesbian groups, women who had been in prostitution and pornography. It was the first time that anyone had tried to make the woman in the photograph part of the issue. She is human. Who is she? Why is she there instead of here, instead of in the law-school class, for instance? And it turned out that there were survivors everywhere, including in our class. I never go into a room now where I don't know that there are survivors of pornography and prostitution. In 1983 those were unarticulated lives, and they are barely articulated now because of the defeat of the civil-rights law that would have allowed these sisters to say, 'This is my life and you have stolen it from me, and this is how you stole it.' The interest in the prostituted woman rarely goes beyond the concern that she may be spreading HIV to men, that she is a medical danger to men. The questions less often asked are: Who is she? Where does she come from? Do you know her? Do you care about her? Do you want to know her? Can she sit next to you? Is she sitting next to you? What a dirty, dirty woman she is. What dirty, dirty things she has done.

The politics of feminism are necessary. One cannot just say, it's bad, it hurts, stop it, don't do it anymore, not good, bad; woman hanging from a tree, bad, circle with a diagonal line through it, do not do it. But women in general do not even have as much authority or place or recognition in this society as a traffic sign would have that signals caution. Being part of a political movement is one way of developing real authority. Authority has to happen on the ground in the real world or it is not happening. You can go to a lecture and hear words with many syllables flowing by, and feel good or righteous or sad on leaving. But if a woman sells herself that night, you have had that lecture at her expense. And it is good that you were moved, but that does not help her. Feminism is not a lifestyle. It is not a party. If you think that everything is all right and women are equal, you do not need feminism; you do not need a political movement. What would it be for? If everything right now is fine, forget about politics. Watch television, do whatever is interesting but not disturbing.

The fact that one talks about women's rights means in part that women do not have the rights women need. And in the United States, every time one brings up the hurt of people, an organized hurt, an organized way of injuring a particular group of people, one is told—and historically this has been true for all oppressed groups—that the rights of those doing the hurting are more important than the rights of those who are being hurt. In the US this has had a direct racial meaning. The slavers are right; Harriet Tubman is wrong. The segregationists are right; those who have to integrate lunch counters are wrong. This is very Amerikan;[1] there is a total individualism that does not take into account anyone else; if things are good for me, I don't have to think about the woman next door.

To begin with, the premise is a lie, because things are not that good for women in the United States. The US Justice Department reports that about 22,000 women experience some form of sexual violence or assault every week in the United States, mostly from male intimates or men they know. Women found out that if the axe-murderer were actually standing where we could see him and if we got all those axe murderers and put them away—which is definitely part of the program—we would not have cut the rape rate very much, nor would we have cut the murder rate of women very much, nor would we have cut the assault rate very much. These are intimate crimes, which is to say that a woman thinks he knows her, and she is very grateful because everyone wants that, and he thinks she belongs to him. But he doesn't know her, nor does he have to, because he has power over her. The power is not just physical; the power is also legal, which is to say this legal system does not help women who are being hurt. It does not. Why is it the women who have to leave their houses? Why are they the ones who are on the run when facing down battering husbands? Why do we talk about keeping the streets safe and then ignore women who are trying to get themselves through another night, whether it's to avoid being beaten up or whether it's to get drugs or whether it's to fill a pimp's money quota. What it is doesn't matter; it really doesn't matter. The weather gets cold in the Midwest. Why are they out there? Most women are not there. Is it because there is a certain group of women who are born not knowing that zero degrees is cold? And those are the women in prostitution? I don't think so.

---

1   In the 1960s some black anti-racist groups spelled 'America' with three k's, Amerikkka, to denote the white-supremacist character of the country. Dworkin's usage of one k comes from Franz Kafka's novel, *Amerika*. Ed.

When one looks for reasons, it turns out that there are reasons all over the world. Reasons change from society to society. In the United States the reasons tend to be child sexual abuse—often with pornography as part of the abuse—poverty, and homelessness. And women are—actually, girls are—easy targets. So-called girl power does not change that. She puts on her miniskirt and does her hair and she is the same dumb bitch when she walks out on the street as all those young men like to sing about in their songs. That's why she needs a political movement.

One needs a political movement because something has to change and what has to change is not individual. It's not something an individual can change without holding hands with someone else and someone else and then another person after that. And in the collectivity of person-to-person, each person cannot do everything, but every person can do something. That is why one has a political movement: because a political movement makes it possible for people to do the thing they can do in a context that gives the doing meaning; because people then can give as much as they can give of what they know, of what they think; because people can give materially. No one has to—or can—do everything. It is appalling that in the United States people believe that an individual must do everything—that if one cannot do everything one need not do anything. She cannot fix it herself so it can't get fixed. But of course a lone woman cannot fix it. Men did not just start selling women. It did not start yesterday and it will not end tomorrow.

One of the worst parts of being an Amerikan is that if something does not happen fast, it does not happen at all; if one cannot make an issue, an atrocity, a tragedy palpable to people in five minutes, or in a sixty-second sound byte, one cannot communicate with other people. Amerikans don't have, or refuse to have, a sense of history, which is necessary in having a sense of endurance, duration—a sense of how hard it is to make change, how long it takes, how incredible it is that one moved forward an eighth of an inch, because then one gets the boot and one is kicked way back to the place where one started, but not quite, because one knows something that one did not know before. Political activism brings knowledge.

One cannot know the enemy, whoever that enemy might be, simply by serving him. One also needs the clarity and the knowledge that comes from defying him—as a movement. Battered women are the most defiant women on the face of the earth. And they get punished for it because they are defiant as individuals. What they do not get is a way out. And prostituted women have been thought not even to deserve a way out.

Question: What keeps us ignorant? Is it just that it is safer not to know? That could be the answer. Twenty-five years ago I would have said that the information about violence against women was not in the popular domain;

that people do not know this vocabulary, this language; that they do not know that all of this abuse stuff is true. Feminists would talk about violence against women and the FBI would say that it doesn't happen. Now the FBI says that the wife-beating they claimed did not exist is the most common form of violence in the country. And gee, they missed it! This is not like missing a terrorist who could be anywhere, any time, any place. This is like missing something that you and your buddies are doing. What they meant was that beating your wife was no crime. That's what the police mean when they refuse to do anything about assaults on women; that's what the FBI meant when they said that wife-beating did not exist.

As a political matter one needs to understand how male dominance works. It does work; it is a system—it has parts and pieces that move in certain ways under certain circumstances. Understanding the system of male dominance requires that one take one's experience outside of oneself so that the experience can be scrutinized: so that one can see how those who hurt do it and where they themselves are vulnerable to attack. Yes, attack. Feminism is the politics of anti-abstraction. The men who hurt you have to be seen objectively as well as known intuitively; and in addition every woman standing on a street corner is your problem. When you see a prostituted woman, you have to know that you are not free, whatever your status in this male-over-female hierarchy.

The ways in which men control women are changing. It used to be marriage and the church that controlled women or that allowed men to control women. Along with the legal system, they were the institutions of male dominance that really mattered. But now those institutions have been rendered ineffective or less effective. What is happening before your very eyes is that the pornography industry has managed to legitimize pornographized sexuality and to make it the duty of every woman to perform sexually as a prostitute. Partly, the voyeurism of the pornography industry changes the way in which women are seen. This includes how we see ourselves. Partly, there is an increasing cruelty of touch. 'Sensual' is a word that has virtually fallen out of usage when people talk about sex and few people know what it means anymore. Women have been chattel property for a long time; but now prostitution becomes the clearest expression of what it means to be a woman, to be sexual, and to be owned, but to think one is free.

A prostituted woman can be owned by a dozen men a night but she cannot be herself. Sex becomes depraved because she is the lowest object or commodity. She has sex over and over again with men she does not know or like; her body and mind have to tolerate that kind of punishment. The mind tries to help: it leaves, watches, induces numbness but does not stay integrated with the body. She can feel her mind hovering in the room near the ceiling in a corner. She tries to get rid of him as fast as she can. Fundamentally, that is what prostitution has in it for women. If there is anything that makes a prostituted woman happy it is the sense that 'He's dumber than I am because he is going to pay me money to manipulate him sexually'. One can get very high on that, because it feels like a form of dominance in a world in which women are constantly demeaned. Women are supposed to be passive, but the prostitute is not passive: she went out, took that guy by his penis, and he pulled out his money. There is nothing passive about that, so she is different from those other women, the ones who won't talk to her when they see her on the streets, the women who think she deserves exactly what she gets.

Most women now are treated as whores; and so are girls growing up, as if their sexuality should be a sexuality of sexual service. It's important to think about the ways in which women have been colonized, because it all has to do with our own bodies. We may also be hurt when men send ships and drop bombs and do all the other really exciting things they do when one takes the remote away from them. But since women are usually hurt by male intimates or acquaintances, and since the hurt takes place in our bodies, it becomes important to realize that the training to accept the hurt is hand-delivered by a man or men to the body of a girl. Sometimes the mother is the instrument through which girls are trained to accept pain and humiliation. In childhood, for most women who are prostituted, the training begins with incest or child sexual abuse, often called molestation. Incest is boot camp for prostitution. Incest makes a prostituted consciousness as well as the compliant and knowing body: a human body in which there is the recognition that you do this and you get a reward, you do this and you get punished, including by the loss of what passes for love. I personally am sick of hearing people being sentimental about children while they are buying and selling them or supporting the trade in children or the so-called privacy of the child rapist.

But one cannot help the children without dealing with the second-class, socially inferior status of women. At the very beginning of the women's movement, Shulamith Firestone wrote in *The Dialectic of Sex* that the connection between women and children is not biological but political. Women and children are in the same place at the same time, and being a woman is foreshadowed by being a child. When a woman is being hurt, there is the likelihood that a child is being hurt. A child can be hurt by a woman; the woman may be half-perpetrator and half-victim, half-battered, half-raped. In families where there is abuse, women and children are on the bottom, and the guy in the newspaper whose sad story is being told when he has killed his wife, children, and himself is painted as a tragic human being, not a mass murderer. The woman and children are not mourned; the man is the one human being in the story. The man is not seen as a bad human being but as a hurt human being, an injured human being. And he may be injured and hurt, but he does not get to kill women and children because of it. What a radical idea. How many more years and how many more marches will it take to make that radical idea a premise rather than a rare, unpopular conclusion?

People hate certain ideas, sometimes with justice, sometimes with no justice. A whole lot of people are willing to march with a swastika even now. Not enough people are willing to march for women and children even now. Women, and increasingly children, need to be desirable to men, need to conform, need to self-police the body by making it into a wanted object. One does it to oneself by responding to an outside command that one carries inside. There does not have to be an army to make one conform and comply. One does it because one has learned to do it and thinks it is the right thing to do. One does not see the consequences, except that when another woman gets hurt, one says, well she was dressed like that, of course it happened to her. This is called denial. And when women are prostituting on street corners they look like what they are doing: to the unprostituted woman, the street-corner women look different, even if one strives to be a sexual object. But women all share a lot: women have all been used in sex; even if a woman has loved truly and greatly, she will also have experienced exploitation or force or manipulation or emotional abuse.

Question: Why is 'love' a dirty word? If this word is a good word, why does it have such a dirty meaning? And why is the dirt in what happens to the woman and what the woman is? Why is the woman the dirt? If one follows male-dominant logic, the answer is that the vagina is dirty. 'Her genitals are dirty. She is dirty. Yeah, I want to get inside her, but then I really have to punish her because she is so dirty; I am driven to get inside her, but when I am done and I get out I check my penis to make sure it is still there; I see that it's there but it is very much smaller; her vagina overwhelmed it.' Then, if the guy is a little hostile and a little worried because he penetrated this dirty thing, he will take it out on the woman. Why is sexual intercourse in our society the central sex act? Why is it a dirty word? How does sex stay dirty and why? Women of my generation—who came of age during the 1960s—have been through sexual liberation, the right to birth control and abortion; and still women remain second-class and sex remains dirty. There is something fundamentally wrong with the way a woman's life is valued. That devaluation is what allows one to accept that the lives of prostituted women are nightmares of insult and injury and that those lives need not be changed.

This question of being dirty really does matter. There is a long history of the woman as dirt and sexual abuse as such being conjoined. And the prostituted woman is the dirtiest woman because she is the most purely sexual woman. When one sees her, one is looking at sex. And when one sees her and is looking at sex, one is looking at dirt. That is why prostituted women are treated the way they are treated, including inside the women's movement. That is why it is almost impossible for women who have not survived prostitution to align themselves for the freedom of women who are prostituting now or who have prostituted. The sense of contamination through association is very deep. The prostituted woman is sex. There are no qualifying clauses. She must be left there to die, because if she is worth anything then male dominance is wrong. If one comes to the conclusion that male dominance is wrong, two things can be done: one can stay quiet or one can tell people that male dominance is wrong. If one tells people that male dominance is wrong, those people might expect one to do something and one might expect them to do something. There are activists who work year in and year out doing everything they can think to do; but there are not a lot of them.

When is the vile subordination of women going to end? Say feminists win victories. Say feminists win a lot of victories in going up against the so-called sex industry—pornography, the international trafficking in women, home-grown prostitution. Say feminists can create places of safety and education and refuge for prostituted women. If feminists can do those things, one is looking at three hundred to four hundred years. This trafficking in women is the largest slave trade that the planet has ever seen. It is larger than the slave trading of the middle passage. It is larger than any race-based slave trading. I am not measuring suffering. I mean to measure the dimensions of the problem. Selling women makes more money than anything else. Prostituted women and children are the main cash crop in the Thai economy. And those women are dead or dying by twenty and that is a long life for a child who is sold into prostitution in this world of man-made murder, man-made rape, and AIDS.

One gets nowhere without taking a first step and a second one and a third one. It is damned hard because every single minute the industry that buys and sells women and children is getting bigger, and more and more women and children are getting hurt. In 1983 Minneapolis decided to do something about pornography and I regard it as a terrible failure of the women's movement that the initiative failed finally. Since the overt attack on pornography, there has been enormous noise about how repressed everyone is who opposes the injury of women in and because of pornography. Those who accuse feminists of being repressed think they know because they measure sex against the photographs that they buy at the store—video store, adult store, magazine store, bookstore, movie theater—or the pornography they download from the internet.

There are choices to be made. One choice is to buy one's sex; another choice is to be one's sexuality inside one's humanity. One never has the right to buy another human being and through one's consumption make that human being do something repugnant, from being an object to having violence used against the body.

The way to look at that three hundred to four hundred years is that one can have an impact on that woman who is on the street corner being sold, hurting not because she wants to be hurt but because she has been deemed worthless except as a sexual convenience for men. There is no humanity in that. There is no dignity in that. No matter how hard those who have been prostituted try to bring meaning and dignity to lost years, it cannot be done.

I am asking everyone here to start organizing again. Make the Democratic Party more accountable for legislation on the status of women. Do direct action against targets that sell woman hating—one has a responsibility to close those targets down no matter how many there are, how mammoth the ambition seems. There is talking and writing and picketing. There is using one's freedom of speech to video men who use sex stores and live sex outlets and strip clubs. The only thing required for these kinds of actions is the belief that the planet belongs to women, to women as much as to men. The men are despoiling our planet by the ways in which they are humiliating and hurting women and children. If one has a right to be here and live here, one has a right not to be treated like garbage, as if women are nothing but receptacles for a male sex act. If one believes that prostituted women are worthless, do nothing. Things will stay the same except that the so-called sex industry will get bigger, big enough to touch every woman, whatever her presumed status.

Say no. Organize. Stand up to the political establishment that protects the so-called sex industry. If the law does not adequately recognize the worth of women, it has to be changed. Slaveholders wrote the Constitution. It had to be changed. Now it has to be changed again to recognize women's equality. It is a Constitution that is remarkably indifferent to the buying and selling of people. It is rooted in that old plantation mentality where property matters and people don't. Pretend that the United States belongs to the women who live here and knock down whatever gets in the way; knock down the barriers that keep prostituted, pornographized women low, so low that sometimes dying seems better. Fight for women's lives.

PART TWO

Resisting the Sexual
New World Order

D. A. Clarke

Prostitution for everyone: Feminism, globalisation, and the 'sex' industry

I. Uphill work: Feminist opposition to the traffic in women

Sex, as it is organized in this society, is the most common way in which human rights violations, injustice, and inequality are acted out. Acts of sexual injustice continue to be protected by the right as moral, and by the left as personal freedom. This difference creates a superficial political opposition over a fundamental agreement.

Both the right and the left have taken an active role in protecting traditional sexuality . . . The left has responded to feminism's success and the breakdown of the patriarchal family not by trying to reassert the traditional family, but by actively defending as freedom, or dismissing as unimportant, its substitute: men's intensified sexual aggression against girls and women via pornography, libertine television and movies, prostitution, private sexual assault, and a culture that imposes sexual demands on girls at a younger and younger age.

—Adriene Sere, 'What if the Women Mattered?' (*Eat the State*, Sept. 23, 1998)

. . . Guan Somyong was no longer ashamed that his fifteen-year-old daughter was the first in their village to enter the sex trade. From the money she sent home, the family now had a brick house, refrigerator, TV and stereo. 'Now all the girls want to go', her mother said.

—William Greider, *One World Ready Or Not: the Manic Logic of Global Capitalism*

A report from western Colombia describes a situation where women headed many of the households and provided, even when married, cash income as agricultural labourers, in addition to crops from their gardens. They were driven out of production with the encroachment of cash crops introduced by Green Revolution technicians. 'Whereas men saw their interests being improved by wage labour available in the mechanised farming sector, women lost control over the variety of crops that had been the mainstay of their subsistence activities and ensured their children food in the face of market values of monocrop cultivation. Some of their coffee trees were ruined by the insecticides dusted over tracks outside the commercial crop and by planes used in

149

the commercial enterprises' . . . Starvation affects men and women differently . . . Previously 'moral' women turn to prostitution to obtain food.

—Marilyn Waring, *Counting For Nothing: What Men Value and What Women are Worth* (quoting Anna Rubbo and referencing research by Rubbo and by Gail Pearson)

Female employees of beleaguered US telecoms firm WorldCom have been invited to pose in *Playboy* magazine as part of a revealing 'Women of WorldCom' piece in an upcoming issue.

Women who choose to participate will be following in the footsteps of the 'Women of Enron' who grace *Playboy*'s July issue . . .

Not to be left out, the women of Arthur Andersen, the auditing firm linked to both the WorldCom and Enron corporate scandals, were also asked to pose nude for the men's magazine.

—Agence France-Presse story republished by News.com.au, Australian online news magazine, July 16, 2002

'I got the shit kicked out of me', she said. 'I was told before the video—and they said this very proudly, mind you—that in this line most of the girls start crying because they're hurting so bad . . . I couldn't breathe. I was being hit and choked. I was really upset, and they didn't stop. They kept filming. You can hear me say, "Turn the fucking camera off", and they kept going'.

—Regan Starr, porn actress, interviewed by Martin Amis in 'A Rough Trade', UK *Guardian* March 17, 2001

Let me tell you what pimping is. Pimping is slavery.

—Police Detective Herman Glass, quoted in 'They Call Their Pimp "Daddy"', *Atlanta Journal-Constitution*, April 8, 2001

Hurting women is bad. Feminists are against it, not for it.

—Andrea Dworkin, personal communication

For well over a century, feminists of various nations have struggled to expose and delegitimise the practice of 'trafficking in women', that is, the business of men selling or renting women and girls (and sometimes boys)—or live voyeuristic views of women and girls—or pictures of women and girls—to other men. Feminists have been trying, in other words, to stop men from selling and buying every kind of access to the bodies of women and children.

Feminists have opposed and exposed various kinds of traffickers. In my view this includes married men who coerce their wives into being 'loaned' to male friends; husbands and boyfriends who take photos of women during sex (with or without their knowledge) and then trade or sell those images among other men; brothers and fathers who coerce or trick women and girls into providing sexual services inside or outside the family; procurers who prey on the naïveté of young women with false offers of jobs, passports, love, security; outright kidnappers who imprison, beat, and 'break' women into sexual slavery; men who think that a dinner or a movie is sufficient 'payment' for forced sex; men who believe their daughters are their personal property and can be sold at their convenience; and many more. Feminists have also exposed and critiqued the male clients and customers of these traffickers.

The harm done to women by these conversions into a tradable commodity is well documented. In this book and others, there is ample evidence of the frequency and severity of abuse that trafficked women survive, or sometimes do not survive. The evidence, both testimonial and documentary, leaves no question that human rights are being routinely violated in this international trade. There is far less secrecy now than there was fifty or even thirty years ago; pimps and pornographers have been driven (or have proudly strutted) into the open. Prostitution can be discussed openly—indeed, romanticised— in film, literature, and theatre, as well as in the press, and pornography is increasingly visible to ordinary people.

Over the last few decades, pornography and prostitution have become more and more socially acceptable, more 'mainstreamed'. We are generally told that this process is a positive sign of the liberalisation of society, a movement away from restrictive social norms associated with the fifties and earlier decades. The acceptability of pornography and pimping is tied closely in the public mind with tolerance for lesbians and gays, improved sex education, improved access to birth control technologies, etc. We are told it is a package deal.

These two threads of social change—to this feminist—seem, on the contrary, quite opposite and contradictory. It's true that much of the greater 'sexual freedom' to which arch-conservatives object so strenuously is generally beneficial to women: sex education in schools helps protect girls from the pitfalls of ignorance, secrecy, and shame; lesbians are spared at least some of the stigma, violence, and discrimination they experienced in earlier decades; and access to birth control—and if necessary, abortion—is a fundamental feminist demand.

However, with the rising popularity and social presence of pornography has come an apparent intensification of its violently misogynist content. From video games aimed at pre-teens, to popular film, to all-porn TV channels and websites, the supply of images and themes reflecting (and appealing to) a sadistic, paedophilic, and generally brutal attitude to women and girls has increased enormously. The 'sex education' offered to contemporary youth via these commercial media is generally an education in contempt and even hatred towards women. Meanwhile prostitution (which according to liberal futurist theory of the sixties should have withered as general sexual freedom flourished and 'repressions' were abandoned) has on the contrary burgeoned into an enormous and increasingly mainstream industry. Nor has there been any marked improvement in the conditions of life and work for the world's prostitutes; they still endure hardship, danger, violence, hunger, drug addiction, official contempt, low wages: every kind of violation of human rights and dignity.

The essential issues which traditionally inspired feminists to challenge and criticise the sex industry have not changed despite decades of effort. It has been remarkably difficult for feminists to make any progress on these issues. It is very difficult even to get the issues taken seriously. Obviously one reason for this is that feminist activity has not changed the fundamentals of social power. Men still control decisive power blocs such as the armed forces, the higher levels of government, big business and media—and the 'sex industry' is a service industry for men. A critique of this industry is bound to be uphill work.

Perhaps more surprising is the difficulty we have had finding allies in this effort. Even though there is a fairly strong consensus among progressive or liberal people about the value of peace, economic justice, and human rights— and about the negative values of corruption and secrecy in government, excessive concentration of wealth in the hands of small elites, and so forth— there is a remarkable non-consensus about issues of gender power and sexual exploitation. The sexual privileges claimed by men under the rules of patriarchy are often still claimed by 'progressive' men marching under the banners of peace and justice.

To clarify: we know that the presumption of access rights to women's bodies leads to predictable abuses by dictators, kings, pharaohs and other 'oppressive monsters' of history whom progressive men, as well as women, deplore. Tiberius and Caligula spring to mind, not to mention the iconic Henry (VIII) Tudor, or even the notorious sons of Saddam Hussein. We recognise *droit du seigneur* as an abominable abuse, symbolic of all that was rotten about feudal aristocracy. Yet we find that most men 'of good will', that is, progressive and liberal men— despite their commitment to democracy and their distaste for feudalism and dictatorships—continue to fantasise about unlimited access to women; to consume access to women in the form of pornography, and/or to imagine that they have 'rights' of some kind to sexual services from a particular woman or all women. Indeed many liberal/progressive men continue to use a privilege-inverting 'poverty' model to understand sex and male behaviour; they see 'sex' (a euphemism for 'access to other people's bodies for my own gratification') as being in short supply and men as being needy, hungry, and somehow *deserving*, thus placing a kind of moral obligation on women to provide.

Male privilege is, we might conclude, the last bastion of those systems of privilege which progressive people generally try to critique or challenge. Men and women can stand together in solidarity along lines of class, race, political belief, or religion; but to talk honestly about male sexual privilege or the mythology of male sexual entitlement drives a wedge between heterosexual couples, threatens the most intimate infrastructure of ego and self-definition for men, and calls into question time-honoured rituals of courtship, mating, pairing, etc. to which most people are deeply attached. It is not, therefore, surprising that as a culture we attempt some rather fancy ideological footwork rather than confront directly the assumptions which even liberal/progressive men (and women) make about male sexual identity and behaviour.

Many feminists have felt baffled, if not completely speechless, in face of the cultural mandate to welcome and applaud the work of the porn industry as a facet of social progress. Violently misogynist websites are reviewed with smug approval in 'liberal' and 'progressive' publications (both virtual and paper); traditional Leftist journals such as *The Nation* continue to support pornographers as some kind of heroes of free speech and secular liberation. The feminist community is further divided by factions of women who claim that pornography and prostitution are in fact empowering for women, and that feminists should support and endorse them as such. Does all this defence of pornography spring only from the stubborn persistence of traditional patriarchal privilege in our cultures?

> Running an online escort directory, it turns out, isn't much different than managing a corporate Web site. The same rules apply: Keep it simple, know your audience, keep the customer satisfied. 'It's just like my regular Internet job was; the only difference is that I'm not hamstrung by the six-month VP review process', says Giorgio. 'I can have a site up in a day and see immediately how it's doing and start fine-tuning it. As a Web professional, it's much more rewarding . . .'
>
> FrugalJohn's upcoming move into Texas is timely and could prove to be a much-needed tonic for a local economy battered by recession and corporate malfeasance. There have to be plenty of out-of-work guys in Houston who would like to do to a reasonably priced escort what Enron did to them.
>
> —Tom McNichol, writing for *Salon Online*, March 11, 2002

In the twenty-some years of my own adult life as a feminist—despite passionate and well-informed efforts and despite limited victories in many other areas of political struggle—we seem to have made zero or negative progress in challenging or restraining the men who buy and sell, rent and lease, women and girls. Nor have we reduced the appetite of men, in America or elsewhere, for grotesque imagery of female humiliation, pain, and fear. The twin industries of pornography and prostitution have boomed worldwide and the degree of misogyny deemed acceptable in everyday cultural life has ratcheted upwards to levels I would not have believed possible. All this has happened 'on my watch'; and I suspect that other feminists may share my feelings of personal failure.

Despite our best efforts, the international traffic in women has grown, not diminished, and it has become harder, not easier, to generate serious public discussion of the violation of basic human rights in pornography and prostitution. In this set of interlocking short essays I try to understand why. Why is it so difficult to bring a critique of prostitution into the public discourse? Why do we seem to be losing political ground? Where might we go from here?

The difficulty of transcending either our historical or primate legacy—we disagree amongst ourselves whether the mystique of the alpha male is a product of nature or culture—might in itself explain our failure to increase the ration of social justice allowed to women and girls by abolishing trafficking. But I believe there is another factor that makes our critique even more difficult to articulate today, and particularly difficult to introduce into serious public discourse.

In these essays I will suggest that over the last three decades an ideological barrier—perhaps a much more perdurable one than even the traditional hurdles of male privilege, right-wing misogyny, and liberal smugness—has been raised with the intent to silence discourse about social justice in general. The ideology of neoliberal economics (also known as 'globalisation' or 'global capitalism' or the 'New World Order') has created a new intellectual, cultural and media milieu in which it's virtually impossible for feminists to create any serious social dialogue about the meaning and implications of the traffic in women and girls. I will suggest that in order to renew a meaningful critique of the commodification of women and girls, we must rediscover a critique of commodification itself—of neoliberal economics in general, of global capitalism, and of the 'consumer model' of politics, life, and reality itself which is now firmly enthroned in academia, government, and business circles.

II. There's never a Leftist around when you need one

> Suppose I decided to rape Catharine MacKinnon before reviewing her book. Because I'm uncertain whether she understands the difference between being raped and being exposed to pornography, I consider it required research for my critique of her manifesto that pornography equals rape and should be banned.
>
> —Carlin Romano, in the US Leftist journal *The Nation*, 15 November, 1993

> In this scene, actor-director Hardcore is having rough sex with Cloey Adams, who is pretending to be under age. 'If you're a good girl, I'll take you to McDonald's later and get you a Happy Meal'. Hardcore then 'proceeds to piss in her mouth'.

Addressing the camera, Cloey Adams says, 'What do you think of your little princess now Daddy?' Nor is Hardcore through with her. Turning to the crew, he calmly says, 'I'll need a speculum and a hose' . . . One of Max's favorite tricks is to stretch a girl's asshole with a speculum, then piss into her open gape and make her suck out his own piss with a hose. Ain't that romantic?

> —*Adult Video News* review of a Max Hardcore video, quoted by Martin Amis in his article 'A Rough Trade', published by the UK *Guardian* (3/17/01) and US *Talk* magazine (3/01)

Max Hardcore is no unpopular aberration. *The Nation*, a known progressive, leftist, noncommercial magazine, ran a fluff piece by pornographer Mark Cromer (February 26, 2001) heralding the work of Max Hardcore as a hero who works to keep porn dirty, 'the way it should be'.

> —*Mediawatch*, Ann Simonton

The agenda of business is simple: to make a profit. Commerce, though it recognises binding legal obligation, treaties and contracts between peers, and (sometimes) limits on the means which may be used in competition, does not otherwise observe the ethical boundaries of community life. One of the world's oldest businesses is the buying and selling of human beings—slavery—of which prostitution, sweatshop labour, kiddie porn clubs, the coyote trade ('people-smuggling'), and other modern exploitations are later and somewhat moderated forms.

When we recognise that buying and selling human beings is wrong—as when we pass laws against slavery—we contradict the fundamental agenda of business. Slave trading has always been a very profitable undertaking, and there are still people in the world who consider it a respectable one. The (partial) abolition of slave trading is a prime example of the defeat of purely business interests by the public or national conscience. Slave trading is *good business*, in the purely business sense: it turns a handsome profit. When we claim that slave trading is in fact *bad* business, we invoke standards and values from outside the marketplace.

Traditionally, the Left or progressive element in national politics has been that which counterbalances the profoundly amoral quest for profit and promotes what we might, in today's commercialised discourse, call 'non-market values'. These are values such as justice, the dignity of the individual, and the notion of civil (as opposed to purely property) rights. In theory, we expect to find the Left opposed to the narrow self-interest of capital, sympathetic to the worker rather than the boss, the exploited rather than the exploiter. We expect the Left to take a stand against the unfettered pursuit of profit at any human cost; if the Left does not take this stand, it has forfeited its position on the political playing field.

For all these reasons, feminists have often been frustrated and infuriated by the fond attachment of the (male) Left to prostitution and pornography. The enthusiasm of good Leftist men for the high principles of *Liberté*, *Egalité*, and *Fraternité* all too often peters out before forging any genuine solidarity with the global *Sororité* of exploited women.

Prostitution, so the weary old cliché goes, is 'the oldest profession'. Many feminists, decade after decade, have protested that pimping, not prostitution, is the 'profession'; in prostitution, the management class is made up of pimps and madams, and the 'girls' are lowly line workers, garnering none of the benefits we associate with 'professional' status. Most do not earn high wages; most have no health benefits; as a group, prostitutes certainly do not enjoy the respect accorded to 'professionals' such as engineers, doctors, lawyers. (To describe prostitution as a 'profession' not only obscures the class and race stratification that characterises the sex trade; it casts an implicit slur on all legitimate professions to which women may aspire.)

The odds always favour the house. The pimps and the higher-level investors get rich; the 'girls' are sometimes lucky (and smart) enough to get out while they are ahead (if they ever get ahead); but the majority of the world's prostitutes—like the rest of the world's sweatshop labour—live and die poor, never collecting more than a tiny fraction of the profits made off their own bodies. Prostitutes are also at even higher risk than female sweatshop and field workers when we consider femicidal and misogynist violence, alcoholism, drug abuse, STDs and police harassment.

The average prostitute, world-wide, is the very paradigm of exploited labour. The barons of the sex sweatshop trade are paradigmatic exploiters.

The international trade in women's and children's bodies, as a marketable commodity for the sexual entertainment of adult men, is a staggeringly large money machine. In the US alone, demi-respectable pornography alone is a multi-billion dollar industry; the global reach and cash-flow of the 'sex industry' is hard to measure, since much of its business occurs 'off the books', conducted by extralegal operators with or without the connivance of government officials. But we know enough to be sure that it is very big business indeed. And we know that very, very few of its line workers ever escape from grinding poverty. The relationship of capital to labour in the sex industry is classically Dickensian, and we are not—as a culture—unaware of this.

The material facts of the relationship between pimp and prostitute are brutally obvious not only to those researchers who study the demographics or economics of 'the trade', but to the average person, through the lens of pop culture. As the language and posturing of gangsters becomes once again romanticised and popularised in film, music, and TV, it is not uncommon to hear young men of the oblivious middle classes say jestingly of an overbearing boss or professor, 'Yup, I'm his bitch all right', or 'He treats me like his ho'. 'Pimp and Ho' has become one of the more popular Halloween his-n-hers costume choices, with the party-goers often acting out 'humourously' the domination of the pimp over his 'property'. 'Official Pimp-Mobile' is a 'joke' sticker seen on the cars of college and high school students. 'Bitch-slap' has become a catch-phrase considered clever and slightly spicy among pop-culture writers.

> This just in: Pimps are greedy, vicious, criminal motherfuckers who make their pay through the exploitation, abuse, torture, and outright enslavement of women. Well, duh.
>
> —*Geekery Today*, April 22, 2001

Whether literate in economics and sensitised to issues of class/race/gender or not, we are not, generally speaking, unaware of the real dynamics of prostitution. That knowledge is deeply encoded in the culture and available to us all.

So where is the (male) Left on this issue? Sadly the answer is usually 'nowhere in sight', or worse, rooting for the 'civil rights' of the pimps and panders. Occasionally the Left stirs itself to advocate unionisation as the solution to the abuse of women and girls in the sex trade. This, we note, is in a country (the US) where as of 1999 less than 10 percent of the private-sector workforce was unionised, and where union-busting is company policy at most of the biggest and most successful corporations (Amazon.com, McDonald's, Wal-Mart, etc). The notion that in this political and economic climate an effective union movement is miraculously going to spring up among prostitutes, seems naïve to say the least. Unions rely on other unions as allies; solidarity strikes are the 'equaliser' that makes government and industry take seriously single-sector strikes. With US trade unions at an all-time low, and mostly male-dominated, who is going to walk out in solidarity with striking prostitutes? Are masses of men going to honour the picket lines by refusing to patronise sex sweatshops until prostitutes achieve some kind of wage and workplace-safety parity?

Alas, a tip of the hat to unionisation is about as far as most of the male Left is willing to go. For the last 30 years and more, I have watched liberals in America and the rest of the G8 nations try to repackage pornography and prostitution as a hip and groovy thing, a liberating thing, something novel and progressive and good for us all, men and women alike. Allegedly 'Leftist', 'progressive' men declare their loyalty (both as customers and partisans) to one of the biggest and most exploitative sweatshop industries of them all. Men who would not be caught dead wearing Reeboks or Nikes, or drinking Starbucks coffee, can still kid themselves into thinking Larry Flynt is some kind of People's Hero.

This self-deception has not, I think, gone unremarked by the captains of other industries; nor have they failed to learn from it. There are suggestive parallels between the re-branding of the sex industry as a fun, wholesome place to work or as an agent of liberation, and the contemporaneous and intensifying hard-sell of market values and the New, Improved Global Economy as the truly groovy, modern solution to all our problems. It seems more than coincidental that pimps and pornographers have been flourishing during the decline and defeat of organised labour and the triumph of both centre-right and far-right policies and rhetoric.

I am convinced there are more than just parallels: the two trends are related. In fact, the two are one. The mainstreaming of prostitution and pornography is, I suggest, at least as much a result of the triumph of neoliberal dogma in politics and economics, as it is one of the mixed blessings of 'sexual liberation'.

III. Corporations R Us?

While IBM was going on the airwaves to proclaim 'I am!', Friedman was virtually asking us to imagine that God was somehow behind the re-engineering programs at AT&T or GE, that God stood in solidarity with strikebreakers everywhere, that it was God who told American management to outsource the jobs to initiate 'change' programs, to send the entire payroll out into the parking lot one fine morning and hire half of them back as temps.

—Thomas Frank, *One Market Under God*

One of the world's biggest advertising agencies has declared that 'brands are the new religion' . . . a new advertising strategy is being adopted in order to win customer loyalty, the tapping of religious yearning. 'Everyone needs something to believe in', a recent advertisement for a car reminded us . . .

—Mark Corner, 'Religion and the Rise of Advertising', *Guardian*, March 2002

According to Active Parenting Publishers, more than three million parents have attended training sessions to make their families more like mini-corporations. Participants learn how to run family 'board meetings' complete with printed agendas, mission statements, and rotating chairmanships . . .

—*Wall Street Journal*, August 10, 2001

[C]ommercialism is *not* making us behave against our better judgment. Commercialism is our better judgment.

—James Twitchell, *Lead Us Into Temptation*

Now that pharmaceutical giant Pfizer sponsors Sesame Street, messages capping off the end of every episode have been replaced. Announcements that the show has been brought to you by, say, 'the letter Z and the number 2', have been replaced with 'Pfizer brings parents the letter Z—as in Zithromax'.

> —Pfizer company press release, October 1999 [see also FAIR Action Alert March 2000, 'The Commercialization of Children's Public Television', and 'Sesame Street Meets Madison Avenue' in *Mother Jones*, March 2001]

From a marketing point of view, you don't introduce new products in August.

> —White House Chief of Staff, Andrew Card, September 7, 2002, referring to the timing of the White House campaign to promote a US invasion of Iraq.

What happens if the commercial ethic (or lack of it) becomes paradigmatic or prescriptive for a society? If profit and business are adopted ideologically as the highest good, then what? What are the implications and consequences for community life and popular culture?

This is the cultural experiment that has been played out for the last 40 years in the United States and its satellite nations (i.e. NATO members and Japan).

America came out of the war years with a 10-year lead over most of the other industrial economies (which had been bombed, burned, and looted into the ground). It was not difficult for America, with its vast natural resources and war-stimulated technological momentum, to leap into a dominant position in the world economy, and for its population to reap the benefits of such rapid economic growth and control of international markets. Combined with strong legislation and social safety nets inherited from the (increasingly disowned) New Deal past, it all added up to prosperity and a jubilant, optimistic ride of several decades' duration for large sectors of the public.

All in all, almost three generations of Americans were treated to a period in history when the nation's barons of industry really did seem to 'bring good things to life'. In relatively easy times produced by economic expansion, hidden government subsidies, cheap energy, and a temporary lack of global competitors, Americans experienced a period of general prosperity which seemed to justify blind faith in capitalism and big business. The ugly realities of the capital/labour skirmishes of the teens and twenties were forgotten; socialist and labour parties had a hard time scaring up anyone with a sufficient grievance to join. America's hot political issues were race and gender, and not without good reason; but even as these issues were courageously struggled over, for decades, the age-old dynamics of capital and labour, wealth and power, were being forgotten in the brief summer of (relative) opportunity and prosperity for all (or most).

America's conservative business and financial community, however, had never forgiven Roosevelt for 'caving in to the Reds'. (As of the time of writing, in 2004, a right-wing initiative seeks even to banish FDR's head from the US dime and replace it with that of Ronald Reagan, the first President of the neoconservative revolutionary calendar.) That business community—which had fought every progressive measure for over fifty years, tooth and nail—had not changed its spots overnight. It was paying more attention than ever before, however, to changing its image; from the post-war years on, an accelerating catalysis between public relations, advertising, and media acquisitions changed the political strategy of capital.

The underlying agenda never changed; the aim of the highest echelons of industry (the ruling class, in an industrialised state) remained constant: to lower wages and remove restrictions on trade and more particularly on capital; to reduce employer responsibilities and employee rights, income taxes and corporate taxes; to sweep away pesky safety and consumer regulations; and generally to eliminate every possible cost of doing business—these have been the self-interested aims of Big Business for as long as there has been Big Business. America's corporate leadership has quietly pursued this agenda, steadily but surely, decade after decade. What with one thing and another, they have by now got almost everything they ever wanted. For people like myself who came of age in the seventies, the speed and success of the rollback are difficult to comprehend.

But there was more to this campaign than open bribery or brute force (though both were, and are, used when expedient). There was also a new mastery of popular culture, mass media, and public relations. The triumphalist culture of management and owners poured a tremendous investment into what (in biz-speak) is known as 'mindshare'. Business was no longer content to be mere commerce, a necessary but sometimes rather vulgar and brutal aspect of a greater civilisation; business was out to redefine *itself* as the pinnacle of civilisation and the ultimate purpose of human evolution.

Only Business, said Business, really knew how to Get Stuff Done. Needless to say, there was widespread agreement from major media wholly owned by Big Business (or beholden to advertising contracts for their revenues), from academics occupying research chairs funded by Business, and from politicians owing their position and influence to generous donations from Business. Business knew much better than government, better than employees, better even than God, how to run the world properly. The professional management classes puffed themselves up into a frankly religious ecstasy over the benevolent world-shaping power of *pure unrestrained commerce*. And the fever was catching.

The metaphor of business, the monetary yardstick, and the overwhelming imperative to show a profit, permeated popular culture and the culture of government. Government departments started referring to the public as 'customers' rather than 'citizens', and calling for cost-benefit analyses of public services. On the assumption that only private enterprise is efficient, public services were massively privatised, and those which remained in the public domain were starved of funding. In the US particularly (and in the UK, practically its client state), the whole style of public and governmental discourse was replaced, with familiar concepts and metaphors like 'family', 'community', and 'brotherhood' (evoking non-market values) giving way to concepts and metaphors drawn from the traditions of public relations, advertising, marketing, and accounting.

Most Americans are familiar with the various downstream effects of the great privatisation and anti-government backlash: Scroogeian slashing of welfare benefits; new 'workfare' programs; the emergence of HMOs to mete out and control the health care offered to employees by employers; metastatic growth of the prison-industrial complex; rollback of environmental safeguards; cuts in community services; degradation of conditions in public schools; a general scarcity of affordable health care; job flight and outsourcing—it is a dismal litany. Given the devastating effect of this backlash on millions of Americans (including the middle-class), many observers both in and outside America wondered how the business/government elites could get away with it. The US is, after all, a country where elections are regularly held and incumbents must defend their seats after fairly short terms of office. As the pain and dislocation of corporate-friendly policy was felt on Main Street, why didn't political heads roll? One fairly convincing answer is 'ownership of mass media'.

In the last twenty years, the process of 'commercialising' mass culture, and of concentrating media control into fewer and fewer hands, has accelerated. Unrelenting, persevering efforts by powerful business interests have paid off; almost every media outlet and press in America is now merely a subsidiary of a much larger commercial organisation whose primary purpose is not publishing or news. This includes our three largest television networks and most of our radio, as well as most newspapers.

The conflict of interest which has always haunted the newsroom—how much news can be honestly reported if it annoys the advertiser whose fees support the paper—is no longer a conflict; the 'advertiser' now owns the paper outright, and the paper is no longer an independent newspaper but a line item in the yearly public relations budget of a much larger outfit. The purpose of the paper (or radio station, or TV station) is to sell the audience, by the hour, by the demographic, to the advertisers. This has its inevitable effect on content. For example, I am not aware of any mainstream daily paper in the United States which still pays a 'labour reporter' for reporting labour issues. By contrast, every paper has a 'business' section reporting the antics, fortunes, and misfortunes of the business-owning class. Increasingly, newsworthy issues are treated strictly from the 'Wall Street point of view', as in early 2004 when a 'mad cow' food scare in the US provoked more newspaper speculation about the effect on stock values than inquiry into the possible risk to public health.

Beyond the ideological control exerted by business interests via the mass media, it also helped that finance capital was having a party on the accumulated wealth of prior decades of industrial productivity. As finance capitalism displaced industrial capitalism in the leading economies, speculation displaced actual building, making, and selling; and money could be 'created' by the usual mechanism of bubble markets. Stimulated by cynical, deliberate crowd-herding on the part of insiders, world stock markets roared upwards— particularly in the US, where the bull market to end all bull markets was in full cry throughout the 1990s.

As in all bubble markets, of course, fortunes were made on paper, based on paper prospectuses, without any actual employment, goods, warehouse, factory, or storefront ever existing to back the paper. But the money (on paper) was rolling in, and American Business hailed itself as the author of all this wonderful prosperity.

Even while the gap between rich and poor was widening every year, steady industrial jobs were vanishing, and consumer debt was ballooning, Americans revelled vicariously in the rising number of youthful millionaires, 'dot com kids', and lottery winners. Respectable financial journals purported to measure the economic health of the nation by the rising number of millionaires, and even proletarian media offered 'millionaire watch' web pages and feature-boxes in which enthralled readers could follow the rising personal wealth of the very uppermost crust. A handful of small investors managed to accumulate wealth during the boom, and their successes were over-reported in the breathless media enthusiasm of the time. Wealth itself re-acquired a glamour and magic which it had not had since the 1920s, and a second 'Gilded Age' seemed to be in full swing. This time, however, skilled spin doctors would avoid the appearance of elitism that might give the game away; the new capitalism was wrapped in a slick populist veneer. Although even at the height of the boom only 25 percent of Americans held any individually purchased stocks or mutual funds, the cultural fantasy being shaped in the corporate media was one of ever-broadening distributed ownership of the nation's wealth. Ironically, the reverse was happening.

It was quite a re-branding of capitalism. Shrewd public relations firms advised their clients to divest themselves of the stuffy suit-and-tie image of business—no pin-stripe trousers for bankers, no Victorian financial *gravitas*. Venture capitalists and fortunate inventors redefined themselves as visionaries, prophets and heroes, some acquiring a pop-star status which in previous decades had only been accorded to popular artists or sports figures of high achievement. This sugar coating of success, a 'growth' economy, and the illusory but mesmerising promise of money for nothing and overnight riches, made the infiltration of commercial values and metaphors into the mainstream culture quite painless. Business was chic, business was hip, business was *radical*, business was *fun*. Business was the real wellspring of democracy, upward mobility, and freedom.

The mass media have been dutifully broadcasting Business' soaring, inescapable love song to itself, to good effect. At this point American public discourse has been reshaped into a mould which, if the public had not had two decades and more to get used to it, would be embarrassing for everyone. After the semi-successful terrorist 'hit' on the World Trade Center in New York, politicians all over the country urged Americans to go out and consume, *go shopping*, to express their *patriotism*. The mayor of San Francisco authorised the distribution of posters in which the American flag was converted, by means of two bold graphic strokes, into a shopping bag, surmounting the legend, 'America: Open For Business'.

There was a time—and it was not too long ago—when large numbers of sincere patriots would have been outraged at the insult offered to the US flag by any graphic artist who turned it into a shopping bag for a corporate marketing campaign. At that time, those serious-minded patriots might well have fulmi-nated about the *prostitution* of their flag (more on this and similar metaphoric uses of prostitution later). But in a culture in which television commercials quite literally compare major corporations to God, it raised few eyebrows.

Traditionally in Western (and other) cultures, commerce and profiteering—the 'worldly' activities of the human race—exist in tension and counterpoise with other social spheres. Sometimes a traditionalist land-owning gentry class scornful of 'mere money', sometimes a powerful religious/charitable tradition, or a strong network of guilds or labour organisations, might defend and protect what we now (tellingly) call 'non-market values'. In later, industrial societies, organised labour and strong socialist or social-democratic parties evolved to carry the burden of social conscience and mutual responsibility. But in America at the tail end of the twentieth century, none of these counterpoises had enough mass to balance the cultural, ideological, political and material forces of commercialism.

Thus the eighties and nineties in America were the culminating decades of an enormous (engineered) cultural shift, from a sensible mistrust of excessive wealth and corporate power towards an open celebration and flaunting of the same—towards a cult-like worship of Business-for-its-own-sake. Such a shift was especially easy in America, where there was already a strong ideological association between capitalism and freedom (the Free Capitalist West versus the Poor, Enslaved Communist East), and where a successful campaign of intimidation and repression had long ago silenced or dispersed the core of a socialist intelligentsia. Rolling back legislation both nationally and internationally, buying politicians both openly and covertly, preaching non-stop the doctrine of the invisible hand and laissez-faire, demonising 'big government' and 'do-gooders' with one hand, and sparing no expense to publicise its own charitable stunts with the other, American big business was (and is) well on the way to creating *truly unrestrained commercialism*.

IV. Neoliberalism: meet the new boss

A general characteristic of neoliberalism is the desire to intensify and expand the market, by intensifying the number, frequency, repeatability, and formalisation of transactions. The ultimate (unreachable) goal of neoliberalism is a universe where every action of every being is a market transaction, conducted in competition with every other being and with every other transaction, influencing every other transaction, with transactions occurring in an infinitely short time, and repeated at an infinitely fast rate.

—from the web site of Paul Treanor, freelance social critic

Neoliberalism is both an ideology and a strategy. Like so many criminals, it has many aliases, 'Reaganomics', 'Thatcherism', 'supply-side economics', 'monetarism', 'new classical economics', and 'structural adjustment'. The ideology of neoliberalism is the worship of the 'market' and subordination of all other economic actors to its demands, including government and individuals. The strategy of neoliberal economics includes privatization, reduced social expenditures, union busting, land enclosure, lower wages, higher profits, free trade, free capital mobility and the accelerated commodification of nature.

—Accion Zapatista de Austin (University of Texas)
position statements on globalisation and neoliberalism

The movement toward the neoliberal utopia of a pure and perfect market is made possible by the politics of financial deregulation. And it is achieved through the transformative and, it must be said, destructive action of all of the political measures (of which the most recent is the Multilateral Agreement on Investment (MAI), designed to protect foreign corporations and their investments from national states) that aim to call into question any and all collective structures that could serve as an obstacle to the logic of the pure market: the nation, whose space to manoeuvre continually decreases; work groups, for example through the individualisation of salaries and of careers as a function of individual competences, with the consequent atomisation of workers; collectives for the defence of the rights of workers, unions, associations, cooperatives; even the family, which loses part of its control over consumption through the constitution of markets by age groups.

—Prof. Pierre Bourdieu, 'The Essence of Neoliberalism', *Le Monde*, December 1998

Deputies of the State Duma's rightist SPS (Union of Rightist Forces) faction have decided to push market reforms to the extreme and legalize prostitution in Russia. If the bill prepared by the rightists is passed in autumn, the prostitutes will turn into civilized 'sex-workers', ridding themselves of pimps and providing services according to the law.

—Viktoria Maliutina, Gazeta.Ru (online Russian news magazine)
July 12, 2002

The overly stringent [IMF] 'adjustment policies' in country after country forced cutbacks in education and health; in Thailand, as a result, not only did female prostitution increase but expenditures on AIDS were cut way back; and what had been one of the world's most successful programs in fighting AIDS had a major setback . . .

Disillusion with the international system of globalization under the aegis of the IMF grows as the poor in Indonesia, Morocco, or Papua New Guinea have fuel and food subsidies cut, as those in Thailand see AIDS increase as a result of IMF-forced cutbacks in health expenditures, and as families in many developing countries, having to pay for their children's education under so-called cost recovery programs, make the painful choice not to send their daughters to school.

—Joseph E. Stiglitz, *Globalization and its Discontents*

The evangelists of globalised capitalism are eager to consign every form of socialism, collective responsibility, even the ancient concept of the Commons, to the proverbial trash-heap of history. They proclaim a brave new world—a pure and perfect Market—in which Capital is the Friend of the People, and Commerce the most progressive force on the planet. Ideological contortions surrounding the traffic in women and children, however, continue unabated on both the Right and the battered Left; if anything they may be amplified, raised to new levels of absurdity, by the new ideologies of neoliberalism.

As noted by those who attempt to define neoliberalism in the pull-quotes above, the keystone of neoliberal ideology is that the most essential—the ideal—model of human interaction and human society is the marketplace. The Market is the perfect and maximally functional mechanism by which all human needs can be met; it is automatically just, fair and free. All imperfections in human society are merely the result of interference with the perfect functioning of a free market, and all interferences of this type will inevitably lead to inefficiency, waste, unemployment, poverty, etc., whereas the removing of artificial restrictions upon the functioning of markets will result in prosperity, wealth, progress, etc. Wealth, prosperity and progress can only be measured in money and in manufactured goods (i.e. only in those quantities and items which can be traded in the marketplace).

In the US, and increasingly throughout the 'advanced' nations, an almost seamless ideology has been constructed which equates 'capitalism' with 'democracy' and both with an idealised Smithian 'free market'—a naïve and oversimplified version of real commerce which conveniently ignores most of what we know about unfettered commercialism—including some of Smith's own astute observations:

> People of the same trade seldom meet together, even for merriment and diversion, but the conversation ends in a conspiracy against the public, or in some contrivance to raise prices.
>
> —Adam Smith, *The Wealth of Nations*

Thanks to this naïveté, neoliberal theorists now enjoy the kind of intellectual hegemony and stature that was once accorded to hard science, or in earlier times to prelates of the Church Militant: their jargon of 'rational agents', 'cost/benefit analysis', and 'optimisation' has infected almost every discipline. It has become received opinion that human beings are inherently selfish, greedy, and amoral. Any attempt to construct more humane public policy, to challenge and limit the malfeasance of powerful men, to question the establishment of money as the only yardstick of productivity, well-being, or social good, even to envision a less brutal society, or suggest that kindness or conscience have any place in public life—is contemptuously dismissed as 'naïve' or 'ideological'.

'Ideology' is the convenient wastebasket into which the neoliberal establishment sweeps any argument which does not enshrine money and power as the ultimate social values. Suppose you suggest that social investment in such infrastructure as universal education, childcare for working mothers, public health, public transit, or (in some extreme cases) even libraries and museums, might enhance the quality of life for all and therefore 'pay back' generously the nation which makes such investments, then you are being 'ideological'. If, on the other hand, you suggest that diverting safely invested Social Security funds into the risky arena of the open stock markets will stimulate the economy, enrich retirees, and generally bring about the promised land, then you are a sound, practical, realistic thinker with no ideology at all. Truly it is said that those who claim they have no politics invariably mean that their politics are of the Right—that is to say, of Business.

This atmosphere of 'tough thinking', with its self-congratulatory contempt for such values as charity, kindness, empathy, justice, self-restraint, and so forth, has engendered backlashes and contradictions of every flavour in every realm of progressive discourse. Some feminists may immediately think of Katie Roiphe's published opinion, that is, that women who suffer date-rape have only themselves to blame (along the lines of *Boys will be boys, and girls should be more careful*) or Camille Paglia's glib dismissal of women's contributions to human history and development (*If civilization had been left in female hands we would still be living in grass huts*), the iFeminists, and various other voices of the 'New Anti-Victim Feminism' who have found it unsurprisingly easy to win media attention and airtime in the last few years.

Much as the architects of the *Zeitgeist* loathe and disown the word, it is a profoundly ideological culture they have created—one in which the fundamental article of faith is that The System Works. If some people can't 'make it' in the system, it is not the system that needs fixing, it is their own fault. The world is as it is—mean, selfish, competitive, and dangerous—and only the fit will survive. This pseudo-Nietzschean, pseudo-Darwinist ethos is of course particularly appealing to the people who have already 'made it' and can now rest assured of their innate superiority as 'survivors'. (I would like to note here in passing the advent of 'survivor shows' and 'reality TV', and their startling popularity—a theme to which I will return later.)

Despite the elitism and brutality implicit in neoliberal ideology, its promoters maintain a thin veneer of populism which perhaps accounts for its hold on the popular imagination. Neoliberal ideology promises that when a 'boom' is experienced (i.e. large profits are reaped or monetary activity increases) in business, this is a Good Thing. The rising tide, as investment bankers and other multi-millionaires often assure us, lifts all boats. In other words, what is good for the Market is good for everyone; what is good for General Motors is good for the country; and what is good for Wall Street is just plain good.

Populist critics such as Michael Moore are quick to point out the fundamental disconnect—while US media pundits congratulated 'us' on a 'booming' stock market, increasing numbers of Americans lost their jobs, household savings dwindled, the rate of personal bankruptcies rose to an all-time high, control over wealth, property and media was concentrated in fewer hands, over 40 million Americans found themselves without medical insurance . . . and so on. The will of the prevailing ideologues to disregard such data (what Herman Daly calls 'feral facts') is notable; the ideological obedience of mainstream pundits and reporters may be measured by their ability to repeat such Orwellian oxymorons as 'jobless recovery' without even cracking a grin.

Many critics have decried this selective perception as amounting to fanaticism in certain sectors of the neoliberal school of economics. Neoliberal theorists are now ensconced in positions of influence and power in centre-right governments and at the World Bank, International Monetary Fund (IMF),

ImEx Bank and similar institutions; to say that they are intolerant of dissent is to indulge in understatement. No matter how negative the outcomes of their utopian theories when applied to real populations, no matter the degree of poverty, dislocation, and desperation caused by their 'shock treatments', 'market reforms', and 'belt-tightening measures' worldwide, they continue to preach that only good can come of adherence to their True Religion.

In Argentina, for example, where the government has meekly obeyed the dictates of the IMF and World Bank for the last decade or more, the results have been disastrous, the toll in human suffering enormous. The disconnect between neoliberal theory and reality on the ground in South America is far more extreme and painful than anything the US has (yet) seen—though our time may come. Nevertheless, the response of wealthy first-world pundits is that the only cure is more of the same. Prosperity, like paradise, is always just around the corner for those who are willing to suffer and have faith. To the true believer, all indicators always demonstrate the correct working of God's (or in this case the Market's) will on Earth; material evidence is irrelevant.

We may seem at this point to have wandered far from the topic of prostitution; but the thesis of this essay is that, in fact, we have not.

Some time in the summer of 2001 (if I recall correctly) I was listening to the BBC World Service and heard a story on AIDS in China, which to me seemed illustrative of the tortuous doublethink of the cheerleaders for global US-style capitalism. With increased prosperity and 'market reform' in China, said the announcer—in the victorious, vindicated tones we have become accustomed to in the West since the collapse of the USSR as a super-power—the new, more democratic China was experiencing a 'boom in the sex industry'. A couple of snide, disparaging references to the 'Puritanism' of the Mao years made it clear that this was to be seen as a Good Thing and a sign of progress and enlightenment.

Except, of course, that over a million 'sex workers' in China had been exposed to AIDS. Western values were being imported via TV and movies, and teenagers were becoming sexually active earlier in life and more promiscuously, so there was concern about the possibility of an AIDS epidemic in China. Most people there, said the announcer, are still ignorant about this disease, and their ignorance can be blamed on (once again) the 'Puritanism' of the Communist past.

Now let us parse this brief news item, as presented. An increase in the number of prostituted girls, boys and women is to be read as an indicator of prosperity and freedom; and if increased prostitution and the sexualisation of youngsters at earlier and earlier ages exposes the population to the risk of AIDS, this should be blamed on the Communists who discouraged prostitution and sexual promiscuity. Globalisation can only bring good; market values are identical with liberation and 'reform'. Not one person interviewed in the course of this story asked whether a resurgence of prostitution might not reflect a resurgence of pre-Communist values such as feudalism and Confucian patriarchy; whether it might indicate a decline of egalitarian ideals and a revival of traditional male privilege; or even whether it might simply indicate an upsurge in poverty and inequity, fuelling economic desperation.

The neoliberal is prevented from perceiving any negative aspects to the boom in prostitution precisely because it is a boom—an upswing in monetist activity, an increase in the number of market transactions. It is *good business*. To me as a feminist, the neoliberals' centre/rightist ideology carries a familiar and unpleasant whiff—it smells rather like the same logic (or illogic) that has consistently been applied to prostituted women by the doublethink of the US (and international) Left.

Though we know, culturally, by experience or by osmosis, that women and children are prostituted most commonly through violence, through poverty, through deprivation or betrayal, Western liberalism has pretended for decades that more prostitution and pornography only mean more freedom, openness, and (just as in the case of neoliberals crowing over the 'softening' of Communist China) more Democracy. The fact that real democracy plays very little part in the day-to-day experiences of the average prostitute, does not seem to register. The ideological fanaticism with which the neoliberal theorist ignores all negative effects of the 'freeing' of markets is not unlike the resolute effort with which the traditional sex-liberal theorist has ignored the negative effects of the so-called 'sexual revolution'.

Inconvenient statistics, feral facts like the average life expectancy of prostitutes, the average age of induction into prostitution, the average income of prostitutes, and so forth—hard demographics—have never disturbed those who defined the sex business as a force of liberation. The fact that the 'freedom' being realised is mostly the freedom of men to access the bodies of women and children—or of G8 nations to access the markets and raw materials of Third World nations—is conveniently overlooked when predation is redefined as progress.

From the perspective of pure laissez-faire capitalist theory—with its convenient intellectual mechanisms of externalised costs and discounted futures, abstract 'rational actors', and other game-theory constructs—there is nothing at all wrong with prostitution. Similarly there is nothing wrong with fixing drug prices too high for AIDS-stricken Africa (or uninsured Americans) to afford, and nothing wrong with relocating production facilities to whatever country offers the cheapest and most docile labour pool. It's nothing personal; it's strictly business. There's a demand, so there's a supply; prices are set by the Market, and by the demand of stockholders for high rates of return on investment capital. We should perhaps note that in the US, corporations are *required by law* to maximise return on stockholder investment.

Most of us are by now familiar with the line taken by corporate CEOs and their apologists with regard to cheap overseas labour. If women in the Philippines or Mexico, they say, are willing to work in FTZ factories for 60 cents (US) a day, then those women are free agents making their individual contracts with their employer. They have chosen the best deal, as all rational actors do in a free market; anyone who questions the terms of the deal is impugning their personhood and their rationality. Anyone who tries to get the transnationals to pay their sweatshop workers more, or to alleviate the brutal conditions under which many labour, is merely working against the women she is trying to help, because the corporations will simply leave if their costs rise too high, and then the women will be jobless again.

The language of 'feminist' and Left-leaning apologists for prostitution eerily echoes the language of the corporate CEOs and their apologists. Prostitutes, we are told, choose their line of work in a free market; they are rational agents. To criticise the industry which exploits them, or even to say that they are exploited, is to deny their agency. To attempt to regulate or restrict it is only to deny them 'opportunities' and 'choices'. The similarity of the language is no coincidence, of course: the incursion of commercial values and beliefs into academia as well as popular culture has been gathering momentum for decades. It is becoming increasingly difficult—and increasingly marginal or disreputable—to think outside the box of the Market.

Popular culture reflects the *Zeitgeist* accurately and unflatteringly in such media excesses as the reality shows to which I alluded earlier, in which 'contestants' are pitted against each other, not unlike Roman gladiators in a bitter contest for wealth. Some radio 'talk shows' now offer their 'guests' money or 'fame' as an incentive to submit to various public humiliations. In one notorious incident, shock-jock Howard Stern convinced a woman to strip in the studio and to eat dog food out of a bowl on the floor, in exchange for his giving air time to music recorded by a friend of hers. The pseudo-Smithian ideology of 'choice', and the rest of the market-populist mumbo-jumbo, would of course emphasise this woman's 'choice' to endure such a scene, rather than questioning the ethics of Stern, the radio station, or its advertisers and listeners. The scene itself is paradigmatic of prostitution: a man holds out the offer of something a woman wants or needs, in order to persuade her to do humiliating things for his amusement.

In an era dominated by neoliberal ideology, it is obviously difficult to mount a successful campaign against the sexual exploitation of women and children. On every front, feminists meet a brick wall.

First, the prevailing Market-worship mocks and devalues any suggestion of altruism; if women fortunate enough to have escaped sexual exploitation in their own lives demonstrate concern and caring for prostituted women, they are dismissed as naïve, unrealistic idealists and (of course) 'ideologues'. The 'sexual liberation' pseudo-progressive ideology then serves to cast women who object to exploitation, profiteering, coercion and other routine practices of the sex industry as 'crypto-conservatives', 'neo-Victorians', 'anti-sex', and so forth. Should either of those barriers fail to discourage the feminist social critic, the neoliberal dogma is trotted out to prove that, for example, the woman eating dog food on the floor of Stern's studio is exactly where she wants to be. Neoliberal dogma will say that any woman who expresses disgust at the men who enacted and enjoyed this ritual of humiliation is actually an *anti*-feminist: she is denying the agency and choice exercised by this 'liberated' female, the 'good sport' who is 'tough enough to take it' and needs no sympathy or interference from well-meaning nannies. Just as, of course, the poor are quite capable of pulling themselves up by their own bootstraps and need no insulting assistance from the smothering hands of Big Government.

V. Economies of scale

An estimated 60 percent of two million tourists visiting Thailand each year are allegedly drawn by bargain price sex.

—Thanh-Dam Truong, 'The Dynamics of Sex Tourism: the Case of Southeast Asia' cited in M. Waring, *Counting for Nothing*

When governments promote tourism as a currency-earning growth strategy, they usually count prostitution as part and parcel of it. Local young women are seen as a sexual pool for tourists, regardless of the social consequences or the risks and side-effects for the women themselves. It is considered officially admissible, indeed desirable, for the national economy, that women's bodies should be thrown onto the world market at a knock-down price.

—Christa Wichterich, *The Globalized Woman*

We [Americans] have 50 percent of the world's wealth but only 6.3 percent of the population. This disparity is particularly great between ourselves and the peoples of Asia. In this situation, we cannot fail to be the object of envy and resentment. Our real task in the coming period is to devise a pattern of relationships which will permit us to maintain this position of disparity without positive detriment to our national security.

—George Kennan, Director, US State Department's Policy Planning Staff, 1948 [from a top-secret memo declassified under FOIA]

Each year approximately ten thousand American troops descend on Thailand for a joint military exercise called Cobra Gold. The military part of these visits is largely make-work for the American and Thai staffs, but the troops love Cobra Gold because of the sex. According to the newspaper *Pacific Stars and Stripes*, some three thousand prostitutes wait for the sailors and marines at the South Pattaya waterfront, close to Utapao Air Base. An equal number of young Thai girls from the countryside, many of whom have been raped and then impressed into the 'sex industry', are available downtown in Bangkok's Patpang district. They are virtually all infected with AIDS, but the condom-equipped American forces seem not to worry. At the time of the 1997 war games, just before the economic crisis broke, sex with a Thai prostitute cost around fifteen hundred Thai baht, or sixty dollars at its then pegged rate of 25 baht to $US1. By the time of the next year's Cobra Gold the price had been more than halved. This is just one of many market benefits Americans gained through their rollback operation against the 'Asian model' of capitalism.

—Chalmers Johnson in *Blowback: the Costs and Consequences of American Empire*

A top-selling video game, 'Grand Theft Auto III', is an exercise in crime and violence ... In 'Grand Theft Auto III', the player works for the mafia, which involves killing police officers and innocent bystanders, stealing cars, and doing drugs. When the player begins to lose his health, he can pick up a prostitute on the street and have sex with her, as indicated by a bouncing car. As a result, the player's health goes up, but his funds go down. Once the hooker exits the car, if the player wants his money back, he can dash after her, beat her to death and recover the cash.

People who have played the game say that the bloody beating is done with a baseball bat that players can 'feel' in their hands through the PlayStation controller.

—MediaWatch campaign newsletter, April 2002

It's nothing personal. It's strictly business.

—Don Vito Corleone, *The Godfather*

Make the economy scream.

—Richard M. Nixon, US president: instructions to CIA, September 15, 1970, for the destabilisation of Chile's new Allende government

We all know about the Mafia—or about organised crime of whatever ethnicity. At least, we have some kind of folk knowledge, a sense of cultural familiarity. We know it's all about a tightly organised extended clan, controlled and operated by men, dealing in 'bad stuff' like guns, drugs, gambling, contract assassination, and (of course) prostitution. It operates in an atmosphere of violence; people who don't cooperate, or who threaten to inform, are likely to be murdered—sometimes in spectacularly gruesome ways—to 'send a message' to others and keep everyone toeing the line. The object of any Mafia is simple: to make money, to secure the best return for their stockholders. It sells whatever will command a price, unfettered by pesky regulatory bodies or public oversight; and the best prices are often to be had for the 'worst' goods, as every drug dealer knows. Sometimes the more traditional families or clans have their own rules, their own 'lines' below which they don't wish to deal; but over time, truly unrestrained commercialism ensures a moral race to the bottom, a marketplace in which just about anything is for sale to the highest bidder.

The Mafia also specialises in 'closed loop' marketing; they sell fire insurance in neighbourhoods where their hired arsonists can be sent out at any time to demonstrate the need for insurance. They provide bodyguards and 'security' to protect business owners from their own thugs. They steal your stuff and then sell it back to you. They ensure that you have to buy from one of their 'family' businesses; sometimes their competitors suffer a series of mysterious 'accidents'.

The operation of the Mafia is the purest form of laissez-faire. Its tactics do not differ substantially from the tactics used by 'above the line' businesses when they think they can get away with it. The only differences are those of degree and scale.

The Mafia can make you disappear if you don't buy what you are told to buy at the price dictated from above; a monopolistic corporation can shut your business down, revoke your lease, terminate your employment. Although the degree of violence and severity of threat involved varies, the basic principle of 'business at gunpoint' is shared. Even the differences of degree are not always observed; there have been many cases—from the hired thugs whose head-bashing and gunfire was unleashed to break strikes in the 19-teens and twenties, to the defamation and removal of third-world leaders whose policies inconvenienced US business interests—where murder has been done in the cause of 'legitimate' corporate profit.

Nor is there a strong and clear dividing line between 'the kind of people' who pursue one form of profiteering considered legitimate, and those who pursue another considered criminal. We read with horror and a sense of shock that the UN is called upon to investigate aid workers in Africa: 'The study of refugees in Guinea, Liberia and Sierra Leone found almost 70 aid workers from 40 agencies had been pushing refugee children into sex in exchange for food, medicine and other supplies sent to save their lives'. (Reuters, February 27, 2002)—or that in Bosnia, employees of Dyncorp, a 'military contractor' (corporatised mercenaries) were implicated in trafficking, and that employees who blew the whistle on gun-running and prostitution rings run by Dyncorp and UN staff were sacked by the corporation (*Observer*, July 29, 2001). The activities of 'legitimate' corporations and agencies, in out-of-the-way places unscrutinised by the First World press, may easily morph into flagrant Mafia-ism; if publicised, these 'lapses' by staff and functionaries will be roundly condemned, and in fact may serve to distract public attention and perception from the equally Mafia-like strategies and methods of the parent corporation. The small-scale operation seems genuinely criminal—how dare these men take advantage of vulnerable women and children?—and in our indignation over their crimes, we tend to forget that much of the world's poverty is engineered, and is often the wreckage left behind by larger scale, more respectable profiteering.

> When I give food to the poor they call me a saint; When I ask why the poor have no food, they call me a communist.
>
> —Dom Helder Camara, bishop and 'liberation theology' activist, Brazil

When we condemn men—corporate employees and NGO functionaries, police, soldiers—for taking advantage of hungry women and children, we stay within the bounds of conventional morality. When we ask why women and children are made hungry and vulnerable in the first place, why their economies or societies have collapsed, why they are abjectly dependent on food aid or why corporate mercenaries are at large in their countries, we risk departing from the conventional by rejecting the camouflaging power of scale, and holding the larger crimes to be as wicked as the smaller ones.

When it comes to scale, in the years since the decline of antitrust legislation and the frenzy of corporate mergers, what is officially called 'organised crime' can hardly compete with the new, globe-spanning corporations. The Mafia buys a politician here and a politician there; the transnational corporations can buy entire governments, and the pursuit of their interests can bankrupt and ruin not merely a city or even a state, but an entire country or several. National economies can be crashed by the deliberate manipulation of cross-border capital flow for the sake of the marginal profits which can be realised on currency exchange rates.

If scale lends legitimacy to crime, then it should be less criminal to murder ten people than one person. But it seems that scale doesn't kick in until some much higher number. You have to murder several hundred or several thousand people before your murders achieve the respectability of 'war'. You have to cheat thousands or millions of people before you are allowed to call your dealings 'business' or 'finance' instead of just plain cheating. I am not the first person to wonder bitterly why it is that when a handful of poor men with dark skins get over-excited during a period of disorder and loot a storefront, that's a deplorable crime and proof of their inherent barbarism and backwardness; yet when a handful of very rich white men with power get over-ambitious and loot an entire country, that's 'Progress' and 'History'—and proof of their inherent Darwinian fitness and superiority. Scale is a wonderful thing.

If we divest ourselves for a moment of the legitimising magic of large scale, we may see the neoliberal economic agenda in a new light. Many critics of globalisation have documented and condemned the 'fire-sale' acquisition, by deep-pocketed G8 or transnational corporations, of essential resources and physical plant from countries whose economies have been crashed by IMF/WB 'austerity measures'. To drive one's competitors into bankruptcy by mailfist tactics, then buy up their properties at deep discount, is something the world's various Mafias have always been good at.

Not as much has been said, except by a few dogged feminists, about the creation of yet another cut-rate exploitable resource in these battered economies: an underclass of attractive young women thrown into sudden poverty.

Wherever the neoclassical economists administer their shock treatments, the pimps clean up. Women from the former Soviet Union, for example, have been for sale all over the Middle East, Asia, and wealthy Europe since the collapse of the Soviet regime which took down with it their chances of an education or a decent job. The story recurs wherever a country which once enjoyed some kind of social safety net has it ripped away.

Above the line, the transnational vultures acquire physical plant, rolling stock, mines, land, warehouses full of goods, all for pennies on the dollar. Local 'entrepreneurs' (usually the ruling elite who since colonial times have owned most of the land and other resources) snap up public services and public property in an orgy of privatisation, and sign sweetheart deals with foreign corporations.

Meanwhile, below the line, the pimps scoop up the 'surplus' women at bargain prices, and drug dealers open whole new markets among the newly miserable and despairing. Everybody wins—the predators and parasites, anyway. As in conventional wars, so in economic warfare: women and children generally lose.

Imagine for a moment that someone did this to your family: suckered you into 'easy money' loans with their best hard-sell techniques, let's say; got you in over your head at ruinous rates; crashed your credit rating; drove you into bankruptcy. Then the same people, or their very good friends, bought up your home at ten cents on the dollar when you were down and desperate, *and* enticed your teenagers into prostitution when you were unable to feed or clothe them properly. We would have little difficulty identifying this as the work of loan sharks, thugs, gangsters, Mafia, whatever they are called in your community. But when the IMF and first-world corporations do it to an entire country it is called 'politics' or 'policy' or 'reform' or even Progress. In both cases it is *good business*. Fortunes are made.

That hungry women are prostituted is one of the ground rules of human history. It seems obvious to the average person of common sense that relatively few women would ever spontaneously or casually decide to service multiple men per day for very low wages. Mass prostitution flourishes where poverty and hunger flourish—particularly where wealth flaunts itself in the near vicinity.

Thanks to globalisation, of course, wealth is always flaunting itself in the near vicinity. The obscene wealth and luxury of the G8 nations does not even require air transport to make its presence felt abroad. Every television in the Third World brings it close enough to touch—*almost*—makes it more immediate, more intrusive, more insistent even than the wealth of native elites. All that wealth, flagrantly flaunted, out of reach, tantalising, serves to make pimps greedier and girls more deluded.

> In most cases, it was an experience of violence in the family or in a circle of acquaintances that first drove the women into commercial sex work. They are helped to get through the 'programme with a gringo' by the dream of a 'fairy prince', preferably from Germany, and by drugs that deaden their feelings of repulsion. More than half the girls had already been once to Europe with a client, in the hope that a marriage might come out of it . . .
>
> —Christa Wichterich, on prostitution in Recife, Brazil

Moreover, cheap air transport ensures that wealthy men from the G8 (and almost any man from the G8 is wealthy compared to most women from the rest of the world) can easily seek bargain sex in the poorer nations. There is of course nothing new about this. Men have always traded in 'exotic' women across national and international borders. The Vikings and Goths in their day captured Irish people (women, kids, men) and sold them a long, long way down river—to the Ottoman Empire and beyond. Wealthy men of all the ancient empires prided themselves on the exotica of their harems just as they stocked their private zoos with rare and costly fauna.

Like cheap international travel, internet access has proved to be far more about men's access to the bodies of women and girls, than about women's and girls' access to resources, education, employment, empowerment. 'Hot teen girls' of almost every nationality are now available to web-surfing men, only a few clicks (and perhaps a credit card charge) away. The vulgarisation of privilege that Engels foresaw has taken strange new directions; every man wealthy enough to own a computer and pay an ISP can enjoy an infinite virtual harem in the seclusion of his home.

The new technologies of travel and communication increase the scale and the ease of trading in access to women's bodies. It is a conceit of capitalist culture to believe that these improvements in ease and scale of access to women's bodies represent Progress and liberalism; but the wholly illiberal fundamentals of the business have not changed.

The current boom in prostitution and pornography is not a passing phenomenon generated by a localised war or famine; it is happening on a vast scale, in response to ever-increasing inequities of wealth and never-ending fiscal crisis and dislocation, in a world whose values are informed and shaped by mass production and monetism—a world where vast scale lends respectability, where the mass replication of a crime seems to render it less, and not more, criminal, and where cash value is the only value.

What does scale really mean for prostitution and pornography? Does the inconceivable scale of internet pornography, for example, normalise and legitimise pornography and prostitution in the same way that the sheer scale of destruction and murder legitimises warfare? Does selling a woman to a potentially infinite number of johns somehow diminish the badness of each individual sale? Does replicating the videotape of her rape or humiliation ten thousand times diminish the affront to her personhood? Surely it is the reverse: mass production, mass distribution, only intensifies our sense of commodification, depersonalisation, reification of the female body and soul. The affront is amplified, not diminished. The industrialisation and mass-production of 'access to women's bodies' affront the humanity of the individual woman in a way quite symmetrical with other affronts to human nature and human dignity resulting from the intrusive ideology of industrialisation and mass production.

What of the large-scale distribution of 'freeware' internet porno, hailed by some (naïve) cyber-leftie types as a radical and positive development? If there is no monetary transaction, does this make the granting of access to a woman's body, by one man to another man or to all comers, a less offensive proposition?

Suppose for a moment that such amateur, self-published porno—'open source' or Gnuporn—started to displace the commercial variety. If cyber-voyeurs, for example, place web cams in hundreds of thousands of women's restrooms, changing cubicles, and locker rooms, charging nothing for viewing access online, is this 'free porn' somehow less destructive than corporate porn? My personal feeling is that whether the currency is hard cash, or the more nebulous yet quite measurable currency of 'web hit rates' and online reputation, we are still seeing men selling women to other men; the relationship of Seller (male), Buyer (male) and Product (female) still obtains. Even if the only return for the pimp/pornographer is being able to brag about how many voyeurs visit his site as opposed to someone else's, a woman is still being marketed.

Scale (and distance) operate strangely here to distort perception, as they do with other Mafia-like activities. If in the average workplace one man turned to another and offered him nude pornographic pictures of 'my wife', my guess (based only on the workplaces and the male colleagues I have known) is that the recipient of the offer would be embarrassed, disturbed, and even offended. Yet the same men might (perhaps furtively) visit amateur porn websites offering 'hot pictures of my girlfriend'. Perhaps the web-hit counter is reassuring—to look at a picture of a woman stripped and paraded seems less harmful if one knows that 'this page has had 20,195 visitors so far'.

Yet the woman—supposing that (a) she was unaware of being photographed in the first place, (b) she later wished she had not permitted the photography, or (c) she cooperated in the photography as 'love play' but had no idea the pictures would be published online—I suspect would feel rather differently about that web counter and its implications.

Perhaps the effect of scale here reflects the old masculinist belief that a woman can only lose her 'honour' once—that once a woman is raped or seduced she is 'dirty' and it no longer matters what happens to her. If so, it is a familiar theory, an attitude millennia-old and still thriving not only in the 'backward' traditional patriarchies of the pre-industrial world, but at the heart of 'modern' capitalist societies which claim to be their polar opposite.

Neither vastness of scale nor technological modernity should be allowed to distract us from the man behind the curtain.

VI. Metawhores: Whore as metaphor, prostitution as market model

> The site that set out to bring the media to their knees—but found out they were already there.
> —motto of mediawhoresonline.com, a media criticism site

> Politics is supposed to be the second oldest profession. I have come to realize that it bears a very close resemblance to the first.
> —Ronald Reagan, March 2, 1977

During the US presidential campaign of 2000—which ended so dubiously— many progressive voters felt that both the major parties had become so corrupted by corporate/business influence that there was little to choose between them any more. That fall I went to hear the 'hopeless outsider', Ralph Nader, speaking at a small civic auditorium. Outside, on the steps, a small group of activists cheerfully chanted 'Albert Gore, Corporate Whore', to the tune of 'Frère Jacques'.

What they meant, of course, was that Democratic candidate Al Gore was for sale. They referred to the Democratic party's acceptance of huge 'soft money' contributions, but specifically to Gore's own family and its fairly large stake in Occidental Petroleum—a company with (like most oil companies) a shady record in both the environmental and human-rights arenas.

At the time, and when the first draft of this essay was written, 'Oxy' (as it is affectionately called by managers and stockholders, and contemptuously by activists) was facing opposition from an indigenous group in Colombia, the U'Wa tribespeople, who did not want oil exploration and drilling to happen on their ancestral territory. The Colombian government, of course, was keen on a profitable contract with Oxy, and the company's deep pockets were said to be funding a brutal campaign of repression and intimidation against the stubborn indigenous resisters.

In other words, Oxy's money was buying the Colombian government; it was trying to buy the land out from under people whose livelihood, culture, and very life is in their land. The chanting critics asserted that Oxy and companies like it had also bought and paid for not only the Republican candidates in US elections, but the other party as well. Al Gore, critics said, should sell his Oxy stock and sever his family's association with this dirty money, rather than allow such a conflict of interest where traditional Democratic party values (like human rights and social justice) were involved. The fact that a few years earlier a book on environmental ethics had been published under Gore's name only intensified the perception of his hypocrisy and venality.

All this was implied and contained in the terse chant calling Al Gore a 'corporate whore'. So, of course, was a legacy of misogyny which blames *women* for prostitution. Presumably some chant could have been devised which would dwell on Occidental Petroleum as a 'thug and pimp', but the immediate goal was to confront/insult Gore or his supporters. To call Gore a 'whore' worked on the gut-level as a slur on his masculinity, by ascribing to him a 'female' subservience and spinelessness (or mercenary amorality), as well as on the more intellectual level by calling attention to his dubious financial connections and lack of probity.

And yet, as weary feminists know, in liberal and even in radical American circles, prostitution and pornography (the literal rather than metaphorical kind) continue to be for the most part redeemed and defended, even if lukewarmly, on the grounds of free speech or sexual liberation. It struck me at the time as deeply interesting that one could make a public statement that 'the relationship between Oxy and Al Gore is like that of a john (or a pimp) and a whore, and this is despicable', to fairly good effect, yet the same demographic segment who were more or less receptive to this statement would almost certainly be wary of (or even hostile towards) radical feminist critiques of porn and prostitution.

The brutal face of capitalism—profiteering with the mask off—is loathsome to progressives and liberals when it is embodied in Oxy's cynical use of violence and corruption to further its commercial aims. The analogy with prostitution is on some level perceived, and used to criticise the corruption by wealth of a better relationship that should exist between government and business, between government and people, between people and commerce. One risks, however, being called prudish or neo-Victorian if one suggests that the sexual relationship between free persons is also corrupted and damaged by money influence.

The way we use metaphors of pimping and whoring reveal a profound mistrust, a perception (valid, in my view) that the intrusion of 'market values' into community life or intimate life is not a healthy thing. Yet we persist simultaneously in the fantasy that the relationships of literal prostitution, the trade itself, the original from which our metaphorical distaste is drawn, are somehow harmless.

The disconnect is remarkable; it is as if we could thoughtlessly describe something wicked or corrupt as 'as bad as racism', and in the next breath accept last week's lynching or cross-burning as a commonplace—or even a healthy expression of free speech and democracy.

Despite our loose usage of 'metawhores' in common speech and thought, we do not often consider far deeper correspondences between prostitution and the daily life and culture which is (for most of us) largely defined and shaped by corporate capitalism.

In the world of commerce, the customer is not (despite the best efforts of PR agencies) anyone's best friend. As one corporate honcho memorably put it, 'Our friends are our competitors. Our enemy is the customer.' This is an interesting statement, one which codifies two of the great contradictions of commercial culture.

One is that the 'free market' of theory, in which cut-throat competition assures innovation and puts ultimate power in the hands of the customer, is a myth. One of the first things that corporate power does, just as national powers and Mafia families do, is to make strategic, diplomatic, and contractual alliances with its apparent competitors—dividing up the available supply of prey as amicably as possible and settling down to fix prices. Apparent competitors often turn out to be in reality co-investors, or to have made 'gentlemen's agreements' on or off the books. The customer is the 'mark' as it were, and the corporate powers are the wily old hucksters of the sideshow, wise to each other's tricks and bound by a kind of rogues' fraternity.

But there is another aspect to the customer as prey or enemy, and that is the imperative of marketing. The customer in some cases seems to be less customer than *product*.

Critics of corporate media and culture have often remarked that corporate-controlled newspapers or broadcast media, for example, have entirely changed their nature over the last few decades. Although there has generally been some commercial presence and some advertising in public media, the roles of the media, the public and the advertiser have changed significantly.

The 'customers' of broadcast television, as I mentioned earlier, are not the viewers. They are the advertising agencies (and by extension their corporate customers) who desire access to the attention span of the audience. The fantastical prices paid for 30 seconds of prime-time major-network advertising slots, and the fabulous budgets of these obsessively overcrafted micro-masterpieces of video production, are the real business of television. The audience is the commodity, to which access is granted for a fee by the broadcaster.

This selling by the media corporations of timed blocks of 'customer' attention span to the advertisers who 'rent' the audience, presents an undeniable analogy to prostitution. Cast the media companies as the pimps, the audience as the whores, the marketing departments as the johns. Television watchers are sold—by the half-minute interval—to avid advertisers, who hope in their turn to permute the relationship, provoking and stimulating the appetites of the consumer so as to part the public from its money.

Several very successful PR agencies now exist whose business it is to write pseudo-reportage for the paper media (mostly newspapers, some magazines). The corporate customer approaches the agency with a product, event or process which it wants publicised; the agency hacks write a 'news article' which just happens to give a high profile to that corporation, its product, or its process. The agency then makes it known to newspaper editors throughout the country, or in a targeted demographic region, that 'news' can be obtained free—in other words, they offer something like a wirefeed, but with no charge. Many newspapers both small and large, eager to cut costs for fear of being downsized out of existence by their new corporate owners, leap at the chance to fire a few reporters and replace column-inches which cost salary money with column-inches which cost nothing.

As a result, some industry analysts estimate that as much as 40 percent of some newspapers' content is 'placed material', that is, it is actually advertising—though not designated as such. Experts in the trade claim that they can tell, when reading a daily newspaper, which pseudo-articles were written by which PR agencies; the different agencies are said to have 'finger-prints' of prose style and content which (if you know which writers are working where and who has which corporate contracts) identify the articles far more accurately than their fictitious bylines. Some journalists refer to working for the 'infomercial' agencies as 'whoring' or 'prostituting oneself'.

In our 'marketised' society, we must expect these analogies with prostitution to abound, and to expand and multiply. Since the working definition of a prostitute is 'someone who will do anything for money', and a monetist society is one in which money is the only thing worth doing anything for, a gradual convergence is inevitable: the 'rational actor' of neoliberal economic theory would never refuse good money for the sake of a mere point of principle. Second only to outright slavery, prostitution has to be the ultimate expression of loyal adherence to 'market values'. What interests me is that the analogies, as in the Albert Gore example, seem to arouse more outrage and distress than real prostitution itself.

The crass commercialisation of childhood, for example, rouses even market-happy G8 denizens to protest. Some commentators say that some American schools have 'prostituted themselves' by signing contracts obliging students to drink only Pepsi, or only Coke, or to participate in public relations stunts for soft drink companies. Schools have taken corporate money in exchange for placing advertising in restrooms, or making students watch a mandatory hour of the infamous 'Channel One' so-called educational TV (a great deal of the content of which is product placement or outright advertising). 'Renting our children to advertisers', as the Channel One contracts have sometimes been described, certainly has overtones of prostitution.

The same BBC World Service which reported a boom in Chinese prostitution as a sign of reform and liberalisation has run a few cautionary stories on the 'disturbing trend in commercialising our schools'.

Children are even recruited as 'secret agents' by toy and clothing companies who pay parents a fee if the child files reports on what his or her playmates like to wear, eat, play with, etc. Corporate sponsors offer 'free' computers to schools, on the condition that the students use the provided web browsing software which (a) exposes them to advertising and (b) keeps track of all their browsing habits for later analysis by demographic marketing experts.

Recently, a video game producer joined forces with marketeers to use a children's video game for information-gathering: kids use a barcode wand to scan labels on food and other household products to 'add strength' to their fantasy dinosaur characters in the virtual world of the game. Meanwhile, the corporate databases are filled with interesting data about what the kids' families buy and consume.

The outrage that many people express about these manifestations of intrusive marketing is remarkably similar to feminist anger about the sexual exploitation of women and children. It is inappropriate, in the moral and philosophical frame inhabited by feminists, to make use of another human being in such an instrumental, calculating way.

It is inappropriate, say outraged parents, to smother the authentic experience of childhood in a blizzard of manipulation and brand-name promotion, to make every experience a child has into a commercial transaction (the end state of neoliberal theory), a matter of selling or being sold to, or being sold. The life in which every experience is one of selling or being sold is of course the experience of the average prostitute; the destruction of the authentic experience of life is even more brutal and overwhelming when one's living depends on faking enthusiasm, or suppressing fear and disgust, during hours of sex with strangers.

In any case, porno is littered—porno is heaped—with the deaths of feelings.

—Martin Amis, 'A Rough Trade'

It is perhaps a similar *death of feeling*—the death of non-market feelings such as affection, sympathy, and joy—that parents fear when they see their children being redefined as consumers, and childhood itself redefined as a marketing opportunity. All human feelings other than competitiveness, greed, fear, and the satisfaction of impulse are 'non-market' values. The death of such feelings is implied by the neoliberal ideal of imposing the conceptual mould of the Market onto all human life, converting every human interaction into a market transaction, every earthly thing into commodity. At some point our human sensibilities rebel, in moral outrage or in simple 'common' sense.

In recent years the commercial concept of intellectual property right, for example, has been stretched to the point of absurdity—the point at which common sense rebels. Monsanto now claims to 'own' the genome of rice. In theory, no one can do research using these genome data, or perhaps even grow rice (the staple food of half the world), without owing Monsanto some kind of copyright fee. At present, Monsanto is being nice about it and offering to share the data; but according to the letter of intellectual property law, they have the option not to be nice.

All through the Third World, First World companies have been prowling, collecting herbs and foodstock which native farmers have conserved and bred for centuries—in some cases millennia—and patenting their genotypes; patenting something, in short, which they (the companies) never invented, never created, never put a lick of effort into, only 'discovered' (much as their predecessors claimed to have 'discovered' lands in which other people had already been living for millennia). In passing, we might consider whether we find a parallel here with the pornographer who can copyright as his own intellectual property the rawest snapshot he manages to take of a woman's body—to be sold and re-sold at his will and at a profit, with or without her consent. We also say of porn and movie stars that they are 'discovered', even though they have existed and led their own lives all along, until the arbitrary moment when someone else decided money could be made from them.

Controversy erupted in Iceland in early 2000 when the government announced its plan to 'sell' the genotype of the Icelandic population to a US-backed corporation—that is, to sell intellectual property rights over the genetic information encoded in living people. Monsanto drew heavy fire in 1999 and 2000 for its plans to implement 'terminator technology', a genetic tweak which would make the seed of agricultural crops monogenerational; if a farmer planted Monsanto's GE seed, next-generation seed collected from the resulting crop would be infertile. (This technology is still being developed by the European biotech giant Syngenta.) The goal is evident: to put a stop to the millennia-old human tradition of seed saving, and make farmers dependent for each year's crop on a fresh purchase of patented seed from the corporation. (I remind the reader here that wherever we wander in the transnational corporate world, we never drift far from the topic of prostitution: the displacement of subsistence and village farmers, worldwide, by corporate agriculture based on expensive Western technologies such as patented seed and tailored herbicides, has dispossessed and impoverished millions of women and girls. What happens to hungry, landless women and girls? We know the answer.)

What these snippets from the news-stream have in common is that they elicited an angry and indignant response from a fairly large proportion of the reading public. These intellectual property claims over life itself induce in the average progressive or humanitarian person a sense of revulsion or indecency, an affront to human feeling, that ominous sense of the death of feeling. Ownership is being asserted over something which it seems not reasonable or right to consider as property. Jokes, those sure indicators of public fear or covert social criticism, started to make the rounds. 'Patent your genome and sue your parents!' was one: a terse comment on the fundamental absurdity of patenting life at all, and on the violation of fundamental human relationships implied by this incursion of Business into intimate life.

Such jokes, and a growing 'consumer' resistance to lifeform-patenting, GMO crops, and so forth, suggest that ordinary 'apolitical' people fully embedded in a neoliberal cultural matrix may become critics of capitalism when Business's strategies of enclosure, expropriation, and control pass a certain threshold, approaching the logical conclusions of neoliberal theory. The outrage, disgust, mockery or disbelief then expressed poses a direct challenge to neoliberal ideology. Public distaste, boycotts and jibes in response to genome patenting and other radical enclosures attempted by corporate culture, assert a contemporary heresy: some things should not be for sale; the Market should not encompass all things.

This is the same heresy asserted by feminists: women's bodies should not be for sale—it is simply wrong to commodify and trade in some things. The values of the Market are not the ultimate human values. Yet this feminist position—despite a long tradition and obvious parallels with other established human rights movements—seems more marginal, less popular, than the recent resistance to Monsanto and its ilk.

The ground rules of the sex industry—which are the ground rules of capitalism—offend and disturb us when they invade 'respectable' people's lives. But looking at contemporary liberal mainstream culture we have to wonder: where is the collective outrage at the accelerating, nearly complete commercialisation of sexuality? Where is the hip 'anti-globalisation' protest against the commodification of women and children—which has so much more extreme immediate, physical, material impacts than the commodification of audiences, schoolchildren, education systems?

VII. Supply and demand

SE: There's no question that the internet is increasingly a territory for consumption. I just talked with someone last week about how all these industries now are studying the pornography industry because pornography is the most successful business on the internet.

CM: Yeah, even a 'family' company like AOL is making all their money off porn. They censor bad words from their 'legit' conferences or whatever and then make all their money off smutty chat rooms.

—Stuart Ewen, interviewed by Carrie McLaren, *StayFree* #14, January 1998

Americans, roughly 4% of the planet by numbers, gulp down more than half the world's illegal drugs, but in all the strident speeches and in all the poorly conceived foreign policy measures, it is always the fault of Mexico or Colombia or Vietnam or Panama or the French Connection or someone else out there. Anyone, that is, but the people who keep gulping and snorting the stuff down, and all the shady American officials who are so clearly necessary to keep the merchandise widely available.

—John Chuckman in *YellowTimes*, an online journal, March 2002

What appeals to the male gaze and what sells is certainly integral to the coin of the realm. That's why the contradiction of a corporate conglomerate like Viacom trying to tame its hip sexual sensationalist subsidiary MTV is rather laughable. While the right will prate on about indecency on television, capitalism will continue to consolidate its media control. The boob tube will, when necessary, respond to the political winds, hoping never to expose too much of its own sordid relationship with the master class of mind managers, whether corporate or political. Only when the body politic reveals the bawdiness of capitalism as the real violator of human beings will the boob tube no longer suckle those who would bite the breast that feeds it.

—Fran Shor, 'Whose Boob Tube? Return of the Culture Wars',
Counterpunch, February 4, 2004

Hovering over the relationship of commerce to society at large—assuming we have not yet accepted the prevalent notion that the two are one and the same—is the question of *legitimacy*, both of supply and demand. It should come as no surprise that three areas in which ethical questions are often artificially restricted to the supply side are the 'Mafia' businesses: arms, drugs, and prostitution. The criminalisation of prostitutes rather than johns is a typical result of deflecting any critique of demand and focusing exclusively on supply. Feminists should take heed, however, of some encouraging indicators that a debate over the legitimacy of demand may be taking shape.

The infamous 'War on Drugs' stands as a premier example of the hypocrisy of a predatory 'free market' society which establishes certain apparently arbitrary limits to the legitimacy of commerce. Certain recreational drugs are legal (notably nicotine in the form of tobacco, and alcohol); other drugs are not (notably cannabis, and the various heroin derivatives). Other psychotropic drugs are prescribed in startlingly large quantities, such as the SSRIs and other behavioural modification medications now routinely administered to children as young as six and seven years of age.

All these drugs have potentially harmful effects. Tobacco smoking alone accounts for some 400,000 American lives per annum, and nicotine is said to be the single most addictive drug in the Western pharmacopoeia. Alcohol is implicated in serious national health problems, as well as in behaviour disturbances which may lead to violence. Yet these drugs are quite legal; the defence invariably offered to critics of the suppliers of these substances is that the consumers know what they are doing and are exercising freedom of choice. The consumers want these items, and the logic of the Market dictates that where there is a demand there must and should be a supply. No one is being forced to smoke or drink, say the tobacco and alcohol companies. If people become addicted, it is due to their own 'misuse' of the products. If people become ill, it is because they 'misuse' the products by consuming them to excess.

The officially proscribed drugs, on the other hand, are demonised with a zeal remarkable in an allegedly secular nation, and in this market sector the drug dealers are presented as public enemies of the first order. The argument that demand exists, and therefore supply naturally arises to meet it, is not deemed acceptable even by the most passionate free-marketeers when it comes to the illegal drugs. The suppliers in this case are held very culpable indeed for the negative outcomes of their customers' preferences. Cultural legitimacy or illegitimacy, rather than actual amount or degree of harm done, seems to determine the extent to which suppliers will be criticised for the end results of their trade. The heroin dealer is considered a vile criminal who preys upon human weakness, but the multinational tobacco or alcohol producer is not.

A similar impasse is reached with regard to small-arms sales. The individualist doctrine on which American political life is based persistently regards private ballistic weaponry as an inalienable right. There is a demand, therefore there is a supply; America has many gun shops. Again, criticism, where it exists, is levelled at the suppliers; it is 'too easy' to buy a gun, gun shop owners are told they should exercise more discretion, and so forth. As mentioned above, debates over prostitution also tend to focus on the supply side. For men to desire and purchase sexual service is considered normal and harmless; for women to provide it is considered immoral, unclean, and criminally culpable by traditional conservatives, and despicable (as our colloquial use of 'metawhores' in conversation and rhetoric clearly indicates) but harmless by sex-liberals. It is noteworthy that 'What a john he is' not only lacks the derogatory punch of 'What a whore she is', but sounds artificial and contrived because 'john' is not a conventionally insulting epithet.

I propose that 'What a john he is' can never be a catchy epithet in the context of hegemonic capitalist ideology. To question the demand side of any market is dangerous ground in contemporary American public discourse. The religion of the Market rests on a fundamental assumption that all desires and appetites are valid, and that to criticise any 'customer preference' is to become that dreadful thing, a judgmental or Puritanical person—committing the cardinal sin of Interfering with the Free Market. However, in each case above we may find grounds for questioning the demand side of the transaction.

Why do so many people rely on alcohol as an excuse to commit acts of violence? *Why* are so many people sufficiently depressed or bored that recreational drugs easily become necessities? *Why* do people indulge in self-destructive behaviours generally, and in specific behaviours such as chain-smoking, heavy drinking, and other drug abuse which are well known to inflict physical harm, impair judgment, etc? *Why* do so many Americans want to own a gun, and what are they planning to do with it once they own it?

Or, in our case, *why* do so many men want to rent or buy a woman, girl or boy?

To critique desire is to render oneself virtually an intellectual outcast in contemporary American discourse. It is acceptable to critique scheming suppliers, but not excessive demanders; to blame the tobacco company, but not the smoker; to blame the prostitute, or perhaps if one is very radical the pimp, but never the john. The thread of discourse which critiques insatiable desire is vanishingly marginal, as one would expect in a hyperconsumer culture. Profits are maximised by maximising consumption. Consumption is maximised by stimulating desire to irrational extremes. Modern capitalism works, irrationally enough, by depriving more than half the world of basic necessities in order that the remainder of the world can go into consumer debt feeding an insatiable hunger for luxuries.

> The values I longed to give my children—honesty, cooperativeness, thrift, mental curiosity, physical competence—were intrinsic to my agrarian childhood, where the community organized itself around a sustained effort of meeting people's needs. These values, I knew, would not flow naturally from an aggressive consumer culture devoted to the sustained effort of inventing and engorging people's wants.

> —Barbara Kingsolver, 'A Good Farmer', *The Nation*, November 3, 2003

Nevertheless, a slender but tenacious thread in American public discourse over the last quarter century and more is deeply contrarian—as contrarian as anti-prostitution feminism. At the very margins of this 'consumer society'— branded kooks, 'neo-Puritans' (a label certainly familiar to anti-prostitution feminists!) and so forth by mainstream pundits—is an eclectic group of people questioning the primacy of material acquisition and the sanctity of the Market.

These people ask not (as the Market dictates), 'How shall we satisfy every desire?' but rather 'Is it necessary to satisfy every desire? Is it even possible?' 'Are all desires justified?' and 'What are the implications of insatiable desire?' More specifically, they ask such important questions as whether it is legitimate to desire a level of luxury and convenience that can only be achieved by bankrupting future generations; whether it is legitimate to desire cheap consumer goods, if they are so cheap that they can only be obtained by exploiting sweatshop labour. These questions are fundamentally homologous with the feminist questions: 'Is the demand for prostitution and pornography a legitimate demand?' 'What is the price of fulfilling it? Is this price justifiable?'

This question of the legitimacy of desires, and whether the fulfilment of desire is the same thing as 'freedom', is at the heart of a feminist critique of pornography and prostitution. Traditionally the defence of such predatory sexual manifestations as sadomasochism and the consumption of pornography and prostitutes has been on the grounds that all desire is *ipso facto* legitimate, and therefore the suppression (or even critique) of desire is *ipso facto* illegitimate and oppressive.

This unconditional defence of desire and appetite is free-market ideology at its finest. It is the basis of the alleged synonymy of Capitalism and Freedom.

Thus it is not possible to critique the various forms of sexual instrumentalism and objectification, without critiquing the fundamental assumptions of neoliberalism; nor is it possible to make neoliberalism the official ideology of the world without making prostitution its official sexuality, and pornography its official medium.

> *Playboy* founder Hugh Hefner is to star as a cartoon superhero fighting evil alongside a bevy of buxom Bunnygirls, it was announced today. He has teamed up with Spider-

Man creator and Marvel Comics guru Stan Lee to develop the TV cartoon. Septuagenarian Hefner will lead an elite crime-fighting team made up of various Playmates of the Month, in the show Hef's Superbunnies, according to Variety magazine. The adult cartoon will take viewers inside the Playboy Mansion, the heart of his operation to fight injustice [. . .]

Lee said: 'As a fan who bought and cherished the very first copy of *Playboy* in 1953, it is an enormous thrill for me to be partnering with a man who has done so much to shape the culture of the times we live in.

'Hugh Hefner has long been one of the great communicators in our society, and I can't think of anyone I'd rather work with'.

—*Breaking News* (online Irish news journal), July 18, 2003

VIII. Allies and prospects

Of course, the usual dynamics of, 'It's not our problem, it's theirs', is going on, as the article totally fails to account for how our political economy drives girls and women into grinding poverty, how our epidemic of child rape provides an easy source of psychologically tormented and economically desperate young girls for pimps to prey on, how our pop culture glorifies pimps, how we either ignore or demonize women caught in the system of prostitution, how perfectly 'ordinary' men continue to pay the pimps to sustain the industry of prostitution, and so on ad nauseam. The only time any recognition of our wide-scale cultural responsibility for these kinds of horrendous crimes is allowed to creep in, is when it is in the mouth of the defendant for the pimps: 'All you have to do today is turn on MTV, turn on any radio station that plays music, and half the songs you hear are about being a pimp. It's just a part of the culture'. True. Too bad that nobody will listen to this person, since he's already been discredited by defending the pimps.

—*Geekery Today*, April 22, 2001

I suppose the drawing and quartering of an individual's dignity is at the heart of the appeal of all reality shows . . .

—Ana Marie Cox, 'Donald's Wannabe Slaves', *In These Times*, February 18, 2004

I am against pornography and against the wars of empire. This confuses some of my left-wing allies, who also oppose the war but think pornography is about sexual freedom, and therefore wonder if I am a closet conservative. It also confuses some of my right-wing opponents, who cheer on the war but think all lefties are pro-pornography, and therefore wonder if I am a closet conservative.

—Robert Jensen, 'Blow Bangs and Cluster Bombs: the cruelty of men and Americans' in *Feminista!* an online journal, v5 n1

The growing polarization of wealth and poverty between nations (a polarization that exists within nations as well) is the system's crowning achievement on the world stage. It is also what is ultimately at issue in the struggle against modern imperialism. As Magdoff argues in 'Imperialism without Colonies', there is an essential oneness to economic, political, and military domination under capitalism. Those seeking to oppose the manifestations of imperialism must recognize that it is impossible to challenge any one of these effectively without calling into question all the others and hence the entire system.

—John Bellamy Foster, 'Imperial America and War',
Monthly Review, May 28, 2003

I suspect that many of the feminists who have contributed their research and writing to this book have often felt painfully marginalised, as though struggling against a smothering hegemony. We are. Commerce, government, and pop culture have merged into a new Orwellian orthodoxy: the ideology of the monetist centre-right; just 'liberal' enough to approve of sex in general, but quite capitalist enough to approve of it even more if it turns a profit.

The Left, or what remains of it, does seem to be rallying feebly to protest the corporate domination of just about everything, but the corporate exploitation of women and children always seems to slip under their radar.

In 'liberal' or 'progressive' circles, pornography and prostitution are either sacralised by a knee-jerk association with freedom of speech (and sexual liberation), or discussed with a kind of sniggering, prurient 'humour' and smug self-satisfaction (at our being so very liberated and worldly and modern as to find the subject amusing rather than shocking or depressing) which obviates any need to take the lives and deaths of prostituted women seriously. Trafficking is at one and the same time regarded as a visible symbol of liberation and progress, and as a dirty joke. It is either above criticism, or beneath notice.

When the subject of pornography or prostitution comes up in polite right-wing circles it is discussed in a framework so misogynist—that is, that wicked, sinful, 'low' women deserve to be shunned and driven out from respectable society—that one almost feels driven to defend the institution itself as a means of defending its victims. Similarly, when the subject of women's oppression in traditional patriarchies is discussed in right-wing circles, it is currently in the context of an anti-Arab racism or an anti-Muslim religious bigotry so offensive that it drowns the allegedly feminist principle being discussed. What these two rhetorical styles have in common is the exploitation of a social justice issue—the violation of women's civil rights and human dignity—to fuel a quite different rhetorical agenda.

Feminists seem to be no closer today to winning widespread support for a critique of prostitution *as an international social justice issue in its own right* than we were thirty years ago.

Some feminists (perhaps in despair?) have sought to forge alliances with the conservative Right. At least, they say, right-wing women have an analysis of prostitution and pornography as degrading to the human spirit. Yet the remainder of the right-wing agenda, in keeping with its long history of commercial and business advocacy, further marginalises non-market values. And while such movements as 'Promise Keepers' may chide men for irresponsible or predatory sex, they also enforce traditional gender roles and male authority over women to a degree that no feminist could view without profound unease and suspicion.

For feminists seeking allies against the traffickers in women and kids, the men of the traditional Left and Right remain fairly useless.

The conservative politician of cliché thunders from his (always his) pulpit about Family Values and premarital sex and indecency. One would think he might be moved to thunder a bit about rich, respectable men who take sex tours to Thailand. But after his speaking engagement he is likely to fly back to the Bohemian Grove or any other exclusive rich-men's-club, where in discreet privacy he can enjoy strippers, call girls, and the other higher-ranking geisha who service the wealthy. He may even take the occasional sex tour of Thailand himself, though of course it will appear on his expense account as a business trip.

The radical activist of cliché thunders against exploitation, sweatshop labour, putting-profits-before-people, corporate propaganda, and so on. He may even want to ban tobacco advertising, or tear down alcohol billboards in Black and Chicano neighbourhoods. But he suddenly turns squeamish when feminists approve of (or commit) non-violent action against porno stores, or argue for limits to the pornographic content of public media. Freedom of speech, and access by men to women's bodies, are for him inseparable. The symbolic destruction of porn videos or magazines strikes at the root of his own male privilege, unlike the destruction of a tobacco billboard; it is usually at this point that he suddenly remembers his absolutist First Amendment principles.

The conservative's staunch pro-business stance, reflected in his stereotypically pro-gun, anti-EPA, anti-labour, anti-OSHA, government-is-bad, laissez-faire, profit-is-good speechifying, always stops just short of publicly supporting the very profitable business of selling or renting women and kids to men for sexual use. *That* business is below the line, beyond the pale. He will not admit that this also is Big Business, the logical conclusion of 'getting government off the back of business', the ultimate in laissez-faire.

The radical's staunch anti-business stance, reflected in his highly developed critique of monetism, the WTO, NAFTA, GATT, IMF, WB, IEB, OECD, biotechnology, HMOs, sweatshops, etc., stops just short of publicly vilifying the sex-sweatshop trade in women and kids. Sex is above the line, inside the pale, a groovy thing—after all, the right-wing bad guys (see above) say it's bad, therefore it must be good.

There's nothing new about this interlocking mirror trick which makes the sex business disappear—*as a business*—from both the pro-business and the anti-business rhetoric. But the new extremes of capitalist ideology, and the new corporate and transnational face of colonialism, have ratcheted up the contradictions to a new level. This intensifying cognitive dissonance may provide a window of opportunity for feminist social critics.

It remains for feminists, the only political thinkers with a fundamental stake in the human rights of women, to connect what has been consistently disconnected; to call down the masculinist ideologues of both the Right and the Left for their hypocrisy. Based on past experience one may be forgiven for wondering whether much change of heart can be achieved among the men themselves—but to what extent we can, surely we must try to disabuse their female constituents and colleagues of the illusion that (left to male leadership) 'family values' will ever include the abolition of so profitable a family-destroying business as the traffic in women, or that 'fighting the power' will ever include fighting the power of the pimp and the john.

Perhaps the best hope for an international challenge to prostitution lies in the anti-globalisation movement. Though this movement is not feminist *per se*, it does uphold a core value without which no challenge to prostitution or pornography can be maintained. The anti-globalisation movement believes that commerce is not the crown and goal of human evolution and civilisation, that market values are not the only values, and that it is immoral and despicable to buy and sell certain things, or to make money in certain ways. This is a sound philosophical basis from which to critique the traffic in live sex toys.

The anti-globalisation movement poses a fundamental philosophical challenge to the current corporate/monetist intellectual and media hegemony in the G8 nations. It is rankly and frankly heretical, and its spirited rejection of commercial control and intrusion might, without great difficulty, be extended to include a rejection of the commercialisation of sex. Its desire to balance the agency and autonomy of Third World nations against the need to protect their resources and populations from First World exploiters is almost exactly analogous to the feminist desire to respect and yet protect the exploited women and children of all nations. It seems promising ground for building a bridge and an alliance.

But whether this movement, still mostly dominated by men, can be made to face facts with regard to commercialised sex—to admit that the sex industry is not merely *parallel to*, but *identical with and implicated in*, the rest of corporate power and profiteering—is an open question. One would think that the connection was abundantly clear between the forcible commercial-isation of just about everything, from genomes to water supplies, and the commercialisation of women's bodies. But for several generations Leftist men have done their best to ignore the obvious, and the WTO generation may be able to do likewise unless and until a strong feminist voice develops in the Green and anti-corporate movements.

It must also be said that for US feminists to build a bridge to the international anti-corporate movement will require a refreshment of our own radicalism. Many US feminists are spending their time on discrimination issues which, while legitimate in their own local context, do not make sense in a wider global justice movement. For example, the campaign to force US auto insurance companies to stop discriminating against women drivers may not win friends in an anti-corporate movement whose members are painfully aware of the connections between the US car-centric lifestyle, petroleum consumption, global warming, and oil wars. If we wish the Greens and the 'Seattle generation' to take pornography and prostitution seriously, then US feminists will have to take anti-capitalism, global resource maldistribution, and global warming seriously.

Where the neoliberal ideology rules unchallenged it is not possible to challenge the traffic in women and girls: the official sexuality of capitalism is prostitution. It is my hope that feminists, Greens and other progressives will seize the historical moment—this modest, but possibly growing groundswell of populist disgust with crass commercialism, hyper-exploitation of human and natural resources, and the naked brutality of unfettered profiteering. I hope that we will manage to make, or re-forge, the connections between the Commodification of Everything, the corporate colonisation and enclosure of both private life and the public sphere, the neo-colonial agenda making itself embarrassingly plain in current US foreign policy, and the commodification of women and the colonisation and expropriation of the female body. Truly, 'it is impossible to challenge any one of these effectively without calling into question all the others and hence the entire system'. Feminists have been saying for over a century that some things should not be for sale. This may be the right time to say it again—and to challenge the entire system.

Notes

For typical 'left-liberal' enthusiasm over prostitution and pornography in various forms, the trendy online journal *Salon* is an inexhaustible source and may serve as a typical instance representative of many other publications. The online journal *Feminista!* (www.feminista.com, volume 3 number 10) featured a discussion provoked by the enthusiasm of a 'liberal feminist' columnist for a necrophilia web site. The track record of such 'mainstream lefty' institutions as *The Nation* and the ACLU speaks for itself.

An excellent short introduction to media ownership and its implications is 'Free Press for Sale', Derrick Jensen's interview of media critic Robert McChesney in *The Sun* magazine. For more eerie parallels between corporate/advertising culture and prostitution, see Jim Rutenberg's disturbing 'The Way We Live Now: The Secret Agents of Capitalism are All Around Us', *New York Times*, July 15, 2001. For my analysis of the 'poverty model' of male sexuality as used to justify abuse, see 'Scandals of Sexual Greed', *Z Magazine*, October 2002. My thinking as of about 15 years ago on the nexus of capitalism and sexuality is preserved in the essay 'Consuming Passions' in the anthology *Unleashing Feminism* (HerBooks 1990, out of print), or online at www.nostatusquo.com courtesy of N. Craft, webmaster.

Neoliberalism has many near-synonyms. It's known as 'Chicago School' economic theory because of the enormous influence of neoliberal economist Milton Friedman during his tenure at the Chicago School of Economics; many contemporary neoliberal pundits were Friedman's disciples in their younger days. It's also known as 'the Washington Consensus' due to the strong influence of American economists and to the tacitly understood role of the IMF and World Bank as enforcers for US financial/corporate interests. 'Globalisation', which might legitimately apply to any world-wide phenomenon such as the world-wide anti-war movement which responded to the US invasion of Iraq, or a world labour movement, has been 'branded' by the neoliberal economists to mean the imposition of their theories, by coercion or by armed force, on all the world's economies. Hence 'anti-globalisation' activists are actually 'anti-neoliberalism' activists; they are themselves *global activists*, with strong international connections.

A word or two of heartfelt thanks is due to the readers who bravely waded through many drafts early and late: Irene Reti, John Burke, Vicki Behrens, Sarah Pheral, Robert Jensen, Rebecca Whisnant (more or less in chronological order). Their comments, caveats and questions were often like a flashlight in a very dark cave.

Further reading

Rather than weigh down this text with a blizzard of footnotes, I've compiled a *partial* list of sources which have strongly influenced my thinking about prostitution, pornography, commerce, and globalisation over the last ten years. I am no longer able to compartmentalise these topics; readings in capitalism, colonialism and globalisation seem to be 'about' prostitution and pornography as much as readings in prostitution and pornography are 'about' globalisation, colonialism and capitalism. (I am reminded of the brief scandal when British troops in Iraq were found to have staged and photographed pornographic scenes using Iraqi POWs; how can these threads be neatly disentangled?)

A Green History of the World: The Environment and the Collapse of Great Civilizations (Clive Ponting)

Affluenza (John de Graaf, David Wann, Thomas H. Naylorde Graaf *et al.*)

Amusing Ourselves to Death: Public Discourse in the Age of Show Business (Neil Postman)

Bananas, Beaches and Bases: Making Feminist Sense of International Politics (Cynthia Enloe)

Counting for Nothing: What Men Value and What Women Are Worth (Marilyn Waring)

The Cultural Contradictions of Capitalism (Daniel Bell)

The Culture of Make-Believe (Derrick Jensen)

Energy and Equity (Ivan Illich)

For Adult Users Only: The Dilemma of Violent Pornography (Susan Gubar *et al.*)

For the Common Good: Redirecting the Economy toward Community, the Environment, and a Sustainable Future (Herman E. Daly and John B. Cobb, Jr.)

The Globalized Woman (Christa Wichterich)

Globalisation and its Discontents (Joseph E. Stiglitz)

Hegemony or Survival: America's Quest for Global Dominance (The American Empire Project) (Noam Chomsky)

No Logo: No Space, No Choice, No Jobs (Naomi Klein)

One Market Under God: Extreme Capitalism, Market Populism, and the End of Economic Democracy (Thomas Frank)

One World Ready or Not: The Manic Logic of Global Capitalism (William Greider)

Shovelling Fuel for a Runaway Train: Errant Economists, Shameful Spenders, and a Plan to Stop Them All (Brian Czech)

The Sorrows of Empire: Militarism, Secrecy, and the End of the Republic (The American Empire Project) (Chalmers Johnson)

Tools for Conviviality (Ivan Illich)

Upside Down: A Primer for the Looking-Glass World (Eduardo H. Galeano)

See also: many essays by Arundhati Roy, Vandana Shiva, George Monbiot, Bill McKibben, John Adams and other critics of Market-worship too numerous and various to list here. The web site socialcritic.org offers a varied hoard of dissenting essayists. I've been inspired by many bloggers and online news and editorial websites; in these days of tightening corporate media control, access to international and independent news is not merely refreshing but a necessity.

If I had a particular goal in mind when writing this set of essays, it was to encourage feminists to explore both the new and older literatures of anti-capitalist thought, and to encourage anti-globalisation and anti-corporate activists to explore feminist critiques of sex-capitalism. I believe we can and should make common cause against the hegemony of the hucksters; now's the time.

Addendum

This essay was begun before 9/11, and was in near-final draft before the American invasion of Iraq. The introduction to 'Further reading' indicates that hints of the sexualised abuse of prisoners were emerging in late 2002 or early 2003. By May 2004 the Abu Ghraib scandal had been officially broken by veteran US journalist Seymour Hersh in *The New Yorker*, and as of final copy-editing, the scandal continues to spread upwards into the Bush administration. Two things happened which compelled me to expand the terse comment which appears in the paragraph above.

When the first photographs were made available by the *Washington Post* and other media outlets, some images alleged to be of Iraqi prisoner abuse were found to be, instead, commercial 'war porn'—pornography which specialises in military imagery. Specifically, they were of the gang rape of women dressed in flowing black robes and veils, apparently in a barren desert environment, by a group of men dressed in US-style military fatigues. In an online discussion group I read the comments of one angry American, shocked by the Abu Ghraib revelations, who said s/he was 'relieved' to find that at least some of the pictures were 'just ordinary commercial porno'. Apparently it was possible for this person to disconnect—utterly—the existence of a thriving sub-genre of porno devoted to racist depictions of the gang rape of 'Arab' women by US soldiery, from the fact of actual US soldiery abusing and raping actual Arabs. This honest and naive expression of relief haunted me for weeks afterwards.

Then, in correspondence with a feminist colleague, the inevitable question was raised about the US troops at Abu Ghraib and the many digital pictures they took of prisoner abuse—pictures that were traded, collected, shared via email, stored on personal and work-related computers, and finally 'leaked' to the American public after months of ongoing torture and sexual abuse had been documented. 'Why,' asked my colleague, 'Why on earth did they take pictures? I mean, they're doing this stuff and it's horrible enough as it is,' she wrote, 'but by taking pictures they are just leaving evidence. Why do it, except that it adds to the sexualised thrill to be making porno?'

This is a good question, deeply thought-provoking, deeply connected to the first troubling incident. This question applies across the board. Why did the Nazis take pictures and meticulously document the atrocities committed in the camps? Why did a generation of White Hunters take pictures of themselves standing on wild animals they had shot? Why do hunters hang trophy heads on their walls? Why did white people take pictures of lynchings and make them into postcards that were then collected, traded, etc.? Why did GIs in Vietnam collect ears (and other more private body parts) from their victims? Why did 'Indian fighters' and bounty hunters in the old American West collect body parts from dead Indians? And—lastly—why do men make documentary pornography? Reverting to our first question again: Why is one kind of documentary pornography reassuring and normal, whereas another (like the Abu Ghraib pictures) is deeply shocking and horrible?

'Documentary pornography' is a term I am using to try to distinguish, for my own clarity, pornography of the imagination (such as literature, paintings, animation) from pornography that is photographed or filmed, using real people—real women, children, real male and female models. It is pornography that, while details of it may be 'faked' or simulated, *purports to be a document* of actual events. The fact that it is photographic—still, film or video—lends it, even in these digital times, an aura of verisimilitude. The use of live models required by this genre makes it documentary in other senses, which I'll address in a moment.

Structural similarities between the documented humiliation of prisoners and the conventions of 'normal' pornography are many and strikingly obvious. The prisoners were made to masturbate for the camera; images and footage of women masturbating are a stock theme in commercial porn. The prisoners were made to pose in tableaux suggestive of homosexual activity such as fellatio. A large and profitable sub-genre of commercial porn is 'girl/girl', in which (presumably heterosexual) models are posed in tableaux mimicking lesbian sex, or directed to engage in sexual behaviour with each other while the camera rolls. These models usually bear little resemblance to real-life lesbians, being selected (like most porn models) for their conformity to commercial and male-defined standards of heterosexual attractiveness.

In these forms of documentary porn there are surely two gratifications: one overt and one tacit. The overt gratification is the fantasy of violation of privacy, of spying on the intimate and private acts of another person. But the Abu Ghraib pictures should illuminate for us a further, tacit or covert gratification: the gratification of knowing or believing that the persons depicted were compelled or persuaded or paid to submit to a violation of privacy in reality, to strike poses and perform acts in reality which most people would not care to have seen or photographed by others. This is one sense in which this genre is genuinely documentary.

The 'kick' of girl/girl porno lies partly in its catering to the fantasy of violating the privacy of lesbians, of making even sex between women—something quite threatening to male sexual prerogative—serve a male agenda; the other, tacit element is the kick of seeing 'normal girls' made to emulate homosexual activity. The assumption is that homosexual activity is repulsive, and that therefore the models are disgusted by it and endure it under some compulsion—whether the compulsion of money, force of personality, or physical threat. Pictures of real lesbians—at Gay Pride rallies, for example—kissing, necking and flirting are often considered 'disgusting' and 'ugly' by the same men who enjoy 'girl/girl fantasy' porn. Lesbians in the public world who kiss, hold hands, or otherwise behave like a sexually intimate couple (in a restaurant, in a park, at a movie) have often been subjected to abuse, threats, and violence from hetero men—the same men who constitute the market for ever-popular girl/girl porno. What is *disgusting* in the case of real lesbians in the real world seems to be the women's autonomy; what is *attractive* in the case of commercialised, fictionalised documentary porn is the evidence of reduced autonomy, the dissonance between what the porn consumer assumes are the real wishes and feelings of the model, and the actions she is being bribed or forced to perform. If the model were a real lesbian she would experience violation and humiliation due to the invasion and exploitation of her sexual privacy by men; if the model is conventionally heterosexual then she is presumed to experience a degree of humiliation in being made to commit, or mime, homosexual acts.

Ironically (being otherwise deeply opposed in many ways) Arab men and Western lesbians both represent an Uppity Other, in their different ways claiming a private culture and personal pride, defiantly separate and distinct from white male Euro-American power. It's not surprising that a parallel to girl/girl porn is found in the pictures from Abu Ghraib, in which Arab men were forced to pose in suggestively homosexual tableaux. The covert kick of documentary porno is that the viewer/purchaser believes it genuinely documents some violation of the will and autonomy of the subject. In the Abu Ghraib images this feature has become overt.

Our reaction—as a nation and a public—to the use of Iraqi prisoners in amateur pornography shows that we believe this was a deeply humiliating experience for them. Our media have made much of the 'special' characteristics of Arabs, to explain why this experience is so very humiliating for them in particular—whereas it is of course perfectly harmless and good for the women and girls spread, splayed, stripped and mocked throughout our commercial advertising/porn media nexus. This neocolonial cultural essentialism deserves an entire essay or book unto itself, of course, starting with a no-holds-barred critique of *The Arab Mind*. (Appallingly enough, this racist classic appears to have been used as a serious planning document by the Bush regime.) But our space here is limited and we cannot afford to digress.

To summarise: no matter what degree of fakery may be involved in some documentary pornography, it is still presented and consumed as a document of humiliation; even if the actresses or models are inured to their trade, take it casually or even take pride in it, the consumer is still buying the *idea* or *concept* of a document of humiliation. This explains the enduring market—despite an astounding glut of every variety of 'normal' pornography available in many media—for 'real' porno, as in the 'real incest, real rape' porn sites and videos which claim to document real abuse. The primary fantasy is the purported story of voyeurism, homosexual humiliation or rape. When this fantasy is no longer sustained by a willing suspension of disbelief, the secondary fantasy provides the thrill. The secondary fantasy involves the humiliation or constraint of the people used to create the primary fantasy. When this secondary fantasy is weakened by a conventional belief that porno is a Good Thing and the actresses/models in it are all well-paid and happy, then 'really real' pornography fills the gap by purporting to be a *genuine* document of abuse—*We mean it this time, really.* Unfortunately we know from survivor testimony and police records that at least some substantial chunk of it is all too genuine.

The Abu Ghraib pictures fall squarely into this last 'outlaw' category of documentary porn. But they are not distinct or separate from the rest of the industry. The taste for porn pretending to be a documentary of rape or torture, combined with the underlying taste for an inferred real humiliation or pain involved in acting out the pretended rape, humiliation or torture, lead logically to a taste for documentation of unambiguously real rape, humiliation or torture. Or, alternatively, it is the same taste being indulged with *varying degrees of impunity*. The Abu Ghraib pictures are pornography made in a culture of total impunity.

Let us now return to the second vexing question: *Why?* What is this compulsion of men to purchase or share documents of other men's sexual exploits; to be—or to court—the peeping-tom, in what is conventionally described as a most private and secretive activity; or to consume the documentary evidence of other men's acts of violence or domination? Why do they take pictures? Why do they like to look at these pictures? Why do they document their own crimes?

I'll put forward a theory. Suppose (for argument's sake) that there is a durable, venerable form of male (primate?) sexuality which is wholly male-oriented; suppose that the structural, social, functional and emotional point of this sexuality is men engaging with, showing off for, gratifying, other men. Call it the sexuality of gang rape—in which a woman is the prop or target for a ritual among men, possibly a hazing or manhood-testing ritual, possibly a primate resource-sharing ritual not unlike passing food around. This aggressive, vicarious homoeroticism might be dignified and ritualised—as in the ancient Viking funerary rite in which the dead man's friends gathered, drank to his memory, and 'shared' (i.e. raped) one of his servant girls, who was then killed and burned along with the body of her 'lord and master' (the Viking equivalent of *sati*). Or it might be impromptu; a gang of youths getting drunk and raping any passing girl, or frat boys[1] (or football players) 'getting out of control' at a party. My point is that the men, acting together, overpower (with muscle or money), rape, humiliate, and perhaps kill a victim, and they do so primarily not because of anything about the victim, but to enact a social and emotional ritual amongst themselves.

The act of violence, however, is not the end of the ritual. Part of the ritual is that they brag about it afterwards. I'm thinking now of locker-room jocks, boasting about their (sometimes imaginary) sexual conquests; of the endless barracks anecdotes about what the guys did on their liberty nights; of sailors' stories about shore leave; of 'dirty joke' contests and boys sniggering together over centrefolds. Men, among other men, traditionally practise a kind of oral pornography that consists essentially of bragging about their masculinity and dominance, their genital size, how they 'put women in their place', what 'base' they got to, what they talked (or forced) a girlfriend or prostitute into doing or permitting. Trophy display and bragging, as a ritual of male bonding, are cultural traditions crossing boundaries from hunting to tourism, name-dropping to warfare to sex.

A more benign form of this competitive sexual talk might be a man's jovial boasting about what a great lover he is, how 'the ladies' love him, how happy he can make a woman, how married women can't resist him, etc. But there's a more dismal, savage side that comes down to—basically—bragging about rape. One point of this bragging may be that it clearly defines the braggart himself as an aggressor and not a victim (lest his fellows get any wrong ideas).

---

1   For non-US readers: 'frat' is short for 'fraternity', a name for an all-male social club of the type formed in high schools and colleges. 'Frat houses' are apartment or boarding houses exclusively occupied by members of one fraternity. Fraternities vary in tone and purpose from casual social or sports clubs, to charitable organisations, to more sophisti-cated and elitist clubs which serve (like the British 'old school tie') to connect and cement complex Old Boys' networks later in life. Some require would-be members to undergo a ritual ordeal before acceptance. These ordeals, known as 'hazing', vary from juvenile foolery to genuinely dangerous stunts and physical torture.

At the same time the braggart offers, for the collective consumption of the peer group, his own pornographic narrative—shared as one might share food or drink, in a ritual of social bonding and fellowship. (The British comedy team French and Saunders have produced a painfully percipient series of skits which illustrate this dynamic in an archetypically pathetic form: the transparently imaginary misogynist boastings and fantasies of a couple of sad old men.)

It seems obvious that a substantial subset of men[2] get off on listening to this kind of bragging, on hearing or watching male dominance exercised. (It's hard to determine whether a majority of men actively enjoy 'locker room talk', and how many endure it or participate only for fear of losing status.) It seems to me a kind of male/male sexual encounter: some men listen while another man brags, or a group of men relive their 'adventure' as a gang by telling the story over again. Male peers in our version of patriarchy cannot have sex with each other: that would require someone to lose his 'manly status' by taking on the passive or victim role. But they can create intimacy and shared sexual thrills by sharing their sexual dominance over someone else. Prison rape survivor (and researcher) Stephen Donaldson has written about being raped by two men at once (orally and anally) while incarcerated; his perception at the time was that the two men were having sex *with each other* far more than with him—he was just the 'medium of exchange' (to take a note from Levi-Strauss). His notes on male definitions and perceptions of heterosexuality are also worth mulling over: in prison culture, a man who rapes other men is 'straight'. Only a man who is raped, or who consents to being penetrated, is 'gay'. There is little distinction between consent and force; 'gayness'—functional gender—is an attribute of the receptive role, regardless of volition or physical gender.

The idea of 'sharing a woman' has a mythic quality in patriarchal male thinking—the woman (or in Donaldson's case the victimised male) being the connection that permits sexual intimacy, while avoiding 'forbidden acts' which would necessarily demote one man to 'woman status'. If we are willing to posit the existence of a male/male sexual dynamic based on this 'sharing', then we would expect the acquisition of 'sex partners' to be motivated not solely by their own value or pleasure but just as importantly by their value as 'offerings' to a male peer group (whether anecdotally or literally, physically). Now the obsession with documentation starts to make sense. In this model, men would make documentary porn as a valued commodity to be shared, bartered, offered to other men in social bonding.

This deepens our understanding (above) of the dual nature of the attraction

---

2 Let us ignore women for the moment; though there may be a female 'girlfriend gossip' version of trophy bragging, it seldom involves violence.

of documentary porn. In light of the 'sharing' dynamic, we might view it as material produced literally in this spirit of 'sharing the rape', i.e. produced as a form of trophy or bragging: *Look what we did to her! We can show you!* We might see it as a commercialised, ersatz, sanitised substitute for the showing/ sharing of trophies from a rape. Or it might be both at the same time: deniable/ acceptable/sanitised because it is 'pretend', yet satisfying because it is still consumed and appreciated as a document of (perceived) humiliation.

The come-ons for online porn rely heavily on the braggart style: 'You Won't Believe What These Girls Can Handle' [read: *What we did to these girls*], etc. The tone is (to my ear) not strongly differentiated from the sniggering of high school jocks over what they got some girl drunk enough to endure at last night's party: the social/ritual continuity between violation and bragging is consistent.

The fact, then, that the tortures and humiliations committed by the US troops at Abu Ghraib and elsewhere were documented, and were evidently committed in a 'party hearty' atmosphere with clowning around, big stupid grins, etc., shouldn't surprise us. It's the logical extension of the frat-house or barracks male bonding experience, the use of the body and person of some third party as the medium for expressing an intimate sexual and social connection among men. When Rush Limbaugh commented that the upset over the Abu Ghraib photos was excessive, that these were just a bunch of guys 'blowing off steam' and no worse than a frat hazing, the Left responded with (appropriate) outrage. But after all, what Rush said about Abu Ghraib is what conventional men have been saying about the rape of women by frat boys ever since there have been frat boys: namely, that it's no big deal.

Real rapes—sometimes gang rapes—do happen at frat parties. Hazings occasionally result in real deaths or permanent scars. The overexcited, giddy atmosphere of the frat party 'out of control' is notable in first-hand accounts of lynch mobs, who tellingly referred to their social bonding events as '*necktie parties*' [emphasis mine]. Violence and the party atmosphere are by no means incompatible. The irony is painful: the US Left leaps to vilify Rush for daring to trivialise the Abu Ghraib abuses by comparing them to something unimportant or benign—like rape and abuse at frat parties. Some commentators did make the connection with 'lynching postcards', photographs of lynchings made into postcards and traded/sold/collected in the US. These photos have sometimes been referred to *metaphorically* as 'lynch mob porn', but this is merely another metawhore—the essential connection with commercial porn and its various structural purposes is obfuscated, not illuminated.

The participation of women always shocks the general public—whether in lynch mobs, management positions in the prostitution industry, or the Abu

Ghraib pictures. Their presence and participation suggest several possibilities to me (perhaps a complex blend of them all):

1. The women were grateful to have their male cohorts' sadistic/aggressive gang-bang impulses safely diverted to some other target;
2. The women were trying very hard to be 'one of the boys', as the support/approval of the unit/tribe is very important to surviving military service in a hostile environment—and as we know, a woman has to try twice as hard to succeed in 'a man's job';
3. The women were already strongly racist, and were bonding racially with their troopmates in a mode parallel to male bonding, through pack violence;
4. The women had themselves been victimised or intimidated (rape is quite common within the US armed forces) and were themselves being used as porn models, told where and how to stand, when to smile, etc.

Some of the Abu Ghraib pictures (which the public has not yet seen) are said to show 'group sex' among soldiers, not involving prisoners. One Congressman commented that these pictures seemed to be 'consensual'—but this is what men traditionally say about sex, in the absence of overwhelming forensic evidence of force. Whether female troops participated willingly in consensual orgiastic group sex (perhaps with the aid of recreational drugs), or whether these other pictures are yet more trophy porn documenting gang rape, we may never know.

I don't rush to claim victim status for the female troops. Female Nazis existed, and demonstrated ideological enthusiasm in excess of what mere survival would require. White women were prominent in the crowd at many lynchings, laughing and cheering the men on. While their mere presence in the crowd could be compelled by domineering husbands or fathers, raucous enthusiasm is harder to explain. The female troops at Abu Ghraib may have been fully complicit in the abuses, as they appear to be from the photographic record. I preserve a reasonable sliver of doubt because we know that the millions of women apparently smiling, laughing, and enjoying themselves in documentary porn from around the world, are often smiling and laughing on command. To what extent they may have 'gone along' as weaker men sometimes have—cooperating in a gang rape even though stomach and conscience rebel, lest they themselves become the target of the gang-rape party mood—and to what extent they actively enjoyed humiliating and hurting helpless prisoners, is known only to them. They have to live with their complicity, as do we with ours.

There was a howling silence at the heart of US liberal discourse on 'the Abu Ghraib thing'. That silence was the protective shell built around our multi-billion-dollar porn industry and the ideology of neoliberal capitalism that enables it.

Throughout all media discussion of the torture pics and revelations, the doublethink caused by the mainstreaming of porno made itself painfully obvious. Pundit after pundit referred to the Abu Ghraib pictures with evocative phrases: 'like a bad porno flick', 'the S&M war', 'dirty pictures from Iraq', etc. Predictably, the conflicting necessities of responding to the Abu Ghraib documents with appropriate revulsion and outrage, yet continuing to maintain the received definition of pornography as a Good Thing, tied left/liberal commentators in knots. (See www.spinifex.com.au for some typical samples of left/liberal commentary on the Abu Ghraib scandal.)

To take just one example, one leftist pundit's Abu-Ghraib-inspired discussion of the American 'culture of suffering' includes a wholly unself-conscious reference to pornography:

> 'America's Funniest Home Videos'—the once-backchannel program where we became comfortable in snickering at people's pain like a kid thumbing through porno locked in the bathroom—has now come out of the closet and moved into the mainstream.
>
> —http://www.alternet.org/story.html?StoryID=18659

The kid thumbing through porno in the bathroom *is* snickering at people's pain; how much porno can we dig up that is not somehow predicated on women's (or kids') pain—or if not outright pain then at least shame and embarrassment—or if not shame then at least poverty and harshly limited opportunities? The viewer/purchaser knows that s/he would not like to strip naked and pose in front of cameras, to be displayed to thousands of strangers—and that some extraordinary inducement must be offered to convince anyone to consent to such vulnerability and exposure. The more humiliating or offensive the poses and props, the more obviously uncomfortable or painful the activities photographed, the more dubious the probability of genuine consent—the stronger becomes the voyeuristic thrill of watching the documentary evidence of abuse.

I have come slowly to believe that documentary pornography of the most prevalent kind—i.e. highly misogynist, often racist, definitely cruel and demeaning, hateful of the human body and particularly of female bodies, the kind of pornography promoted by spam mailers every day in email-boxes all over the world—is part and parcel of the social dynamics of gang rape. It's all about 'taking pictures of what we did to her', even if 'what we did to her' is as structural and generic as the reduced economic opportunities available to women, the impact of poverty on women, etc.

Feminists have documented several ways in which men use pornography on/against women in their lives. Documentary pornography may be socially functional not only in male bonding, but also as a social tool for emphasising and enforcing women's lower social status. It might serve as an impossible standard of sexiness and beauty that no living woman can measure up to, as a message of intimidation and hostility to female employees trying to enter traditionally male workplaces, as a 'how to' manual which men coerce or wheedle their lovers/wives into imitating for them—or (and I suspect this is a more important function than we realise) it may be a veiled threat: this is what can happen to women without money, without the protection of a man. Certainly this parallels the use of State-sanctioned torture; one need not torture very many individuals to send a cautionary message to the general population: *This is what can happen to you.*

Misogyny drips from all accounts of Abu Ghraib, and from all attempts to analyse it. The outrage of Arab men that the Americans 'treated our brothers like women'. The idea that making men wear 'women's undies' is a form of torture. The overarching, stunning hypocrisy of the world's largest pornography-exporting nation acting so dreadfully shocked when its line troops treat POWs in the same ways that its prison guards and stronger inmates treat weaker men, and that its pornography and prostitution industry treats women, every single day.

For this radical feminist the Abu Ghraib pictures merely elucidate what porn is really about. The essence is not obfuscated for once, because the victims are men, and literally prisoners behind bars and facing guns (instead of behind economic bars, facing hunger/homelessness). Therefore we can suddenly perceive that they are victims, that they have personal pride and dignity which have been assaulted, that they have rights which have been violated. The nameless, traceless women posing for websites like 'See Asian Sluts Get What They Deserve' or 'Farm Girls And Their Pets'—whether guns are pointed at them in the course of their work or not—arouse no such outrage or compassion. Even with such a searing illustration and example before us, the connection was made by only one or two marginalized feminist voices: Linda Burnham and Susan Brison, for example, whose essays at least started to address the connection between 'Bush porn', Abu Ghraib, male supremacy and US imperial supremacy.

Nor does anyone (except me?) wonder why we would expect any other behaviour from the troops of a nation so completely addicted to pornographic imagery, or indeed from any group of men forced into close bonding by immediate physical danger, indoctrinated with race hatred, trained in brutality and violence, and isolated in a culture of impunity.

What no one wants to face—in America, anyway—is that these pictures are not just *like* pornography. They *are* pornography, the raw essence of pornography: taking trophy pictures of people being stripped, sexually humiliated, raped—so that you can brag about it afterwards.

Joyce Wu*

Left Labor in bed
with the sex industry

Background

On July 1st, 2001, a Left Labor Conference was held at the Melbourne Trades Hall. It was meant to provide a speaking forum for 'left Labor activists and their supporters to force progressive reform'. The first session, entitled 'Our Bodies Our Rights', was meant to address issues of civil liberties and free speech. Two of the speakers in this session, Peter Tourney and Maureen Mathews, are members of the Eros Foundation, a lobby group for Australia's $1.2 billion a year sex industry.

Why is Left Labor in bed with mainstream business lobbyists and asking for their opinions on Human Rights, free speech and personal freedom but not including an independent feminist representative to provide a criticism of the sex industry?

Initial response

Local feminists, both within and outside of the Left Labor, were asking the above question when we saw the email promoting the conference. Many of us emailed or phoned the conference organiser to express our concern at this omission; we also recommended a feminist speaker to be included. In response, he claimed that feminism is merely a 'sectional interest' rather than of 'universal concern'. Furthermore, he viciously attacked us in a public internet newsgroup by describing the feminists who contacted him as 'a tiny group of reactionaries' who have the 'gall' to meddle when 'it's not their bloody conference'.

Despite his cavalier dismissal, the issue of autonomy over women's bodies has long been of central concern to feminists, and it should be of concern to everyone who cares about social justice. As one feminist from Left Labor commented:

> I find it both alarming and disappointing that a Labor conference which professes to build a left alternative within Labor, does not have a contemporary feminist view

---

* I would like to thank Del, Heather Benbow, Helen, Kelly, Shankari, and many others for their support, contributions, and/or participation at the protest; also Nikki Craft for her inspiring and supportive emails, as well as feminists from email lists who followed our activities closely.

represented. Far from being a "sectional interest", feminist theory has much to say about the ways in which the discourses of both capitalism and socialism serve to perpetuate the status quo and limit the economic and therefore social choices available to people.

Feminism in action

When it became apparent to us that the organiser was adamant in his wilful denial of feminist speech, we decided it was time to take action. We wrote a leaflet and contacted local feminists to participate in or support our protest at the conference. Feminists from other countries extended their support and encouragement. It was a wonderful thing to see feminist solidarity in action. Amidst those activities, we had a sense of hope: surely people will realise the inconsistency of the Left not seeking the views of industry bosses on issues of workers' rights, while deeming sex industry lobbyists to be qualified to speak on behalf of women. Surely, we thought, the pornographers' speech is not more important than the lives of women and children harmed by pornography.

On the day of the conference, we met half an hour before the conference began to pass out leaflets to the attendees as they arrived. After that, three of us including myself entered the conference; the plan was to listen to the speakers and then articulate our thoughts during the discussion period.

Jim Cairns, the first speaker, was right-on when he observed that 'Labor works within capitalism'. But when it came to discussing sex and the sex industry, all awareness of power relations seemed to vanish: according to Cairns, human eroticism is intrinsic to human biology and should be completely unrestricted 'free-flowing energy'. Cairns might want to consider that biology itself is a human discourse which is not free from the influences of the socio-political context from which it arises. *Those in power often justify their sexual exploitation of those with less power* by defensively appealing to their 'natural', biologically determined sexual urges.

Peter Tourney, member of the Eros Foundation, then talked about publishing rights and censorship. But he seemed to be more interested in portraying all anti-pornography perspectives as supporting censorship, right-wing conservatism and religious fundamentalism. As is common with such libertarian arguments, his accusations were not backed with any factually based evidence. He obscured the issue of pornography's harm against women and children (and sometimes men), instead issuing dire threats about the loss of 'free speech' and of 'personal freedom' to engage in sexual expression. While personal freedom is a privilege taken for granted by many middle-class Western white males, the same is not true for women and minority groups for whom personal freedom often depends on protection from abuse. *For these groups, social and political equality is a necessary precondition to freedom.*

Maureen Mathews, member of the Eros Foundation and Emily's List, as well as the storeowner of Bliss for Women, began by saying that she wished to provide a feminist perspective on the sex industry. As far as we could tell, the central point of her 'feminist' analysis was that women can, and indeed must, fuck their way to social freedom and justice. She showed no awareness that sexuality is fused with male dominance in our society and that this affects the workability of 'liberation through sex'. But in a world where vicious and pervasive sexism intersects with other forms of discrimination (such as racism, classism, homophobia, ageism and many others), anyone who assumes that women can ignore all those issues and blissfully sleep our way to liberation is either politically naïve or has another agenda. What is especially dangerous about 'feminist' representatives such as Mathews is that the sex industry will prop her up as their 'feminist speaker' whenever there is a public forum of debate on the sex industry, and members of the general public who are not familiar with feminism will learn about feminism only what the sex industry wants them to learn, thereby discrediting the arguments of actual feminists against pornography.

We did manage to speak a little during the discussion period. (As one of the feminist activists present commented, she felt as though we were in the suffragette movement—literally begging the men to grant us speech.) Heather pointed out the inconsistency of Left Labor in asking representatives of the sex industry to talk about free speech and personal freedom while denying feminists a platform to speak. I rebutted the tired sexual-libertarian sophistry of Tourney's statement that 'sexual repression . . . leads to rape and assault', pointing out that pornography itself contributes to the social construction of a particular version of masculinity and sexuality, one which eroticizes male power and dominance, including rape. We also showed a horrific picture of a woman being vaginally and anally raped which was found in an internet porn site, to illustrate that pornography is not all (or even mostly) the fun, liberating experience that the speakers had portrayed. Finally, I spoke about the similarities between racism and sexism, and asserted that as a woman of colour, I do not find dominance and subordination to be erotic.

Surprisingly, some audience members applauded. Mathews quickly stepped in to characterise our position as merely based on 'emotion', without addressing the arguments we had made. (I had been choking back tears at the end of my comments.) We left the conference in disgust, feeling betrayed and manipulated by people who should be our political allies.

Conclusion

Our experience demonstrated, once again, that people often wilfully hold onto their ignorance of social reality when that ignorance allows them to maintain and justify their privileges. Doing so is much easier than challenging the status quo.

Furthermore, as an Asian radical lesbian feminist, I was disgusted by how the sexual libertarians and pornographers present at the conference presumed to impose their predominantly Eurocentric, Western ideology and understanding about sexuality on a multicultural society such as Australia. Sexism is the dehumanisation of women as sexual objects, and racism is a 'flesh-coloured' dildo.

Although we did not attend the rest of the conference, I think the first session speaks volumes about what Left Labor is about: while talking about the evils of capitalism, it invites business entrepreneurs to enlighten us about free speech, personal freedom, and what our political priorities and alliances should be. It purports to give a platform to Left Labor supporters and activists, yet denies the speech of young women activists and of feminists within Left Labor.

In short, Left Labor has decided to be in bed with the sex industry. According to them, that is sufficient lip service to feminism and women's rights.

Lee Lakeman, Alice Lee and Suzanne Jay

Resisting the promotion of prostitution in Canada: A view from the Vancouver Rape Relief and Women's Shelter*

Since 1973 the Vancouver Rape Relief and Women's Shelter has been an organizing centre and a 24-hour phone line for women raped and battered. Since 1980 it has also been a feminist transition house. We house women running from abusive men—usually husbands and fathers, but sometimes pimps, johns, landlords, and sons. At any given time some thirty women collectively deliver these services and advocate for the women calling. Only ten are paid. We consider that the women who call us for help in their individual lives are also purposefully connecting with a feminist collective in order to document violence against women and in order to join forces with other women to make a better world. Besides doing what we can for each woman in turn, we collect those stories of sexist horror and women's resistance and pass them on to other women who call. We mean to spread examples, but also to inform and reinforce those women—including but not limited to ourselves— who are writing theory, designing tactics and executing strategies to end violence against women.

We organize collectively and usually commit a year at a time in groups of about thirty women. Some members have stayed for over a decade, and a couple for more than fifteen years. We are usually about one third lesbian, usually about a third are from working class backgrounds, and usually we have a higher proportion of women of colour in our group than does Vancouver's population generally. A small aboriginal membership has been steady for many years now. Although we do not have quotas, we work to keep those percentages of marginalized women as high as we can.

As a group we participated in and have often led campaigns in the Canada-wide coalition of such centres called the Canadian Association of Sexual

---

* Developed from the report *Canada's Promises to Keep: The Charter and Violence Against Women* by Lee Lakeman for The Canadian Association of Sexual Assault Centres (CASAC) 2004. The author is Lee Lakeman except where otherwise noted.

210

Assault Centres (CASAC). As in our case, the women who founded and work in those centres are largely from working class backgrounds. Women of colour have held leadership positions within major centres for at least fifteen years. Our delegate to the UN Conference on Women in Nairobi in 1985, for instance, was chosen on an affirmative action strategy for black women. Most centres have at most one woman with a university degree, for instance. Our structures are still largely cooperative, if not collective: Montreal, Toronto, and Vancouver are all collectives.

As CASAC we also take part in several other progressive feminist alliances, including the Feminist Alliance For International Action (FAFIA) and the Canadian wing of The World March of Women (Marche Mondiale des Femmes).

During the five years spanning the new century (1998–2003), our Vancouver collective participated in and hosted a research project called CASAC LINKS to examine why cases of sexual violence do so poorly in the criminal justice system. We asked ourselves and we asked our callers (and women in ten sister centres across the country asked another ten callers each) how criminal convictions were discouraged and even blocked.[1] In reporting that research, we found it necessary to speak not only about the individual acts of male violence against women, but also to examine numerous aspects of their social, political, and economic context in order to begin to fight for a better future.

Even to win the relatively few cases that are brought before police and/or the courts, we need massive social change. Two decades ago Canadian feminists won the Charter of Rights and Freedoms[2] (which functions somewhat like the Equal Rights Amendment hoped for in the USA). In reporting our research, we meant to increase the pressure on the Canadian system to comply with those Charter Rights to equality. We examined the forces that are acting on us and on other women living in Canada that hold us back from a future of peace, equality, and justice.[3]

Since the Charter is a domestic instrument that carries the human rights thinking of the United Nations as expressed in the United Nations Declaration of Human Rights, we examined strategies such as the promotion of human rights through the United Nations, especially using CEDAW (the Convention on the Elimination of all forms of Discrimination Against Women). Unlike the USA, Canada has signed the CEDAW agreement and agreed to the optional protocol that will allow a Canadian to appeal to the UN if her rights are

---

1 Copies of the full report, *Canada's Promises to Keep*, are available through
   http://www.casac.ca
2 See http://canada.justice.gc.ca/Loireg/charte/const_en.html
3 Feminists have always argued that Charter Rights apply to any women in Canada and
   not just citizens.

ignored or trampled within Canada and she has exhausted possible remedies within the country. We joined a coalition that offered to the UN committee overseeing CEDAW a version of the recent and current conditions of Canadian women quite different from the one presented by our government as to the progress made for women in this five-year reporting period.[4]

We did not rely solely on these lobby efforts either internationally or nationally but also participated in processes of building the international grassroots women's movement, such as gathering in The World March of Women at Puerto Allegro in Brazil and Mumbai in India. That work took the form of membership in the Canadian Women's March Committee.

We gathered our membership and some 800 allies at a national conference in Ottawa—Women's Resistance from Victimization to Criminalization—to discuss all these facets of our work and of the stories of our lives.[5] We digitally recorded those proceedings, stories and debates for future consideration and have made samples of them available online at both our local site, www.rapereliefshelter.bc.ca, and our national site, www.casac.ca .

Each member centre of CASAC, including ours in Vancouver, continues to apply our understanding and our hopes in each community. Our centre has engaged in a local debate about the importance of welfare, about prostitution in our city, and about the need for local women's service/organizing centres that are autonomous both of political parties and of limiting professional disciplines. We have been defending these tactics as part of our overall strategy to reduce—indeed to end—violence against women and to advance the status of women as a group.

What follows are excerpts from this whole range of our work regarding prostitution as violence against women. All three pieces are works in progress.

1. Structural adjustment comes to Canada

Author's note: Under pressure from international capital, and propelled by both a right-wing economic theory (neo-liberalism) and a whipped-up public frenzy about the economic deficit, the Canadian federal government recently gutted two sets of federal policies that were vital to the interests of Canadian women.

They eliminated national standards partly by ending the federal provincial economic deal called CAP (Canada Assistance Plan) which used to fund and thereby standardize across the country women's access to welfare, health care and education (including transition houses). Canada once had nationwide entitlements to survival incomes that could be appealed to in law. Now each province is setting separate policies mostly

---

4   The FAFIA alternate report and the BC CEDAW Group alternate reports are at
    http://www.fafia-afai.org/index_e.htm
5   See http://www.casac.ca (Go to the order form to access the recordings.)

copying the welfare 'reforms' of the USA: time limits, cuts, regional disparity and other punitive and regressive policies.

They effectively ended federal funding to national women's groups, especially those that were founded and maintained by the feminist movement with the support of the community to address women's equality. Funding has been removed from anti-violence work unless it is either a service (and explicitly not advocacy) paid for by the province, or an educational or research opportunity for professionals. There is no longer a federal policy to fund anti-violence work as a means to achieve the end of women's oppression.

In examining the application of legal concepts of equality to the legal cases of women complaining of violence, we found ourselves up against the regressive changes to our country's social safety net and to global economic relations. We have tried here to connect our crisis calls to those other grave considerations. What follows is the part of our national report used as the basis of a presentation to the Federal Standing Committee on Finance as it traveled the country in pre-budget hearings during the fall of 2003.

Some effects of restructuring Canada on the nature,
severity and incidence of violence against women
'The poor will always be with us', 'prostitution is the oldest profession', and 'men are just naturally that way'. These stereotypical assumptions and essentialist positions or attitudes are not promoted in CASAC centres.[6] Rather, we see that each corporate move, social policy, and interaction of the state with its subjects moves us toward or away from the desired future. Class, race and gender division and domination are social and economic constructions always in the making . . . as is equality.[7]

The end of the welfare state and the social welfare it sometimes provided is part of the globalization process in which Canada has played a role and that has engulfed women living in Canada. We have rarely had the opportunity to express, in our own way, the connections that are part of our daily lives between those international economic forces, federal laws and policies, and what is happening in anti-rape centres. Rare indeed is our opportunity to express the link between global/federal forces and our advocacy supporting women, especially those violated women trying to engage the power of the state against the power of their male abusers.

---

6   We are saying that there is nothing intrinsically different about the women and children who end up poor or violated. And the men who violate them are not biologically compelled; they make choices to do so.
7   Professor Dorothy Smith's work has helped us to keep seeing this. Her early analysis of the United Way struggle in Vancouver from the 1970s to 1990s was followed by conversations with us about class and the women's movement over the years.

The CASAC LINKS project offered possibilities for renewing our alliances with other anti-rape centres and for speaking out together about the lives of women; but in any case we were compelled to do so by the changes in our daily work brought by the changes in Canadian society.

We are not the best ones to articulate, and there isn't space in this report to fully express, the devastating impact on Canadian women of the loss of public sector jobs and services.[8] But from our point of view, it is clear that there are few women who have not been made more vulnerable to criminal sexual assault. There is no criminal violence against women in Canada that has not been negatively affected. There is no liberatory and/or ameliorative process affecting violated women that has not been damaged and undermined.

CASAC's goal of a social economy that values women's labour and fairly shares wealth with women has been set back drastically. The trajectory of reforms toward those ends that had been won by our grandmothers, mothers, and ourselves—from the vote to unemployment insurance, from pensions to childcare, from self determination to settling land claims, from welfare to more humane immigration policies, from criminalizing sexist violence to the inclusion of women in a living Charter of Rights and Freedoms—has been reversed in the service of grotesque individualism and corporate wealth.

CASAC wishes to express our understanding of those effects which we have encountered most often in our crisis work during this five-year period, and which affect anti-violence work most profoundly: the loss of women's right to welfare, the promotion of prostitution, the use of the Divorce Act in such a way as to uphold the permanence of the patriarchal family, and in short the restructuring of Canada (from the shape of the justice system to the structure of civil society). These effects appear to CASAC to amount to a refusal by our national government to apply The Charter of Rights and Freedoms; to apply the Charter would require a diligent application of the current knowledge of women's oppression and an appropriate commitment to women's advancement.[9]

There are those who see it differently.[10] We have had to defend our positions rather rigorously in the last few years. The government has applied only formal

---

8   We have learned a lot from Penni Richmond, Madelaine Parent, Sharon Yandel, and Linda Shuto, and suggest their work as a source of that history and its importance to women.

9   According to our Supreme Court Rulings that support substantive equality approaches rather than merely formal equality (since sometimes by treating different groups exactly the same way causes more inequality) and support contextual understandings.

10 It remains to be seen whether the Social Union Framework Agreement can and will be an improvement on the Meech Lake Accord or the lost CAP and Health regimes. Certainly the process so far has barred non-government involvement. We have no reassurance, either, that our particular identities will be recognised or that our collective or universal needs and entitlements will be met. While there seems to be some consensus that the framework can be adjusted to serve us as citizens and specifically as women, we should not be satisfied with less than the language that encodes those promises in enforceable national standards and oversight mechanisms.

equality when attending to equality at all. It has sometimes ignored both the Supreme Court rulings against formal equality and the reverse impact of the application of these polices. Huge economic and political forces have been mounted to oppose any government role beyond armies and prisons. Sometimes we have found ourselves reeling from many simultaneous blows.

At the same time, there was a big push, supported by government, to promote the rights of victims, even a possible new national victim's association. The government promotion of the notion of 'victim' as a legal policy category plus the changes to community policing, sentencing changes to confinement in the home rather than jails, and the promotion of prostitution, opened up a number of key questions within criminal justice. Who, for instance, defines community and how? And who is considered part of the community? What is the relationship between the state and the community? What is the relationship between women's anti-violence groups, social change and the state?[11] We were interested in those conversations that might affect our understanding of our options as the nature of the Canadian state changed.

The bottom line: the loss of the women's welfare
Most members of the community realize that we are contending with mean-spirited welfare reductions and restrictions that make life more difficult for the poor. Although it is difficult to keep track of the specifics, some changes have been publicized. In British Colombia, for instance, we know that 'women with children will lose one hundred dollars a month from their already inadequate cheques by April 1, 2004' (Duncan 2003).

No government declared honestly to its citizens before election either the nature of welfare cuts it intended or the further feminization of poverty that would be imposed by those cuts. It is simply not true that Canadians voted for those attacks on the poor.

And no government within Canada has been given a mandate to end welfare. Any such mandate would be legally questionable in any case, given the Charter and human rights law and conventions. This is perhaps why no government makes public those whom it is refusing subsistence. But CASAC women are witness to the fact that women across the country have no guaranteed, or even likely, access to a promised minimum standard of living. No matter how poor, women have no guarantee of welfare in any form. As women consider their options for improving their lives, they certainly learn this, and so do we.

With the end of national standards of welfare, we have lost a small but significant recognition and amelioration of the historically disadvantaged

---

11 Dobash and Dobash best introduce these issues in 'State Public Policy and Social Change' (Dobash, E. and R. Dobash. (1992)).

economic condition of women's lives. But as predicted in feminist accounts of the end of CAP funding and as recorded in our alternate reports to CEDAW, women in Canada have also lost what application we had of this encoded economic human right (Brodsky and Day 1998). CASAC is most concerned that we are losing this benchmarked redistribution of income toward equality.

In each province and community the attacks and erosion have been different, ranging from workfare to 'man in the house' rules, age limitations, rate decreases, time limited access, lifetime bans, immigration and settlement restrictions, punishment bans after and through criminalisation, to bans based on health requirements.

Not only has the formal policy been degraded, but the positive discretionary power in applying procedures and enforcing regulations has also been curtailed. Management and sometimes the remaining staff too often interpret rules with the same anti-entitlement attitudes.

There is a plain abdication of the federal role in assuring women and others who need a guaranteed dignified income, and it is Canada-wide. This includes the downward pressure of shrinking transfer payments and block funding without national standards (Brodsky and Day 1998). That abdication encourages provinces to set welfare, education and health needs of the community against the needs of business for roads and bridges, to ship goods, and transport tourists. We don't win.

Transition houses in Canada emerged partly to deal with the limits that existed in the welfare policy of the 1970s. Welfare departments would refuse to grant women welfare cheques when they came to the state for assistance in dealing with abusing husbands. Welfare workers were directed to tell women that the state could not be responsible 'for the break-up of families' (Lakeman 1993). If a woman left and established residency on her own, then welfare might be granted since it was an assumed economic right of Canadians to not starve or be homeless. Since they usually had no money, women moved to transition houses, where they didn't need rent or deposits, not only for immediate safety, but to establish a separate residence to prove to the state that they had left the marriage/family/couple. During their stay with us, they qualified for welfare.[12]

Women still come. Transition houses are full. Shelters for the homeless and other emergency facilities are also full. But now these women 'qualify' for welfare less and less often, and they do not ordinarily receive benefits without aggressive advocacy from someone independent of government. They are told constantly that it is not a right and cannot be relied on. Welfare, they are told,

---

12 Between 1975 and 1995 it was rare for women to have trouble getting welfare after living in a transition house.

can be reduced, withdrawn, and denied temporarily. A woman could be banned for life.[13]

Women, especially poor women, have always had to make extra-legal deals with the men in their lives. When ex-husbands or lovers are taking responsibility by sliding women money under the table for childcare, we are all glad. But in women's position of extra dependence created by the state withdrawal, sometimes those deals are dangerous underground contracts, which the women cannot enforce, and which subjugate them to the very men they are trying to leave for the sake of themselves and their children.

Any welfare granted currently is so inadequate and insecure as to force the women into subsidizing it with an informal economy: housework for others, childcare for others, personal health care for others, food preparation and production for others, drug sales, and/or prostitution.[14] If the woman finds a way to subsidize her income legally, then it is either clawed back through mechanisms that 'allow' recipients to keep only pittance earnings above the welfare cheque, or the subsidizing activity is declared illegal. To be poor is to be criminalized.

Women who complain to the state of rape, sexual harassment, incest, sexual exploitation and trafficking face the denial of security: no exercisable right to welfare. If by some cleverness, accident or kindness a woman gets welfare and is subsidizing it to get by, she is vulnerable to blackmail by her attacker. If she reports criminal sexual abuse, she will quickly be threatened (directly and indirectly) by the defence bar. Exposure can cause either a loss of informal income or the loss of her credibility as a complainant. She can and will be painted as a liar, thief, con, drug dealer, prostitute, unworthy of the protection of the law.

The fourteen- or eighteen-year-old incest victim leaving home, the worker on minimum wage or making her way in the informal economy, the dislocated woman pulled from her small town or native Indian reserve into the city for work or education, the immigrant woman struggling to survive or trying to transition into lawful citizenship and a reasonable life . . . all are frustrated. If the normalcy of male violence against women were not known, one might think this was something other than state collusion with violence against women.[15] Access to the rule of law and equal protection under the law become meaningless.

---

13 In both BC and Ontario, lifetime bans have been imposed. Temporary refusals have been instituted. Time limits—for instance, of being eligible for only two years out of five—have been imposed. Health criteria have been imposed. Rate reductions have been imposed.
14 All welfare rates as well as minimum wage rates in the country are below the poverty line.
15 Federal-Provincial-Territorial Ministers Responsible for The Status of Women. (2002).

Predictable access to welfare was a power used by more than the destitute. It was a power in the hands of all women: the knowledge that we could (in a very modest amount) pay for food and shelter for ourselves and our kids by right. It was a power used to fend off attackers and to take advantage of opportunities. It was a basis on which to build one's self respect: the organizing in the 1930s, resulting in the legislation of welfare rights, had declared that everyone in Canada was entitled to at least this minimal share in the community and in the commonwealth.

We have no romantic memories of the days when welfare was great. We learned early in our herstory, and as we discussed our lived experiences, a critique of the welfare state as social control, especially of women.[16] We needed much more income redistribution and much less regulation of women's lives (Sidel 1996). Still, we share with many second- and third-wave feminists[17] a critique of the dismantling of the welfare state and the social safety net that it sometimes provided.[18]

In anti-rape centres we now face daily many women who judge that they simply cannot leave or escape men who criminally abuse them: husbands, fathers, bosses, pimps, johns, landlords, and sometimes social or welfare workers.[19] Since they cannot afford to actually leave, they cannot afford to effectively stand up to their abusers either. Those that do leave those economic positions are on their own with their children, and they know it.

Canadians have been deceived and manipulated to achieve this reversal of social policy. Clearly national standards are necessary as are achievable protections for women across the country.

When we redesign 'welfare', as we surely will, we must revive and improve the Guaranteed Annual Income concepts that generated the welfare reforms from the 1930s to 1975. Feminists will not tolerate going back to notions of family income or of the worthy and unworthy poor, to disentitling immigrant workers, divisions of minimum wages from disability rights, disassociated child poverty, or to mothers' allowances, aboriginal disentitlement, forced work camps, or age restrictions even when disguised as age entitlements. We will certainly not tolerate going back to the intrusive state supervision of the private lives of women.

In this desperate time for so many women, perhaps we should take heart that most Canadians have not yet realized our loss of welfare and will surely rise to the occasion.

---

16 See CASAC newsletters (1978–1982) available at Vancouver Rape Relief library.
17 Such as the member groups of FAFIA and the BC CEDAW group.
18 See online http://www.fafia-afai.org/index_e.htm
19 Welfare workers and social workers are sometimes reported to us as abusers of their clients. They have much more power to abuse if the women know they have no enforceable right to welfare: they are dependent on the discretion in his hands.

A global economy: the promotion of prostitution

Can anyone still believe that there is no connection between the economic redistributive functions of the state, including within the social safety net, and the staggering increase in the informal economy? Are we meant to say the emperor is clothed? The economic division of the peoples of the world is staggering. The economic division among Canadians is growing exponentially.

Child and street-level prostitution and the so-called 'adult entertainment' industry are booming. This is globalization being brought to Canada. Drug trafficking and prostitution are replacing welfare, health care, and education as the hope of the destitute.

Professor Dara Culhane at Simon Fraser University describes 'a process that moves women farther and farther out from under whatever small protections working people and women have been able to construct within the state.'[20] While they have for many years been prey to the law and order agenda and remain so, at the same time some are now moving out past the reach of law to the no-woman's land of the urban and suburban informal economies.

Aboriginal women have been talking about this for years as a factor in violence against women on and off reserve. We remember Teresa Nahanee at an Ottawa LEAF conference in the early 1990s describing the condition of aboriginal women in many parts of Canada as having to live without any basic rule of law. Now these are the conditions for many women in every major Canadian settlement.

Many women are being driven into the hands of global traders in labour, flesh and drugs. They are trafficked into and throughout Canada by those global traders on the one hand and, on the other, within Canada by Canadian gangs, particularly the motorcycle gangs.[21] As protection we are offered racist immigration practices that jail the people trafficked, and legalization of the prostitution industry. Of course, we don't want the criminalization of the victims, including all those at the bottom of these rigid hierarchies.[22] But surely we are all aware now that this multi-billion dollar prostitution industry is actively involved not only in the trade itself, but also in the promotion of the legalization of the trade in women and drugs.[23]

---

20 Personal communication, October 2001.
21 In our work we have become aware of the ownership and prostitution dealings of (at least) The Hell's Angels in every province except the Maritimes, the Big Circle Boys gang, the Lotus gang, Fukianese, the Russians, the Mafia-related gangs, and the Vietnamese gangs.
22 Most of the Canadian women's movement has agreed that prostitutes and low-level drug dealers should not be jailed or even criminalized. We have also agreed that those women trafficked as indentured labour or sex slaves should not be criminalized or deported. Our debates are about how to deal with the men and how to interfere with the trade.
23 Gunilla Eckberg, personal communication, September 2003. She is special advisor to the government of Sweden on prostitution.

As with our struggles against the rest of the inhumane multinational trade agenda, we must expose, confront, and interfere with the managers, owners, profiteers and consumers. The leadership of Sweden in this matter of human rights and women's rights is impressive and hopeful.[24] Sweden has criminalized the seller and begun to protect the victimized.[25] It regards prostitution as violence against women. It is no accident that Sweden is not building an economy on tourism or the sex tourism that goes with it.

To ignore women's equality aspirations and the current unequal status of women in Canada and in the world will undermine any progressive efforts to protect prostituted women from criminalization. Naïve good intentions to protect the individual women should not be used to tolerate the development of this grotesque industry. In our efforts to address the needs of women trafficked into and throughout Canada, CASAC has come to the conclusion that we can only serve them by protecting their gender rights, their status as women, and the status of all women. No one is disposable or worthy of any lesser rights.

In our centres we are contending with women trafficked from abroad as indentured labour, mail-order brides, domestic workers, and street-level prostitutes. Sometimes we are asked to support beaten and raped exotic dancers, as well as women working in 'escort' services and 'massage' parlours. Daily we are dealing with women dislocated from remote territories within Canada and trying to make their way in the cities. We are taking calls from, housing, and referring women who have been supplementing their incomes with prostitution and who want protection, both legal and political, from their pimps, johns, boyfriends, lovers and fathers, and sometimes from the government officials to whom they try to report incidents of violence.

The public provision of exit services to women leaving prostitution is inadequate. From our centres in the early 1980s we supported the development of both the ASP (The Alliance for the Safety of Prostitutes) and POWER (Prostitutes and Other Women for Equal Rights) networks.[26] Both were spin-offs, in both membership and politics, of anti-rape centres that wanted to specialize in serving women prostituted.

During this project we participated in Direct Action Against Refugee Exploitation (DAARE)[27] and have provided financial and political support for Justice for Girls[28] and many other initiatives across the country. But we remain

---

24 For instance, see online
    http://www.naring.regeringin.se/fragor/jamstadlldhet/aktuellt/trafficking.htm
25 And here we mean the pimps. We rarely see the women as the sellers.
26 See online: http://wwwrapreliefshelter.bc.ca/herstory/rr_files86.html
27 For those who wonder, the extra A is because the cookie company DARE threatened us
    with lawsuits if we used their trademarked name.
28 Justice for Girls is a group focusing on feminist intervention against the exploitation of
    young women.

convinced that to use the easier provision of services as an argument for legalization is misguided. As Cherry Kingsley says:

> If we want to set up areas to protect women, to give women dignity and police protection, appropriate childcare, housing, and job training, and so on, then we should do that. Why should women have to service men sexually to be offered those things needed by all women?[29]

Certainly, among the women who call us and come to us, most do not choose prostitution except as a highly available way to survive. We speculate that the few women in the world who do choose it are short-time participants with privileges that allow them to leave. The provision of services specific to women trapped in or wanting to leave prostitution is inadequate everywhere. But to think that such services alone will curtail the harm of prostitution in the midst of this economic agenda is ridiculous. And for the federal government to refuse to try to curtail the domestic and international prostitution of women is barbarous.

The recognition of the so-called 'rights of prostitutes' or the new talk of decriminalization (meaning legalization) is a self-serving policy ploy.[30] It legitimizes men's right to abuse women and also legitimizes Canada's refusal to redistribute income to women, some of whom are the most needy women, both within her borders and in the international community.

Sex tourism is surely a cash cow for many a government, both national and city. 'The sex industry now accounts for five percent of the Netherlands' economy' (Daley 2001). 'Prostitution has become an accepted side of the tourism and casino boom in Victoria, Australia, with government sponsored casinos authorizing the redeeming of casino chips and wheel of fortune bonuses at local brothels' (Sullivan and Jeffreys 2001). Is it any wonder that Canadian rape crisis centres protested the mega-tourism plans as far back as Expo 1986 and up to the current Olympic plans (Lakeman 1985)? Before both those tourism events, there was a heightened promotion of prostitution in Vancouver.

Men who buy women, on the streets of Canadian cities and in the third world, are almost always situated in higher class and race designations.[31] In Canada, most of the men buying the sex services of women on the street, for use there or in their cars, could afford to purchase sex in more comfortable surroundings, but they prefer the street trade where the degradation, humiliation,

---

29 Cherry Kingsley, personal communication, October 2001. Cherry Kingsley works in the International Centre to Combat Exploitation of Children.
30 Decriminalization used to mean preventing charges against the women. Now it is shorthand for the legitimating of the trade. We continue to stand with the women and against the trade.
31 Professor Dara Culhane, personal communication, October 2001.

and violence are part of the purchase.[32] CASAC and many others have discredited the ineffective and silly use of John Schools to divert these men from the consequences of criminal activity (Lowman 1998). CASAC has long held the position that criminalizing men's behaviour requires that they be convicted of the crimes they have committed. And no diversion should occur before conviction. The illusion that this trade will simply move indoors and be tamed by the legalization of prostitution is ridiculous. It hasn't worked anywhere else in the world and it won't work here.[33] Women who are so trapped as to be part of that disastrous practice will not be incorporated into the imagined self-organized bawdy house or the call girl trade of the 'Pretty Woman' propaganda. More than 50 percent are aboriginal women raised in poverty and racism who are dislocated from their communities to the urban ghettos.

In any case, the phoney division in law and practice between the attitudes and approaches to different 'kinds' of prostituted women—innocents victimized by sexual exploiters (the adolescents, the so-called survival trade women, 'forced' trafficking of mentally handicapped women) versus women somehow deemed complicit in their own victimization—is reminiscent of the traditional virgin/whore dichotomy used to divide and conquer each group of women who tried to use law to address other violence issues: the raped, the beaten, the impoverished, the racialized, the disabled, those women thought rightly or wrongly to be lesbians.

Nor will their dignity, body integrity or human right to a life without violence and a reasonable standard of living be assured by legalizing prostitution. Pretending to accept prostitution as a viable option for our sisters and daughters by protecting men from social and criminal sanctions for buying and selling women and sex, presents us with a grim version of women's equality under the law. To use a woman in this state of desperation as the example of protecting women's agency is to make a mockery of the concept.[34]

CASAC women fear that we are facing an era when women will be designated, numbered and regulated by city health departments as prostitutes. They will cooperate in order to evade immediate and punitive criminalization.[35]

---

32 Professor Dara Culhane, personal communication, January 2003, in conversation about the research she was conducting in the Downtown Eastside of Vancouver.

33 'Amsterdam's Street Prostitution Zone to Close'. (2003, October 21). *Expatica News*.

34 CASAC women note that the most destitute and violated are always invoked as a reason we should accept legalization, and then the most uncommon and privileged are invoked as the proof of agency. We say we should look at and set policy based on the most common experiences and the unromantic version of prostitution.

35 We imagine them charged with nuisance charges or other offences. So far the regulating processes of Harm Reduction are not made to answer even indirectly to Charter rights. For instance, how would we keep the records of past sexual history out of the case of sexual assault against a registered prostitute, when the state already would own those health records and the legal practice would make those records vulnerable to disclosure obligation claims?

That designation will remain with them for life and will affect every aspect of their lives and futures. Those who are sick, drug addicted, or who rebel against this trade regulation will be further forced into the illegal informal economy and will simply be the 'bad' prostitutes and 'bad' drug addicts who have refused the 'harm reduction' model and therefore are even less worthy of the protection of law.

The current public policy debate about adult prostitution is constructed around the wishes of men, the big city interest in real estate development, and the interests of international capital, including their interest in cheap migrant labour. In those debates, pro-prostitution voices use the women subject to prostitution in their rhetoric. They try to box us into a discussion limited to anecdotes about individual women and their individual adaptation to a horrible situation: about their 'choices'. It is as though political concepts of disadvantaged groups are silenced. The public is confined in these debates to giving our approval, or not, of how women and their children live in the belly of the beast of international trade.

Responsibilities for the well-being of citizens and for the safety net programs and policies have been downloaded from the national to the provincial level, and then to cities. This has put a tremendous burden on cities. There is a long-standing Canadian political strategy of gathering political party power at either city or provincial levels in order to set the stage for that party's affecting federal power. In this moment of Liberal party dominance at the federal level and conservative dominance at our and other provincial levels, it should come as no surprise that politicians argue for a new government relationship between the federal and city levels.[36] Notably in Ottawa, Toronto, Montreal and Vancouver, city officials trot out urban decay, including the debauchery of the informal economy in the sale of drugs and flesh, as a rationale for this new relationship. In one example called The Vancouver Agreement, millions of federal dollars are injected directly to the city. Instead of welfare, education and health commitments to the whole population (some universal programs across Canada and national standards for others) being met by the federal provincial agreement, money-short local services are bribed with short-term funds to their own programs so obviously that local people refer to them as 'poverty pimps' and the 'poverty industry'. So far those federal-provincial-municipal negotiations do not invite or even tolerate participation from equality-seeking groups (those committed to redistribution, not just services) and are not in any meaningful way public and transparent processes. The misery of the people on the

---

36 'Municipalities Urge Martin to give Cities a Fair Share of Funds: Heads of Municipal Organization Tours Downtown Eastside and Calls Its Problems A Canadian Issue, Not a Vancouver Issue'. (2003, September, 24). *The Vancouver Sun*, p. B5.

streets is cynically used to justify new and questionable, if not bad, governance processes.

These changes are further weakening women's access to Charter rights. A renewed federal legal and social policy approach is needed to address the plight of prostituted women and girls. This approach must be based on an equality-driven attack on the beast that is prostitution: a hugely profitable form of violence against women.

The basic social unit: enforcing the private domain and upholding the patriarchal family after divorce

> **Author's note:** From the earliest conversations between transition house workers and residents, it has been clear that incest and wife assault are closely related and that women forced into prostitution have often experienced sexual coercion from their male guardians. I heard it from women in one of the first shelters in 1973. Sometimes those guardians were their institutional or stand-in fathers—teachers, priests, athletic coaches, foster fathers, residential school staff—but most often they were their every-day fathers, both biological and custodial. We will not solve prostitution without solving incest. And we will not solve incest without allowing and aiding women socially and financially to leave the families of men who use sexual violence to enforce their status.

When we began this CASAC LINKS project, we were worried by the imposition of the 'law and order' public policy agenda, the promotion of insubstantial and false 'restorative justice' as an alternative to that agenda, the funding cuts to already inadequate legal aid and legal services, and the pressure to label and shape our work as merely victim assistance, rather than as initiatives toward the equality of women and the prevention of women's sexualized victimization (Lakeman 2000).

While these concerns remain and must be dealt with, these past five years have dramatically changed the picture. We contend with the privatization of police to such a degree that we now have as many private police as public police, and often armed just as lethally. We face the privatization of courts in 'community based' diversion programs that authorize religious groups (both Moslem and Christian) to rule on the fate of women. We have police serving as judge and jury of aboriginal children without legal counsel. Mediators, both regulated and unregulated, are replacing legal advisors and legal advocates. Courtrooms, which are obliged by law to be public, are being replaced with private closed venues where each victim is told she is the centre of activity, but where she is in fact isolated from other victims and from other equality advocates in the name of privacy and where her rights are balanced against the rights of the accused. Victim Rights approaches accept crime and oppression as inevitable at best and as the functions of weirdos, monsters, or freaks at worst. They never demand more than the 'right' to be treated with some politeness, and they certainly never encompass the right not to be a victim or the hope that one might be the last such. The Victim Rights Movement is too often a tool of the right wing to call for more law and order— that is, more guns, more police, longer sentences, and less civil rights beginning but not limited to the accused. The Victim Rights Movement is used to undermine already scarce community support for state-supplied social programs, state-organized social sharing, state-delivered policies of humane compassion, and the overarching commitment to equality for all that is required to support effective social change.

Under the new pressures and in the new policies we can see a different use of the state emerging. It is questionable what privatizing public roads, rails, and airlines may be doing to Canada, but it now seems obvious to us that devastating equality losses result from privatizing criminal and civil law, legal assistance to individuals, and consultative processes of law reform, as well as what we normally understand as 'cops, courts and corrections'. Many Canadians are not yet aware that we are experimenting with privately owned and privately run jails. And most are not aware that for a decade, policing has become more and more a matter of private companies guarding private property and private interests. (We are, however, all getting inured to the image of security guards in shopping malls and building lobbies who are armed with handcuffs, clubs, stun wands, sometimes guns . . . but never with the Charter.)

This newly adjusted state carries with it the danger of further reinforcing the patriarchal family, including the violent ones. When women are threatened by having to face their religious leaders for permission to leave, warned that they must appear friendly to the parenting of the men they are leaving, deprived of their rights to social services and welfare payments to support them in the likelihood of their being poorer after divorce, denied legal aid or pro-bono legal representation on family matters or on poverty law, faced with an organized fathers'-rights right-wing lobby and no well-funded support for equality law to counter it, faced with threats to the custody orders they need to protect their children, faced with property settlements that must be yielded in order to protect custody interests, faced with the pervasive assumption that men must have unrelenting access even after abusive behaviour, warned that they may lose mobility rights and have unenforceable child support payment schedules . . . how is divorce an option? For that matter, even if a woman persists against all these obstacles, how does divorce actually get her out of this marriage? She is likely to be tied to him for years by the initial and forever-ongoing court settlements of economic and custody and access orders.

CASAC claims that violence against women is not simply or best understood as a crime against one woman, but as an individuated incident or stream of incidents in the campaign of sexist violence that terrorizes and contains most women. It has some of the character of hate crime against a minority, or racialized group, and some of the character of violence that we categorize as terrorism. That is, it affects all women and all women's freedom. And this is no less true when the violence is committed in the family.

Sometimes both progressive prison abolitionists[37] and capitalist privatization promoters challenge us to consider whether the adversarial justice system (either criminal or civil) is an appropriate vehicle for women to use. They apparently agree with each other that the state is suspect on the issues of freedom and oppression. One side fears direct repression by the state, and the other fears wasteful expenses and 'social engineering'.

Still others point out that this is a time of the 'shrinking of the state' and so our worries about the imposition of the law and order agenda and victim's rights approaches are ill placed. Our insistence on the positive obligations of government, they claim, is dated and doomed. But some of the same people support aggressive federal government intervention in urban redevelopment in the name of health or so-called 'harm reduction strategies'. Some do not see the government intervention involved when, in divorce settlements of property, mobility, custody, and access, the government falsely claims gender neutrality while upholding the apparently perpetual paternal, social, and economic interests in the family.

Anti-violence workers continue to argue that women must have the power of the state and the legal system added to ours, to protect ourselves and as part of the struggle for equality. We are not naïve. We know that we must also be careful of the ways courts and laws and legal processes can be used to exploit and exacerbate the inequalities among women as well as the inequality between men and women. We have already learned that race and class oppression have to be considered and fought in any plans we make for reforms and in any analysis of the changes needed. We must never sacrifice women's freedom or the full range of women's human rights—especially our privacy, agency or autonomy—in our search for safety.

Seeking protection through family courts
Most violence against women that enters the courts does so at family court level, where it is dealt with as civil and not as criminal law. This is not only

---

37　See Julia Sudbury, 'Locating this Conference in the Wider World—2001', opening plenary in the proceedings of *Women's Resistance: From Victimization to Criminalization*. And, for an example of a corporation profiting from mediation, see online: http://www.mediate.ca

because much of the violence done to women is committed in the family, but also because of the history of law and policing, and because those designing the justice system prefer it that way. It is important to remember here that civil law contends with struggles between individuals or private parties, and criminal law was developed to deal with offences against the community or the state.

All through the 1970s, feminists interfering with sexist violence negotiated with the welfare state. We were funded by it. We relied on it to guarantee income to women leaving abusive men. We referred women by the thousands to legal services. As assistants to women beaten (especially by their husbands), we were in constant contact with the courts.

Those of us who worked with women raped by strangers were constantly aware of the differences in criminal justice offered to wives. We always debated the acceptability of diverting wife assault and child incest from criminal court rooms to civil law units where often it meant settling for mediation, and counselling rooms. We sometimes agreed that family court was a solution women could sensibly try when police offered no court at all.[38] Women could appeal to those courts without convincing the police to charge their abusers with a crime. In our debates, one side protested the acceptance of this diversion. The other side argued that it was useful to women and children that they be spared the rigors of criminal court, including the burden of legally proving violence, and that relaxed and specialized methods could be applied in family courts, which might serve women well. But we agreed then and agree now that mediation and counselling must never be mandatory.

Some 'specialized family courts' incorporated a criminal as well as civil stream; some of these improved the criminal conviction rate and the response to women's complaints for a year or more. In the early days of those experiments, the concentration of professionals particularly interested in the problem and the coordination of their energy paid off. As long as the original personnel are present, the conviction improvements are likely to hold. Too often, however, these specialized courts became job ghettos and policy pockets.

---

38 By not arresting and/or laying criminal charges. Coroners are provincially appointed officials. Coroners are mandated to investigate deaths of people while in the care of the state, and they also have discretion to investigate other deaths in order to determine and recommend measures to prevent similar types of deaths. Coroner's inquests are a formal court proceeding open to the public and allow for examination of evidence relating to a death. Inquests were conducted in the highly public murders of Gillian Hadley and Arlene May, both killed by ex-husbands. Both juries took education from front-line feminists in their deliberations killings and made a series of important and wide-ranging recommendation to government, police and other government agencies. The Hadley inquiry reinforced the findings and recommendations of the May/Iles inquiry. The recommendations are yet to be applied.

The overall contempt for women in the legal system (Wilson 1993) carried over into a lack of respect for these woman-identified legal venues and proceedings. At the same time, these venues replicated the racism and class biases of the wider legal systems. Men of colour and aboriginal men were much more likely to be tried and convicted of wife and incest assault than their white neighbours. Generally, the Specialized and Unified Family Courts also suffered a lack of financing from both federal and provincial budgets after the first years. Any initial success was usually sabotaged.

Whatever the motivation for their creation and maintenance, family courts often seemed to us to be torture chambers for battered and raped wives and for children sexually assaulted by their fathers. The problems ranged from the victim having nowhere to sit or stand that wasn't vulnerable to his gaze, harassment, following, verbal assault, and/or silent intimidation, all the way to her having no way to make her message understood by staff and professionals (and no assistance in doing so) because of language, culture and class, but most of all because of gender biases.

Information and public support does not seem to be the answer to improving the state response to wife murder. After two very high-profile cases of wife murder, Canadian coroners' inquests have recommended useful state interventions in the inequality imposed on women and improvements on the state response to sexist violence. But we do not hold out much more hope. One provincial government, Ontario, claims to be responding by instituting 56 new Domestic Violence Courts funded with some 24 million dollars. The May/Iles and Hadley inquest jury demands cannot possibly be satisfied in this way.[39]

As one example of the faulty practices in family courts, women (before they were denied lawyers by the cuts to legal aid) were told by their legal aid lawyers to be careful not to breach the 'friendly parent' or 'maximum contact' rule for fear of appearing uncooperative with the court. This 'rule', which may well be encoded in the new divorce law, claims to favour the interests of the child by presuming that the ideal situation for a child is to have both parents involved and cooperating with each other as equals. It of course contradicts reality in that the parents are not equal socially, financially, or legally. But since the rule dominates the decorum of the court, it was unwise to mention violent incidents against either the wife or the child unless they had winnable criminal cases of violence. And who did!

Alternatively, women and children might be heard as truthful in this family court if they had professional authorization of their voice as the officially raped and battered. That authority could only be attached by a medical or

---

39   May/Iles and Hadley Jury recommendations from the coroner's inquests.

social work professional. Without such professional authorization, their lawyers were not free to assert that criminal assault had occurred, and there was no police or crown responsibility for checking out the criminal activity, even if abundant evidence was still available.

In fact, in family courts most decisions have always been made by professionals other than legal ones and then confirmed by the judge. In our minds, this created enormous problems regarding the place of legal equality concerns in the proceedings. Even after the Charter and the discussions fostered by it, the staff and professionals—including the few who were legally trained—didn't see themselves as being guided, much less bound, by the Charter, Human Rights law, or any other legal concept of equality. And their personal or collectively held view of equality was never declared or open to challenge or review.

These courtrooms were (and are still) finally technically answerable to the criminal justice accountability and appeal systems. With expert legal counsel, with a fund for legal challenges or a topnotch advocate, or with highly trained and committed family court staff, some women could make their way. But that is rarely the situation. And like many other 'special' venues offered to women, it often turns out to be a ghetto or dead end in efforts to assert a right to be free of violence.

If a woman is lucky and the professionals believe her, she might get a separation settlement that protects both mother and children, but no criminal procedure against the abuser: criminal immunity for him in return for autonomy and/or safety for her. Otherwise, she is better off remaining silent about such criminal abuse and fighting for custody and access, supervised visits, and autonomy as though the abuse had never happened. That is, of course, a difficult case to make once she has had to leave the most important facts out of her story. To reveal abuse (unproven in criminal law) is considered by some professionals within the system, and by the law, an unfair use of the police and courts. It might well cost a mother sole custody of her children or result in an access order that eliminates the safety plan of the protesting ex-wife.

It can also increase the risk to the daughter. The children of an abused woman are left to observe the abuse of their mothers and suffer it as training for themselves in their future roles as women and men. This moment of legally disarming and abandoning mothers who try to protect their daughters from incest (by leaving abusive men or by telling on them to the state) is key in the creation of young women ready for the prostitution trade. Displaying to daughters and sons the state's contempt at worst and disregard at best for their mothers propels both young men and young women into harm's way. Research clearly shows that the girl children of abused mothers are more likely to be abused as girls and as women and that the young men are more likely to become abusive to their future partners and to their mothers.

There were always many pitfalls, even for those women granted custody. The victory might be limited to having the abusive husband or father ordered to see the child only under supervised conditions. But supervision was privatized and, most of the time in most of the country, had to be bought. Often men would claim inability to pay, but the legal order stood and had been hard-won, so usually the abused wife paid. Even then, the supervisor was neither under her contractual control nor ordered by the court to secure her safety or her equality interests.

Not every marriage break-up is the end of an abusive, battering or incestuous relationship, of course. But of the ones that go before the state, most are troubled if not abusive. Otherwise, the two individuals would just resolve things themselves with less bother and expense for both of them. And the trouble is between two who are unlikely to be of equal position, resources or status in the world. Clearly it is wiser to make our knowledge of women's current unequal status, and of the current frequency of violence against women in marriage, central to shaping policy, law, and procedure for everyone.

Most women in family court do not choose to be there in the sense of asking for mediation in a struggle between two individuals. Many have called on the state because they are told by welfare departments, and sometimes by legislation, that they will not receive welfare unless they do. Staff members of child protection agencies—often motivated by the knowledge that men who abuse their wives often also abuse their children (Edelson 2003; Jaffe, Baker and Cunningham, in press)—do blackmail abused women, often aboriginal women, with threats to take away (that is, to take state control of) their children if they do not formally sever violent marriages.

The destructive pressure on our relationship with battered women by social workers bullying women into shelters for the sake of the children is short-sighted, counter-productive, and an infringement on women's equality. The same is true of the co-opting pressure on us (introduced through protocols, coordination models, and funding standardization) to screen or monitor the mothering of women who come to shelters. The autonomy of these women is essential to their children's safety, and the voluntary relationship of trust between us and the women who call us is an essential ingredient of both the children's safety and the women's autonomy.

For many reasons, usually less noble than an interest in the safety and freedom of the women and children, state officials demand that women (especially poor women) formally settle child custody and access agreements. It is part of the ideological change that claims to reduce welfare payments by holding individual men responsible for their obligations. Actually it functions by criminalizing more poor men than rich men for the same behaviour, meanwhile excusing the state for eliminating the collective economic responsibility we have to the women and children in need.

Police almost automatically press women to engage civil restraining orders and other family law processes, because once they do so the pressure for criminal investigations is over for the police.

The poorest, the racialized women, those most vulnerable to state apprehension of their children, and those who have tried to involve police and criminal law are often those who enter the family courts. These are the mothers whose daughters, while in the public state care of group homes and foster homes, are at increased risk of entering prostitution.

The women from these and other overlapping categories often don't distinguish between civil and criminal law, but they do understand themselves to be completely overpowered and unfairly treated. They seek fairness and security. State officials instruct them that family court is the appropriate place to invoke the protection of the state for their children and themselves from inequality and sexist domination by their intimate enemy. They have no idea that, practically speaking, it could mean they are dependent on convincing some untrained person—who may well be empathetic or kind, but who is not Charter-literate, never mind equality-literate or equality driven—to see the danger or unfairness in their situation.

This family court process shirks the state's responsibility to create equality and to enforce criminal law against violence, even as it forces women to accept more and more state intrusion and imposition of inequality.

Sometimes what has been missing is the intervention that can be made in criminal court to assert the social interests of women as a group. As friends of the court, women's groups have been able to request an opportunity to put their interests in the case before the courts. This is a role that should expand. The domestic violence courts in Ontario and the Yukon conceive of women's groups only as low cost service-delivery systems for women's emergency housing and comfort while their cases are handled by the courts. Both courts reduce women's groups to advisory committees outside the formal processes, which can legitimate the court's authority but not affect its outcomes, and on which the courts rely to keep women acquiescent. These courts are created by the same provincial governments that refuse to provide shelters with the core funding and political independence they require.

Often programs to counsel men (out of illegal abusive behaviour) are tied to these courts as diversions from jail. But because men lie about the criminal violence they do even while in these diversion programs that promise them criminal evasion, the presence and ongoing assistance of the wives and ex-wives is an essential source of information to the therapeutic diversion plan. They become the monitoring assistants to the counsellors, reporting on the advance—or more likely the failure—of men to change. In this impossible job they are not only unpaid but at risk of revenge. Both courts plan to spend inordinate amounts of time and money on these therapeutic approaches, which so far have very limited results, and which do not in any way address the equality issues of the women.

We might expect, then, that for a while these courts will improve some women's safety, but in the long run they will fail. The independence of the women's services from the state and the men, which was reinforced by their connection to the wider independent women's movement, will be compromised and weakened. Their embodiment as a kind of women's auxiliary to the courts will render them merely victim service providers directly under the control of the courts. The chance of women's groups maintaining enough independence to advocate for Charter rights from that position is not very good. If not us, then who?

The proposed divorce law changes

Author's note: The interconnections between economics, divorce law, the virtual impossibility of legally proving incest, and pressure toward prostitution (and other informal or illegal economic activity) are complex, intense, and never unimportant. The poorer women are, the more they are forced to rely on fair divorce law, especially if welfare and minimum wages do not protect them. Divorce law for poor women is about custody and access, about parental responsibility and women's mobility. More and more women find themselves trapped by men's abandonment in the form of lack of child care payments and parental responsibility, or on the other hand by paternal control of and endangerment of the children. If he is exploiting the economic situation by refusing to pay, or abusing the sexuality of the children, or abusing the woman directly, it all becomes pressure on her. If a young girl wants to escape from an abusive father, knows that criminal law will fail her, and cannot rely on her mother's access to effective divorce law, she will struggle to find a source of income; and since usually the state will refuse her help unless she can prove incest or has her father's permission, it will be either a new man or the illegal economy.

This year, CASAC women and all other anti-violence workers have had to examine the proposed amendments to the *Divorce Act, Bill C-22*, for their implications for women raped and battered by their husbands, and for women mothering children who have been incestuously attacked by their fathers. Coalitions formed all across Canada to look at the issues from an equality perspective and to prepare proposals for the Standing Committee on Justice this fall.

There is a high level of resentment about this. We have been forced into this work by the government pandering to the agitation of the fathers' rights groups.

They went into full gear in response to the small victory of the changes to support payments and tax breaks that Allan Rock, then Minister of Justice, introduced to the Child Support guidelines in 1997. Those changes eliminated an unfairness in which men could claim tax breaks for paying child support and women were taxed as receiving extra income when they got child support payments. In a dispute within his political party over supporting that bill, the minister agreed to support a reconsideration of the whole Divorce Act after a public hearing process under the control of an anti-feminist senator.

According to the National Association of Women and the Law, the introduction of *Bill C-22 (An Act to Amend the Divorce Act)* significantly altered the terms that govern the custody and access to children of divorcing parents. It contends with key issues of woman abuse, access to justice, parenting after separation, the best interests of the children, and women's equality rights in family law.

The draft proposal of the law re-opens the question of support payments by challenging ideas about custody and access. To save themselves from paying for a fair share of the costs of raising children, the fathers' rights organizers challenge the recognition that women do most of the nurturing of children. The bill presses 'joint parenting' principles similar to those imposed in the USA and could entrench them in law.

But in May 1995, the Federal and Territorial Minister Responsible for the Status of Women had already agreed 'on the importance of gender-based analysis undertaken as an integral part of the policy process of government'; later that year, Status of Women Canada published *Setting the Stage for the Next Century: The Federal Plan for Gender Equality (Status of Women in Canada 1995)*, which says that 'the federal government will where appropriate ensure that critical issues and policy options take gender into account'. CEDAW and in fact all Human Rights Law requires this.

The international agreements, the decisions of Parliament in declaring the Charter, the Supreme Court adjudication of cases that interpreted it, and the legal precedents set in cases women have brought should be implemented. Otherwise the oft repeated election promises of providing aid to violated women and 'mainstreaming gender' meant nothing.

Having allowed the senator to stir up right-wing sentiment against divorcing women, the government refused to handle the furor without jeopardizing women's equality concerns. At least one reading is that women and our safety and freedom are being sacrificed as unimportant chattels in the negotiations for the imagined right-wing votes. This strategy is destructive to everyone. CEDAW, the Charter and the policy of gender mainstreaming were supposed to override such banal politicizing.

Yet not one politician, jurist or bureaucrat effectively interfered with this sexist backlash while conducting the hearings of the Joint Committee in 1997, preparing the critique of the current legal practice and law, preparing the *For The Sake of The Children* report in 1998, preparing research and drafting in the next year, preparing the Federal/Provincial Territorial Family Law Committee report released in 2001, or the new report in November 2002 and in the work of the drafting staff that proposed the amendments announced in December 2002. As drafted, this Divorce Law:

* refuses to name gendered inequality;
* acknowledges violence—but not who does what to whom—including by stating the obvious: that men commit the violence in the family and that they use the family structure to do it;
* does not assure or attempt to assure women's equality at the time of divorce;
* does not allow women to be assured that divorce ends the patriarchal relationship; in fact the amendments could keep her more married;
* does not assure women of safety and security in divorce proceedings;
* does not contribute to women's ability to plan for safety and security in the months after separation/divorce, which we know are potentially dangerous for women in tense or abusive relationships;
* does not assure women legal representation in legal processes that require representation to assure equality interests;
* is not consistent with Charter obligations;
* is not consistent with Canadian positions or agreements taken and promoted internationally;
* is not consistent with election promises;
* is not consistent with commonsense versions of equality and safety.

The proposals in the draft to assert, exempt, screen, identify, or isolate cases of violence against women and treat them differently are unworkable. Officials know it, and therefore it is only a cynical recognition of the violent reality. There is no workable plan to redress the violence or redistribute power. The government-proposed draft leaves unchecked both male power and the power of male violence to enforce inequality.

It is still very unevenly wise for women to reveal to the state or the community the violence committed against them by husbands and fathers. They get blamed for the violence, labelled as attackable women, discredited in the storytelling of their own lives, and belittled with facile advice about how they could or should have protected themselves. They may well be abandoned by the state to a more angry man. The justice system still grossly under-convicts the violence against women that is reported to it. It is therefore unreasonable to base a divorcing woman's access to equality interests on whether she can prove or convince others about violence in her life. Women should not have to prove violence or even expose violence against them or their children in order to secure their right to safety and autonomy. The process and the law should assure that universally.

Nor should they be invited to relinquish privacy and autonomy in a search for safety from sexual violence and security for themselves and their children. We have not achieved any reasonable level of proving violence in any court yet. Revealing incest or wife assault may well backfire in the woman's loss of custody or in the lack of fair economic settlements that provide the children with proper care. The loss of status and income involved in divorce already undermines the power women need to keep their sons and daughters safe. The draft, like all new family law initiatives, proposes to step even further back from equality law. It implements ADR approaches with no plan for how these approaches will meet equality obligations to women, even as determined by the Charter law and rulings.[40]

'But don't worry,' says the draft: 'First we accept inadequate universal entitlement to the rule of law, then we build in an exception designed to deal with violence.' So now we could easily and often be put in the position of having to prove violence in order to apply for equality.[41]

Two responses are likely: one is that non-feminists and humanists will be tempted to widen and soften the definitions of violence, in hopes that more women (whether or not they have suffered violence) can qualify for equality practices—practices which are considered exceptions to the norm and only to be applied to violent marriages. There will then be a backlash against that tactic. The backlash forces will cite the widening of the definition of violence as a further excuse for the state's withdrawal from assisting women against violence at all.

The other is that most women seeking fair custody and access agreements at the end of marriages will still get pushed through the screen that was supposed to catch their stories of violence, because no one will believe them (and because there is no money or legal initiative to help them, and in general because all women continue to get unequal application of the law at divorce). In those few cases where the people doing the screening do believe the women to be victims, the women will lose control over decisions about how to proceed, by virtue of being victims. That is, they will predictably face unwanted state

---

40 Alternate Dispute Resolution has been the overarching policy of the Department of Justice at least since George Thompson was deputy minister in Allan Rock's administration.

41 The Canadian Divorce Act reforms are on hold now. The Attorney General has announced they will wait. We think that is because the Supreme Court rulings on same-sex marriages will so affect any definition of marriage that the government will have to reconsider the laws again. So this process is not over, and the danger for women and their children has not diminished.

intervention. Some women stand to lose even more agency, privacy, and dignity and sometimes security.

There are many practices of law applied to the family in which we could demonstrate the same degrading and sometimes lethal mix of abandonment and overpowering of women and children. The withdrawal of aid to the oppressed and the simultaneous insistence on intrusion into and control over the lives of the oppressed are practices that move away from the responsibilities of welfare and redistributive justice for individuals and groups of individuals within the state. They also move away from any equality-seeking protection of individuals (including the most historically disadvantaged) from the unfair intrusions of the state.

This is obvious to CASAC in the flip-flop application and reversal of the 'mandatory' arrest practices as well as in the abandonment of any useful contextualizing policy such as the Violence Against Women Policy in British Columbia (Gulyas 2002). It is clear in the apprehension of adolescents from the streets under 'secure care acts' (Justice for Girls 2001) and in the well-documented failure to protect young women who are in the care of child welfare authorities from prostitute training.[42] It is clear in the continued disproportionate apprehension of the children of aboriginal women, and the consequent damage to both women and children while maintaining an economic program that assures those women, on and off reserve, of destitution and impossible parenting conditions. Too often we are offered a trade: recognition of victim status and identity in place of rights and equality.

2. Trafficking across the Pacific

Vancouver, British Columbia, Canada sits on a shelf below the mountains on the Pacific coast an hour or two north of the American border. Vancouver Island is a three-hour ferry ride off our coast.

Of course almost our whole population base is immigrant, in the sense that this land was settled originally by aboriginal people and First Nations. Our country has recently increased the difficulty both of immigrating and of being legally authorized. Thus, immigration—especially what is legal and illegal in Canadian immigration, and how to treat illegal immigration—is a big issue here, as it has been in California and Washington. People are debating how to handle immigration policy, trafficking, and economic refugees, among other things. Feminists are bringing attention to the role of sex and gender in these debates.

---

42 Cherry Kingsley, personal communication, October 2001, in discussion of children in care.

These are clearly matters of individual lives as well as of international trade, of the aspirations of women and those of international capital. For us it has been a crisis call. Alice took some of the work of that call, and this is her account of it to the federal government and the anti-rape movement.

Alice Lee
Ever since July 20, 1999 when the first boat from China arrived on the shores of B.C. with 123 Chinese refugees, Vancouver Rape Relief and Women's Shelter has been grappling daily with the issue of trafficking (Lee 2000). In the months following that summer, three more decrepit boats arrived, depositing a total of 599 Fujian Chinese refugees into B.C. Traffickers from the second boat had dumped its passengers in the cold waters of the North Pacific near Vancouver Island as they fled from authorities.

The arrival of refugees in Canada is not a new thing, but the arrival of several boatloads in a row gave many people in B.C. a sense of urgency, and they wanted to give material aid to the women, men, and children.

In contrast, the Canadian government engaged in a systematic punitive response to the refugees. With the end goal of deportation, the government encouraged a racist media campaign, introduced incarceration as an appropriate immigration policy, and actively suppressed the legal rights that are the entitlement of all persons who come to Canada.

Upon arrival on B.C. shores, the refugees were 'welcomed' by local police. They were immediately detained under military guard and checked by doctors for disease and general health. Most were strip-searched, fingerprinted, and handcuffed. After the first boatload, many were automatically detained and remained in jail until their deportation; some were jailed for more than a year and a half. Children under eighteen were apprehended and placed in government group homes. Out of the 599 refugees, 90 were women, and 96 were under the age of eighteen.

Because Zhen was nineteen, she was jailed with the women. According to Zhen and other women who eventually lived in our shelter, solitary confinement was a common punishment. Zhen herself was isolated there for crying. After being in solitary confinement for days, she felt unable to cope any more and attempted suicide by jumping and hitting her head on the concrete.

In response to the first boatload of refugees, the Immigration Department designated the Canadian Forces Base at Esquimalt as a port of entry to process them. The Fujians were confronted with a process that jeopardised the likelihood that they would be rightly recognized as political refugees. They were detained illegally and denied legal counsel during their initial interviews with Immigration Canada. This made them extremely vulnerable, because the interviews became part of their refugee application. As a result, many exclusion orders (legal determinations that individuals could not apply for refugee status) were issued (DAARE 2001). Denied access to counsel, the claimants were unaware that, under B.C. law, they could assert refugee status and engage legal aid to assist them with the immigration process.

A media that branded and isolated them supported the government strategy. Messages carried in local and national media embodied predictable, negative judgments that prevented humanization of the people. We were not informed of the conditions of their lives and the reasons why they would take such dangerous risks. We were encouraged to participate in the construction of racist and classist stereotypes. As the boats arrived, the media continued to sensationalize the story, evoking strong racist anger and causing a split in my Asian community as well as in the general public. The distancing of the refugees was enhanced by the structure of current immigration laws that have opened the borders to those who are wealthy or hold professional standing; these people clearly did not fit into those categories. Headlines such as 'Go Home' fuelled the debate, distorting the public discussion by focusing it on the matter of costs, on the 'relaxed' Canadian immigration laws, and on the illegal refugees having 'jumped queue'. A demand for deportation without legal process was loudly and repeatedly expressed in the media. There was no discussion of why the people had been illegally detained, or of the reasons for a substantive shift in legal criteria whereby group profiling was utilized as a just reason for detention. The refugees were deemed guilty without a fair hearing.

We at the centre were horrified to hear about the conditions the refugees had endured trying to get here and, along with other women, we struggled for an effective response. We soon confirmed that the trafficked women were being subjugated to indentured labour, including prostitution—and that apprehension and jailing did not save them from the traffickers.

Women around us were outraged and rallied against the detention on International Women's Day, March 2000. That summer, women's groups at a Legal Education Action Fund (LEAF) conference heard Direct Action Against Refugee Exploitation (DAARE) recount the plight of the refugee women who were jailed. Calling for their immediate release, we challenged the argument that the government was only protecting them from dangerous traffickers and that there was no place for them to go.

My shelter collective quickly offered space and a welcome to the trafficked women. Our efforts, together with those of DAARE, aided in the release of several Fujians and created opportunities for them to group with other women to share and plan for their survival. Zhen was released to us from prison, pending her refugee hearing.

The Fujians were eventually allowed legal representation, either through legal aid or individual lawyers paid by the province. By providing inadequate translation services and insufficient and overworked legal counsel, the government ensured that most refugees would lose their claim for refugee status. Since that time, even our own justice system has recognized the unfair treatment the Fujians received and has acted to overturn many of the exclusion orders in court. Of course, it is too late for some of those people to benefit . . . justice delayed.

In the process of offering what we hoped would be useful and appropriate aid, we were confronted with many challenges, some successfully resolved, others regrettably not.

The primary difficulty we faced was the collection of useful information regarding the trafficking of women. During the months that followed the arrival of the first boat, it was almost impossible to get any accurate information regarding how many refugees there were, why they chose to take this incredible risk, who had trafficked them, and who benefited from the trafficking of women.

Zhen knew very little about her traffickers. She had contact with one person and she only knew his alias. He told her not to bring any belongings, as everything she needed would be provided for her, and that she would be traveling for only a few days. He had assured her that the ship was fully equipped and included her own private room and bed. Zhen was on the ship for over a month. She did not want to talk much about it.

Zhen came from a poor family in Fujian province in China, and lacked formal educational training, characteristics shared with many of the refugees trafficked by boat. Her mother had remarried, but her stepfather was in jail, and she could barely keep up with the living expenses of Zhen and her brother. One day a stranger asked Zhen if she would like the opportunity to come to Canada. It would cost her $US35,000. She was not required to make a deposit but had the understanding that work would be set up for her when she arrived to repay that debt. She had no idea what kind of work she would be doing, but she decided to come since she had always heard that Canada was a land of opportunity and freedom. When I asked what made her take such a risk, she replied that she was her family's only hope for any future.

Almost all the refugees were escaping either political repression or extreme poverty. Women are subjected to severe birth control measures under China's One Child policy. Forced abortions and sterilization continue to be common enforcement methods. The push for globalization in the West is an impetus for China's change in economic policy, resulting in extreme poverty and massive unemployment. It is estimated that by 2002, over twenty million public sector workers had lost their jobs as China moved toward privatization. China's 'floating population' is now around 70 to 100 million people (James and Price 1999), with many people migrating to the cities in search of work. Both women and men end up working for little pay at exploitative jobs as day labourers, factory workers, restaurant cooks and servers; many women end up working as prostitutes. Although prostitution is not legal in China, during a recent trip I observed that prostitution is rampant. It is very much a part of the local economy.

In Jinan, China, people I talked to noted that changes in municipal government policies have greatly encouraged the growth of 'night entertainment'. The growth of 'night entertainment', restaurants and bars has been accompanied by a tremendous increase in prostitution. Some believe this is deliberately overlooked as part of the government's plan for increased tourism and investment. With no social safety net, women are forced to service men. Canada, along with other Western countries, actively promotes such conditions by aggressively pressing for economic trade agreements that benefit only the wealthy few. By moving their businesses to the developing world and demanding outrageously low wages and poor working conditions, the businesses not only control the world's resources but they have also succeeded in commodifying human lives and migration opportunities.

Even the Criminal Intelligence Service of Canada acknowledges that international migrants are highly extorted and that women are often gang-raped and sold into prostitution. Zhen was unaware that she was a likely young candidate. The federal government, however, is aware of the presence of various gangs in Vancouver trafficking women like Zhen. To close the borders more and more, and then to jail the trafficked women, seems the least effective way to manage the situation.

Often women like Zhen are sent on to Toronto and New York, both destinations with large Fujianese populations (Criminal Intelligence Service Canada 1998). Many remain there without status and become part of the economy providing cheap illegal labour in the sweatshop industry and prostitution. Without legal standing in our country or the US, trafficked refugees are helpless, intimidated and controlled by real threats to them and/or to their families back home.

In this environment, helping the refugees is difficult. In China, women's services are often controlled and operated by the state, not by an independent women's movement; as a result of this (in conjunction with their treatment by the Canadian government), women are often suspicious of services offered for their aid. A guarantee of Landed Immigrant status would increase the willingness of at least some to testify against their abusers. If Canada and we were seen to be obeying our own laws, it might help to make us trustworthy.

Zhen told me that she had no idea what the journey would be like and that she would never have imagined being put in jail by the Canadian government. If she had known, she might not have come. Having women visit her in jail was a great encouragement, and having a place to stay at Rape Relief and Women's Shelter was a tremendous relief for her. After her stay at our shelter, along with DAARE, we found her more permanent housing while she waited for her hearing. Zhen grew more and more restless as she waited. She grew increasingly scared of being deported, as she knew prison would be waiting for her in China. Any future that she might have had back home would no longer be an option. The media was full of stories of other refugees' deportations. In the end, Zhen disappeared before her hearing. We have only clues of her whereabouts from a phone call she made before crossing the US border.

Our collective found that the individual experiences of the Fujianese women were not so different from those of other battered women staying in our transition house. Isolation is a primary factor in all of these women's lives, and extreme poverty always makes women even more susceptible to male violence. But the refugee women had the extra burdens of language barriers, cultural differences, and being born in the global south.

Both the traffickers and the State acted to isolate these women from each other and from the community—that is, they created and sustained conditions where women remain desperate and can be duped by promises of a 'better life'. In such an environment, it is little wonder that women are apprehensive and find it difficult to navigate their way toward autonomy and freedom. We regret that we could not offer Zhen any guarantee that staying in Canada for her hearing would mean a fair chance to achieve her autonomy and a 'better life'.

3. Vancouver women resist the red-light district as a solution to violence against women

Author's note: Vancouver has suffered a quickly growing ghetto of squalor, unemployment, drug addiction and prostitution and a series of serial killers that have preyed on the women there. We handle crisis calls from this area every day (although we serve the whole city and many of the women who call us are not economically desperate). Gentrification, land values, the need for social worker jobs, Puritanism and vigilantism all play a part in the debates. So does the revulsion of ordinary people who want to see drug addicts and prostitutes treated with dignity and compassion. In early 2003, our city had just elected a 'progressive left leaning' city council to address these and other local issues, but also as a beach-head against the more right-wing provincial and federal governments. The legalization or criminalization of the drug trade and of sex trade were and are key parts of the public discourse.

Our collective was active in a local coalition that organized an event in March 2003 called the Raging Women's Conference. It was meant to re-engage many of the activists who had fought for women in this city from the 1970s through the 1990s, with the hope of also pulling new young women into feminist activity. Rape Relief women judged that the most important issues that needed a feminist voice at this conference were welfare, prostitution and the need for women's groups to re-establish themselves. We were trying to enter the discussion in a way that could unite women to fight for a fair and just world while we all grapple with our immediate violent and sexist realities. What follows is a version of our presentation.

Suzanne Jay

I have spent hours in the courtroom with Robert William Pickton.[43] I was there for his first day in court. I've watched him sit in the bullet-proof glass case that was built especially for him. I've heard his voice on tapes that the police made of their interrogations. Reporters refer to the case as the case of the century. That may well be true for Canadian women.

When Pickton was first arrested, I called a press conference so that feminists could claim a voice about the case. I've been to the Pickton farm many times, I've talked with family members of missing women, and I've talked to women who escaped the Pickton Farm.

While I was in the courtroom, I started to think about Jack the Ripper. I think about how Jack the Ripper's violence has been promoted to us and kept in the public consciousness of westerners, usually through commercially made movies, documentaries, books and tourism (Caputi 1987). I think about how the circumstances that allowed Jack the Ripper to kill, escape and become legend are mostly forgotten. Millions of dollars are being spent on the Pickton Farm case. There are media reports, books are being written and probably movies will be made as well. This case is a massive money-maker. But the money is not being distributed in ways that could challenge another man's ability to create another pig farm, and it isn't even going towards preventing you or me from being beaten or raped tonight.

William Robert Pickton may or may not stay in our collective memory. But we need to understand the circumstances that helped Pickton rape, beat, drug and kill so many women. I'm at the beginning of analyzing what the global corporate agenda, the provincial cuts, and sexism have to do with the creation of monsters like Pickton and Jack the Ripper, and how women are delivered into their hands. I'm going to base my analysis on some examples from the last three months of Vancouver Rape Relief's work. Some of the situations are severe, but I chose them because they expose a lot about women's oppression through violence.

Two months ago, Jane moved into our transition house. She had been charged with assault. Her husband picked a fight and wouldn't let her walk

---

43   Robert William Pickton is criminally charged with the first degree murder of fifteen prostituted women. All of the women were on a list of now over sixty 'missing women'. It is possible that seven additional charges will be brought.

away, and she knew he was building up to hit her. She says she grabbed a knife in self-defence and he cut himself when he lunged at her. He says she stabbed him.

Jane is from the Philippines. She is part of the global migration of women that results from that country's policy of exporting women to earn foreign currency. And she is part of Canada's policy of bringing in low-paid labour to provide domestic services, mostly childcare. Canada has established particular labour laws for domestic workers and other guest workers so that their employers don't have to follow the same standards (for instance, regarding wages and hours of work, rights to change employers, or obligations to live-in) as for Canadian workers, and so that the Canadian government isn't obliged to provide these workers with medical or welfare services. It has also made it very difficult for domestic workers to get citizenship. (Guest workers can be sent home whenever the companies or individuals hiring here no longer want them.)

Jane has Canadian citizenship now. She has asked Vancouver Rape Relief to help her defend against the criminal charges and get custody of her children. Her husband has the children and says he wants to keep them.

Now if the government was interested in protecting and advancing women's equality, Jane would be guaranteed to have a lawyer—someone who is trained to understand and interpret the law and defend Jane's freedom and her rights. Instead, the provincial government cut legal aid by 40 percent. They made this cut to a budget that the NDP (New Democratic Party) had already weakened by almost $18 million. The $18 million was from a tax on lawyers' fees that was supposed to be added to the federal contribution to legal aid, but the NDP put that money into general revenue.

Jane does have a lawyer to defend her on the criminal charges, but I don't know about custody yet. Women can get legal aid for family matters in cases of male violence, but remember, the police charged her. The other complication is that a social worker could get involved and decide that neither parent is acceptable as a carer, and take the children into care. There is no legal aid for anyone trying to prevent the apprehension of their children by the government.

Jane should have been able to stay in the Philippines and have a happy life there. Or she should have been able to immigrate here without having to live in servitude and constant danger of deportation if she didn't please her employer. At a minimum, Jane's immigration should have included immediate landed status and entitlement to all social services, settlement help including training in English as a second language, and an introduction to civics and to civic services. With these things she might have been able to make her husband change right in the beginning, or she might not ever have needed him.

Margaret has not lived in our transition house, but she did live in another one last year. I met her at the Pickton trial. She's a very attractive 44-year-old woman who has been married and has adult sons; she works out in the gym every day. Right now she is living on welfare. Last week I found out that she hadn't been going to AA for the past month because she didn't have enough money for the bus fare. She has to decide between spending her welfare money on bus tickets and spending it on food.

Margaret split with her husband six years ago. She worked in a hair salon and had her own apartment. A couple of years later, her boyfriend introduced her to crack cocaine. She was addicted for two years, and during that period she lost everything she had. The boyfriend was also using crack. He started to pressure her to act in porn movies and to go with other men at parties. He told her she could earn them some money to pay for the drugs. She refused and ran away. It's more complicated than this, but you need to know that she got away. Margaret has been off crack for two years. She says that it was easier for her to get off it because she was in her late thirties when she started. She had a life to go back to.

In the last three months that I've known Margaret, she has lived in four different places with four different roommates. She can't find her own place at the welfare rate. One of the roommates expected to be her boyfriend. He monitored her calls and questioned her whenever she went out. After he told her that he had people watching her, she moved out. She asked Vancouver Rape Relief to be with her when she went to the police to tell them what she knew about Pickton and the pig farm. We also offered to help get her money for the bus fare so she can go to AA.

Despite the North American war on drugs, the international drug trade has increased. In fact, the United States is the biggest importer of illegal drugs in the world. Americans and Canadians demand access to drugs. Poor people of colour are targeted by the large-scale dealers and turned into users and street-level dealers. The addiction makes people easier to control. Power and resources continue to flow away from women, people of colour and the working class. Corporations depend on a controlled population to be their market and to be their labour pool. Corporations exert enormous pressure on national government agendas, and poor countries have come to rely on the export of drugs to support their economies.

If the government were committed to protecting and advancing women's equality, Margaret would have enough money to eat and get to her AA group. The provincial Liberal government cut Margaret's welfare cheque from $521 to $510. If I were to give Margaret a gift of $10.00 or $100.00, it would be taken off her cheque. She is not allowed to have more than $510.00 per month. She can't earn any money, either. If I give her a gift and she doesn't tell her welfare worker, she has committed fraud. Anyone committing welfare fraud can now be banned from receiving welfare for the rest of her life. This is the first time in Canada since welfare was put in place that someone could be banned for life. Somehow it's become acceptable to leave someone to starve to death.

I don't think that welfare will bring about feminist revolution, but we can't make feminist revolution if half of us are starving to death or have no safe place to live. Welfare should be guaranteed to anyone who walks into a welfare office. The welfare rate must be enough for food and shelter at market rates and must include access to public utilities, like a telephone service, heating and hot water, and bus fare money. Women should be able to walk away from a violent husband and know that welfare will be enough to live on. A woman should also be able to quit a job where the boss is abusive, and get welfare. A woman should be able to provide for herself and her kids without having to commit the poverty crimes of stealing or prostituting or drug trafficking. This would be the start of fair income redistribution in one of the richest countries in the world. There is no reason to force women into the degradation of breaking the law in order to eat.

Sara lived in the transition house two years ago. She was 26 and had grown up in a small town. She came to the transition house to get away from her husband. He had punched her in the stomach repeatedly after finding out that she was pregnant. Sara thought she could go on welfare while she had the baby, but welfare disqualified her. Even before this last round of provincial welfare cuts, a battered pregnant woman with no means of support could not get welfare. The cuts were being implemented even before the changes had been legislated. The welfare worker told Sara that she should go into adult entertainment if she needed quick money. When Sara questioned her, the welfare worker told her that escort services have business licenses and are perfectly legitimate work.

Some of you might know that some members of Vancouver City Council support the idea of establishing a red-light district. A red-light district would be a designated area of town where men can buy prostitutes legally. It's supposed to protect us from seeing prostitution in our neighbourhood, while keeping it easy for men to find prostitutes. In other cities, like Amsterdam, Bangkok, Tokyo and Melbourne, the red-light district is also called an 'adult entertainment district'. There is a debate going on around the globe about prostitution. Capitalists are pushing for red-light districts in cities all over the world. Whole countries, like Thailand, have been turned into red-light districts. It is an enormous pressure on government to create the conditions that would push women into prostitution.

On December 28, 2002, the *Financial Post* ran a front-page story about Daily Planet, a brothel in Australia, going public. People could buy shares in the brothel on the stock market. At the time, two men owned the brothel, which has operated since 1971. It has been legal since 1985 when brothels were legalized in parts of Australia. Investors are promised 10 percent return on their investment. The company is debt-free and is projecting earnings of $AUS1.1 million per year. The owners expect that people will buy a minimum of $AUS6.2 million worth of shares. The women who work at Daily Planet are not employed by the brothel. They are considered free agents, and the hotel has little to no obligation to any of the women. The 150 women are free agents in an 18-room brothel. The brothel owners charge each man $115 for every hour he spends in each room. It seems that fire regulations are the only limit on the number of men allowed in each room with a woman.

The Daily Planet will be the model for any new brothel anywhere in the world. It isn't a new model; it's just the most public of them right now. And as of December 2002, when the story was written, there were plans for expansion into different cities in Australia, but the brothel owners are already talking about how poor countries like Colombia and Brazil are desperate for their expertise.

People buying registered retirement savings plans or making any kind of investment that involves mutual funds may eventually be buying shares in brothels.

Here in Vancouver, the Pickton farm is used to provide the background and justification for arguments about establishing a red-light district. Pickton was a well-known john, and the fifteen women he is charged with killing were prostituted. The chief argument for a red-light district is that it will be safer for prostitutes. People who are worried about the safety of women in prostitution are being told that the police will come faster and more reliably in a red-light district.

At this time, Vancouver police are looking for a man who targets prostitutes. He hires a prostitute from the street, drives her out of town and strangles the woman while he rapes her. The police are describing him as 'the guy with the wonky eye'. The first report to the police was in February 2002, right after Pickton was arrested. In March 2003 the police started telling the public about this man. A CBC reporter asked the Vancouver police why they waited so long to release information. In their own words, the police said they 'didn't think he was a danger because he limited his attacks to prostitutes'. Since February 2002, he has raped and strangled at least four more women. I'm not convinced that police will suddenly start protecting prostitutes because they work in a red-light district where prostitution is legalized.

Some people argue that even if the police won't respond to a prostitute, they will respond when the brothel owners call. The rationale is that brothel owners will want to maintain a reputation that is acceptable to the men using the area. In other words, the message is, 'Don't worry, capitalism will make women safe.'

But in fact, Daily Planet shareholders will not be happy if there are any publicized situations that make the brothel look bad. Most cases become public because they are recorded by the police. The media generally depend on police to release information about violence cases. It is far more likely that places like the Daily Planet will have a private security firm to take care of any incidents. The police will not be alerted, and any attack on a woman in the red-light district will be hidden by the privatized security. The official police record of violence against women, and by extension the official media record of violence against women, will be reduced—but not because the attacks are not happening.

Dara Culhane's research shows that most of the men who buy street prostitutes can actually afford to buy women through escort agencies or in massage parlours. The question is, why would a man who has enough money to buy sex in a safe, clean setting choose otherwise? Dara's research shows that the men are actually buying the degradation of women, not sex. Robert William Pickton had money. He could have bought women from escort agencies, but he didn't. Historians speculate that Jack the Ripper was from the upper class and that he may even have been part of the extended royal family. If women's degradation is what the consumer demands, the capitalists are sure to provide it.

If the government was committed to protecting and promoting women's equality, they would have given Sara welfare at a liveable rate. Feminist advocacy centres would be core funded to work without government control. Government would stop all planning for a red-light district and instead would be talking about how to stop women from being turned into prostitutes. They would seek our advice about how to promote women's escape from violence. They would plan with us about how to prevent the rapes and the assaults that will come with the Winter Olympics in 2010. (COPE members met with women's groups during the election campaign and agreed that provision of money from the city to women's groups was 'doable'. Since the election, that offer has disappeared.)

Jack the Ripper and Robert William Pickton both operated in a time when there was a huge redistribution of people, power and resources. In the Ripper's time, the economic agenda was shifting from agriculture to industry. In Pickton's time, the economic agenda is shifting from national control to globalized corporate control. Then as now, women were in a mass migration to get to jobs that paid very low wages and of which there weren't even enough to go around. Women were disconnected from their regular social networks. In the Ripper's time, social services were minimal, and mostly church-based.

And we all see what is happening to our social services in Pickton's time.

For both killers, there were red-light districts. Jack the Ripper's was the downtown of London, and in the case of Pickton I would argue that it was his farm that served as the red-light district. Mass media was well developed for both men, using the mystery and luridness of the murders to sell newspapers or advertising time. Media itself is now globalized under a corporate agenda. Neither government at the time was actively invested in protecting or promoting the status of women. Fear of these men was used to control women in each time period. In our time, the fear of Pickton is generating the localized pressure to create a red-light district in Vancouver. This is a plan that proposes a gross level of control over women. This control will be exercised most obviously on the women who are prostituted in the district, but every woman will feel it. The lower the status of the most destitute woman the lower the potential status of us all.

Feminists won laws on violence, affirmative action, and Charter protection for equality. A government-approved red-light district will reverse that legal ground. Anti-sexual harassment policies are impossible to apply when the woman's job is to be nude and available to any man in the establishment. When the sexual assault law was written, the government recognized that a man had to get a woman's consent to sex without using coercion. In a red-light district, women will provide sexual contact they wouldn't otherwise agree to if they weren't being coerced by their need for money. As for the Charter of Rights and Freedoms, the Charter's guarantee of security of the person becomes meaningless when a woman must be penetrated in order for her to have access to food or shelter.

If the government does create a red-light district, it will be delivering women into the hands of killers like Pickton and Jack the Ripper, because we are now living in circumstances that allow that kind of man to emerge.

In closing, I'm asking you to foment dissent against a red-light district and smash back at patriarchy.

Note: A temporary conclusion

The women at Vancouver Rape Relief and Women's Shelter fight all violence against women and fight its function in holding women down. So in a sense we expect to offer the same support to all women and we know from experience that all women abused by men will be harmed in similar ways.

Still, we do see that rape of a young girl by her father, or the beating of that girl's mother, is observable violence with the extra character of pressing the girl into prostitution. The lack of welfare for that mother, and the low rates and insecurity of welfare, make prostitution more of a consideration for both the mother and the daughter, and render them and all other women more vulnerable to the violence that men think they are negotiating in prostitution.

There are particularities in the combinations of global economics and world wide sexist violence that increase the likelihood of women being abused at young ages, of dislocated women migrating from the third world to the first or from the rural to the city as mail-order brides or guest farmworkers, and of women being trafficked for sweatshop work or sexual slavery.

We do regard a woman as carrying an extra burden if she has been raped and beaten by a man on the streets of our city, who pretends to himself that he has bought the right to do this. The difference we see is that she needs intervention not only against his physical power and the superior male status assigned him that allows him to get away with the violence, but also against the economic powers that put her in harm's way and gave him the permission to buy her exploitation.

We do not usually distinguish between the way we treat women who cross our borders to find a way to live and those who come down the coast from Prince Rupert (on our north coast near Alaska) or from remote or impoverished reserves. Others would say one group is trafficked and the other is choosing prostitution. We see that in addition to facing sexist norms, both are migratory populations of women in search of a better life for themselves and their families, and both are prey to men who will exploit their vulnerabilities, including their love of their families and their love of their homelands and their loneliness. Both populations are denied their rightful share of the common wealth of society, and both are denied legal equality. Otherwise good people often romanticize the lives of both populations rather than assisting them.

Of course there are differences to be addressed between women. We find it impossible to work for women violated without daily confronting the issues of violence against prostitutes, and without facing the fact that the women available on the streets and in the massage parlours and strip clubs are disproportionately aboriginal First Nations and women of colour. Often they are also disabled women.

It is also impossible for us to avoid the reality that the women on our streets and in our legalized prostitution sites (massage parlours) are only manageable to the men if they are heavily drugged and brutalized. Drug addicts are forced to prostitute, and prostitutes are unable to continue without drugs. The stories may begin differently, but this reality almost always imposes itself at some point.

We know that prostitution will not end without the end of women's economic and social enslavement; without an end to the racializing of women; without an end to class and poverty. The hope we see is to continue our work to assist women who resist the abuse heaped on them and who join with us to fight for the others.

References

Brodsky, G. and S. Day. (1998). *Women and the Equality Deficit: The Impact of Restructuring Canada's Social Programs.* Ottawa: Status of Women Canada.

Caputi, Jane. (1987). *The Age of Sex Crime.* Bowling Green, OH: Bowling Green State University Popular Press.

Criminal Intelligence Service Canada. (1998). 'National Organized Crime Priorities'. Available at http://www.cisc.gc.ca/AnnualReport1998/Cisc1998en/asian98.htm

Daley, S. (2001, August 12). 'New Rights for Dutch Prostitutes, but No Gain'. *New York Times.*

Direct Action Against Refugee Exploitation (DAARE). (2001). *Movement Across Borders: Chinese Women Migrants in Canada.* Vancouver: DAARE.

Dobash, E. and R. Dobash. (1992). *Women, Violence and Social Change.* London and New York: Routledge.

Duncan, C. (2003, October). 'Raging Women: Fighting the Cutbacks in BC'. Paper presented at the Raging Women's Conference by Vancouver Women's Health Collective. Vancouver, Canada.

Edelson, J. (2003). 'Should Childhood Exposure to Adult Domestic Violence be Defined as Child Maltreatment Under The Law?' In Jaffe, P.G., L. Baker and A. Cunningham (eds). *Ending Domestic Violence in the Lives of Children and Parents: Promising Practices for Safety, Healing and Prevention.* New York: Guilford Press (pp. 8–29).

Gulyas, M. (2002, December 31). 'Proposed Abuse Policy Changes Worry Chiefs: Amendment Would No Longer Make Charge Automatic'. *Delta Optimist.*

Harnett, C. (1999, August 15). 'Go Home: We asked you to have your say about the latest wave of migrants to reach our shores. Your response was huge, the message was clear: send them back immediately'. *Times Colonist.*

Jaffe, P.G., L.L. Baker and A. Cunningham (eds). *Ending Domestic Violence in the Lives of Children and Parents: Promising Practices for Safety, Healing and Prevention.* New York, NY: Guilford Press (in press).

James, A. and J. Price. (1999, November). *No Safe Harbour: Confronting the Backlash against Fujian Migrant Workers.* (Working Paper Series, Series #1, Working Paper #2). Vancouver: Canada Asia Pacific Research Networks.

Justice for Girls. (2001). 'Statement of Opposition To The Secure Care Act'. Available at http://www.justiceforgirls.org/publicactions/pos_securecareact.html

Lakeman, L. (1985, February 27). 'Who killed Linda Tatrai?' A speech delivered in Vancouver (available at www.rapereliefshelter.bc.ca/herstory/rr_files85_linda.html#02) and at the meeting in October 2002 between women's groups and COPE candidates for Vancouver city election.

Lakeman, L. (1993). *99 Federal Steps Toward an End to Violence Against Women.* Toronto: National Action Committee on the Status of Women.

Lakeman, L. (2000). 'Why Law and Order Cannot End Violence Against Women and Why the Development of Women's (Social, Economic, Political, and Civil) Rights Might'. *Canadian Woman Studies,* 20 (3), 24–33.

Lee, A. (2000). 'Working with Refugee Women'. *Canadian Woman Studies,* 20 (3), 105–107.

Lowman, J. (ed.). (1998). 'Prostitution Law Reform in Canada'. In *Toward Comparative Law in the 21st Century.* Institute of Comparative Law in Japan, Tokyo: Chuo University Press, pp. 919–946.

Sidel, Ruth. (1996). *Keeping Women and Children Last: America's War on the Poor.* New York: Penguin.

Special Joint Committee on Child Custody and Access. (1998). *For the Sake of the Children: Report of the Special Joint Committee on Child Custody and Access.* Ottawa: Special Joint Committee on Child Custody and Access.

Status of Women in Canada. (1995). *Setting the Stage for the Next Century: The Federal Plan for Gender Equality,* cat. SW21-15/1995. Ottawa: Status of Women in Canada.

Sullivan, M., and S. Jeffreys. (2001). 'Legalising Prostitution is Not the Answer: The Example of Victoria, Australia'. Coalition Against Trafficking in Women, Australia and USA. Available on CATW Web Site at: http://action.web.ca/home/catw/attach/AUSTRALIAlegislation20001.pdf (Last accessed May 2004).

Wilson, B. (1993) *Touchstones for Change: Equality Diversity and Accountability.* Ottawa: Canadian Bar Association.

Mary Lucille Sullivan

Can prostitution be safe?: Applying occupational health and safety codes to Australia's legalised brothel prostitution

Introduction

Prostitution has been legalised or decriminalised in four Australian states and territories beginning with Victoria in 1984. Legalised prostitution is regarded as work and, as such, is governed by Occupational Health and Safety (OHS) codes formulated by state and territory governments in association with sex work organisations. These OHS codes provide a unique resource for analysing the power relations that are involved in prostitution.

Much of the literature on health and safety in prostitution has as its premise that legalisation or decriminalisation[1] minimises work-related harms for prostituted women. Ine Vanwesenbeeck makes this point in her discussion of prostitution in the Netherlands, arguing that some form of regulation is 'needed to contest the power and dominance of employers over prostituted women, which remains invisible because of the illegality of their business' (Vanwesenbeeck 1994, p. 157). The weakness in her position is that she does not consider the male consumers who purchase women's bodies as an inherent source of harm. Moreover, as her study was undertaken prior to the formal legalisation of prostitution in the Netherlands in 2000, there existed no Occupational Health and Safety codes in countries other than Australia to test her views against. Australia's experience of treating prostitution as work demonstrates that prostitution can never be made into a safe and acceptable industry.

Australia's 1985 Occupational Health and Safety Act guarantees the right of all workers not to have their health put at risk through carrying out the ordinary requirements of their work. Prostituted women working in Australian licensed brothels or for escort agencies, as 'legitimate' workers, share these

---

1 *Legalisation* is when the state recognises prostitution as a lawful activity. In effect this involves the regulating and licensing of brothel prostitution, which permits some women to work in a limited way, while street prostitution, for example, remains illegal. *Decriminalisation* means that prostitution is treated as a commercial activity, with no restrictions other than those that apply to other businesses.

252

rights. An examination of Victoria's OHS strategies for the state's sex industry exposes that normalising the violence of prostitution as just another workplace safety issue ignores that this population of 'workers' is vulnerable to very specific and unique kinds of harm due to the nature of the 'work' they are doing. In practice, the application of OHS to the sex industry makes acceptable the violence of prostitution.

I will argue that Victoria's legislators and state health authorities have constructed OHS policy for the sex industry as being about public health. They have never been overly concerned with the safety and health of prostituted women. OHS policy and its implementation are focused on 'safe sex' and the containment of sexually transmitted infections (STIs). This will be shown to be a strategy to protect the health of male consumers and the general community. Women's health and safety is considered only when it can be fitted into this public health framework. The narrow focus on safe sex diminishes prostituted women's right to healthy and safe work, while ensuring that the right of men to purchase women for their sexual gratification remains unchallenged. The state's safe sex agenda also dismisses the power dynamics that exist between the 'buyer' and the 'bought'. Are women in prostitution in a position to negotiate how the prostitution act will be conducted, and, if they are not, how does this impact on OHS outcomes?

STIs, AIDS and public health

The state government operates within a framework of harms minimisation that accepts the inevitability of prostitution. OHS codes and practices prioritise 'safe sex' and the containment of sexually transmitted infections (STIs). This agenda is concerned with protecting the buyer's health and stemming the spread of STIs and AIDS, which since the mid-1980s has increasingly been perceived as a public health emergency. Such emphasis disregards the male role in the spread of STIs and places the responsibility for safe sex on women in the sex industry. Where STIs are treated as a legitimate occupational risk of prostitution, measures adopted to minimise the inevitable harm to women's health and safety are inadequate and often more debilitating than the initial infection.

OHS in Australia is monitored and regulated through state authorities such as WorkCover Victoria. OHS principles place responsibility for workplace safety on the employer. Codes of practice developed through consultation with workers provide practical guidelines that reflect various work-related risks that workers face according to the specific type of work they do, as well as a number of options for eliminating harm from the workplace. While codes of practice are not themselves legally binding, they provide regulatory authorities with a standard to measure whether employers are meeting OHS responsibilities.

Codes of practice for the sex industry suggest that the violence experienced by women in prostitution as part of their normal working day is located outside of the sex industry and therefore can be eliminated or at least minimised. Such violence is thought to be about male power and aggression that some men exhibit, the product of aberrant criminal behaviour, unrelated to work procedures or the prostitution work environment. Thus the violence of prostitution is portrayed as something that a few aberrant men might do, rather than as endemic to the power dynamics of prostitution.

The *Victorian Health (Infectious Diseases) Regulations 2002* is the major set of laws dealing with health and safety for the state's licensed brothels and registered escort workers. Ostensibly the health and safety of prostituted women is considered within this legal framework, but the regulations are stated as being principally designed to protect 'public health by containing the spread of infectious diseases, particularly STIs in brothels' (Victoria 2001, p. 56). Clauses that stipulate appropriate storage and handling of condoms, the right of prostituted women to refuse service to men suspected with STIs, provision of safe sex information and health inspection, merely represent, 'one part of the total package to prevent and minimise the spread of infectious diseases in various settings' (Intergovernmental Committee on AIDS 1991, p. 49). This bias not only narrows the harm of prostitution to STIs, but also views such harm primarily as an issue of public health, not about the right of women to safe work practices and a safe work environment.

The fact that Victoria's key prostitution legislation, the *Prostitution Control Act 1994*, requires mandatory testing of prostituted women for STIs, implies that women's interests have never been a concern of the state's public policy makers. The government penalises prostitution 'service providers' who knowingly allow a prostituted person to work while infected with STIs (*Prostitution Control Act*, section 19: 1a and b). In parallel to this, a 'sex worker' who works knowing she has a STI will be penalised (*Prostitution Control Act*, 20:1). Both groups are considered to know of the infection unless it can be shown that women have undergone regular health checks as set out by the Act, thus forcing women to comply with the regulations. There is no legal coercion for the buyers to undergo similar testing.

Men's invisibility in safe sex agendas

There has been considerable controversy over mandatory testing of prostituted women for STIs, which many view as a form of discrimination against women. Feminists, sex workers' groups and AIDS organisations have been unyielding in their opposition to the practice. Criticisms include that mandatory testing stigmatises prostituted women as 'diseased' and 'irresponsible' and isolates workers, rather than their 'clients', as vectors of disease (Banach and

Metzenrath 2000, p. 6). A further point is that this discrimination against women in the sex industry ignores the fact that HIV is overwhelmingly transmitted via male-to-female vaginal and anal intercourse, not vice versa (Farley and Kelly 2000, p. 35). A 1999 study of 4000 people undertaken in Melbourne, Victoria's capital, found that 'clients represent a multiple risk population with respect to HIV and other STIs [and that] men who use prostitution are twice as likely to have had unsafe sex with twice as many people as non-client men' (Moore 1999, p. 32).

Mandatory testing represents an abuse of prostituted women's human rights and inevitably must fail as a means of protecting either women or men, or the public health. The obvious question, then, is what is the government's motivation in its continuance? Mandatory testing, in my view, simply creates the semblance that the Victorian government is responsive to the perceived public health crisis related to STIs and AIDS, while keeping intact men's right to use and abuse women in prostitution. Unless governments challenge the concept that prostitution is inevitable, they must continue with this duplicity.

Do the limitations of the Victorian legislative model for OHS change if we shift our attention away from mandatory testing to educative, peer-based approaches to health and safety for prostituted women?

Peer-based approaches to safe sex

Peer-based approaches to OHS advocate developing educational strategies for reaching prostituted women, providing accurate information about the most effective ways of preventing workplace health risks, and supporting them in their efforts to utilise these measures consistently (Cohen, Alexander, Wofsky 1988). The avenue for peer consultation within the sex industry was well established by the late 1990s in the state of New South Wales, which decriminalised prostitution in 1995. This contrasts to the state regulations in Victoria discussed above. The New South Wales WorkCover Authority worked in conjunction with the state's Health Department to establish workplace training for people in prostitution. One of the products of the project was the sex industry-based publication *Getting on Top of Health and Safety in the Sex Industry* (Sex Workers Organisations Project 1996). A similar manual, *A Guide to Best Practice: Occupational Health and Safety in The Australian Sex Industry* (2000), was produced by the Scarlet Alliance, a national forum of sex workers. The relevant New South Wales OHS authorities have recommended both these publications to be used as codes of practice for the state sex industry. As stated above, while codes are not themselves legally binding, they provide regulating bodies with a measure of compliance with health and safety standards. Both guides allow us to study the extent to which sex worker organisations' OHS initiatives can eliminate the exploitation and violence involved in prostitution.

What is particularly new in the above material is the breadth and diversity of the OHS prostitution workplace issues being addressed. While these documents covered safe sex practices, other fields for evaluation were building safety and cleanliness, client screening procedures, violence in the workplace, alarm systems and bedroom lighting, repetitive movement injuries and drugs in the workplace (Tucker 1999, p. 3). Still, *Best Practice* argued that the practice of safe sex should continue to be 'the basis on which workplaces operate' (Scarlet Alliance 2000, p. 20).

This emphasis on safe sex is predictable as Australian sex worker organisations receive public monies only to the extent that their campaigns and activities reflected the goals of public health discourses on AIDS and other STIs. In an interview with Jocelyn Snow from the Victorian sex worker organisation, the Prostitutes Collective of Victoria, she made clear that the Collective's main role was to educate sex workers about STIs. 'A lot of people think we are a union, but we are not a union', she said. 'We are here to support and refer on behalf of sex workers . . . and we get funding from the Health Department. We get matched funding from federal and state governments and that comes under the HIV-AIDS strategy' (Snow 1999). By the late 1990s most sex worker organisations accepted that their principal role was unambiguously that of a service provider in the area of sexual health (Scarlet Alliance 2000, p. 3). A distinctive feature of the New South Wales system, nonetheless, is that it situated safe sex practices outside of public health discourses and viewed them as an issue of workplace safety and a legitimate occupation risk for women in the sex industry.

Ostensibly the New South Wales approach to OHS for the sex industry appears progressive, as it makes the health of the prostituted woman the issue, rather than how she might contaminate others. This view is, however, still severely damaging to women's health as it accepts that STIs are a legitimate occupational risk to be dealt with 'in a similar fashion to silicosis, asbestosis and chemical sensitivity' (Toms 2000, pp. 4–5). Moreover, the provision of condoms, water-based lubricants, dams, gloves and safe disposal equipment—all part of personal protective equipment (PPE)—does not safeguard prostituted women from the harms associated with STIs.

The process of risk management, as suggested in *Getting on Top of Health and Safety*, is: to 'identify the foreseeable hazards', 'assess the risk(s) to people's health and safety arising from the hazards', 'use appropriate control measures to eliminate or reduce the risk', and lastly to 'monitor and review the control measures to ensure continual safety' (Sex Workers Outreach Project 1996, p. 19). The aim here is to adapt working conditions and the working environment to the physical and mental capacity of all workers as opposed to traditional OHS strategies which demanded that workers modify their behaviour while dangerous work practices remain intact.

Best Practices reinforces the role of brothel owners and managers in supplying safe sex resource information and equipment. 'Employers should ensure that all employees are well informed of the need to use condoms . . . and that ongoing access to information and training regarding safe sex practice is provided' (Scarlet Alliance 2000, p. 20). There also exists an array of practical advice on how employers can put OHS principles into practice. A typical example is for them to ensure that prostituted women are able to conduct examinations of their clients for STIs. Under the risk management approach, employers are required to provide '100-watt lamps for employees to perform thorough examinations of their clients' (ibid., p. 65). In the case of outcalls, prostituted women should 'carry a small torch' (ibid., p. 56). Ultimately the liability for ensuring safe sex in the prostitution workplace stays with the prostituted woman, and the precautions recommended would be nonsensical if the situation was not so dangerous, even life-threatening.

The prostituted woman's role is based on a supposed expertise in identifying STIs. Recommended procedures are to 'visually inspect the client' then 'gently squeeze along the shaft of the client's penis to see if discharges emerge' (ibid.). Following the examination, the sex worker has the right to refuse service if she suspects the buyer has an STI. The question is, can 'examination of clients' be considered an 'appropriate control measure to eliminate or reduce risk'? The measure of success is whether a prostituted woman without either medical or nursing qualifications has sufficient expertise to identify at a minimum, twenty-three STIs, the number listed in the Commonwealth-sponsored *STD Handbook* for prostituted women under 'quick reference' (Snow 1998, p. 27).

The available evidence from both government sources and sex workers' organisations is that inspection for detection of STIs is a defective strategy. The *STD Handbook* cites a series of STIs that cannot be detected through such examination. Hepatitis A, B, and C, for instance, frequently have no symptoms in the initial stages, although these infections may lead to death (ibid., pp. 37–38). The Australian Capital Territory's sex workers' group, WISE, makes the critical observation that 'There is no sure way to tell if your client is free of STDs including HIV/AIDS' (WISE 1997, p. 11). At most, WISE can only conclude that 'a visual check . . . is one way to find some of the more obvious symptoms of STDS' (ibid.).

The limitations of visual checks for STIs suggest that a more reliable safeguard for women is the use of condoms and other personal protective equipment. Again, a search of safe sex literature demonstrates that a reliance on such methods is flawed and dangerous to women's health. The immediate drawback of personal protective equipment is that it fails to protect fully against STIs. Herpes is a common infection that may be transmitted irrespective of whether a person uses condoms. The Commonwealth's reference book shows that commonly the virus occurs on a man's balls, while a condom only protects what it covers, that is, the shaft of the penis (Snow 1998, p. 34). Thus, while occupational risk may be reduced through condom use, herpes is an occupational risk that 'cannot be avoided no matter how careful they [the prostituted women] may be' (ibid.).

Moreover, skilled use of condoms and other personal protective equipment can only have minimal benefit, as there exists an extremely high risk of condom breakage and slippage. *Getting on Top* lists condom breakage and slippage as severe health risks that can cause death or disability. Its probability is 'anytime' and the need for action to counter the problem is 'immediate' (Sex Workers Outreach Project 1996, p. 22). This failure of personal protective equipment is considered by sex worker organisations to be 'one of the most stressful' occupational risks for prostituted women. The caption is followed by the words, 'You want it all OUT. Immediately' (Sex Workers Outreach Project (NT) n.d.). Several methods are promoted to deal with condom breakage and slippage, but for the women at risk of STIs, the initial problem will most likely be exacerbated by such procedures.

Sex worker organisation information on coping with condom breakage and slippage contains two main plans of action. The first relates to STIs in general, the other exclusively to HIV/AIDS. The guidelines deal with vaginal, neo-vaginal, anal and oral sex, but an evaluation of treatment for condom failure during vaginal sex is sufficient to illustrate the debilitating effect of such treatments. The risk management procedure promoted in the section 'Action to be taken in the event of condom breakage and/or slippage' is to remove excess semen 'by squatting and squeezing it out using vaginal muscle exertion'. Follow-up procedures are that 'Fingers can be used to scoop out any remaining excess semen, though care must be taken to avoid scratching the lining of the vagina with fingernails' (ibid.). The above procedures are totally inadequate for preventing STIs once a prostituted woman has come in contact with a male's infected genitals.

Douching, scouring or flushing, which are thought to be common practices amongst prostituted women after a condom breaks, are not recommended in any instance. *Best Practice* lists a range of health risks related to the above procedures. Douching is hazardous as it makes the vagina more susceptible to infections by getting rid of naturally occurring bacteria (Scarlet Alliance 2000, p. 67). Further, it can push semen up the vagina towards the cervix, causing pelvic inflammatory disease (PID) and ectopic pregnancy (ibid., p. 67). Spermicides such as Nonoxynol-9 are claimed to be beneficial against

STIs as they kill sperm and infections in the vaginal tract. Their detrimental effects include genital irritation, vaginal and cervical ulcers and recurring yeast infections. Women at risk are warned that 'These conditions—were they to occur—would result in a greater risk of STI taking place' (ibid.). In addition, both scouring and flushing lower the pH content of the vaginal wall, creating a pre-cancerous condition. All that therefore remains for prostituted women is to have a health check as soon as possible.

Safe sex literature highlights that health checks are inadequate as a treatment and also causes psychological harm to women who must resort to their use. Medical testing is firstly inaccurate due to the different window periods it takes to reveal STIs. Prostituted women must consequently face the onerous experience of constant testing—'straight away after condom breakage for gonorrhoea . . . two weeks . . . for a swab for chlamydia', as well as HIV and syphilis tests, to be tested again within three months (Sex Workers Outreach Project (NT) n.d.). The Prostitutes Collective of Victoria has pointed out that the experience of waiting itself is highly stressful for the prostituted woman. With HIV, a potentially life-threatening organism, 'concerns are exaggerated by the asymptomatic and unpredictable nature of the virus itself, and by the fact that you must wait at least three months after transmission-risk activity until you can receive an accurate HIV-antibody test result' (Gilbert 1992, p. 9). However, knowledge that one has contracted an STI is simply a precursor to treatment.

Post-exposure prophylaxis (PEP), an anti-viral treatment, is recommended in safe sex literature as a follow up to condom breakage or slippage where HIV is suspected (Scarlet Alliance 2001, p. 25). In a work-related environment such as a hospital, PEP is normal procedure for health care workers who have been at risk of contacting the HIV virus. At the present time, New South Wales is the only Australian state or territory where PEP is available to women in the sex industry under the Pharmaceutical Benefits Scheme. In Victoria, prostituted women must still bear the cost of such drugs (ibid). Even if the drugs were to become more cost effective, their benefits for women in the sex industry remain unproven due to the difficulty 'with maintaining the necessary treatment program as well as the uncertainty regarding its effectiveness' (ibid.). At best the application of OHS for women in prostitution offers an assortment of inadequate risk management procedures for STIs that frequently prove to be as hazardous as the initial infection.

It can be argued that any measure that may minimise or at least decrease the harm of prostitution is beneficial. However, such concepts relate to traditional male-dominated workforces and industry, which consider that OHS is about removing, or protecting against, potential workplace accidents and injuries. There is a basic assumption that the work environment is not inherently harmful (Quinlan 1993). Contemporary OHS research and policy development focuses more on the right of all workers to a safe and healthy work environment and are thus more relevant for the prostitution work environment (Forastieri 2000). For example, where it was established that asbestosis in buildings meant that workplaces could not be made hazard free, its further use was banned. OHS strategies should not demand that workers modify their behaviour while dangerous work practices remain intact. What other categories of workers have to accept STIs as an 'inevitable'—not an accidental—consequence of just going to work? Defining STIs as an occupational health hazard does nothing to ameliorate the physical and psychological harm they cause to prostituted women. The underlying principal that the work environment must not be inherently harmful to workers, simply cannot be applied to prostituted women.

However, in those Australian states and territories where prostitution is legitimised as 'sex work', OHS strategies must fall back on making it incumbent on the workers to wear protective equipment and be prepared to handle occasional emergencies. These strategies disregard the gender power dynamics that define who controls the prostitution act. The harms of prostitution are distinguishable from other work-related harms because the very idea of prostitution is constructed out of male dominance and male violence, so work-related harms cannot be avoided. In any other work context such acts would be considered abuse. Dealing with STIs as just part of the job dismisses the concept that prostitution is about men's abuse of women's bodies.

Who controls the prostitution act?

On the basis that the primary health goal of OHS should be harm prevention, sex worker organisations have responded to the limitations of the current safe sex agendas by focusing on programs aimed at increasing worker responsibility for health and safety. Information sheets on condom breakage and slippage produced by The Sex Workers Outreach Project (SWOP), for example, advises:

> Have a number of different sizes of condoms in supply . . . **Do not let the client put the condom on** [SWOP's emphasis]. It is best you do this, as you are aware of the possible damage to the condom and feel confident that it is properly on (Sex Workers Outreach Project).

The assumption that prostituted women can themselves minimise the harms of prostitution in relation to safe sex is immediately problematic. Firstly, it presupposes a willingness by male buyers to agree to a safe sex agenda. The other presumption is that prostitution is worker-controlled, that is, that prostituted women are in a position to negotiate the manner in which the prostitution act will be conducted.

There is a growing body of evidence to indicate that men who us
titution take no responsibility for safe sex and in fact many demaɪɪu tne
opposite. A 1997 New Zealand pilot health study of buyers' behaviour by
sociologists Chetwynd and Reed revealed that male users take no initiatives for
condom use (quoted in Plumridge and Abel 2001, p. 79). These results parallel
the results of studies of the behaviour of men who purchase women in the
Victorian sex industry, despite nearly two decades of legalised prostitution. A
1998 report by the MacFarlane Burnett Centre for Medical Research found
there was a continuing reluctance by buyers to use condoms. The researchers
concluded that one in five men have unsafe sex (Louie 1998, p. 23). Thus the
government's proposed educative role for prostituted women around safe sex
is immediately compromised by the buyers' perception that their purchasing
power entitles them to demand any type of sex they envisage.

Sex worker organisations maintain that prostituted women are not victims
but negotiators involved in business transactions. This point was central to the
1992 submission by the Prostitutes Collective of Victoria's to the Law Reform
Commission Victoria, *Regarding Sentencing Practices in Rape Cases* (Gilbert
1992). It considered violence against prostituted women resulted from a few
aberrant 'clients' and that clients in general should not be stigmatised as
violent. Moreover 'Sexual acts with commercial sexual transactions are,
commonly, more clearly negotiated than other sexual acts [as] the role of a
client of a sex worker is clear within commercial sexual transactions' (Gilbert
1992, p. 4). But just how much leverage do prostituted women have in negotiating with men who demand unsafe sex?

Several studies have suggested that the power relationship between the
prostituted woman and the buyer is a crucial factor in the safety of commercial
prostitution encounters. Recent research on the sexual and personal safety
of New Zealand prostituted women concluded that 'issues of violence and
coercion . . . require attention to the power relationships between individuals'
(Plumridge and Abel 2001, p. 80). These researchers concluded that 'More
than half the women (58 percent) in the study reported that they had felt
pressure to accept a client when they did not want to (53 percent of street
workers and 59 percent indoors)' (ibid.). Similar observations have been made
in Australia in relation to legal brothels.

A 2001 report by the Federal Occupational Health and Safety Commissioner, Jocelyn Plovits, found that prostituted women were being pressured to
have full sex without condoms in unhygienic and often unsafe conditions in
the Australian Capital Territory (Clack 2002).The fragmented nature of the
Victorian sex industry which is made up of both legal and illegal sectors makes
it difficult to determine the prevalence or nature of violence experienced by
prostituted women where unsafe sex is refused. The Victorian government,

in its 2001 impact statement on new brothel health regulations, did note that condoms 'were not always acceptable to some users of specific sex worker services' (Victoria 2001 p. 61). The report confirmed too, that when buyers are refused sexual demands they would seek other avenues for unsafe sex (Victoria 2001 p. 61).

One prostituted woman, responding to a Prostitutes Collective of Victoria questionnaire, agreed that buyers were not deterred by legal regulations from getting the type of sex they wanted. Her comment was that 'when someone has attacked a worker on the street, it's not guaranteed but there's a fair chance they're going to be accessing sex workers in other sectors of the industry' (Chambers 1995, p. 21). These views have been supported by a recent sociology study (Pyett and Warr 1999) on women at risk in the Victorian sex industry. The researchers revealed that 'client resistance, whether in the form of threats or enticements, was a continual obstacle to be overcome by negotiation in the sexual encounter' (ibid., p. 4). Street prostituted women were more vulnerable to physical coercion to perform sex without condoms. Pyett and Warr further disclosed that 'in some licensed brothels where, although in contravention of the law, management did not insist on condom use for all services, women experienced competition from other workers and considerable pressure from clients' (ibid.).

Women accede to men's demands for sex without condoms for diverse reasons. The Victorian Health Centre for Transmitted Diseases put forward the view that women who are economically vulnerable often have little choice to refuse sexual demands which they find unacceptable or, from a health aspect, likely to cause diseases such as hepatitis, chlamydia and genital herpes, let alone AIDS (Pyett *et al.* 1997, pp. 539–547]. *The Effects of the Prostitution Regulation Act on Victorian Sex Workers* (Keogh 1992), a research project undertaken by Sarah Keogh for the Prostitutes Collective of Victoria, drew attention to the economic precariousness in which women in legal brothels could find themselves. One interviewee made this comment:

> There are a lot of women who don't get picked all night; you sit around for eight hours, or you may even do a double shift and be in the one place for sixteen hours, and you earn $40. And that is really hard (Keogh 1992, p. 20).

Feminists Farley and Kelly extend such analysis as to why prostituted women are susceptible to male pressure, to homelessness, drug abuse, or because women are 'seasoned' to accept male demands through childhood sexual abuse and as women in prostitution (see, for example, Farley and Kelly 2000, pp. 11–14).

Even when coercion is not overt, women in the sex industry remain disempowered. The prostituted woman must appear to agree to any sexual

acts a buyer demands to obtain a booking. She then is forced
renegotiate the way the sexual act will be performed later wher
has commenced and she is alone with the buyer. Ingrid B
(Barclay 2001), which looked at the experience of four women in one of
Melbourne's legal brothels, underscores this point well. Statements reflecting
women's inability to set boundaries on the prostitution act included, 'I'm
always having to say that I will do something in the booking that I don't want
to, that is normally outside the service that I like to provide. It's hard because
if the client has asked me, I know that he will ask everyone. If you want to
get booked you have to do these things' (Barclay 2001, p. 32). Another
interviewee reported that 'To get regulars you have to conduct the booking
all about him. You have to indulge in his type of conversation, his type of sex'
(Barclay 2001, p. 32). These women's perspectives support the view that it
is the buyer who sets the parameters for what a prostituted woman's work
is supposed to entail.

Prostituted women obviously have no autonomous control over the prostitution act in rape. The Prostitutes Collective of Victoria's *Hussies Handbook*,
a self-help manual for prostituted women, stresses that rape is an occupational
hazard. 'Sex workers can be, and are, raped' (Prostitutes Collective of Victoria,
n.d., p. 19). Similarly, *Best Practice* says 'Unfortunately, incidents—for
example, rape—occur where workers are forced by clients to have sex without
a condom against their will' (Scarlet 2000, p. 22). Prostituted women
commonly make statements to the Collective like ' He [the rapist] didn't use
a condom and how do I know if he's got AIDS?' (Keogh 1992, p. 20). Despite
the extensive evidence confirming the power imbalance that exists between the
prostituted woman and her client, OHS literature, in accepting prostitution
as no different than other occupations, continues to risk the lives of women
in the sex industry.

Training in communication and negotiation skills is highly recommended
in OHS guides for the sex industry. The Commonwealth-sponsored *STD
Handbook* stipulates that:

> It is important that you and your client clearly understand your boundaries and
> expectations of the service. You need to take control of the situation, tactfully, politely
> and yet firmly (Snow 1998, p. 9).

The Professional, SWOP's industry magazine, goes further in promoting
the importance of worker control. 'Negotiating condom use' gives emphasis
to the positive advantage of attaining negotiating skills. The article's recommendation is that women in the sex industry, 'Be prepared to be a health
educator and share [their] knowledge' (Sex Workers Outreach Project 1995,
p. 7). It further states that 'dealing with stubbornness and ignorance will also

build your own confidence and strength' (Sex Workers Outreach Project 1995, p. 7). The caveat that appears in this piece is that a woman must 'Be careful and suss the client out, as you can be much more vulnerable without clothes on' (Sex Workers Outreach Project 1995). How the prostituted woman is to 'suss the client out', and what she should do if she is concerned, is not made clear.

Specialist groups offer programs on self-defence and conflict resolution for the sex industry that potentially provide some avenue of defence against the violence of prostitution. The services of Pacific Martial Arts are a typical example. The company offered sex industry employers a short course in which prostituted women are taught to handle threatening situations. Excerpts from the company's promotional material explain that its course:

> Allows employees in the sex industry to react to threatening situations in a number of ways, often behind submissive but protective postures and teaches them how to create a common vision with an aggressor, which can often lead to a compromise of initial harmful intentions (Brental n.d.).

Other advertising catch phrases include 'controlling self-violation, that pre-empts negative outcomes'; 'creating a common vision that shares an empathetic rapport with the violator'; 'de-escalation negotiation'; 'maintaining 'first strike' advantage' (Brental n.d.). This program is suggestive of crisis management for hostage situations. In what other non-military profession can hostage negotiations be deemed necessary to cope with the normal workday? Radical feminist Sheila Jeffreys has made the point that, 'It is surprising that prostituted women are seen to have such power. In other situations in which women find themselves alone with unknown men who expect to use them sexually, they are more likely to feel vulnerable. Payment does not make a difference . . . employment, marriage and prostitution create social relations of subordination, not equality' (Jeffreys 1997). OHS strategies, in treating prostitution as no different than other forms of work, operate as if this power differentiation is irrelevant.

It is perhaps inevitable then that when all other strategies fail to protect women from violence, duplicity becomes an acceptable work skill for prostituted women to acquire. SWOP's safe sex guidelines instruct prostituted women when dealing with men's unwillingness to engage in safe sex to, 'Tell the client you want to change positions' (Sex Workers Outreach Project n.d.). 'Certain positions' they say, will 'allow you [the prostituted woman] to check the condom discretely, for example if you are doing it from behind, you can reach underneath and check the condom without the client noticing' (Sex Workers Outreach Project n.d.). Apart from the unknown consequences for the woman if the man discovers the deception, no other work environment demands fraudulence as essential to being able to conduct work and avoid assault.

The most critical problem with negotiation and duplicity, as means of diffusing a potentially violent situation, is that such methods may in fact exacerbate the harm done to prostituted women. Citing a 1995 study by Karim *et al.*, Farley and Kelly claim that women were at a higher risk of physical violence when they attempted to insist on condom use with buyers whose violence contributed to their relative powerlessness. 'It would be more appropriate to view all prostituted women at risk, as it has been established that women were unable to prevent johns' demands for unsafe sex, and were often physically assaulted when they requested condoms' (Farley and Kelly 2000 p. 10).

Rape must be recognised as a high risk factor for STIs and HIV/AIDS; in fact the World Health Organisation (WHO) has argued that violence is the primary risk factor for HIV (Pyett 1999, p. 7). Clearly there are serious, indeed fundamental, contradictions in the current OHS priorities as outlined above. This is true irrespective of whether the issue of safe sex is managed from a regulatory perspective or whether it is about peer-based education. OHS guidelines can suggest and encourage condom use, for example, but cannot enforce their use, and neither can the prostituted woman. The buyer controls the prostitution interaction.

The expectation that prostituted women's bodies become available to the buyer for him to use at his will, is sustained by similar expectations held by many brothel owners and managers. Despite the principal OHS requirement that employers must maintain a safe and healthy working environment for workers, there is evidence that brothel owners and managers collude with buyers in maintaining women's unequal position in the prostitution transaction. Keogh's research cited above provided some disturbing insights about the role of brothel and escort management. One interviewee reported that her 'option' to reject a client whom she was seriously uncomfortable about servicing, had to be weighted against pressure from her workplace and her own financial needs:

> I had one regular client [the woman says] and I didn't want him to be my regular client at all. But the agency said 'if you don't go, we'll fine you and we will still take the booking for you' and he was really horrible. He was abusive, he was always drunk and always threatened physical violence and I didn't want to be there. But he kept ringing up for me and the agency kept sending me—and I couldn't afford to be fined for those bookings, because he rang up four or five times and, well, it was $300 I'd have to pay [in fines] for that many bookings (Keogh 1992, p. 22).

Keogh's conclusions were that the legalisation which created the potential for OHS to be applied to the legal sex industry had in fact exacerbated the lack of choice for prostituted women. As another interviewee explained:

The legal system has done nothing for the women in terms of improving their working conditions, in fact, it has done the opposite . . . There is definitely far more competition, the clients are extremely demanding, the control over what the women will and won't do is often taken out of their hands . . . We're put in a position where the type of service we offer is stipulated to us . . .There is a range of fantasy line work you can do, but for women who have just started working, this can be a somewhat daunting prospect (ibid., p. 7).

The employment of OHS in the sex industry cannot be in the interests of prostituted women. The experience of Victoria is an overt demonstration that public policy supports the idea of health and safety for prostituted women only to the extent that it correlates with the interests of the male consumer and the state's public health strategies. By studying the supposedly more responsive OHS codes developed by sex worker organisations, we find that they too prioritise 'safe sex'. Sex worker organisations, in leaving unchallenged the prostitution behaviour of the 'normal client', continue to promote the idea that violence is located outside of the prostitution work environment. The best that can be offered to ameliorate the harm of prostitution is a set of wholly inadequate techniques that in some cases are themselves life-threatening. Women in prostitution must ultimately resort to psychological tactics that would be applicable to hostage situations in order to avoid such 'occupational hazards' as contracting life-debilitating infections, assault, rape or death. In any other workplace these abuses of women's human rights have nothing to do with labour regulations, but are considered a criminal offence. Nothing could more clearly illustrate the fact that prostitution is not, has never been, and can never be an occupation comparable to other forms of legitimate work. It is at its core a manifestation of male violence against women.

References

Banach, L. and S. Metzenrath. (2000). *Principles for Model Sex Industry Legislation.* A joint project of the Scarlet Alliance and the Australian Federation of AIDS organisations. Red Hill, ACT.

Barclay, I. (2001). *Practices of Negotiating Between Sex Work and their Clients.* Melbourne: The Department of Political Science, The University of Melbourne.

Brental, S. (n.d.). 'Dealing with Menacing and Violent Behaviour in the Sex Industry'. Canberra: Eros Foundation Archives (Flinders University, Adelaide, South Australia).

Chambers, C. (1995). 'Who Cares for Whores? An Evaluation of Ugly Mugs: A Self-Help Approach Used by Prostitutes to Make their Work Safer'. St.

Kilda, Melbourne: Prostitutes Collective of Victoria, pp. 1–33.

Clack, P. (2002). 'Brothels fail health, safety test'. *The Canberra Times*. Eros Publications and Archives, Flinders University Library, Adelaide, Reference file: ACT 2000.

Cohen, P. Alexander and C. Wofsky. 'Prostitutes and AIDS: Public Policy Issues'. *AIDS & Public Policy Journal*, 1988; 3 (2):16–22

Farley, M. and Vanessa Kelly. (2000). 'Prostitution: A Critical Review of the Medical and Social Sciences Literature'. *Women and Criminal Justice*, 11 (4), pp. 29–64.

Forastieri, V. (2000). *Information Note of Women Workers and Gender Issues on Occupational Health and Safety*. Geneva: International Labour Office.

Gilbert, K. (1992). *Submission to the Law Reform Commission in Victoria Regarding Sentencing Practices in Rape Cases*. Melbourne: The Prostitutes Collective of Victoria, pp. 1–16.

Jeffreys, S. (1997). *The Idea of Prostitution*. Melbourne: Spinifex Press.

Keogh, M. (1992). *The Effects of the Prostitution Regulation Act on Victorian Sex Workers*. Melbourne: Prostitutes Collective of Victoria, pp. 1–29.

Louie, R. *et al.* (1998). *Project Client Call*. Melbourne: Macfarlane Burnett Centre for Medical Research.

Moore, S. (1999). 'Characteristics, Attitudes, Behaviour of Australian Men Who Visit Female Sex Workers'. *Venereology, the International Journal of Sexual Health*, 12 (1).

Plumridge L. and G. Abel. (2001). 'A "Segmented" Sex Industry in New Zealand: Sexual and Personal Safety of Female Sex Workers'. *Australian and New Zealand Journal of Public Health*, 25 (1), 77–83.

Prostitutes Collective of Victoria. (n.d.). *Hussies Handbook*. St Kilda, Victoria: Protitutes Collective of Victoria.

Prostitution Control Act 1994 (Victoria, Act No. 102).

Pyett, P. and D. Warr. (1997). 'Vulnerability on the Streets: Female Sex Workers and HIV Risk'. *AIDS Care*, 9 (5), 539–547.

Pyett, P. and D. Warr. (1999). 'Women at Risk in Sex Work: Strategies for Survival.' *Journal of Sociology*, 35 (2).

Quinlan, M. (ed.). (1993). 'Women's Occupational Health and Safety: A Conceptual Framework'. *Women's Occupational Health and Safety: The Unmet Needs*. Brisbane, Queensland: Women's Consultative Council, School of Management, Human Resources and Industrial Relations.

Scarlet Alliance. (2000). *Best Practice Occupational Health and Safety in the Australian Sex Industry*. Sydney, NSW: The Australian Federation of Aids Organisation.

Sex Workers Outreach Project. (1995). 'Negotiating Condom Use'. *The Professional*, 15.

Sex Workers Outreach Project. (1996). *Getting on Top of Health and Safety in the NSW Sex Industry*. Sydney: Workcover NSW.

Sex Workers Outreach Project. (n.d.). When a Condom Breaks or Slips (Fact Sheet). Darwin, Northern Territory: Sex Workers Outreach Project.

Snow, J. (ed.). (1998). *STD Handbook*. Canberra, ACT: Commonwealth Department of Human Services and Health, Education Section of the AIDS/STD Unit.

Snow, J. (1999). Interview. Mary Sullivan. Melbourne.

Toms, M. (2000). 'Health and Workplace Safety in the NSW Sex Industry'. *Safety at Work*. 12 December.

Tucker, S. (1999). 'Prostitutes to get on top of safety issues'. *The Newcastle Herald*. 4 November. p. 3.

Vanwesenbeeck, I. (1994). *Prostitutes' Well-Being and Risk*. Amsterdam: VU University Press.

Victoria, (2001). *Proposed Health (Infectious Diseases) Regulations 2001: Regulatory Impact Statement*. Melbourne: Public Health Division, Victorian Government Department of Human Services.

WISE. (1997). *Sell Safe Sex*. Australian Capital Territory. Eros Publications and Archives, Flinders University Library, Adelaide. Reference: Sex Industry 1997.

Adriene Sere

Sex and feminism:
Who is being silenced?*

Leftist publications have a problem with radical feminism. They have long maintained an informal ban against publishing radical feminist writers. They refuse to grapple with radical feminism's critique of male supremacist sexuality as a system of oppression of women. They generally pretend radical feminists don't exist, except for Andrea Dworkin and Catharine MacKinnon, whose names they try to weld into keywords for 'censorship', 'anti-sex', and 'bad kind of feminist'.

Leftist publications do publish liberal feminists and leftist women, thanks in part to the pressures of the feminist movement. There's a tiny bit of space given to women in *The Nation*, a little bit more in *Z Magazine*, and a generous bit more in *The Progressive*. But whatever the ratio, all publishing access comes under the provisions of an underlying contract: 'We will publish your writing. We will even allow you to be stars. Just don't go *there*—where Catharine MacKinnon, Andrea Dworkin, and those nameless radical feminists go. That's taboo territory. Don't even think about respectfully engaging with these feminists. If you join their ranks, we will treat you the way we treat them. If you even look like their friend, you will no longer be welcome here. We will reward you, so long as you don't cross that line.'

After decades of this divide-and-conquer strategy, radical feminists might hope that sexist men on the left would simply tire themselves out. After all, how can they keep pummeling those who are made invisible? How can they both bash and erase, year after year? How can they keep getting liberal and leftist women to follow their rules, almost without exception?

Unfortunately, no one is getting tired—except perhaps radical feminists. Women who move in leftist and liberal publishing circles know the rules of the contract, and more and more of them make these rules their own. Many of them take the initiative to bash and erase the 'bad feminists' (the two that exist) as a pledge of allegiance to the men and the system around them.

Laura Flanders, a leftist-feminist journalist and founder of the Women's Desk at Fairness and Accuracy in Reporting, provided an example in the May

---

* This article was first published in July 2001 in *Said It: feminist news, culture, politics*. Available at http://saidit.org/archives/jul01/mediaglance.html.

2001 issue of *The Progressive* (Flanders 2001). In 'Living on the Wrong Side of Sex', Flanders profiles Amber Hollibaugh, a 'pro-sex' writer and activist who, like celebrated writers Dorothy Allison and Joan Nestle, argues that people shouldn't have to suppress their enjoyment of a 'politically incorrect' sexuality to fit a feminist politics (Hollibaugh 2000). That's a valid message that should be heard. Like so many other 'pro-sex' writers, Hollibaugh also argues incessantly that the feminist movement is sexless, prudish, 'the last rock of conservatism'; that egalitarian sexuality, referred to as 'vanilla sex', isn't really sex at all; and that sadomasochism is a working-class sexuality. These are arguments that should be openly discussed, as part of a fair dialogue, when they are made in progressive political forums.

The problem is that these arguments are put forth in an ongoing monologue that not only suppresses dissent, but contemptuously dismisses those who would object. What is called 'pro-sex'—sadomasochism, butch/femme role-playing, and the selling of sex as a commodity—is put forth not just as a personal preference that one should be able to choose without shame, but as cutting-edge politics itself. In *The Progressive*, such a depiction of 'pro-sex' is featured, in all seriousness, alongside coverage of workers' rights, militarism, US imperialism, and deteriorating inner city schools.

Capitalizing on the aura of taboo, 'pro-sex' advocates tend to characterize themselves as oppressed in a way that is on par with racism, sexism, and classism. This notion has been widely accepted in popular alternative media, even though the explicit themes of 'pro-sex' are ritualistically hierarchical and often fascist—slave owner and slave, Nazi and prisoner, etc. Advocates also tend to depict themselves as silenced and censored, in spite of their access to the popular alternative publishing world, from *Salon* to local weeklies, to *Bust* and *Sojourner*.

The ones who are, in fact, denied speech by almost all alternative (not to mention mainstream) publications, are radical feminists, specifically in their attempts to critique what they see as a male supremacist sexuality. Leftist publications (unlike a few mainstream publications) also seem to be uninterested in offering space to popular liberal feminists such as Pepper Schwartz or the more cutting-edge Shere Hite, both of whom explore the possibilities of egalitarian relationships and sex. (Review of Shere Hite's work has appeared in leftist pages only for the purpose of scrutinizing the imperfect methodology of her studies.) The male-established leftist media, eager to portray women's participation in hierarchical sex as 'cutting-edge', are simply not interested in promoting egalitarian sexuality as a politically progressive or liberatory venture.

The extent of censorship of radical feminists in particular is difficult to calculate, since it consists of what the public doesn't see or hear. However, the suppression of speech, direct or indirect, can be measured by the absolute absence of radical feminist thought in the leftist media—though radical feminism is, even now, not uncommon in the grassroots, and tends to flourish when women are exposed to its ideas.

Occasionally, deliberate acts of censorship are exposed. For instance, in *Letters from a War Zone*, Andrea Dworkin recounts several attempts to get her (exquisitely written) essays published in *The Nation, Mother Jones, The Village Voice*, and many other publications (Dworkin 1993). Colleen McGuire's articulate letter to *The Nation*, taking columnist Katha Pollitt to task for her ignorance of grassroots feminist activism, was published only after editors nonsensically omitted the writer's brief reference to pornography as a tool of oppression (*off our backs* 1994).

By keeping radical feminism out, leftist media allow the promoters of 'pro-sex' to make virtually any assertions about those who would challenge them, without fear of accountability, challenge, or correction. Certainly Flanders was able to publish her article without worrying excessively about account-ability for facts or balance. One would hope that as a journalist who has dealt extensively with the unfairness of the corporate media, Flanders would make sure to give critical viewpoints a fair shake, and radical feminists accurate representation, if she is going to represent them at all. No such luck. Leftist concern for media fairness simply does not apply when it comes to radical feminists. As is predictable in the 'pro-sex' monologue, Flanders points to and then contemptuously dismisses Andrea Dworkin who, she says, sees 'prosti-tution and pornography as the root of all evil'. More accurately, Dworkin sees prostitution and pornography as male supremacy's main playing fields. Shouldn't Flanders and *The Progressive* treat a complex and original thinker like Dworkin in a more constructive manner—for instance, by arguing with her actual ideas? Instead, they simply sneer, as if Dworkin were nothing more than an anti-intellectual, anti-leftist propagandist like Rush Limbaugh.

Ironically, while misrepresenting and excluding the ideas of radical femi-nists, Flanders attempts to characterize 'pro-sex' advocates as the ones raising the critical questions. She quotes Hollibaugh as asking, 'If the forbidden is connected to taboo, how can we resist oppression without destroying our means to excitement? . . . Is there feminist sex?' Well, some of us would like to answer that question in a forum like *The Progressive*. In fact, there is a large body of work by radical feminists that has, for decades now, explored such questions; it is the analyses these feminists put forth, and the answers they discover, that have gotten them effectively banned from the leftist media.

As is also predictable in this monologue, Flanders characterizes anti-porn activists as historically having wanted to silence those with a more brave and honest sexuality. She writes, 'Demanding inclusivity brought Hollibaugh into direct conflict with the just-then burgeoning anti-porn movement in New York.' She refers to the 1981 Barnard Conference on Sexuality, and claims that 'alongside novelist Dorothy Allison, Joan Nestle of the Lesbian Herstory Archives, and sociologist Gayle Rubin, Hollibaugh was picketed and denounced by anti-porn feminists'. A caption below an accompanying photo of Hollibaugh and Allison reads, 'Amber Hollibaugh and novelist Dorothy Allison were denounced by anti-pornography feminists in 1981.'

As always, there is no representation of the viewpoints of the denounced anti-porn activists. A younger feminist would have to do some serious research to learn about the anti-porn activists' version of events. Fortunately, the radical feminist paper *off our backs* revisited the controversy in several issues during the early '90s. Both sides were represented, alongside an extensive interview with Joan Nestle, belying the accusation that anti-porn feminists are the ones obsessed with wanting to suppress speech.

Carol Anne Douglas, who was a reporter for *off our backs* during the conference, recounts, 'I was astonished and pained that a group of women who identified as feminists would hold a conference on sexuality where virtually every radical feminist and lesbian feminist I respected—from Ti-Grace Atkinson to Adrienne Rich to Andrea Dworkin—was heavily criticized, with no voice to counter those attacks. I didn't hear anyone [among the protesters] criticize the speakers as perverts, but I heard a great deal of dismay that [the conference organizers] did not permit any feminists who have a critique of sexuality rather than an 'anything goes' perspective to speak' (Douglas 1993). In other words, radical feminists, not 'pro-sex' advocates, were the ones who were silenced. *The Progressive* continues the exclusion twenty years later, with the extra bonus of portraying anti-porn feminists as the ones who were trying to suppress dialogue.

Douglas also states in her account, 'I don't think we should target particular individuals' practices, but I do think it is very important for us to hold each other accountable for what we defend theoretically. Specifically, I think it is very relevant that an individual defends sadomasochism theoretically; that certainly does not mean that she practises it, and whether she does is not a subject that reporters should investigate.' 'Pro-sex' writers such as Hollibaugh and Allison have written extensively on the shame they were made to feel by 'rigid' feminists because of their enjoyment of hierarchical and 'taboo' sexuality. No doubt, there were many feminists who failed to make the distinction that Douglas makes, and carried their politics into others' personal territory— judging, condemning, even excommunicating. By exposing and criticizing such behavior, Allison and Hollibaugh have made an important contribution to the feminist movement. However, the legitimate objection to inappropriate peer pressures should not be used as an excuse to eliminate from public debate feminist analyses of the history, context, and larger meaning of what is called 'pro-sex'.

It must also be acknowledged that peer pressure and the demand for conformity within political movements are hardly exclusive to feminists. Leftist culture, particularly during the 1960s and 1970s, put incredible pressure on people to conform to certain forms of behavior—including what to eat, how to dress, what language to use, and how to earn and spend money. Perhaps the most stringent demand for conformity was made on women's sexuality. For a woman to be considered acceptable within leftist culture, she had to have a 'good attitude' about sex. She was supposed to be sexually accessible, go along with casual sex, and be open to 'sexual experimentation'. If a woman rejected the demand for sexual conformity, she would face ferocious male wrath in the form of exclusion, harassment, and stigmatization.

Strangely, Flanders criticizes leftists, as well as feminists, for their role in 'oppressing' those who are 'pro-sex'. Many leftists, of course, still carry prejudices they learned from the establishment, such as homophobia and disrespect for sex workers. But by and large, the left's attitudes toward sexuality have been extremely compatible with the taboo-breaking 'pro-sex'. In fact, it could be said that the left uniquely influenced today's mainstream culture in its intolerance for 'prudishness'.

The Progressive must delight in publishing an article that criticizes the left for being too sexually uptight. They would be far less likely to use up three pages of the slim publication for an article examining the peer pressures that actually characterized leftist culture. While feminists are criticized without end for their 'repressive' peer pressures, real or imagined, the leftist media have better things to do than examine themselves in this way.

If they did ever allow certain aspects of the left's rigidities to be criticized, it is certain that they would not exalt those who gleefully participate in the status quo. Meat-eaters, for instance, would never be characterized as cutting-edge liberators, just because they enjoy eating meat and are rebelling against rigid vegetarians. Critics of the meat industry and meat consumerism would never be slandered for their positions, portrayed as 'anti-appetite', and denied a voice in the leftist media.

But such is the treatment that radical and anti-porn feminists receive. Leftist publications characterize the anti-porn movement (when they acknowledge it at all) as a censorship-monger with no meaningful points to make; nothing of substance to communicate. The only significance of the movement is that it 'oppresses' those who have a good time being sexual.

Or so the monologue goes, without end. Everyone knows there will be no retorts, no corrections, no arguments and counterarguments made by radical feminists. There is simply no criticism allowed, and no built-in system of accountability when it comes to the terrain of male supremacist sexuality. These publications just pretend that radical feminism doesn't really exist— except to occasionally warn women away from the 'bad' feminists, or to portray the never-heard-from radical feminists as the all-powerful oppressors of those who in fact monopolize the 'discourse' on the politics of sexuality.

References

Douglas, Carol Anne. (1993) 'A response to "Interview: Joan Nestle: A fem reflects on four decades of lesbian self-expression"'. *off our backs*, 23 (8, Aug/Sept).

Dworkin, Andrea. (1993). *Letters from a War Zone*. Brooklyn, NY: Lawrence Hill Books.

Flanders, Laura. (2001). 'Living on the Wrong Side of Sex'. *The Progressive*, 65 (5).

Hollibaugh, Amber L. (2000). *My Dangerous Desires: A Queer Girl Dreaming her Way Home*. Durham, NC: Duke University Press.

McGuire, Colleen. (1994). Letters column. *off our backs*, 24 (6, June).

'Sex: Let's shed some light on this issue'. (1993). *off our backs*, 23 (8, Aug/Sept).

Trimberger, E. Kay. (1995). 'Family Matters—The Hite Report on the Family: Growing Up Under Patriarchy by Shere Hite'. *The Nation*, 260 (24).

Kirsten Anderberg

No more 'porn nights'

Mainstream pornography is not empowering to fat women's self-esteem. The mainstream pornography industry has relegated fat women to a strictly fetish standing. It has also rendered fat women constructively invisible. It is not surprising, in a society whose media are obsessed with one body type for women, that the trend would continue on to porn also. The amazing part for me is how little room there is for constructive criticism on this topic within the 'sex-positive' community. Thus, even when a woman ventures out into a more open sexual lifestyle, the pornography industry will keep reminding her of whom she is here to serve.

I am a proponent of free speech and nudity; I am anti-censorship. But I still maintain that pornography hurts fat women. I have experienced this directly and this is my story.

In my quest for a broader sexuality, I began to associate with several 'sex-positive' groups in 1997. These included groups focusing on bisexuality, polyamorism (loving more than one), 'sacred sexuality', tantra, sex education, and lesbianism. In this 'erotic community' there was an unspoken rule of acceptance, where one was not to judge another's sexual preferences. I became involved, eventually, with one of the nation's polyamory poster boys, a man who had a 'pro-sexuality' website with some of the highest traffic in the sexual education genre. Many times we argued on topics related to feminism, but it was the topic of pornography that ended our relationship.

My partner's 'sexual society' had organized a 'porn night'. People would go to a member's house and watch porn together. I had avoided pornography my whole life as the little I had seen made me feel degraded, but since I trusted the people involved, I decided to give it a chance. But this 'porn night' was the end of my relationship with that community.

My partner and I arrived to find twelve people present—six men and six women—of whom I knew all but two. The first movie they showed was called *Daring Debutantes*. This movie consists of a middle-aged, fat, bald guy in socks asking young women to masturbate for him. He tries to touch them at times, and they back away in horror. After some time of watching this man sexually harass these young, naïve women, I asked the group of 'friends' why all of the women in the movie were thin, blonde and young. 'Because it is a fantasy', one man blurted out. I commented that not one woman in the room looked like those women. I asked why we weren't considered fantasy bodies. People in the room became extremely irritated, as if I were Andrea Dworkin, their arch-enemy.

I tried to shut up, but I watched these young girls and could only imagine that in several years they would deeply regret doing these scenes. Watching a very young woman masturbate for a drooling man, for money, did not seem sexy to me. It seemed sad. It felt like I was watching sexual abuse. I wanted to talk to the women in the video. *Daring Debutantes* made me feel violated somehow.

The next movie had a cast of older women having sex together. I again infuriated my friends when I asked, 'Since we have seen two hours of only women having sex, is the rest of the night going to be male-exclusive sex?' In response, someone yelled, 'This isn't gay porn night!'

I revisited the issue of why none of the women in these videos looked like the women in the room. I asked why the man in *Daring Debutantes* was allowed to be fat and old and 'unattractive' while all the women had to be thin, young and 'beautiful'. One of the men present said that it was to give the men something to 'identify with' in the video. I asked what the women in the room were supposed to relate to in the video. By now, people wanted me to leave.

I honestly found nothing sexual about these videos. They overtly objectified women's bodies for men. It was political, not sexual. Erika Jong once said that the first thirty minutes of porn makes her want to have sex and then the next thirty minutes makes her never want to have sex again. I never wanted to have sex again after three minutes.

Soon after this second video came a third. It was a light BDSM video, where a woman was being paddled and making sounds like it hurt. It was disturbing and finally I asked to leave. We left and my boyfriend was furious with me. The people at the apartment were laughing at me like I was immature and ignorant, which added to my boyfriend's shame.

In the car home, I tried to explain that the porn made me suddenly feel fat, ugly, old, and undesirable. He said I was being stupid and making up problems. I asked if he could name his favorite fat women porn stars, since he was an encyclopedia of porn titles, authors, and production companies, due to his writings and industry involvement. He could not name one fat porn star he liked. He began to yell at me, and I started to cry. I could not understand why, if my body type was beautiful, it was never in porn. It made me realize this was not about sex, or women's sexuality, but about controlling women. In this respect, it is like the weight slavery industry.

The next day I found myself hating all men and not wanting to interact with them at all. I felt they all relegated me to a second class status. I felt invisible.

I knew I was not their fantasy. I was just an old, fat woman in the way of men
. . . worse, one who asked disturbing questions. Young, thin women also
made me wince. Knowing they were often ignorant of the dynamic did not
ease the reality that these women mattered in a way that I did not. I began to
feel hatred—toward men, certain women and my own body. I decided to just
go home and stay home that day.

When I got home, I took some time out. I realized I was having extreme
body hatred due to the 'Society for Human Sexuality Porn Night'. I was caught
between wanting to starve myself, wanting to never have sex again, wanting
to hide, and wanting to become a separatist lesbian. I decided to work on my
body esteem instead of trying to fit in with the 'sex-positive' community any
more. I decided to find body-diverse environments where I would be included.

In the days and weeks following 'porn night', I was systematically ostracized from the 'erotic community' for my 'sex-negative' views. I was labeled
a 'knee-jerk feminist' who thinks 'all sex is rape'. Although I tried to explain
my position, there was no room for discussion.

I quit my involvement with the 'sex-positive' community because they were
not open to discussion about how what they were doing made women like me
feel, and because they attacked me when I tried to discuss it. I have no desire
to watch mainstream porn again. All of the reasons I avoided pornography
in the past were reconfirmed at the 'porn night' event. I hope I never have
to watch women be sexually abused, whether by others, or by themselves at
the prodding of others, again in this lifetime. In addition to the feeling that
the women were being degraded as some form of entertainment, there is also
the body esteem issue. There are no fat women in porn, except in fetish
capacities, and that degrades fat women to the status of sideshow attractions.

I do not support porn because it is damaging to fat women's body esteem;
because there are double standards regarding what is gay porn, which has
sexist implications; because porn is hidden a lot—you never see people openly
reading *Playboy* in public for those articles! So this is about hiding and
keeping women as silent victims, and the 'sex-positive' community is as guilty
of silencing women with sincere questions, like me, as the porn industry is.
No open discussion is allowed. That is the first sign of an unhealthy situation:
no one is allowed to discuss the problem. I see no benefit to me in going to
'porn nights' ever again.

Christine Stark

Girls to boyz: Sex radical women promoting pornography and prostitution

It might be kinda like playing with bugs . . . [t]orturing a girl, yeah, that could be fun.

—'A Night Out With The Boyz'

The sex radical perspective

In the last twenty years, a great deal has been heard in feminist circles from queer and heterosexual women who define themselves as sex radicals. Sex radicals promote pornography and prostitution (as well as sadomasochism and other supposedly deviant sexual practices) as a lifestyle, a sexual identity, and an expression of feminism. Portraying themselves as rebelling against a traditional and repressive culture, they embrace pornography and prostitution as sites of freedom, adventure, and rebellion. To sex radicals, any political critique of pornography and prostitution as violence against women and children is deemed anti-sex, anti-male, censoring, prudish and judgmental.[1]

In the sex radical analysis, there are good girls and bad girls. The good girls are those—whether heterosexual, lesbian, or bisexual—who engage in 'vanilla' (that is, non-commercial and non-sadomasochistic) sex. The bad girls are whores, women who use pornography, women who sexualize children, and women who buy prostituted women: 'Whores, sluts, and dykes are bad girls, bad because we're sexually deviant' (Queen 1997a). Sex radicals define prostitution as a sexuality and then link that to homosexuality, the sexual use of children by adults, and sadomasochism, calling them all 'sexual outlaws'. They claim to be censored and discriminated against, not by pimps, tricks, wife beaters, racists, corporations, and daddy rapists, but by feminists fighting sexual violence, racism, and poverty. The sex radicals' 'good girl/bad girl'

---

1 The sex radical claim that feminism is judgmental toward prostituted women is especially specious. Much of feminist theory and activism against pornography and prostitution has been and continues to be developed by formerly prostituted women, who are not judging or otherwise maligning prostituted people, but rather exposing pimps and tricks as rapists, and the sex industry as an institution of male violence and racial and economic privilege.

analysis is nothing new or radical; it merely reproduces the conservative patriarchal dichotomy between madonna and whore.[2] Sex radicals simply reverse the valuation attached to the two sides: here bad girls are to be celebrated for their rebellion and audacity, while good girls are scorned and mocked as boring, repressed, and obedient.

In using the term 'radical' to describe their position, sex radicals invoke the meaning of radical as 'marked by a considerable departure from the usual or traditional.' In contrast, feminists use the definition of radical as a means of getting to the root of an issue—seeking fundamental rather than superficial change. Feminism is a truly radical perspective on pornography and prostitution, understanding them to be institutionalized sexual violence inseparable from racism and other forms of oppression. In this view, pornography and prostitution do not constitute a lifestyle, sexual identity, or type of feminism any more than does domestic violence or incest. Feminists oppose the institutions of pornography and prostitution, but do not blame or stigmatize the women and children in them. When sex radicals promote pornography and prostitution as feminist, they are acting against the sexual freedom of women and children and they become complicit in the abuse of women and children.

Queen of the sex radicals

Carol Queen's writings provide a useful illustration of some central sex radical themes. Queen writes that 'Sex radicalism means to me that I am automatically on the side of the minority sexual viewpoint or behavior . . .' (Queen 1997b). This quote reveals her refusal to be analytical about who is being hurt and who is doing the hurting: she is *automatically on the side of the minority*. Queen's claim to be on the side of the minority is simply not true. Given the magnitude of the sex industry and the rampant use of pornography among men of all political persuasions, women who automatically align themselves with the sexual minority would not be sidling up to tricks and porn users. Queen is on the side of the majority, the male majority, which sexually abuses women and children, consumes billions of dollars worth of pornography each year, and then attacks the feminists who speak out against sexual violence.

2   One of the ways sex radical women misrepresent feminist work against pornography and prostitution is by claiming that feminists are in bed with conservative religious groups. This accusation is false and the sex radicals use it as a red herring. The accusation that feminists are in league with religious groups is especially noteworthy given that sex radicals are not critical of abortion rights groups or pro-prostitution groups when they work with religious groups. COYOTE (Call Off Your Old Tired Ethics) held their First Annual Hooker's Convention at Glide Memorial Church in San Francisco. Glide Memorial Church (and *Playboy*) gave money to Margo St. James to begin COYOTE. Apparently, they consider that 'networking'.

Queen and other sex radicals have a rebellious, adolescent-style reaction to sex: what they perceive as being 'different' or rebellious is good, period. What sex radicals lack in thoughtfulness and feminist analysis they make up for by appealing to emotion. They channel women's valid anger and desire to rebel against patriarchy into their political camp by misrepresenting the term sex radical. True sex radicalism would mean recognizing structures of inequality and oppression, working toward egalitarian relationships, and aligning with those (whether minorities or majorities) who do not have social or political power—such as women and children hurt in pornography and prostitution or lesbians against lesbian pornography.

Sex radicals deride feminists for being prudish and judgmental and claim to reject all judgment of people's sexual practices and desires. However, Queen herself judges some people and not others. Queen situates herself in 'the whores' world I have known', then goes on to distance herself from those prostituted women 'who do not work voluntarily, who are underage, who are not sex-positive, and who act out the negative expectations imposed on them by a sexist and sex-negative culture' (Queen 1997b). In this way she blames and stigmatizes prostituted women and girls, the vast majority of whom are coerced, controlled by pimp/batterers, underage, raped, beaten, homeless, drug addicted, survivors of childhood sexual abuse, and disproportionately American Indian and African-American. In Queen's view, their resistance, courage, and survival are 'not sex-positive'. In a similar vein, Queen ridicules Linda Marchiano (known in the porn industry as Linda Lovelace) who was forced into prostitution and pornography by her pimp husband, Chuck Traynor. Traynor raped Marchiano, beat her, sold her to other men, forced her to make *Deep Throat*, and to have sex with a dog on film. Queen says Marchiano 'embrace[s] the victim role' and refers to her as 'Linda 'He-Had-To-Put-A-Gun-To-My-Head-To-Get-Me-To-Fuck-That-Dog' Lovelace' (Queen 1997a). Queen is only too happy to dismiss and judge women who speak out against the abuse in pornography and prostitution.

Queen also mocks and pathologizes anti-pornography feminists, whom she calls 'the girls down at Women Against Practically Everything' (Queen 1997a). She even goes so far as to suggest that feminists opposed to pornography and prostitution are 'absexual' (a term made up by her doctor-husband). Queen says, 'The crusading absexuals are fundamentally nonconsensual, for their goal is to impose their standards of sexuality on the rest of society' (Queen 1997a). She proposes that women against pornography and prostitution have a smaller hypothalamus: 'If the hypothalamus is injured or atrophied, one result can be a condition called 'anhedonia', in which pleasure in orgasm is lost . . . anhedonia might plague a high percentage of absexuals' (Queen 1997a). Queen flippantly dismisses life and death work against rape, racism, and poverty by claiming an absurd biological condition causes feminists to fight pornography and prostitution.[3] In classifying women's political resistance as the result of frigidity, Queen once again reveals how much sex radicals have in common with conservative woman-hating beliefs.

Queen lashes out at women, and her solicitude for men is striking. In her view, men must be able to experience their sexual desires without being judged: 'Will [the prostituted woman] honor the desires of her clients or trash them as perverted? Does she believe everyone has the right to access sexual satisfaction? Does she honor sexual service and feel positive about providing it?' (Queen 1997a). This smarmy litany would be enough to make someone gag if its tone were used to weed out applicants at Burger King, but when one considers that she is talking about prostitution it is astonishingly woman hating. Queen goes on to say that she:

> has known too many whores who put down clients that are common (or uncommon, it doesn't matter); how must it affect their self-esteem to be the ones to provide that sort of sexual release? The extreme version of this, of course, is the whore who does not like or respect sex at all: who thinks sex is dirty or at least overrated and men are pigs (Queen 1997a).

She emphasizes that dyke whores are in particular danger of disliking men or prostitution, but that they too must be sure to be sex-positive. According to Queen, it's all in the attitude of the women: the dykes and heterosexual whores must be sex-positive at any cost to themselves and their sisters. Those poor tricks and pimps feel bad if they are judged (they are such sensitive souls), but Queen never mentions the everyday violence prostituted women and girls endure at the hands of tricks and pimps or the extreme stigma prostituted women and children experience which often causes them to lose their jobs, housing, children, and lives. Obviously, to Queen, the rapists, racists, and batterers who buy and sell women and children are more important than prostituted women and children.

COYOTE

The duplicity evident in Queen's writing is also apparent in the activities of COYOTE, a prominent US-based sex radical organization dedicated to promoting prostitution. COYOTE advances the image of the prostitute as an independent, in-charge professional despite enormous amounts of testimony

---

3   Valerie Jenness states that the prostitutes' rights movement targeted contemporary feminism and its representatives throughout its national and international crusade. Other examples include Suzie Bright's and Nadine Strossen's blatant misrepresentations of the work of Andrea Dworkin and Catharine MacKinnon.

and studies that prove otherwise.[4] Its founder, Margo St. James, and others portray the organization as being the true voice of prostituted women, and claim that COYOTE has 'supported prostitutes in trouble'. Yet much of their energy goes into protecting pimps and tricks. COYOTE testified to the New York State Bar Association that 'The laws against pimping (living off the earnings of a prostitute) and pandering (encouraging someone to work as a prostitute) should be repealed . . .' (Jenness 1993). They refer to pimps, who are among the most brutal batterers and rapists, as 'managers' (Jenness 1993). It is telling that an organization that purports to be 'of and for prostitutes', that portrays prostitutes as independent professionals, would work to make it easier for pimps to sell women.

COYOTE derives much of its perceived legitimacy from its claim to be an organization of current and former prostitutes. According to Janice Raymond, however, 'COYOTE is represented by several women who claim to be prostitutes but who were never in prostitution or who equate being in prostitution with multiple casual sexual encounters, some of which may have included receiving monetary favors. This equation trivializes the experiences of millions of women who have actually lived in systems of prostitution' (Raymond 1995). Even supporters of COYOTE question the organization's claim of authenticity. Valerie Jenness wrote:

> Contrary to COYOTE's public image, only a small percentage of its members have worked as prostitutes, and an even smaller percentage are active prostitutes who are also active in the organization . . . St. James has admitted that COYOTE is not an organization constituted by prostitutes: That has always been the myth, the media's terminology for their idea of COYOTE. I'm not a working prostitute. I haven't worked for many, many years (Jenness 1993).

COYOTE has not worked to 'debunk the notion that it is an organization *of* prostitutes. On the contrary, organizational leaders have been central in creating and promoting the image of COYOTE as an organization *of and for* prostitutes' (Jenness 1993).

Sex radical Priscilla Alexander, former director and spokesperson of COYOTE and the National Task Force on Prostitution (NTFP), 'has never been in prostitution' (Jenness 1993). According to one formerly prostituted woman, 'neither organization ha[d] a visible membership or board of directors'

---

4   In a peer-reviewed study conducted in nine countries with 854 prostituted people, 95 percent experienced sexual harassment; 68 percent of 827 people in several different types of prostitution met criteria for PTSD; and 89 percent of 785 people in prostitution wanted to escape prostitution. From 'Prostitution and Trafficking in Nine Countries: An Update on Violence and Posttraumatic Stress Disorder', by Farley *et al.* in *Prostitution, Trafficking, and Traumatic Stress*, edited by Melissa Farley.

(Jenness 1993). She assumed that COYOTE and NTFP 'are, in fact, one and the same and as such reflect primarily Alexander's philosophy' (Jenness 1993). Jenness agreed: 'In another move to nationalize its campaign, COYOTE declared itself the National Task Force on Prostitution (NTFP) in 1979 . . . In essence, COYOTE and the NTFP became the same organization . . .' (Jenness 1993).

According to M. Hanson, COYOTE procured her into legal prostitution and extracted pro-prostitution statements from women in the legal brothels of Nevada. Hanson, who was in legalized prostitution in Nevada for 20 years, was introduced to the Nevada houses by a woman from COYOTE immediately after Hanson turned 18. Hanson had run away from an abusive home, been prostituting on the streets of San Francisco since the age of 12, and been gang-raped. She had had contact with COYOTE women from the age of 14. The woman with COYOTE knew that she had just turned 18 and would be able to legally 'work' in the Nevada houses. Instead of getting real help for this young, abused woman, they delivered her to the legal brothels of Nevada, where twenty more years of her life would be taken from her. Hanson never had a pimp like many of the women in the Nevada brothels; rather her pimp 'was the house'.[5] After twenty years in legalized prostitution, she nearly committed suicide. She ended up in a hospital and escaped to another state with 'only the shirt on [her] back'.[6] She had no money because all the money she made at the houses went back into the houses for expenses. According to Hanson, this was true for all the women. Hanson also said that women came into the Nevada houses periodically and made the women prostituting sign statements saying that they were there willingly and that they enjoyed being prostitutes. She said the women were with COYOTE (Stark and Hanson 1998).

COYOTE is perceived by many to be the authentic voice of prostituted women, despite their lack of credibility and research. This is largely because they articulate prostitution as a legitimate profession and a victimless crime which fits in with the mainstream view of prostitution and is an easy and comfortable belief for privileged people with generally liberal mindsets. Such

---

5   Hanson talked about how some pimps brought women into the legal brothels of Nevada and collected the women's money every Sunday morning inside the brothel. She also said, 'I know women [in the Nevada brothels], their husbands are pimps. They go in and work and their husbands get the money.'

6   Hanson received assistance from an organization that assists prostituted women (founded by a survivor of prostitution) and a battered women's shelter. She is now out of prostitution. Hanson said, 'I'm lucky. I'm lucky to be alive and be here.' She said that she's been so suppressed [from her time in prostitution] that sometimes she feels like she's 'a bottle ready to explode'. She has difficulty simply interacting with people. She doesn't 'know how to talk with her neighbor'.

people view COYOTE and other sex radical women as the authentic voice of prostitutes in large part *because* they are espousing this mainstream understanding of prostitution. For this reason, it can be very difficult to discuss prostitution as a system of violence, even when one speaks as a survivor of prostitution. Survivors are often dismissed because their opposition to conventional understandings of prostitution prevents their being perceived as 'real' or 'authentic' whores.[7]

Sex radicals as prostitutes, tricks, and porn users

Some advocates of pornography and prostitution claim they are sex radicals not only because they use pornography, but also because they have been involved in the sex industry as 'whores'. They attempt to speak from a point of authenticity as 'bad girls', but these women are not representative of the majority of prostituted women and girls, and they admit this themselves. Jill Nagle wrote in *Whores and Other Feminists* that, 'Like many of the contributors to this volume, my racial and economic privileges afforded me the opportunity to choose participation in the sex industry from among many other options' (Nagle 1997). In an article about setting up a butch sex service for lesbians, Les Von Zoticus wrote, 'Unlike many sex workers, I had the comfort of a day job to pay my bills . . .' (Von Zoticus 1997). Many of the sex radicals are white, privileged academics who have made their careers championing the sexual exploitation of women by regurgitating age-old woman-blaming lies. Their promotion of pornography and prostitution helps maintain the social and political structures that literally keep millions trapped world-wide in pornography and prostitution.

Some sex radical women are tricks who buy prostituted women or otherwise get pleasure from the harm prostituted women and girls experience. This should not be entirely surprising—it is, after all, the meaning of sadism, and sex radical women are advocates of sadomasochistic sex. Wendy Chapkis

---

7   Ward Churchill's analysis of a similar situation in American Indian politics resembles the inability of mainstream culture to grasp prostitution as violence against women and children. Churchill says that some 'Indian professionals' closely aligned with the government and other anti-Indian groups 'have proven themselves quite willing to publicly dismiss bona fide native rights activists, usually in the face of overwhelming evidence to the contrary . . .' He cites one of the effects of these 'leaders' is to foster '"mainstream" perceptions that, since we Indians ourselves cannot agree on the nature of our oppression, or even whether we are oppressed, then non-Indian intervention on our behalf is pointless at best' (*Fantasies of the Master Race*, XV, Ward Churchill). Another effect is that mainstream society recognizes the 'only "genuine", "authentic", "representative", and therefore "real" Indians are those who have elected to "fit in" most comfortably . . . "Real" Indians provide "voluntary" and undeviating service to those "greater interests" associated with the Euroamerican status quo' (*Fantasies of the Master Race*, XVI, Ward Churchill).

'arranged to pay for sexual services in the form of hands-on sexual instruction from two professional sex workers' (Chapkis 1997). Self-proclaimed 'sexpert' Suzie Bright 'has said that the best jerk-off book she ever found was the compiled evidence of the Meese Commission', which 'focused on the most hard-to-obtain stuff . . . the extra kinky' (Queen 1997a). In other words, Suzie Bright masturbates to women's testimony about the degradation and harm they suffered in pornography and prostitution. Veronica Monet believed all her life that 'if a man could do something, so could a woman' (Monet 1997). In her view, this included using prostituted women, which was 'another male bastion [she] wanted to force [her] way into' (Monet 1997). Monet, along with her husband, 'sought out a prostitute' at the Mustang Ranch (Monet 1997). For Monet, buying a prostituted woman was an attempt to prove her equality with men by becoming one of the boys, even though, as she talked with the woman, Monet admitted the legal brothel 'started to sound like prison' (Monet 1997).[8] It is one thing to want privileges traditionally relegated to men that do not oppress women or children, and quite another to adopt the oppressive behaviors used against women and children. This distinction is conveniently obscured and ignored in the writings of sex radicals.

Self-congratulatory sadism reaches new heights in the actions and writings of Patrick Califia (a former lesbian who is now a transgendered man). Califia supports the North American Man Boy Love Association and sex between children and adults, which he euphemistically calls 'intergenerational love'. In an article published in *Paidika*, a Dutch pedophile magazine, Califia wrote, 'I support *Paidika* and enjoy working with the editors of this special issue' (Califia 1994). Sixty-odd pages later he wrote, 'The bottom can be shaved. A

---

8   Monet's view coincides with the testimony of M. Hanson. She 'worked' in numerous legal brothels in Nevada, including both Mustang Ranches. She stated that the women were 'being monitored all the time. The floor maid sits in different places and keeps track of everything you do. You're being watched.' She also stated that there were intercom systems in each room and 'they can listen anytime'. Hanson had to get an abortion to continue working in the legal brothel. She said an employee at the house asked her if she wanted the baby. 'Of course I wanted the baby. They really turned it around. I saw the house doctor and had an abortion . . . the house doctor took care of the abortion.' The house doctor also prescribed pills for the women. Hanson typically worked one week on and one week off. When she was working she stayed at the brothel the entire week. On her week off she went to her apartment and 'lay down on my bed and sle[pt] for three days. I [was] so worn out that [my] body [didn't] realize until [I was] out of the environment. I had a bed that no man has ever been in so that was even more comfortable to me. The fourth day I'd get up and wash my costumes. The fifth day I'd go back to sleep. The sixth day maybe I go back to work . . . because you had nothing else to do. Your life totally revolved [around the house].' In one of the brothels where she worked all the windows were boarded up, the women had to wear black and the women even had to watch the tricks go to the bathroom. Hanson stated that the houses were 'all about control. Total control. Total disrespect.'

razor removes the pelt that warms and conceals. My lover/slave has her cunt shaved. It reminds her that I own her genitals and reinforces her role as my child and property' (Califia 1994). In his writing, Califia has repeatedly glorified sexual objectification, incest, Daddy/girl, and master/slave sex scenes. He describes women's approach to sex as unfavorable in comparison with men's approach to sex, reporting that he 'loved the fact that men would walk into bars, grab each other's nipples, and pat each other on the crotch. They could have this ten-second conversation and then go off and fuck . . . You wouldn't get that far with a girl if you bought her dinner for six weeks in a row!' (Califia 1997). In 1993, Patrick Califia carved a swastika into a woman's arm. The woman and her friends retaliated against Califia for carving the swastika into her arm. In response Califia filed charges against the woman and the woman's friends (Califia Attacked . . . 1983).

Sex radicals vociferously assert that prostitution consists of consensual sex in an attempt to legitimize prostitution, which indicates they think it is important for sexual activities to be consensual. However, their lip service to consensual sex is questionable at best. Annie Sprinkle did not allow women to say no to sex partners at a women-only orgy. According to Wendy Chapkis, who was present at the orgy, group sex 'wasn't about choosing a sexual partner, it was about consenting to a collective, group, commercial, sexual experience' (Chapkis 1997). Chapkis goes on to say that 'Shock passed through the room as we realized that we would have no further choice in sex partners . . .' (Chapkis 1997).

Donna Minkowitz describes masturbating to descriptions of a mentally retarded girl who was gang-raped. 'The 1992 gang rape trial of college football players in Glen Ridge, New Jersey, was a bonanza for my fantasy life, with both a baseball bat and a mocked-at, retarded victim' (Minkowitz 1995). She also describes 'trawling' Andrea Dworkin's novel, *Mercy*, searching for depictions of sexual violence. *Mercy* includes descriptions of a woman brutally raped and beaten in jail and prostitution, and by her husband. 'Late at night, I turn the lights down low, uncap some Astroglide, and pull out Andrea Dworkin, trawling for passages . . .' (Minkowitz 1995). The passage Minkowitz quotes from *Mercy* ends with the words: '"he kept tearing me to pieces"' (Minkowitz 1995).

According to sex radicals, if a woman masturbates to the description of a mentally retarded girl gang raped or a woman raped by jailers, tricks, and her husband, well, such is life. Too bad for the women and girls whose pain, death, and humiliation are the impetus for orgasm. Too bad for the millions of women and children around the world who are trafficked in prostitution, beaten by husbands, and raped in their homes. Too bad for the woman torn to pieces. The sex radical wants her porn and her orgasm is more important than anything or anyone else. In the sex radical world, orgasms rule, and 'the bottom line . . . is the need to honor desire' (Queen 1997a).

Lesbian pornography: On Our Backs

Lesbian pornography is often promoted as feminist and as separate and distinct from heterosexual pornography. However, the content of lesbian pornography, as well as its connections with mainstream heterosexual pornography, reveal its anti-feminist and woman-hating politics.

Today, the best-selling lesbian magazine is *On Our Backs*, a purportedly feminist pornographic magazine for lesbians modeled after mainstream pornography such as *Playboy*, *Penthouse*, and *Hustler*. The name is a play on *off our backs*, the oldest feminist periodical still in existence. *On Our Backs* and other lesbian pornographic magazines feature articles and advertisements for mainstream and 'woman-run' sex phone lines; barely legal centerfolds; instructions on how to burn your girlfriend; bondage equipment; floggers; Gay travel guides; lesbian sex bars; fetish auctions; dildos; butt plugs; anal beads; medical sex tools; Bungee sexperience bondage (as seen on Playboy.com); pornographic web sites, magazines, and videos; advertisements for a photolist of Russian women; fetish clothing stores; short stories; photographs; cartoons; interviews; letters to the editor; oversized nude posters; reviews of lesbian bondage and 'daddy/incest' videos; genital piercings; personals; sado-masochistic sex advice; astrology columns; classifieds; and political articles. The articles discuss topics ranging from disabled lesbians and sex, to attacks against individual feminists who oppose pornography, to information on the sexual uses of specula, wartenberg wheels, Str8-Edge Razors, scissors, blind-folds, Str8-jackets, and gags.

On Our Backs claims to offer 'the best of lesbian sex'. However, the standards by which the magazine is determined to be the best of lesbian sex are clearly not feminist. When the best of lesbian sex includes pictures of a white woman pushing a knife into an Asian woman's nipple, it is clear that lesbian pornography holds de Sade and Hitler in higher esteem than feminist principles (On Our Backs 2000).

On Our Backs is now sold at mainstream bookstores such as Borders, where any number of men buy it. (The author worked at a leftist bookstore in the early 1990s where *On Our Backs* was sold. Men purchased the magazine almost exclusively.) *On Our Backs* has direct economic and theoretical ties to the mainstream pornography industry, especially *Playboy*. Lesbian pornography is financially supported by mainstream pornography because it carries advertisements and articles lauding mainstream pornography, especially *Playboy*'s multi-million dollar empire. Individual lesbian sex writers are also financially tied to mainstream pornography. Suzie Bright, former lesbian and editor of *On Our Backs*, writes a column for Playboy.com.

Mainstream pornography and woman-made lesbian pornography have similar themes. In mainstream pornography, lesbian sex as titillation for the male viewer is a common theme. Mainstream pornography says that women can never be sexual with other women unless a male presence is involved as voyeur, physical participant, or in the form of an artificial phallus. In mainstream pornography, lesbian sex gratifies men sexually and politically because lesbian sex is often portrayed as women being cruel to other women. In comparison, in lesbian pornography, the 'female' lesbian in high heels and mini skirt is on her knees sucking the cock dildo of the 'male' lesbian, who pulls the female lesbian's head back by her long hair. There is a look of pain on the 'female' lesbian's face. In other lesbian pornography, women put other women into bondage using handcuffs, masks, ropes, and chains. A chain saw as phallus is next to a breast. A woman in a welder's mask aims a lighted blowtorch at another woman's genitals. Women whip, claw, scratch, and spank each other. Lesbian pornography carries articles and advertises books that detail torture methods for women to use on other women, including how to set one's partner on fire. Woman-made pornographers acknowledge their commonality with mainstream pornography. *Femme Fatale*, a lesbian pornography production company, advertises that the difference between lesbian-produced pornography and mainstream lesbian-themed pornography 'is the lesbians'.

Lesbian pornography, especially *On Our Backs*, is a significant part of contemporary lesbian culture. Thanks in large part to *On Our Backs*, today's lesbians are much more likely to read anti-anti-pornography puerile diatribes written by lesbians against what they call mainstream vanilla feminism than they are to read about and organize against racism and male supremacy. *On Our Backs*' name, the magazine itself, and the politics it endorses, indicate the intentions of lesbian pornographers: to attack feminist politics, collude with straight and gay male pornographers, and put women right back where they have been for centuries: on their backs with their legs spread wide.

Girls to boyz

The short story 'A Night Out With The Boyz' is a stunning example of the complicity of lesbian pornography with male perpetrators. In 'A Night Out With The Boyz', Daddy, Tidbit, and the boyz, Muss and Ben, engage in sado-masochistic sex. All of the characters are biological women, but the boyz and Daddy are referred to by both male and female pronouns. Tidbit is the only 'girl' and the one whom Daddy and the boyz torture. At various points Daddy grabs Tidbit by the hair, plays with her nipples while she is in his lap, orders her to 'Take your shirt off, slut', grabs her by the hair again, calls her 'You, Cunt', slaps her three times, and reddens 'her pate pink nipples' with lipstick. The boyz watch, enthralled. Daddy grabs Tidbit's hair again and asks the boyz, 'I bet you wouldn't mind torturing one, would ya?' The boyz become excited because 'It might be kinda like playing with bugs . . . [t]orturing a girl, yeah, that could be fun.' Ben gets so excited she rubs her cock. Daddy slaps Tidbit again, who is now referred to as Cunt. Cunt starts to cry because it is not fair. Cunt begins to dissociate, 'floating away from Daddy and the boyz.' Tidbit (Cunt) wants the night to be over. Cunt crawls to the center of the room . . . her face just below Ben's crotch'. She notices how big Ben's bulge is and she is surprised because she 'always thought she'd have a skinny, short, little-boy dick'. Ben unzips her leather pants and lets out her cock. Daddy tells Ben to make Cunt beg for the cock. Ben says, 'Whatever the slut's Master wants.' Ben rubs her huge, veined cock against Cunt's cheek until Cunt licks it. This makes Cunt wet. Ben smacks her cock against Cunt's face. Ben makes her beg until Cunt finally calls Ben 'Sir'. Ben makes Cunt bark for her cock. Cunt barks because she wants 'the taste of Ben's cock in her mouth'. Ben has an orgasm when Cunt sucks her cock. The night of sex torture continues until Ben's master shows up to take the boyz home. The sex torture story ends by saying they 'will all see each other the next day at their softball game' (A Night Out . . . 1999).

This story and others like it are considered subversive by sex radicals, apparently because women (transformed into boyz) are portrayed as sexually degrading another woman. This a disturbing and pathetic expression of internalized misogyny, but what makes it worse is that sex radical queers are so totally aligned politically with men who buy and sell women for sex that sex radicals defend them, front for them, and act like them. Sex radicals' collusion with men makes it more difficult for prostituted women and children to get out, gives men an excuse to continue to sexually use women and children, and makes lesbian battering sexy, thereby blurring the line between perpetrator and victim in lesbian battering.

For a woman to masturbate to, or enact, the rape and torture of women and girls she must disassociate from the one being hurt, thereby dissociating from any part of herself that is, has been, or could be victimized. Finding pleasure in another woman's pain is a way to not feel one's own vulnerability or hurt and to do that a woman must get over on other victimized women. The abuse is compounded when a lesbian gets off on a woman being degraded as a lesbian. Both are disassociations from the self as woman and as lesbian in an attempt to identify with not women/lesbians and with men. This is no new, radical sex order. It's just women abusing women.

Boyz is premised upon the negation of women and lesbians; and for a woman or lesbian to dissociate from her gender class she must first dissociate from herself, from her body, especially the pain, embarrassments, and humiliations put upon her for being a girl, woman, and lesbian. In *Bad Girls, Good Girls*, Doyle and Lacombe argue that porn is subversive because 'it reveals how the female viewer does not necessarily automatically identify with the female subject position provided by the text' (Doyle and Lacombe 1996). This is precisely the problem.

The men in the pornography and prostitution industry would like nothing better than for women to use pornography, identify with the sexist and racist sexuality of pornography, and orgasm to the sexual humiliation of women. Celebrating or accepting the sexual degradation of women and girls in pornography and prostitution is connected to what happens in the 'rest of the world'. It is especially harmful when lesbians get off on sexual torture because they are (at least) twice oppressed: as women and as lesbians. In a world where one out of three girls are sexually abused before they turn eighteen; and lesbians are targeted for hate crimes; and lesbians live with disabilities, racism and poverty; and lesbian women and girls are used in pornography, prostitution and battered in relationships; violence against lesbians is not a fantasy. Resistance is crucial to the survival of lesbians, and lesbian pornography negates lesbian existence.

Conclusion

Sex radical women do the pornographers' dirty work by promoting pornography and prostitution as work, freedom, fun, and choice in both lesbian/bisexual communities and mainstream society. They front for rapists and racists. They attack and misrepresent individual feminists and feminist work against pornography and prostitution. Under sex radicalism, the pornography and prostitution industry disappears along with a class-based political analysis of sexism, racism, heterosexism, and classism—leaving a few select, privileged women to write about how they can 'choose' to oppress and be oppressed. Sex radicalism turns away from feminism, embracing a captor/captive mentality as revolutionary. No matter how many cute ways one spells 'boys', celebrating the objectification of women is dehumanizing and reactionary, whether it's men or women doing the objectifying.

When women defend and promote pornography and prostitution, they attach themselves to a politics that hates them and negates their existence. Sex radicals are not rebels; they are dupes of the massive global sex industry, selling out women and by extension themselves. When women sexually use or defend the sexual use of other women, they are complicit with abusers or abusers themselves. They must be held accountable for their part in perpetuating the sexual exploitation of all women and girls. It is radical in every sense of the word when women stand against the pornography and prostitution industry and for the women and girls who are hurt in and because of pornography and prostitution. Anything less is unacceptable.

References

'Califia Attacked for Carving Swastika on S&M Partner'. (1983, January). *off our backs.*

Califia, P. (1994). *Public Sex: The Culture of Radical Sex.* San Francisco: Cleis Press.

Califia, P. (1997). 'Identity Sedition and Pornography'. In C. Queen and L. Schimel (eds). *PoMoSexuals: Challenging Assumptions About Gender and Sexuality.* San Francisco: Cleis Press (pp. 87–106).

Chapkis, W. (1997). *Live Sex Acts: Women Performing Erotic Labor.* New York: Routledge.

Doyle, Kegan and Dany Lacomb. (1996) 'Porn, Power: Sex, Violence and the Meaning of Images in 1980s Feminism'. In N. Bauer Maglin and D. Perry. *Bad Girls, Good Girls: Women Sex and Power in the Nineties.* New York: Rutgers University Press (pp. 188–204).

Jenness, V. (1993). *Making It Work: The Prostitutes' Rights Movement in Perspective.* New York: Aldine De Gruyter.

Minkowitz, D. (1995). 'Giving It Up: Orgasm, Fear, and Femaleness'. In R. Walker (ed.). *To be Real: Telling the Truth and Changing the Face of Feminism* (pp. 77–85). New York: Anchor Books.

Monet, V. (1997). 'No Girls Allowed at the Mustang Ranch'. In J. Nagle, *Whores and Other Feminists.* New York: Routledge (pp. 167–169).

Nagle, J. (1997). Introduction. In Nagle, J. (ed.). *Whores and Other Feminists.* New York: Routledge. (pp. 1–15).

'A Night Out With The Boyz'. (1999). *Bad Attitude: Lesbian Erotic Fiction,* 12 (1).

On Our Backs. (2000) (lesbian magazine).

Queen, C. (1997a). *Real Live Nude Girl: Chronicles of Sex-Positive Culture.* San Francisco: Cleis Press.

Queen, C. (1997b). 'Sex Radical Politics, Sex-Positive Feminist Thought, and Whore Stigma'. In J. Nagle (ed.). *Whores and Other Feminists.* New York: Routledge. (pp. 125–135).

Raymond, J. (1995). *Report to the Special Rapporteur on Violence Against Women: The United Nations, Geneva, Switzerland.* N. Amherst, MA: Coalition Against Trafficking in Women.

Stark, C. and M. Hanson. (1998). Personal communication.

Von Zoticus, L. (1997). 'Butch Gigolette'. In J. Nagle. *Whores and Other Feminists.* New York: Routledge. (pp. 170–176).

PART THREE

Surviving, Conceiving, Confronting

Margaret A. Baldwin

Strategies of connection: Prostitution and feminist politics*

Feminist activists confront profound challenges in crafting feminist strategies against prostitution, and for prostituted women. Those challenges require putting into action the greatest and most demanding strengths of feminism: forging connections among women, confronting the political meaning of our silences, and refusing to abandon any woman by the side of the road. A feminist political approach to prostitution must begin from these strengths, and be tested against the standards set by them. How can we use these strengths to guide our vision of resistance to prostitution? How can we translate these strengths into concrete action? This paper attempts some modest answers to these large questions.

On connection

In feminism, we are committed to promoting solidarity among all women. We do this based on the belief that our experiences as women are linked, and our destinies shared. Yet the divide between 'prostitute' and 'non-prostitute' is thought to describe something meaningful and real, no less in feminist advocacy than in society at large. We assume an antithesis, or at least a difference, between prostituted women and 'other women'. We should know to be cautious about these kinds of assumptions. The history of women's oppression is likewise a tale of fine distinctions made among us: who deserved it, who asked for it, who is made for it, and so on. The history of feminism is, in turn, the history of our resistance to those distinctions. So we need to ask carefully whether, and how, the division between 'prostitutes' and 'other women' has a place in feminist politics. Is prostitution something *distinct* in the experience of women? Or is prostitution but another example of the many practices of sexual subordination—like rape, incest, sexual harassment, and pornography—that are challenged by feminism?

To many of us this may seem a very abstract discussion, lying somewhere between 'so what?' and 'who cares?' That men hurt, despise, and exploit

* This article is an edited version of an article that appeared originally in the Michigan Journal of Gender and the Law 65 (1993). I thank Lily McCarty for editing assistance, and Pearl Seafield, Jonquil Livingston, and Mike Cunningham for technical support.

295

women and girls in and by prostitution should be enough reason for solidarity with survivors. My question, though, is whether *more* is demanded of us in forging a connection between prostitution and other sexual abuse—and between prostitutes and other women—beyond an initial understanding that prostitution is abusive, too. We must, in addition, challenge how prostituted women are seen and treated as 'other': the assumption that whoever we are, the prostitute is not, and vice versa. We have long examined how men's treatment of women as 'other' operates as a practice of domination. Likewise, we need to explore whether prostituted women are treated within feminism as 'other' in this political sense, and if so, how those relationships can be transformed into genuine bonds of solidarity.

This is not to suggest that all women are the same, or experience the same kinds of victimization as women. Certainly, not all women are prostituted, and that is a good thing. Not all women, that is, turn tricks for money, five times a day, thirty-five times a week, with two thousand men a year,[1] while suffering at least the usual incidence of incest, rapes, beatings, and sexual harassment that other women do.[2] The prostitution is on top of that. Many women have to endure only pieces of prostitution. Many women are subjected to unwanted sex from men who objectify us, but not typically from two thousand men a year. Many women suffer serial battery from husbands or lovers, but not typically also at the hands of hundreds of relative strangers. Many women receive money from a harassing boss in the form of a paycheck, but not typically in a context where the harassment *is* the job. Each of these transactions shares something in common with prostitution, but none of them *is* prostitution. We might observe, too, that none of these transactions is exactly like the others, either. Rape is one thing, domestic battery another thing, sexual harassment another, prostitution another. All of them, nevertheless, involve

---

1   For data on the number of prostitution transactions a prostituted women typically experiences weekly or daily, see Perkins and Bennett's (1985) study of prostituted women in Sydney, Australia, reporting an averaged 40 to 50 johns per week, and research conducted by Freund *et al.* (1989) in Camden, New Jersey, indicating that women averaged 4.13 johns per day.

2   Susan Hunter's analysis of the histories of women involved in the Council for Prostitution Alternatives (CPA) program documents the prevalence of abuse suffered by prostituted women. See generally Hunter (1993). Other available data suggests that between 60% and 70% of women in prostitution were sexually abused as children. See Silbert and Pines' (1982) analysis of data from interviews with 200 'street prostitutes'. See also Silbert's (1980) data indicating that 65% of her survey sample of prostituted women had been raped, 85% of them before the victim was 15. For a summary of the data reporting incidence of rape and battery, see Weisberg (1985) at 108–110; see also Silbert and Pines' (1981) report that 70% of the street prostitutes they interviewed had been raped by johns, and 65% had been beaten by them; see also Nancy Erbe's (1984) summary of data on sexual and physical abuse of prostituted girls and women.

some expression or manifestation of sexual ownership. Each of these practices, understood this way, is like a particular tactical weapon in the arsenal of male dominance—each can be deadly, even if differently deployed.

On this understanding, the political 'otherness' of prostitution can be dispelled simply by 'adding on' prostitution to our existing feminist reform agenda. Much of the groundwork developed by prostitution support agencies founded in the 1980s represented 'add on' efforts of this kind, providing prostituted women with safe space, material support, health resources, collective encouragement and avenues for political confrontation. These groups organized brilliantly to extend battered women's services to women in prostitution, challenging practices that excluded prostituted women and girls from shelters and from the vision of the anti-sexual violence movement. The National Coalition Against Sexual Assault and individual and statewide rape crisis organizations also worked to recognize prostitution as a practice of sexual violence and exploitation of women. The Coalition Against Trafficking in Women has advocated similar interventions at the international level. This work was not easy to accomplish, and needs the continued support of survivors and their allies to sustain and move forward.

In Florida, the state where I live, there is an enormous prostitution industry. On the 'demand' side, the industry is fueled by the usual local suspects, by the vast tourist contingent on vacation at Disney World, and by the residents of several naval and air force bases. Yet we do not have even one shelter or support program specifically for prostituted women and girls in Florida. But in the spirit of 'adding on' prostitution to the feminist agenda, about ten years ago a handful of us were able to persuade our state Supreme Court Gender Bias Commission to address prostitution as an issue of discrimination against women in Florida.[3] The effort proved sadly fruitful. The commission concluded that 'the justice system's present response to prostitution exhibits some of the most egregious gender bias to be found anywhere' (Tannen 1990, p. 892). The commission rejected the commonly held view of prostitution as a 'victimless crime'.[4] Rather, it found that prostitution exploits the isolation and vulnerability of sexually and physically abused girls, and is maintained through coercion, while 'enforcement practices hold women culpable for the offense' (Tannen 1990, p. 906).

The commission's reform recommendations echo the strategies historically pursued on behalf of other victims of sexual violence: advocacy support for

---

3 So far, Florida's commission is the only state commission that has done so. See Tannen (1990).
4 The commission consequently refused to endorse the legalization of prostitution. Legalizing abuse, in the commission's view, is clearly not an appropriate response to discrimination against abuse victims. See Tannen (1990) at p. 905.

victims and criminal intervention against perpetrators. Victim advocacy suggestions include establishment of support programs for women and girls in prostitution, increased funding for both battered women's shelters and victim services outreach organizations for prostituted women and girls, and staff training for meeting victims' needs (Tannen 1990, p. 907). Enhanced penalties for pimping and procuring are encouraged, and enforcement of existing prostitution sanctions against johns are urged (Tannen 1990, p. 907–908).

The commission's findings also implicitly challenge the basic presumption dividing prostitutes from other women: the presumption that prostitutes 'consent' to prostitution. Another recommendation, that the legislature enact a statutory civil remedy for women and girls pimped in prostitution (Tannen 1990, p. 908), opened the door for that challenge to be articulated even more directly. I was asked by State Representative Helen Davis to draft the substantive provisions of a bill creating effective civil remedies more broadly for any 'nonconsensual' prostitution. The proposed bill became law in Florida in 1992, and affords compensatory and punitive damages for girls and women coerced in prostitution.[5] The process of defining 'coercion', as that term was used in the statute, created a rich opportunity for developing a feminist concept of consent in the context of prostitution.

In drafting the definition of coercion, I was again aided by feminist reform work on behalf of other victims of sexual violence. For if the presumption of prostitutes' consent is especially entrenched, every other feminist reform initiative against sexual violence has confronted similar victim-blaming obstacles. The litany is familiar: rape victims ask for it, battery victims provoke it, sexual harassment victims manipulatively sleep their way to the top. Where name-calling fails, the victim's judgment is questioned. Again, the litany is familiar: What was she doing there? Why didn't she leave? What did she get out of it? In the domestic battery context, feminists have responded to the 'why did she stay?' question by detailing how repeated battery impairs a woman's ability to take action, and how male violence usually escalates when a woman does attempt to leave. More assertively, we have questioned why a woman has to leave her own home anyway, as the price of proving she did not consent to being routinely beaten there.

I approached the task of defining coercion in the prostitution statute from a similar perspective. Like other forms of sexual abuse, prostitution is often compelled by physical force or its threat, by physical and mental torture, and by kidnapping. The statute thus prohibits prostitution induced by those means.[6] Tactics of control exploiting the legal and related social vulnerabilities

---

5   FLA. STAT. ANN section 769.09 (Harrison 1992).
6   Section 796.09(3) (a)–(c).

of girls and women in prostitution are also defined as non-consensual, including prostitution induced by threats of legal complaint, promise of legal benefit, threat of report of delinquency, extortion, blackmail, and threat of legal interference with the woman's relationship with her children.[7] In addition, the statute defines as coercive those sexual 'bargains' which exploit women's isolation, deprivation, and despair. Thus, the statute prohibits inducement to prostitution by:

(k) Restraint of speech or communication with others.

(l) Exploitation of a condition of developmental disability, cognitive limitation, affective disorder or substance dependency.

(m) Exploitation of victimization by sexual abuse.

(n) Exploitation of pornographic performance.

(o) Exploitation of human needs for food, shelter, safety, or affection.[8]

These provisions affirm simply that women and girls are not available for prostitution, and do not consent to it, by the fact of being human, with real needs, real vulnerabilities, and real wounds. They also pose the question, and answer it in the negative, whether prostitution should be the price that women are expected to pay for being homeless, unloved, jobless, and afraid. Taken together, these provisions also describe the conditions under which most, if not all, prostitution occurs.

You can do this kind of work in solidarity with prostituted women, whether in law reform, through advocacy, or in providing important recovery services. Contact the staffs and boards of your local shelters, rape crisis services, and statewide coalitions. Find out whether women in prostitution are being provided services and whether staffs are trained to assist girls and women in prostitution, and insist that they contact a prostitution recovery agency for knowledge about how to do it. Explore the possibilities of funding and staffing a support service for girls and women in prostitution in your hometown. Lobby your legislatures to enact new statutory remedies for women and girls in prostitution, and to order enforcement of sanctions against johns. Educate yourself and other women about how sexual harassment claims might be crafted on behalf of women in prostitution, in strip clubs, and other 'live sex' operations. In any forum in which violence against women, women's poverty, or the sexual exploitation of children is on the table, take initiative in

---

7   Section 796.09(3) (d)–(h).

8   Section 796.09(3) (k)–(o). Also prohibited are inducements by 'promise of greater financial rewards'. Section 796.09(3) (i). This would include acting or modeling contracts conditioned on acts of prostitution. Prostitution induced by 'promise of marriage' is also prohibited. Section 796.09(3) (j).

addressing the victimization of women and girls in prostitution as a necessary focus of political action against those practices.

These 'add-on' strategies, though, are not complete ones. There is more at stake in the 'otherness' of prostitution than simple ignorance or neglect, as in 'Oops, we forgot prostitution'. For underlying each of our principal strategies in rape law reform, in domestic battery and self-defense work, and in sexual harassment resistance, is an assertion crying out to be believed—we are *not prostitutes*. Our rape shield rules are crafted to distinguish in a juror's mind between the woman testifying that a man raped her, and the prostitute who presumably has sex with anyone, consensually. Our domestic battery reforms have hinged on descriptions of the love and intimacy connecting a woman to an intimate other, explaining in sanitized 'good girl' terms both why women do not abandon abusive men and why they sometimes kill them. The leading premise of anti-sexual harassment advocacy—that sex as work injures women—falters in the case of prostitution, which is seen by non-prostitutes as a consensual 'job' and therefore harmless.[9] These are all strategies of *disconnection*—put bluntly, of trying to get the best deal we can from a legal system that only has time and sympathy for women who are not identified as prostitutes, by distancing 'us' from 'them'. There is simply no way for women in prostitution to be 'added on' to these strategies respectfully.

I have thought a lot about this business, and I have come to think of the expulsion of prostitutes from the mainstream feminist legal agenda as the prostitution of the feminist movement by law. I say this with love, with as much love as I have for myself as a feminist and for prostituted women. Like women in prostitution, feminism too has been channeled, deprived, punished, and cajoled to maintain certain limits, to please in certain ways—conditions which may have come to seem normal for us, and which some of us will at times enthusiastically say we chose. An essential term of this sexual-political bargain is a tacit agreement to certain discrete silences: silences about men, silences about women in prostitution, and silences about the experience of women who are not prostituted. I would suggest that by politicizing these silences—by understanding how certain relationships of power are maintained by them—we may begin to develop a more liberating, and genuine, connection between prostitutes and other women.

On silences

The biggest silence maintained by the anti-prostitute design of our sexual violence work is silence about johns. In reality, they are mostly white, married men with at least a little disposable income—real people, that is. Empirical

---

9   For a more complete analysis of these difficulties, see Baldwin (1992), p. 47.

research on johns is almost non-existent.[10] Since johns are rarely arrested, their identities remain shielded from public disclosure, as well as from criminal sanction. Even johns themselves try to avoid the label. In prostitution transactions, johns frequently adopt a variety of sexual roles—as boyfriend, as lover, as father, sometimes as punitive avenger of the public good. By insisting on these roles, a john avoids seeing himself as just a trick. On all of these fronts—academic, legal, and personal—who johns are, why they buy women, and their culpability for doing so, are evaded questions.

Two important potential sources of information about johns do exist: data that emerges from enforcement of car forfeiture ordinances, and information supplied by prostituted women themselves. Car forfeiture laws allow the police to seize any vehicle used by a john in the course of a prostitution transaction. Forfeiture sanctions have been very effective in both deterring men from buying women, and identifying johns to the communities they value, including their families and employers. Forfeiture ordinances enacted in Portland, Oregon; St. Paul, Minnesota; Minneapolis, Minnesota; and Wayne County, Michigan have been enforced to dramatic effect. Elizabeth Sipe reports that the 'first year the St. Paul ordinance was in effect more than 130 vehicles had been seized', while the county attorney in Wayne County has a staff of three committed to prostitution car seizures (Sipe 1992). A Michigan forfeiture law was upheld by the United States Supreme Court in 1996, opening the door for other municipalities and states to enact and enforce similar forfeiture measures across the country.[11]

However, few other states have chosen to do so. The St. Paul forfeiture ordinance was declared unconstitutional by the Minnesota Court of Appeal in 1992, because the court interpreted state law to prohibit cities from enacting such ordinances without state-level authorization.[12] Likewise, the Florida Gender Bias Commission rejected a recommendation that the state legislature adopt similar legislation, concerned that the penalty would affect johns too harshly. A proposed forfeiture bill, introduced in the Florida Legislature in the 1992 session, was never passed out of committee.[13] To date, then, johns are still largely protected from the community disclosure that car forfeiture penalties bring about, except in the few jurisdictions that enforce them.

---

10 For a survey of research on johns, see Holzman and Pines (1982).
11 *Bennis v. Michigan*, 116 S. Ct. 994 (1996). The case was brought by the john's wife, who was a co-owner of the seized car.
12 *State v. Gonzalez*, 483 N.W.2d 736 (Minn. Ct. App. 1992).
13 Florida law does provide for revocation of johns' drivers licenses when they are arrested for prostitution using their cars. See FLA. STAT. ANN. section 322.26(7) (mandating license revocation for conviction for prostitution offenses effected through the use of a motor vehicle).

Prostituted women and girls themselves, who have the most insight and information on johns, have also been silenced. The prostitution itself takes its toll: in despair, depression, denial, drug abuse, isolation, torture, and murder. Many women do not survive. Women who do survive prostitution usually find recalling and retelling their experiences enormously painful and disturbing. The law, too, plays a role in silencing survivors. Criminal records, mental health treatment histories, and substance abuse issues compromise a prostituted woman's credibility, assuming she ever gets to talk at all about the men who buy her. The occasions where she might talk are few enough, anyway, under a legal regime always ready to justify the abuse of 'real' prostitutes. The obvious beneficiaries of the suppression of prostituted women's voices, again, are the johns who use them.

We need to begin to understand the stake that men have in not being named as johns, whether by themselves, by other men, or by prostitution survivors. Perhaps non-prostitutes, especially white, middle-class, married women, have some stake in this separation, too. It is uncomfortable to think of your nice husband or retired dad as a guy who buys women and girls for sex. Maybe this is a reason, however unconscious, for non-prostituted women, especially white, middle-class, married women, to keep separating themselves from prostitutes and their own abuse from prostitution. In any case, there is an obvious historical continuity available for understanding these arrangements, permitting mostly white men to buy 'bad' women for sex, while their wives and daughters avert their eyes in complicity and shame. I am referring to the institutionalized prostitution of African-American women in slavery.[14] In real life, women of color, particularly African-American and American Indian women, and poor women of all races, are disproportionately targeted for prostitution[15] and most likely to be seen as consenting to it. Thus, to say that prostitution is 'just like' other forms of sexual abuse is to ignore the racism and classism that supports the mass prostitution of women and girls, especially of young Black women, in this country. The 'otherness' of prostitution, then, is part and parcel of the otherness of race and class and needs to be confronted as such.

Moreover, we know that some of the realities of prostitution are not confined to prostitution itself. I have been thinking and talking with women for many years about how we experience sexual exploitation as 'incomplete' prostitution—exploring incest as a practice of pimping, rape as an act of

---

14 See White's (1985) description of the prostitution of enslaved women and the response of white women; also see Giddings' (1984) analysis of the consent-based justifications used to support the prostitution of enslaved women.

15 For analysis of the data on the racial demographics of prostitution, see Weisberg (1985), at 87–88. On the economic dimension, see Romenesko and Miller (1989). See generally Carter and Giobbe (1999).

attempted prostitution, sexual harassment as recruitment to prostitution, and domestic violence as one long, bad, ugly trick. Each of these forms of sexual exploitation often entails some measure of sexual bargaining: for survival, for some remnant of control, even—God forbid—for something we might be able to *use*. At the bottom of many women's deeply felt belief that they asked for or deserved abusive treatment, I believe, is the shame of the deal. We need to take the first step to acknowledge this, and then take the further step to acknowledge prostitution as both the model and measure of its harm. Until we do, we will not adequately grasp the harm of prostitution, or the silence of women's unarticulated confusion in the face of it. Moreover, this approach demands real political accountability *to* prostituted women, rather than simply acknowledging a passing acquaintance among us. This connection not only concedes that prostituted women are hurt; it also affirms that the voice and participation of prostituted women are necessary to understand the conditions of all women's lives.

In addition, the example of prostitution also helps us take into account the number of men from whom women sustain these injuries, in every arena of our lives simultaneously. The legal segmentation of domestic battery from rape, and both from sexual harassment, suggests that women are abused by only one man, and only in one locale, at a time. In prostituted women's lives, these boundaries are not so fixed. Whether a woman is on the street, turning tricks, or at whatever place she calls 'home', sexual exploitation and abuse is a given. I think this is true in most women's lives, at different intensities. One man is not the same as two thousand. Nor is one man the same as the 20, or 30, or 50 men any woman could probably name as directly contributing to her history of sexual abuse by the time she is thirty years old. The example of prostitution helps us all to grasp the significance of this day by day, man after man, home-work-street abuse that 'one man/one place' legal descriptions overlook. Moreover, forging these connections challenges the real separations to which male supremacy devotes its deepest commitments: separating normal men from johns, and separating both (who are in reality often the same person) from incesting fathers, alcoholic husbands, not-getting-it bosses, and violent, gun-wielding rapists who do 'real' harm. Prostituted women face all of these men every day, day after day, undefended and alone.

The road

On October 9, 2002, a prostituted woman named Aileen Wuornos was executed by the State of Florida. She had been arrested in 1990 and charged with killing seven johns over a two-year period. She said she killed these men in self-defense; seven of the probably 4000 men who bought her over that time. With maybe one exception, each of these johns was a 'nice' white married guy—one a child abuse investigator, another a former missionary. She stood alone at the side of the road—literally, for twenty years.[16] It is time for us to join her.

References

Baldwin, Margaret A. (1992). 'Split at the Root: Prostitution and Feminist Discourses of Law Reform'. *Yale Journal of Law and Feminism*, 5.

Carter, Vednita and Evelina Giobbe. (1999). 'Duet: Prostitution, Racism and Feminist Discourse'. *Hastings Women's Law Journal*, 10.

Chesler, Phyllis. (1993). 'A Woman's Right to Self-Defense: The Case of Aileen Carol Wuornos'. *St. John's Law Review*, 66.

Erbe, Nancy. (1984). 'Prostitutes: Victims of Men's Exploitation and Abuse'. *Law and Inequality Journal*, 2.

Freund, Matthew *et al.* (1989). 'Sexual Behavior of Resident Street Prostitutes with their Clients in Camden, New Jersey'. *Journal of Sex Research*, 26.

Giddings, Paula. (1984). *When and Where I Enter: The Impact of Black Women on Race and Sex in America*. New York: William Morrow.

Holzman, Harold R. and Sharon Pines. (1982). 'Buying Sex: The Phenomenology of Being a John'. *Deviant Behavior*, 4.

Hunter, Susan Kay. (1993). 'Prostitution is Cruelty and Abuse to Women and Children'. *Michigan Journal of Gender and Law*, 1.

James, Jennifer and Jane Meyerding. (1977). 'Early Sexual Experience and Prostitution'. *American Journal of Psychology*, 134.

Perkins, Roberta and Garry Bennett. (1985). *Being a Prostitute: Prostitute Women and Prostitute Men*. Boston, MA: Allen and Unwin.

Romenesko, Kim and Eleanor M. Miller. (1989). 'The Second Step in Double Jeopardy: Appropriating the Labor of Female Street Hustlers'. *Crime and Delinquency*, 35.

Silbert, Mimi H. (1980). 'Sexual Assault of Prostitutes: Phase One' p. 85, cited in D. Kelly Weisberg. (1985). *Children of the Night: A Study of Adolescent Prostitution*, p. 136, note 89.

Silbert, Mimi H. and Ayala M. Pines. (1981). 'Occupational Hazards of Street Prostitutes'. *Criminal Justice and Behavior*, 8.

Silbert, Mimi H. and Ayala M. Pines. (1982). 'Entrance Into Prostitution'. *Youth and Society*, 13.

---

16 See *State v. Wuornos*, 644 So. 2d 1000 (Fla. 1994). For a feminist analysis of the Wuornos case, see Chesler (1993).

Sipe, Elizabeth. (1992). 'Car Confiscation Ordinance Overturned'. *WHISPER Newsletter*, 1. Minneapolis, MN: WHISPER.

Tannen, Ricki Lewis. (1990). 'Report of the Florida Supreme Court Gender Bias Study Commission'. *Florida Law Review*, 42.

Weisberg, D. Kelly. (1985). *Children of the Night: A Study of Adolescent Prostitution*. Lanham, MD: Rowman and Littlefield.

White, Deborah Gray. (1985). *Ar'n't I a Woman: Female Slaves in the Plantation South*. New York: Norton.

Sherry Lee Short

Making hay while the sun shines: The dynamics of rural strip clubs in the American Upper Midwest, and the community response

> I asked the then president of [the] bank . . . what he thought about Teddy's having dancers . . . He said I would have to be crazy if I didn't: 'You have to make hay while the sun shines'.[1]
>
> —Teddy Bellmore, co-owner of Teddy's strip bar in Wahpeton, North Dakota

Across the country, in both urban and rural areas, the stripping industry is rapidly expanding. Forty new clubs have opened each year since 1986.[2] The growth of the stripping industry parallels the expansion of other industries and businesses profiting from the economic and political status of women and children. It parallels the growth of internet pornography, Hooters restaurants,[3] and Howard Stern-style radio and television.[4] The increased patronage of the stripping industry also reflects the American cultural tolerance for social inequality and the growing popular resistance to feminism and other avenues for achieving equity.

Many of the new strip clubs are the so-called gentlemen's clubs that are located in metropolitan areas. Many of these clubs cater to businessmen who may spend upwards to $2000 a night on drinks, food, and private contact dances. Through website advertising, promotional advertising in mainstream press, and listings with chambers of commerce, such 'upscale' clubs have con-

---

1 Statement made at Wahpeton City Council meeting, August 5, 1996. Videotape recording of the meeting on file at the Women's Network of the Red River Valley, Moorhead, Minnesota.
2 Estimates vary regarding the number of new clubs that open each year. According to the ABC News program, 20/20, 250 clubs opening between 1987 and 1997 (see Stossel, 'A Day at the Office'. ABC News. 20/20. September 26, 1997). According to *Working Woman* magazine, 300 clubs opened during the six-year period between 1986 and 1992 (see 'The New Old-Boys Clubs'. *Working Woman*. August 1992, p. 18).
3 Hooters is a national American chain restaurant. 'Hooters' is American slang for 'breasts'. The restaurants hire only young, female waitresses. The uniforms are mini-shorts and tight T-shirts with 'Hooters' written across the chest.
4 The Howard Stern Show is a popular raunchy, liberal radio and television broadcast.

306

tributed to the mainstreaming of stripping into American culture and social practices. Nested in urban downtown business districts, they have blended themselves into the American business scene in an attempt to camouflage— or alternatively, legitimize—the industry's connection to other aspects of commercial sexual exploitation such as pornography and prostitution.

Rural communities also host their share of these new strip bars. Rural bars are both different from and similar to metropolitan bars. Unlike metropolitan clubs, rural clubs cater largely to tourists, truckers, hunters and fishermen, military personnel, as well as local community men. Rural clubs are typically smaller and less lucrative, nevertheless, they form a significant part of the growing stripping industry. In addition, rural strip bars, like metropolitan bars, have a significant relationship to the economy of the communities in which they are established. Indeed, the dynamics of rural strip clubs are intimately bound with the dynamics of the rural economy. Many small communities are no longer able to depend on agriculture or seasonal attractions such as fishing or hunting to sustain them. New businesses need to be established, in particular businesses that bring in a dependable flow of outside capital to revive and sustain the local economy. Such economic hardship is a magnet for the sex industry.

The economic hardships experienced by women are particularly attractive to sex industry businesses. In fact, the poverty of women is a necessary condition for the establishment and survival of the sex industry. Economic opportunities for women in many rural areas are extremely limited. Often, jobs simply are not there. Most of the opportunities that do exist are at minimum wage levels or just above. Poor women who live in isolated rural areas may not be able to afford a car, its insurance, and the gas needed to travel to and from such low-paying jobs. In addition, opportunities for higher education are very limited for all rural women unless they can afford to travel and leave their families. This creates a pool of women vulnerable for recruitment into the sex industry.

As a result, a disproportionate number of strip clubs exists in a number of Upper Midwest communities (seven largely rural states in the upper-midsection of the United States). For example, Aberdeen, South Dakota, with a population of 25,000, has five strip bars. Remarkably, Aberdeen is a hundred miles from any town of comparable size. Clearly, neither the size of the community nor its proximity to other communities determines the number of sex industry businesses that may be established. The dynamics of the economy, compounded by local and regional cultural and social practices regarding women and men, historical factors, and other characteristics, lay the foundation on which the sex industry is built. The number of strip bars in Aberdeen attests to the fact that social and political characteristics of small and mid-sized communities in the Upper Midwest are inviting to sex industry entrepreneurs.

Nevertheless, rural community members are often unprepared for the development of such businesses and startled when the prostitution of women traveling on the stripping circuit makes the local press. Many of these communities have wrongly believed that 'traditional' rural values create an immunity to sex industry exploitation, consequently, these communities find themselves in disorganized public debates over 'the legislation of morality' and 'free speech' and have little understanding either of the local dynamics that laid the foundation for sex industry businesses, or of the greater context of the sex industry as a whole. Rural farming communities, park and recreation areas, and hunting and fishing towns tend to define the growing rural stripping industry as an external invasion from urban areas, and do not recognize the industry's connections to the history and internal dynamics of rural communities themselves. As a result, the sex industry businesses often get the upper hand in organizing when threatened by community resistance.

The purpose of this paper is two-fold. First, it is to analyze the dynamics of the stripping industry in rural areas. As part of this analysis, the paper will briefly examine the collective rhetoric espoused by pro-sex industry academics, activists, and pimps—rhetoric that upholds the industry and manipulates political and personal tolerance and support for the sexual exploitation of women and children. It will then overview the ways in which the rural stripping industry is part of, tied to, supported by, and contributes to the greater network of the sex industry on a regional, national, and international scale. It will also explore how the dynamics of the rural economy affect both recruitment and entrapment of women in the industry.

Second, this paper will examine both anti-strip club and pro-strip club organizing efforts in rural communities. Specific case studies from communities in North Dakota will be used. These sections will also show how the dynamics of the rural economy create a fundamental and growing acceptance in communities for new and existing clubs.

This paper is not intended to be a comprehensive analysis. Indeed, it is an introductory analysis describing a new field of activism, organizing, and research.

Rhetoric

He said, 'You'll be in power. You'll be in control' . . . This is what is called 'pimp propaganda.'[5]

—Heidi Somerset, former dancer, describing the man who recruited her into stripping

---

5   Comment made by Heidi Somerset during a public talk at the Moorhead Public Library, October 11, 1996. Videotape recording of the presentation is on file at the Women's Network of the Red River Valley, Moorhead, Minnesota. Talk was co-presented with Vicki Smiley. Both presenters were survivors of the sex industry and had been prostituted in rural communities.

Much of the organizing efforts for and against strip clubs take place concurrently with a public exchange of rhetoric, whether through letters published in local papers, statements before city commissions, or the publication of articles, essays, and books. Regardless of the source, the arguments of pro-sex industry advocates and proponents have a common theme: the industry springs from a liberal mindset and frees women and men, sexually, politically, and spiritually.[6] Part of this logic is that sexuality—particularly women's sexuality—has been oppressed historically and that the sex industry offers women and men the liberating possibility of unbridled sexual expression.

This logic ignores the fact that the use of women in prostitution as well as other forms of human sexual commodification has existed for as least as long as there has been an historical record. Thus, if sexual commodification were freeing, then sexual oppression would be uncommon or, more likely, exist only as some curious historical fact.

This logic also ignores the reality that the sex industry thrives where the political, social, and religious milieu is fundamentally conservative. It thrives where beliefs about women and children and their roles are the most traditional. Trafficking patterns on a global scale involve women and children being recruited or sold to traffickers from countries that have entrenched patriarchy. They are then sold to brothel owners, club managers, and pimps in a second country that also has entrenched patriarchal ideas about gender roles.[7]

Thus, 'liberal' support for the sex industry is only a mask for the traditional face of prostitution. A sexually freeing or liberating industry offering unique and new experiences of choice and revolutionary change for women and

---

6   Examples are too numerous to adequately cite. For reference see McElroy, W. (1995). *XXX: A Woman's Right to Pornography* (New York: St. Martins Press: 'Pornography benefits women, both personally and politically', p. i; National Coalition Against Censorship. (1993). 'The Sex Panic: Women, Censorship and "Pornography"' [conference proceedings]. New York: NCAC: '. . . if women's ignorance and shame are to be lessened and new attitudes and behaviors submitted . . . what's needed is more [pornographic] materials, p. 10; Stubbs, K.R. (1997). *The New Sexual Healers: Women of the Light.* California: Secret Garden Press: 'The [modern prostitutes] in this book are contemporary human beings serving a significant sexual function in our culture: we see them walking in grace and beauty on a sacred sexual path', p. 239; Flynt, L. '21st Century Flynt: Larry Flynt on *Hustler*, Hollywood And How to Save the Country' *Larry Flynt*, April 7,1997: 'It's hard to fathom something with more socially redeeming value than pornography', p. 80; Quan, 'The VOX Fights', *Vox*, Winter 1991: 'Prostitutes have furthered the cause of women's independence . . . In essence, it is the prostitute's ability to *control* her sexuality . . . that is key to her independence, her source of strength within society', p. 32.

7   For analyses of traditional values and cultural beliefs about women and children in relationship to international trafficking, see Fund for Women. (1996). *Sisters and Daughters Betrayed: The trafficking of women and girls and the fight to end it* (videotape). See also Brock, R.N. and Thistlewaite, S. (1996). *Casting Stones: Prostitution and Liberation in Asia and the United States*, Minnesota: Augsburg Fortress Publishers.

children would not be characterized by bodies being exchanged for money or other payment. Indeed, the exchange of bodies for money or other payment is a very old and un-revolutionary practice. Prior to sex industry rhetoric, this was referred to as bondage, slavery, or indentured servitude.

Nevertheless, the rhetoric of the sex industry has been highly successful, in part because it has co-opted the language of feminism. The phrases 'women's rights', 'sexual liberation', 'sexual equality', 'power', and 'choice' are commonly used both by writers defending the sex industry as well as recruiters for strip clubs, prostitution, and pornography. For example, the titles of a number of recent books defending the sex industry utilize the language of equality, including Nadine Strossen's *Defending Pornography: Free Speech, Sex, and the Fight for Women's Rights* and Wendy McElroy's *XXX: A Woman's Right to Pornography*. The use of the language of equality has not only made the sex industry, including strip clubs, more acceptable to communities but also has contributed to breaking down women's resistance to commercial sexual exploitation. For many women who become involved with stripping, sex industry rhetoric about choice and power, including economic power, has everything to do with their recruitment. Take, for example, the following excerpt from an internet ad:

> This can be an ideal position for college students seeking a stable part-time income, or even a way to pay for their entire college education. If you've ever wondered what it might be like to be onstage, here's your golden opportunity'.[8]

However, other pages from the same website, pages recruiting *patrons* to the establishment, reveal the reality under the recruitment rhetoric: the dancers are trained in bondage and domination, 'virtually any fetish that you can imagine', and are available to patrons in 'fantasy suites'.[9] Dancers become involved in the industry through promises of lucrative careers and empowering experiences. Many dancers find otherwise.

Global patterns/local lessons

> Filipina women are . . . friendly and extremely affectionate . . . At the end of the day, they hope to meet the man of their dreams, who will sweep them off their feet, and transport them magically to a land far away from the poverty they are used to . . . in other words, if you go to a bar and find a girl you like at 8 p.m., you pay a

8   'Girls Wanted to Become Highly Paid Entertainers', 1997. Available at
   http://www.fantasysex.com/helpwant.html
9   'Welcome to Club Can Can', 1997. Available at
   http://www.fantasysex.com/cancan.html

total of 600P,[10] and she'll fuck and suck you until 10 a.m. the next day! . . . This has got to be the best deal in earth![11]

—Philippines strip club review from the internet

I strongly recommend Milano's . . . the dancers are much more willing to spend (uncompensated) time with the customers . . . Lawrence also has a new place . . . but it's more expensive . . . with mandatory tipping if next to the stage. Not recommended.[12]

—Kansas strip club review from the internet

Regardless of how women become involved in systems of prostitution, the sex industry has no intent of allowing women to make enough money to pull themselves free, even though some may. Sex industry 'businessmen', pimps, managers, film producers, and strip club owners do not run their businesses on equitable philosophies and practices. Prostituted women do not receive health care benefits, paid vacations, social security, or retirement benefits. Instead, the industry sets up systems that ensure women's servitude. Poor women on the local and global scale are recruited into an industry that only benefits by their entrapment. In the Netherlands, women trafficked from eastern and central Europe are literally locked into clubs until they can pay off their debt to the club that recruited them.[13] In Toronto clubs, newly trafficked Thai women work for just $1 a dance; the other $9 goes straight to the club.[14] On the rural strip circuits in the American Midwest, many dancers also work to pay their 'debts' to their pimps:

I am going to give an example of a bar in South Dakota. The situation was one woman had her pimp along . . . and she had to meet the quota. So she had to do whatever it takes to get that money. The men shoved bullets up her, beer bottles, shoved dollar bills up her, and this was the situation that I encountered.[15]

---

10 At the time this comment was posted on the internet (1996), 600P in the Philippines was equivalent to approximately $US25.00.
11 'World Sex Guide Document: Angeles-City', February 1999. Available at http://www.smutland.com
12 'Grimace Nudie Club Listing', 1996. Was available at http://access.digex.net/~Idgrim/ks.html. Grimace Nudie Club Listing no longer posts patron comments. Printouts of Grimace Nudie Club Listing patron comments for North Dakota, South Dakota, Kansas, Iowa, and Wisconsin from 1996 are on file with the author.
13 International Organization for Migration. (1995). 'Trafficking and Prostitution: The Growing Exploitation of Migrant Women from Central and Eastern Europe'. Available at http://www.iom.int/DOCUMENTS/PUBLICATION/EN/MIP_traff_women_eng.pdf
14 *MacLeans*, 'A No to Dirty Dancing', July 17, 1995, pp. 34–35.
15 See Somerset (Note 5).

Examining who has and who has not goes a long way in completing an understanding of the dynamics of the sex industry. Globally, individuals, communities, and even governments seek to cash in on the economic subordination of women and children. Indeed, many communities and governments have found an 'economic miracle' in marketing the bodies of the economically disenfranchised: the phenomenon known as 'sex tourism'.

The dynamics of sex tourism have been examined by a number of researchers in a variety of important, recent books on the international trafficking of women and children. These books primarily focus on the major trafficking centers of Thailand and the Philippines as well as Vietnam, Korea, Japan, and western and central Europe. Domestic issues of trafficking continue to be understudied, including the dynamics of trafficking and sex tourism in rural America. Rural strip circuits throughout the US may be accurately defined as a form of trafficking. In addition, rural strip circuits have connections to other forms of trafficking in women and children in North America.

Although the individual experiences of women on the stripping circuit vary, there are also some identifiable patterns. Typically, most dancers strip in more than one bar. The reasons for this are numerous. For example, a dancer may move from working in one bar to another in hopes of finding a better working environment. Alternatively, a dancer is typically not booked for enough hours in one bar to be able to make a satisfactory living and, therefore, will work in one or more other establishments. Moreover, patrons are not entertained by seeing one woman dance all evening. Instead, patrons prefer to have many dancers competing with each other for tips. This creates a much more exciting environment for the patrons and increases their power over the strippers (patrons withhold tips from dancers who are not willing to accommodate their requests, and pay those who do). Club owners facilitate this by over-booking dancers. Within this competitive environment, few dancers can make enough money by working in only one bar.

Women who work in strip clubs in rural areas often have to travel great distances between each club. In a typical month, dancers may cross several state lines, living transient lifestyles. Some women travel independently or with other dancers. Other dancers will travel with husbands or boyfriends, who are best identified as pimps as they are the economic and other beneficiaries of the sexual servitude of their 'partners'. Yet other dancers may be driven from club to club by employees of the establishments, never having control of where they are going or how they are getting there.

Once working in a club, each dancer is controlled by club rules and by a manager who enforces them. Club rules may include not being allowed to use the bathroom without permission, or paying a fine for having gained weight.[16]

---

16 See Somerset (Note 5) and for more detailed statistical and other research on customer and management harassment and abuse, see Holsopple, K. 'Strip Clubs According to

Part of the unwritten contract between the manager and a dancer—or her pimp—may be that she has to perform a sexual act with the manager to bind the contract, an experience reported by dancers in urban and rural areas alike:

> One thing that I wanted to mention that I found extremely sick and sticks out in my mind with the job interview for these jobs . . . and it basically was if the person that was interviewing you decided that you were supposed to do something sexual, if you wanted the job, you'd better do it.[17]

During her week of performance at a club on the rural strip circuit, the dancer may be set up on 'dates' (prostitution) by the manager who may also schedule her at his discretion for bachelor and retirement parties. This degree of sexual servitude and control, combined with the trans-state migration of women working on the circuit, is aptly defined as 'trafficking'.

The rural strip circuit in the Upper Midwest is also tied to trafficking in children. Some Midwest states are documented as key recruiting areas within the United States for pimps looking for children to traffic into prostitution in urban areas.[18] Many children are also trafficked *within* rural areas. Evidence from dancers' anecdotes indicates that rural clubs are more likely to have underage children performing than urban ones. At times, a pimp will have a number of children that he will drop off at the beginning of the week at one club, pick them up at the end of the week, then drive them to another club for the following week. Some dancers in rural clubs are as young as 12, with the average age of underage dancers estimated at 16.[19]

Trafficking in women and children on the rural strip circuit is profitable business for small communities. Local businesses gain income from tourists drawn to town by the stripping industry. Local businesses also profit from the dancers, who shop in the stores and sleep in the hotels.

A thriving sex industry may also be tied to corruption within local government and law enforcement, which seek in various ways to benefit from the exploitation of women and children. At the time of writing this paper, for

Strippers: Exposing Workplace Sexual Violence', 1998. Available at http://www.uri.edu/artsci/wms/hughes/stripc1.htm.

17 'K. T.', interview transcript on file at the Women's Network of the Red River Valley, Moorhead, Minnesota.

18 Clayton, M. (1998). 'Prostitution "Circuit" Takes Girls Across North American'. *The Christian Science Monitor*, Friday August 23, 1996. (Available at http://www.csmonitor.com/atcsmonitor/specials/children/p-part2a.html) In this article, Kansas is identified as a key recruiting state for traffickers bringing children to New York and other major US cities. Somerset and Smiley (see Note 5) also identified Minnesota as a key trafficking state.

19 *Analysis of the Stripping Industry*, videotape documenting public speech by Kelly Holsopple, researcher and former dancer, at Moorhead State University, October 25, 1996. On file at the Women's Network of the Red River Valley.

example, two law enforcement officers from Bemidji, Minnesota—a popular hunting and fishing tourist community in the northwest corner of the state—are on trial for 'aiding the solicitation of prostitution, aiding the promotion of prostitution and conspiracy to promote prostitution'.[20] On trial are a deputy sheriff and a police sergeant who organized a party for other law enforcement officers. Testimony from the trial alleges that police officers engaged in various degrees of paid sexual contact with strippers hired for the party, including sexual intercourse.[21]

These patterns are reflective of the dynamics of the sex industry on an international scale. Corruption of government and law enforcement is a predictable pattern from Thailand to Bemidji. Trafficking in children is intimately bound with the bar and nightclub scene in tourist and sex industry hot spots throughout the world. The existence of an impoverished population of women and children is fundamental to the industry. Traditional values—values which confine the roles of women and children to that of servers—provide the fundamental belief system on which all sex industry practice is based. Many parts of the rural Upper Midwest have all of these characteristics.

Wahpeton

Our business brings a lot of people from the rural area as well as other business people and dancers and they shop, eat and often stay in the local hotels that will lose income if we close up. Topless Dancing . . . [is] our income, our kids [*sic*] future, their education and dreams.[22]

—Barry and Nola Pausch, owners of The Oasis
strip club in Wahpeton, North Dakota

. . . [T]he Oasis is a must-see. Why? Because it's the only place where you can play 'beaver basketball' . . . . To tip the girls you stand at the bar and shoot baskets into their panties . . . FUN[23]

—Oasis patron comment posted on the Ultimate Strip Club List

---

20 'Prostitution trial under way: Prosecution calls first three witnesses'. *The Pioneer* (Bemidji, Minnesota), December 12, 1998.
21 'Day 2 Prostitution trial: Photos used to make case'. *The Pioneer* (Bemidji, Minnesota), December 15, 1998.
22 'We needed to stand up and speak out'. *The Daily News* (Wahpeton, North Dakota), November 29, 1996.
23 *The Ultimate Strip Club List*, May 14, 1999, available at http://www.tuscl.com/tuscl-bin/n_cityclubs.asp?state_id = 34 & state_ name = North +Dakota & city_ name = Wahpeton&city_id.-386

As long as others shove their immorality on the community, and make the community pay for it . . . then those of us who are against that conduct will continue to 'promote' morality. [24]

—Brad Friesen, Wahpeton community member

. . . but there are many, many people out there, for them, whether they are participating or whatever, it's a freedom of choice issue and I think that in fairness, you know, it needs to be argued in those terms.[25]

—Wahpeton City Council member, Warren Meyer, in response to Friesen

Approaching the I-29 turnoff to Wahpeton, North Dakota, from the south you will pass a 'Welcome to Wahpeton' billboard. The only graphic on the billboard is a camel, a reference to this small town's zoo. Ironically, it also symbolizes another key attraction in this rural community of 8700—The Oasis, the town's long-standing strip bar.

The Oasis strip bar was established in Wahpeton 25 years ago during a period of prosperity. During the 1970s, the small community was thriving, experiencing a population increase of 28 percent during that decade. The 1980s, however, were difficult for North Dakota. The farm-based economy of the Red River Valley and other farming regions across the country was—and is—threatened. Every year, dozens of family farms in the Upper Midwest close due to financial hardship. The stress of competing with the weather, a fluctuating market, and the development of agribusiness has overtaken many independent farmers. As a result, many small towns in North Dakota have experienced a significant drop in population as community members have moved to larger metropolitan areas. Many have moved out of state in search of jobs or educational opportunities. This phenomenon has also impacted Wahpeton.

Therefore, 1994 was a unique year for Wahpeton. Construction of a large ethanol plant was taking place and a significant number of new community members moved into the area.[26] This provided an economic opportunity for Wahpeton businesses, and one that was not going to be missed by Teddy and Lenore Bellmore, who decided to expand the entertainment format of their bar, Teddy's, to also include strippers on a regular basis.

---

24 Wahpeton City Council meeting, July 1, 1996. Audio tape recording of the meeting on file at the Women's Network of the Red River Valley, Moorhead, Minnesota.
25 Ibid.
26 In his statement to the Wahpeton City Council (refer Note 1, above), Teddy Bellmore stated that the Pro Gold plant had brought 1300 new community members to Wahpeton. This author, however, was unable to verify this number.

The opening of a second strip bar in Wahpeton resulted in widespread community concern. Local citizens began organizing and approached the Wahpeton City Council requesting that an ordinance be developed that would regulate stripping. Interestingly enough, even though stripping had existed in the community for two decades, there was little law that directly regulated it.

Testimony before the Wahpeton City Council during the ensuing several months of debate revealed the impact that the stripping industry had had on the community. The local crisis center reported that since the opening of the second club there had been a 96.6 percent increase in domestic violence and sexual assault cases.[27] Representatives of the center reported that many victims had stated that they had been abused after their husbands or boyfriends had returned home from one of the strip bars.[28] Other community members also expressed concerns about a diminishing quality of life in their small rural community.

Testimony revealed disparate perspectives regarding the fundamental issue at stake. Some of the community members condemned the dancers, rather than the establishments: 'Hell is for sinners, and nude dancing is a sin',[29] while others offered a social-political explanation that condemned the sex industry: '. . . historically women have been treated as property.'[30]

The initial ordinance drafted by the Wahpeton City Council in April 1996 was highly problematic. The primary intent of the Council was to consolidate 13 existing ordinances regarding liquor licenses. Clauses that specifically addressed stripping were peripheral. Not carefully designed, these clauses would have created more problems than they would have solved. For example, the ordinance would have required the clubs to videotape performances of the dancers and to make the videotapes available to law enforcement when requested; the videotapes were intended to be an instrument for measuring the clubs' compliance with other stipulations within the ordinance. Videotapes, however, have been a common way for strip clubs to exploit women. Strip clubs have been known to videotape performances and sell or offer these tapes to customers.[31] In fact, Barry Pausch, owner of the Oasis, informed the Council that videotaping the dancers was already a standard practice at his bar. Moreover, by specifying that the cameras were to be directed to the

---

27 Minutes of the Wahpeton City Council, May 2, 1996.
28 Minutes of the Wahpeton City Council meeting, July 1, 1996.
29 See Minutes of the Wahpeton City Council, May 2 (refer Note 27, above).
30 'Council holds liquor ordinance hearing: residents protest strip bars in Wahpeton'. *The Daily News*, May 3, 1996.
31 See Somerset (Note 5, above). In addition, the first strip club to become unionized (1996) was the Lusty Lady in San Francisco; dancers at the Lusty Lady organized after the management refused to stop videotaping the private dance rooms.

performance area, the ordinance was clearly targeting the dancers, not the abusive and violent behavior of patrons in clubs. Further, cameras directed at the stage would not document staff and management abuse, much of which takes place in the dressing rooms, offices, and other unmonitored areas. Clearly, the ordinance defined the dancers as the 'problem'.

The ordinance also specified that the customers, unless they were conveying tips, were not to touch the dancers. Yet the ordinance would have penalized the dancers, not the patrons, for being touched; the ordinance stated that the 'licensee' (strip bar) was to 'put each performer on notice that a violation of the restrictions would result in termination of their services'. However, the ordinance did not significantly penalize patrons for violations; patrons would simply have had to leave the premises for an unspecified period of time.

Ironically, many strip clubs penalize dancers in various ways—for example, by imposing fines—for being touched by customers when there are club rules against it. The logic of clubs is to have women always feeling that they are responsible for the abuse that they receive. This is a typical ploy that abusers of all types use against their victims. The proposed Wahpeton ordinance would not only have become party to it, it would have mandated it. Interestingly enough, the owners of Teddy's stated that they did not have an objection to the ordinance's language.[32]

Community members, however, were not satisfied with the proposed ordinance because it would not curb the expansion of the sex industry in the community nor address the secondary harmful effects—such as the increase in crime and the decline in property values—in any meaningful way. Nevertheless, the ordinance was passed by the Council in July. It was vetoed by the mayor, however, who commented that 'this is an issue of great substance and it should be further reviewed'.[33]

While the ordinance was back on the drafting board, the strip bars made the press for another reason. Two extraordinarily violent fights, unrelated to each other, erupted at The Oasis and at Teddy's on the same evening. The fight at The Oasis bar involved 12 or more people. One person was left with a broken leg. By time the ambulance arrived at The Oasis, club patrons from Teddy's were fighting in that bar's parking lot. This second fight was nearly life-threatening, with one of the men suffering severe knife wounds to the face, neck, and abdomen.

Club owners, already under fire from local community members after months of intense debate on the ordinance, quickly dismissed the violence as

---

32 See Minutes of the Wahpeton City Council, May 2 (Note 27, above).
33 'Wahpeton's liquor ordinance is still contentious: Mayor Rood vetoes ordinance pending new review', *The Daily News* (Wahpeton), July 2, 1996.

being irrelevant to the fact that these fights took place at stripping establishments. The Wahpeton Chief of Police also stated that he believed the fights had simply taken place because the bars were overcrowded. Nevertheless, these two fights escalated the public controversy to a new level. The already-heated public debate became particularly volatile.

The Bellmores presented to the Wahpeton City Council on August 5, 1996, a protracted statement that attacked individual community members and representatives of local organizations that had been organizing against the bars. Following the Bellmores' statement, several community members raised their hands in a request to respond. Curiously, Warren Meyer, council member chairing the meeting in the absence of the mayor, did not give the community members an opportunity to speak.

During their statement, Lenore and Teddy Bellmore also emphasized the economic assets of their business, tapping into the community's uncertainties about its economic future. They detailed their annual city sales taxes and the amount they paid to the city for their liquor license. They outlined their annual donations to local programs and services: $3000 to the carousel in the local park, $1000 to the Korean and Vietnam Memorial, $1000 to United Way, and $500 to the North Dakota State College of Science. They also argued that their bar was one of the features of the town that attracted the many Pro Gold construction workers and encouraged them to spend their money locally.

By fall, a final draft of the liquor license ordinance was completed. The final draft of the ordinance included provisions that would prohibit 'cabaret types of entertainment' beginning July 1, 1997. Weary from months of public debate, the Wahpeton City Council scheduled an 'advisory vote'. In December, community members would tell the Council whether or not they wished to have the strip clubs in their community.

In response, the Pausches launched an advertising campaign in the local paper, *The Daily News*. Three advertisements were placed in the November 29 edition, each formatted as a letter. The first was signed by Barry and Nola Pausch:

To the Citizens of Wahpeton:

Tuesday, Dec. 3, may not be a very important day for all citizens in Wahpeton, but it is for us, our family, the people we employ and several businesses we support to remain in business . . . if they succeed in banning 'Topless Dancing', our yearly income will drastically decrease and this may force our family to move from town. Where are they going to make up this money? From you home owners and other businesses . . . we need to stand up and speak out. It just may be your job, business, or rights that will be the next target for someone to end.[34]

---

34 See *The Daily News* (Note 22, above).

The following two advertisements were signed by their children. The first was signed by their three eldest:

> . . . we need your vote to keep our family's business going so we can fulfill our hopes and dreams and maybe someday come back to Wahpeton and raise our families and work in whatever job career we can get into . . .[35]

The last, by their 11-year-old son:

> My grandfather had the Oasis for 18 years and my dad has had it for over two years and someday I would like to buy it from my dad and keep it in my family . . . I only wish that they would let 11-year-olds vote because I would go vote and vote 'Yes'.[36]

The strip bars owners' organizing strategy emphasizing the economic fragility of this small rural North Dakota community was successful. On December 3, 1996, Wahpeton citizens voted by a close margin to keep the strip clubs in town. A week later, the decision of the Wahpeton City Council followed the advisory vote.

Anytown, USA

> . . . it can very easily happen in a small town.[37]
>
> —community member from Crosby, North Dakota

Crosby, North Dakota, lies along the Canadian border in the far northwest corner of the state. In 1992, a local bar began to host strippers a couple of times each week. Shortly after, Crosby considered adopting an ordinance that would ban 'male/female go-go dancers, exotic dancers, and strippers from performing in local licensed liquor establishments'.[38] As in Wahpeton, the ordinance was voted down in the public election, primarily for economic reasons.[39] In 1998, local law enforcement arrested four dancers on prostitution charges. The population of Crosby is 1500.

The stripping industry continues to grow in rural communities. Nevertheless, rural strip bars in smaller communities cannot thrive without networks of support from sex industry businesses in metropolitan areas. Crosby is two hours northwest of Minot. Minot has three strip clubs, patronized by a large population of military personnel from the air base, college students, and local

---

35 '"It's really not fair" for me and my parents'. *The Daily News*, November 29, 1996.
36 '"My family needs your help" Dec. 3'. *The Daily News*, November 29, 1996.
37 'Exotic dancers arrested in Crosby on prostitution charges'. *The Fargo Forum*, June 6, 1998.
38 Minutes of Crosby City Council, March 2, 1992.
39 See *The Fargo Forum*, June 6, 1998 (Note 37). Voters who turned out for the election voted 64% to 36% in support of stripping in Crosby establishments.

community men. Dancers who work in Crosby travel on the circuit through Minot. Only one of the dancers arrested in Crosby was from the local community. Another dancer was from a small town outside of Minot. The other two were from Bismarck, North Dakota, and Milwaukee, Wisconsin. The dynamics of Wahpeton are similar to those of Crosby. Wahpeton is 45 minutes south of Fargo. Dancers working in Fargo's strip bars often appear in Wahpeton the following week.

Urban sex industry businesses support strip bars in rural areas in other ways as well. For example, some small towns have bars that have strippers only seasonally. During hunting season, for example, it is not uncommon for a small town bar to host strippers. These bars capitalize on the large population of men temporarily visiting the area, traveling without their families, seeking to be entertained in the evenings. This phenomenon however, would not be possible if women were not already being trafficked through the area. Some women report dancing during hunting season in towns with populations of less than 200. Such small bars could not afford to bring women in from long distances unless the women were already traveling on a rural circuit—and the rural circuit is stabilized through its connections to the metropolitan sex industries that feed it.

> If you want a real Corn Belt experience, check out the Peacock Bar in Winner SD. It's too late for this year, but time your trip to coincide with the hunting season. They import some good talent from around the country and the place really rocks.[40]

In the Upper Midwest, '[strip] bars out in the middle of nowhere, bars that no one knows anything about'[41] are supported by the lucrative sex industry businesses in such large to mid-sized metropolitan areas as Minneapolis, St. Paul, Duluth, Superior, Madison, Ames, Green Bay, Milwaukee, Oshkosh, Des Moines, Davenport, Sioux City, Topeka, Lawrence, Kansas City, Wichita, Omaha, Lincoln, Rapid City, Mandan, Minot, and Fargo.

Fargo

> One question I often ask people is 'Did I go to the [strip club] last night?' It's a question they can't answer, because it doesn't have an effect on their lives. It's my life. What I do with my life doesn't affect theirs.[42]
>
> —Bruce Bernstein, chairman of Citizens Against Censorship, Fargo, North Dakota

---

40 See *Grimace Nudie Strip Club Listing* (Note 12, above).
41 See Somerset (Note 3, above).
42 'Question and Answer: Is ordinance about censorship or standards?'. *The Fargo Forum*, January 15, 1998.

Protect Women
—Slogan of the anti-strip club campaign organized by
the Coalition for Public Sexual Standards, Fargo

As voters go to the polls, they must realize that the outcome will not simply impact 'speech' or public nudity, but will also determine the workplace and civil rights of many women and community members.

—excerpt from letter submitted by the Women's Network
of the Red River Valley to the *Fargo Forum*[43]

Although Fargo is only 45 miles north of Wahpeton, it differs from Wahpeton in significant ways. The population of Fargo is 90,000, making it the largest city in North Dakota. Fargo hosts a major university, North Dakota State. Immediately across the river is Moorhead, Minnesota, where there are three colleges. During the school year, the twin cities of Fargo and Moorhead swell with college students. An abundance of movie theaters, bars, coffee shops, and restaurants are patronized by college students—students who also fill many of the communities' service jobs. In addition, Fargo has benefited from the population exodus from the more rural areas of the state. Over the past decade, Fargo has experienced a boom in construction, particularly in housing.

Nevertheless, Fargo and Wahpeton share similar characteristics. Fargo is also surrounded by flat, fertile farmland and much of the business and industry in Fargo and Moorhead is agriculturally based. Additionally, the social and political makeup of the community is conservatively oriented, reflecting the area's rural history. Indeed, the Fargo-Moorhead community can be aptly defined as 'rural-urban'.

'Exotic dancing' has existed in Fargo and surrounding communities for some time. Early bars, however, were closed because of ongoing legal problems, many involving assaults and prostitution. In the mid-1980s, the Four-Ten Lounge opened in Fargo. The club featured exotic dancers on an irregular basis, primarily on weekends. Although Fargo residents at that time circulated petitions urging commissioners to ban topless dancing, the commissioners approved the license for the Four-Ten Lounge with a vote of 3–2. In the early 1990s, the Four-Ten became Northern Exposure and strip dance became its nightly feature. By 1995, it went through its final name change, becoming simply The Northern. Other bars in Fargo also sponsor strippers on a sporadic basis. One popular college hangout for women is Cactus Jacks, which hosts male revues.

---

43 This letter was submitted to, but not published by, *The Fargo Forum*. On file at the Women's Network of the Red River Valley.

Similar to what would occur in Wahpeton the following spring, it was the possibility of an additional bar opening as a strip club in the fall of 1995 that precipitated widespread community response. At that time, a former employee of The Northern, Thomas Grandbois, applied for a liquor license that would enable him to open an exotic dance bar. Within a week, a citizen-driven petition drive was underway requesting that the city commissioners deny Grandbois a license. Soon after, a second petition was developed asking the commissioners to change the existing cabaret ordinance to prohibit stripping in Fargo altogether.

The Commission denied Grandbois his license. He sued. As the suit was in process, the Commission developed an ordinance that would prohibit stripping in bars that sold alcohol. There was an existing ordinance on the books that prohibited stripping in 'juice bars'. Therefore, passage of the additional ordinance would end stripping in Fargo in all public establishments.

The Fargo Commission received more mail and telephone calls during the debate on this ordinance than it had ever received before. Conservative, religious community members were concerned about public nudity and community values. The local feminist organization, the Women's Network of the Red River Valley, cited statistics about violence against women working in strip clubs. That fall, a representative of a new Fargo group, Citizens for a Free Thinking Society, also spoke before the commission. CFTS's basic platform was that the proposed ordinance was regressive and non-liberal and that the primary issues were 'free choice' and 'respect for rights'.[44]

Supporters emphasized that The Northern was a 'good' club—a club with very few police reports and one of the more popular clubs among the dancers traveling on the circuit. Nevertheless, community members who worked or lived near The Northern expressed concerns about their safety and that of their families. A former patron of The Northern alleged that he had been solicited for prostitution by dancers, had seen drugs on the premises, and knew of underage dancers.[45]

The City Commission meetings were volatile. An exhausted Commission passed the ordinance late in December. The ordinance was to be enacted on January 1, 1997.

During that period, however, the Commission had become concerned that Grandbois would win his lawsuit. Grandbois was suing for infringement of his free speech rights, arguing that by denying his liquor license while also having an ordinance that prevented him from opening a strip club without alcohol, the City of Fargo had denied his constitutional right to freedom of expression,

---

44 Minutes of Fargo City Commission, December 4, 1995.
45 Minutes of Fargo City Commission, November 20, 1995.

that is, to be a strip club owner. Therefore, under the advice of the Fargo City Attorney, who also signed a petition supporting the existing strip club, the Fargo City commission repealed the existing 'juice bar' ordinance. Thus, on the same night that the Commission passed the ordinance that would prevent stripping in alcohol bars, it repealed the ordinance that prohibited stripping in non-alcohol bars. With that, stripping establishments remained legal in Fargo, but the nature of the bars would change—they could not sell alcohol beginning in 1997.

This shifted the debate. It required each group actively organizing around strip club issues to re-evaluate its strategies. Over the next year, Citizens for a Free Thinking Society retained much of its basic platform but also underwent a name change. Likely recognizing that it needed to appeal to a broader segment of voters, the group became Citizens Against Censorship. This was a wise political maneuver, as the word 'censorship' carries significant connotative power. CAC also began a petition drive to prevent the alcohol bar ordinance from being enacted on January 1, 1997. If the petition drive were successful, it would bring the ordinance to a community vote.

The Women's Network also underwent some political and philosophical changes over the next year. The organization had originally lobbied for the alcohol bar ordinance with the anticipation that its passage would end stripping in Fargo. With stripping now legal in bars not selling alcohol, the Network undertook research to analyze the impact this would have on the local stripping industry, women working within the industry, and the greater community. Over the next year, the Network also became more connected with women who had been in the industry. Their voices shaped the Women's Network's activism in significant ways.

Members of the conservative religious community also organized. Eventually they became the Coalition for Public Sexual Standards and developed the 'Protect Women' campaign that emerged in 1998.

Although the debate over the alcohol bar ordinance monopolized much of the public dialogue regarding sex industry businesses for over a year, another ordinance regulating the sex industry was introduced and passed in the fall of 1996.

This was a zoning ordinance that originated in the fall of 1995 through a motion by City Commissioner Arlette Preston, who felt that additional ways to restrict the sex industry in Fargo were needed. A year later, a draft of the ordinance was presented to the City Commission by the Planning and Development Director with the following comments:

> . . . research collected clearly demonstrates . . . that such businesses have a negative effect on the use and value of nearby property, on the quality of life on nearby

neighborhoods, and ultimately have an effect on crime and violence near such businesses . . . the Planning Commission's own experience with adult entertainment businesses has already shown a negative effect on potential land-use and value . . .[46]

Therefore, the proposed ordinance was designed to zone future sex industry businesses in Fargo a given distance from any other existing sex industry businesses or bars, as well as schools, parks, or churches. The planning Commission recommended 1000 feet.

Community members who presented their perspectives to the City Commission expressed the expected plate of concerns. A member of the conservative religious community spoke in support of the ordinance, encouraging commissioners to move ahead with 'marginalizing these kinds of commercial activities that appeal to the lessons of the flesh'.[47] The Women's Network of the Red River Valley gave its support to the ordinance with a caveat: that the maximum legal distance possible be written into the ordinance to best ensure that poor communities and communities of color were not disproportionately impacted. The ordinance for the most part zoned future sex industry businesses into industrial park areas, which were sections of town in proximity to some poor neighborhoods. The Women's Network argued that a minimum of 1250 feet would be necessary to create a buffer zone between sex industry businesses and poor neighborhoods. Supporters of the stripping industry also spoke before the City Commission, expressing concerns of 'censorship' and the right of women and men 'in their choice to entertain' and to 'display their art'.[48]

On September 23, 1996, the City Commission unanimously passed a 1250-foot zoning ordinance. The ordinance including a 'grandfather clause', exempting existing sex industry businesses; therefore, The Northern as well as other Fargo sex industry businesses, such as The Adult Bookstore and Cinema, were not impacted by the ordinance.

Shortly after, in December 1996, just before the earlier alcohol bar ordinance was to go into effect, Citizens Against Censorship submitted its petitions to the City of Fargo. A large number of signatures had been acquired, many more than needed to put the alcohol bar ordinance on hold. Therefore, the City Commission slated a public vote on the ordinance for April 1998. With that, the stripping debate fell out of the public dialogue for over a year.

Early in 1998, widespread public debate re-emerged. Citizens Against Censorship launched a community-wide 'Stop Censorship' campaign backed by sizable donations—some in the five digits. Its campaign involved extensive

---

46   Minutes of Fargo City Commission, September 24, 1996.
47   'Fargo panel revises restriction on strip clubs'. *The Fargo Forum*, August 27, 1996.
48   See Minutes of Fargo City Commission (Note 46, above)

displays of posters in local bars, billboards and marquees, numerous advertisements in the local papers, and promotional events. Citizens Against Censorship also capitalized on the fact that the ordinance was poorly worded and might impact other forms of entertainment in non-stripping establishments.

The Women's Network had spent the year consulting with dancers who had worked in juice and alcohol bars. The Women's Network had determined that *either* outcome of the April 21 vote was problematic. It concluded that if the ordinance were passed, it might increase the likelihood of juice bars opening in Fargo. The organization was concerned that juice bars were highly exploitative; for example, dancers in juice bars may be 18 and, because the bars do not make money from alcohol, they typically take as much as 40 to 50 percent of dancers' tips to compensate. However, dancers working in *any* strip bar, whether alcohol or non-alcohol, routinely experience a degree of sexual harassment and sexual violence unparalleled in any other workplace environment.[49] If the ordinance were not passed in Fargo, stripping would remain legal in both alcohol and non-alcohol bars.

Therefore, the organization concluded that it 'cannot support harm against women and we refuse to accept violence against women simply because there are no positive choices available. Therefore, we cannot and do not support either option . . . It should be clear to citizens as they cast their votes that workable solutions to the harm of the sex industry are not yet available.'[50] The organization titled its campaign 'Your Choice'. The campaign was informational and educational, focusing on the industry as a form of violence against women for which there were no substantive legislative options available.

The Coalition For Public Sexual Standards also increased its organizing as the April poll date pressed closer. The Coalition utilized radio talk shows by sponsoring guests to speak on behalf of the Coalition and placed paid advertisements in local papers. The Coalition, like the Women's Network, had significantly less financial backing than the Citizens Against Censorship and, therefore, significantly less exposure.

Citizens Against Censorship's well-financed publicity campaign was very influential. Support for the 'Stop Censorship' campaign was reflected in the *High Plains Reader*, a local arts publication. The editor wrote:

> Granted, some people are opposed to stripping in bars . . . But they can stay home . . . [T]o effectively convince the Fargo City Commission to pass an ordinance that

---

49 See Holsopple (Note 19, above).
50 *Long Position Statement of the Women's Network*. On file at the Women's Network of the Red River Valley.

would prohibit nude dancing and other forms of adult entertainment in liquor establishments is a violation, a serious one . . .[51]

The 'Stop Censorship' campaign also convinced many community members that the ordinance would have wide-ranging impacts on their lives. The Chair of CAC made a number of ambiguous public statements implying that there would be significant and undetermined ramifications from this ordinance: 'It would have a much broader effect than most people think';[52] 'Once you start chipping away at these freedoms, where do they stop?'[53] The CAC ads also engendered fear of widespread censorship: 'The government seems to want to control all aspects of our lives';[54] 'If we let them take this freedom, they will take it all, one word, one action at a time.'[55]

The Women's Network was also attacked, even though it had pulled its support for the ordinance after the juice bar ordinance had been repealed. Some community members were suspicious that the Women's Network's 'Your Choice' campaign was camouflage, concealing an intent to erode a wide range of rights. Witness the following exchange of letters to the *High Plains Reader*, the first from the Women's Network:

. . . by simplistically reducing this complex set of issues to a single-issue debate about censorship, Citizens Against Censorship is clearly hoping that the public will not consider other, vitally important aspects of the debate . . . community members must be aware . . . [of] the typical differences between such bars that sell alcohol and those that do not . . . the amount of violence dancers experience . . . that violence typically increases significantly outside of clubs where sex industry activities and alcohol are in close proximity . . . [that with juice bars] recruitment of local young women into stripping increases . . . [therefore] either outcome, a yes or no vote, will not address the critical issues of exploitation and violence in the sex industry. The outcome will simply be a vote for one type of harm over another.[56]

The second from a community member the following week:

The most important thing that voters need to understand is exactly how this proposed ordinance will impact their day-to-day lives, regardless of how they feel about

---

51   'A Tale of Two Cities'. *High Plains Reader*, April 16, 1998.
52   'Fargo voters consider banning adult entertainment in bars, clubs'. *The Spectrum*, April 16, 1998.
53   See *The Fargo Forum* (Note 42, above).
54   Source of advertisement unknown, probably *The Fargo Forum*. On file at the Women's Network of the Red River Valley.
55   Source of advertisement unknown, probably *The Fargo Forum*. On file at the Women's Network of the Red River Valley.
56   'Be informed before you vote on the stripping ordinance'. *High Plains Reader*, April 9, 1998.

nudity or strip clubs . . . it would be illegal for . . . women to wipe themselves after urinating at an establishment that sells alcohol . . . I urge everyone to get off their ass on April 21 and vote 'no' . . . I would ask that . . . the Women's Network of the Red River Valley quit spreading their mistruths under the guise of 'informing the public . . .'[57]

The *High Plains Reader* also fueled anti-feminist sentiment. In the same publication on the same day, one week before the vote, next to an illustration of a giant, scowling farmer pitchforking a helpless strip club patron, the editor endorsed a 'no' vote and patronizingly commented: 'We suggest we give the proponents of anti-stripping a hug for speaking up.'[58]

The 'Stop Censorship' campaign also garnered the support of *The Fargo Forum*. Two days before the vote, the editorial staff of the *Forum* wrote that the 'ballot is a hypocritical sham', that the ordinance 'is only marginally about 'exotic' dancing', that the ordinance 'is a form of censorship', and 'finally, the Fargo ordinance is, in effect, an antibusiness measure'. The editorial concluded:

> We might not like the so-called sex trade. We might believe women who earn a living by stripping are pathetic victims. We might not like the idea of men slobbering in their beer as female dancers disrobe. But our dislikes and biases are not enough to endorse the blatant misuse of government power. Vote no on the stripping ordinance.'[59]

On April 21, 1998, citizens of Fargo voted down the ordinance by a significant margin. Therefore, the status of strip clubs in Fargo remained unchanged. Stripping continues to be legal in both alcohol and non-alcohol bars. However, future sex industry businesses will be 1250 feet away from any residential area, existing bar, or existing strip industry business.

Causes and effects

Pretty college student will dance. Specials.[60]

—Adult Entertainment classified advertisement, *The Fargo Forum*

The protracted debates over the zoning and alcohol bar ordinances kept Fargo's principal strip bar, The Northern, under public scrutiny for over two years. During that time, unlike other bars in North Dakota, The Northern maintained a clean public record. Unlike Mandan, North Dakota, no dancer

---

57 'Get out on April 21—stop this tyranny'. *High Plains Reader*, April 16, 1998.
58 See *High Plains Reader* (Note 51, above).
59 'Ordinance a misuse of city government power'. *The Fargo Forum*, editorial, April 17, 1998.
60 *The Fargo Forum*, classifieds, January 10, 1999.

was arrested for assaulting another dancer with a knife.[61] Unlike Wahpeton, no police reports of patron violence related to the bar made the front page of the local paper. Unlike Crosby, no dancers were arrested on reports of prostitution. Although a former patron had initially made accusations of underage dancers, drugs, and prostitution at The Northern, no additional accusations were made. Therefore, editors of the *Forum* wrote with confidence: 'There is no compelling evidence—from police records or any other credible source—that suggest criminal activity.'[62]

In addition, dancers who worked at the bar spoke out against closing the establishment. Dancers emphasized that 'Northern has a great reputation among dancers as the best place to work in the Midwest'[63] and as 'one of the most professional run clubs'.[64] Dancers stated that The Northern's patrons were 'friendly and interesting',[65] like 'neighbors'.[66] Indeed, The Northern had a positive reputation among dancers. It was, and is, seen as a 'good' club.

Interestingly, during the two years of debate, the owners of The Northern—two brothers—never spoke at Fargo City Commission meetings. Although their attorney, a man, briefly spoke in public on a couple of occasions, all others who spoke as representatives of the club were women. The Northern elected to have its female managers as spokespersons. In addition, late in 1996, The Northern was put up for sale; the interested buyer was a woman. Although the club was not sold and, therefore, continues under the same management, the interested buyer spoke in public on numerous occasions against the ordinances and for the strip club.

This had several effects. First, the public witnessed a significant number of women supporting the sex industry. Second, this strategy of the local sex industry, to keep men associated with the bar out of the public eye, effectively pitted women representing the industry against women from the Women's Network, some of whom had been in the industry and many of whom had not. The president of the Coalition for Public Sexual Standards was also a woman. Although the chair of the Coalition Against Censorship was a man, he emphasized that he was not a patron and brought letters of support from female dancers to read at his speaking engagements. Therefore, male patrons

---

61 'Argument between dancers lands one in jail'. *The Fargo Forum*, January 25, 1998. It must be noted that media coverage on strip club-related violence is typically about dancers or patrons. The violence perpetrated by staff and management does not make the press. Staff and management are the least scrutinized in the press, public debate, and research.

62 See *The Fargo Forum* (Note 59, above).

63 'Stop defining all women as weak victims'. *The Fargo Forum*, April 28, 1998.

64 'Fargo should remain an open and free place'. *High Plains Reader*, April 16, 1998.

65 Ibid.

66 See *The Fargo Forum* (Note 63, above).

of the bar, male owners of the bar, male managers of the bar, and men involved in myriad other aspects of the sex industry in Fargo were never in the spotlight. They were never held accountable for *their* 'choices'. Anonymous male patrons watched the debate unfold on the bar television while dancers stepped forth and spoke out in public. One of the bar's female managers was on the nightly news. The male owners were never seen on television or quoted in the press. Therefore, the messy sex industry debate about women's 'rights' and women's 'choices' was presented as a collision between women. Men from the bar were invisible bystanders who, by not appearing in the debate, appeared to have nothing to do with creating the mess, orchestrating the mess, sustaining the mess, nor benefiting from it.

Thus, in many ways, The Northern and its patrons sustained 'good' reputations. This opened the gates for the sex industry in Fargo.

As recently as 1996, 'rent-a-stripper' businesses or 'escort services' were rarely advertised in *The Fargo Forum*. At the time of writing, several such businesses advertise regularly. In fact, late in 1998, *The Fargo Forum* had to open up a new classified column, 'Adult Entertainment', to accommodate the increasing number of advertisements for the sex industry. These new businesses also advertise in the local college papers, as college students under 21 can rent strippers even though they cannot go to the local strip bars. Representatives of these businesses also walk the campuses and recruit college students to work as dancers.[67] Women and men who are 18 can dance for private stripping agencies.

The presence of a 'good' club, accompanied by the successful defeat of an ordinance that had been at the center of controversy for over two years, has made the sex industry palatable to the community of Fargo. The future of the sex industry in Fargo is predictable. It will grow. Rapidly.

Commentary and conclusions

Fargo, Minot, and other larger communities with established sex industry businesses are important links in the economic chain of support for the sex industry in rural areas. However, small communities are not passive victims of an urban sex industry invasion. The sex industry has existed in rural areas in the Upper Midwest since frontier times. Many pioneer towns, including Fargo, had numerous brothels. Small towns may no longer have brothels, but they have gas stations with magazine racks holding *Playboy*, *Penthouse*, and *Hustler*. Small video selections at the same gas stations include 'unrated', 'adult theme', and hard-core videos.

---

67 Anecdotal information shared with the author by female college students during talks given to classes at North Dakota State University and Minnesota State University.

Men in bars in communities of all sizes buy women drinks and provide women with drugs in exchange for sex. Poor women in communities of all sizes exchange sex for fundamental needs such as food, shelter, and transportation. The internet now links johns and pimps all over the world. Manifestations of prostitution exist in all communities, urban and rural.

Small communities in the rural Upper Midwest will coexist with and tolerate existing forms of prostitution until a visible, tangible business, such as a strip club, opens in town. Initially, a group of citizens will organize to resist. Then they will be startled by the resiliency of the business. They will be puzzled as to why the strip club cannot be closed. They will be concerned that city council members, local business owners, representatives of the local press, and neighbors support the club. Yet the 'new' strip club will bring nothing new to town. It will only expand upon what is already there. It will only be the most recent manifestation of an industry that is already rooted in rural America. Rural strip clubs can not survive if there are not community members willing to run them and patrons willing to visit them. They can not survive without preexisting, entrenched patriarchal ideas regarding women's roles and men's rights. They can not survive without a poor class of women vulnerable for recruitment into systems of prostitution.

Therefore, rural community members need to begin their resistance to the sex industry *before* a strip club opens in town. They must exert pressure on the local gas station that sells pornography. 'Boycott' is a word that must enter the rural vocabulary. Rural communities must ensure that social services, health care practitioners, law enforcement, churches, and other agencies that may be accessed by women who have been prostituted are well-educated regarding the issues of exploitation and violence experienced by women and children in the industry. Rural communities must work to provide educational and employment opportunities for women who are poor. And, most important, local churches, schools, and families must examine and rewrite the lessons they teach women and men, girls and boys about their rights and identities.

Rus Ervin Funk*

What does pornography say about me(n)?: How I became an anti-pornography activist

I hate pornography. I hate what pornography does to women, what it does to men, what it says to men to do to women and other men.

In spite of my current convictions about pornography, I have not always felt this way. For much of my life I supported and actively used pornography. This essay examines my process from pro-pornography consumer to anti-pornography activist. As a bisexual man, I've consumed—and have since become critical of—both heterosexual and gay male pornography. As I'll explain, my experiences indicate how both are similar forms of men's sexist violence. Through the lens of my experience as a pornography consumer, I will look at what pornography says to and about men, and in particular what pornography says to men about what to do to women and other men. Finally, I will offer some observations on organizing men to become more actively involved in efforts against pornography, prostitution and other forms of men's sexist violence.

I am a European-American, thirty-something, queer-identified male from a working-class Texas background. I am an activist in the feminist movement to end men's violence as well as in the bisexual movement, in anti-racist struggles, and in the movement for anti-militarism and nonviolence. As a social worker, I have also provided therapeutic services to women and men who have been victimized by men, as well as intervention services with men who batter, and with adolescent and adult men who sexually offend. Still, my primary focus is on community organizing, direct action, and policy analysis. It seems to me that working to end men's abuse and violence, and to transform the context in which men's violence and abuse occurs (i.e. institutionalized misogyny) through social change, is as essential as providing direct services to support the women and men who are harmed.

* The author would like to thank John Stoltenberg, Amy Mudd, Robert Jensen, Dr. Robert Miller, and Jon Cohen for their support, encouragement and editorial comments in the drafting of this chapter. I also want to thank Christine Stark and Rebecca Whisnant for taking the initiative for this book, and Rebecca for her editorial comments and support for this article.

For men to be involved in combating sexism, men's violence, and men's exploitation of women and other men through pornography and prostitution, men must see these issues as relevant for and to us—we need to define these issues as *men's* issues, while simultaneously keeping those who are harmed in and by pornography and prostitution at the center of our thinking, analysis and activism. Rather than doing this work to benefit women (which too easily slips into a form of paternalism and protectionism that only maintains male supremacy), men need to partner with women—to do the work that men need to do in ways that are accountable to feminist leadership and that ultimately enhance gender justice.

Before I go further, I should note the danger in using autobiographical narrative to expand or explain theory. As Michael Awkward (2001) explains, on the one hand, autobiographical narrative allows me to describe and account for my experience of using and coming to reject pornography, and more generally my relations to white and male privilege. This process, one that John Stoltenberg describes as 'revolutionary honesty', is essential for men wishing to expose the processes of male privilege, male bonding, and male oppression of women. On the other hand, autobiographical exploration by definition places me (as a European-American man) at the center. The danger of this process is at least twofold: first, that the focus of attention is on me, rather than on the pornography and its harm to women and men; and second, that it reproduces the pornographic, male supremacist paradigm by once again placing men at the center. My hope, then, is to use a self-conscious, self-critical autobiographical forum to focus attention on pornography and the harm that it does, while simultaneously de-centering myself and subverting the pornographic, male supremacist paradigm. Ultimately, you, the reader, are the judge of how well I do.

Getting here from there

I was born into a liberal family, with parents who were very open about sexuality. One of their main goals in relation to their children was that we would never feel ashamed about who we were as sexual beings. The shame and embarrassment I learned about sex did not come from home, but from school, peers, and elsewhere. For my parents, almost no questions were out of bounds. We were actively encouraged to talk about sex and sexuality (even at times when we didn't want to). Mom and Dad supported gay male and lesbian rights long before it become politically correct to do so, and invited out gay men and lesbians into our home—no one was ever asked or expected to 'closet' themselves in any way around us as kids.

Periodically, during my pre-adolescent and adolescent years (the seventies and early eighties), my parents taught classes on human sexuality in the community, through local colleges, and in churches. They designed these classes to be open and challenging. For example, they would ask their students to switch gender roles for a whole day (not just in class). My parents also took the class to visit the local strip joint, arranging to meet and interview one or more of the strippers before their performance. After each of these experiences, the class period would be spent processing the students' reactions.

It was in this context that pornography was a part of my life. Pornography was openly a part of our home—not on the coffee table or as a 'center piece', but it was in the family room bookshelves. Like other books in the house, we had access to the pornography, as well as to *Our Bodies, Ourselves* and other books on human sexuality. Pornography was so acceptable and normalized in our family that, when I was 18, my older brother gave me a subscription to *Penthouse* as a Christmas present.

I learned much later that my father brought the pornography into the house and that, in fact, my mother was somewhat uncomfortable with it being there and being so open. But given the efforts they were trying to make together for us to be as comfortable as possible with sexuality and nudity, any misgivings she had about the pornography were countered by her desire to be as open and accepting as possible.

I was raised to understand that people are inherently sexual beings and that our sexuality is something sacred and beautiful. I grew up understanding that pornography was the depiction of nudity and that looking at pornography was one way to appreciate the beauty of sexuality. It never entered my mind to critically examine *how* women, men and sex were depicted in the pornography that we saw, or to explore *which* women were shown and how different women were differently depicted. It never occurred to me to examine the lessons I learned as a result of looking at pornography—the lessons about men and masculinity, women and femininity, relating to (and with) women as a man, being sexual, having sex, etc. What I learned was that looking at naked women and masturbating to those pictures was part of 'normal' male sexual development. What I learned was that looking at women as sexual beings and 'appreciating their beauty' was natural, healthy, expected . . . and a right that I could expect as a man.

After I left home and went to college, my use of pornography continued and escalated, reflecting the acceptability and normalcy of men's use of heterosexual pornography. In the men's dorms that I lived in at a south Texas university (as in most male dorms and other environments), not only was pornography tolerated, it was actively promoted. Pornography was seen as a right, almost a necessity, that was above reproach or question; along with our textbooks, backpack, pens and notebooks, we had our pornography. Most of the men, I suspect, bought or otherwise had regular access to pornography—

mostly through magazines (this was the early to mid-1980s, prior to the advent of the world wide web and the explosion of internet pornography). Pornographic pictures decorated our dorm rooms and the bathrooms; pulling out a pornographic magazine during a party was common, and it was not unheard of for us to show pornographic videos in the lobby on the campus-supplied TV and VCR.

In general, men's use of pornography is a private matter, although publicly known, acknowledged and accepted. So it was for me and the other men in my dorms. We looked at pornography quite openly, yet there was also a sense in which our looking was a private matter. Defining men's use of pornography as 'private' allowed us to use pornography with no real consequences. Our viewing of pornography was constructed and understood as a 'personal (and therefore private) choice' and one that therefore was beyond any debate or deliberation. We used heterosexual pornography as a way to bond with each other—and the assumption of privacy congealed the bond. By agreeing (or at least playfully arguing) about which women were attractive and what we would like to do with those women, we developed a camaraderie and increased our affinity with each other. As a public event, using pornography advertised our views of women, sex, and ourselves. Women were on notice about how they were going to be looked at when they came to the dorm. As a private matter—defined as a 'choice' that men have the right to—our use of pornography was exempt from criticism.

I suspect that I was no different from the other men in that I would look at the pornography in public settings, and discuss it openly, but would masturbate privately. This private envelope around using pornography was where I created my fantasies about the women in the pornographic pictures and the women I knew (or wished I knew) who I would replace the women in the pornographic pictures with while masturbating. Again, I suspect that I was no different from the other men in this respect. We all had women that we came across on campus whom we wanted to use like the women in pornography were used. For example, I picked women from campus that I was attracted to and who looked like they would do the things that I wanted to do with (or to) them. Then I'd find pictures of them (in the student newspaper, the school album, etc.) and masturbate to their pictures and those in pornography. I would, in effect, re-create these women in my mind to be the women in pornography—that is, women who liked having done to them exactly what I liked doing to them. I chose women who I thought would be more willing to comply with my sexual demands—and who I fantasized (again, based on their image) would enjoy the particular sexual activities as well. I never fantasized about women whom I liked, or with whom I had any kind of relationship. I always fantasized about women I didn't know or knew only peripherally.

It was while living in this context that I slowly (and reluctantly) began making connections between pornography and the rape and domestic violence to which I bore witness at the shelter. During my first year in college, I began volunteering at the local Women's Center (a joint domestic violence/rape crisis program). The year was 1983, and I was seventeen and living in an all-male dorm. The Hays County Women's Center operated from an overtly feminist perspective that identified domestic and sexual violence as weapons of sexism as well as violence perpetrated by individual men. My work at the Center was where I first began examining men's violence, and this was the first time that I was exposed to feminist literature and theory on violence and oppression. It was also where I first began considering my use of pornography.

I slowly began to accept the feminist analysis of pornography as harmful to women, but I also continued to enjoy looking at pornography, held onto the connection it provided with the other men in the dorm (a connection that was growing increasingly tenuous as a result of my developing feminist consciousness), and felt entitled to the sexual release I got by masturbating to pornography. So I continued looking at pornography even for the first few years that I worked in the movement, and at the Center.

As I became increasingly critical of pornography, this bond I had with other men became increasingly threatened. Looking at pornography with them was one of the few ways that I maintained a connection with them. I wasn't sure what kind of man I was becoming (there were painfully few role models) and I didn't know how to be a man, much less bond with other men, outside of the only kind of connection that I had with men—which had as much to do with looking at and sexualizing women as with anything else. I wanted to maintain this bond. So even if my bonding with other men came at the expense of justice—at the expense of women—initially it was a cost I was willing to pay. Even though I claimed that I knew better, I continued to look at pornography even after I began to understand it as a form of men's sexist violence.

As I continued to grow into a pro-feminist consciousness, my commitment to maintain this bonding with other men became increasingly tenuous, and finally broke. For the more than two years that I continued to live in the dorm after adopting an anti-pornography, pro-feminist stance, my connection with the other men in the dorm was virtually non-existent. I simply lived there. My friends, supporters, and comrades became exclusively women. There was no specific act or moment that moved me to finally stop looking at pornography and throw it away. Rather, it was the culmination of what I was learning about feminism, pornography, and men's violence; what I was learning about myself; and my growing commitment to bring my personal behaviors in line with my developing political beliefs. Becoming pro-feminist—in lifestyle as well as politically—is a process. As with most processes, my own growth was in fits and starts. Coming to understand pornography from a feminist perspective and then moving to actually stop using pornography was a matter of taking 'two steps forward and one back'.

As I began to openly question our use of pornography (at least using publicly funded equipment), one other man also raised his voice. Marshall's objections were based on his religious beliefs and seemed to have nothing to do with gender justice. While neither of our objections was ultimately heeded, his position was at least acknowledged, tolerated and to some degree respected; my position, on the other hand, was mostly ignored and ridiculed. When the men were discussing a pornographic movie or image that they had seen and Marshall came into the room, they would politely change the subject or at least lower their voices. When I came into the room, they would often continue the conversation, watching for my reaction. I had pornography images taped to my dorm door and stuffed into my mailbox, and was frequently taunted into arguments or debates with a group of men (never one-on-one) about my views. Given that my views were still developing and therefore not fully thought-out or articulate, I was an easy target for this kind of harassment.

What remains one of my most painful memories is of a Christmas 'gift' I received during my last year of living in the dorm. One of the traditions in the dorm was to draw names and exchange gag gifts. The night of the dorm party, I had been out with feminist friends, and came in late. Over a dozen of my dorm mates were hanging out; they quickly gathered around to watch as I opened my gift. To my shock and horror, my 'gift' was a naked girl baby doll covered in ketchup. I was so dismayed that I initially didn't know how to react. I went numb, let the 'gift' drop to the floor, and quietly walked to my room. From that point forward, I remained utterly disengaged from the men in the dorm and from any of the dorm activities. Although that last assault was not specifically targeting my views about pornography, it was clearly an attack on my views of violence against women and children. It exposed the level of utter contempt the other men had for me and my work.

It was through working at the battered women's shelter that I most clearly began recognizing the connections between pornography and other forms of men's violence against women. Most of the women who came to the center (or whom I accompanied to the hospital or police station)—the majority of whom were Latina—were reluctant to disclose the details of their abuse and victimization to a 17–20-year-old white man. Even still, some of the women did share with me the remarkable gift of their stories—often much more than I ever wanted to know. Some of their stories included the ways that the men who battered them used pornography. Initially, I maintained the facade that there was a fundamental difference between those men, who put the women they loved in the shelter or the hospital, and me. As I become more involved in the movement, and came to better understand the dynamics of power and control, I increasingly came to realize just how similar I was (and am) to the men who choose to abuse the women they claim to love. My commitment to continue looking at pornography was, perhaps, one of the most striking ways I was like 'them'. As I listened to the women who stayed in the shelter or who came to the center, and heard them describe the ways that their men treated them, I began to hear some common themes—themes of expectations, rights, and entitlements. As I began recognizing these themes, I also began seeing them in the ways that I acted with the women I dated, and in the ways that we as men talked about the women we dated and were attracted to.

The often brutal stories these women shared, coupled with the analysis I was beginning to understand, led me to look more critically at how my use of pornography poisoned my view of women, undermined my commitment to social justice, disturbed my view of sex and sexuality, damaged my view of men, and ultimately undermined my humanity. Thanks largely to my early feminist mentors (including Delma Gomez, Cindy Medina, Linda Webster, Dr. Ramona Ford, Debby Tucker, Loretta Ross, and others), I began to criticize what I had always taken as normal, healthy and a right. I began to recognize the stories that some of the women from the center told me in the stories I read in the pages of those magazines, and in the fantasies that I myself created.

The women whom I fantasized about having sex with (on, at, in . . .) became strikingly similar to the women with whom I sat at the hospital, in the shelter or at the police station. The women that I fantasized about began to lose their anonymity and they started to become more real. This is not to say that I got to know any of the women whose images I jacked off to, but rather that their images began to hold real human meaning for me. Rather than being anonymous names and pictures of 'women who looked like they would like to . . .', they became women who were sisters, friends, girlfriends and daughters of someone, and who might have been abused as kids, raped by a date, abused by a boyfriend, or who watched their father beat up their mother. As I began to see through the pornographic imagery of these women— my school-mates—my ability to masturbate to their images became increasingly difficult. The sexualized image I had created of them began to fade into the real women that they were. My experience mirrors that of the men in my parents' classes, when they interviewed the women strippers before watching the show. They reported that they couldn't enjoy the show as much any more because the women had become real to them through the interview.

I gradually, and painfully, began to realize that my sexual fantasies (encouraged by pornography) were more about violation than about sexual discovery and relating. The 'sex' promoted by pornography is not based on mutual exploration and satisfaction, and does not hold respect, dignity, and justice as core values. Rather, pornography is about men doing what we will to women, and women depicted as deserving and liking what we do to them—enjoying the position of being done to (or on, or in, or at). So long as it is called 'sexual' and understood as purely personal (and therefore private) behavior, and as long as sex is defined as the sexual satisfaction of me(n), then what is actually done is defined as beyond debate. Ultimately, my participation in pornography was my participation in violation and abuse.

It was somewhere in this process that I began reading Andrea Dworkin. Her work was a profound influence on my developing pro-feminist/anti-pornography position. Although I can't remember who or what originally led me to her work, I do remember vividly the first book of hers that I read (*Our Blood*) and its immense impact on me.[1] One of the segments that spoke to me follows:

> I want to suggest to you that a commitment to sexual equality with males, that is, to uniform character as of motion or surface, is a commitment to becoming the rich instead of the poor, the rapist instead of the raped, the murderer instead of the murdered. I want to ask you to make a different commitment—a commitment to the abolition of poverty, rape and murder; that is, a commitment to ending the system of oppression called patriarchy; to ending the male sexual model itself. (p. 12)

Reading this, as a nineteen-year-old, was challenging and difficult, but Andrea's prophetic call to justice resonated in me and called me to a deeper commitment—a commitment that included re-examining my use of pornography.

I did not want to hear or believe what she had said in that book—or in some of her later books. I cried at the stories she shared and the enormity of the pain that they uncovered. I became enraged—not only at the horrible injustice that was committed, but also at Andrea for the conclusions that she drew. I was, after all, still committed to my own use of pornography and did not want to have to connect my buying of *Penthouse*, or watching of *Debbie Does Dallas* with the pain and horror that she described. I was not like them . . . I was a kinder, gentler pornography consumer—a pro-feminist reader of *Penthouse* and *Playboy*.

Reading Andrea Dworkin ripped off the blinders of denial and minimizing that I had constructed around my use of pornography—and ripping was exactly what it felt like, as if a portion of my eyelids were being slowly torn away. I had, by then, done enough work myself to allow the ripping to happen,

---

1   Although *Our Blood* does not itself directly examine pornography, the analysis Dworkin offered in this book began to influence my developing pro-feminist analysis and the way that I looked at pornography. *Our Blood* was also my introduction to Andrea Dworkin, and my entree into the rest of her works.

but I truly believe that had I not read Andrea's work, I would not have come to understand the depth of degradation, humiliation and pain that I was a party to through my participation in pornography. I learned to hate pornography thanks to Andrea Dworkin.

I did have the choice to close my eyes again once they had been opened—to continue to deny, minimize or ignore the pain and harm that I had become witness to, but that level of self-deception became exceedingly difficult, and the self-denial involved was a huge price to pay. As I began to understand the harm of pornography, and thus, the harm of *my* use of pornography, I struggled with the tension between denying what I was learning—thus allowing myself to continue to look at pornography—and striving to be true to myself. I came to realize the direct connections. I looked at *Penthouse*; the women who were shown in *Penthouse* were harmed by the pictures that I paid for, and the women that I looked at on campus and in the streets of that small south Texas college town were harmed by the change in how I looked at them.

Perhaps most basically, I came to understand, via Dworkin, how pornography represented the most grotesque forms of male self-centeredness. The sex that I learned—and I agree with Dworkin that all men learn, whether heterosexual, bisexual, or homosexual—is a sex with *me* at the center. The discourse of pornography is that sex is about *my* (read 'male as the subject') sexual pleasure and release. If my sexual 'partner(s)' achieve sexual pleasure, it is secondary to mine, and occurs as a result of the degree to which they have successfully sexualized their subordination.

Lessons from [heterosexual] pornography

While looking at pornography, I developed a way of looking at women. I developed, if you will, a pornographic ethic. After looking at pornography, I did not look at women as colleagues, potential friends, or allies, or with any kind of gaze based on justice or caring. I looked at women based on how I compared them to the man-made images of women I saw in the magazines or on the videos. The women I saw on the street, in classes, at meetings, etc. became simply 'fuck-able' to varying degrees. I looked at them and thought about the things that I would like to do *to* (not *with*) them sexually—things that I fantasized they would enjoy, but the ultimate focus of which was my own sexual fulfillment.

Heterosexual pornography offers messages to men not only about *how* to relate to women, but also about *which* women to relate to, and how to relate to different women differently. Not all women are displayed in pornography, and different kinds of women are displayed differently. Lesbians, for example, are depicted as male-focused and still 'really' only wanting penetrative sex. Women of color are depicted more often with multiple men having sex with (on or in) them, and very often are depicted with animals, being tied up, or with weapons. This pattern reinforces racist gender stereotypes in male consumers—that Latina women are 'hot' and insatiable, that African-American women are aggressive and insatiable, that Asian women are submissive and insatiable, and that European-American women are still the 'real' prize of sexual conquest. Heterosexual pornography's messages about different kinds of women reinforce the messages that are already imbedded in our society, and have real ramifications for the real women who are living in communities along with men who look at pornography.

I certainly found this to be true in my experience on the college campus. When I dated women of color or had women of color as friends who came up to my room, the imagery that my dorm mates created about the kinds of sex that I shared with these women was straight out of the pornography that we looked at. For example, when a European-American dorm mate was dating a Latina woman, other men in the dorm would comment on how 'hot' she must be, and in other ways expanded upon very sexualized and racialized themes. Granted, this was the way that we conversed about all women—all were rated on the degree to which we saw them as 'fuck-able'—but for women of color and Latinas in particular, these conversations were intensified.

Perhaps even more telling is my experience (much later) of working with adolescent and adult men who sexually offend. In my experience, and according to most of the literature, most men who sexually offend use pornography on a regular basis. Their pornography use not only defined for them an image of women or children, and created sexualized images which they projected onto other women or children; pornography also helped them construct an image of themselves as men—as virile, powerful, sexually attractive and desired by women or children. Men who sexually offend generally differentiate themselves from 'rapists' or 'sex offenders', indicating that what they did is not the same thing, because (they think) the women or children they assaulted liked what happened. This belief is based in part on their denial and minimizations, but it is also based in part on their pornography use.

As much as any single experience, my work with men who sexually offended confirmed for me the ways that pornography creates and enforces messages about men's sexualized use of violence with women. I can't describe the number of times I heard men describe, utterly sincerely, how the women or children they raped 'really liked it'—in spite of their having been arrested and convicted, in spite of the victim's tears, her pushing him away, her attempts to get away from him. This belief is identical to the fantasies in so much hard-core pornography—pornography that depicts women being forced to do sexual things and 'liking it'. The message from pornography is that women want sex, often and indiscriminately, and they only need to be reminded (by men, often forcibly) that they do, after all, want sex.

Pornography taught me these lessons: 'be in control', 'be a top',[2] 'your sexual pleasure is tied to the degree to which you can maintain yourself as a top'. Women are depicted as a compilation of holes in which, and body parts on which, to unload men's cum. Pornography also teaches that men become (and remain) men by penetrating women or other men—in both heterosexual and gay male pornography; that the 'best sex' is depicted as involving multiple penetrations. Either a woman or man is penetrated several times at once by different men, is penetrated by a penis and a finger (or dildo, or fist, or some other object) at the same time or is penetrated several times (and in multiple positions) over the period of a sexual encounter. Images of non-penetrative, exploratory, experimental sex are so rare as to be almost nonexistent in pornography. As Dworkin (1987) has convincingly argued, penetration under patriarchy—and especially in pornography—means more than penetration. A man's act of putting his penis into another's body connotes that he now owns that person, and once owned, the 'woman' relinquishes any right to say no. The more times and ways one is penetrated, the more owned one becomes.

As I reflect upon the lessons I learned through pornography, this lesson stands out. Having sex meant penetration—and once I had penetrative sex with a woman I felt that I then had greater access to her in more situations, at more times, and in more ways. In short, I came to see her as 'mine.'

'Flirting' without the pornographers' gaze

As I began to better understand pornography, I realized that the masculinity depicted in pornography was not the kind of masculinity—indeed, the kind of personhood—I wanted for myself. I began to develop a view of my own personhood that was fluid, flexible, and allowed for multiple kinds of relationships with both women and other men. I wanted the ability and encouragement to experience sexuality in ways that include softness and pleasure not necessarily derived from genital stimulation. Pornography does not allow these images of masculinity and in fact, it teaches men that being manly requires the dissolution of such 'wimpy' characteristics.

I realized that I had to develop a new way to flirt with and date women (I was not at this point out, even to myself, about my bisexuality). Giving up the pornographer's gaze towards women was hard enough; developing a new gaze that allowed me room to be attracted to women and to express that attraction in non-degrading ways was something else again. I had little

---

2   In the US (at least) gay culture refers to sexual partners as 'top' or 'bottom' to reflect their preferred position in sexual encounters. There is often also an underlying suggestion as to one's preference in terms of being more submissive (a bottom) or more dominant (a top) in a relationship in general.

support, except for my female feminist friends (with whom, of course, there was little room to talk about how I could flirt or be attracted in a way that subverted the pornographic paradigm). Without any support or models, I found no way to resolve the dilemma, other than to give up dating altogether. While far from a perfect solution, this did provide me with the room and distance I needed to begin re-constructing my gaze towards women in a way that highlighted their humanity while also allowing for any attraction I felt. For several years, then, I did not flirt—at least not consciously. This does not mean that I wasn't attracted, only that I didn't know how to act on those attractions in a way that honored the women to whom I was attracted. Thus, I stopped acting on them at all.

Slowly, I did begin to develop a way to find women attractive outside of the pornographic mindset. I learned to notice the beauty of women and men in a way that was not sexualized and objectified. Beauty is just beauty. I came to realize that the pornographic gaze was a sexualized gaze—seeing beauty only in sexualized terms that in turn were linked to my access. Pornography had taught me not only to notice and appreciate women's beauty, but to sexualize it—and by sexualizing it, I made 'it' something that I had the right, or at least should have the opportunity, to claim. Once sexualized, a woman's beauty became some-*thing* (a thing distinct and separate from her *self*) that I was then entitled to—to look at, make comments about, touch, have sexual release to (either directly or through my fantasies), etc.

As I became better able to notice and acknowledge the beauty of the people around me without sexualizing it, it lost this key element of entitlement and access. You will also note that I included men in this discussion. As women's beauty became less sexualized for me, I was able to notice and acknowledge men's beauty. Thus, this was the time when I began exploring my bisexuality.

For me, it was only through not participating in flirting while I continued to divest myself from the pornographic gaze, that I was finally able to develop a way to look at women and men, to flirt, and to appreciate beauty that felt respectful. I found that I was able to see and appreciate a wider range of 'beauty'—not just the physical attributes that are so highlighted in pornography, but the real beauty of human beings—his eyes, her smile, the way he carries himself, how her joy floods out of her body. These forms of beauty are not even acknowledged under the pornographic gaze, and as long as I continued to look with this gaze, I could not notice them.

Coming out and coming to confront gay male pornography

I began to explore my bisexuality, in part, by looking at and masturbating to gay male pornography. This occurred after I had already come to reject heterosexual pornography. Initially, I believed the pro-pornography hype that describes gay male pornography as inherently different from heterosexual pornography. According to this view, gay men are subject to what Adrienne Rich (1980) describes as 'compulsory heterosexuality'—the notion that we are pressured and coerced to act (only) heterosexually. Within such a culture, any depiction of same-sex sexual behavior is a direct affront to compulsory heterosexuality and is therefore understood as an act of rebellion and liberation.

For me, gay male pornography was one way to begin exploring my sexual feelings towards other men and to educate myself about different forms of same-sex sex. I used gay male pornography and had it used on me in order to explore different kinds of sexual expression, and to begin defining my boundaries for sex with other men. By definition, this boundary-setting process means that there were times when I learned what I was comfortable with or enjoyed by engaging in behavior that I later realized I did not like. I understand that this is often part of the process that we go through to learn our limits— sometimes you have to cross a line to figure out where that line is. However, gay male pornography made this limit setting, as a baby queen, much more difficult, and my limits much easier to manipulate by some of the men I dated who were more interested in their sexual pleasure than in my defining limits.

Some of the men I dated would show me gay male pornography as a way of demonstrating what they wanted to do, or thought that I would enjoy. Luckily, I had very few experiences of men being overtly mean or abusive— forcing me to do what I clearly wasn't interested in doing. But the use of gay male pornography was a way to show me that it was 'okay' and that I 'might' like it. Having gay male pornography used with me in this way left me feeling vulnerable and rather limited in my options. There was a pressure to comply, to go along with whatever was suggested, because I liked the men I was with, I wanted them to ask me out again, and I didn't know if I would like what they were describing or not unless I tried it. Being new to the gay/bi male scene, I was unsure about possible ramifications if I chose not to go along (Would he not ask me out again? Would he spread the word to other men? Would I have a hard time finding other men to date? etc.). I was already somewhat suspect because I also dated women, so I feared that any hesitation in going along with the gay male pornographic ethos would be further evidence of my 'not belonging'.

The use of gay male pornography, combined with my own feelings of inadequacy and doubt, meant that the option to say 'no'—or to say 'yes but'—was not clear to me. This is not to say that I was somehow victimized, but rather that the way that gay male pornography was used with me made it more difficult to see the full array of sexual options in front of me, which means that my ability to truly consent was limited.

In retrospect, I also realized how gay male pornography set the tone for these sexual encounters. In gay pornography, there is a top and a bottom. The possibility of partner (i.e. side-by-side, mutual) gay male sexuality is not depicted. What is normalized and eroticized is the 'top' dominating and the 'bottom' enjoying being dominated, or at least being the one that is done to (on, in, at). Most of the men I dated, at least initially, were interested in my being the bottom. It was only after being in the gay scene for a while that I began to meet men who were more interested in a partner kind of sexual relationship.

It's clear, then, that the pornographic ethic I described earlier is not exclusive to heterosexual pornography or to heterosexual men. Gay and bi men learn the very same ethic, only with other men as the target of our gaze. As I began accepting my attraction to men, gay male pornography taught me which men were—and how to present myself as—fuck-able. The men that are done-to in gay male pornography are presented as different from the men who are doing. This difference is often gendered and raced—the men who are done-to are 'feminized' in many ways, including through the use of language. The one done to becomes the 'woman', 'bitch', 'cunt', 'whore', 'pussy' (Kendall, 2002). By looking at gay male pornography, I learned which of these two options I wanted to be—the top ('man') or the bottom ('woman'). In the gay male pornography that I saw (unlike most of the gay sexual activity that I engaged in), these roles were rigidly maintained—the top was not penetrated and the bottom did no penetrating. In this way, gay male pornography maintains the very same social oppression—of women and queer men—that it allegedly rebels against.[3]

Through gay male pornography I learned not only how to 'gaze' at other men, but also how to be gazed at—and to like it. The gaze itself was no different than the gaze I had grown up learning how to direct at women. Turning that gaze to other men took some additional learning and self-exploration, but the gaze, and its objectifying of its target, was the same. If our goal is to create and sustain justice in our relationships, to treat others and be treated with the respect and dignity that every body deserves, then we need to look at other men and women, appreciate their beauty, and be turned on by them without the pornographic gaze.

Currently, as an out bisexual involved in queer activism, I have found very limited opportunities to offer a perspective critical of gay male pornography. The scorn and contempt I face suggests that by 'daring' to criticize gay male pornography, I am challenging sacred territory. As I mentioned above, I am

---

3   For a more detailed development of this argument, see Kendall and Funk, 'Gay Male Pornography's "Actors": When Fantasy Isn't'. In Melissa Farley (2003). *Prostitution, Trafficking and Traumatic Stress*. Binghamton, NY: Haworth.

already suspect within many queer communities for being bisexual, and my exploration of the harm perpetrated by gay male pornography fuels these suspicions. I've been called a man-hater (a charge that has some different meaning and power when made by gay men) and have found myself excluded from queer rights organizing (for example, from projects combating violence against queer people).

Gay and bisexual men's use of pornography, it seems, is sacrosanct. Any suggestion that some (most, all, any) of the men involved in gay male pornography may be harmed, or that gay and bisexual men's use of pornography runs counter to sexual justice and ultimately undermines the queer rights struggle, is utterly unwelcome. As the message is unwelcome, so too is the messenger.

My experiences in gay male communities and movements are, in the end, not dissimilar to my experiences of developing an anti-pornography analysis while living in the all-male dorm in Texas. It seems that men, regardless of their sexual orientation, hold very tightly to their dearly felt 'right' to look at and use other people's nudity. The sexual liberal cult within gay and bisexual male communities functions to negate any critical thinking about 'dirty pictures'.

Despite this environment, I have found that I still need to raise my voice. As a result, I have developed some very strong positive relationships with queer women. Every time I speak up, it builds upon the times that I have spoken out before, and there is a little more awareness, sensitivity and room for questioning. Sometimes allies are discovered in the most unlikely places. As with any other effort for social change, each episode of 'speaking out' is a drop against the boulder of previously held beliefs.

Men of color in pornography

Men of color are rarely depicted in either gay or straight pornography (although this may be changing with the continuing development of the on-line pornography industry and the development of several sites that focus specifically on inter-racial sex). When they are depicted, the image is that they are 'well endowed' and sexually driven. These depictions maintain and reinforce the racist stereotypes of men of color. Heterosexual pornography conveys to European-American men that men of color (particularly African-American men) are threatening competitors for the 'finest prize' of European-American women's sexuality. It reinforces a white and male supremacist view of men of color as a threat to 'white womanhood', in addition to portraying 'white women' as objects to be desired, protected, taken, had, used, etc. As a liberal 'white boy' in South Texas, I considered myself to be anti-racist and had men of color as friends, dorm mates, and roommates; still, I found myself looking at men of color (including my male friends) and wondering if they really were as I had seen them depicted in pornography.

Similar images of men of color are found in gay male pornography, although with the complicating factor that men of color are also depicted, in interracial sex, as the 'bottom'. When men of color are depicted as the bottom, it is often with multiple 'partners' or with the same kinds of weapons and penetrative objects that women of color are depicted with in heterosexual pornography. Men of color are shown as insatiably sexualized (even more so than European-American men) and as willing to do anything for a good lay. This imagery, maintained, reinforced and strengthened by pornography (both heterosexual and gay male), could have been produced during slavery and reconstruction, during the Texas independence wars (in relation to Latino men), during the Indian wars, or during the building of the rail line (in relation to Asian men). It is a dangerous white supremacist fantasy, and it is alive and well in pornography.

As these differing portrayals imply, men from different backgrounds have different relationships with pornography and prostitution, as well as different experiences with male privilege and sexist violence. The ways that men from various groups are portrayed in pornography, the use of men in prostitution, the ability of men to control women and other men in pornography and prostitution (i.e., as producers, promoters, director, owners, etc.) all have an impact on how men from different backgrounds relate to pornography. This is not to say that all men don't benefit and don't abuse women, or that men's use of women or other men in pornography and prostitution is not always harmful; this is to say that men's use is more complicated than blanket statements suggest, and it is deserving of a more complex and nuanced analysis and a broader range of activism.

Implications for organizing men

The main goal of this essay is to suggest means of mobilizing men to take action against pornography, sexism, and men's violence. This means, in organizing men, that we work with men from where they are (not from where we want them to be). By better understanding men's different relationships with various forms of men's violence and sexism, as described above, we are better equipped to support men as they begin working for gender and sexual justice.

There are three key questions that flow from this analysis and that affect efforts to mobilize and organize men. First, how do pornography and prostitution keep men from being involved actively in ending men's sexist violence against women? Second, how do pornography and prostitution interfere with men's ability to create and sustain loving, passionate and just relationships with women and other men? Third, what does it say about men that these forms of sexual exploitation exist in the first place?

Unpacking this last question results in a host of additional questions. What does it say about men that these forms of sexual exploitation have become huge multi-billion dollar industries? What does it say about men that these specific forms of sexual exploitation of women have resulted in the development of a huge underground international network that traffics women for the purposes of men's sexual satisfaction—a trafficking network that is, reportedly, third in size after drug and weapons trafficking? What does it say about men that these forms of sexual exploitation are not seen as exploitation—the harm denied, the pain ignored—but are so firmly entrenched as forms of sexual expression, and thus as a right? What is the connection between men's participation in pornography and prostitution, and men's involvement in rape and sexual harassment? What is the relationship between men's participation in pornography and prostitution and men's racism, homophobia, anti-Semitism, and ageism?

Most organizing and activism is based primarily on identity politics—getting people mobilized and increasing their skills to more effectively take action to address those issues that directly affect them. This approach has also been used, at least initially, in many of the efforts to organize 'allies' (such as white folks against racism, heterosexuals against homophobia, and men against sexism). Organizing men against pornography, prostitution, and other forms of sexist violence often begins by organizing men as allies, and examining and exposing the ways that pornography and prostitution affect men. Thus, one part of organizing men against pornography and prostitution requires showing how men—individually and collectively—are harmed by the production, distribution and consumption of pornography. In such efforts, we must always take into account the different relationships that different populations of men have with pornography and prostitution. We must also be extremely careful not to pit men's harm and pain related to pornography against that of women. To more effectively mobilize and organize men, part of our work is to develop deeper analyses of how men are harmed by pornography within an overall context that focuses on women's experiences and needs.

These kinds of tactics can be useful as a way to begin engaging men in a discussion about pornography and prostitution (as well as about other forms of men's sexist violence). Some such attempts have emphasized that using pornography (and/or prostituted women or men) inhibits men's healthy sexual development and growth, undermines men's abilities to maintain healthy and just sexual relationships with women and/or other men, and increases their likelihood of committing sexual assault. However, these harms are often difficult to identify and articulate. Many men have a hard time recognizing this harm on other than an intellectual level; there is little emotional connection and 'buy in'. Furthermore, any harm that men identify must be weighed against the immediate, concrete, and dramatic benefits that they receive from pornography and prostitution (directly from their own use, as well as indirectly from the existence of these industries). Organizing men from this perspective is based on men's self-interest and thus requires that organizers identify a greater self-interest for men in stopping their pornography use than in continuing it. For these reasons, men's self interest is a tenuous foundation for mobilizing and organizing men against prostitution and pornography. While it may be useful in opening the door for men, it does not seem effective in creating an ongoing movement of men committed to eliminating pornography, supporting women and men who have been victimized, and creating sexual and gender justice.

Thus, as anti-pornography activists, we need to create tools and analyses that move beyond identity-based organizing. While some have argued that men aren't capable of being involved for reasons beyond their self-interest, our experiences as activists, and my personal experiences depicted here, suggest otherwise. As I have described in this chapter, my own movement to an anti-pornography position was based on my growing understanding of the harm caused by pornography, my empathy with the women and men who are harmed, and my increasing awareness of the ways that pornography undermined my personal commitment to justice, freedom and liberation. Although my sex life improved dramatically as I began critiquing and dissecting the pornographic ethos I had grown up with, this element of self-interest served to reinforce my growing commitment to justice as the primary motivator.

On a broader level, many men are leaders and involved participants in anti-globalization, anti-racism, and anti-militarism movements, as well as in other social justice and human rights causes that do not benefit them personally. They (like the women in such movements) are motivated primarily not by self-interest or identity politics, but by a broader moral commitment. It is this same sense of moral commitment that needs to be developed for men in confronting pornography.

I broke with pornography when I recognized the inherent immorality and hypocrisy of my working for gender justice on the one hand, while using my other hand to jack off to the imagery of women created by other men for me(n) to sexualize. Being committed to justice and using pornography is inherently contradictory, because one cannot look at others as fully equal, empowered, dynamic human beings if one is also looking at them through the pornographic gaze.

Developing creative and effective tactics for mobilizing men means, in part, re-claiming the morality of gender justice and human rights. The conservative right has been extremely successful in organizing from a 'morality' perspective, and in the process, they have hijacked the language of morality. But ending pornography through anti-woman, anti-choice, anti-sexuality, anti-gay perspectives is neither just nor moral. Organizing men against pornography requires that we continue to develop a pro-feminist radical morality—one that is sex positive, that supports equality of rights for people of all sexual orientations, and that supports a full array of reproductive rights for women and reproductive responsibilities for men. It is morally correct for women to be seen and celebrated for their full humanity, and to be supported and encouraged to express that humanity.

Organizing men against pornography from a morality angle can be seen in the 'pose exercise' developed by John Stoltenberg and Men Against Pornography. In this exercise, men are invited, in front of other men, to 'strike a pose' in the way that women are depicted in pornography (the men are allowed to keep their clothes on and the 'props' are not a part of the exercise). The men posing are then asked to describe how they feel in general, and in particular how empowered and comfortable they feel while taking the pose. Invariably the men describe feeling disempowered, uncomfortable, vulnerable, anxious, and so on. The exercise thus builds their empathy with the women in pornography, and appeals to their sense that it is morally right for each person to feel empowered and morally wrong for anyone to be systematically disempowered.

Additionally, by exploring how the men in heterosexual pornography (either as 'co-stars' or as producers) view the women in pornography; and how they themselves view the women in pornography, men can begin to see how pornography strips women of their multi-dimensional humanity, creating a sexualized uni-dimensional caricature that is depicted as always open, available and desirous of men. This view of women is morally wrong, and an industry that systematically portrays women in this way is morally bankrupt.

Pornography is hate propaganda, and prostitution is exploitation. If we want a world that is based on justice—gender justice, racial justice, class justice, justice among people of various sexual orientations—then pornography and prostitution must be eliminated. To eliminate pornography and prostitution requires that men be involved—not only because men are half the population, but more importantly because men are the main producers, distributors, and consumers of women and men in pornography and prostitution. The morality of justice is our morality, and it cannot coexist with pornography and prostitution.

References

Awkward, Michael. (2001). 'A Black Man's Place in Black Feminist Criticism.' In Byrd, Rudolph P., and Beverly Guy-Sheftall (eds). *Traps: African American Men on Gender and Sexuality.* Bloomington, IN: Indiana University Press.

Barry, Kathleen. (1995). *The Prostitution of Sexuality.* New York: New York University Press.

Dines, Gail, Robert Jensen and Ann Russo. (1998). *Pornography: The Production and Consumption of Inequality.* New York: Routledge.

Dworkin, Andrea. (1976) *Our Blood: Prophecies and Discourses on Sexual Politics.* New York: Pedigree Books.

Dworkin, Andrea. (1979). *Pornography: Men Possessing Women.* New York: Pedigree Books.

Dworkin, Andrea. (1987). *Intercourse.* New York: The Free Press.

Dworkin, Andrea. (1988). *Letters From a War Zone: Writings 1976–1989.* New York: E.P. Dutton Books.

Dworkin, Andrea. (2002). 'A Human Rights Framework for Addressing Pornography'. Presentation at the *Centers for Disease Control's Sexual Violence Prevention Conference,* Chicago, IL.

Dworkin, Andrea and Catharine A. MacKinnon. (1988). *Pornography and Civil Rights: a New Day for Women's Equality.* Minneapolis, MN: Organizing Against Pornography.

Farley, Melissa (2003). *Prostitution, Trafficking and Traumatic Stress.* Binghamton, NY: Haworth.

Funk, Rus Ervin. (1993). *Stopping Rape: A Challenge for Men.* Philadelphia, PA: New Society Publishers.

Itzin, Catherine. (1992). *Pornography: Women, Violence and Civil Liberties.* Oxford: Oxford University Press.

Jeffreys, Sheila. (1997). *The Idea of Prostitution.* North Melbourne, Vic., Australia: Spinifex Press.

Kendall, Christopher. (2002). 'The harms of gay male pornography: A sex equality perspective post Little Sisters Book and Art Emporium'. *Australasian Gay and Lesbian Law Journal,* 10.

Lovelace, Linda. (1980). *Ordeal.* New Jersey: Citadel Press.

MacKinnon, Catharine A. (1989). *Toward a Feminist Theory of the State.* Boston, MA: Harvard University Press.

MacKinnon, Catharine A. and Dworkin, Andrea. (1997) *In Harm's Way: The Pornography Civil Rights Hearings.* Boston, MA: Harvard University Press.

Rich, Adrienne. (1980). 'Compulsory Heterosexuality and Lesbian Existence'. *Signs: Journal of Women in Culture and Society,* 5 (4) p, 63.

Russell, Diana E.H. (1993a). *Against Pornography: The Evidence of Harm.* Berkeley, CA: Russell Publications.

Russell, Diana E.H. (ed.). (1993b). *Making Violence Sexy: Feminist Views on Pornography.* Buckingham, England: Open University Press.

Stoltenberg, John. (1990). 'Gays and the Pro-Pornography Movement: Having the Hots for Sex Discrimination'. In Kimmel, Michael (ed.). *Men confront pornography.* New York, NY: Crown Publishers.

Who are women in pornography?: A conversation

Ann: Carol Smith is currently a volunteer with the Mary Magdalene Project. She is a full-time student, and she hopes to start a new organization called 'Porn Star', helping women involved in pornography who want to get out. Can you tell us, Carol, how did you get into this business?

Carol: I got into pornography 11 years ago. I was highly addicted to drugs, and I had been sexually abused as a child. But at that time I hadn't remembered any of that. And here I am 10 years later. After recovering those memories, I put two and two together—the childhood sexual abuse and pornography—and realized, something needs to be done about this.

Ann: You say you were drug addicted. How old were you when you started using drugs?

Carol: I started drinking and doing drugs when I was about ten. By the time I was fourteen, I went to a rehabilitation center. I was nineteen when I got involved with pornography.

Ann: How did you get involved in pornography? You live in the Los Angeles area?

Carol: Yes, I grew up in Calabasas.

Ann: Was it through a friend, or were you modeling?

Carol: I was highly addicted to cocaine. I was doing drugs and living in a house with a bunch of drug dealers, and we were getting evicted. So I was looking in the paper for a job, a regular job. I saw the ad and I went in, and at first I was really scared because I didn't want to do film. I just wanted to do photos. They offered in the ad to just do nude photos. Then the owner of the agency offered me a home—a place to live—and a lot of work if I did film. At that point in my life I really didn't have any other options.

Ann: Describe your experience being in pornography.

Carol: It was awful. It was horrible.

Ann: In what way?

Carol: The way I felt. The way I felt about myself. The way I was abused by men. The way I let people treat me. And even the effects of it now are awful.

Ann: Were you ever physically hurt?

Carol: Yes, I was. A few times.

Ann: Was it on camera?

Carol: One time was on camera and the other time . . . I'm not quite sure of because I was given that date rape drug, so I don't remember much of it.

Ann: The film makers gave you a date rape drug?

Carol: Yes.

Ann: Tell me about the money. A lot of people have the misconception that women in pornographic films make a lot of money.

Carol: Yes, that's a myth. This was ten years ago, back in the early nineties. What I got paid was about $200 to $300 for one scene. You could be in the movie three or four times and get paid more. But that money doesn't last very long when you have a $200-a-day cocaine habit, which probably 80 percent of the women in the industry do.

Ann: You would say 80 percent?

Carol: In the early nineties, yes. Some of the companies now have a policy that you can't be on drugs, but I don't know for sure if that is happening. I'm sure the women use drugs in the amateur films, some of the lower budget films and some films done by new producers.

Ann: Are you familiar with an article Martin Amis wrote on the pornography industry? It ran in the UK *Guardian* and in *Talk* magazine in February of 2001.

Carol: No.

Ann: He describes the pornography industry in detail and talks about how the women are 'used up' quite quickly. He explains how after about a year of being in porn films, the women are often asked to do double anals and more hard-core stunts in the films. It sounded like the pornography audience increasingly wants for the women to be hurt; that it isn't about having sex, but about women being humiliated and in pain. Amis wrote that young eighteen-year-olds who were fresh on the scene would get top money, notoriety and better parts. Then as they got more exposure, they would end up doing lower-budget films and then in two years' time, often be done with the industry or 'used up'.

Carol: That happened to a lot of the women I knew in the industry—mainly because they were so addicted to drugs and it was very difficult for them to function.

Ann: What got you out of the industry or made you want to leave?

Carol: What made me want to leave was that I was totally against doing anal sex. What I didn't remember at the time was that as a child I was abused in that way. So I wouldn't do it. I was afraid to do it. It got to the point where I wasn't getting any work because I wouldn't do it. When it got to the point . . . when you are used up, and they want the women to do gang bangs, I just . . . I couldn't do it. I attempted suicide. I hit bottom. I couldn't do it any more.

Ann: Was it the suicide attempt that made you get out?

Carol: Yes. After two really serious suicide attempts, I finally thought, 'OK. Either die or get out.'

Ann: Did you have any supportive people around to help you?

Carol: I had one aunt who was very supportive. Unfortunately she was an alcoholic, so I had a very difficult time staying sober. And the thought of going back and allowing my parents to help—the people who abused me from the very start—delayed my recovery in a lot of ways. If I had had a program available to me that would've helped me stay clean and sober and given me the services I needed, to provide me with the right type of counseling, education, and to get the skills I needed to function in society, I would have been where I am today—probably eight years earlier.

Ann: What program was it that helped you see there was some other way for you to live?

Carol: It took me a while. I ended up going into a halfway house. I finally just turned my back on everything that had happened to me. I pretended like it had never happened. I sort of reinvented myself and stayed sober. Someone was watching out for me because there aren't many women who have been able to do that on their own. I started working for my father. I met a man, ended up getting pregnant and married him. I started going to church and lived this 'stay-at-home, community mom' sort of life, and pretended that none of that had ever happened to me.

Ann: Can you talk about the harm that you saw and why you feel it is so important to provide services for women to get out of this industry?

Carol: What I saw were women just like myself who were desperate, addicted to drugs, homeless and I'm sure probably at least 80 percent of them suffered from sexual abuse as children. I saw them re-living their childhood experiences by getting into that industry. They were looking for attention, pleasing men, and being abused. And that's all they know. They think it's great. They think it's wonderful. I could've looked you in the eye ten years ago and told you that I loved being in pornography, was proud of what I was doing and that I was having a great time. But now I can tell you that it's so far from the truth. I was very convincing. I could convince you. I mean, I could walk up to a porn star today and she could tell me the same story and I can remember being in that place.

Ann: Why do you think there is so much denial? Is it the myth of the happy whore and the 'pretty woman'? It is certainly a popular myth in today's society.

Carol: I think a lot of it is post-traumatic stress disorder. When you suffer from childhood sexual abuse or were severely abused as a child, you usually repress those memories. You are unable to say, 'I am doing this because I was abused as a child and this is all I know how to do. This is all I know how to feel.' I think a lot of the women are in denial . . . and they don't realize what post-traumatic stress disorder is. You either totally go a whole different direction and turn your life around and get as far away from that abuse as you can—or you re-live the experience, and a lot of these women are re-living what they know how to feel.

Ann: That's a good point. When I was gang raped, like many survivors of sexual abuse, I left my body. At the time this happened to me I was working as a professional model in New York City. I was already good at pretending not to be in my body so I didn't have to feel the harsh judgments of how I looked that were part of my job. To maintain any dignity I tried to disappear—but not existing meant I had to re-invent myself. It was confusing.

Looking back I see similarities between modeling and prostitution. Listen to a model's booking agent pitching the female merchandise to potential clients. In both professions women sell their bodies to make money, and a lot of models use drugs on the job. Although when a model does drugs it's viewed by society as somehow glamorous or exciting.

Carol: Right. Well, you get paid more and it's more acceptable.

Ann: Exactly. Why do we, as a culture, elevate one job and put the other into the gutter? There were many times I had to be naked or change my clothes in front of people, like being in a crowd in the middle of Central Park while they held towels up to try to hide you. They expected models to have no inhibitions about being naked. We embrace one job as terrific and see the other as despicable, when really, they have similarities—except, obviously, posing in outfits is not as invasive as having sex with some stranger.

Could you tell us more about your own experience?

Carol: Yes. I was twenty-seven and a half when I recovered memories from my childhood. Feeling those memories, feeling the pain of them . . . I just wanted to die inside. I think women who are only nineteen or younger are so vulnerable, and no one teaches the young girls in pornography and prostitution how to get through the pain, or to get over it. Not that it ever goes away . . . but being able to deal with it rather than hiding from it, doing drugs and finding other outlets to escape from it.

Ann: What's your understanding of the connection between prostitution and pornography? People often view the two as very different.

Carol: Pornography is prostitution that is legalized as long as someone gets to take pictures or watch. Actually, pornography is much worse than prostitution because it will harm you in a different way the rest of your life. I'm still exploited all over the internet ten years later. It follows me around. People recognize me. I'm harassed because of it. My kids are being harassed at school because of it. So it's going to affect me for the rest of my life. It's not like I just went out onto the street, had sex with a john, collected my money and went home. This will affect my children for their entire life. If one of them wants to become a public figure or an actress, or whatever she wants to be, she's going to be harmed because of who her mother was.

Ann: Hopefully our culture will be more informed about this by the time your children grow up. Maybe that's a good segue for you to tell us about the group you're organizing entitled 'Porn Star', and what your ideas are for that.

Carol: Well, I'm a volunteer for Mary Magdalene Project, and what they do is rescue street prostitutes and provide a long-term facility for them to get care, education, anything they need they get—to be able to recover and function in society. What I would like to do is to eventually have the same type of shelters for women who are involved in the making of pornography. Another thing I will be doing is education in schools, churches, and other organizations about pornography and its root causes. I want to expose what really happens—the danger, the corruption and what's really going on with many of the women involved. I'd also like to go to strip clubs and hand out flyers and pamphlets to strippers, because a lot of women in pornography are recruited through stripping. Strippers make more money if they get involved in pornography and get pictures and box covers, that kind of thing.

Ann: Are you familiar with Julia Query's movie *Live Nude Girls Unite*? She's a stripper from San Francisco who tried to form a union to protect the strippers. The union was meant to address some of the problems for women who strip. One of the problems is that the men carry video cameras into strip booths and film the strippers through the one-way glass. The nude dancers in these booths can't see their audience and have no idea they are being filmed. Then the men post their images or film clips on the internet. There are so many levels of abuse that people aren't aware of. Unfortunately, this film portrays stripping as if it were a terrific job, and helps to legitimize it as a viable job option. The film ignores the harms and how strippers are lured into pornography, as you mentioned.

Carol: The public is so unaware of one of the root causes of what drives women to do this. In our society, we're the objects of desire for men and our job is to please them and make them happy while hurting ourselves. A lot of people don't understand that. And that's what my project will be about— going out and educating kids in junior high and high schools.

Ann: What would you say to a group of young students?

Carol: I would tell them my story. It would grab their attention and they would understand from my personal experience that I know what I'm talking about. It's about educating them and making them aware of how to protect themselves, so that when they do encounter situations like that and they see pornography, they will know what is going on. 'That woman was raped, battered and beaten as child and she's reliving her experiences on film to survive.' They'll have to ask themselves, 'What's wonderful about that? What's glamorous about that? Why would you want to see something like that?'

Ann: That would be a powerful message to young boys. Young girls are possibly already questioning their image in the media. But the boys rarely question these portrayals of women. Most of them haven't even thought about the women as being real people. What a powerful message to our youth, coming from someone like you.

Carol: I would educate the parents first and then the kids. I would get parent groups together and say, 'Here's what I'm going to talk with your kids about— and it is likely you don't know much about this either.' The number one consumers of free internet pornography are boys between the ages of twelve and seventeen, and the rate that children are being molested by boys in that age bracket is rising at an alarming rate and I wonder why?

Ann: It's not surprising, when all they see is oversexed females who appear to want sex all the time. An ad ran during *South Park* recently for a video that featured dozens of women lifting their shirts and showing their breasts, pulling down their pants and showing their rear ends in thongs, and gyrating—all in a 30-second ad. Boys can easily assume women are a different kind of species who constantly and for no apparent reason bare their breasts and jiggle their rear ends.

Carol: And that's so wrong.

Ann: It's certainly distorted. The media sells young boys this message; the billboards say it, everything in our media says it. And who is teaching them that women are humans who deserve respect and who do more than have sex 24/7? No one is. In the home, when mothers, sisters, or wives ask for dignity and equality and respect from their families . . . it becomes nearly impossible in this environment.

Carol: There are so many high school girls I've been involved with here, junior and senior high kids in the community, who want to be porn stars. It's amazing. They have no idea what they're getting into. I think that pornography . . . has desensitized generations of girls to think it's OK.

Ann: Exactly. And not just that it's OK but it's glamorous. The point you made earlier—that what all young girls want is attention and to please men, and it doesn't matter if they're hurt in the process because at least they're getting attention and pleasing men—is a really good point.

Carol: There are other ways to get attention in this world as a woman rather than taking [your] clothes off. How about getting an education or raising children in a healthy family?

Ann: As an activist, I explain that I'm not against sex and nudity but that women do more than just have sex. It's a no-brainer on one level. But on the other hand, when 90 to 95 percent of the images that surround us portray women flat on their backs with their legs open—whether it's *Vogue*, or pornography or beer ads—the message is that women get power through our sexuality and this is how women excel. Sure it's good to be smart, but you'd better look good in a thong—because if you don't, it's as if you don't exist.

Well, Carol, your project sounds incredible . . .

Carol: I'd like to do a lot of outreach and to find other women who are in the same shoes as myself because they're very hard to come by. I haven't found anyone yet, but I want to seek them out personally. . . People have a lot of questions about this. I was in a seminar the other day and there was a group of people who were starting non-profit organizations. Many were coming up to me and asking all kinds of questions, and they were astonished at the information that I was giving them. A lot of the women had children in junior high and high school, and they couldn't believe what they were hearing.

Ann: Well, the bottom line is we live in a sexually repressed culture. Sex is a marketable commodity, not something that we celebrate or rejoice in. We don't teach that the best sex involves an emotional connection with another human being. It has so much to do with having women for sale, how much can you make, what's the gimmick . . . and when the gimmick becomes boring, then pornographers provide something more explicit or violent or bizarre. I've been working as an anti-pornography activist for twenty years, and today kids are one click away from free internet rape, child abuse, bestiality, and worse.

Carol: They don't even have to click!

Ann: Our culture promotes violence, rape and abuse as if it were normal and acceptable.

Carol: Showing healthy sexual relations, or even just a friendship between two adolescents of opposite genders that doesn't have any sexual charge to it, is rare. There was that Pepsi ad with Cindy Crawford where young six or seven-year-old boys were shown staring at her rear end—teaching that little boys are supposed to look at women's 'cans' and say, 'Whoa! Look at that can.'

Ann: Tell me more about your goals.

Carol: Well, I eventually want to go to law school because I am now trying to find a way to remove my material from the internet. The material I only made $200 from, and they made $200 million. I'm trying to get that off the internet, and there are no laws like this that protect women. And who writes and makes the laws? Men.

Ann: Yes, and these same men diligently work to protect their right to view women in every position imaginable—at their leisure.

Carol: Pornography is not free speech.

Ann: Can you explain that?

Carol: For example, in my case, my free speech would allow me to take those [original] tapes and burn them [so they couldn't be sold any more]. Do I have a right to do that? No, even though I am in them and now I realize what their content actually is. I haven't any rights as long as someone else thinks it's OK, even though I'm in them. Where are my rights? Where are my rights to protect my kids? They don't exist.

Ann: I don't think enough people are aware of the legal loophole in a woman's right to own her own image. Once it hits the marketplace, it's not only available for everyone to download and copy but is protected as free speech.

Carol: That is another big reason I want to go to law school, to help reform that industry. The government needs to step in and say, 'OK, if you're going to do this and you are going to have young girls sign contracts—then here's how the contracts have to be written.' It should be illegal to use their image for longer than a certain period of time and it should be illegal for pornographers to only pay the women 0.02% of the profits made from the woman's image.

Ann: It's amazing that our 'civilized' culture can use the signatures of young drug-addicted girls who have been sexually abused on legally binding contracts, then pay them some pittance, and then allow these pimps to own the woman's image forever.

Carol: You know, after I left that industry I never turned back. But in the process of my divorce, my ex-husband decided to inform the neighborhood of my past. He found me online and told the whole neighborhood; my whole community knows, and it's a very small town.

Ann: That is so awful. It provides even more incentive for you to get the information out about what is going on in this industry, who you are and what you are doing now. The fact that you are volunteering for the Mary Magdalene Project is great. What is it like working with them?

Carol: It's an awesome experience. The women who run it are incredible. It's helping me understand what it takes to run an organization. Those women do the work of ten men. It's unbelievable what they get done, the amount of work they have to do and they have a great attitude about it. They enjoy doing it. Their success rate in that program is about 90 percent. That's really rare. The long-term stability they've had with their employees is also very rare. I'm getting great experience from it because I hope to have a similar program. Also, it's important that Mary Magdalene does not accept government money, because the government puts restrictions on how long a woman can stay in the program.

Ann: Some need longer than others, especially those who have been sexually abused as children.

Carol: Right, and some people don't even remember the abuse. I was eight years sober, had two kids, had been married, gotten away from the industry, had somewhat of a relationship with my family . . . until one day my father wanted to take my kids fishing alone. I started waking up with nightmares and my memories came back. It took me that long to get those memories back.

Ann: People don't understand how common that is, and that the memories won't surface until one is ready—or when something triggers them, like when your father asked to be alone with your daughters overnight.

Carol: I could have turned my back on the nightmares and gone back into the same mode I was in when I got myself into pornography. But then I would have repeated the cycle with my own kids. I could never ever watch my kids being hurt like that. It pains me to see other people's kids have to face that kind of stuff too. I cry a lot when I see other kids being hurt.

Ann: Of course. It's a natural instinct, given what you have been through.

Carol: Yes, you know, for me it is natural and for a lot of women it is, but not for my family. I mean they did nothing; they didn't care. They didn't wonder. They don't care what happens to their grandchildren. My mother watched me being sexually abused and did nothing about it.

Ann: Do you have a relationship with her?

Carol: No, because I confronted them. They wanted to know why they couldn't take them fishing and I said, 'Here's why. Let's talk about this.' But they refused and didn't want to have anything to do with me any more. They tried to have a relationship with my children through my ex-husband and tried to visit them at his house. I had to put a restraining order on them.

Ann: Can you talk about what is going on with your lawsuit against the pornographers?

Carol: Well, I have talked to probably twelve lawyers in depth about the issues of the case. And because I have 36 different [porn companies as] defendants, 90 percent of the lawyers don't want to touch it. Most of them don't have experience with it. I don't want to say that they don't care, but to do this on contingency is a lot of work. A lot of them say, 'Oh, there's got to be another case like this.' If I could find a similar case to mine there would be no problem, but there hasn't been one. There has not been another woman who's come back and said, 'What you did was wrong. You're going to pay for it and you are going to take my images off of the internet.' There are no cases in California that we have found using several lawyers, and I'm a paralegal myself and still we haven't found a case like mine. So this would be putting a case on the books.

Ann: Which is essential for women's human rights. We need to regain our rights over our bodies and images. The fact that others haven't tried is frightening. There could be images of you when you were given the date rape drug; that's clearly not something you consented to. Your case is vital to all women and I wish you the best.

Carol: I just talked to Catharine MacKinnon. She has exhausted the law herself. She was Linda Lovelace's attorney, and there was nothing she could do for that poor woman. And Linda had not signed any contracts—I signed over a hundred contracts that gave them the rights to my life to do whatever they wanted, whenever they wanted. And even without contracts there was nothing Linda could do. A lot of lawyers don't want to stand up against the pornography industry, because they would have to go up against some of the most well-paid lawyers in the world. But at some point things will have to change.

Ann: Exactly; there are always new angles we can take to try to rethink the situation.

Carol: Yes, there are a couple of angles in my case that I have developed with the attorney that I've retained. Unfortunately, I can't speak about the details yet.

Jane Caputi

Cuntspeak: Words from the heart of darkness*

This is the place our stories come from—
Tales of break and entry

. . .

This is where the songs, pictures, poems
no one wants to know about happen—
here,
between our legs.

. . .

This is where our stories come from—
from our bearded mouths.

—Heide Eigenkind (1991, p. 24), 'Cunt Song'

'I'm gonna fuck your brains out, cunt!'
My no comes from the goddess
Deep inside the dark cave of my body,
From my blood and bones and womb,
For once my father is silent.

—Alison Stone (in Harris 2000, p. 285)

What the survivors said was speech; the pornography had been throughout their lives,
a means of actively suppressing their speech. They had been turned into pornography
in life and made mute; terrorized by it and made mute. Now the mute spoke.

—Andrea Dworkin (1997, p. 91), 'Beaver Talks'

In her 1987 work, *Intercourse*, Andrea Dworkin invites her readers to
consider how heterosexual coitus, defined and delimited by male power,
operates as a sexually political practice, a ritual that positions women as space

* Parts of this article first appeared in Caputi (2003). I want to thank Jennifer Rycenga
and Brooke Bailey for their generous and most helpful critical readings of this piece.

to be invaded, that bonds eroticism to dominance and submission, that requires female objectification, that works to destroy female freedom, and induces women to collaborate with our oppression.

In a review of *Intercourse* published in the left-wing magazine, *The Nation*, the visual artist Maureen Mullarkey (1987) blasts Dworkin's ideas as, among other things, lunatic and fascist. So outraged is Mullarkey that she reaches deep for a word that can convey the very essence of Dworkin's offense. Finding it, she avers: 'Dworkin's strong-arm specialty is cuntspeak' (p. 721). What exactly is she saying? That Dworkin sounds like a 'cunt'— stereotypically stupid, mindless and irrational? That Dworkin herself is pornographic, obscene? Mullarkey doesn't really define this evocative term, using it loosely to castigate what she feels to be Dworkin's crudity, 'hate-mongering', and error.

Mullarkey's brand of female-, sex- and body-negative invective is not unique. A similar rhetoric characterizes those who are hostile to women's freedom and women's speech. For example, in 2001 some male members of the French Parliament, rancorous about female membership in what they wanted to be a purely male governmental body, made sneering remarks about 'vaginal verbosity', slurs that were meant to silence a female colleague as she stood to make a speech (Otis 2000, p. 9).

A parallel slur informs a comic selection from the pornographic magazine *Hustler*. It simultaneously provides a rather astonishing vindication of Dworkin's argument about the sexist dimensions of intercourse. Under a caption reading 'Lip Service', there is a photograph of a woman's face; a hairy vulva has replaced her mouth; the text below the picture reads:

> There are those who say that illogic is the native tongue of anything with tits . . . It comes natural to many broads; just like rolling in shit is natural for dogs . . . They speak not from the heart but from the gash, and chances are that at least once a month your chick will stop you dead in your tracks with a masterpiece of cunt rhetoric . . . The one surefire way to stop those feminine lips from driving you crazy is to put something between them—like your cock, for instance (cited in Russell 1998, p. 65).

Hustler warns of the danger of 'illogic' or 'cunt rhetoric' to the patriarchal logos or worldview. It recommends the appropriate remedy: to shut the offending 'mouth' through intercourse/rape.[1] Ironically, Dworkin is accused of 'cuntspeak' precisely when she dares to interrupt patriarchal intercourse— not only the sexual but also the discursive kind (*intercourse* means not only

---

1 Visual representations of this same intent can be found readily, and free, on pornographic websites. A standard image is of the mid-section of a woman with legs spread wide, labia wrenched apart by clamps, vagina and anus stuffed with thick electrodes, and wires attached to electro-shock and torture her.

a sexual interchange but also 'communication', 'communion', and the 'exchange of thought and feeling'—*Webster's*). As Dworkin so vividly argues throughout all of her works, the logic of domination enacted in patriarchal intercourse is the very 'logic' that drives the patriarchal logos or general worldview. Indeed, once you understand, as Kate Millett (1970) also does, the ways intercourse is a paradigm of 'sexual politics', you also can begin to notice that such intercourse functions as a paradigm for a series of linked abuses—for example, the atrocities on the female body committed by serial sex killers like Jack the Ripper and his brethren (Caputi 1987), the development and proliferation of nuclear weapons (Caputi 1993), and imperial conquest, or what Andrea Smith (2003) terms 'sexual colonization'.

Dworkin further ponders the ways that male-prerogative sexual intercourse denies women voice, space, and a site of radical articulation. Drawing upon the nineteenth-century US feminist Victoria Woodhull, Dworkin argues that women must have complete dominion, authority and control over intercourse. She must have 'sexual sovereignty' (1987, p. 137) and a *language* to call this reality into being:

> We know only this one language of these folks who enter and occupy us: they keep telling us that we are different from them; yet we speak only their language and have none, or none that we remember, of our own; and we do not dare, it seems, invent one, even in signs and gestures. Our bodies speak their language. Our minds think in it. The men are inside us, through and through. We hear something, a dim whisper, barely audible, somewhere at the back of the brain; there is some other word, and we think, some of us, sometimes, that once it belonged to us (p. 135).

Indeed. Somewhere, there *is* another word, another voice, another intelligence, another language, another intercourse, an utterly other *logos*—that is, a sexual/spiritual/cultural/political imagination other than the patriarchal one. With no apologies to Mullarkey, I suggest that we strategically think of this alternative and resistant logos as *cuntspeak*.[2] For, however much Mullarkey intends *cuntspeak* to function as a pejorative, the word itself defies this trajectory.

The pornographic worldview is utterly dependent on a mind/body split, one linking thought to the realm of the superior ethereal and figuring the body as the site of all that is 'low', dirty, dumb and inferior. Feminism resists this deceptive split and insists that the body instead is a 'unique means of access to

---

2   Whenever anyone, male or female, speaks of listening to or having 'guts' or tells us that they are speaking from the 'heart', we catch a whisper of the cuntspeaking tradition. *Webster's* tells us that the etymology of *bowel* is akin to IE *cwith*, belly womb, OHG *quiti* vulva, ON *kvithr* belly, womb and Goth *quithus*, stomach, womb. The archaic meaning of *bowel* is 'the seat of pity or tenderness or of courage, GUTS, HEART'.

knowledge and ways of living' (Grosz 1994, p. 15), a 'talisman' connecting us to the body of knowledge that is the living Earth (Allen 1990). Such ways are denied and/or trivialized by the rationalist, objective, abstract and dispassionate model of thought that is valorized in patriarchal systems. Of course, it is bodily/ earthy knowing, that yields the recognition that pornography, in both everyday and overt forms (Caputi 2004), epitomizes the disconnected and soulless patriarchal logos or worldview.[3] Cuntspeak, unlike pornography, is rooted in the convictions that the personal is political and that the body (female and male) is knowledgeable. But before thoroughly reclaiming *cuntspeak*, we will have to give some attention to that problematic word and concept—*cunt*.

The cunt issue

> Whoever despises the clitoris despises the penis
> Whoever despises the penis despises the cunt
> Whoever despises the cunt despises the life of the child . . .
> Who will speak these days,
> if not I,
> if not you?
>
> —Muriel Rukeyser, 'The Speed of Darkness' (Levi 1994, p. 228)

Some women to whom I have mentioned the concept of *cuntspeak* react with appreciation. 'That's juicy!' one proclaimed.[4] Others flinch. For *cunt* can be used as the most vicious of misogynist epithets (Greer 1971). I remember the moment I heard it for the first time. A neighborhood boy looked at my older sister (who was probably about 12 at the time), wearing tight jeans of which she was very proud, and pronounced for all to hear: 'Wow, you can really see her cunt.' Her pride plummeted, as did mine. In his feminist-friendly *Guide to Getting it On* (2000, p. 13), Paul Joannides abhors the use of *cunt* as a slur and recalls learning it when he was young as the very worst thing that he could call another boy.

In the pornographic context, *cunt* disappears women's subjectivity. It renders all women as utterly interchangeable, vulnerable and perpetually

---

3   'Pornography' as I am using it here is not synonymous with sexually explicit and/or erotic representations. Pornography is the representation and endorsement of male supremacist and phallocentric sexuality. It is a way of representing, as well as thinking and acting, that sexualizes and genders domination/conquest and submission-making domination masculine (even when a woman plays that role), and submission feminine (even when a man plays that role) and making both the essence of sex (Dworkin 1988, pp. 253–275). Pornography and its variants condition both women and men to have a substantial sexual and gender investment in maintaining the status quo—from interpersonal relationships to international politics.

4   Thanks to Juba Ometse Clayton.

available, and reduces us to our supposedly 'lowest', most 'disgusting' and 'inferior' parts. When directed at a male, it reduces him to the status of females with just a word. Its misogynist use sets up women as something to be voyeuristically consumed: the 'beaver shot' in *Hustler*, the 'monster shot' in porn films. Defaming women as *cunts* is meant to strip us physically and metaphysically, ritually divesting us not only of full humanity but also of protection from harms both material and energetic. And the common opposition of the genitals to the brain is a fundamental one in the mind/body dichotomy that underlies both patriarchal religion and pornography.

But *cunt* was not always so defamed and some feminists argue for its reclamation (Walker 1983; Muscio 1998). There is historical validation for this. In *A Dictionary of Slang* Eric Partridge notes that *cunt* was once part of Standard English but, 'owing to its powerful sexuality the term has since the C15th been avoided in written and polite English . . . and been held to be obscene, i.e. a legal offence to print it in full' (cited in Mills 1989, p. 60). Partridge himself prints it as C*NT. *Cunt*, he details, isn't really slang at all, but an ancient word. Its etymological origins are in dispute, though Partridge links it to *queen*. *Cunt* is, another linguist tells us, 'a true language word, and of the oldest stock' (J.S. Farmer cited in Dames 1977, p. 110). Michael Dames (1977, p. 112) says that the cunt was named obscene due to patriarchal dread of the feminine (Dames 1977, p. 112). He etymologically links *cunt* to such wonderful, if now obsolete, words as *cunctipotent* (all-powerful), and *cunning* (possessing a magical knowledge or skill).

Another word for *cunt* can be found in the discourse of religious studies—*yoni*, an ancient Sanskrit sacred word with various meanings such as 'womb, vulva, vagina, place of birth, source, origin, spring; abode, home, lair, nest; family, race stock, caste' (Marglin 1987, p. 330). The yoni symbol references *Shakti*—elemental female energy inherent in all growth and life, often understood through the metaphor of *goddess*. *Yoni*, significantly, is derived from *yu*, to join and unite. The yoni signifies the force of connection. It evokes the divine energy circulating amongst all being, human and other than human. It bespeaks the power that is generated through the inter-relationship of all beings.

Many cultures in the ancient world—and some today—venerate icons representing overt depictions of *yonis*, female figures spreading their legs, as well as symbolic ones (downward pointing triangles, caves, concentric ovals, spiral patterns, sea shells, fruits), recognizing in these the original animating, generative and transformative matrix (Marglin 1987, p. 333). In *Goddess: Myths of the Female Divine*, David Leeming and Jake Page (1994) trace an ancient history of goddess worship followed by systematic denigrations during the patriarchal era. The original female divine had to be profaned and demonized so that the male could become 'God' (Harris 1977, p. 8). Arguably, it is pornography (in both its overt and everyday manifestations) that most contains and then degrades the yoni as well as other characteristic features of goddess-centered spiritualities. Some of these include: sexual exuberance and orgiastic, including same-sex, activity; an honorific association between sexuality and 'nature'—animality, dirt, the elements, the night sky; nakedness to indicate potency; the honoring of male femininity, female masculinity and ceremonial transvestitism; the naked dance to invoke power (Omolade, 1983; p. 350); whipping as part of a same-sex initiatory ritual (Reis, 1995, pp. 206–212); the spread legs of a woman or goddess—a sign of *yoni* worship (Marglin, 1987, p. 330). Mythic narratives commonly contain proscriptions against gazing unbidden or unceremoniously on a goddess's nakedness, which is understood as symbolizing her unshielded power (Chevalier and Gheerbrant 1994, p. 200). All of this suggests that we might understand pornography as the deliberate appropriation and distortion of imagery and practices that previously signified and activated female potency, turning these, instead, into signs of degradation. This accomplishes two aims. A source of power, which we might think of as *cunctipotence*, is forbidden to women but is simultaneously made exclusively available to men. Indeed, this sexual/spiritual force, akin to what Audre Lorde (1984) spoke of as the *erotic*, is exploited and used as a source of energy powering the patriarchal system itself.

Pornography, along with conventional morality, teaches both women and men to view the body and sexuality, especially the female body and female sexuality, as being 'lower' than the rationality that is associated with men, and, ironically enough, signified by the 'phallus'. This results in a generalized anxiety if not paranoia among many academic feminists about any female focus in our language, our theory, our art, and our religion. Rather than being accused of 'cuntspeak' or any such equivalent, many choose to train their (often worshipful) attention on the phallus and either insult or pussyfoot around the female body, deliberately dis-identifying with female anything, including female spaces and languages.

The phallus issue

In Sanskrit, the masculine correspondent of *yoni* is *linga* and symbols of the *linga* or penis marks religious and cultural history around the world—and not always in a patriarchal context. Susan Bordo (1999) notes that the origins of symbols of the penis were explicitly biological and based in worship of fecundity. But, in response to the rejection of sexuality and the body cultivated by patriarchal religion, and in keeping with modern forms of racist and rationalist systems, the 'phallus' was disconnected from the 'lower' biological body and associated not with fecundity but with the superiority of (the usually white) 'male intellect, rationality, mind' (p. 90).

This (always erect) phallus thus dishonors not only the cunt but also the fleshy, real penis. Patriarchs prefer the phallus because the penis, in truth, has downright 'feminine' qualities: it is more often soft than hard, extremely sensitive, and seems to have a veritable 'mind of its own', not subject to the masculine will. The almighty phallus is associated with permanence, potency, authority, rationality, and domination. It is identified with 'power over' or 'domination'. It invokes the 'Law of the Father'—the language and history from which women have been disappeared. Catholicism overtly refers to the patriarchal god as 'The Omnipotent', language that suggests that god himself is another version of the phallus. On a more mundane level, taking familiar shape in skyscrapers, monuments, cameras, power tools, pens, paintbrushes and steeples, the phallus is the ubiquitous symbol of male supremacy. In a direct inversion of the former association with fecundity, the phallus now is mirrored in weapons and highly destructive technologies (Caputi 1993) as well as in dry and tedious abstract thought.

The higher the phallus soars, the lower the cunt descends. *Hustler* calls women 'cunts' one way but there are other, more erudite, ones as well. For Aristotle, woman 'is as it were an impotent male, for it is through a certain incapacity that the female is female' (cited in Agonito 1977, p. 44). Sartre (1966, p. 782) looks down on woman as an obscene 'hole'. For both Freudian and Lacanian schools, woman is defined as an absence, a negation lacking the luster of penis or phallus. Conceptually, then, she is disappeared.

For Lacanians, the phallus is supposed to be a concept, not necessarily linked to the penis. This supposedly conceptual phallus is spoken of, nonetheless, quite reverently as the 'mythic, omnipresent, invulnerable signifier' (Zita 1998, p. 224). Indeed, even feminist theorists (and sexual entrepreneurs) often direct attention far more to phallic matters than to any exploration of a female imaginary.[5] Judith Butler (1992 p. 164) argues that women, lesbian and straight, can possess what she calls the 'plastic and transferable' phallus. But why bother? Why not, instead, shift the terms of the argument, taking to heart Barbara Christian's (1997, p. 56) powerful reminder that Black feminist traditions advise us to look not only 'high', but also to 'look low, lest we devalue women in the world . . . [and] our voices no longer sound like women's voices to anyone.' An essential component of cuntspeak is the inclination to go down, to look low. Taking our eyes off the phallus, we go 'down there' in search of a female symbolic.

---

5   This ubiquitous phallic focus has incited one unruly lesbian to point to the operation of a pervasive if veiled 'male identification' (Walters 1996, pp. 847–848) coursing through queer theory and cultural studies.

In the discourse of elite psychoanalytic and cultural theory there is no symbolic female equivalent of the phallus. One psychoanalytic feminist thinker, Jessica Benjamin (1988), believes female 'representation at the same level as the phallus' (p. 124) to be an impossibility, due to fearfulness associated with the mother as well as to the fact that our psyches are already pre-occupied by and with the phallus. As she sees it, because representation of the body 'is organized and dominated by the phallus, woman's body necessarily has become the object of the phallus' (Benjamin 1988, p. 124). And the phallus is always the 'doer', except, Benjamin notes, when the phallus is 'done to' in castration anxiety.

Of course, in this psychodrama described by Benjamin, we find the basic script of pornography: a 'woman' (or a feminine subject) is presented as an absence, already castrated, that is, impotent. She is a passive object for the 'man' to 'do it' to (that is, have intercourse with) with no fear of him losing anything important in the process. Alternately, in the pornographic psychodrama, the 'woman' stars as a high-heeled dominatrix/castratatrix, entertaining the companion phallic fantasy of being 'done to' by a castrating cunt. Either way, the pornographic 'woman' has no real agency or presence. One way or the other, she remains defined by her relationship to the phallus. Sexual violence against women is inevitable according to either of these scripts: in the first case because she invites it, in the second because she deserves it.

Mary Gossy (1994, p. 23) issues this challenge: 'Let those of you who are not lesbians just try to imagine a response to a cunt that is not determined by castration anxiety.' And let us simultaneously try to imagine a reality not determined by the (lifeless/deathless) phallus. To do so, we might consider the symbolic value of the cunt/yoni. Once again, the phallus is said to ordain separation. But *yoni* is derived from a word that means to unite or connect. If we focus on the cunt (and penis), we find, instead of the familiar sex-gender divide, an understanding of sexuality as a continuum and a recognition of sexual *correspondence* and not *difference* between males and females (who are both formed from the originally female fetus). Sexuality is experienced as a mode of *connection* and not objectification, a practice that connects not only to the sexual partner but to the body of knowledge in the psychophysical self as in the energetic-material world.

In the worldview informed by the image of the (cold, hard, and artificial) phallus, the female and feminine are stigmatized, rendered paradigmatically obscene, unmentionable and veritably unspeakable. To counter this silencing, cuntspeakers become utterly shameless.

Impudicity

[Phallic power is] really womb power that men stole. A man standing with his legs apart is impersonating a woman. Men all have womb envy. We don't have penis envy. My psychic penis is way larger than any man's. My attitude is, I have a vagina and therefore I have the bigger penis . . . I was the filthiest act ever. I would do anything. People say to me, 'You're not very feminine'. Well, they can suck my dick.

—Roseanne (quoted in Lahr 1995, p. 44)

Cuntspeak is nothing if not a vulgate. In her immortal *SCUM Manifesto*, Valerie Solanas (1967) challenges women to 'trust only their own animal, gutter instincts' (p. 177). Conversely, ladylike propriety enjoins girls and women to keep our minds and language 'out of the gutter'. Yet that metaphorical site may well deserve our devotion. Frankly, in a phallocentric culture, it is inevitable that women speaking suppressed truths regarding our sex will be perceived as speaking a form of 'gutter language', dirty, vulgar, impudent and shocking (Woolf 1977, pp. xxxix–xxxx). Yet, impudent is exactly what we should be.

The word *impudence* is derived from the L. *pudendum*, the vulva, which in turn is derived from *pudere*, to feel shame. And shame is invariably created and enforced by silence.[6] In their sex education guide for parents, Dr Justin Richardson and Dr Mark A. Schuster (2003) cite a study finding that while 95 percent of boys (36 months to 15 years old) had been taught the word 'penis', only 52 percent of girls in the same age group had been given a specific name for their genitals; '40 percent had been given no word at all. In fact, girls were more likely to have been taught the name for boys' genitals than for their own.' 'Wordlessness', they conclude, 'significantly limits a child's ability to understand her body (2003, p. 74). It also might lead her to believe that there is something wrong with her.

Unable to name our own space, women can hardly claim it. Mortified, generations of women modestly/shamefully referred to our genitals as 'down there' (Steinem 1998, p. vii) or referred to them as nothing at all. A revelatory moment occurs in Colette's (1952) *Gigi*. The teenaged Gigi refers to her 'you know what'. Madame Alvarez vehemently cuts her off: 'Silence! Aren't you ashamed to call it your you-know-what?' Gigi replies that she wouldn't 'mind calling it by any other name, only . . .' [ellipsis in the original]. Madame doesn't even let Gigi finish her sentence. '"There is no other name"' she tells her (cited in Callander 1996, p. 53). Colette here is explicitly making a con-

---

6 Being silenced is one of the most recurring ways that women describe the effects of rape and other forms of sexual abuse (e.g. Pierce-Baker 1998; Raine 1998).

nection between the imposition of female modesty and its attendant social institutions—marriage and enclosure for 'good' women; pornography, prostitution and exposure for 'bad' ones. Literary critic Margaret Callander analyses this scene. Because Gigi's '"you-know-what"' is about to be 'sold intact to a male owner, it must remain outside language', for naming it would 'subvert the proprieties of that world' (Callander 1996, p. 53). To aid in counteracting centuries of sexual sales, silencings, alienations, and shamings, cuntspeakers naturally gravitate to the loud, the *impudent*, the guttural, the base, the vulgar, the earthy, the shameless. We name it; we get down and dirty.

Playwright Eve Ensler describes the liberating effect of what she calls 'vagina-talking' in an interview regarding her 1995 play, *The Vagina Monologues*, a title which suggests not only talking about, but *with*, vaginas. The play, which has become a popular phenomenon, consists of a series of vignettes, shaped by Ensler from stories and perceptions she collected from women whom she had asked to think about (and, implicitly, *with*) their vaginas. Ensler told the *New York Times* that she has been pondering what she calls:

> 'the vagina brain' a separate brain, she said, whose 'understanding of the world comes through the body. The reason we're in so much trouble on earth is that the vagina intelligence has been damaged by rape, battery, sexual abuse and terror' (Boxer 1998, p. A23).

In her 'Introduction' to the play, Ensler writes:

> I say 'vagina' because when I started saying it I discovered how fragmented I was, how disconnected my body was from my mind. My vagina was something over there, away in the distance. I rarely lived inside it, even visited. I was busy working, writing; being a mother, a friend. I did not see my vagina as my primary resource, a place of sustenance, humor, and creativity. It was fraught there, full of fear. I'd been raped as a little girl, and although I'd grown up, and done all the adult things one does with one's vagina, I had never really reentered that part of my body after I'd been violated. I had essentially lived most of my life without my motor, my center, my second heart (1998, p. xxi).

In order to reclaim her integrity, and as part of a process of stopping the shame and the violation, Ensler found herself saying *vagina*, over and over, no matter how 'dirty' it sounded.

Other resistant speakers invent words. Emma Pérez reports that at some of the liveliest meetings of a group of Chicana/Mexicana lesbians, 'women invented cultural vocabulary, making up words and poems with transgressive connotations' (1994, p. 114). Significantly, most of these deliberately reversed what she terms *phallogocentrism* and performed an outrageously obvious cuntspeak: '*Chingar* (fuck) has phallocentric implications. Tired of the phallogocentric, the women improvised with *panochear*, from the Nahuatl root, *panocha*, which is contemporary slang for vagina. Instead of using *chingon*, which implies a herculean man, we invented *panochona*, representing a formidable, impressive, women, whether lesbian or straight' (1994, p. 114).

An extensive feminist literature addresses the issue of the transformative powers of female language, writing, and voice. Several of these thinkers link that empowering language metaphorically to the vulva and to the need for women to reclaim sexual discourse. Literary critic Alicia Suskin Ostriker (1986, p. 92) recognizes that women still under the 'thumb' of phallocratic culture are prohibited from direct reference to female bodies:

> One of the ways we recognize a poetess—which is to say a woman poet locked into sentimentality by her inhibitions—is that she steers clear of anatomical references. As womanly inhibition declines, we grow aware of its sources in dualistic ideology, gender polarization, and the dread of female sexuality. One of the ways we recognize that a woman writer has taken some kind of liberating jump is that her *muted parts begin to explain themselves* (emphasis added).

Artist and filmmaker Carollee Schneeman, has since the 1960s invoked an anti-pornographic eroticism in her performances and writings. She deliberately invokes a cunctipotent female mythic tradition and challenges the mind/body dichotomy. For example, in a performance work, 'Interior Scroll', she stands naked, pulls a scroll out of her vagina and begins to read a text that references a tradition of women's knowledge. Schneeman comments on the work's conceptual background: 'I thought of the vagina in many ways—physically, conceptually, as a sculptural form, an architectural reference, source of sacred knowledge, ecstasy, birth passage, transformation' (2002, p. 229). And, in Schneeman's work there is actually a recurrent exhortation to what we can immediately recognize as *cuntspeak*:

> For many years I researched depictions of the power of genital sexuality found in cultures nominally excluded from Western art history. In the mid-nineties . . . I had accumulated reams of notations . . . and had been struggling for weeks to compose and edit this material. One night I had a dream, with an instructing voice that stated: "you will never be an artist back in your studio working with your hands while you have that great mess-up pile of notes all over the floor. WHY DON'T YOU LET VULVA DO THE TALKING?" (Schneeman 2002, p. 299).

The vulva also is associated with transformative speech and knowledge in the philosophy of Luce Irigaray (1985), particularly in her suggestive essay, 'When Our Lips Speak Together'. The title refers explicitly to both the oral and the vaginal lips. Here the metaphoric evocation of a voluble vulva suggests once again the possibility of a language with which it is impossible to support or replicate phallocentric/pornographic reality, but with which one may speak otherwise inaccessible truths.

The truths of cuntspeak

The divinity of woman is still hidden, veiled. Could it be what 'man' seeks even as he rapes it?
—Luce Irigaray (1993, p. 71)

'What is the truth?' Dr. Holly asked me, and knowing that I could not answer him he answered himself through a Voodoo ceremony in which the Mambo, that is the priestess, richly dressed, is asked this question ritualistically. She replies by throwing back her veil and revealing her sex organs. The ceremony means that this is the infinite, the ultimate truth. There is no mystery beyond the mysterious source of life.
—Zora Neale Hurston (1983, p. 137)

I was drawing before I could speak . . . That sense of formation was linked to the excitement of my body, of my sexuality being sacred. I was masturbating when I was four, and that experience was where Santa Claus and Jesus lived, in that pleasure in the body. I had that all worked out. By the time the culture moved in to try to get the pencil out of my hand and my hand off my body, it was too late. I knew where the truth was! The rest was not the truth.
—Carolee Schneeman (2002, p. 202)

The Clitoral Truth
—book title (Chalker 2000)

Cuntspeak is a variously literary, mythic, poetic, comedic, ritual, and prophetic tradition of truth-telling. In the passage cited above, Zora Neale Hurston describes a Voodoo ritual in which the priestesses' vulva is identified ceremonially with the truth. A consanguineous insight comes through in the narrative of a former slave, recounted by Dorothy Roberts (1997, p. 45) in her powerful work, *Killing the Black Body*:

A common recollection of former slaves was the sight of a woman, often the reporter's mother, being beaten for defying her master's sexual advances . . . . Minnie Folkes remembered watching her mother being flogged by her overseer when she refused 'to be wife to dis man'. Decades after her emancipation, Minnie repeated with pride her mother's teaching: 'Don't let nobody bother yo principle; 'cause dat wuz all yo' had'.

The use of the word 'principle' for vulva is exceptionally rich in association. *Webster's* (1986) defines 'principle' as 'a general or fundamental truth . . . on which others are based and from which others are derived . . . basic or primary source of material or energy: ultimate basis or cause . . .' The mother's use of 'principle' understands the vulva to be precisely that: an incarnation of the truth; a physical manifestation on the female body (as the penis is on the male body) of the cosmic source, the basis and cause of life. Is this, as Luce Irigaray conceptualizes, part of the underlying motivation of rape? Is it also, we can wonder, the reason why castration, of both women and men, features so prominently in such hate crimes as lynching and sexual murder?

In *The Pure and the Impure*, Colette refers to a female-to-female 'half-spoken' language, composed of words and a 'small but infallible number of signs' (cited in Callander 1996, p. 63). Similarly, cuntspeak is composed not only of words but also of infallible signs, formations, and gestures. The principal sign is that of the vulva itself. In Voodoo as well as numerous other religious traditions, the exposure or symbolic evocation of the cunt or *yoni* is a sacred gesture (Marglin 1986), an icon, having nothing to do with pornography but instead signifying divine energy. A few examples will suffice.

Most of us know the story of Medusa, the snaky-haired Gorgon whose face Freud (1955) and nearly every subsequent commentator identify as an ancient representation of vulva. Medusa has a protruding tongue and a toothy, fanged mouth. Sometimes she is represented only as a face; at other times she sits with legs widely spread in the typical iconography of *yoni*/cunt veneration. Uninvited male trespass results in the intruder being turned to stone, due, variously, to gazing upon her, or to a dart of light from her all-powerful eye.

But Medusa's *voice* is equally important. The word 'gorgon' is from an Indo-European root *garj*, denoting a fearful shriek, roar, or shout (Segal 1994, p. 18). Medusa's epithets include 'Gorgon voiced'. We might not be surprised to find that she represents, according to one scholar, the 'maternal throat/vagina' (Segal 1994, p. 30). No wonder the culture 'hero' Perseus felt the need to decapitate/castrate/silence her. Still, Medusa is immortal. She remains a central figure in feminist reclamation (Caputi 1993). Her visage, states Emily Culpepper (1986), enables women to tap 'deep and ancient symbolic/mythic power to change our lives'. Though characterized by patriarchs as both hideous and castrating, cuntspeakers easily see that Medusa is beautiful and that she is vocalizing, speaking and laughing (Cixous 1975), coming and becoming.

Another provocative vulvic figure from Greek myth is an old woman figure called variously Baubo and Iambe, sometimes called the Goddess of Obscenity due to her association with lewd jokes and the exposure of the vulva. Images of Baubo show her sometimes as a full-bodied woman lifting her skirt, other times only as a vulva, and other times as the lower half of a female body with a face in place of a vulva. Baubo figures prominently in the myth of the Goddess Demeter who, bereft at the rape and loss of her daughter Persephone, wanders the Earth. During this wandering she changes into an old woman and refuses to eat or drink. Fertility ceases. Eventually, the seemingly inevitable apocalypse is forestalled when Baubo makes the Goddess smile and even belly laugh out loud. Variations on the story present her either as a talkative old woman who tells Demeter dirty jokes, or the dancing Baubo, who lifts her skirt, revealing her vulva, and, again, making the Goddess crack that beatific and world-saving smile (Lubell 1994).

The magical or sacred power of the vulva continues to be recognized by the Baule people of the Ivory Coast. Female figures with spread legs are highly unusual. When they occur, their 'aggressive nudity may express an implied threat'. For 'the female body as the source of life is one of the most potent *amuin* (energetic or spirit force) the Baule have, and clandestine or brazen looking at a woman's sexual organs can be fatal to men' (Vogel 1997, p. 60). The most powerful *amuin* is recognized as belonging to the women's deities, notably *Adyanun*.

> The women dance *Adyanun* as a last recourse in times of impending calamity— epidemics, war, drought, a president's death—because it is more potent than all the other *amuin* . . . The women's *amuin* is danced 'naked' because its locus of power is every woman's sexual organs (Vogel 1997, p. 59).

Shirley Ardener, a British anthropologist living in Cameroon, found that Bakweri women, in defense of their sexual honor, would employ a type of sacred obscenity. For example, when a man insults a woman's vulva—perhaps 'by saying that it smells', that woman calls out all the other women of the village.

> Converging upon the offender, dressed in vines, they demand immediate recantation and a recompense of a pig, plus something extra for the woman who has been directly insulted. The women then surround him and sing songs which are often obscene by allusion, and accompany them by vulgar gestures (1987, p. 115).

Another Cameroonian people, the Balong, employ even more extravagantly vulgar gestures. If a man insults his wife's lower parts 'it is like insulting all women'. The women gather and 'they will take all their clothes off. They will shame him and sing songs . . . the term used for this phenomenon (*ndon*) is probably derived from a root meaning "beautiful"' (1987, p. 117).

Ardener is concerned with tracing an historical phenomenon whereby women employ deliberately vulgar '"ritual games" and gestures . . . in an *idiom* which reverberates across time and space, to defend their corporate identity' (1987, pp. 114–115). Her essay begins with examples of African women collectively signifying sexual dignity and ends with the visual art of such women as Judy Chicago, Suzanne Santoro, Niki de Saint-Phalle who deliberately use honorific vulva images in their work in order to, in Chicago's words (1981, p. 63), represent the 'active feminine principle' to counter the insults of the patriarchally religious and pornographic world. Ardener concludes that this traditional use of deliberate vulgarity constitutes a form of oppositional discourse invented by groups who are 'muted' and negated by dominant others. Of course, women who try to take back this power are themselves charged with being 'pornographic'. Significantly, right-wing politicians soon condemned Chicago's art as pornography. At the same time, an academic elite pejoratively labeled her 'essentialist', and derided such art as the very lowest of the low— 'cunt art'.

Another work that honors the cunctipotent tradition, though also generally 'dissed' and dismissed by academics, is the popular *Women Who Run With the Wolves* by Clarissa Pinkola Estés (1992). Estés tells Baubo's story, urging her readers to reclaim the 'Dirty Goddess', the female divine who is both sexual and sacred. Estes advocates what we can recognize as cuntspeak:

> There is a powerful saying: *Dice entre las piernas*, 'She speaks from between her legs' . . . 'speaking from the vulva' . . . is, symbolically, speaking from the *primae materia*, the most basic, most honest level of truth—the vital *os*. What else is there to say but that Baubo speaks from the mother lode, the deep mind, literally the depths' (pp. 339–340).

Estés's words directly inspire novelist and essayist Sandra Cisneros in her exquisitely brazen essay, 'Guadalupe, the Sex Goddess' (1996). Trained by Mexican Catholicism to be alienated, estranged and ashamed of her female body, coming into adulthood she at first rejects Guadalupe as a lofty, unrealistic, asexual 'goody-goody meant to doom me to a life of unhappiness' (p. 48). Overcoming those prohibitions leads to sexual sovereignty, literary creativity and spiritual becoming. Thus awakened, she critically reinterprets the *Virgen* and her pre-Columbian antecedents—a pantheon of sex, life, and death Goddesses who were deemed obscene by the Church—Tonantzin, Coatlicue, Tlazolteotl (see also Anzaldúa 1987, pp. 27–28). She affirms that Guadalupe is herself a continuation of 'the sex goddess, a goddess who makes me feel good about my sexual power, my sexual energy, who reminds me I must, as Clarissa Pinkola Estés so aptly put it, "[speak] from my vulva" . . . and write from my *panocha*' (p. 49).

A few years earlier, and with a most impressive impudicity, Chicana lesbian Victoria de los Santos Mycue reinterpreted the iconic image of *La Virgen de Guadalupe* as her own vulva. In 1993, de los Santos Mycue published and later performed 'A Little Prayer' as an erotic reading, understanding *La Virgen de Guadalupe* in this way:

I could understand and love you better once I understood you in relation to my love for other women, once I understood you in relation to myself . . . Your gently tilting face, your beautiful visage, is my clitoris. Our sensors of head and pleasure are one. Your flowing garment and folded arms are the wings of my vagina, the labia. Your belly, framed by your hands held in prayer is your womb, like the precious entrance to me . . . Once I began to see you as my vagina, I began to see you as the symbol for all women, as a deity advocating our empowerment on earth, and not as a repressive silencing force . . . I begin to understand you as advocating 'Pussy Power' and thus advocating for both my sex and sexuality (Trujillo 1993, p. 1).

De los Santos Mycue reverses the reversals of phallocentric imagery, decolonizing sacred imagery and intimate space, loudly interrupting silencing by understanding the vagina as speaking/advocating. She shamelessly locates the Godhead in female sex and lesbian sexuality.

While de los Santos Mycue responds with ecstasy to her vision of the vulva in *La Virgen*, Cisneros reacts with terror at the image of the vulva proffered to her by a porn movie: 'The film star's *panocha*—a tidy, elliptical opening, pink and shiny like a rabbit's ear. To make matters worse, it was shaved and looked especially childlike and unsexual . . . my own sex has no resemblance to this woman's. My sex, dark as an orchid, rubbery and blue purple as *pulpo*, an octopus, does not look nice and tidy, but otherworldly' (p. 51).

Significantly, the signs and gestures of cuntspeak superficially resemble those of pornography—the goddess or priestess with spread legs, the focus on the cunt, the striptease, the obscene joking. These surface correspondences between the signs of cuntspeak and those of pornography do not reflect some implicit or explicit female power or feminist practice behind stripping, prostitution or pornography. To the contrary, these patriarchal practices deliberately mimic and devour erotic or cunctipotent energies. Those of us— feminist theorists, artists, performers, and entrepreneurs—who seek to take back and reinvent female erotic practice and representation, to use sexual practices and imagery to advocate and educate for female sexual sovereignty (Chalker 2000), need to take great care to ensure that we do not end up replicating pornographic misogyny, objectification, disconnection, and deception (of self and of others).

Words from the heart (of darkness)

. . . the sexual life of adult women is a 'dark continent' . . . we have learnt that girls feel deeply their lack of a sexual organ that is equal in value to the male one; they regard themselves on that account as inferior, and this 'envy for the penis' is the origin of a whole number of characteristic feminine reactions.

—Sigmund Freud (cited in Doane, 1991, p. 210)

I don't want their language . . . I'm not trying to be another Shakespeare or Henry James—I'm trying to find the blackest, bloodiest, female-est form of expression I can! I am not aiming to be as good as a white man; I'm aiming to find the Heart of Darkness, the very thing they've tried to suppress . . . which they claim is ugly and valueless then spend half their time imitating and murdering.

—Sapphire (Juno and Vale 1991, pp. 172–173)

We are the modern cunt
Positive anti reason
Unbounded unleashed unforgiving
We see art with our cunt we make art with our cunt
We believe in jouissance madness holiness and poetry
We are the virus of the new world disorder
Rupturing the symbolic from within
Saboteurs of big daddy mainframe
The clitoris is a direct line to the matrix

we are the future cunt

—VNS Matrix, 'Cyberfeminist Manifesto'

The word 'matrix', from the Latin *mater*, means 'uterus' as well as any place of origin or development. One of the most famous oracles of the ancient world was found at what was commonly understood to be the matrix of the Earth, found at *Delphi*, a Greek word which often is euphemized as meaning 'belly' or 'navel', but which actually means, as Mircea Eliade (1978, p. 21) politely puts it, 'the female generative organ'. Female oracles in ancient Greece were known as 'belly talkers', accessing truths from the earthly matrix that were otherwise inaccessible. As these ancient forms suggest, cuntspeak, then, is a form of concourse with the Source. It is the voice of nature, pejoratively characterized as mere 'instinct' or 'intuition'. It is a tradition of speaking from the heart, listening to the gut, and attending to the messages issuing from the very bowels of the Earth, the holy, not horrific, heart of darkness.

The 'dark continent' as a referent for Africa was immortalized by Joseph Conrad (1999) in his 1901 classic, *The Heart of Darkness*, and picked up later by Freud to refer to the female sex. This image reveals the intertwined racism, sexism, imperialism, and heterosexism that perceives darkness and femaleness to be inextricable and also to be irredeemably 'low', primitive, uncivilized, horrific, and beyond logic and reason. But this is again pure reversal. It is that Dark Heart that is the source and origin of all light and life. That dark source or matrix, as Sapphire perceives, is feared, scorned, raped, hated, denied, but also profoundly envied by phallocrats. At the heart of their fear of the Dark is fear of their own darkness, their own participation in the female principle, and perhaps also their own desire to worship the cunt for they too originate in (and will return to) the intelligent, lubricious darkness of the Earth.

Sapphire avows that she is 'aiming to find the Heart of Darkness'. The cosmic or archetypal cunt is not only dark; it is a heart, a divinely bleeding heart. Eve Ensler referred to her vagina as her 'second heart'. Avatara, in Paule Marshall's *Praisesong for the Widow* (1983), describes 'the other heart at the base of her body' (p. 128). Judy Chicago titles one of her works of cunt imagery, 'Did You Know Your Mother Had a Sacred Heart?' Cherríe Moraga (1983), who consistently merges the mouth and the cunt in her poetry and essays, ultimately joins heart, mouth, and cunt:

> My mouth cannot be controlled. It will flap in the wind like legs in sex, not driven by the mind. It's as if la boca [the mouth] were centered on el centro del corazón [center of the heart], not in the head at all. The same place where the cunt beats (p. 142).

In gynocentric and tribal oral traditions, the Laguna poet and essayist Paula Gunn Allen explains that in indigenous traditions, in the Americas and elsewhere, 'Heart often means 'womb', except when it means 'vulva'. But this cannot be understood to mean sex as sex; rather sexual connection with woman means connection with the womb, which is the container of power that women carry within their bodies' (1986, p. 24). Allen cautions against understanding sex as we usually do, as a wholly physical act, an 'it' stripped of its energetic dimensions.[7] Rather, the essence of sex and the female principle is 'Thought'. And, Thought is divine. In Laguna philosophy the creator is called 'Thought Woman.

From that imaginary place that is not centered around the phallus, we can begin to understand and experience sexuality itself as a manifestation, in our bodies, of the exuberant/ecstatic/generative power of the universe.[8] Though we experience that potency in a living body, the power itself, Allen cautions, 'is not really biological at base; it is the power of ritual magic, the power of Thought, of Mind, that gives rise to biological organisms as it gives rise to social organizations, material culture, and transformations of all kinds' (1986, p. 28).

Pornographic thinking of all kinds splits body from mind and deems the lowly genitals, both cunt and penis, as mindless. But this is a profound reversal. The

---

7   See Mary Pellauer's (1994) article on the cosmic implications of orgasm.

8   This power is not 'generative' only in a heterosexist sense but part of what biologist Bruce Bagemihl (1999) understands as 'biological exuberance'. He writes, 'Natural systems are driven as much by abundance and excess as they are by limitation and practicality. Seen in this light, homosexuality and nonreproductive heterosexuality are 'expected' occurrences—they are one manifestation of an overall 'extravagance' of biological systems that has many other expressions' (p. 215).

cunt, both physical and metaphysical, is quintessentially *not* dumb—neither silent nor stupid. The idea that our genitals, both female and male, are manifestations not of a thinking, generating, speaking divine, that the powers of Mind are akin to, not opposed to, the powers of Sex, is not a familiar one to those schooled in sex-, women- and body-negating philosophical and theological systems. Yet, that is the crucial revelation of the mythic and popular traditions of cuntspeak discussed here. Let us then take heart from the response of a six-year-old girl interviewed by Ensler and included in *The Vagina Monologues*. When Ensler asked her, 'What's special about your vagina?' she replied: 'Somewhere deep inside I know it has a really really smart brain' (1998, pp. 88–89).

References

Agonito, Rosemary. (1977). *History of Ideas on Woman: A Source Book*. New York: Berkeley Publishing Group.

Allen, Paula Gunn. (1986). *The Sacred Hoop: Recovering the Feminine in American Indian Traditions*. Boston: Beacon Press.

Allen, Paula Gunn. (1990). 'The Woman I Love Is a Planet; The Planet I Love Is a Tree'. In Irene Diamond and Gloria Feman Orenstein (eds). *Reweaving the World: The Emergence of Ecofeminism*. San Francisco: Sierra Club Books. (pp. 52–57).

Allen, Paula Gunn. (1991). *Grandmothers of the Light: A Medicine Woman's Sourcebook*. Boston: Beacon Press.

The American Heritage Dictionary of the English Language. (1981). Edited by William Morris. Boston: Houghton Mifflin.

Ardener, Shirley. (1987). 'A Note on Gender Iconography: The Vagina'. In Pat Caplan (ed.). *The Cultural Construction of Sexuality*. New York: Tavistock. (pp. 113–142).

Awiakta, Marilou. (1993). *Selu: Seeking the Corn Mother's Wisdom*. Golden, Colorado: Fulcrum Publishing.

Bagemihl, Bruce. (1999). *Biological Exuberance: Animal Homosexuality and Natural Diversity*. New York: St. Martin's Press.

Benjamin, Jessica. (1988). *The Bonds of Love: Psychoanalysis, Feminism, and the Problem of Domination*. New York: Pantheon.

Bordo, Susan. (1999). *The Male Body: A New Look at Men in Public and in Private*. New York: Farrar, Straus & Giroux.

Boxer, Sarah. (1998, Feb. 14). 'From Cringing to Comfort: A Word Has Its Day'. *The New York Times*, pp. A13, A23.

Butler, Judith. (1992). 'The Lesbian Phallus and the Morphological Imaginary'.

Differences: A Journal of Feminist Cultural Studies, 4 (1), pp. 133–171.

Callander, Margaret. (1996). 'Colette and the Hidden Woman: Sexuality, Silence, Subversion'. In Alex Hughes and Kate Ince (ed.). *French Erotic Fiction: Women's Desiring Writing, 1880–1990*. Washington, DC: Berg. (pp. 49–68).

Caputi, Jane. (1987). *The Age of Sex Crime*. Bowling Green, Ohio: Bowling Green State University Popular Press.

Caputi, Jane. (1993). *Gossips, Gorgons, and Crones: The Fates of the Earth*. Santa Fe, NM: Bear & Company.

Caputi, Jane. (2003). 'The Naked Goddess: Pornography and the Sacred'. *Theology and Sexuality*, 9 (2), 180–200.

Caputi, Jane. (2004). *Goddesses and Monsters: Women, Myth, Power, and Popular Culture*. Madison: University of Wisconsin Press.

Chalker, Rebecca. (2000). *The Clitoral Truth*. New York: Seven Stories Press.

Chevalier, Jean and Alain Gheerbrant. (1994). *The Penguin Dictionary of Symbols*. Translated by John Buchanan-Brown. New York: Penguin Books.

Chicago, Judy. (1981). 'A Female Form Language: Interview with Judy Chicago'. In Gayle Kimball (ed.). *Women's Culture: The Women's Renaissance of the Seventies*. Metuchen, NJ: The Scarecrow Press. (pp. 60–71).

Christian, Barbara. (1997). 'The highs and lows of black feminist criticism'. In Robyn R. Warhol and Diane Price Herndl (eds). (1990). *Feminisms: An anthology of literary theory and criticism*. New Brunswick, NJ: Rutgers University Press. (pp. 51–56).

Cisneros, Sandra. (1996). 'Guadalupe the Sex Goddess'. In Ana Castillo (ed.). *Goddess of the Americas La Diosa de las Américas: Writings on the Virgin of Guadalupe*. New York: Riverhead Books. (pp. 46–51).

Cixous, Hélène. (1975, 1997). 'The Laugh of the Medusa'. In Robyn R. Warhol and Diane Price Herndl (eds). (1991, 1997) *Feminisms: An Anthology of Literary Theory and Criticism*. New Brunswick, NJ: Rutgers University Press. (pp. 347–362).

Colette. (1952). *Gigi. Julie de Carnelhan. Chance acquaintances*. New York: Farrar, Straus and Young.

Conrad, Joseph. (1901, 1999). *The Heart of Darkness*. New York: Penguin.

Culpepper, Emily. (1986). 'Gorgons: A Face for Contemporary Women's Rage'. *Woman of Power*, (3), 22–24, 40.

Dames, Michael. (1977). *The Silbury Treasure*. London: Thames and Hudson.

Doane, Mary Ann. (1991). *Femmes Fatales: Feminism, Film Theory, Psychoanalysis*. New York: Routledge.

Dworkin, Andrea. (1987). *Intercourse*. New York: The Free Press.

Dworkin, Andrea. (1989). *Letters From a War Zone*. New York: EP Dutton.

Dworkin, Andrea. (1997). 'Beaver Talks'. *Life and Death: Unapologetic*

Writings on the Continuing War Against Women. New York: The Free Press. (pp. 77–101).

Dworkin, Andrea and Catharine A. MacKinnon. (1988). *Pornography and Civil Rights: A New Day for Women's Equality*. Minneapolis: Organizing Against Pornography.

Eigenkind, Heidi. (1991). 'Cunt Song'. In Louise M. Wisechild (ed.). *She Who Was Lost Is Remembered: Healing from Incest Through Creativity*. Seattle: Seal Press. (pp. 24–25).

Eliade, Mircea. (1962, 1978). *The Forge and the Crucible: The Origins and Structures of Alchemy*. Translated by Stephen Corrin. Chicago: University of Chicago Press.

Ensler, Eve. (1998). *The Vagina Monologues*. New York: Villard.

Estés, Clarissa Pinkola. (1992). *Women Who Run with the Wolves: Myths and Stories of the Wild Woman Archetype*. New York: Ballantine.

Freud, Sigmund. (1922). 'Medusa's Head'. In James Strachey (ed. & trans.). (1955). *Standard Edition of Complete Psychological Works of Sigmund Freud*, Vol. XVIII. London: The Hogarth Press. (pp. 273–74).

Gossy, Mary. (1994). 'Gals and dolls: Playing with some Lesbian Pornography'. *Art Papers* 18: 21–24.

Greer, Germaine. (1971). *The Female Eunuch*. London: Paladin.

Grosz, Elizabeth. (1994). *Volatile Bodies: Toward a Corporeal Feminism*. Bloomington: University of Indiana Press.

Harris, Bertha. (1977). 'What we Mean to Say: Notes toward Defining the Nature of Lesbian Literature'. *Heresies: A Feminist Publication on Art and Politics*, (Sept.), 5–8.

Hurston, Zora Neale. (1938, 1983). *Tell My Horse*. Berkeley, California: Turtle Island.

Irigaray, Luce. (1977, 1985). *This Sex Which Is Not One*. Translated by Catherine Porter. Ithaca, NY: Cornell University Press.

Irigaray, Luce. (1993). 'Divine Women'. In *Sexes and Genealogies*. New York: Columbia University Press. (pp. 55–72).

Joannides, Paul. (2000). *Guide to Getting it on!* Waldport, OR: Goofy Foot Press.

Jones, A. (1996). 'The "Sexual Politics" of The Dinner Party: A Critical Context'. In A. Jones. *Sexual Politics: Judy Chicago's Dinner Party in Feminist Art History*. Berkeley, CA: University of California Press. (pp. 81–118).

Juno, Andrea and V. Vale (eds). (1991). *Angry Women*. San Francisco: Re/Search Publications.

Lahr, John. (1995, July 17). 'Dealing with Roseanne'. *The New Yorker*. (pp. 42–61).

Leeming, David and Jake Page. (1994). *Goddess: Myths of the Female Divine*. New York: Oxford University Press.

Levi, Jan Heller (ed.). (1994). *A Muriel Rukeyser Reader*. New York: WW Norton.

Lorde, Audre. (1984). 'Uses of the Erotic: The Erotic as Power'. *Sister Outsider*. Trumansburg, NY: The Crossing Press. (pp. 53–59).

Lubell, Winifred Milius. (1994). *The Metamorphosis of Baubo: Myths of Women's Sexual Energy*. Nashville, TN: Vanderbilt University Press.

Marglin, Frédérique Appfel. (1987). 'Yoni'. In Mircea Eliade (ed.). *The Encyclopedia of Religion*, Vol. 15. New York: Macmillan. (pp. 530–535).

Marshall, Paule. (1983). *Praisesong for the Widow*. New York: Dutton.

Matrix, VNS. (2003). 'Cyberfeminist Manifesto'. In Amelia Jones (ed.). *The Feminism and Visual Culture Reader*. New York: Routledge. (p. 530).

Millett, Kate. (1970). *Sexual Politics*. Garden City, NY: Doubleday.

Mills, Jane. (1989). *Womanwords: A Dictionary of Words About Women*. New York: The Free Press.

Monaghan, Patricia. (1994). *O Mother Sun! A New View of the Cosmic Feminine*. Freedom, CA: The Crossing Press.

Moraga, Cherríe. (1983). *Loving in the War Years*. Boston: South End Press.

Mullarkey, Maureen. (1987, May 30). 'Hard Cop, Soft Cop'. *The Nation*. (pp. 721–726).

Muscio, Inga. (1998). *Cunt: A Declaration of Independence*. Seattle: Seal Press.

Omolade, Barbara. (1983). 'Hearts of Darkness'. In Ann Snitow, Christine Stansell and Sharon Thompson (eds). *Powers of Desire: The Politics of Sexuality*. New York: Monthly Review Press. (pp. 350–367).

Otis, Ginger Adams. (2000, January). 'Chienne de Farge: French Feminists Vigilant against Sexist Language', *Sojourner: The Women's Forum*. (p. 9).

Pellauer, Mary. (1994). 'The Moral Significance of Female Orgasm'. In J.B. Nelson and S.P. Longfellow (eds). *Sexuality and the Sacred*. (pp. 149–168). Louisville: Westminster/John Knox Press.

Pérez, Emma. (1994). 'Irigaray's Female Symbolic in the Making of Chicana Lesbian Sitios y Lenguas (Sites and Discourses)'. In Laura Doan (ed.). *The Lesbian Postmodern*. New York: Columbia University Press. (pp. 159–184).

Pierce-Baker, Charlotte. (1998). *Surviving the Silence: Black Women's Stories of Rape*. New York: WW Norton.

Raine, Nancy Venable. (1998). *After Silence: Rape & My Journey Back*. New York: Three Rivers Press.

Reis, Patricia. (1995). *Through the Goddess: A Woman's Way of Healing*. New York: Continuum.

Richardson, Justin, and Mark Schuster. (2003). *Everything You Never Wanted*

Your Kids to Know About Sex (But Were Afraid They'd Ask). New York: Crown.

Roberts, Dorothy. (1997). *Killing the Black Body: Race, Reproduction, and the Meaning of Liberty*. New York: Pantheon.

Russell, Diana E.H. (1998). *Dangerous Relationships: Pornography, Misogyny, and Rape*. Thousand Oaks, CA: Sage Publications.

Sapphire. (1991). Interview. In Andrea Juno and V. Vale (eds). *Angry Women*. San Francisco: Re/Search Publications. (pp. 163–176).

Sartre, Jean-Paul. (1966). *Being and Nothingness*. Translated by Hazel E. Barnes. New York: Washington Square Press.

Schneemann, Carolee. (2002). *Imaging her Erotics: Essays, Interviews, Projects*. Cambridge, MA: The MIT Press.

Segal, Charles. (1994). 'The Gorgon and the Nightingale: The Voice of Female Lament and Pindar's Twelfth Pythian Ode'. In Leslie C. Dunn and Nancy A. Jones (eds). *Embodied Voices: Representing Female Vocality in Western Culture*. New York: Cambridge University Press. (pp. 17–34).

Smith, Andrea. (2003). 'Not an Indian Tradition: The Sexual Colonization of Native Peoples'. *Hypatia*, 18 (2), 70–85.

Solanas, Valerie. (1967, 1968, 1996). 'The SCUM Manifesto'. In Mary Harron and Daniel Minahan (eds). *I Shot Andy Warhol*. New York: Grove Press. (pp. 157–190).

Steinem, Gloria. (1998). 'Introduction'. In *The Vagina Monologues*. New York: Villard. (pp. vii–xvii).

Stone, Allison. (2000). 'She Said No!' In Miriam Kalman Harris (ed.). *Rape, Incest, Battery: Women Writing Out the Pain*. Fort Worth: Texas Christian University Press. (pp. 285–286).

Trujillo, Carla. (1998). 'La Virgen de Guadalupe and Her Reconstruction in Chicana Lesbian Desire'. In Carla Trujillo (ed.). *Living Chicana Theory*. Berkeley: Third Woman Press. (pp. 214–231).

Vogel, Susan M. (1997). *Baule: African Art, Western Eyes*. New Haven: Yale University Press.

Walker, Barbara G. (1983). *Woman's Encyclopedia of Myths and Secrets*. San Francisco: HarperSanFrancisco.

Walters, Suzanna Danuta. (1996). 'From Here to Queer: Radical Feminism, Postmodernism, and the Lesbian Menace (Or, Why Can't a Woman Be More Like a Fag)'. *Signs: Journal of Women in Culture and Society*, 21 (4), 830–859.

Webster's Third New International Dictionary of the English Language Unabridged. (1986). Edited by Philip Babcock Grove. Springfield, MA: Merriam-Webster.

Williams, Patricia. (1985). *The Rooster's Egg: On the Persistence of Prejudice*.

Cambridge: Harvard University Press.
Woolf, Virginia. (1977). *The Pargiters: The Novel-Essay Portion of 'The Years'*. Edited by Mitchell A. Leaska. New York: The New York Public Library and Readex Books.
Zita, Jacquelyn N. (1998). *Body Talk: Philosophical Reflections on Sex and Gender*. New York: Columbia University Press.

Sheila Jeffreys
Prostitution as a harmful cultural practice

In the last two decades arguments that prostitution should be seen as ordinary work or women's choice have been used as the basis for legitimising the growth of a burgeoning international sex industry (Jeffreys 1997). I shall argue here that prostitution should, on the contrary, be placed within United Nations understandings of what constitutes a harmful traditional/cultural practice.

With the legalisation of brothel prostitution that has taken place in Australia, Netherlands and New Zealand, prostitution has become a very profitable business. In Australia the industry of brothel prostitution has been legalised or decriminalised in Victoria, New South Wales, Australian Capital Territory and Queensland, and legalisation legislation is being considered in Tasmania. Street prostitution, which is less easily turned into a profitable industry, remains illegal except in tolerance zones in New South Wales. New Zealand legalised brothel prostitution in June 2003. Where brothel prostitution is legalised it quickly becomes a booming business for those who skim the profits from this harmful cultural practice, both pimps and governments. A 1998 International Labour Organisation (ILO) report called for the recognition of the important role of prostitution in the economies of countries in South-East Asia in which it accounted for between 2 and 14 percent of GDP (Lim 1998). *The Age* newspaper devoted the front page of its business section to SEXPO (the sex industry exhibition) in 1998 alongside a profile of Australia's sex industry, said to have an estimated annual turnover of $A1.2 billion.

Meanwhile, the traffic in women and children to provide the raw materials of this industry is growing at an alarming rate. It was recognised by the United Nations as a major issue of international crime in the protocol to the UN Convention on Transnational Organised Crime (2000). The number of women and children trafficked internationally each year is estimated as between 700,000 and 2 million (Richard 1999). A 2003 report from Europap estimates that well over half of all prostitutes in the EU were not born in the country where they work, a figure which has doubled since 1990. Today three-quarters have travelled from outside the EU (Stewart 2003). As the industry grows the import of vulnerable women from poorer countries is required because there are not enough women from within the EU who can be induced to enter the expanding number of brothels. There is more and more

386

convergence between trafficking and prostitution, so that they become hard to separate.

Whilst trafficking in women is recognised by most governments and international agencies as a problem, the industry to which the victims are delivered is increasingly being normalised. I will suggest here that the distinction between trafficking and prostitution that those who wish to protect the profits coming from the industry are so keen to maintain is unsustainable, and that prostitution in all its forms should more properly be included within UN understandings of what constitute harmful cultural/traditional practices against women. Once prostitution is understood as a harmful cultural practice then the eradication of the attitudes that create and maintain this practice should become the responsibility of states rather than the effective exploitation of a new economic 'sex' sector.

What is a harmful traditional/cultural practice?

Since the 1970s there has been considerable development in the recognition of what are called in United Nations documents 'Harmful traditional/cultural practices'. The words 'traditional' and 'cultural' are used interchangeably in UN literature on this subject. This development is the result of feminist campaigning and was kickstarted by concerns about female genital mutilation, which can be considered the paradigmatic 'harmful cultural practice'. This concern was written into the 1979 United Nations Convention on the Elimination of all Forms of Discrimination against Women. Article 2(f) of CEDAW states that parties to the Convention will 'take all appropriate measures, including legislation, to modify or abolish existing laws, regulations, *customs and practices* which constitute discrimination against women' [my italics]. Article 5(a) similarly states that 'all appropriate measures' will be taken to 'modify *the social and cultural patterns of conduct* of men and women, with a view to achieving the elimination of prejudices and *customary* and all other practices which are based on the idea of the inferiority or the superiority of either of the sexes or on stereotyped roles for men and women' [my italics].

The definition of 'harmful traditional practices' was developed in 1995 in UN Fact Sheet No 23 entitled 'Harmful Traditional Practices Affecting the Health of Women and Children'. The definition offered in the introduction covers several aspects that, I shall argue below, fit prostitution very well. Traditional cultural practices are said to 'reflect values and beliefs held by members of a community for periods often spanning generations' and are said to persist because they are not questioned and take on an aura of morality in the eyes of those practicing them (UN 1995, pp. 3–4). The practices are 'performed for male benefit' (Idem). They are 'consequences of the value placed on women and the girl child by society', and they 'persist in an environment where women and the girl child have unequal access to education, wealth, health and employment'.

In one part of the Fact Sheet prostitution is listed as a form of violence, and indeed prostitution fits the criteria for the recognition of harmful cultural practice very well. Radkhika Coomaraswamy, the UN Special Rapporteur on violence against women, has been instrumental in developing international understanding of the seriousness of harmful cultural practices and the ways in which they are created by harmful attitudes for men's benefit. It is perhaps surprising then that she has chosen, in her reports, to exclude prostitution from this category. She has adopted the forced/free distinction favoured by the sex industrialists and those who take a free market, American liberal individualist position, and excludes 'free' prostitution from her concern (Coomaraswamy 2000). She suggests in her 2000 report on trafficking that international organisations now have a consensus that trafficking in women should be understood to require force and should not be seen as connected with prostitution but simply to cover any kind of labour. In her bibliography Coomaraswamy chooses only to include the names of sources which uphold her forced/free distinction and separate trafficking from prostitution. She does not for instance, include the Coalition against Trafficking in Women despite its considerable international profile. Coomaraswamy identifies harmful cultural practices in the causation of the traffic in women:

> The preference for male children and the culture of male privilege deprives girls and women of access to basic and higher education and, consequently, illiteracy rates among women remain high. In addition, certain religious and customary practices, reinforced by government policies, further entrench and validate discrimination and perpetuate the cycle of oppression of women (2000, p. 20).

She specifically does not, however, see prostitution as arising from or constituting a harmful cultural practice in its own right.

Coomaraswamy allies herself with the position that 'sex work is often a personal choice, and thus a private matter between consenting adults', a view which should, she explains, lead to seeing 'relationships between sex workers and pimps, brothel owners, clients and landlords and the acts arising out of such relationships' as 'outside the purview of criminal law' (ibid. p. 11). She has thus adopted the 'choice' approach to prostitution which understands it to be the result of and exercise of women's free choices. This is an approach which I discuss elsewhere as exemplifying American liberal individualism which, at its most extreme, such as in the work of Milton Friedman, demands freedom from, for instance, wearing car seatbelts (see my chapter on choice in Jeffreys 1997). Coomaraswamy can be seen as having chosen a particular cultural approach, one which arises from American free enterprise capitalism, in relation to prostitution.

Coomaraswamy's liberal individualist approach to prostitution, and her decision to ignore or exclude the views of those who see prostitution as a result of women's subordination and a form of violence against women, shows the extent to which this American view has influenced international thinking in the past 10 years. During this period, led by certain American 'feminist' intellectuals, the view that prostitution should be seen as women's choice has been taken up by some prostitutes' organisations in the US and in many Western countries (Chapkis 1997; Nagle 1998; Jeness 1993; Kempadoo 1998). It has also been taken up by governments keen to justify their legalisation of men's rights to sexually buy women, and the benefits this brings economically, with the idea that it is in women's interests. It is a view that reflects the burgeoning strength and influence of the international sex industry on economies and legislatures.

How prostitution fits the definition of harmful traditional practice

Damage to the health of women and girls
Prostitution clearly fulfils the basic criterion on which UN documents base their definitions of harmful cultural practices, that is, damage to the health of women and children. The notion that prostitution is damaging to the health of children is not controversial. The ILO report, for instance, which was founded upon a strict distinction between child and adult prostitution, states categorically that prostitution is damaging to the health of children, but sees this as one way in which child prostitution can be distinguished from the prostitution of those over 18 (see Jeffreys 2000b). The report states:

> Commercial sexual exploitation is one of the most brutal forms of violence against children. Child victims suffer extreme physical, psychosocial and emotional abuse which have lifelong and life-threatening consequences. They risk early pregnancy, maternal mortality and sexually transmitted diseases. Case-studies and testimonies of child victims speak of a trauma so deep that many are unable to enter or return to a normal way of life. Many others die before they reach adulthood (Lim 1998, p. 177).

But because this report is built around a distinction between child prostitution and the prostitution of adult women which is defined as a matter of choice and entirely different, the effects of prostitution on the health of adult women are not considered.

However it is interesting to note that UN understandings of HTPs bracket women and girls together as the victims of these practices. In many cultures there is not such a strict demarcation between the statuses of childhood and adulthood as there is in the West. Both female children and adult women are subjected to and suffer from similar harmful cultural practices based upon their subordinate status. When children are separated out as different from adult women, then it is an understanding of women's oppression which is sacrificed in favour of a sentimentalised view of what is special about children.

In fact both women and children who suffer prostitution abuse experience similar damage, though to different degrees. One way in which prostitution damages women's health is through sexually transmitted diseases. Though venereal disease can be more readily contracted by children as a result of the undeveloped nature of the mucous membranes in the orifices the buyers use, they are also undoubtedly a severe scourge of adult women in prostitution too. A 1994 study of prostituted women in the United States found that only 15 percent had never contracted a sexually transmitted disease (Parriott 1994). The gynaecological problems that prostituted women and girls suffer, often as a result of sexually transmitted diseases, include chronic pelvic pain, pelvic inflammatory disease, unwanted pregnancy, miscarriages, high infertility rates, and increased risk of reproductive system cancers.

The inherent power imbalance of commercial sexual exploitation—the gulf that exists between the buyer and the bought—means that the prostituted woman or child is simply not in a position to demand 'safe sex' practices. As a result, exploitation in the commercial sex industry is increasingly a death sentence. A 1998 study published in the *International Journal of STDs and AIDS* revealed that prostituted women and girls in many parts of the world are more likely than not to contract HIV: 58 percent of the prostituted women in Burkina Faso; 52 percent of the prostituted women in Kenya; nearly half the prostituted women in Cambodia; 34 percent of the prostituted women in Northern Thailand; and 50 percent of the prostituted women in Bombay. Fifty to 70 percent of trafficked Burmese women were infected with HIV/AIDS and of 218 girls rescued from a Bombay brothel, 65 percent were HIV positive. Prostituted women in the global West and North, where AIDS education is widespread, also show a far higher incidence of AIDS than women who have not been subjected to commercial sexual exploitation. In Italy, for example, the incidence of HIV/AIDS among prostituted women grew from 2 percent to 16 percent from 1988 to 1998 (Leidholdt 1999). Other sexually transmitted diseases are common. One study found that 38.3 percent of prostituted women in 'low priced brothel areas in Denpasar' suffered human papillomavirus infection (Ford *et al.* 2003). 95 percent of the women in the brothels took part in the study. The rate of infection amongst those under 18 years was 69.2 percent.

Another form of damage to health is the violence prostituted women and girls suffer. Research suggests that prostituted women and girls are subjected to extremely high levels of violence such as beatings, rapes, torture, and murder. Much of the violence they suffer comes from partners or pimps, categories that are not always easily distinguished (Dalla, Xia and Kennedy 2003). I distinguish this violence, which is not part of the ordinary abuse that the men who buy women actually pay, from what prostitution survivors have called 'commercial sexual violence' or 'bought rape', that is, the routine violence that the male users pay to inflict, such as unwanted sexual intercourse, sexual harassment. A 1998 study, 'Prostitution in Five Countries', of 475 prostitutes in South Africa, Thailand, Turkey, the United States, and Zambia, revealed that, across countries, 73 percent of the subjects reported physical assault in prostitution and 62 percent reported having been raped in prostitution, 46 percent at least five times (Farley *et al.* 1998). A 1985 Canadian report on the sex industry in that country reported that women in prostitution suffer a mortality rate forty times the national average (Leidholdt 1999).

An important element of the damage caused to health by men's abuse of women in prostitution is the psychological harm associated with the practice of dissociation that prostituted women and children use to survive. Dissociation is a mind/body split employed to protect the self from the violation of the abuse. One thing about which prostitution researchers with diverse political agendas agree, is that prostituted women, as well as children, dissociate to survive (McLeod 1982; Hoigard & Finstad 1992). Dissociation is routine and achieved by various means documented by prostitution survivors: drink, drugs, cutting off. This dissociation may be learnt by prostituted women to survive childhood sexual abuse or in the early stages of prostitution abuse. Research on prostituted women suggests that between 60 percent (Silbert & Pines 1981) and 90 percent (Giobbe 1990) have experienced child sexual abuse, though there are different interpretations in the literature as to the directness of the connection between such abuse and entry into prostitution. Those who do not learn the technique of dissociation survive less well (Vanwesenbeeck 1994). The effects of dissociation are to injure women's relationships with their bodies and their selves and their relations with others. Some feminist researchers have identified the effects of prostitution abuse as resembling post-traumatic stress disorder. This range of symptoms of trauma, originally associated with combat veterans, has also been found in the victims of child sexual abuse (Herman 1994). Melissa Farley uses the notion of PTSD to investigate the effects of prostitution abuse (Farley *et al.* 1998).

> Adult prostitution survivors speak of guilt, shame and feelings of worthlessness just as the child victims do. One of the prostituted women interviewed by Hoigard and

Finstad in Oslo described feeling like 'a piece of shit' (Hoigard & Finstad 1992, p. 109). Another said that her emotional relationships failed because when embarking on them she starts 'hating myself, my body is filthy' (ibid. p. 113). Two women in this study are quoted at length on the difficulties of carrying on a life outside prostitution, such as taking exams and standing up and speaking at meetings when they feel they are still, underneath the facade, the persons who were prostituted. They feel they live a double life.

Evelina Giobbe, founder of the prostitution survivors' organisation WHISPER (Women Hurt in Systems of Prostitution Engaged in Revolt), defines prostitution as 'bought rape'. She found that prostitution survivors who contacted the organisation suffered harms similar to those that result from other forms of sexual violence, such as negative effects on their sexuality, flashbacks and nightmares as well as lingering fears and deep emotional pain that often resembled grieving (Giobbe 1991, p. 155).

One significant consequence of prostitution for the health of women and girls is suicide. A 2002 report of research into involvement in prostitution and suicide amongst street youth in Ontario, Canada, showed a strong connection (Kidd & Kral 2002). Interviews were conducted with 29 young women and men from 17 to 24 years. Responses indicated that 69 percent were involved in prostitution; 76 percent reported once suicide attempt and of these 86 percent had made more than one attempt. When asked about their feelings in relation to these attempts, 'many described feelings of being merely an object for someone to "get off on" or "just some hole" (ibid. p. 421). Prostitution brought back earlier experiences of child sexual abuse that was connected in their minds with their entering prostitution in the first place. Suicide attempts were regularly preceded by a 'bad date' which meant 'not getting paid, a trick that takes too long or is too demanding, being beaten up, raped, or tricks who make offensive, demeaning comments' (ibid.).

The research findings as to the harm of prostitution are challenged by some individual prostituted women who speak of how prostitution is, for them, a good and reasonable job. One example is Annie Sprinkle who has made a career out of promoting prostitution publicly (Juno 1991). In order to understand such protestations it is important to apply to prostitution the insights that feminist researchers have developed about 'minimisation' in relation to other kinds of violence against women. Liz Kelly and Jill Radford point out that women victims of violence in many forms, such as domestic violence and sexual harassment, tend to say that 'nothing really happened' and consistently minimise the extent of the abuse and the harm they suffer (Kelly & Radford 1996). The pressure to minimise can be exacerbated by economic dependence on the continuation of the abusive behaviour as in prostitution.

Reflects values and beliefs held by members of a community for periods often spanning generations
Prostitution is a practice which fulfils this part of the definition very well. Defenders of prostitution tend to say that it is 'the oldest profession' and often use examples from prehistory to justify the view that prostitution should be honoured and celebrated (Shannon Bell 1994). One problem with this celebration of 'sacred' or 'temple' prostitution is that the proponents assume a golden age in which women were equal and in which the form of prostitution that existed was empowering to women rather than abusive. But there is no good evidence to suggest that prostitution had its origins in an egalitarian society. Gerda Lerner, for instance, attributes prostitution's origins to the practice of slavery itself in Mesopotamia where extra slave women were placed in brothels (Lerner 1987). The historical evidence of the longevity of prostitution in different forms might more easily be used to support the idea that prostitution should be categorised as a harmful traditional practice.

For the benefit of men
All the sound and fury that emanates from the debates presently raging in the international community of non-government organisations and feminist academics about prostitution concentrate upon women as if men were not involved in prostitution at all. The forced/free distinction encourages the exclusion of the men who use women in prostitution and those who make profits from that abuse from consideration. It is a socially constructed masculine sexual desire that provides the stimulus to the industry of prostitution. Women can exercise no 'choice' to be in prostitution without the sex of male supremacy and men's demand to exercise that sexuality in the bodies of women bought for that purpose. The prostitution industry exploits the economic, physical and social powerlessness of women and children, in order to service what is an almost exclusively male desire. In Western cultures women are seen as freely choosing prostitution whilst the male abusers are invisible. The men need to remain invisible if the social harm of their prostitution behaviour is to be hidden from their women partners, relatives and workmates.

A comparison can be made here with female genital mutilation, which is often represented as something that women choose for their female children. This practice is usually carried out by women alone and men are absolved of responsibility. However, feminists campaigning against FGM have consistently stressed that FGM occurs so that women may conform to male ideas of female sexuality, and it is indeed men's requirements that underlie the practice (Dorkenoo 1994).

Takes on an aura of morality

Prostitution is also starting to take on an aura of morality. Although it has traditionally led to punishment and social isolation for women (although not for the men for whose use and benefit it exists), it is now being legalised in many places such as the Netherlands and Australia. When the 1998 ILO report on prostitution (Lim 1998) can call for the recognition of the usefulness of prostitution to the economies of South-East Asia, then the status of prostitution as an industry starts to take on the appearance of a positive good, rather than a social evil. The status of prostituted women does not necessarily change, however, even though the business of making a profit from the industry can become respectable. Even if prostitution is not always seen as wholly good, it is certainly seen as inevitable in most countries of the world, an inevitability which shows the deeply rooted nature of its acceptance, its embeddedness as a practice in male-dominant cultures.

The sex industry is a powerful educator and creates its own morality through pornography. Pornography consists of photographs and moving images of women being paid to perform sexual acts, that is, prostitution. It teaches important messages which legitimise men's prostitution abuse. It teaches that women like and crave to be sexually used, despite the fact that the women are in fact simulating desire or even enslaved and clearly bruised. It teaches the practices of prostitution as what sex is. Pornography is, I would agree with Kathleen Barry, the 'propaganda of womanhatred', but it is also the force which propels the prostitution industry to expand and teaches new generations of men a morality in which the abuse of women in prostitution is a conceivable option (Barry 1979).

Prostitution is given an aura of morality by academic justifications which represent it as good for women, as representing women's 'choice' and 'agency' and even 'feminism in action' (Nagle 1998). Thus prostitution takes on the aura of contributing to women's 'empowerment' and those who continue to want to point out the brutality involved in men's prostitution behaviour can be said to be acting against women's interests (Roberts 1992). Mentioning the men whose interests create and maintain prostitution becomes a social solecism.

Western bias

It may be precisely on the grounds of the idea of choice that the UN documents on harmful traditional practices omit, apart from the general issue of violence against women, all such practices in the West. The Western bias is a major obstacle to the inclusion of prostitution. The practices specifically referred to in the definition in the UN Fact Sheet are as follows:

. . . female genital mutilation (FGM); forced feeding of women; early marriage; the various taboos or practices which prevent women from controlling their own fertility; nutritional taboos and traditional birth practices; son preference and its implications for the status of the girl child; female infanticide; early pregnancy; and dowry price (UN 1995, pp. 3–4).

The only practice in the UN Fact Sheet that is clearly cross-cultural is violence against women, and that seems to have been added almost as an afterthought. This is problematic since it could imply that Western culture is devoid of practices harmful to the health of women and children. That is demonstrably untrue, for there are a number of practices that could be seen to fit the UN definitions and which relate directly to the 'non-Western' practices that are recognized (Wynter, Thompson and Jeffreys 2002). The mutilation of women and children to fit them into the dictates of patriarchal society is alive and well in Western countries. One example is intersexual surgery, in which the genital organs of newborns and young children who are considered not to exhibit sufficiently clear biological sex differences are mutilated to place them in the political categories of male and female (Kessler 1998). Intersexual surgery, transsexual surgery and labiaplasty can be considered analogous to female genital mutilation.

The absence of these Western practices from the lists needs to be explained. It could be that this reflects a common bias in Western commentators towards seeing the West as not having a culture, whereas non-Western societies do (Narayan 1998). Or it could be that Western practices are excluded because Western culture is founded upon liberal individualism. Thus practices that could be understood as expressing degrees of coercion or lack of choice in other cultures are seen in the West to express 'choice' and 'agency'. Western culture is based upon some other important values too which are involved in justifying Western harmful practices, such as valuing consumerism and the profit motive such that women are encouraged to shop for forms of mutilation which will make surgeons rich. Another important Western value is respect for two industries involved in the marketing of such practices: the fashion industry and the medical industry. Both are culturally valued and treated with respect, indeed medicine is given considerable authority. The cutting up of women in breast implant surgery and labiaplasty are attributed to women's desire to be beautiful, represented as the exercise of choice and freedom, and carried out under medical authority (see Jeffreys 2000a and forthcoming 2005).

It is these Western cultural values that exclude prostitution too from consideration as a harmful cultural practice. The tendency amongst governments and feminist theorists in the 1990s has been to apply liberal individualism and the profit motive to prostitution in their own Western backyards, whilst maintaining some concern for prostitution in other countries in which it is harder to maintain the fiction of 'choice'. Distinctions are regularly made in thinking about prostitution presently in international fora on the basis of the ability of the prostituted women to exercise choice. Thus child prostitution is distinguished from adult prostitution, Western prostitution from Eastern prostitution, brothel prostitution from street prostitution, 'forced' trafficking from 'labour migration'.

The advantage of analysing prostitution as a harmful cultural practice is that it is a way to sidestep the obstacle to serious theory and practice on the issue that is presented by such narrow, and culturally specific, liberal individualism. The UN notion of 'harmful cultural practices', despite its present restriction to non-Western practices, is useful because it incorporates an understanding of how harmful attitudes arising from the subordination of women can create practices which can seem to be chosen by women and represented as being in their interests.

Business opportunity or harmful traditional practice

One element that distinguishes the harmful practices of the West is the extent to which vested interests make huge profits from them. The fashion and cosmetics industries, medicine, and the sex industry represent powerful interests which then shape cultural understandings of the practices they profit from. Thus even the ILO is promoting the idea that prostitution is a good business opportunity that can usefully contribute to the gross domestic product of a nation. It is hard to imagine that the practices identified as harmful to women in non-Western contexts could be turned into nice little earners in this way without some outcry from the human rights community.

Prostitution fits the criteria for recognition as a harmful traditional/cultural practice extremely well. This approach helpfully takes us beyond the discussion of whether women 'choose' to engage in prostitution, since 'choice' is not relevant to the definition of such practices. It makes the forced/free distinction irrelevant. It illuminates the harm involved in the present determination by some governments and international agencies to develop national and international industries of prostitution. It is an approach that allows change by recognizing that the beliefs and behaviours of men that cause them to abuse women and girls in prostitution are cultural, not natural, and can be brought to an end.

References

Barry, Kathleen. (1979). *Female Sexual Slavery.* Englewood Cliffs, NJ: Prentice-Hall.

Bell, Shannon. (1994). *Reading, Writing and Rewriting the Prostitute Body.* Bloomington, Indiana: Indiana University Press.

Chapkis, Wendy. (1997). *Live Sex Acts. Women Performing Erotic Labor.* New York: Routledge.

Coomaraswamy, Radhika. (2000). *Integration of the Human Rights of Women and the Gender Perspective. Violence Against Women.* Report of the Special Rapporteur on violence against women, its causes and consequences, Ms Radhika Coomaraswamy, on trafficking in women, women's migration and violence against women, submitted in accordance with Commission on Human Rights resolution 1997/44. United Nations Economic and Social Council. 29 February 2000. E/CN.4/2000/68.

Dalla, Rochelle L, Yan Xia and Heather Kennedy. (2003). 'You Just Give Them What They Want and Pray They Don't Kill You'. *Violence Against Women,* 9 (11), 1367–1394.

Dorkenoo, Efua. (1994). Cutting the Rose. London: Minority Rights Group.

Farley, Melissa *et al.* (1998). 'Prostitution in Five Countries: Violence and Post-Traumatic Stress Disorder'. *Feminism and Psychology,* 8 (4), 405–426.

Ford, Kathleen, Barbara D. Reed, Dewa Nyoman Wirawan, Partha Muliawan, Made Sutarga and Lucie Gregoire. (2003). 'The Bali STD/AIDS Study: Human Papillomavirus Infection among Female Sex Workers'. *International Journal of STD and AIDS,* 14, 681–687.

Giobbe, Evelina. (1990). 'Confronting the Liberal Lies about Prostitution'. In Dorchen Leidholdt and Janice Raymond (eds.). *The Sexual Liberals and the Attack on Feminism.* New York: Pergamon Press.

Giobbe, Evelina. (1991). 'Prostitution: Buying the Right to Rape'. In Ann Wolpert Burgess (ed.). *Rape and Sexual Assault III. A Research Handbook.* New York: Garland Publishing.

Herman, Judith Lewis. (1994). *Trauma and Recovery: From Domestic Abuse to Political Terror.* London: Pandora.

Hoigard, Cecilie and Liv Finstad. (1992). *Backstreets. Prostitution, Money and Love.* Cambridge: Polity.

Jeffreys, Sheila. (1997). *The Idea of Prostitution.* North Melbourne: Spinifex Press.

Jeffreys, Sheila: (2000a). 'Body Art': Cutting, Tattooing and Piercing from a Feminist Perspective. *Feminism and Psychology,* 10 (4), 409–429.

Jeffreys, Sheila. (2000b). 'Challenging the Child/Adult Distinction in Theory and Practice on Prostitution'. *International Feminist Journal of Politics,* 2 (3), 359–379.

Jeffreys, Sheila. (2005 forthcoming). *Beauty and Misogyny: Harmful Cultural Practices in the West*. London and New York: Routledge.

Jeness, Valerie. (1993). *Making it Work: The Prostitutes' Rights Movement in Perspective*. New York: Aldine de Gruyter.

Juno, Andrea. (1991). 'Interview with Annie Sprinkle'. In *Angry Women*. *RE/SEARCH*, 13. San Francisco: Re/Search Publications.

Kelly, Liz and Jill Radford. (1996). '"Nothing Really Happened": The Invalidation of Women's Experiences of Sexual Violence'. In Marianne Hester, Liz Kelly and Jill Radford (eds.). *Women, Violence and Male Power*. Buckingham, UK: Open University Press.

Kempadoo, Kamala and Jo Doezema. (eds.). (1998). *Global Sex Workers: Rights, Resistance and Redefinition*. New York: Routledge.

Kessler, Suzanne J. (1998). *Lessons from the Intersexed*. New Brunswick, NJ: Rutgers University Press.

Kidd, Sean A. and Michael J Kral. (2002). 'Suicide and Prostitution among Street Youth: A Qualitative Analysis'. *Adolescence*, 37 (146), 411–430.

Lerner, Gerda. (1987). *The Creation of Patriarchy*. New York: Oxford University Press.

Lim, Lin Lean (ed.). (1998). *The Sex Sector: The Economic and Social Bases of Prostitution in South-East Asia*. Geneva: International Labour Office.

Mcleod, Eileen. (1982). *Women Working: Prostitution Now*. London: Croom Helm.

Nagle, Jenny (ed.). (1998). *Whores and Other Feminists*. New York: Routledge.

Narayan, Uma. (1998). 'Essence of Culture and a Sense of History: A Feminist Critique of Cultural Essentialism'. *Hypatia*, 13 (2).

Parriott, Ruth. (1994). Health Experiences of Twin Cities Women Used in Prostitution: Survey Findings and Recommendations (unpublished). Available from Breaking Free, 1821 University Avenue, Suite 312, South, St. Paul, MN 55104, USA.

Richard, Amy O'Neill. (1999). *International Trafficking of Women to the US*. Washington: State Department.

Roberts, Nickie. (1992). *Whores in History*. London: HarperCollins.

Silbert, M.H. and A.M. Pines (1981). 'Sexual Child Abuse as an Antecedent to Prostitution'. *International Journal of Child Abuse and Neglect*, 5, 407–411.

Stewart, David. (2003, October 20). 'Organised Crime is Flooding Europe with Migrant Sex Workers'. *Time* magazine, 162 (15).

United Nations. (1995). 'Harmful Traditional Practices Affecting the Health of Women and Children'. Fact Sheet No. 23. Geneva: United Nations.

Vanwesenbeeck, Ine. (1994). *Prostitutes' Well-Being and Risk*. VU University

Press: Amsterdam.

Winter, Bronwyn, Denise Thompson and Sheila Jeffreys. (2002). 'The UN Approach to Harmful Traditional Practices: Some Conceptual Problems'. *International Feminist Journal of Politics*, 4 (1, April), 72–94.

John Stoltenberg
Pornography and international human rights*

The country I come from has been profoundly and uniquely affected by its civil-rights movement. I am an activist in the radical-feminist anti-pornography movement there, but I also speak as one who came of age in the United States during a time of intense social upheaval and struggle, a time of radical change in human consciousness, as regards interpersonal ethics and racial identity. The US civil-rights movement occurred when descendants of slaves confronted those whose social status and very identity as 'whites' was dependent upon prejudice, discrimination, and political persecution—all backed up by entrenched economic policy and the law of the land that bound states together. Racial identity for 'whites' had necessarily meant oppression of 'blacks', and US law was written by eighteenth-century slaveholders in part to secure white rights.

From this historical perspective, the concept of civil rights, or human rights, cannot be abstracted away from identity politics—the domination done to have a dominant identity. Human rights are what identity politics must always deny. There can be no dominant identity apart from domination.

This legacy of the US civil rights movement has been inherited by the radical-feminist anti-pornography movement to which I proudly belong. This legacy is a keen, scalpel-like insight into the roots of identity politics—in this case oppression done to construct gender identity. The legacy of the US civil rights movement has prompted a comprehensive and liberatory political analysis that could potentially inspire real human freedom globally—freedom from being in any oppressed class, and freedom from belonging to any oppressor class. There is no greater freedom imaginable. There is no more important freedom to be fought for.

---

* Out of concern for the influx of pornography into Britain that seemed likely as Western Europe became a unified economy, the Gracewell Institute—a registered charity for the study and treatment of sex offenders—sponsored an international conference in Birmingham, England, on November 12, 1992, entitled 'Pornography . . . and Sexual Crime (Implications for an Integrated Europe)'. The profeminist writer and activist John Stoltenberg—cofounder of Men Against Pornography in New York and author of *Refusing to Be a Man*—was among the invited speakers. This essay is based on his conference address.

400

The legacy of the US civil-rights movement is the clear and dynamic recognition that identity oppression is done in order to define and defend the oppressor class's identity: by dominating others on the basis of pigmentation or genitalia—wondrous variations on the human theme—the categories 'white' and 'male' obtain whatever credible social and individual meaning they can possibly have. Without such personal and political oppression, those identities are utterly devoid of palpable content.

'Male' and 'white' are hierarchical, class-based identities that result from acts, not anatomy. The identities 'male' and 'white' are due far more to dominance than to difference. You can't be 'the man there' without someone 'nonmale' underneath. Nor can you be 'white' without someone 'nonwhite' underneath.

These radical lessons of history are being learned the hard way in the country I call home, thanks to the ongoing civil-rights movement and the more recent radical-feminist critique of gender. From both these perspectives, I want to explain why the traffic in pornography must be viewed internationally as a civil-rights, or human-rights issue, not as a trade issue. I will explain why in the context of the historical meaning of civil rights, plus the biographical meaning of male sexual identity and the international meaning of male supremacy. In short, I will explain how pornography works in the world of 'real men among men'.

To begin, it's important to explore why pornography is now viewed internationally in the European Community as a trade issue, and why most governing authorities—who are obviously men—probably think there is nothing inappropriate about viewing the traffic in pornography in just that way.

The trade model for talking about pornography, after all, seems a logical and reasonable way for talking about anything that has to do with production and product, with property and distribution, with commerce and profits. Not incidentally, whenever talk is about money and property, the talk does not have to be about human rights—especially the human rights of women and children. The trade model is intrinsically an ownership model—owners get to talk it—and there is a reason that ownership obliterates human rights: Ownership obliterates human rights because of the biographical meaning of male identity politics.

The traffic in pornography is treated as a trade issue in part because the buying and selling of pornography services male sexual identity. And that's because male sexual identity is fundamentally invested in what I call the eroticism of owning. That eroticism is key. It gets to the guts of the problem of pornography posed by a common market among diverse nation states.

The eroticism of owning and male sexual identity

There is much circumstantial evidence that the eroticism of owning exists. For instance, from the testimony of women who are or have been sexually owned in marriage, taken in rape, and/or sexually used for a fee in prostitution, it seems that for many men, possession is a principal part of their sexual behavior. Many men can scarcely discern any erotic feelings that are not associated with owning someone else's body. In English—as in many other languages—the verb 'to possess' is a pun. It means both 'to own' and 'to fuck', and that semantic coincidence appears to be no accident. Apparently many men—at all points along the political spectrum, from left to right—equate standard 'male' sexual behavior with literal ownership of another human being's body. Whether the ownership shall be private or collectivized, it must be personalized at the point of sexual possession. To have sex with someone and simultaneously to be 'a real man' is necessarily and subjectively to *have* that person, to *take* that person, to *possess* that person. To have sex correctly and to have *a* sex correctly—if you were born into male supremacy with a penis—requires a property relation of some sort.

Now, I was born penised, I was raised to be a man in male supremacy, but I count myself a radical human-rights activist too, and I do not believe that anyone has the right to own someone else's body ever—not in order to *have* sex, not in order to have *a* sex.

No one is born with the eroticism of owning—it is learned. By rights we are all sovereign sexual beings. But everyone is born into a society that is organized both to serve and perpetuate the eroticism of owning. For example, the eroticism of owning completely pervades the laws of most countries. Proprietary sexuality wrote the patriarchal lawbook.

Patriarchal laws preserve men's proprietary relation to other people's bodies in sex. That's what patriarchal law has always been for. Essentially the law has been an instrument of ownership of human flesh by selectively entitled human beings. The law codifies phallic possession, sorts it out, sets forth which human flesh *can* be owned and fucked, which human flesh *cannot* be owned and fucked, and which human flesh *must* be owned and fucked. Thus the law administers heterosexuality and keeps the bodies of women and children the property of men.

The phenomenon of pornography occurs in the broad context of this eroticism of owning, and if we imagine or delude ourselves that it does not, we shall not honestly help any human who is hurt by it. Pornography mass-produces sexual ownables for a market of men who become real men only in the act of sexual owning—of one sort or another.

Sexual owners can be heard to offer many justifications for their proprietary sexual proclivity: 'It's men's nature . . . it's women's nature . . . it's

God's will . . . it's her fault . . . it's manifest heterosexual destiny . . . she wants it . . . I need it . . . she loves it . . . she deserves it . . . whatever turns me on . . . she's getting paid for it . . .' But rarely does a sexual owner tell the gender-identity truth: Unless he feels like a sexual owner, he can't feel like a real man.

There is a fundamental connection between property and sexuality and gender identity. And the traffic in pornography is a system of human-rights violations that helps to forge that connection. Pornography democratizes the property relation in male-supremacist sex. The traffic in pornography keeps all women targeted for sexual possession by all men—and it keeps wealthy men safe from the rage of men with less money. Pornography redirects that rage and shows men how to take it out on someone lower down—especially someone whose flesh is female or juvenile.

Along with many other radical feminists, I believe that gender is a political and social construction, a social fiction. Gender identity resonates within our human bodies and brains emotionally and physically, but it is a phenomenon based on no essential anatomical or metaphysical reality. The social fiction of gender has a material reality only to the extent that it resonates in between human bodies economically. To feel real, to be made flesh, the social fiction of gender identity has attached to the property relation.

The economic relation of owner and owned can be found throughout human history in slavery and in the slave trade, in the family and in fathers' ownership of human breeding stock. What is not often noted is the way the economic relation of owner and owned has become the substance and substructure of all sexual relations that construct social gender. For the social fiction of gender to make emotional and physical sense in human bodies and brains—for certain human beings to feel they really belong to the sex class 'men'—an eroticism must be learned, an eroticism of owning, and this eroticism must be experienced with the same urgency as social gender itself. For one human being to 'own' another human being does not otherwise reinforce gender identity. But owning a human being through sex makes gender make sense; it lends owning an emotional and physical resonance; it lodges social gender in bodies and brains. The social fiction of gender feels subjectively real only within the erotics of economics—when 'owning' becomes the same sexual turn-on as 'being the man there'.

Pornography mass-produces ownables so that penised humans can have a sex. The traffic in pornography offers penised humans commoditized bodies to possess in order to feel like a real man.

To 'be the man there' is a meaningless proposition unless that person is committing effective acts of disparagement and domination, relational acts that will incontrovertibly establish a gender identity somewhere over and above someone else who is not the man there, or subordinating someone through sex. One cannot rest on the laurels of one's physiology; one must constantly do derogating deeds in order to be the man there.

There can be no dominant identity apart from domination. The social fiction of gender is always a matter of dominance, not difference—of acts, not anatomy.

Conveniently, the economic relation of owner to owned helps one avoid having to make so many day-in-and-day-out nuisance decisions. The economic relation of sexual owner to someone else's sexually owned body is a great expedient. You don't have to decide every little detail of every relational act to assert and believe you're the man there. Instead, with your ownership of another human being's body established in the proprietary way you have sex, you can know you're the man *there*, at least in clear-cut contrast to the body you sexually own. But owning that body in and through sex has to make you feel closer to manhood; owning has to make you believe in your physical and emotional reality as a man; owning has to convince you erotically that you have an authentic and superior sexual identity.

The erotics of economics have emerged in male-supremacist history in the private-property sense of the word 'to own'. And they also arise in the biography of nearly every penised human—through his personal erotic adaptation to life in male supremacy—in the proprietary sense of the word 'to fuck'. In no other way could the economic relation between owner and owned come to feel so sexy to so many human beings. In no other way could some selected human beings find their way to a socially convincing sexual identity with such apparent passion, flushed with such a prideful sense of power.

From the point of view of someone born penised into male supremacy, this means learning a physical imperative to have sex in a specifically proprietary way in order to feel one has a social gender at all. To personally perpetuate the erotics of economics, to do your part, you must learn to feel you have to *have* someone, you have to *take* someone, you have to *possess* someone— otherwise you're not legitimately a man and therefore you're less than nobody. A penised human may go so far as to feel the other person's body is literally his—to do with whatever he wants. Like an ownable object. Like an ownable thing. Like his private personal property. He may feel that if he wants to have it, then obviously he should just be able to buy it or take it. He may feel packed solid with the emotional and physical feelings of owning. He may feel utterly terrified to experience any other, nonproprietary kinds of emotional and physical communications and sensations, or to act sexually in any ways that do not stake his claim to someone else's flesh—for fear that if he does so he himself will feel owned, and therefore not a real man.

For countless humans raised to be a man, that's what having sex means: Having it. Having someone. Having someone—owning them—as an 'it'. Then having more of it—having more its—to feel more real, to feel more real a man. Having sex to have a gender.

The pornography market is driven by this gender-identity urgency, and this gender-identity urgency is significantly driven by the traffic in pornography. At a time when institutions such as marriage, the church, and professions closed to women no longer reliably shore up the gender identity 'men' for humans whose penis gives them that birthright, pornography offers low-cost gender insurance in the form of mass-marketed consumables. Marriage, rape, and prostitution are still available for the purpose, of course. But modern, technologized pornography takes much of the trouble out of feeling like the man there. When you buy it, when you masturbate to it, when you replay it in your mind's eye, you get a quick fix for your manhood—gender identity cheap.

Marriage, rape, and prostitution may appear to be very different ways of 'being the man there', and the women experiencing each of them may be known by different names as well (wife, rape victim, whore), and the practices may fall into three different categories legally. But seen from the point of view of an acculturated male-supremacist sexuality—witnessed through sexual feelings rigorously conditioned to own, to respond sexually only to selected human bodies as ownable objects—these practical distinctions have a visceral common theme, one that could not be plainer than when a man joins the pornography consumer market.

Subjectively marriage, rape, and prostitution may feel quite dissimilar to the owned—and the relational particulars quite distinct to owners too. But to penised human beings correctly committed to manhood, the eroticism of owning feels all alike in the dark: it is the feeling of owning someone else's body in sex. It is the feeling of being the man there. It is the feeling of having a certifiable and superior social gender. It is the passion of sexual possession. It is the subjectivity of having sex like a real man.

The practical particulars of the economic arrangement may vary: whether the ownership is long term or short term, whether there is purchase or theft, whether the owner has sexual access to more than one ownable at a time, whether the ownable has been optioned or leased or mass-produced or agented, or whether the ownable is an independent contractor. But the eroticism of owning is a constant. The eroticism of owning is how penised human beings get to feel like the man there.

There will be no real escape from oppression until gender itself has ended. There will be no freedom, no equality, no human dignity, no justice, until the time comes when owning someone in sex is no longer what anyone needs or wants in order to feel they belong to a sex class. And when that time comes, there will be no sex classes to belong to. There would, in effect, be as many sexes as there are people—as many sovereign sexual selves as there are human beings.

We cannot grapple with patriarchal law's protection of trafficking in pornography—or the law's regulation of prostitution or the law's administration of heterosexuality or the law's jurisdiction in rape—without keeping absolutely clear about patriarchal law's continued investment in proprietary sexuality. Patriarchal law is a social institution designed to create, maintain, and enforce the sex-class system by maintaining and enforcing the eroticism of owning—in order that humans born penised shall have a socially superior sex class to belong to.

Man-to-man conflict and international male supremacy

To understand yet more deeply the international human-rights issues in the pornography traffic, I want to look next at the way male-supremacist governance works. I want to sketch a personal picture showing how all male-supremacist governance is actually modeled on what happens between humans raised to be a man—when one of them challenges the other's manhood.

All humans who grow up to be a man are raised to pass tests of loyalty to manhood. These tests can be routine ones; these tests can be episodically treacherous. However great or small, these tests have one theme in common: they almost inevitably cancel out loyalty to someone's human rights. Perhaps the most terrifying test of loyalty to manhood occurs when one is confronted by another man who intimidates or scares you. I invite those of you who were raised to be a man to remember just such events in your own life.

In the moment of the confrontation—when another man's threat rears up, when his opportunity to hurt or humiliate becomes clear to you both—no amount of mental or physical preparedness seems to prevent your falling for the test and somehow attempting to prove your loyalty to manhood. Naturally, you wish to save your neck. But more important, you wish to pass the test: the test of your loyalty to manhood, which another man may have impugned.

There is a classic dramatic plot line that occurs virtually every time two humans raised to be a man—flush with fight-or-flight fury—decide to lock horns, go *mano a mano*, or 'step outside' in order to pass the manhood test. The plot is so familiar that it would be utterly boring if not for the emotional investment so many men have learned to have in it—and if not for the high stakes for various offstage human beings whose fate may hang on the outcome of the duel at downstage center. This is how the drama goes:

When you and another man are both in combat defending your manhood act, there are three and only three possible resolutions to the conflict:

One: You lose. He manages to humiliate you or he manages to hurt you in such a way that he comes off more manly.

Two: He loses. You manage to humiliate or hurt him in such a way that he will have learned not to mess with you.

Three: You both agree to pick on someone else. You end up in a truce, a tacit treaty that must have a third party—someone you both agree has a relatively inferior manhood act or someone else who is simply female. With (and only with) that third party for contrast, you both become comfortable enough to concede that your mutual manhood acts pass muster.

These are the inevitable sexual politics of confrontations between individual manhood acts, and these are exactly the sexual politics that define international relations between male-supremacist nation states: one loses, the other loses, or they both somehow gang up on one or more third-party losers.

Condoning human-rights violations is the way male-supremacist nation states forge male-supremacist truces. It's the price of penised peace. These sexual politics of male-supremacist governments are laid bare in both the proliferation of pornography and in existing methods to 'control' it. In the name of 'nationalism' and 'national independence', male-supremacist governments make truces that essentially condone one another's rights to commit human-rights violations, one another's rights to domination and exploitation over women and ethnic minorities within their respective borders. When the traffic in pornography is treated as merely a trade issue, the *mano-a-mano* model of male-supremacist governance is exposed: the pornography traffic is governmentally regulated, and therefore tacitly condoned, because the people whose lives it is made from do not matter as much as the men whose sexual identities are secured in the interface truce between male-supremacist states. The traffic in pornography between nations becomes a male-supremacist bond—a pact against third parties—against the people whose human rights are violated to make it and sell it.

Driven by the acculturated eroticism of owning, plus the structurally predictable consequences whenever manhoods clash, the sex industry has grown more and more to become an international cartel. The prostituted human beings from whose lives the pornography is made become like flies to wanton war lords, who buy and sell them as much for sport as for gender-identity security—a line of gender defense that maintains boundaries between real men and borders between male-supremacist states.

You see, the way to be the man there when there's another man threatening to invade your space or to blow you away is always to bond with him against a third party, preferably a woman or a feminized male; that way the other man will respect your manhood; that way the other man will leave you alone.

In the international arena, where manhood vies with manhood and state vies with state and they sell out women and ethnic minorities as a first line of gender defense, the profligate traffic in pornography emerges also as a conduit of wealth and seminal wealth, a quasi-homoerotic medium of exchange of economic liquidity.

Note the way that the international trafficking in women generally, and the traffic in pornography in particular, has in the new world order become a conduit of Western, or harder, currency. Note the way that pornography— the literal documentation of sexual abuse and human-rights violations—has come to function commercially as an exportable and importable product, with money passing from consumers' hands to pornographers' hands, from johns' hands to pimps' hands, from man to man, keeping currency hard as safe homosex.

I do not mean to get too elliptical here—but I must completely break down the frame of reference that takes traffic in pornography for granted as a trade problem. I must emphasize in all seriousness why the human-rights issues in prostitution and pornography necessarily become completely obscured in wrangles among men and male-supremacist states over import policies and trade rights. Such policies and perspectives not only fail to solve the social problems presented in pornography—the human-rights violations in the production, traffic, and consumption of pornography; these trade policies also reflect a model of governance that merely manages hegemonies among male supremacists—policies that protect the identity oppression but never remedy the human-rights violation without which the identity could not persist.

The history of civil rights in the United States and the future of human rights in an integrated Europe

I come from the United States, where a very important political lesson was learned about the human-rights violation that was racial segregation: The US learned—painfully—that racial segregation could not be addressed as a problem of states' rights. Racial segregation could not be addressed solely as a problem of interstate commerce. Racial segregation had to be addressed— in conscience, by the nation as a whole—as an issue of civil rights. To address racial segregation, the US had to get down to basics: there are inalienable human rights, rights to equality, that may not be abridged by any government or by any individual.

I come here to tell you: the European Community must begin looking at pornography as if its human victims matter—and as if human rights matter more than monetary unity or manhood.

The alternative to treating pornography as a trade issue is not only radically democratic legislation—such as the civil-rights approach to pornography, which originated in the US and which would give individuals harmed in or through the production and traffic of pornography a right to fight back through civil lawsuits. I cannot underestimate how crucial this human-rights model of legislation is. Its application and implementation in the European Community must be given immediate priority.[1] But I want to say more: I want to urge consideration of a different model of governance as well.

The challenge for those who would confront the deleterious impact of pornography on human society is twofold:

1. legislation must be enacted that will empower those whose human rights have been violated, so that they may seek meaningful justice, and
2. a new, more responsive model of governance must be pressed for: governance that respects the human rights of the most vulnerable, governance that does not concede any other government's authority to violate the human rights of its citizens.

This means that international agreements must be designed so that they do not, in effect, simply secure within separate borders the rights to shield sexual exploitation and the commercial rights to profit from sexual abuse. The European Community has an historic opportunity to esteem universal human rights—by empowering those whose human rights have been violated in and through the traffic in pornography. But influence over such international agreements cannot be unduly wielded by nations whose state-protected sex industries have most extensively exploited populations vulnerable to sexual abuse, nations where documentations of sexual torture most originate as export 'entertainment'. Those countries that have most evidently licensed human-rights violations through pornography shall have to defer. Countries desiring to make human rights central shall have to set the terms. Otherwise the truce is corrupt—and the unified European market will be destined to become yet another male-supremacist pact against powerless third parties.

Fundamentally, the baseline for humane governance—now and in the future—must be whether any society takes seriously what happens when someone is harmed so that someone else can have 'sex'.

Interpersonally, no one has a right to violate someone else's human rights— not to *have* sex, not to have *a* sex. Internationally, there is an irreconcilable contradiction between protecting pornography as a trade problem and furthering principles of equality and human rights.

I call upon the uniting European nations to regard pornography not as a trade issue but as a human-rights issue. A trade policy for pornography is a *commitment* to identity oppression: negotiation among owners about who gets to own whom. A human-rights approach to pornography is a commitment to cohesion in real human freedom.

---

1 See *Pornography: Women, Violence and Civil Liberties*, edited by Catherine Itzin (Oxford University Press, 1992).

Carol Davis

Against their will: Nepal's activist theatre fights girl-trafficking*

Against their will, girls and young women from rural Nepal are coerced into prostitution. Transported across borders and estranged from people and languages they know, they are pressed into slavery in the miserable brothels of India. The magnitude of the girl-trafficking problem is staggering as, annually, more than five thousand Nepali women are kidnapped, lured, tricked, sold, and married into the business of sex. His Majesty's Government maintains that the number of Nepali prostitutes in India is nearly 200,000, though exact figures are impossible to obtain.

Nepal's theatre community has turned its spotlight onto the girl-trafficking crisis, and troupes of dedicated artist/activists battle this problem using theatre as their only weapon. To raise awareness and mobilize policy makers, police, and the general public toward stopping the sale of girls and young women for sex, actors portray the causes and consequences of the girl-trafficking dilemma. In Nepal, the rural literacy level is extremely low, poverty is rampant, electricity is scarce, terrain is arduous, and roads are few. Consequently, live, mobile, entertaining, and free theatre proves a powerful means of raising awareness about issues, such as domestic prostitution and girl-trafficking, which have few alternative routes of discourse.

While Nepal's current system of prostitution and girl trafficking has complex origins, it also has historical precedents; culture and religion have played significant roles in the development of the sex trade. The *deuki*, for example, in practice for hundreds of years, is the tradition of offering girls to temples to appease deities or gain their favor. An impoverished family may give their daughter to a temple or may sell her to a wealthy family, who will dedicate her to temple service. In either case, the poor family is rid of the responsibility of raising and marrying off their daughter, and both they and the wealthy family gain merit and honor for the sacrifice they have made. While *deukis* may be held in respect for their implied relationship to the deities, they are generally not given financial support. Burdened by the common conception that *deukis* should not become wives, these temple

* I am grateful to the Asian Cultural Council for the generous support that enabled me to conduct research for this article in Kathmandu.

denizens turn to prostitution to survive. Children born to *deukis* 'cannot obtain citizenship since they have no legal fathers, and without acceptable social status they become marginalized by society. The tendency nowadays is for daughters [born to *deukis*] to enter into the same profession' (Sattaur 1993, p. 58). While both the *deuki* system and prostitution are illegal in Nepal, certainly both are practiced there today.

For hundreds of years the professional entertainment and semi-nomadic *Badi* caste members earned their living as dancers, singers, and musicians, performing for Nepal's kings and wealthy landlords. The popularity of their entertainments now replaced by television and film, the landless and poor *Badi* settle in urban centers and *Badi* women turn to prostitution to support their families.

> An interesting phenomenon among the *Badi* is that in contrast to the rest of Nepal where the birth of a boy is welcomed and that of a girl is considered a burden, *Badi* girls are cherished as they may be certain to provide security for the parents in their old age. It has been said that the status of women in the *Badi* family is high because the responsibility for the survival and well being of the family rests on the shoulders of the female members. (Ghimre 1998, p. 6)

It is accepted that girls born of the *Badi* community will become prostitutes and, that while they are between the ages of thirteen and forty-five (Sattaur 1993, p. 58), they will support their families in this way.

Until only fifty years ago, when Nepal first flirted with democracy, young and beautiful girls were brought from throughout the country to serve as attendants, servants, and cooks in royal palaces. Many of these girls learned to dance or sing in order to please their patrons, and many were used and traded as objects of recreation and sexual pleasure. Some palaces had harems with thousands of these pleasure girls. Such sexual exploitation, sanctioned and practiced by Nepal's rulers, established the precedent for the disregard and abuse of young women throughout society in general.

People from Nepal's hills have long migrated to India for seasonal or permanent work. Over a century ago the British recruited Nepali men to fight in their army and, indeed, it became glamorous and lucrative to be selected to serve as a *Gurkha* soldier in the British Army, and remains so today. The Indian army also offers an enticing opportunity to young Nepali men disenchanted with the hardships of agrarian life, and other armies, such as that of the Sultan of Brunei, continue to recruit armed forces from among the young men of Nepal. Such historical and contemporary work-motivated migrations of people from every part of the country provide an easy opportunity and an accepted pretext for agents to take Nepali girls across the borders to the Indian prostitution markets.

Nepal's theatre activists, who, for the past twenty years have dramatized pressing social issues, challenge these historical traditions of commodifying young women for sexual pleasure. They strive to raise public awareness by questioning the tradition-laden current cultural system that permits the sale of women and girl children at home and abroad. Theatre troupes in urban and rural areas work to sensitize the government and the public toward essential social change that includes the re-valuation of women and girls.

Nepal's theatre artists began using theatre for social change during the 1980s pro-democracy movement. Theatrically embodying the situations they sought to change, rather than making speeches, proved a successful means of attracting large audiences. Initially, university students performed *agit-prop* (agitation-propaganda) plays before a populace unfamiliar with formal education. The political struggle between government and people was temporarily resolved by the declaration of a constitutional monarchy in 1990. Since then, Nepal's theatre activists have turned their attentions to social and cultural problems, most notably focusing on the issues of women's rights.

Nepal's multifarious society, with its complexity of religious practices and cultural traditions, does not easily permit generalization about the status of women, yet, as Prativa Subedi writes in *Nepali Women Rising*, 'it can be stated without reservation that Nepali women from the communities high in the Himalayan region to those of the lowlands in the southern *terai* region are exploited and oppressed' (Subedi 1997, p. 1). According to a common Nepali saying, and one referred to in virtually all plays that focus on the consequences of the devaluation of Nepali women, investments in a girl's future, such as education and nutritional care, are 'like watering a neighbor's field'. A pervasive conception is that a girl child is merely held in custody for her future husband and his family, and that women have no intrinsic status, but gain value only through their service to fathers, brothers and husbands.

> The inequality in treatment between boys and girls begins with a preference for the birth of a boy and develops into inequality in treatment that continues through life. Girls are valued less, fed less, educated less, worked harder and deprived of opportunities to broaden their personal, social and intellectual horizons (Sattaur 1993, p. 51).

Theatre makers take aim at various sources of this problem, including the notion that girls are valuable to their families only as workers, be it menial labor or prostitution. The play, *Sabadhan*, created and performed throughout the country by the Art Group of ABC Nepal (a non-government organization begun in 1987 by two Nepali women), shows ramifications of the misconception that it is more important to keep a girl working than to educate her. ABC's play demonstrates that educational deprivation renders girls functionally illiterate and less aware and thus, more easily duped into the sex trade. As *Sabadhan* dramatizes, village girls are regularly held home from school to help with agrarian and household chores. Rural enrollment of girls in primary school is approximately half the enrollment of boys, and by high school there are approximately six boys to every girl in school. Such disparate access to education obviously results in a far lower level of literacy among women than men. Currently, only 25 percent of females over six years of age are literate, as compared to 55 percent literacy among males over six years (UNICEF 1996, 114). This average figure varies from region to region with some rural areas demonstrating a female literacy rate of less than 4.7 percent (INSEC 2000, p. 225).

Combating the educational deprivation of women, other activist theatre artists play scenes that emphasize the importance of sending girls to school and show ways in which the education of girls benefits the child, the family, and the community. The Nepal Swastha Pariyojanaa Naatak Samuha (Nepal Health Project Theatre Troupe) encourages rural families to educate their daughters by emphasizing essential hygiene and first aid information girls may learn in school. In their play, *Haamro Swastha, Haamro Haatma Chaa* (*Our Health is in Our Hands*), a schoolgirl shows her mother how to lower her baby brother's fever (without medicine), teaches her mother how to treat a bad burn (without medicine), and counsels her mother on the necessity of washing hands before eating and cooking for the family—a novel idea to her mother. By using health issues of concern to all villagers, the scene demonstrates that a girl's education offers advantages to her parental family as well as to the family into which she marries. In a 1993 survey of nearly 500 Nepali prostitutes in Bombay, it was found that most were illiterate (UNICEF 1996, p. 106). In both *Sabadhan* and *Haamro Swastha, Haamro Haatma Chaa*, education is shown to be a means of instilling the self-confidence, awareness, and skills by which girls may resist trafficking and entry into prostitution.

Still, many rural families hold the traditional view that a girl's education takes her away from useful service and makes it more difficult for the family to find her a husband. This view is expressed in an ancient Sanskrit play, Kalidasa's *Shakuntala*, in which a father rejoices at giving away his daughter in marriage:

> The daughter is a thing to give away
> For someone else she is kept
> What a relief to send her away today
> I'm light as a feather and free from debt.

> (Act IV)

Sadly this attitude, that daughters must be married off as quickly as possible, has changed little in Nepal in the approximately 2300 years since *Shakuntala* was written and, sadly, this attitude still contributes to child marriage and girl trafficking. Syndicates involved in girl trafficking prey on the eagerness of poor families wanting to rid themselves of daughters without having to pay dowries.

ABC's play *Sabadhan* shows a family eager to marry their daughter to a seemingly wealthy man who has come to their village in search of a young bride. Promising a life of ease and wealth, the stranger pays the father a small amount of money and takes away his daughter. This fraud husband has no intention of honoring marriage vows and, instead, sells his unsuspecting bride to an Indian brothel. Clearly, sham marriages perpetrated on the impoverished and illiterate in remote villages provide an abundant source of girls for the sex industry. Large poor families marry off especially young girls when their attempts to produce a son have yielded many daughters.

Girl trafficking syndicates value young girls and, as *Sabadhan* shows, Nepal's high incidence of child marriage creates fertile ground for their aims. Although underage marriage has been illegal in Nepal for almost four decades, studies have found that approximately 40 percent of rural girls marry before the age of 14 (Ghimre 1998, p. 4) and even in relatively urban centers, 44 percent marry by the age of 19 (Nepal South Asia Center 1998, p. 7). (My Nepali language teacher's elder sister and mother were both married at the age of 11, one of them to a man 30 years her senior). A recent article in the *Kathmandu Post* (November 28, 2000) states that in the village of Balami, girls as young as eight are married and sent to live with their husband's families. The principal of the local school says that most girls drop out of school once they are married. Only a dozen girls attend the large local high school and only three have attained the School Leaving Certificate that declares they have completed the ten grades offered by public schooling.

Girls are often married at a young age so that a daughter-in-law may be brought into the home as free labor. Made the servant of her in-laws, a girl-bride often shoulders the majority of the burden of household tasks. Once handed over to her husband, a young bride faces not only the pressure of having to perform all types of physical labor for her in-laws, but also the pressure of having to bear a son as soon as possible, for until she does so, her place in the home is not secure. Should she be unable to produce a son, a wife may be discarded, returned humiliated and unmarriageable to her parents, or forced to live shunned by her husband, under the thumb of a new son-bearing wife. Consequently, 40 percent of rural women bear their first child between the ages of 15 and 19. Childbirth at such a young age puts both baby and mother at greater health risk. Nepal's infant mortality is 98 per every 1000 live births, and Nepal's maternal mortality rate of 875 per 100,000 women aged 15 to 49 years (Nepal South Asia Center 1998, p. 58) is among the very highest in the world.

Child marriage is one reason for maternal mortality, yet other indicators of poverty contribute as well, including the lack of pre-natal and post-natal care, lack of trained midwives, unsanitary birth conditions, and malnutrition. Two thirds of all pregnant women in Nepal suffer from iron deficiency and are anemic. Nepal Health Project Theatre Troupe performs a scene that attempts to rectify this situation. The scene takes place in *Yamlok*, land of the dead. To *Yamraj*, the lord of death, a pregnant woman explains that in her husband's home she functioned as a servant for the large extended family. Saddled with responsibility for the crops, animals, wood gathering, water collecting, housekeeping, laundry, child minding, and cooking, the young wife was exhausted by the day's work. As custom dictates, daily, she served meals first to her husband, his father and brothers, and when they had eaten their fill, she served her mother-in-law and sisters-in-law. If, at the end of their meal, only a handful of rice remained, that is all she would eat; if none remained, she would go hungry. Malnourished and too weak to survive labor, she died giving birth. This moving scene points to one of the major causes of the exceptionally high maternal mortality rate in Nepal, and underscores the dangers of the low status of women. Life expectancy in Nepal is lower overall than in other South Asian countries and, in stark contrast to the global pattern in which women live considerably longer than men, women in Nepal, on the average, have a life span shorter than men. This points to the developmental deprivations Nepali women encounter throughout their lives.

The play *Kumji Aagyan Garnu Huncha* (*Thus Spoke Kumarki*), created and performed since 1999 by the theatre troupe Sarwanam, dramatizes one of the ways in which history continues to oppress and undervalue women and pave the way for entry into prostitution. In this play, an older and authoritatively powerful man rapes a very young woman and, when called to account, he cites a well-known legend as justification for his behavior and successfully escapes punishment. In his defense, the rapist recounts the story of a god who took human shape to rape and then abandon a young virgin, and claims that in all things men strive to be like the gods. This play demonstrates the menace of rape and suggests the way in which it often leads to prostitution. It conveys the powerlessness of the rape victim in a society where age is valued over youth, where men are valued over women, and where women are taught to be docile, submissive and cooperative, as is illustrated in the text of the ancient play *Shakuntala*:

Respect your superiors, Shakuntala.
Never be angry with your husband, no matter what happens.
In everything be humble.
These qualities make a woman; those without them are black sheep in their families.

(Act IV)

While most young rural women recognize the threat of rape and attempt to thwart it by rarely being alone, rape is a significant problem in rural Nepal, although numbers of rapes are impossible to obtain as most go unreported. Gang rape is a major problem and is perpetrated on girls who find themselves vulnerably alone while gathering firewood or water, or walking the hours it may take them to reach school. Where vehicle roads come close to mountain villages, truck drivers are known to climb to the outskirts of hill villages to rape young women and then dash back to the safety of their trucks and drive off before the crime has been reported. If rapists cannot be certainly identified there is no recourse for vindication. Even if the identity of the rapist is known or suspected, low-*caste* families and families of meager financial means have no agency to pursue their daughters' rapists and even reported rapes most often go uninvestigated.

Most rapes are unreported,[1] for once a woman is known to have been raped, she may be outcast from her community and branded unclean and a whore. It may be fruitless for a woman to take such a risk and report her rape anyway, for often the police or relatively powerful public servants are the rapists themselves or are paid off by the rapists to keep them quiet. Should a woman be so bold as to report a rape and find herself in police 'protection', she may encounter even more danger there. In the Sarwanam play, a few members of the young rape victim's village express outrage at the crime, yet, because the rapist has greater standing in the village and some political clout, he manages to manipulate the law and escape retribution. One aim of these plays is to raise awareness with the public who may, in turn, put pressure on policy makers, for 'research and surveys have revealed that there is a close link between the police, politics and prostitution' (Pradhan [undated], p. 38).

Publicly humiliated and condemned by her violation, a young rape victim often sees no alternative but to leave her home and pursue the vocation that seems to have hunted her down. The various plays that attempt to raise awareness about girl trafficking show clearly how historical precedence, educational deprivation, poverty, the low status of women, child marriage, and violence perpetrated against women, pave the way for the trafficking of young women and girls to domestic prostitution and the hell of India's brothels.

ABC's play *Sabadhan* also shows the devastating effects of forced prostitution when a young woman returns to her village after managing her escape from an Indian brothel. The physically and emotionally shattered young woman describes to appalled villagers her brutal experiences in India. With the pain of memory strong in her voice, she recounts the process of

---

1   In 1999, fewer than 150 rapes were reported to official authorities, this in a country of nearly 30 million people. Nepal Human Rights Yearbook (p. 241).

'seasoning',[2] which aims to tame women by imprisoning and isolating them, starving, threatening, abusing, raping, and torturing them. The more this woman resisted and tried to escape, the more she was tortured.

This character, given the name Kaila in the play, is typical of women who find their lives horribly altered by being sold into the sex market. To her former friends, Kaila recounts her life in hell. She describes her customers and her agents, who all took advantage of her vulnerable powerlessness. Every kind of man visited her, some older or more affluent than others, some more drunk, more sickly, or more brutal. The stage make-up scars and bruises attest to the physical abuse suffered by women in her position and suggest the psychological and emotional scars that may never heal. Kaila considers herself lucky to have gotten out alive and laments that many of her captive 'sisters' were not nor will be so lucky.

Kaila's life, however, is not destined to be long, because the final humiliation and degradation she suffers due to her internment and enslavement is her infection with a sexually transmitted disease. Studies have made it clear that the major source of HIV/AIDS entry into Nepal is via the more than 200,000 Nepali girls who are in Indian brothels. According to Shanta Basnet Dixit, 'a striking aspect in Nepal's confrontation with the AIDS syndrome is the lack of data, and the government's almost complete inability to tackle the problem (a countrywide AIDS prevention strategy has not been developed)' (Dixit [undated], p. 49).

The typical Nepali villager knows little about the facts of HIV/AIDS transmission, and other plays, performed by such troupes as Sarwanam and Aarohan, attempt to educate the populace about the realities of the disease. Yet irrational fears of infection serve to alienate further the women who manage an escape from their sex slave drivers. Already shunned by her community, Kaila's infection severs any hope of regaining a normal life for the time she has left. She is forced to leave her village and becomes the dependent of a charitable organization that helps her live until they help her die.

The story of Kaila, as told by the ABC Art Group, is taken from real life experiences and the stories of those girls and women who have returned from the misery of India's brothels. ABC has taken their play to the rural villages where the girls were born and where they lived until they were tricked or sold into prostitution. In destitute places, such as Sindhupalchowk in the mountains north of Kathmandu, which have become rich sources of girls, awareness campaigns, including the use of street theatre, have met with denial and violence. In other districts, however, performances have been more successful in generating awareness and action. After the presentation of their play, parents

---

2   For more information on 'seasoning', see Brown (2000), p. 97.

have approached ABC's actors and asked for help in tracking down their missing daughters. Suddenly aware of the fate that may have befallen the young women, family members take the first steps that initiate the process of trying to rescue their daughters from prostitution.

The ABC Art Group, like all the socially engaged troupes of Nepali theatre activists, use the rough magic of their street-theatre to catch their audience unaware, to lure them with the promise of entertainment and to startle them with the facts of life faced by thousands of their sisters and daughters. Nepal's theatre artists use their creative talents and determined energies to reach the hearts and minds of those who might otherwise not know or would choose to forget.

References

Brown, Louise. (2000). *Sex Slaves: The Trafficking of Women in Asia*. London: Virago Press.

Dixit, Shanta Basnet. (undated). 'Impact of HIV/AIDS in Nepal'. In *Red Light Traffic: The Trade in Nepali Girls*. Kathmandu: ABC/Nepal.

Ghimre, Durga. (1998). *Sexual Exploitation of Nepalese Girls*. Kathmandu: ABC Nepal.

INSEC. (2000). *Nepal Human Rights Yearbook 2000*. Kathmandu: Informational Sector Service Centre (INSEC).

Nepal South Asia Center. (1998). *Nepal Human Development Report*. Kathmandu: Nepal South Asia Center.

Pradhan, Gauri. (undated). 'The Road to Bombay: Forgotten Women'. In *Red Light Traffic*. Kathmandu: ABC/Nepal.

Sattaur, Omar. (1993). *Child Labor in Nepal*. Kathmandu: CWIN.

Subedi, Pratiya. (1997). *Nepali Women Rising*. Kathmandu: Sahayogi Press.

UNICEF. (1996). *Children and Women of Nepal: A Situation Analysis*. Kathmandu: UNICEF Nepal.

Leslie R. Wolfe

Fighting the war against sexual trafficking of women and girls*

Sex trafficking is the third-largest underground economy in the world. More than two million women and children are sold, tricked, or forced by poverty into sexual slavery or indentured servitude every year. Of these, more than 50,000 are brought into the United States.

Despite the horrifying numbers, the issue of trafficking can seem remote—until its victims are threatened and killed in your own city. Such tragedies are occurring here in Seattle. In 1995, Susana Remerata Blackwell, brought from the Philippines to Seattle as a mail-order bride, was shot to death by her purchaser/husband, Timothy Blackwell. Last year, 20-year-old Anastasia Solovieva King, who was brought to Seattle from the former Soviet Union as a mail-order bride, was found dead in a shallow grave. Her husband has been charged with first-degree murder.

On November 3, 2001, the conference 'Trafficking of Women and Children: Challenges and Solutions' was held at the University of Washington to educate the public and develop a plan of action to fight trafficking at the local and regional levels. Members of the Washington state legislature Velma Veloria (D-Seattle), who initiated the organizing of the conference, worked with Senator Jeri Costa (D-Marysville), and Senator Jeanne Kohl-Welles (D-Seattle), to introduce a bill into the Washington state legislature that is modeled on the Trafficking Victims Protection Act of 2000. Leslie R. Wolfe, President of The Center for Women Policy Studies in Washington, DC, is a leader in the fight against trafficking as a United States policy issue, and educates US state-level lawmakers and the public about the issue. She was the keynote speaker for the Seattle conference.

It is a great honor and delight to be here with you for this groundbreaking conference. I am especially honored to join my colleague, friend and hero, Representative Velma Veloria, on this podium and thank her for including me

---

*   This speech was first published in the Seattle-based online journal *Said It: feminist news, culture, and politics* (http://www.saidit.org/archives/feb02/article1.html). It was prefaced by the above introduction by *Said It* editor Adriene Sere. It has been slightly revised for its publication in this volume.

and the Center for Women Policy Studies in this incredible event, and for her new proposed legislation on trafficking. I also want to recognize the leadership of [Washington state] Senators Jeri Costa and Jeanne Kohl-Welles, who remain stalwarts in the struggle to bring these issues to public debate.

I come to you today from the other Washington, a city on high alert and fearful of what tomorrow will bring. I, too, am fearful—but my fear is for our movement for women's human rights in the United States and around the world, in the context of the new war on terrorism that now is the central focus of United States policy, both foreign and domestic.

But today, we are talking about a different war on terrorism—the one we have been fighting for many years, against the oppression of women and girls as exemplified by the horrors of sexual trafficking. In this most appalling violation of their most basic human rights, thousands upon thousands of our young sisters live in unspeakable conditions of sexual slavery throughout the world—and in our country. This we cannot permit. And we are the ones to stop it.

My sisters, we all are links in the golden chain of the global feminist revolution that is changing the institutions that govern our lives. We are guided and inspired by the earth-shaking UN conferences—from the Vienna Human Rights Conference to the Beijing Women's Conference—at which women's groups forced governments to take the great leap forward to recognize that women's rights are human rights and essential to the sustainable development of all our nations.

I am excited to be here to learn from all of you in our sessions throughout the day. And I promise you that the Center for Women Policy Studies will take up the plan of action you develop here today and continue to focus our laser beam of policy analysis and advocacy on this national emergency, to bring it to our national network of women state legislators, to our colleagues in Congress, and to the State Department.

But first, I must share with you my own—and the Center's—guiding principles. I spoke of the global feminist revolution because I believe that we truly *are* revolutionaries—in the best possible sense of the word. And that best possible sense comes from Che Guevara, who said: 'Let me say, at the risk of seeming ridiculous, that the true revolutionary is guided by great feelings of love.'

And from my dear friend Bella Abzug, who left us a powerful legacy of activism and courage. She reminded the world at Beijing that we are not simply trying to join the mainstream—because it is a polluted stream. As Bella said: 'We want to change the stagnant waters into a fresh flowing stream, making it safe and life enhancing for everyone.' And that is what you are doing here today.

We, dear sisters and brothers, are the lucky ones. Because we have the luxury to be here today. Most of our sisters worldwide and in our own country do not. But we are here today because we work for them. And we know that women in this world are all in the same boat. Some of us—by virtue of our race, ethnicity, immigration status, class, sexual orientation, marital status, disability status—are in first class cabins, some of us are working in the kitchen, some of us are locked in the cargo hold, enslaved. Most of us have never had the chance to be the captain. But we will be.

You already know a great deal about sexual trafficking of women and girls, but I believe we must always reflect on what it means for us and for our sisters worldwide. Because this is our problem, in every part of our nation. Between 50,000 and 100,000 women—the data are far from precise—are trafficked into the United States each year, primarily from impoverished communities in Asia and eastern Europe, but also from Africa and Latin America. In 1998, more than 200 international mail-order bride businesses operated in the United States, bringing up to 6000 women each year into this country for marriage to American men—and many end up as battered, or murdered, wives.

Sexual trafficking of women and girls across borders, within countries, across state lines, is a big business that generates enormous profit for the traffickers.

Trafficked women and girls are forced into prostitution and sexual slavery that takes a variety of forms—from virtual imprisonment in brothels to participation in the production of pornography to commercial or exploitative marriages, often as mail-order brides. And women who are trafficked for other forms of exploitative labor—as domestic workers in private homes and as laborers in sweatshops—are subject to sexual violence as well.

Sexual trafficking is a disease of our patriarchal society, the quintessential violation of women's autonomy and human rights, and the ultimate reflection of our status as the property of men and as creatures who exist primarily to service men's sexual desire.

There is no analogy that truly reflects the underlying truth of this trade—not the analogy to the trade in illegal commodities such as drugs and guns, not the analogy to illegal immigration for work and economic betterment which brought so many of our grandparents and parents to the United States to create a better life.

No. Trafficking in women and girls is the soul of our oppression. Trafficking in women often is fueled by the extreme poverty that many women and children face and is more common in countries and communities where women lack viable economic opportunities—in large part because of their traditionally lower status in law and custom. The traffickers make an appealing and persuasive case, therefore, that other countries offer better opportunities.

And it is a clear case of gendered racism. In fact, racist and sexist stereotypes drive international trafficking patterns across borders—because men, euphemistically called 'the customers', express preferences for women or girls they define as more appealing. In the United States, for example, this often translates into a preference for women from Asia and eastern Europe—because men think they will be more passive and subservient than those dreadfully liberated American women. In fact, this racist and sexist stereotype is a key selling point in the US for mail-order brides.

Further, men who participate in sex tourism in various countries, traveling on vacation to 'try' prostitutes in other countries, demand younger and younger girls—virgins—because they believe that they can thereby avoid HIV infection, or even be cured of AIDS by sexual contact with a virgin. And so, we find young girls forced into the sex trade, infected with HIV by these men, and then tossed aside by the traffickers and brothel owners when they are sick and therefore useless as money makers.

But young women do not know any of this when they are first recruited by traffickers, who employ a variety of appalling deceptive and often coercive strategies to lure desperately poor young women and their families with false promises of money, jobs, and better opportunities abroad.

Severe economic hardship beyond anything we can imagine in this country may encourage families to accept the traffickers' false promises and send their daughters away—for the survival of the family. This tactic works especially well for desperately poor families because traffickers lie to women and their families about the work the women will be offered. Traffickers present fake employment contracts and false visas, and some go so far as to marry their victims—either as a way to recruit them or as a way to protect themselves and their victims from prosecution for illegal immigration. But these contracts, visas, and marriages are always shams.

Once in the United States, women and girls find themselves trapped into sexual slavery without money or legal help to escape. They are victims of terrorism and subjugation. Just try to imagine it.

Imagine that you have left home for a new country and new economic opportunity. You have been brought to this new country by a man or men you fear or even trust, to work and earn money for your family—only to find yourself imprisoned in a brothel or sweat shop. Imagine your terror: you cannot speak the language; you fear the local police, who may be complicit in the trafficking; and you legitimately fear arrest, imprisonment, and deportation to your home country, where you likely will be ostracized because of the sexual nature of your exploitation.

The nature and extent of sexual trafficking in this country are reflected in a few recent cases. For example, after they were promised good paying restaurant jobs in the United States, a group of Thai women were forced into prostitution upon their arrival in New York. A group of Mexican teenage women were told that they were going to jobs as waitresses, landscapers, child care and elder care workers—but they were held in sexual slavery upon their arrival in Florida and the Carolinas, and threatened with harm to themselves and their families if they resisted.

A syndicate of smugglers and pimps brought hundreds of young Asian women—some as young as thirteen—into the United States and forced them to work as prostitutes in brothels, where they lived in bondage until their so-called 'contracts' were paid off. These young women, who also believed the traffickers' false promises of economic opportunity, not only were trafficked into the United States. They also were trafficked across state lines within this country—sent to other brothels in at least twelve other states and the District of Columbia. Why? Because their so-called clients 'got tired of the same women', according to the assistant US attorney in charge of the case against the syndicate. This case is not unique; similar gangs have been charged in New York, Los Angeles, and San Francisco, and the victims have been women from both Asia and Latin America.

What has our federal government done so far? There is good news and, of course, bad news. First, some of the good news is reflected in the cases I have just mentioned, because the FBI and prosecutors at least are arresting and charging some traffickers. And last year the Congress passed, and President Clinton signed, Public Law 106-386, the 'Victims of Trafficking and Violence Protection Act of 2000'—an omnibus bill that includes both the reauthorized Violence Against Women Act and the new 'Trafficking Victims Protection Act'.

The new law requires our government to produce annual reports on trafficking by countries that receive foreign assistance from the United States, to create an interagency task force to monitor and combat trafficking, to protect and assist victims of trafficking, to establish minimum standards and provide assistance to other countries to meet these standards for elimination of trafficking, and to take action against governments that fail to meet the standards and to strengthen prosecution of traffickers. This is a key victory.

But I am reminded of what our sister/friend and hero Shirley Chisholm said when she was a Member of Congress—and one of our most outspoken women's rights activists in the Congress: 'The law cannot do the major part of the job of winning equality for women. Women must do it for themselves. They must become revolutionaries.'

As with all anti-discrimination laws, we must use this imperfect statute as our great weapon for change. For example, Secretary of State Colin Powell expressed a powerful commitment to ending sexual trafficking when he announced the release of the State Department's first report on trafficking in persons, which the new law required the Department to produce. While this does demonstrate the law's importance as a weapon, we should note that—as our sisters of Human Rights Watch pointed out—the report was five weeks late, it glosses over the role of official complicity and corruption in the persistence of trafficking, it does not focus enough on forced labor trafficking, and it does not report sufficiently on how countries are protecting the women and children who have been trafficked.

Funding is insufficient; only $30 million was included in the House-passed 2002 Foreign Operations Appropriations Bill, for example. So we must fight to ensure that our government commits sufficient funds to transforming rhetoric into action to end trafficking.

We also must ask: how strong is the interagency task force? How is the State Department working with the Departments of Justice, Labor, and Health and Human Services on the mandated interagency task force to fight trafficking *in* the United States?

And, since the United States is defined by the State Department as a 'destination country', how will the crossing of state lines within our country be addressed? Will the State Department and domestic departments make the war on trafficking a top priority in the current context of the war on terrorism?

These questions bring us, at last, to our own mandate. We must force the issue by all means and methods available to us.

I know you will agree that our focus as policy makers and advocates should be on protecting women who have been trafficked into the United States. We must not allow our criminal and immigration laws to be used to punish women as criminals, and we must prevent their deportation. We must ensure that women get the help they need to escape.

Indeed, in the United States, despite federal and state opposition to sexual trafficking, we also prosecute women who are arrested for prostitution as felons—and often deport women who have been trafficked—without regard for the circumstances that led the women to this life. This creates a serious legal and policy conflict that must be resolved.

I think we must recognize that existing laws in the United States, as in many other countries, are inadequate to punish traffickers and to protect and help the women and girls who are their prey. Then, we can move on to develop creative responses.

And we must continue our advocacy at the federal level. For example, we can put the pressure on our government to implement existing international agreements in our states and nation, particularly the 1949 UN Convention for the Suppression of the Traffic in Persons and the Exploitation of Others, and the 2000 UN Protocol to Prevent, Suppress and Punish Trafficking in Persons, Especially Women and Children, which supplements the UN Convention

Against Transnational Organized Crime adopted by the UN General Assembly in November 2000. The United States (and 80 other countries) signed the Protocol last December. We now must ensure Senate ratification.

And while we are at it, please keep urging the US Senate to ratify the Convention on the Elimination of All Forms of Discrimination Against Women— CEDAW.

At the state level, you can do what state legislator Alma Adams did in North Carolina: introduce a resolution endorsing CEDAW, and urge the Senate to ratify it. Alma's bill actually passed!

We also can and must make our voices heard in Congress and the Administration to insist that in this post-September 11 era, we maintain a high level of alert and attention to attacking the continuing and increasing sexual trafficking of women and girls. We must urge our federal government to focus on punishing traffickers and governments that support or allow them to flourish—even if those governments are our allies—while increasing our assistance to women and girls who are suffering these horrific abuses of their human rights.

Insist that the Bush Administration implements the 'Trafficking Victims Protection Act of 2000' with extreme vigor and funding and commitment within the United States as well as against other nations.

In addition, insist on increased funding under the 'Violence Against Women Act of 2000' for programs nationwide that protect immigrant women and children trapped in exploitative, commercial and/or abusive marriages— including mail-order brides. Indeed, the Violence Against Women Act of 1994, which the current law reauthorized and expanded, for the first time allowed battered immigrant women to apply for permanent resident status for themselves and their children without the cooperation or assistance of their husbands.

And we must continue to find creative ways to use other federal laws as well—including such ancient statutes as the 1948 Mann Act, which is now used as the basis for current federal prosecution of traffickers who transport women across state lines or US borders for illegal sex work. For example, in *US v. Winters*, the defendant beat and raped a woman he picked up hitchhiking and then forced her into prostitution at a migrant labor camp so that he could receive the profits. He did the same thing to a second woman. He was convicted under the Mann Act for transporting the women across state lines for interstate commerce to engage in prostitution, and the conviction was upheld by the Ninth Circuit Court of Appeals.

Finally, you can urge your state attorney general and prosecutors to use three types of state criminal statutes currently on the books to prosecute some traffickers right away. These are laws that criminalize involuntary servitude, promotion of prostitution, and forced or commercial marriages. Some states, for example, can use statutes prohibiting prostitution and the promotion of prostitution to prosecute traffickers instead of the women and girls they coerced into prostitution. In several states, it is a felony offense to use threat or force or intimidation to compel a person into prostitution and to profit from another's prostitution.

However, such laws do not cover all forms of trafficking and do not offer protections for trafficked women and girls—or provide the services they need so desperately.

The Center for Women Policy Studies has made a serious of recommendations to state legislators for specific state-level responses to trafficking.

We recommend that efforts to address sexual trafficking at the state level focus on criminalizing the activities of the traffickers with appropriately harsh punishments—by defining trafficking as a Class A felony offense. Each state should prohibit all forms of trafficking and should prohibit traffickers' assertion of the woman's alleged consent to be trafficked to be used as a defense.

We also propose that each state legislature mandate creation of a commission of experts—specifically including advocates for refugee and immigrant women and providers of domestic violence and sexual assault services.

We propose that states enact legislation that implements and strengthens the new federal law at the state level—just as Washington led in the 1970s in passing a state educational equity law that implemented and strengthened the federal Title IX prohibition of sex discrimination in education. And finally, we urge legislators to ensure protection from prosecution and deportation for any and all trafficked women and girls, as well as funding for a range of services for women and girls who have been brought to our country under such horrific conditions. Let us welcome and support these sisters with protection and well-funded programs that will speed their recovery from the horrors inflicted upon them. These programs should include all forms of health care services, housing, education and training, and personal emotional support from women's groups in the community.

We share your commitment to finding ways to respond to the horrors that women and girls face in the United States and around the world. We have both a moral and a legal obligation to eliminate these crimes from our states and nation. Together we can truly save the lives and spirits of thousands of young women and girls, and lift our own spirits as well.

I remind you, in conclusion, of Bella Abzug's spirit and commitment as we go forth to act both locally and globally. She reminded us to 'never underestimate the importance of what we are doing here. Never hesitate to tell the truth. And never, ever give in—or give up.'

Contributors

Kirsten Anderberg is a political activist and freelance journalist based in Seattle. Her articles have appeared in *Utne Reader Online*, *Alternative Press Review*, *Infoshop.org*, *Alternet.org*, *Slingshot Zine*, *CompleatMother Mag*, *ZNet/Mag*, etc. Visit her website at www.angelfire.com/la3/kirstenanderberg.

Margaret (Meg) Baldwin is an Associate Professor of Law at Florida State University College of Law in Tallahassee, Florida. Her legal scholarship and advocacy activities have long centred on advancing justice for prostituted women and girls. Professor Baldwin has represented prostituted women in civil rights and clemency cases, authored the first statute in the United States creating compensation claims for women and girls coerced in prostitution, and has written extensively on legal strategies benefiting prostituted women and girls.

Jane Caputi teaches Women's Studies at Florida Atlantic University. She is the author of *The Age of Sex Crime*, a radical feminist denouncement of the heroization of the serial killer, and *Gossips, Gorgons and Crones: The Fates of the Earth*, on nuclear myth and female powers. Her new book is *Goddesses and Monsters: Women, Myth, Power and Popular Culture*. She also collaborated on *Websters' First New Intergalactic Wickedary of the English Language* with Mary Daly.

Vednita Carter is Founder/Executive Director of Breaking Free, an Afrocentric agency that provides services to assist prostituted women and other battered women who have been through the criminal justice system to make healthy changes in their lives. Ms. Carter developed and directed the Women's Services Program for six years at WHISPER (Women Hurt in Systems of Prostitution Engaged in Revolt). She counselled incarcerated women for five years at the Rivers of Life prison ministry program. Ms. Carter is the author of 'Prostitution: Where Racism and Sexism Intersect,' published in the *Michigan Journal of Gender and Law*, and the co-author of 'Prostitution, Racism, and Feminist Discourse,' published by the Hastings Women's Law Journal. Many of her articles on African American women and prostitution have been published nationwide in feminist newspapers and newsletters. She is featured in the documentary *Rape Is* (produced by Cambridge Documentary Films) and has appeared on local and national talk shows addressing prostitution as a form of violence against women and girls.

D.A. (De) Clarke, born 1958 in the UK, became a feminist in the late 1970s. She is a software engineer by trade, an independent scholar by inclination, and

427

a sporadic essayist. She has lived in the US for many years. Visit her website at http://www.ucolick.org/~de

Carol Davis is associate professor of theatre at Franklin and Marshall College where she teaches acting, directing, and theatre history. She holds a Ph.D. from University of California at Berkeley, has taught at Pomona College and Lehigh University, and has acted and directed at major theatres in California. She is the founding artistic director of an educational street theatre troupe that has performed for more than 500,000 villagers throughout rural Nepal. Her articles on Nepali theatre have appeared in *Asian Theatre Journal*, *Mime Journal*, and *Theatre Symposium*.

Gail Dines is a Professor of Sociology and Women's Studies at Wheelock College in Boston. She has written extensively on the nature and effects of pornography and is co-author of *Pornography: The Production and Consumption of Inequality*.

Andrea Dworkin is a radical feminist writer. She is the author of the novels *Mercy* and *Ice and Fire* and the classic feminist works of non-fiction *Intercourse* and *Pornography: Men Possessing Women*. Her other books include the memoir *Heartbreak* and the collections *Letters from a War Zone* and *Life and Death: Unapologetic Writings on the Continuing War Against Women*. Her book *Scapegoat: Israel, Jews, and Women's Liberation* won an American Book Award.

Samantha Emery is Anishinaabe and lives on the White Earth reservation in northern Minnesota. As she grows into elderhood she feels the need to tell her story with those who will listen. She wants to bring hope to those who have been adopted and sexually abused, in order to help them find balance in their own lives.

Melissa Farley is a clinical and research psychologist whose research on prostitution has been used by state governments, as well as by advocates and organizations providing services to prostituted and trafficked women. She completed the edited volume *Prostitution, Trafficking, & Traumatic Stress* in 2003. She can be contacted at mfarley@prostitutionresearch.com.

Rus Ervin Funk, MSW, currently works for the Center for Women and Families in Louisville, Kentucky, and is on the board of directors of the National Center on Domestic and Sexual Violence. He is co-founder of the Baltimore Alliance Against Child Sexual Abuse and M.E.N. (Mobilizing to ENd violence). He is also founder of Men for Gender Justice, the Louisville Teen Dating Violence Network and the on-line discussion group Feminists Against Pornography and Prostitution. He can be reached at rfunk@cwfempower.org.

Donna Hughes is Professor in the Women's Studies Department, Eleanor M. and Oscar M. Endowed Chair, at the University of Rhode Island. She does research and writing on trafficking, sexual exploitation, violence against women, women's organized resistance to violence, and religious fundamentalism and women's rights. She also works on issues related to women, science and technology.

Suzanne Jay's front-line anti-violence organizing includes working with women connected to the Vancouver 'Missing Women' list. She was an organizer of a recent public forum on ending prostitution. Suzanne is a collective member of Vancouver Rape Relief and Women's Shelter.

Sheila Jeffreys is an Associate Professor in the Department of Political Science at the University of Melbourne. She is the author of five books on the history and politics of sexuality including *The Idea of Prostitution* (Spinifex Press, 1997). Her most recent book is *Unpacking Queer Politics: A Lesbian Feminist Perspective* (Polity, 2003). She is a founding member of the Coalition Against Trafficking in Women Australia. Contact her on: sheila@unimelb.edu.au.

Robert Jensen is a Professor of Journalism at the University of Texas at Austin and a member of the board of the Third Coast Activist Resource Center (www.thirdcoastactivist.org). He is the author of *Citizens of the Empire: The Struggle to Claim Our Humanity* and *Writing Dissent: Taking Radical Ideas from the Margins to the Mainstream*, and co-author of *Pornography: The Production and Consumption of Inequality*.

Chong N. Kim is a survivor of child sexual exploitation and prostitution. She currently volunteers as a Legal Advocate assisting other crime victims in getting legal help, and is launching a new non-profit organization for minority and immigrant women who are victims of sexual exploitation and human trafficking. Some of her poetry can be found at www.feministjournal.com. To learn more about her memoir *Silent Cries*, contact her at ckim@wbiav.org.

Lee Lakeman established one of the first transition houses in Canada in the early 1970s. She continues to be a frontline anti-violence organizer as a collective member of Vancouver Rape Relief and Women's Shelter. Lee is a regional representative to the Canadian Association of Sexual Assault Centres and was the co-ordinator of the 5-year pan-Canadian CASAC LINKS research project.

Alice Lee's frontline anti-violence organizing includes working with the Fujianese women refugees who arrived in British Columbia. Alice immigrated to Canada with her family as a child; she studied as an adult in China and travels to Asia regularly. Alice is a collective member of Vancouver Rape Relief and Women's Shelter.

Taylor Lee worked in men's clubs until 1995. She now has a master's degree in social work with a mental health specialization. She currently provides therapy services to children and families facing emotional and behavioral issues often related to abuse, neglect, and other forms of trauma.

Jacqueline Lynne is a woman of Metis ancestry and a social worker currently working in the addictions field. She is a prostitution researcher who views prostitution, in all its forms, as violence against women, and who is committed to ending it.

Seiya Morita is a Lecturer teaching Economics at the Tokyo Metropolitan College. The author of *Capitalism and Sex Discrimination* (Aoki-shoten, Tokyo, 1996), he is a member of the Anti-Pornography and Prostitution Research Group (www.app-jp.org).

Joe Parker is a retired psychiatric nurse. A former Vietnam medic and former reserve deputy sheriff, he has worked on skid row, in a clinic for street youth, on a large state hospital unit which included sexually abused and prostituted adolescents and adults, in a two-county mobile crisis intervention service, and as a County Health Department psychiatric nurse in a maximum security jail. He has cared for both prostituted women and men, and had extensive contact with street level pimps. After retiring, he co-founded the Lola Greene Baldwin Foundation, which serves prostituted men and women of any age and provides community and professional education.

Adriene Sere is the former editor of *Said It*, an online feminist magazine published from 1999 to 2003 (www.saidit.org). She is also a poet, screen-writer, and short story writer.

Sherry Lee Short is an artist, teacher, and activist. She has served as executive director, board member, and volunteer for numerous rural social justice organizations. This work has included the fight for legal, personal, and political justice for individuals and communities affected by the sex industry, and advocacy involving issues surrounding HIV/AIDS in rural areas. She finds balance through organic gardening, backpacking, and running.

Ann Simonton is a lecturer and media activist. She founded Media Watch in 1984, which works to challenge racism, sexism and violence in the media through education and action. She wrote and helped produce two bestselling media literacy films used in schools across the nation.

Carol Smith lives in California and is the mother of two children. She enjoys playing with her kids best. She hopes to contribute in whatever ways she can to ending the exploitation of women in the pornography industry.

Christine Stark is a feminist writer, artist, speaker, and activist of American Indian and European ancestry. She has spoken nationally and internationally on issues of rape, race, poverty, homelessness, prostitution, and pornography and organized many community events, including *Amerika: Land of Rape and Genocide*. Her writing and art have been published in numerous periodicals and anthologies and she has appeared on National Public Radio and various television and radio shows. She was interviewed for *Dirty Little Secret*, a documentary on sexual violence. She is a member of the Minnesota Indian Women's Sexual Assault Coalition and completing her MFA in Writing from Minnesota State University. Christine is a survivor of incest and a racist prostitution and pornography ring. She may be reached at cstark1@visi.com.

John Stoltenberg is a long-time radical feminist activist against sexual violence and philosopher of gender. He is the author of *Refusing to Be a Man: Essays on Sex and Justice* (rev. ed. UCL Press, 2000), *The End of Manhood: Parables on Sex and Selfhood* (rev. ed. UCL Press, 2000), and *What Makes Pornography 'Sexy'?* (Milkweed Editions, 1994), as well as numerous articles and essays in anthologies. In addition to speaking and writing, John works professionally in publishing in New York City, where he has been Managing Editor of five national magazines and served as editorial and creative consultant to many other publications. For *Men Can Stop Rape*, he conceived and creative directs the 'My strength is not for hurting' media campaign. He holds a Master of Divinity degree in theology and literature from Union Theological Seminary and an M.F.A. in theatre arts from Columbia University School of the Arts.

Mary Lucille Sullivan is undertaking her Ph.D. in the area of sexual politics at the University of Melbourne, Australia. The focus of her study is the implications of legitimising prostitution as work in Victoria, Australia. Mary's research interests relate to her feminist activism. She is a member of CATW Australia. She has also worked and published in the area of community history and on issues related to Australia's cultural diversity.

Rebecca Whisnant received her doctorate in philosophy at the University of North Carolina at Chapel Hill, and is visiting Assistant Professor of Philosophy at the University of Dayton. In addition to teaching and publishing in ethics and feminist theory, she is an anti-pornography educator and peace activist who has done public speaking on topics ranging from same-sex marriage to the US wars on Afghanistan and Iraq. Her current work focuses on intersections and tensions between feminist theory and the philosophy of non-violence.

Leslie R. Wolfe is President of the Center for Women Policy Studies, a national non-profit, multi-ethnic and multicultural feminist policy research and advocacy organization founded in 1972. Under Dr. Wolfe's direction the Center has been a leader on many critical women's issues, including:

addressing AIDS policy issues from women's diverse perspectives; defining violence against women and girls in the context of bias-motivated hate crimes; producing landmark research on gender bias on the SAT college entrance exam; conducting research on how women of color define and experience work/family and workplace diversity issues; promoting welfare reform that enables low-income women to attend college; and examining the connection between violence against, and violence committed by, girls and teen women.

Joyce Wu is a worker at the Women's Domestic Violence Crisis Service of Victoria. She is also a member of the Committee of Management at Project Respect, an Australian feminist organisation dedicated to ending sexual exploitation and the trafficking in women. Joyce is completing her honours degree at Melbourne University, Australia.

Index

If you would like to know more about Spinifex Press,
write for a free catalogue or visit our website

Spinifex Press
PO Box 212 North Melbourne
Victoria 3051 Australia